# *Fundamentals of*
# ACCOUNTING

## Robert M. Swanson

*Professor Emeritus of Business Education
and Office Administration
Ball State University
Muncie, Indiana*

## Kenton E. Ross, CPA

*Professor of Accounting
East Texas State University
Commerce, Texas*

## Robert D. Hanson

*Associate Dean
School of Business Administration
Central Michigan University
Mount Pleasant, Michigan*

BA50EA
PUBLISHED BY
SOUTH-WESTERN PUBLISHING CO.
CINCINNATI, OH          DALLAS, TX

ISBN: 0-538-70227-3

5 6 7 8 9 10 11 12 13 14 15 16 17 18 19 20 D 0 9 8 7 6 5

Printed in the United States of America

Developmental Editors: Bill Lee/Carol Volz
Production Editor: Mary H. Draper
Associate Editors/Production, Textbooks: Kimberlee Kusnerak/Leslie A. Kauffman
Associate Editors/Production, Supplements: Bradley C. Ellis/Vince Patton/Edna Stroble
Designer: Jim DeSollar
Production Artist: Steven McMahon
Designer, Simulations: Darren K. Wright/Jim DeSollar/J.E. Lagenaur
Production Artist, Simulations: Sophia Renieris
Photo Researcher: Fred M. Middendorf
Marketing Manager: Ben Willard

Photo Acknowledgments

Courtesy of Coit, 3; Photo courtesy of Windsor Ind., Englewood, Colorado, 8; Larry Allan/The Image Bank, 197; Photo courtesy of Apple Computer, Inc., 219; Tandy Corporation, 246; Eric Meola/The Image Bank, 251; Location courtesy of Wooster Pike Auto Parts, 271; Tandy Corporation, 311;© Jose Carrillo, Ventura, CA, 337; Courtesy of Reynolds and Reynolds, 349; Location courtesy of Wooster Pike Auto Parts, 412; Don Carroll/The Image Bank, 436; Courtesy of International Business Machines Corporation, 463

Cover Photo: © FPG International Corp

# FUNDAMENTALS OF ACCOUNTING

To meet the needs of accounting classes with different curriculum patterns and different proficiency standards, the fifth edition of FUNDAMENTALS OF ACCOUNTING is available in two parts: a short basic course and an advanced course. These two separate modules permit flexible scheduling to meet individual and class differences, and they provide logical cutoff points to meet the requirements of any course organization. The following materials are available for the course in basic accounting.

## BA50E8—FUNDAMENTALS OF ACCOUNTING, Fifth Edition

BA50EA—Textbook (Chapters 1–19)

BA50ED—Working Papers and Study Guides (Chapters 1–19)

Chapters 1–11 cover the accounting cycle for a service business organized as a proprietorship and the procedures for converting from a manual to an automated accounting system.

Chapters 12–19 cover the accounting cycle for a merchandising business organized as a partnership.

## BA51E8—FUNDAMENTALS OF ACCOUNTING, ADVANCED COURSE, Fifth Edition

BA51EA—Textbook (Chapters 20–29)

BA51ED—Working Papers and Study Guides (Chapters 20–29)

Chapters 20–29 cover the accounting cycle of a merchandising business organized as a corporation and selected specialized activities performed by entry-level accounting employees.

# Preface

A universal need exists today for a knowledge of the principles of accounting. A knowledge of accounting contributes to (a) a person's ability to earn a living, (b) a person's understanding of the economic activities of the business world, and (c) a person's competence in managing personal business affairs.

This package of instructional materials, consisting of a textbook and a book of working papers and study guides (workbook), is designed to help you understand the basic principles of accounting. The text material and problems should give you the knowledge needed to keep your personal records. Also, they should give you the skills required for initial employment as a bookkeeper in a small business or an accounting clerk in a large business.

## FEATURES

The following are some of the features of this fifth edition of FUNDAMENTALS OF ACCOUNTING.

**Suitable for self-instruction.** Normally, students in adult classes spend a considerable amount of time studying outside the classroom. For this reason, all of the explanations in the textbook are presented in a nontechnical manner. You can work through the materials with a minimum of help from the instructor. Also, the application materials are ideally suited to permit you to progress at an individual rate of speed. This rate of progress will depend upon the amount of time you devote to study and practice outside the classroom.

**Discussions move from simple to complex.** Great care has been taken to make sure that simple accounting principles are presented first. For example, the records kept by small businesses are discussed first. The basic principles and practices are expanded as more complicated records are introduced. This approach makes the learning task easier.

**Step-by-step presentations.** New principles are introduced in a step-by-step manner. Because of this manner of presentation, you can follow the discussions logically, moving from one step to the next. You can stop at any step and go back to review if necessary. Step-by-step presentations help you understand the explanations with a minimum of instructor interpretation.

**Illustrations keyed to step-by-step discussions.** Appropriate, realistic illustrations aid your learning. Illustrations are keyed to the step-by-step discussions so that each step explained is easy to find in the illustrations. This careful coordination of discussions with illustrations helps you understand the basic principles. Entries for transactions being explained are highlighted in the illustrations in dark black type while entries discussed previously are faded into the background. Background tints on accounting forms are different colors for each kind of form. The same color coding is used throughout the text to help you recognize the different forms being discussed.

**Simulation.** The main vehicle of instruction is simulation. Realism is created through the use of standard forms, standard procedures, approved business practices, and standard accounting terminology. But the most important simulation is through the problems, reinforcement activities, and business simulations. Problems are small-segment simulations that pinpoint specific applications of principles and procedures. Reinforcement activities are minisimulations that provide more in-depth practice and strengthen basic learnings from several chapters. Business simulations give you the feeling of actual experience in realistic business situations. The business simulations are the capstones of your learning process. A variety of business simulations is available. Your instructor will obtain for you any of the simulations you desire.

# STUDY SUGGESTIONS

Many features are built into this educational package to provide maximum aid to you as you study. In addition to what your instructor recommends, the following suggestions are provided to help you learn:

1. Read the textbook discussions carefully; underline important points.
2. Pay careful attention to the step-by-step explanations.
3. Examine each illustration carefully. Notice how each step in the text discussion is keyed to a related illustration. As you read each step, find the step on the illustration.
4. Carefully examine each summary illustration, including any that occur at the end of a section within a chapter. Make sure you understand the summary before proceeding with other end-of-chapter materials.
5. When you finish reading a chapter, define the accounting terms and answer the questions to check your understanding of the chapter. Complete the chapter study guide in the workbook as a further check of your knowledge of the chapter. If you are unable to answer all the questions in a study guide, reread the chapter.
6. When you have a thorough understanding of the theory presented in a chapter, complete the drills and application problems for the chapter. Use the forms provided in your working papers. These forms are keyed to specific problems and pages in the textbook.
7. If you desire additional work to assure mastery of theory, complete the enrichment problems. Use the forms provided in your working papers. Recycling problems are provided at the back of the textbook for extra practice. Forms are not provided for these problems.
8. At appropriate intervals throughout the textbook, your instructor will test your knowledge of the material presented. If you have satisfactorily completed the study guides and application problems, you should have little difficulty with the tests.
9. Your instructor may ask you to complete a business simulation that is available for use with this textbook. If a simulation is required, your instructor will guide you in its use.

# Contents

## ■ PART 3
## PARTNERSHIP ACCOUNTING FOR A MERCHANDISING BUSINESS

# Welcome to Accounting

Managers and owners use accounting information as the basis for making business decisions. Accurate accounting records contribute to a business' success and help to avoid failure and bankruptcy. Failure to understand accounting information can result in poor business decisions. Training in accounting helps managers and owners make better business decisions.

This textbook is the first in a two-volume series for use in a business curriculum with two years of accounting study. The first-year text is for students who have a variety of career objectives. (1) Accounting knowledge and skill needed for beginning accounting careers. (2) Accounting knowledge and skill needed for careers in related business fields. (3) Accounting knowledge and skill to serve as a foundation on which to continue the study of accounting at the college level. The advanced text is for students with determined career objectives in accounting.

One of the most important decisions people make is how to earn a living. Individuals use accounting information to make personal financial decisions about how to earn a living and how to use their personal income. Many young people choose to prepare for a career in the exciting field of accounting.

## WHAT IS ACCOUNTING?

Accounting serves people in business and in their personal lives. Accounting helps people understand business in their careers and in their personal lives.

**Accounting — the language of business.** Accounting is the language of business. Owners, managers, and accounting workers must understand and use this basic language. Salesclerks and general office clerks complete accounting forms and prepare accounting reports. Secretaries take dictation that includes accounting terms. These workers can do their work more efficiently if they know the language of business — accounting.

**Accounting in everyday life.** Nearly everyone in the United States earns money and must submit income tax reports to the federal and state governments. Everyone, personally or for a business, must plan ways to keep spending within available income. Many persons use accounting as a means of earning a living, and all persons must keep personal financial records. All persons can use accounting information and skills.

# JOB OPPORTUNITIES IN ACCOUNTING

Accounting jobs fit into several classifications, including general accountants, bookkeepers, accounting clerks, and other office workers. An increasing amount of accounting work is done using computers. However, the estimated future increase in the use of computers does not appear to be decreasing the need for all kinds of accounting personnel. Computer operators are needed in addition to accounting personnel.

**Accountants.** Accountants plan, summarize, analyze, and interpret accounting information. Some accountants, referred to as public accountants, work as members of accounting firms that sell accounting services to other businesses. Private accountants are employed by a single business.

> **SENIOR ACCOUNTANT.** Person with accounting degree and experience. Duties include general and cost accounting supervision.

> **ACCOUNTANT.** Local business needs an accountant to supervise all accounting functions.

**Bookkeepers.** Bookkeepers do general accounting work plus some summarizing and analyzing of accounting information. In some businesses bookkeepers may supervise the work of accounting clerks. In small to medium-size businesses, bookkeepers may also help owners and managers interpret accounting information. Often these smaller businesses employ a public accountant to plan the accounting system.

> **FULL CHARGE BOOKKEEPER** Work without supervision. Experience in general ledger and payroll.

> **BOOKKEEPER-CLERICAL** Accounts receivable, general office, typing a must.

**Accounting clerks.** If a business has a large amount of accounting information to be recorded, accounting clerks may be employed to record, sort, and file accounting data. Accounting clerks are often given a title, such as payroll clerk or accounts payable clerk, to describe the specific accounting activities they perform.

> **PAYROLL.** Opening for responsible payroll clerk. Coordination of all payroll activities. Salary depends on training and experience.

> **ACCOUNTS PAYABLE CLERK** Retail store. Automated systems. Will train right person.

**Other office workers.** Many other office clerks and computer operators perform some accounting tasks. Regardless of who completes the accounting activities, the work must be done according to established accounting concepts and procedures. Office workers with some knowledge of accounting will better understand the importance of the accounting tasks they complete.

**SECRETARY.** Require 4 yrs secretarial expr., word processing, type 50 wpm, 1 yr bookkeeping training or experience in similar position.

**TYPIST.** For all phases of office work. Bookkeeping training or experience desirable.

# A CAREER IN ACCOUNTING

The following career ladder represents the educational requirements and promotional possibilities in accounting careers.

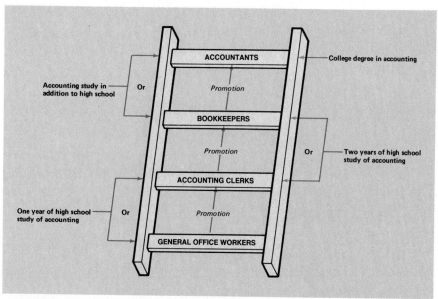

Immediately after high school graduation, individuals may start an accounting career as accounting clerks or general office workers. A few of the better students may start as bookkeepers. High school study in accounting is useful as preparation for these accounting positions. The study of high school accounting also is good preparation for the study of accounting in college.

Almost all persons seeking positions as accountants must complete some study of accounting beyond high school and must gain accounting experience. Most professional accountants also earn the Certified Public Accountant (CPA) designation. Each state sets the standards for earning a CPA certificate. Usually, the requirements include the study of college accounting, some accounting experience, and a passing score on a professional test covering all aspects of the accounting field.

With experience and additional accounting study, accounting personnel can earn promotion to higher positions on the career ladder.

# Accounting for a Service Business

**1**

### GENERAL BEHAVIORAL GOALS

1. Know accounting terminology related to an accounting system for a service business organized as a proprietorship.
2. Understand accounting practices related to an accounting system for a service business organized as a proprietorship.
3. Demonstrate accounting procedures used in an accounting system for a service business organized as a proprietorship.

# RUGCARE
## Chart of Accounts

The chart of accounts for Rugcare is illustrated
above for ready reference as you study Part 1
of this textbook.

# Starting a Proprietorship

ENABLING PERFORMANCE TASKS

After studying Chapter 1, you will be able to:
a. Define accounting terms related to starting a service business organized as a proprietorship.
b. Identify accounting concepts and practices related to starting a service business organized as a proprietorship.
c. Classify accounts as assets, liabilities, or owner's equity.
d. Analyze how transactions related to starting a service business organized as a proprietorship affect accounts in an accounting equation.
e. Prepare a balance sheet for a service business organized as a proprietorship from information in an accounting equation.

Many decisions are made during a person's lifetime. One important decision is how to earn a living. A person may work for others or start a new business. When a person chooses to start a business, that person must make many decisions. To make these decisions, a businessperson needs much information about the business. To provide the information, many records relating to the business must be kept.

## STARTING A NEW ACCOUNTING SYSTEM

A successful business is involved in numerous financial activities. Summary reports of these financial activities are needed by several people. These reports provide the information to help the owners and managers make business decisions. *How much should be charged for the product or service? Are profits sufficient? Should new products be sold? Should new services be provided? Can costs be decreased?* The business' banker uses these reports to make loan decisions. *How much should the bank allow the business to borrow? Is the business likely to be able to repay the loan?* The government requires that the business report financial information when it pays taxes.

In order to create useful reports, financial information must be maintained in an organized way. Planning, recording, analyzing, and interpreting financial information is called accounting. A planned process for providing financial information that will be useful to management is called an accounting system. Organized summaries of a business' financial activities are called accounting records.

## THE BUSINESS

A business that performs an activity for a fee is called a service business. Ben Furman worked for a service business that cleans carpets for a fee. Mr. Furman wants to be in control of his hours and his earnings. Therefore, he decided to start his own carpet-cleaning business. A business owned by one person is called a proprietorship. A proprietorship is also known as a sole proprietorship. Mr. Furman has named his new proprietorship *Rugcare*. Rugcare will rent office space and the equipment used to operate the business.

Since a new business is being started, Mr. Furman must design the accounting system that will be used to keep Rugcare's accounting records. In the accounting system, Mr. Furman must be careful to keep Rugcare's accounting records separate from his own personal financial records. For example, Mr. Furman owns a house and a personal car. Rugcare's financial records must *not* include information about Mr. Furman's house, car, or other personal belongings. For example, Mr. Furman must use one checking account for his personal expenses and another checking account for Rugcare. The financial records for Rugcare and Mr. Furman's personal belongings must be kept separate. The accounting concept, *Business Entity*, is applied when a business' financial information is recorded and reported separately from the owner's personal financial information. *(CONCEPT: Business Entity)*

Accounting concepts are described throughout this textbook when an application of a concept first occurs. When additional applications occur, a concept reference, such as *(CONCEPT: Business Entity)*, indicates an application of a specific accounting concept. A brief description of each accounting concept used in this text is also provided in Appendix A.

## THE ACCOUNTING EQUATION

A business has many items that have value. Rugcare will own items such as cash and supplies that will be used to conduct daily operations. Anything of value that is owned is called an asset. Assets have value because they can be used to acquire other assets or be used to operate a business. For example, Rugcare will use cash to buy supplies for the business.

Rugcare will then use the asset, supplies, in the operation of the rug-cleaning business.

Financial rights to the assets of a business are called equities. A business has two types of equities. (1) Equity of those to whom money is owed. For example, Rugcare may buy some supplies and agree to pay for the supplies at a later date. The business from whom supplies are bought will have a right to some of Rugcare's assets until Rugcare pays for the supplies. An amount owed by a business is called a liability. (2) Equity of the owner. Mr. Furman will own Rugcare and invest in the assets of the business. Therefore, he will have a right to decide how the assets will be used. The amount remaining after the value of all liabilities is subtracted from the value of all assets is called owner's equity.

The relationship among assets, liabilities, and owner's equity can be written as an equation. An equation showing the relationship among assets, liabilities, and owner's equity is called the accounting equation. The accounting equation is most often stated as:

$$Assets = Liabilities + Owner's\ Equity$$

The accounting equation must be in balance to be correct. Thus, the total of the amounts on the left side of the equation must always equal the total of the amounts on the right side. Before Mr. Furman actually starts the business, Rugcare's accounting equation would show the following amounts.

| Assets | = | Liabilities + Owner's Equity |
|---|---|---|
| Left side amount | | Right side amounts |
| $0 | = | $0  +  $0 |

## HOW BUSINESS ACTIVITIES CHANGE THE ACCOUNTING EQUATION

Business activities change the amounts in the accounting equation. A business activity that changes assets, liabilities, or owner's equity is called a transaction. For example, a business that pays cash for supplies is engaging in a transaction. After each transaction, the accounting equation must remain in balance.

The accounting concept, *Unit of Measurement*, is applied when business transactions are stated in numbers that have common values — that is, using a common unit of measurement. *(CONCEPT: Unit of Measurement)* For example, in the United States, business transactions are recorded in dollars. In Switzerland, business transactions are recorded in Swiss francs. The unit of measurement concept is followed so that the financial reports of businesses can be clearly stated and understood in numbers that have comparable values. For example, reports would not be clear if some information was reported in United States dollars and some in Swiss francs.

## Received cash from owner as an investment

Mr. Furman uses $10,000.00 of his own money to invest in Rugcare. Rugcare should only be concerned with the effect of this transaction on Rugcare's records. The business should *not* be concerned about Mr. Furman's personal records. *(CONCEPT: Business Entity)*

*Transaction 1.*
*August 1, 19--.*
*Received cash from owner as an investment, $10,000.00.*

A record summarizing all the information pertaining to a single item in the accounting equation is called an account. The name given to an account is called an account title. Each part of the accounting equation consists of one or more accounts. For example, one of the asset accounts is titled Cash. The cash account is used to summarize information about the amount of money the business has available.

In the accounting equation shown in Illustration 1-1, the asset account, Cash, is increased by $10,000.00, the amount of cash received by the business. This increase is on the left side of the accounting equation. The amount in an account is called the account balance. Before the owner's investment, the account balance of Cash was zero. After the owner's investment, the account balance of Cash is $10,000.00.

| | Assets | = | Liabilities | + | Owner's Equity |
|---|---|---|---|---|---|
| | Cash | = | | | Ben Furman, Capital |
| Beg. Balances | $0 | | $0 | | $0 |
| Transaction 1 | +10,000 | | | | +10,000 (investment) |
| New Balances | $10,000 | | $0 | | $10,000 |

Illustration 1-1
Receiving cash from owner as an investment changes one asset and owner's equity

The account used to summarize the owner's equity in business is called capital. The capital account is an owner's equity account. Rugcare's capital account is titled Ben Furman, Capital. In the accounting equation shown in Illustration 1-1, the owner's equity account, Ben Furman, Capital, is increased by $10,000.00. This increase is on the right side of the accounting equation. Before the owner's investment, the account balance of Ben Furman, Capital was zero. After the owner's investment, the account balance of Ben Furman, Capital is $10,000.00.

The accounting equation has changed as a result of the receipt of cash as the owner's investment. However, both sides of the equation are changed by the same amount, $10,000.00. The $10,000.00 increase on the left side of the equation equals the $10,000.00 increase on the right side of the equation. Therefore, the accounting equation is still in balance.

## Paid cash for supplies

Rugcare needs supplies to operate the business. Ben Furman uses some of Rugcare's cash to buy supplies.

*Transaction 2.*
*August 3, 19--.*
*Paid cash for supplies, $1,577.00.*

The effect of this transaction on the accounting equation is shown in Illustration 1-2. In this transaction, two asset accounts are changed. One asset, cash, has been exchanged for another asset, supplies. The asset account, Cash, is decreased by $1,577.00, the amount of cash paid out. This decrease is on the left side of the accounting equation. The asset account, Supplies, is increased by $1,577.00, the amount of supplies bought. This increase is also on the left side of the accounting equation.

For this transaction, two assets are changed. Therefore, the two changes are both on the left side of the accounting equation. When changes are made on only one side of the accounting equation, the equation must still be in balance. Therefore, if one account is increased, another account on the same side of the equation must be decreased. After this transaction, the new account balance of Cash is $8,423.00. The new account balance of Supplies is $1,577.00. The sum of the amounts on the left side is $10,000.00 (Cash, $8,423.00 + Supplies, $1,577.00). The amount on the right side is also $10,000.00. Therefore, the accounting equation is still in balance.

|  | Assets | | = | Liabilities + | Owner's Equity |
|---|---|---|---|---|---|
|  | Cash | + Supplies | = |  | Ben Furman, Capital |
| Balances | $10,000 | $0 |  | $0 | $10,000 |
| Transaction 2 | −1,577 | +1,577 |  |  |  |
| New Balances | $ 8,423 | $1,577 |  | $0 | $10,000 |

Total of left side:
$8,423 + $1,577 = $10,000

Total of right side:
$10,000

Illustration 1-2
Paying cash for supplies
changes two assets

## Paid cash for insurance

Insurance premiums must be paid in advance. For example, Rugcare pays a $1,200.00 insurance premium for future insurance coverage.

*Transaction 3.*
*August 4, 19--.*
*Paid cash for insurance, $1,200.00.*

In return for this payment, Rugcare is entitled to insurance coverage for the length of the policy. The insurance coverage is something of value owned by Rugcare. Therefore, the insurance coverage is an asset. Because insurance premiums are paid in advance, or *prepaid*, the premiums are recorded in an asset account titled Prepaid Insurance.

The effect of this transaction on the accounting equation is shown in Illustration 1-3. In this transaction, two assets are changed. One asset, cash, has been exchanged for another asset, prepaid insurance. The asset account, Cash, is decreased by $1,200.00, the amount of cash paid out. This decrease is on the left side of the accounting equation. The asset account, Prepaid Insurance, is increased by $1,200.00, the amount of insurance bought. This increase is also on the left side of the accounting equation.

|  | Assets | | | = Liabilities + | Owner's Equity |
|---|---|---|---|---|---|
|  | Cash + | Supplies + | Prepaid Insurance = | | Ben Furman, Capital |
| Balances | $8,423 | $1,577 | $0 | $0 | $10,000 |
| Transaction 3 | −1,200 | | +1,200 | | |
| New Balances | $7,223 | $1,577 | $1,200 | $0 | $10,000 |

Total of left side:
$7,223 + $1,577 + $1,200 = $10,000

Total of right side:
$10,000

Illustration 1-3
Paying cash for
insurance
changes two assets

Since two assets are changed by this transaction, both changes are on the left side of the accounting equation. Since one account is increased, the other account on the same side of the equation must be decreased. After this transaction, the new account balance of Cash is $7,223.00. The new account balance of Prepaid Insurance is $1,200.00. The sum of the amounts on the left side is $10,000.00 (Cash, $7,223.00 + Supplies, $1,577.00 + Prepaid Insurance, $1,200.00). The amount on the right side is also $10,000.00. Therefore, the accounting equation is still in balance.

## Bought supplies on account

Rugcare needs to buy additional supplies. The supplies are obtained from Butler Cleaning Supplies, which is located in a different city. It is a common business practice to buy items and pay for them at a future date. Another way to state this activity is to say that these items are bought *on account*.

*Transaction 4.*
*August 7, 19--.*
*Bought supplies on account from Butler Cleaning Supplies, $2,720.00.*

The effect of this transaction on the accounting equation is shown in Illustration 1-4. In this transaction, one asset and one liability are changed.

| | Assets | | | = Liabilities | + Owner's Equity |
|---|---|---|---|---|---|
| | Cash + | Supplies + | Prepaid Insurance = | Butler Cleaning Supplies + | Ben Furman, Capital |
| Balances | $7,223 | $1,577 | $1,200 | $0 | $10,000 |
| Transaction 4 | | +2,720 | | +2,720 | |
| New Balances | $7,223 | $4,297 | $1,200 | $2,720 | $10,000 |

Total of left side:
$7,223 + $4,297 + $1,200 = $12,720

Total of right side:
$2,720 + $10,000 = $12,720

The asset account, Supplies, is increased by $2,720.00, the amount of supplies bought. This increase is on the left side of the accounting equation. Butler Cleaning Supplies will have a claim against some of Rugcare's assets until Rugcare pays for the supplies bought. Therefore, Butler Cleaning Supplies is a liability account. The liability account, Butler Cleaning Supplies, is increased by $2,720.00, the amount owed for the supplies. This increase is on the right side of the accounting equation.

Illustration 1-4
Buying supplies on account changes one asset and one liability

This transaction changes both sides of the accounting equation. When changes are made on both sides of the equation, the change on the left side must equal the change on the right side. After this transaction, the new account balance of Supplies is $4,297.00. The new account balance of Butler Cleaning Supplies is $2,720.00. The sum of the amounts on the left side is $12,720.00 (Cash, $7,223.00 + Supplies, $4,297.00 + Prepaid Insurance, $1,200.00). The sum of the amounts on the right side is also $12,720.00 (Butler Cleaning Supplies, $2,720.00 + Ben Furman, Capital, $10,000.00). Therefore, the accounting equation is still in balance.

## Paid cash on account

Since Rugcare is a new business, Butler Cleaning Supplies has not done business with Rugcare before. Butler Cleaning Supplies allows Rugcare to buy supplies on account but requires Rugcare to send a check for one-half of the amount immediately. Rugcare will pay the remaining liability at a later date.

*Transaction 5.*
*August 11, 19--.*
*Paid cash on account to Butler Cleaning Supplies, $1,360.00.*

The effect of this transaction on the accounting equation is shown in Illustration 1-5. In this transaction, one asset and one liability are changed. The asset account, Cash, is decreased by $1,360.00, the amount of cash paid out. This decrease is on the left side of the accounting equation. After this payment, Rugcare owes less money to Butler Cleaning Supplies. Therefore, the liability account, Butler Cleaning Supplies, is decreased by $1,360.00, the

| | Assets | | | = Liabilities + Owner's Equity | | |
|---|---|---|---|---|---|---|
| | | | Prepaid | Butler Cleaning | | Ben Furman, |
| | Cash + | Supplies + | Insurance = | Supplies | + | Capital |
| Balances | $7,223 | $4,297 | $1,200 | $2,720 | | $10,000 |
| Transaction 5 | −1,360 | | | −1,360 | | |
| New Balances | $5,863 | $4,297 | $1,200 | $1,360 | | $10,000 |

Total of left side:  
$5,863 + $4,297 + $1,200 = $11,360

Total of right side:  
$1,360 + $10,000 = $11,360

Illustration 1-5
Paying cash on account
changes one asset and one
liability

amount paid on account. This decrease is on the right side of the accounting equation.

This transaction changes both sides of the accounting equation. When changes are made on both sides of the equation, the change on the left side must equal the change on the right side. After this transaction, the new account balance of Cash is $5,863.00. The new account balance of Butler Cleaning Supplies is $1,360.00. The sum of the amounts on the left side is $11,360.00 (Cash, $5,863.00 + Supplies, $4,297.00 + Prepaid Insurance, $1,200.00). The sum of the amounts on the right side is also $11,360.00 (Butler Cleaning Supplies, $1,360.00 + Ben Furman, Capital, $10,000.00). Therefore, the accounting equation is still in balance.

## REPORTING FINANCIAL INFORMATION ON A BALANCE SHEET

Periodically a business reports details about its assets, liabilities, and owner's equity. The financial details about assets, liabilities, and owner's equity could be found on the last line of the accounting equation. However, most businesses prepare more formal financial statements that may be copied and sent to interested persons. A financial statement that reports assets, liabilities, and owner's equity on a specific date is called a balance sheet.

When a business is started, it is expected that the business will continue to operate indefinitely. For example, Ben Furman assumes that he will own and operate Rugcare for many years. When he retires, he expects to sell Rugcare to someone else who will continue its operation. The accounting concept, *Going Concern*, is applied when financial statements are prepared with the expectation that a business will remain in operation indefinitely. *(CONCEPT: Going Concern)*

### Body of a balance sheet

A balance sheet has three major sections. (1) *Assets* are on the left side of the accounting equation. Therefore, Rugcare lists its assets on the left side of the balance sheet. (2) *Liabilities* are on the right side of the accounting equation. Therefore, Rugcare lists its liabilities on the right side of the balance sheet. (3) *Owner's equity* is also on the right side of the accounting equation. Therefore, Rugcare lists its owner's equity on the right side of the balance sheet.

Rugcare's balance sheet, prepared after the transaction on August 11, is shown in Illustration 1-6.

| | Assets | | = Liabilities | + Owner's Equity |
|---|---|---|---|---|
| | Cash + Supplies + | Prepaid Insurance = | Butler Cleaning Supplies + | Ben Furman, Capital |
| Balances | $5,863      $4,297 | $1,200 | $1,360 | $10,000 |

**Rugcare**
**Balance Sheet**
**August 11, 19--**

| Assets | | Liabilities | |
|---|---|---|---|
| Cash | 5 8 6 3 00 | Butler Cleaning Supplies | 1 3 6 0 00 |
| Supplies | 4 2 9 7 00 | *Owner's Equity* | |
| Prepaid Insurance | 1 2 0 0 00 | Ben Furman, Capital | 10 0 0 0 00 |
| Total Assets | 11 3 6 0 00 | Total Liab. and Owner's Eq. | 11 3 6 0 00 |

Illustration 1-6
Balance sheet for a service business organized as a proprietorship

## Preparing a balance sheet

Rugcare's balance sheet is prepared in six steps.

1  Write the *heading* on three lines at the top of the balance sheet. Center each line. The heading for Rugcare's balance sheet is:

*Name of the business:*    Rugcare
*Name of the report:*      Balance Sheet
*Date of the report:*      August 11, 19--

2  Prepare the *assets section* on the LEFT side. Center the word *Assets* on the first line of the wide column on the left side. Under this heading, write each asset account title and amount. The asset accounts are: Cash, $5,863.00; Supplies, $4,297.00; and Prepaid Insurance, $1,200.00.

3  Prepare the *liabilities section* on the RIGHT side. Center the word *Liabilities* on the first line of the wide column on the right side. Under this heading, write each liability account title and amount. Rugcare has only one liability account to be listed, Butler Cleaning Supplies, $1,360.00.

4　Prepare the *owner's equity section* on the RIGHT side. Center the words *Owner's Equity* on the next blank line of the wide column on the right side. Under this heading, write the owner's equity account title and amount. Rugcare's owner's equity account is Ben Furman, Capital, $10,000.00.

5　Determine if the balance sheet is *in balance*. Use a calculator, if available, or a sheet of scratch paper. Add all the asset amounts on the LEFT side. The total on the left side of Rugcare's balance sheet is $11,360.00 ($5,863.00 + $4,297.00 + $1,200.00). Add the liabilities and owner's equity amounts on the RIGHT side. The total on the right side of Rugcare's balance sheet is $11,360.00 ($1,360.00 + $10,000.00). The total of the LEFT side is the same as the total of the RIGHT side, $11,360.00. Therefore, Rugcare's balance sheet is in balance.

　　If the balance sheet is NOT in balance, find the errors before completing any more work.

6　*Complete* the balance sheet. Rule a single line across both amount columns. A single line means that amounts are to be added or subtracted. On the next line, write *Total Assets* in the wide column on the left side. On the same line, write the total asset amount, $11,360.00, in the left amount column. On the same line, write *Total Liabilities and Owner's Equity* in the wide column on the right side. On the same line, write the total liabilities and owner's equity amount, $11,360.00, in the right amount column. Rule double lines below the amount column totals. Double lines mean that the totals have been verified as correct.

　　When possible, words are spelled in full so there can be no doubt about what word was intended. However, in a few situations, where there is insufficient room to spell the words in full, words may be abbreviated. On Rugcare's balance sheet, it is necessary to abbreviate the words *Total Liab. and Owner's Eq.*

## SUMMARY OF HOW TRANSACTIONS CHANGE THE ACCOUNTING EQUATION

Changes in the accounting equation caused by Transactions 1 to 5 are summarized in Illustration 1-7.

Four basic rules relate to how transactions affect the accounting equation.

1. Each transaction changes at least two accounts in the accounting equation.
2. When all the changes occur on one side of the accounting equation, increases on that side must be matched by decreases on the same side. In Illustration 1-7, Transactions 2 and 3 are examples of this rule.
3. When a transaction increases one side of the accounting equation, the other side of the equation must also be increased by the same amount. Transactions 1 and 4 are examples of this rule.

4. When a transaction decreases one side of the accounting equation, the other side of the equation must also be decreased by the same amount. Transaction 5 is an example of this rule.

Illustration 1-7
Summary of how transactions change the accounting equation

| Transaction | Assets | | | = Liabilities + | Owner's Equity |
|---|---|---|---|---|---|
| | Cash | + Supplies + | Prepaid Insurance | = Butler Cleaning + Supplies | Ben Furman, Capital |
| Beginning Balance | $0 | $0 | $0 | $0 | $0 |
| 1. Received cash from owner as an investment | +10,000 | | | | +10,000 (investment) |
| New Balances | $10,000 | $0 | $0 | $0 | $10,000 |
| 2. Paid cash for supplies | −1,577 | +1,577 | | | |
| New Balances | $8,423 | $1,577 | $0 | $0 | $10,000 |
| 3. Paid cash for insurance | −1,200 | | +1,200 | | |
| New Balances | $7,223 | $1,577 | $1,200 | $0 | $10,000 |
| 4. Bought supplies on account | | +2,720 | | +2,720 | |
| New Balances | $7,223 | $4,297 | $1,200 | $2,720 | $10,000 |
| 5. Paid cash on account | −1,360 | | | −1,360 | |
| New Balances | $5,863 | $4,297 | $1,200 | $1,360 | $10,000 |

Total of left side:
$5,863 + $4,297 + $1,200 = $11,360

Total of right side:
$1,360 + $10,000 = $11,360

## ■ ACCOUNTING TERMS

What is the meaning of each of the following?

1. accounting
2. accounting system
3. accounting records
4. service business
5. proprietorship
6. asset

7. equities
8. liability
9. owner's equity
10. accounting equation
11. transaction

12. account
13. account title
14. account balance
15. capital
16. balance sheet

## ■ QUESTIONS FOR INDIVIDUAL STUDY

1. How are financial reports used by business owners and managers?
2. How are financial reports used by a business' banker?
3. Which accounting concept is being applied when a business records and reports financial information separate from the owner's personal financial information?
4. What are the two types of equities of a business?
5. What is the accounting equation?

6. What must be true about the accounting equation after each transaction?

7. Which accounting concept is being applied when a business in the United States reports financial information in dollars?

8. What accounts are affected, and how, when the owner invests cash in a business?

9. What accounts are affected, and how, when a business pays cash for supplies?

10. Why is Prepaid Insurance an asset?

11. How are liabilities affected when a business buys supplies on account?

12. How are liabilities affected when a business pays cash for a liability?

13. Which accounting concept is being applied when financial statements are prepared with the expectation that a business will remain in operation indefinitely?

14. What are the three major sections of a balance sheet?

15. What three items are included in the heading of a balance sheet?

16. What six steps are followed in preparing a balance sheet?

17. What do double lines below a column total mean?

18. What are the four basic rules relating to how transactions affect the accounting equation?

## ■ CASES FOR MANAGEMENT DECISION

**CASE 1** James Patton starts a new business. Mr. Patton uses his personal car in the business with the expectation that later the business can buy a car. All expenses for operating the car, including license plates, gasoline, oil, tune-ups, and new tires, are paid for out of business funds. Is this an acceptable procedure? Explain.

**CASE 2** At the end of the first day of business, Quick Clean Laundry has the following assets and liabilities:

| Assets | |
|---|---|
| Cash | $3,500.00 |
| Supplies | 950.00 |
| Prepaid Insurance | 1,200.00 |
| Liabilities | |
| Smith Office Supplies | $ 750.00 |
| Super Supplies Company | 1,500.00 |

The owner, Susan Whiteford, wants to know the amount of her equity in Quick Clean Laundry. Determine this amount and explain what this amount represents.

## ■ DRILLS FOR UNDERSTANDING

### DRILL 1-D1   Classifying assets, liabilities, and owner's equity

Use a form similar to the following.

| Item | Asset | Liability | Owner's Equity |
|---|:---:|:---:|:---:|
| 1. Cash | ✓ | | |

**Instructions:** Classify each item listed below as an asset, liability, or owner's equity. Place a check mark in the appropriate column. Item 1 is given as an example.

1. Cash
2. Alice Jones, Capital
3. Prepaid Insurance
4. Steward Supply Company
5. Supplies
6. Any amount owed
7. Owner's capital account
8. Anything owned

## DRILL 1-D2  Determining how transactions change an accounting equation

Use a form similar to the following.

| Trans. No. | Assets | = | Liabilities | + | Owner's Equity |
|------------|--------|---|-------------|---|----------------|
| 1. | + | | + | | |

*Transactions*
1. Bought supplies on account.
2. Paid cash for insurance.
3. Received cash from owner as an investment.
4. Paid cash for supplies.
5. Paid cash on account to Konroy Company.

**Instructions:** Decide which classification(s) are changed by each transaction. Place a plus (+) in the appropriate column if the classification is increased. Place a minus (−) in the appropriate column if the classification is decreased. Transaction 1 is given as an example.

## DRILL 1-D3  Determining where items are listed on a balance sheet

Use a form similar to the following.

| 1 | 2 | 3 |
|---|---|---|
| **Items** | **Balance Sheet** | |
| | **Left Side** | **Right Side** |
| 1. Cash | *Asset* | |

**Instructions:** Classify each item as an asset, liability, or owner's equity. Write the classification in Column 2 or 3 to show where each item is listed on a balance sheet. Item 1 is given as an example.

1. Cash
2. Gretchen Murphy, Capital
3. Supplies
4. Prepaid Insurance
5. Action Laundry
6. Anything owned
7. Any amount owed
8. Owner's capital account

# ■ APPLICATION PROBLEMS

## PROBLEM 1-1  Determining how transactions change an accounting equation

Frank March is starting March Repair Shop, a small service business. March Repair Shop uses the accounts shown in the following accounting equation. Use a form similar to the following to complete this problem.

| Trans. No. | Assets | | | = | Liabilities | | + Owner's Equity |
|---|---|---|---|---|---|---|---|
| | Cash + | Supplies + | Prepaid Insurance | = | Swan's Supply Company + | York Company + | Frank March, Capital |
| Beg. Bal. | 0 | 0 | 0 | | 0 | 0 | 0 |
| 1. | +2,000 | | | | | | +2,000 (investment) |
| New Bal. 2. | 2,000 | 0 | 0 | | 0 | 0 | 2,000 |

*Transactions*

1. Received cash from owner as an investment, $2,000.00.
2. Paid cash for insurance, $600.00.
3. Bought supplies on account from Swan's Supply Company, $100.00.
4. Bought supplies on account from York Company, $500.00.
5. Paid cash on account to Swan's Supply Company, $100.00.
6. Paid cash on account to York Company, $300.00.
7. Paid cash for supplies, $500.00.
8. Received cash from owner as an investment, $500.00.

**Instructions:** For each transaction, complete the following. Transaction 1 is given as an example.

a. Analyze the transaction to determine which accounts in the accounting equation are affected.
b. Write the amount in the appropriate columns using a plus (+) if the account increases or a minus (−) if the account decreases.
c. For transactions that change owner's equity, write in parentheses a description of the transaction to the right of the amount.
d. Calculate the new balance for each account in the accounting equation.
e. Before going on to the next transaction, determine that the accounting equation is still in balance.

## PROBLEM 1-2  Preparing a balance sheet from information in an accounting equation

On September 30 the Steffens Company's accounting equation indicated the following account balances.

| Trans. No. | Assets | | | = | Liabilities | + | Owner's Equity |
|---|---|---|---|---|---|---|---|
| | Cash + | Supplies + | Prepaid Insurance | = | Morton Company | + | Steve Steffens, Capital |
| New Bal. | 1,200 | 150 | 300 | | 250 | | 1,400 |

**Instructions:** Using the September 30 balance in the accounting equation, prepare a balance sheet for the Steffens Company.

## PROBLEM 1-3  Determining how transactions change an accounting equation and preparing a balance sheet

Nancy Dirks is starting Dirks Company, a small service business. Dirks Company uses the accounts shown in the following accounting equation. Use a form similar to the following to complete this problem.

| Trans. No. | Assets | | | = Liabilities | + Owner's Equity |
| --- | --- | --- | --- | --- | --- |
| | Cash + | Supplies + | Prepaid Insurance | = Helfrey Company | + Nancy Dirks, Capital |
| Beg. Bal. 1. | 0 +350 | 0 | 0 | 0 | 0 +350 (investment) |
| New Bal. 2. | 350 | 0 | 0 | 0 | 350 |

*Transactions*
1. Received cash from owner as an investment, $350.00.
2. Bought supplies on account from Helfrey Company, $100.00.
3. Paid cash for insurance, $150.00.
4. Paid cash for supplies, $50.00.
5. Received cash from owner as an investment, $300.00.
6. Paid cash on account to Helfrey Company, $75.00.

**Instructions: 1.** For each transaction, complete the following. Transaction 1 is given as an example.
a. Analyze the transaction to determine which accounts in the accounting equation are affected.
b. Write the amount in the appropriate columns, using a plus (+) if the account increases or a minus (−) if the account decreases.
c. For transactions that change owner's equity, write in parentheses a description of the transaction to the right of the amount.
d. Calculate the new balance for each account in the accounting equation.
e. Before going on to the next transaction, determine that the accounting equation is still in balance.
**2.** Using the final balances in the accounting equation, prepare a balance sheet. Use July 31 of the current year as the date of the balance sheet.

# ■ ENRICHMENT PROBLEMS

**MASTERY PROBLEM 1-M**   **Determining how transactions change an accounting equation and preparing a balance sheet**

Gregory Morgan is starting a limousine service called Luxury Limo. Luxury Limo uses the accounts shown in the following accounting equation. Use a form similar to the following to complete this problem.

| Trans. No. | Assets | | | = Liabilities | + Owner's Equity |
| --- | --- | --- | --- | --- | --- |
| | Cash + | Supplies + | Prepaid Insurance | = Limo Supply Company | + Gregory Morgan, Capital |
| Beg. Bal. 1. | 0 +2,000 | 0 | 0 | 0 | 0 +2,000 (investment) |
| New Bal. 2. | 2,000 | 0 | 0 | 0 | 2,000 |

*Transactions*

1. Received cash from owner as an investment, $2,000.00.
2. Paid cash for supplies, $250.00.
3. Bought supplies on account from Limo Supply Company, $300.00.
4. Paid cash for insurance, $600.00.
5. Paid cash on account to Limo Supply Company, $150.00.

**Instructions: 1.** For each transaction, complete the following. Transaction 1 is given as an example.

a. Analyze the transaction to determine which accounts in the accounting equation are affected.

b. Write the amount in the appropriate columns, using a plus ( + ) if the account increases or a minus (−) if the account decreases.

c. For transactions that change owner's equity, write in parentheses a description of the transaction to the right of the amount.

d. Calculate the new balance for each account in the accounting equation.

e. Before going on to the next transaction, determine that the accounting equation is still in balance.

**2.** Using the final balances in the accounting equation, prepare a balance sheet. Use February 5 of the current year as the date of the balance sheet.

**CHALLENGE PROBLEM 1-C**   **Applying accounting concepts to determine how transactions change the accounting equation**

Olson Delivery Service, a new business owned by Jerome Olson, uses the accounts shown in the following accounting equation. Use a form similar to the following to complete this problem.

| Trans. No. | Assets | | | = | Liabilities | | | + | Owner's Equity |
|---|---|---|---|---|---|---|---|---|---|
| | Cash + | Supplies + | Prepaid Insur. | = | Mutual Savings Bank | + | Nelson Supply Co. | + | Jerome Olson, Capital |
| Beg. Bal. | 0 | 0 | 0 | | 0 | | 0 | | 0 |
| 1. | +1,500 | | | | | | | | +1,500 (investment) |
| New Bal. | 1,500 | 0 | 0 | | 0 | | 0 | | 1,500 |
| 2. | | | | | | | | | |

*Transactions*

1. Received cash from owner as an investment, $1,500.00.
2. Paid cash for supplies, $400.00.
3. Paid cash for insurance, $240.00.
4. Bought supplies on account from Nelson Supply Company, $80.00.
5. The owner, Jerome Olson, paid $1,000.00 of his personal cash to Mutual Savings Bank for the car payment on his personal car.
6. Paid cash for supplies. The supplies were bought from a Canadian company. The supplies cost $120.00 in Canadian dollars, which is equivalent to $100.00 in United States dollars.

**Instructions:** For each transaction, complete the following. Transaction 1 is given as an example.

a. Analyze the transaction to determine which business accounts in the accounting equation, if any, are affected. You will need to apply the Business Entity and Unit of Measurement concepts in this problem.

b. If business accounts are affected, determine the appropriate amount of the change. Write the amount in the appropriate columns, using a plus (+) if the account increases or a minus (−) if the account decreases.

c. For transactions that change owner's equity, write in parentheses a description of the transaction to the right of the amount.

d. Calculate the new balance for each account in the accounting equation.

e. Before going on to the next transaction, determine that the accounting equation is still in balance.

# Starting a Proprietorship: Changes That Affect Owner's Equity

ENABLING PERFORMANCE TASKS

After studying Chapter 2, you will be able to:
a. Define accounting terms related to changes that affect owner's equity for a service business organized as a proprietorship.
b. Identify accounting concepts and practices related to changes that affect owner's equity for a service business organized as a proprietorship.
c. Analyze changes that affect owner's equity for a service business organized as a proprietorship in an accounting equation.
d. Prepare a balance sheet for a service business organized as a proprietorship from information in the accounting equation.

A business activity that changes assets, liabilities, or owner's equity is known as a transaction. Chapter 1 describes five transactions involved in starting Rugcare, a proprietorship. Rugcare is now ready to open for business. This chapter presents the transactions that commonly occur during the daily operations of a business. Each of these transactions changes Ben Furman's equity in Rugcare.

## HOW TRANSACTIONS CHANGE OWNER'S EQUITY IN AN ACCOUNTING EQUATION

The accounting equation for Rugcare as of August 11, showing the effect of transactions for starting a business, is shown in Illustration 2-1.

The sum of the balances on the left side of the accounting equation, $11,360.00, equals the sum of the balances on the right side of the equation, $11,360.00. The equation is in balance.

Many transactions involved in the daily operations of a business increase or decrease owner's equity. Detailed information about these

| | Assets | | | = Liabilities + | Owner's Equity |
|---|---|---|---|---|---|
| | Cash + | Supplies + | Prepaid Insurance = | Butler Cleaning Supplies + | Ben Furman, Capital |
| Balances | $5,863 | $4,297 | $1,200 | $1,360 | $10,000 |

Total of left side:
$5,863 + $4,297 + $1,200 = $11,360

Total of right side:
$1,360 + $10,000 = $11,360

changes in owner's equity is needed by owners and managers to make sound business decisions.

Illustration 2-1
Accounting equation after transactions for starting a proprietorship

## Received cash from sales

A transaction for the sale of goods or services results in an increase in owner's equity. An increase in owner's equity resulting from the operation of a business is called revenue. When cash is received from a sale, the total amount of assets and owner's equity is increased.

When Rugcare receives cash for services performed, two accounts in the accounting equation are affected. The asset account, Cash, is increased by the amount of cash received. The owner's equity account, Ben Furman, Capital, is increased by the same amount.

*Transaction 6.*
*August 12, 19--.*
*Received cash from sales, $525.00.*

The effect of this transaction on the accounting equation is shown in Illustration 2-2. The asset account, Cash, is increased by $525.00, the amount of cash received. This increase is on the left side of the equation. The owner's equity account, Ben Furman, Capital, is also increased by $525.00. This increase is on the right side of the equation.

| | Assets | | | = Liabilities + | Owner's Equity |
|---|---|---|---|---|---|
| | Cash + | Supplies + | Prepaid Insurance = | Butler Cleaning Supplies + | Ben Furman, Capital |
| Balances | $5,863 | $4,297 | $1,200 | $1,360 | $10,000 |
| Transaction 6 | +525 | | | | +525 (revenue) |
| New Balances | $6,388 | $4,297 | $1,200 | $1,360 | $10,525 |

Total of left side:
$6,388 + $4,297 + $1,200 = $11,885

Total of right side:
$1,360 + $10,525 = $11,885

After this transaction is recorded, the sum of the balances on the left side of the equation equals the sum of the balances on the right side, $11,885.00. The equation is still in balance.

Illustration 2-2
Receiving cash from sales increases assets and owner's equity

In this chapter, three different kinds of transactions that affect owner's equity are described. Therefore, a description of the transaction is shown in parentheses to the right of the amount in the accounting equation. Transaction 6 is a revenue transaction. Therefore, *(revenue)* is shown beside the $525.00 change in owner's equity in Illustration 2-2.

## Paid cash for expenses

A transaction to pay for goods or services needed to operate a business results in a decrease in owner's equity. A decrease in owner's equity resulting from the operation of a business is called an expense. When cash is paid for expenses, the business has less cash. Therefore, the asset account, Cash, is decreased. The owner's equity account, Ben Furman, Capital, is also decreased by the same amount.

*Transaction 7.*
*August 12, 19--.*
*Paid cash for rent, $250.00.*

The effect of this transaction on the accounting equation is shown in Illustration 2-3. The asset account, Cash, is decreased by $250.00, the amount of cash paid out. This decrease is on the left side of the equation. The owner's equity account, Ben Furman, Capital, is also decreased by $250.00. This decrease is on the right side of the equation.

|  | Assets | | | = Liabilities + | Owner's Equity |
|---|---|---|---|---|---|
|  | Cash + | Supplies + | Prepaid Insurance = | Butler Cleaning Supplies + | Ben Furman, Capital |
| Balances | $6,388 | $4,297 | $1,200 | $1,360 | $10,525 |
| Transaction 7 | −250 |  |  |  | −250 (expense) |
| New Balances | $6,138 | $4,297 | $1,200 | $1,360 | $10,275 |

Total of left side:
$6,138 + $4,297 + $1,200 = $11,635

Total of right side:
$1,360 + $10,275 = $11,635

Illustration 2-3
Paying cash for an
expense decreases assets
and owner's equity

After this transaction is recorded, the sum of the balances on the left side of the equation equals the sum of the balances on the right side, $11,635.00. The equation is still in balance.

*Transaction 8.*
*August 12, 19--.*
*Paid cash for telephone bill, $45.00.*

Most businesses must make payments for goods and services provided by public utilities, such as telephone companies. These goods and services are often referred to as utilities. In addition to telephone services, electricity, gas, water, and sanitation are also considered to be utilities.

The effect of this transaction on the accounting equation is shown in Illustration 2-4. The asset account, Cash, is decreased by $45.00, the amount of cash paid out. This decrease is on the left side of the equation. The owner's equity account, Ben Furman, Capital, is also decreased by $45.00. This decrease is on the right side of the equation.

Illustration 2-4
Paying cash for an expense decreases assets and owner's equity

| | Assets | | | = Liabilities + | Owner's Equity |
|---|---|---|---|---|---|
| | Cash + | Supplies + | Prepaid Insurance = | Butler Cleaning Supplies + | Ben Furman, Capital |
| Balances | $6,138 | $4,297 | $1,200 | $1,360 | $10,275 |
| Transaction 8 | −45 | | | | −45 (expense) |
| New Balances | $6,093 | $4,297 | $1,200 | $1,360 | $10,230 |

Total of left side:
$6,093 + $4,297 + $1,200 = $11,590

Total of right side:
$1,360 + $10,230 = $11,590

After this transaction is recorded, the sum of the balances on the left side of the equation equals the sum of the balances on the right side, $11,590.00. The equation is still in balance.

Other expense transactions might be for advertising, equipment rental or repairs, charitable contributions, and other miscellaneous items. All expense transactions affect the accounting equation in the same way as Transactions 7 and 8.

## Paid cash to owner for personal use

Assets taken out of a business for the owner's personal use are called withdrawals. A withdrawal decreases owner's equity. Although an owner may withdraw any kind of asset, usually an owner withdraws cash. The withdrawal decreases the account balance of the withdrawn asset, such as Cash.

*Transaction 9.*
*August 12, 19--.*
*Paid cash to owner for personal use, $100.00.*

The effect of this transaction on the accounting equation is shown in Illustration 2-5. The asset account, Cash, is decreased by $100.00, the amount of cash paid out. This decrease is on the left side of the accounting equation. The owner's equity account, Ben Furman, Capital, is also decreased by $100.00. This decrease is on the right side of the equation.

After this transaction is recorded, the sum of the balances on the left side of the equation equals the sum of the balances on the right side, $11,490.00. The equation is still in balance.

A decrease in owner's equity because of a withdrawal is not a result of the normal operations of a business. Therefore, a withdrawal is not an expense.

| | Assets | | | = Liabilities + | Owner's Equity |
|---|---|---|---|---|---|
| | | | | Butler | |
| | | | Prepaid | Cleaning | Ben Furman, |
| | Cash + | Supplies + | Insurance = | Supplies + | Capital |
| Balances | $6,093 | $4,297 | $1,200 | $1,360 | $10,230 |
| Transaction 9 | −100 | | | | −100 (withdrawal) |
| New Balances | $5,993 | $4,297 | $1,200 | $1,360 | $10,130 |

Total of left side:                                     Total of right side:
$5,993 + $4,297 + $1,200 = $11,490              $1,360 + $10,130 = $11,490

Illustration 2-5
Paying cash to owner for
personal use decreases
assets and owner's equity

## Summary of changes in owner's equity

After recording the transactions for starting Rugcare as a proprietor-ship, the total owner's equity was $10,000.00. Five transactions have af-fected owner's equity. In Chapter 1, Ben Furman made a $10,000.00 investment. In this chapter, four transactions that changed owner's equity were recorded in the accounting equation.

| Transaction Number | Kind of Transaction | Change in Owner's Equity |
|---|---|---|
| 6 | Revenue | +525.00 |
| 7 | Expense (rent) | −250.00 |
| 8 | Expense (telephone) | −45.00 |
| 9 | Withdrawal | −100.00 |
| | Net change in owner's equity | +130.00 |

A revenue transaction increased owner's equity. Expense and with-drawal transactions decreased owner's equity. These transactions together increased total owner's equity by $130.00, from $10,000.00 to $10,130.00.

> For a business to succeed, revenues must be greater than expenses dur-ing most periods of time. An established business should rarely experience a decrease in its owner's equity.

## REPORTING A CHANGED ACCOUNTING EQUATION ON A BALANCE SHEET

A balance sheet may be prepared on any date to report information about the assets, liabilities, and owner's equity of a business. The balance sheet prepared in Chapter 1, Illustration 1-6, reports Rugcare's financial condition at the end of business on August 11. The transactions recorded in Chapter 2 have changed the account balances of Cash and Ben Furman, Cap-ital in the accounting equation. A revised balance sheet is prepared to re-port Rugcare's financial condition after recording these transactions.

The last transaction on August 12 is recorded in the accounting equa-tion as shown in Illustration 2-5. The new account balances in the accounting equation after Transaction 9 are used to prepare the balance sheet. Rugcare's balance sheet as of August 12 is shown in Illustration 2-6.

The August 12 balance sheet is prepared using the same steps as described in Chapter 1.

| | Assets | | | = Liabilities + | Owner's Equity |
|---|---|---|---|---|---|
| | Cash + | Supplies + | Prepaid Insurance = | Butler Cleaning Supplies | Ben Furman, Capital |
| New Balances | $5,993 | $4,297 | $1,200 | $1,360 | $10,130 |

| Rugcare | | | | | |
|---|---|---|---|---|---|
| Balance Sheet | | | | | |
| August 12, 19-- | | | | | |
| **Assets** | | | **Liabilities** | | |
| Cash | 5 9 9 3 00 | | Butler Cleaning Supplies | 1 3 6 0 00 | |
| Supplies | 4 2 9 7 00 | | *Owner's Equity* | | |
| Prepaid Insurance | 1 2 0 0 00 | | Ben Furman, Capital | 10 1 3 0 00 | |
| Total Assets | 11 4 9 0 00 | | Total Liab. and Owner's Eq. | 11 4 9 0 00 | |

Illustration 2-6
Balance sheet

The accounts on the left side of the accounting equation are reported on the left side of Rugcare's balance sheet. The accounts on the right side of the accounting equation are shown on the right side of the balance sheet. The total of the left side of the balance sheet, $11,490.00, is equal to the total of the right side of the balance sheet. The balance sheet is in balance.

A comparison of the August 11 and August 12 balance sheet totals is shown in Illustration 2-7.

| | Assets | | | = Liabilities + | Owner's Equity |
|---|---|---|---|---|---|
| | Cash + | Supplies + | Prepaid Insurance = | Butler Cleaning Supplies + | Ben Furman, Capital |
| August 11 | $5,863 | $4,297 | $1,200 | $1,360 | $10,000 |
| August 12 | $5,993 | $4,297 | $1,200 | $1,360 | $10,130 |
| | +$130 | $0 | $0 | $0 | +$130 |

Illustration 2-7
Comparison of balance sheet totals

The balance sheet has an increase of $130.00 on the left side (Assets) and an increase of $130.00 on the right side (Liabilities + Owner's Equity).

Few businesses need to prepare a balance sheet every day. Many businesses prepare a balance sheet only on the last day of each month. Monthly balance sheets provide business owners and managers with frequent and regular information for making business decisions.

| Transaction | Assets | | | = Liabilities + | Owner's Equity |
|---|---|---|---|---|---|
| | Cash + | Supplies + | Prepaid Insurance = | Butler Cleaning Supplies + | Ben Furman, Capital |
| Beginning Balance | $0 | $0 | $0 | $0 | $0 |
| 1. Received cash from owner as an investment | +10,000 | | | | +10,000 (investment) |
| New Balances | $10,000 | $0 | $0 | $0 | $10,000 |
| 2. Paid cash for supplies | −1,577 | +1,577 | | | |
| New Balances | $ 8,423 | $1,577 | $0 | $0 | $10,000 |
| 3. Paid cash for insurance | −1,200 | | +1,200 | | |
| New Balances | $ 7,223 | $1,577 | $1,200 | $0 | $10,000 |
| 4. Bought supplies on account | | +2,720 | | +2,720 | |
| New Balances | $ 7,223 | $4,297 | $1,200 | $2,720 | $10,000 |
| 5. Paid cash on account | −1,360 | | | −1,360 | |
| New Balances | $ 5,863 | $4,297 | $1,200 | $1,360 | $10,000 |
| 6. Received cash from sales | +525 | | | | +525 (revenue) |
| New Balances | $ 6,388 | $4,297 | $1,200 | $1,360 | $10,525 |
| 7. Paid cash for rent | −250 | | | | −250 (expense) |
| New Balances | $ 6,138 | $4,297 | $1,200 | $1,360 | $10,275 |
| 8. Paid cash for telephone bill | −45 | | | | −45 (expense) |
| New Balances | $ 6,093 | $4,297 | $1,200 | $1,360 | $10,230 |
| 9. Paid cash to owner for personal use | −100 | | | | −100 (withdrawal) |
| New Balances | $ 5,993 | $4,297 | $1,200 | $1,360 | $10,130 |

Illustration 2-8
Summary of how transactions affect the accounting equation

Total of left side:
$5,993 + $4,297 + $1,200 = $11,490

Total of right side:
$1,360 + $10,130 = $11,490

# SUMMARY OF TRANSACTIONS THAT AFFECT OWNER'S EQUITY

Revenue, expense, and withdrawal transactions affect owner's equity. A revenue transaction increases owner's equity. Expense and withdrawal transactions decrease owner's equity.

The accounting equation has two sides. The left side of the equation shows assets. The right side of the equation shows liabilities and owner's equity. A transaction changes the account balances of two or more accounts. After each transaction, the total of accounts on the left side must equal the total of accounts on the right side. The effects of the transactions analyzed in Chapters 1 and 2 on the accounting equation are shown in Illustration 2-8. After these transactions are recorded, the total of the balances on the left side equals the total of the balances on the right side, $11,490.00. Therefore, the accounting equation is in balance.

The new balances of the accounting equation are used to prepare a balance sheet. The left side of the balance sheet contains asset accounts. The right side contains liability and owner's equity accounts.

## ACCOUNTING TERMS

What is the meaning of each of the following?

**1.** revenue                **2.** expense                **3.** withdrawals

## QUESTIONS FOR INDIVIDUAL STUDY

1. Why do owners and managers need information about changes in owner's equity?
2. What accounts are affected, and how, when cash is received from sales?
3. How does a cash payment for goods or services needed to operate a business affect owner's equity?
4. What accounts are affected, and how, by a cash payment for an expense?
5. What must be true of the accounting equation after each transaction is recorded?
6. What are four expense transactions other than rent and utilities?
7. Which asset is normally withdrawn by an owner for personal use?
8. What accounts are affected, and how, when an owner withdraws $200.00 for personal use?
9. What transactions decrease owner's equity?
10. What must be true of changes in owner's equity if a business is to be successful?
11. What are three accounts that might be found on the left side of a balance sheet?
12. How often might a business be expected to prepare a balance sheet?

## CASES FOR MANAGEMENT DECISION

**CASE 1** Garcia Books receives an investment from its owner, Mrs. Juanita Garcia. This transaction is recorded in the following accounting equation. Is the analysis correct? Explain.

| Assets | | | = | Liabilities | + | Owner's Equity |
|---|---|---|---|---|---|---|
| Cash + | Supplies + | Prepaid Insurance = | | Panther Supply Company | + | Juanita Garcia, Capital |
| $1,000 +750 | $3,000 | $2,000 | | $2,500 | | $3,500 |
| $1,750 | $3,000 | $2,000 | | $2,500 | | $3,500 |

**CASE 2** The manager of Phillip's Department Store prepares a balance sheet at the end of each business day. Is this a satisfactory procedure? Explain.

## ▪ DRILLS FOR UNDERSTANDING

**DRILL 2-D1**  **Determining how revenue, expense, and withdrawal transactions change an accounting equation**

Use a form similar to the following.

| Trans. No. | Assets | | | = | Liabilities | + | Owner's Equity |
|---|---|---|---|---|---|---|---|
| | Cash + | Supplies + | Prepaid Insurance | = | Maxwell Company | + | Susan Sanders, Capital |
| 1. | + | | | | | | + |

*Transactions*
1. Received cash from owner as an investment.
2. Received cash from sales.
3. Paid cash for telephone bill.
4. Paid cash for advertising.
5. Paid cash to owner for personal use.
6. Paid cash for rent.
7. Received cash from sales.
8. Paid cash for equipment repairs.

**Instructions:** Decide which accounts in the accounting equation are changed by each transaction. Place a plus (+) in the appropriate column if the account is increased. Place a minus (−) in the appropriate column if the account is decreased. Transaction 1 is given as an example.

**DRILL 2-D2**  **Determining how transactions change an accounting equation**

Use a form similar to the following.

| Trans. No. | Assets | | | = | Liabilities | + | Owner's Equity |
|---|---|---|---|---|---|---|---|
| | Cash + | Supplies + | Prepaid Insurance | = | Barrett Company | + | Sue Marist, Capital |
| 1. | | + | | | + | | |

*Transactions*

1. Bought supplies on account from Barrett Company.
2. Paid cash for electric bill.
3. Received cash from owner as an investment.
4. Paid cash for insurance.
5. Received cash from sales.
6. Paid cash for rent.
7. Paid cash for supplies.
8. Paid cash for advertising.
9. Paid cash on account to Barrett Company.
10. Paid cash to owner for personal use.

**Instructions:** Decide which accounts in the accounting equation are changed by each transaction. Place a plus (+) in the appropriate column if the account is increased. Place a minus (−) in the appropriate column if the account is decreased. Transaction 1 is given as an example.

## ▉ APPLICATION PROBLEMS

**PROBLEM 2-1   Determining how revenue, expense, and withdrawal transactions change an accounting equation**

Peter Smith operates a service business called Peter's Service Company. Peter's Service Company uses the accounts shown in the following accounting equation. Use a form similar to the following to complete this problem.

| Trans. No. | Assets | | | = Liabilities | + Owner's Equity |
|---|---|---|---|---|---|
| | Cash + | Supplies + | Prepaid Insurance = | Kline Company + | Peter Smith, Capital |
| Beg. Bal. 1. | 625 −300 | 375 | 300 | 200 | 1,100 −300 *(expense)* |
| New Bal. 2. | 325 | 375 | 300 | 200 | 800 |

*Transactions*

1. Paid cash for rent, $300.00.
2. Paid cash to owner for personal use, $150.00.
3. Received cash from sales, $800.00.
4. Paid cash for equipment repairs, $100.00
5. Paid cash for telephone bill, $60.00.
6. Received cash from sales, $650.00.
7. Paid cash for charitable contributions, $35.00.
8. Paid cash for miscellaneous expenses, $25.00.

**Instructions:** For each transaction, complete the following. Transaction 1 is given as an example.
a. Analyze the transaction to determine which accounts in the accounting equation are affected.
b. Write the amount in the appropriate columns, using a plus (+) if the account increases or a minus (−) if the account decreases.
c. For transactions that change owner's equity, write in parentheses a description of the transaction to the right of the amount.

d. Calculate the new balance for each account in the accounting equation.
e. Before going on to the next transaction, determine that the accounting equation is still in balance.

## PROBLEM 2-2   Determining how transactions change an accounting equation and preparing a balance sheet

Doris Becker operates a typing business called QuickType. QuickType uses the accounts shown in the following accounting equation. Use a form similar to the following to complete this problem.

| Trans. No. | Assets | | | = | Liabilities | + | Owner's Equity |
| --- | --- | --- | --- | --- | --- | --- | --- |
| | Cash + | Supplies + | Prepaid Insurance | = | Teale Company | + | Doris Becker, Capital |
| Beg. Bal. 1. | 500 −50 | 260 | 300 | | 100 | | 960 −50 (expense) |
| New Bal. 2. | 450 | 260 | 300 | | 100 | | 910 |

*Transactions*
1. Paid cash for equipment repair, $50.00.
2. Received cash from sales, $325.00.
3. Paid cash for supplies, $200.00.
4. Bought supplies on account from Teale Company, $1,200.00.
5. Paid cash for advertising, $200.00.
6. Received cash from sales, $280.00.
7. Paid cash for water bill, $60.00.
8. Paid cash for insurance, $400.00.
9. Paid cash to owner for personal use, $125.00.
10. Received cash from sales, $260.00.
11. Paid cash for equipment rental, $45.00.
12. Paid cash for charitable contributions, $25.00.
13. Received cash from sales, $300.00.
14. Paid cash on account to Teale Company, $100.00.
15. Received cash from owner as an investment, $1,000.00.
16. Paid cash for rent, $600.00.
17. Received cash from sales, $430.00.
18. Paid cash on account to Teale Company, $750.00.

**Instructions: 1.** For each transaction, complete the following. Transaction 1 is given as an example.
a. Analyze the transaction to determine which accounts in the accounting equation are affected.
b. Write the amount in the appropriate columns, using a plus (+) if the account increases or a minus (−) if the account decreases.
c. For transactions that change owner's equity, write in parentheses a description of the transaction to the right of the amount.
d. Calculate the new balance for each account in the accounting equation.
e. Before going on to the next transaction, determine that the accounting equation is still in balance.

**2.** Using the final balances in the accounting equation, prepare a balance sheet. Use the date July 17 of the current year.

## ■ ENRICHMENT PROBLEMS

MASTERY PROBLEM 2-M **Determining how transactions change an accounting equation and preparing a balance sheet**

Fred Nance operates a service business called Nance Company. Nance Company uses the accounts shown in the following accounting equation. Use a form similar to the following to complete this problem.

| Trans. No. | Assets | | | = | Liabilities | + | Owner's Equity |
|---|---|---|---|---|---|---|---|
| | Cash + | Supplies + | Prepaid Insurance | = | Sickle Company | + | Fred Nance, Capital |
| Beg. Bal. 1. | 1,400 −100 | 300 | 400 | | 1,500 | | 600 −100 (expense) |
| New Bal. 2. | 1,300 | 300 | 400 | | 1,500 | | 500 |

*Transactions*
1. Paid cash for telephone bill, $100.00.
2. Received cash from owner as an investment, $200.00.
3. Paid cash for rent, $500.00.
4. Paid cash for equipment rental, $100.00.
5. Received cash from sales, $895.00.
6. Bought supplies on account from Sickle Company, $600.00.
7. Paid cash for equipment repair, $15.00.
8. Paid cash for miscellaneous expense, $30.00.
9. Received cash from sales, $920.00.
10. Paid cash for advertising, $50.00.
11. Paid cash for charitable contribution, $10.00.
12. Paid cash for supplies, $400.00.
13. Paid cash for advertising, $250.00.
14. Received cash from sales, $795.00.
15. Paid cash on account to Sickle Company, $1,500.00.
16. Paid cash for insurance, $250.00.
17. Received cash from sales, $960.00.
18. Paid cash to owner for personal use, $1,000.00.

**Instructions: 1.** For each transaction, complete the following. Transaction 1 is given as an example.
a. Analyze the transaction to determine which accounts in the accounting equation are affected.
b. Write the amount in the appropriate columns, using a plus (+) if the account increases or a minus (−) if the account decreases.
c. For transactions that change owner's equity, write in parentheses a description of the transaction to the right of the amount.
d. Calculate the new balance for each account in the accounting equation.

e. Before going on to the next transaction, determine that the accounting equation is still in balance.

**2.** Using the final balances in the accounting equation, prepare a balance sheet. Use the date April 30 of the current year.

## CHALLENGE PROBLEM 2-C   Calculating the missing amounts in an accounting equation

Each of the following statements includes four of the five amounts needed to complete an accounting equation.

*Statements*
1. Cash, $400.00; Supplies, $300.00; Prepaid Insurance, $800.00; Dexter Company, $500.00.
2. Cash, $200.00; Prepaid Insurance, $400.00; Dexter Company, $250.00; Pat Bouwman, Capital, $900.00.
3. Cash, $300.00; Supplies, $1,000.00; Prepaid Insurance, $750.00; Pat Bouwman, Capital, $1,200.00.
4. Supplies, $2,000.00; Prepaid Insurance, $1,200.00; Dexter Company, $2,400.00; Pat Bouwman, Capital, $3,500.00.
5. Cash, $100.00; Supplies, $2,700.00; Dexter Company, $1,100.00; Pat Bouwman, Capital, $2,500.00.
6. Cash, $250.00; Supplies, $400.00; Prepaid Insurance, $300.00; Pat Bouwman, Capital, $500.00.
7. Cash, $600.00; Supplies, $2,200.00; Prepaid Insurance, $900.00; Dexter Company, $500.00.
8. Supplies, $100.00; Prepaid Insurance, $400.00; Dexter Company, $150.00; Pat Bouwman, Capital, $500.00.

**Instructions: 1.** Use a form similar to the following. Record the information from each of the statements. Statement 1 is given as an example.

| State-ment | Assets | | | = | Liabilities | + | Owner's Equity |
|---|---|---|---|---|---|---|---|
| | Cash + | Supplies + | Prepaid Insurance | = | Dexter Company | + | Pat Bouwman, Capital |
| 1. | 400 | 300 | 800 | | 500 | | _____ |
| | | Total: _____ | | | | Total: _____ | |

**2.** Figure the sum of the balances on the side of the accounting equation that is complete. The totals of the balances on the left and right sides must be equal for the accounting equation to be in balance.

**3.** For each line of the form, figure the amount of the missing item in the accounting equation. Statement 1 is given as an example.

| State-ment | Assets | | | = | Liabilities | + | Owner's Equity |
|---|---|---|---|---|---|---|---|
| | Cash + | Supplies + | Prepaid Insurance | = | Dexter Company | + | Pat Bouwman, Capital |
| 1. | 400 | 300 | 800 | | 500 | | 1,000 |
| | | Total: 1,500 | | | | Total: 1,500 | |

# Analyzing Transactions into Debit and Credit Parts

## ENABLING PERFORMANCE TASKS

After studying Chapter 3, you will be able to:
a. Define accounting terms related to analyzing transactions into debit and credit parts.
b. Identify accounting concepts and practices related to analyzing transactions into debit and credit parts.
c. Use T accounts to analyze transactions showing which accounts are debited or credited for each transaction.
d. Verify the equality of debits and credits for each transaction.

How business transactions affect accounts in an accounting equation is described in Chapters 1 and 2. Even though the effects of transactions *can* be recorded in an accounting equation, the procedure is not practical in an actual accounting system. Accountants need more detail about the changes affecting each account than will appear in an accounting equation. Also, the number of accounts used by most businesses would make the accounting equation cumbersome to use as a major financial record. Therefore, a separate record is commonly used for each account.

## ACCOUNTS

The accounting equation can be represented as a *T*, as shown in Illustration 3-1.

| Assets | = | Liabilities | + | Owner's Equity |
|---|---|---|---|---|
| Left side | | | Right side | |

Illustration 3-1
Sides of an accounting equation

The values of all things owned (assets) are on the left side of the accounting equation. The values of all equities or claims against the assets

**33**

(liabilities and owner's equity) are on the right side of the accounting equation.

The total of amounts on the left side of the accounting equation must always equal the total of amounts on the right side. Therefore, the total of all assets on the left side of the accounting equation must always equal the total of all liabilities and owner's equity on the right side.

A record summarizing all the information pertaining to a single item in the accounting equation is known as an account. Transactions change the balances of accounts in the accounting equation. Accounting transactions must be analyzed to determine how account balances are changed. An accounting device used to analyze transactions is called a T account. The relationship of a T account to the accounts in the accounting equation is shown in Illustration 3-2.

| Assets | = | Liabilities | + | Owner's Equity |
|---|---|---|---|---|
| Left side | | | Right side | |

| T Account | |
|---|---|
| Left side<br>DEBIT SIDE | Right side<br>CREDIT SIDE |

Illustration 3-2
Relationship of a T account
to the accounting equation

Accountants have special names for amounts recorded on the left and right sides of a T account. An amount recorded on the left side of a T account is called a debit. An amount recorded on the right side of a T account is called a credit. The T account is the basic device used to analyze the effect of transactions on accounts.

The normal balance side of an asset, liability, or capital account is based on the location of the account in the accounting equation, as shown in Illustration 3-3.

| Assets | = | Liabilities | + | Owner's Equity |
|---|---|---|---|---|
| Left side | | | Right side | |

| ASSETS | | LIABILITIES | |
|---|---|---|---|
| Left side<br>Debit side<br>NORMAL BALANCE | Right side<br>Credit side | Left side<br>Debit side | Right side<br>Credit side<br>NORMAL BALANCE |

| OWNER'S CAPITAL ACCOUNT | |
|---|---|
| Left side<br>Debit side | Right side<br>Credit side<br>NORMAL BALANCE |

Illustration 3-3
Relationship of asset,
liability, and capital
accounts to the accounting
equation

Asset accounts have normal debit balances (left side) because assets are on the left side of the accounting equation. Liability accounts have normal credit balances (right side) because liabilities appear on the right side of the accounting equation. The owner's capital account has a normal credit balance (right side) because the capital account appears on the right side of the accounting equation.

The sides of a T account are also used to show increases and decreases in account balances, as shown in Illustration 3-4.

| Assets | = | Liabilities | + | Owner's Equity |
|---|---|---|---|---|
| Left side | | | Right side | |

| ASSETS | | LIABILITIES | |
|---|---|---|---|
| Left side<br>Debit side<br>Normal balance<br>INCREASE | Right side<br>Credit side<br><br>DECREASE | Left side<br>Debit side<br><br>DECREASE | Right side<br>Credit side<br>Normal balance<br>INCREASE |

| OWNER'S CAPITAL | |
|---|---|
| Left side<br>Debit side<br><br>DECREASE | Right side<br>Credit side<br>Normal balance<br>INCREASE |

Illustration 3-4
Increase and decrease sides of asset, liability, and capital accounts

Two basic accounting rules regulate increases and decreases of account balances. (1) Account balances increase on the normal balance side of an account. (2) Account balances decrease on the side opposite the normal balance side of an account.

Asset accounts have normal debit balances; therefore, asset accounts increase on the debit side and decrease on the credit side. Liability accounts have normal credit balances; therefore, liability accounts increase on the credit side and decrease on the debit side. The owner's capital account has a normal credit balance; therefore, the capital account increases on the credit side and decreases on the debit side.

# ANALYZING HOW TRANSACTIONS AFFECT ACCOUNTS

Before a transaction is recorded in the records of a business, the information is analyzed to determine which accounts are changed and how. Each transaction changes the balances of at least two accounts. In addition, debits equal credits for each transaction, as shown in Illustration 3-5.

| Supplies | | Cash | |
|---|---|---|---|
| Left side<br>Debit side<br>Normal balance<br>Increase      1,577.00 | Right side<br>Credit side<br><br>Decrease | Left side<br>Debit side<br>Normal balance<br>Increase | Right side<br>Credit side<br><br>1,577.00      Decrease |

DEBITS ---------------------------------- equal ---------------------------------- CREDITS

Illustration 3-5
Debits equal credits for each transaction

The total debits, $1,577.00, equal the total credits, $1,577.00, for this transaction.

Four questions are used in analyzing a transaction into its debit and credit parts.

1  *What accounts are affected?* A list of accounts used by a business is called a chart of accounts. The account titles used by Rugcare are found on the chart of accounts on page 2.

2  *How is each account classified?* Rugcare's accounts are classified as as-sets, liabilities, owner's equity, revenue, and expenses.

3  *How is each account balance changed?* Is each account increased or decreased?

4  *How is each amount entered in the accounts?* The amount is either debited or credited to the account.

## Received cash from owner as an investment

*August 1, 19--.*
*Received cash from owner as an investment, $10,000.00.*

The effect of this transaction in the accounting equation is shown in Illustration 3-6.

| Assets | = | Liabilities | + | Owner's Equity |
|---|---|---|---|---|

| | | |
|---|---|---|
| Left side<br>Cash<br>+10,000.00 | | Right side<br>Ben Furman, Capital<br>+10,000.00 (investment) |

| Any Asset | | | Owner's Capital | | |
|---|---|---|---|---|---|
| Left side<br>Debit side<br>Normal balance<br>Increase | Right side<br>Credit side<br><br>Decrease | | Left side<br>Debit side<br><br>Decrease | Right side<br>Credit side<br>Normal balance<br>Increase | |

| Cash | | | Ben Furman, Capital | | |
|---|---|---|---|---|---|
| Left side<br>Debit side<br>Normal balance<br>Increase    10,000.00 | Right side<br>Credit side<br><br>Decrease | | Left side<br>Debit side<br><br>Decrease | Right side<br>Credit side<br>Normal balance<br>Increase    10,000.00 | |

Illustration 3-6    DEBITS-----------------------------equal------------------------------------------------CREDITS
How debits and credits
affect accounts when                 Four questions are used to analyze this transaction.
receiving cash from owner
as an investment             1  *What accounts are affected?* Cash and Ben Furman, Capital.

2  *How is each account classified?* Cash is an asset account with a normal debit balance. Ben Furman, Capital is an owner's equity account with a nor-mal credit balance.

3  *How is each account balance changed?* Cash is increased. Ben Furman, Capital is increased.

**4** *How is each amount entered in the accounts?* The asset account, Cash, has a normal debit balance and is increased by a debit, $10,000.00. The owner's equity account, Ben Furman, Capital, has a normal credit balance and is increased by a credit, $10,000.00.

For this transaction, the total debits, $10,000.00, equal the total credits, $10,000.00.

## Paid cash for supplies

*August 3, 19--.*
*Paid cash for supplies, $1,577.00.*

The effect of this transaction is shown in Illustration 3-7.

Illustration 3-7
How debits and credits affect accounts when paying cash for supplies

Four questions are used to analyze this transaction.

**1** *What accounts are affected?* Cash and Supplies.

**2** *How is each account classified?* Cash is an asset account with a normal debit balance. Supplies is an asset account with a normal debit balance.

**3** *How is each account balance changed?* Cash is decreased. Supplies is increased.

**4** *How is each amount entered in the accounts?* The asset account, Supplies, has a normal debit balance and is increased by a debit, $1,577.00. The asset account, Cash, has a normal debit balance and is decreased by a credit, $1,577.00.

For this transaction, the total debits, $1,577.00, equal the total credits, $1,577.00.

## Paid cash for insurance

*August 4, 19--.*
*Paid cash for insurance, $1,200.00.*

The effect of this transaction is shown in Illustration 3-8.

| Assets | | = | Liabilities | + | Owner's Equity |
|---|---|---|---|---|---|
| Cash<br>−1,200.00 | Prepaid Insurance<br>+1,200.00 | | | | |

**Any Asset**

| Left side<br>Debit side<br>Normal balance<br>Increase | Right side<br>Credit side<br><br>Decrease |
|---|---|

**Prepaid Insurance**

| Left side<br>Debit side<br>Normal balance<br>Increase          1,200.00 | Right side<br>Credit side<br><br>Decrease |
|---|---|

**Cash**

| Left side<br>Debit side<br>Normal balance<br>Increase | Right side<br>Credit side<br><br>Decrease          1,200.00 |
|---|---|

DEBITS --------------- equal ------------- CREDITS

Illustration 3-8
How debits and credits
affect accounts when
paying cash for insurance

Four questions are used to analyze this transaction.

**1** *What accounts are affected?* Cash and Prepaid Insurance.

**2** *How is each account classified?* Cash is an asset account with a normal debit balance. Prepaid Insurance is an asset account with a normal debit balance.

**3** *How is each account balance changed?* Cash is decreased. Prepaid Insurance is increased.

**4** *How is each amount entered in the accounts?* The asset account, Prepaid Insurance, has a normal debit balance and is increased by a debit, $1,200.00. The asset account, Cash, has a normal debit balance and is decreased by a credit, $1,200.00.

For this transaction, the total debits, $1,200.00, equal the total credits, $1,200.00.

## Bought supplies on account

*August 7, 19--.*
*Bought supplies on account from Butler Cleaning Supplies, $2,720.00.*

The effect of this transaction is shown in Illustration 3-9.

| Assets | = | Liabilities | + | Owner's Equity |
|---|---|---|---|---|
| Supplies<br>+2,720.00 | | Butler Cleaning Supplies<br>+2,720.00 | | |

| Any Asset | | Any Liability | |
|---|---|---|---|
| Left side<br>Debit side<br>Normal balance<br>Increase | Right side<br>Credit side<br><br>Decrease | Left side<br>Debit side<br><br>Decrease | Right side<br>Credit side<br>Normal Balance<br>Increase |

| Supplies | | Butler Cleaning Supplies | |
|---|---|---|---|
| Left side<br>Debit side<br>Normal balance<br>Increase    2,720.00 | Right side<br>Credit side<br><br>Decrease | Left side<br>Debit side<br><br>Decrease | Right side<br>Credit side<br>Normal balance<br>Increase    2,720.00 |

DEBITS ---------------------------- equal ---------------------------- CREDITS

Illustration 3-9
How debits and credits affect accounts when buying supplies on account

Four questions are used to analyze this transaction.

**1** *What accounts are affected?* Supplies and Butler Cleaning Supplies.

**2** *How is each account classified?* Supplies is an asset account with a normal debit balance. Butler Cleaning Supplies is a liability account with a normal credit balance.

**3** *How is each account balance changed?* Supplies is increased. Butler Cleaning Supplies is increased.

**4** *How is each amount entered in the accounts?* The asset account, Supplies, has a normal debit balance and is increased by a debit, $2,720.00. The liability account, Butler Cleaning Supplies, has a normal credit balance and is increased by a credit, $2,720.00.

For this transaction, the total debits, $2,720.00, equal the total credits, $2,720.00.

## Paid cash on account

*August 11, 19--.*
*Paid cash on account to Butler Cleaning Supplies, $1,360.00.*

The effect of this transaction is shown in Illustration 3-10.
Four questions are used to analyze this transaction.

**1** *What accounts are affected?* Cash and Butler Cleaning Supplies.

**2** *How is each account classified?* Cash is an asset account with a normal debit balance. Butler Cleaning Supplies is a liability account with a normal credit balance.

| | Assets | | = | | Liabilities | | + | | Owner's Equity | |
|---|---|---|---|---|---|---|---|---|---|---|

Cash
−1,360.00

Butler Cleaning Supplies
−1,360.00

| Any Asset | | | Any Liability | | |
|---|---|---|---|---|---|
| Left side | Right side | | Left side | Right side | |
| Debit side | Credit side | | Debit side | Credit side | |
| Normal balance | | | | Normal balance | |
| Increase | Decrease | | Decrease | Increase | |

| Cash | | | Butler Cleaning Supplies | | |
|---|---|---|---|---|---|
| Left side | Right side | | Left side | Right side | |
| Debit side | Credit side | | Debit side | Credit side | |
| Normal balance | | | | Normal balance | |
| Increase | Decrease  1,360.00 | | Decrease  1,360.00 | Increase | |

CREDITS ------ equal ------- DEBITS

Illustration 3-10
How debits and credits
affect accounts when
paying cash on account

**3** *How is each account balance changed?* Cash is decreased. Butler Cleaning Supplies is decreased.

**4** *How is each amount entered in the accounts?* The liability account, Butler Cleaning Supplies, has a normal credit balance and is decreased by a debit, $1,360.00. The asset account, Cash, has a normal debit balance and is decreased by a credit, $1,360.00.

For this transaction, the total debits, $1,360.00, equal the total credits, $1,360.00.

### Received cash from sales

Revenue increases the owner's capital. The increases from revenue could be recorded directly in the owner's capital account. However, to avoid a capital account with a large number of entries and to summarize revenue information separately from the other records, Rugcare uses a separate revenue account.

*August 12, 19--.*
*Received cash from sales, $525.00.*

The effect of this transaction is shown in Illustration 3-11.

The owner's capital account has a normal credit balance. A revenue account shows increases in capital. Therefore, a revenue account also has a normal credit balance. Revenue accounts increase on the credit side and decrease on the debit side. Rugcare's revenue account is titled Sales.

Four questions are used to analyze this revenue transaction.

**1** *What accounts are affected?* Cash and Sales.

**2** *How is each account classified?* Cash is an asset account with a normal debit balance. Sales is a revenue account with a normal credit balance.

| Assets | | = | Liabilities | + | Owner's Equity | |
|---|---|---|---|---|---|---|

**Cash**
+525.00

Owner's Capital
+525.00 (revenue)

| Owner's Capital | | | Any Revenue Account | |
|---|---|---|---|---|
| Left side | Right side | | Left side | Right side |
| Debit side | Credit side | | Debit side | Credit side |
| | Normal balance | | | Normal balance |
| Decrease | Increase | | Decrease | Increase |

| Cash | | | Sales | |
|---|---|---|---|---|
| Left side | Right side | | Left side | Right side |
| Debit side | Credit side | | Debit side | Credit side |
| Normal balance | | | | Normal balance |
| Increase    525.00 | Decrease | | Decrease | Increase    525.00 |

DEBITS ------------------------ equal ---------------------------------------------------------------- CREDITS

**3** *How is each account balance changed?* Cash is increased. Sales is increased. Illustration 3-11

**4** *How is each amount entered in the accounts?* The asset account, Cash, has a normal debit balance and is increased by a debit, $525.00. The revenue account, Sales, has a normal credit balance and is increased by a credit, $525.00.

How debits and credits affect accounts when receiving cash from sales

For this transaction, the total debits, $525.00, equal the total credits, $525.00.

## Paid cash for an expense

Expenses decrease the owner's capital. Expenses could be recorded directly in the owner's capital account. However, to avoid a capital account with a large number of entries and to summarize expense information separately from the other records, Rugcare uses separate expense accounts.

The titles of Rugcare's expense accounts are shown on the chart of accounts, page 2. The expense account, Utilities Expense, is used to record all payments of utility bills. These include payments made for electricity, telephone, gas, water, and sanitation.

*August 12, 19--.*
*Paid cash for rent, $250.00.*

The effect of this transaction is shown in Illustration 3-12.

The owner's capital account has a normal credit balance. Decreases in the owner's capital account are shown as debits. An expense account shows decreases in owner's equity. Therefore, an expense account has a normal debit balance. An expense account increases on the debit side and decreases on the credit side.

| Assets | = | Liabilities | + | Owner's Equity |
|---|---|---|---|---|

Cash
−250.00

Owner's Capital
−250.00 (expense)

| Any Expense Account | | Owner's Capital Account | |
|---|---|---|---|
| Left side | Right side | Left side | Right side |
| Debit side | Credit side | Debit side | Credit side |
| Normal balance | | | Normal balance |
| Increase | Decrease | Decrease | Increase |

| Cash | | Rent Expense | |
|---|---|---|---|
| Left side | Right side | Left side | Right side |
| Debit side | Credit side | Debit side | Credit side |
| Normal balance | | Normal balance | |
| Increase | Decrease   250.00 | Increase   250.00 | Decrease |

Illustration 3-12
How debits and credits
affect accounts when
paying cash for an
expense

CREDITS----- equal ------ DEBITS

Four questions are used to analyze this expense transaction.

1 *What accounts are affected?* Cash and Rent Expense.

2 *How is each account classified?* Cash is an asset account with a normal debit balance. Rent Expense is an expense account with a normal debit balance.

3 *How is each account balance changed?* Cash is decreased. Rent Expense is increased.

4 *How is each amount entered in the accounts?* The expense account, Rent Expense, has a normal debit balance and is increased by a debit, $250.00. The asset account, Cash, has a normal debit balance and is decreased by a credit, $250.00.

For this transaction, the total debits, $250.00, equal the total credits, $250.00.

## Paid cash to owner for personal use

Assets taken out of a business for the personal use of the owner are known as withdrawals. Withdrawals are considered to be part of the owner's equity taken out of a business. Therefore, withdrawals decrease the owner's equity. Withdrawals could be recorded as decreases directly in the owner's capital account. However, common accounting practice is to record withdrawals in a separate account to provide a separate record of the withdrawals for each fiscal period. In this way, the owner knows how much has been withdrawn from the business each fiscal period.

An account that reduces a related account on a financial statement is called a contra account. The drawing account is a contra capital account because the account shows decreases in capital.

*August 12, 19--.*
*Paid cash to owner for personal use, $100.00.*

The effect of this transaction is shown in Illustration 3-13.

| Assets | = | Liabilities | + | Owner's Equity |
|---|---|---|---|---|
| Cash<br>−100.00 | | | | Owner's Capital<br>−100.00 (withdrawal) |

| A Contra Capital Account | | Owner's Capital Account | |
|---|---|---|---|
| Left side<br>Debit side<br>Normal balance<br>Increase | Right side<br>Credit side<br><br>Decrease | Left side<br>Debit side<br><br>Decrease | Right side<br>Credit side<br>Normal balance<br>Increase |

| Cash | | Ben Furman, Drawing | |
|---|---|---|---|
| Left side<br>Debit side<br>Normal balance<br>Increase | Right side<br>Credit side<br><br>Decrease   100.00 | Left side<br>Debit side<br>Normal balance<br>Increase   100.00 | Right side<br>Credit side<br><br>Decrease |

CREDITS----- equal ----- DEBITS

Illustration 3-13
How debits and credits affect accounts when paying cash to owner for personal use

The owner's capital account has a normal credit balance. Decreases in the owner's capital account are shown as debits. Because a drawing account shows decreases in capital, a drawing account has a normal debit balance. A drawing account increases on the debit side and decreases on the credit side.

Four questions are used to analyze this transaction.

1 *What accounts are affected?* Cash and Ben Furman, Drawing.

2 *How is each account classified?* Cash is an asset account with a normal debit balance. Ben Furman, Drawing is a contra capital account with a normal debit balance.

3 *How is each account balance changed?* Cash is decreased. Ben Furman, Drawing is increased.

4 *How is each amount entered in the accounts?* The contra capital account, Ben Furman, Drawing, has a normal debit balance and is increased by a debit, $100.00. The asset account, Cash, has a normal debit balance and is decreased by a credit, $100.00.

For this transaction, the total debits, $100.00, equal the total credits, $100.00.

## SUMMARY OF ANALYZING TRANSACTIONS INTO DEBIT AND CREDIT PARTS

The total debits and total credits for a transaction must be equal, as shown in Illustration 3-14.

| Supplies | | Cash | |
|---|---|---|---|
| Debits<br>1,577.00 | Credits | Debits | Credits<br>1,577.00 |

DEBITS-------------------- equal --------------------CREDITS

Illustration 3-14
Equality of debits and credits for a transaction

A summary of how debits and credits affect account balances is shown in Illustration 3-15.

| Assets | = | Liabilities | + | Owner's Equity |
|---|---|---|---|---|

| Equation's left side | | | | Equation's right side |
|---|---|---|---|---|

| Asset Accounts | | Liability Accounts | | Owner's Capital Account | |
|---|---|---|---|---|---|
| Left side | Right side | Left side | Right side | Left side | Right side |
| Debit side | Credit side | Debit side | Credit side | Debit side | Credit side |
| Normal balance | | | Normal balance | | Normal balance |
| Increases | Decreases | Decreases | Increases | Decreases | Increases |

| Owner's Drawing Account | |
|---|---|
| Left side | Right side |
| Debit side | Credit side |
| Normal balance | |
| Increases | Decreases |

| Expense Accounts | | Sales | |
|---|---|---|---|
| Left side | Right side | Left side | Right side |
| Debit side | Credit side | Debit side | Credit side |
| Normal balance | | | Normal balance |
| Increases | Decreases | Decreases | Increases |

Illustration 3-15
Summary of how debits
and credits affect
accounts

A summary analysis of transactions is shown in Illustration 3-16.

Illustration 3-16
Summary analysis of
transactions into debit and
credit parts

| Transaction | Accounts Affected | Account Classification | How Is Account Affected? | | Entered in Account as a | |
|---|---|---|---|---|---|---|
| | | | Increase | Decrease | Debit | Credit |
| Received cash from owner as an investment | Cash | Asset | X | | X | |
| | Ben Furman, Capital | Owner's Equity | X | | | X |
| Paid cash for supplies | Supplies | Asset | X | | X | |
| | Cash | Asset | | X | | X |
| Paid cash for insurance | Prepaid Insurance | Asset | X | | X | |
| | Cash | Asset | | X | | X |
| Bought supplies on account | Supplies | Asset | X | | X | |
| | Butler Cleaning Supplies | Liability | X | | | X |
| Paid cash on account | Butler Cleaning Supplies | Liability | | X | X | |
| | Cash | Asset | | X | | X |
| Received cash from sales | Cash | Asset | X | | X | |
| | Sales | Revenue | X | | | X |
| Paid cash for rent | Rent Expense | Expense | X | | X | |
| | Cash | Asset | | X | | X |
| Paid cash to owner for personal use | Ben Furman, Drawing | Contra Capital | X | | X | |
| | Cash | Asset | | X | | X |

## ◼ ACCOUNTING TERMS

What is the meaning of each of the following?

**1.** T account
**2.** debit

**3.** credit
**4.** chart of accounts

**5.** contra account

## ◼ QUESTIONS FOR INDIVIDUAL STUDY

**1.** What basic accounting device is used to help analyze transactions?
**2.** What determines which side of a T account will be the normal balance side?
**3.** What is the normal balance side of an asset account? Of a liability account? Of a capital account?
**4.** What two basic accounting rules regulate the increases and decreases of an account?
**5.** On which sides of a T account are increases and decreases recorded for asset accounts? For liability accounts? For the capital account?
**6.** What is the relationship between total debits and total credits in accounting records?
**7.** What are the four questions used in analyzing a transaction into debit and credit parts?
**8.** What accounts are affected, and how, when cash is received from an owner as an investment?

**9.** What accounts are affected, and how, when cash is paid for supplies?
**10.** What accounts are affected, and how, when cash is paid for insurance?
**11.** What accounts are affected, and how, when supplies are bought on account?
**12.** What accounts are affected, and how, when cash is paid on account?
**13.** What is the normal balance side of a revenue account?
**14.** What accounts are affected, and how, when cash is received from sales?
**15.** What is the normal balance side of an expense account?
**16.** What accounts are affected, and how, when cash is paid for rent?
**17.** What is the normal balance side of a drawing account?
**18.** What accounts are affected, and how, when cash is paid to an owner for personal use?

## ◼ CASES FOR MANAGEMENT DECISION

**CASE 1** When Carol Zueker invested in a business, she analyzed the transaction for her $5,000.00 investment as shown in the following T accounts.

Did Miss Zueker analyze the transaction correctly? Explain your answer.

**CASE 2** Sharon Morris records *all* cash receipts as revenue and *all* cash payments as

expenses. Is Miss Morris recording her cash receipts and cash payments correctly? Explain your answer.

**CASE 3** Thomas Bueler records all investments, revenue, expenses, and withdrawals in his capital account. At the end of each month, Mr. Bueler sorts the information to prepare a summary of what has caused the changes in his capital account balance. To help Mr. Bueler prepare this summary in the future, what changes would you suggest he make in his records?

## ▮ DRILLS FOR UNDERSTANDING

### DRILL 3-D1   Determining the normal balance, increase, and decrease sides for accounts

Jeff Dixon owns a service business called HouseClean. HouseClean uses the following accounts.

| | |
|---|---|
| Cash | Sales |
| Supplies | Advertising Expense |
| Prepaid Insurance | Miscellaneous Expense |
| Miller Supplies | Rent Expense |
| Wayne Office Supplies | Repair Expense |
| Jeff Dixon, Capital | Utilities Expense |
| Jeff Dixon, Drawing | |

**Instructions: 1.** Prepare a T account for each account. Label the debit and credit sides of each account. The T account for Cash is given as an example.
  **2.** For each account, label the side of the T account that is used for each of the following. The T account for Cash is given as an example.
  a. Normal balance
  b. Increase side
  c. Decrease side

| Cash | |
|---|---|
| Debit side | Credit side |

| Cash | |
|---|---|
| Debit side | Credit side |
| Normal balance | |
| Increase | Decrease |

### DRILL 3-D2   Analyzing how transactions affect accounts

Use a form similar to the following. Transaction 1 is given as an example.

| 1 | 2 | 3 | 4 | 5 | 6 | 7 | 8 | 9 |
|---|---|---|---|---|---|---|---|---|
| Trans. No. | Accounts Affected | Account Classification | Account's Normal Balance | | How is Account Affected? | | Entered in Account as a | |
| | | | Debit | Credit | (+) | (−) | Debit | Credit |
| 1. | Cash | Asset | ✓ | | ✓ | | ✓ | |
| | Jeff Dixon, Capital | Owner's Equity | | ✓ | ✓ | | | ✓ |

*Transactions*
1. Received cash from owner as an investment.
2. Paid cash for supplies.
3. Paid cash for insurance.
4. Bought supplies on account from Miller Supplies.
5. Received cash from sales.
6. Paid cash on account to Miller Supplies.
7. Paid cash for rent.
8. Paid cash for repairs.
9. Paid cash for miscellaneous expense.
10. Paid cash for telephone bill (utilities expense).
11. Paid cash to owner for personal use.

**Instructions: 1.** Use the account titles given in Drill 3-D1. In Column 2, write the accounts changed by each transaction.

**2.** For each account title, write the account classification in Column 3.

**3.** For each account title, place a check mark in either Column 4 or 5 to indicate the normal balance.

**4.** For each account title, place a check mark in either Column 6 or 7 to indicate if the account is increased ( + ) or decreased ( − ) by this transaction.

**5.** For each account title, place a check mark in either Column 8 or 9 to indicate if the account is changed by a debit or a credit.

## ■ APPLICATION PROBLEMS

### PROBLEM 3-1  Analyzing transactions into debit and credit parts

Dixie Conastar owns a business called Conastar Company. Conastar Company uses the following accounts.

| | |
|---|---|
| Cash | Sales |
| Supplies | Advertising Expense |
| Prepaid Insurance | Miscellaneous Expense |
| Bales Office Supplies | Rent Expense |
| Dixie Conastar, Capital | Utilities Expense |
| Dixie Conastar, Drawing | |

*Transactions*

Apr.  1. Received cash from owner as an investment, $5,000.00.
     2. Paid cash for supplies, $50.00.
     3. Paid cash for insurance, $75.00.
     6. Bought supplies on account from Bales Office Supplies, $100.00.
     7. Received cash from sales, $400.00.
     8. Paid cash for water bill (utilities expense), $25.00.
     9. Paid cash for advertising, $40.00.
    13. Paid cash on account to Bales Office Supplies, $50.00.
    14. Received cash from sales, $400.00.
    15. Paid cash for miscellaneous expense, $5.00.
    16. Paid cash to owner for personal use, $50.00.
    18. Paid cash for rent, $250.00.

**Instructions: 1.** Prepare two T accounts for each transaction. On each T account, write the account title of one of the accounts affected by the transaction.

**2.** Write the debit or credit amount in each T account to show how the transaction affected that account. T accounts for the first transaction are given as an example.

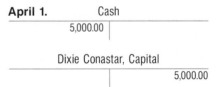

### PROBLEM 3-2  Analyzing transactions into debit and credit parts

Buelah VanBorne owns a business called VanBorne Services. VanBorne Services uses the following accounts.

| | |
|---|---|
| Cash | Sales |
| Supplies | Advertising Expense |

Prepaid Insurance                              Miscellaneous Expense
Fortune Supplies                               Rent Expense
Herdle Office Supplies                         Repair Expense
Buelah VanBorne, Capital                       Utilities Expense
Buelah VanBorne, Drawing

*Transactions*

May   1. Received cash from owner as an investment, $2,000.00.
       4. Bought supplies on account from Herdle Office Supplies, $500.00.
       6. Paid cash for rent, $500.00.
       7. Received cash from sales, $400.00.
      11. Paid cash on account to Herdle Office Supplies, $250.00.
      13. Paid cash for repairs, $80.00.
      14. Received cash from sales, $500.00.
      15. Paid cash for supplies, $600.00.
      19. Paid cash for insurance, $240.00.
      20. Bought supplies on account from Fortune Supplies, $50.00.
      21. Paid cash for supplies, $500.00.
      21. Received cash from sales, $750.00.
      25. Paid cash for telephone bill (utilities expense), $90.00.
      26. Paid cash for advertising, $130.00.
      28. Paid cash for miscellaneous expense, $15.00.
      28. Received cash from sales, $520.00.
      29. Paid cash to owner for personal use, $600.00.
      31. Received cash from sales, $400.00.

**Instructions: 1.** Prepare a T account for each account.

**2.** Analyze each transaction into its debit and credit parts. Write the debit and credit amounts in the proper T accounts to show how each transaction changes account balances. Write the date of the transaction in parentheses before each amount. The amounts for Transaction 1 are given in T accounts as an example.

|  | Cash |  |
|---|---|---|
| (1) | 2,000.00 |  |

|  | Buelah VanBorne, Capital |  |
|---|---|---|
|  |  | (1)  2,000.00 |

##  ENRICHMENT PROBLEMS

**MASTERY PROBLEM 3-M**   **Analyzing transactions into debit and credit parts**

James Lands owns a business called LandScape. LandScape uses the following accounts.

Cash                                           Sales
Supplies                                       Advertising Expense
Prepaid Insurance                              Miscellaneous Expense
Janitor Supplies                               Rent Expense
Derner Office Supplies                         Repair Expense
James Lands, Capital                           Utilities Expense
James Lands, Drawing

*Transactions*

June 1. Received cash from owner as an investment, $3,000.00.
2. Paid cash for supplies, $60.00.
4. Paid cash for rent, $200.00.
4. Received cash from sales, $350.00.
5. Paid cash for repairs, $10.00.
9. Bought supplies on account from Janitor Supplies, $500.00.
10. Paid cash for insurance, $100.00.
11. Received cash from owner as an investment, $900.00.
11. Received cash from sales, $300.00.
12. Bought supplies on account from Derner Office Supplies, $50.00.
15. Paid cash for miscellaneous expense, $5.00.
16. Paid cash on account to Janitor Supplies, $50.00.
18. Received cash from sales, $400.00.
22. Paid cash for electric bill (utilities expense), $35.00.
23. Paid cash for advertising, $30.00.
25. Received cash from sales, $220.00.
26. Paid cash to owner for personal use, $600.00.
30. Received cash from sales, $100.00.

**Instructions: 1.** Prepare a T account for each account.

**2.** Analyze each transaction into its debit and credit parts. Write the debit and credit amounts in the proper T accounts to show how each transaction changes account balances. Write the date of the transaction in parentheses before each amount.

**CHALLENGE PROBLEM 3-C  Analyzing transactions recorded in T accounts**

Edward Burns owns a business for which the following T accounts show the current financial situation.

| Cash | | | | | Sales | | |
|---|---|---|---|---|---|---|---|
| (1) | 5,000.00 | (2) | 80.00 | | | (6) | 475.00 |
| (6) | 475.00 | (4) | 15.00 | | | (8) | 350.00 |
| (8) | 350.00 | (5) | 16.00 | | | (9) | 400.00 |
| (9) | 400.00 | (7) | 900.00 | | | | |
| | | (10) | 150.00 | | | | |
| | | (11) | 95.00 | | | | |
| | | (12) | 50.00 | | | | |

| Supplies | | | Advertising Expense | |
|---|---|---|---|---|
| (3) | 300.00 | | (5) | 16.00 |
| (11) | 95.00 | | | |

| Midwest Supplies | | | Miscellaneous Expense | |
|---|---|---|---|---|
| (10) | 150.00 | (3) 300.00 | (4) | 15.00 |

| Edward Burns, Capital | | | Rent Expense | |
|---|---|---|---|---|
| | (1) | 5,000.00 | (7) | 900.00 |

| Edward Burns, Drawing | | | Utilities Expense | |
|---|---|---|---|---|
| (2) | 80.00 | | (12) | 50.00 |

**Instructions: 1.** Use a form similar to the following.

| 1 | 2 | 3 | 4 | 5 | 6 |
|---|---|---|---|---|---|
| Trans. No. | Accounts Affected | Account Classification | Entered in Account as a | | Description of Transaction |
| | | | Debit | Credit | |
| 1. | Cash<br>Edward Burns, Capital | Asset<br>Owner's Equity | ✓ | ✓ | Received cash from owner as an investment |

**2.** Analyze each numbered transaction in the T accounts. Write the titles of accounts affected in Column 2. For each account, write the classification of the account in Column 3.

**3.** For each account, place a check mark in either Column 4 or 5 to indicate if the account is affected by a debit or a credit.

**4.** For each transaction, write a brief statement in Column 6 describing the transaction. Information for Transaction 1 is given as an example.

# Journalizing Transactions

ENABLING PERFORMANCE TASKS

After studying Chapter 4, you will be able to:
a. Define accounting terms related to recording transactions in a journal.
b. Identify accounting concepts and practices related to recording transactions in a journal.
c. Record selected transactions in a five-column journal.
d. Prove equality of debits and credits in a five-column journal.
e. Prove cash.
f. Forward totals from one journal page to another.
g. Rule a five-column journal.

As described in Chapter 3, transactions are analyzed into debit and credit parts before information is recorded. A form for recording transactions in chronological order is called a journal. Recording transactions in a journal is called journalizing.

Transactions could be recorded in the accounting equation. However, generally accepted accounting practice is to make a more permanent record by recording transactions in a journal.

## A JOURNAL

Each business uses the kind of journal that best fits the needs of that business. The nature of a business and the number of transactions to be recorded determines the kind of journal to be used.

### Journal form

Rugcare uses a journal that has five amount columns, as shown in Illustration 4-1.

| | | | JOURNAL | | | | PAGE | | |
|---|---|---|---|---|---|---|---|---|---|
| | | | | 1 | 2 | 3 | 4 | 5 | |
| DATE | ACCOUNT TITLE | DOC. NO. | POST. REF. | GENERAL DEBIT | GENERAL CREDIT | SALES CREDIT | CASH DEBIT | CASH CREDIT | |
| 1 | | | | | | | | | 1 |
| 2 | | | | | | | | | 2 |
| 3 | | | | | | | | | 3 |
| 4 | | | | | | | | | 4 |
| 5 | | | | | | | | | 5 |

Illustration 4-1
Five-column journal

The five amount columns in Rugcare's journal are General Debit, General Credit, Sales Credit, Cash Debit, and Cash Credit. A journal amount column headed with an account title is called a special amount column. Special amount columns are used for frequently occurring transactions. For example, most of Rugcare's transactions involve receipt or payment of cash. A large number of the transactions involve receipt of cash from sales. Therefore, Rugcare uses three special amount columns in its journal: Sales Credit, Cash Debit, and Cash Credit.

Using special amount columns eliminates writing an account title in the Account Title column. Therefore, recording transactions in a journal with special amount columns saves time.

A journal amount column that is not headed with an account title is called a general amount column. In Rugcare's journal, the General Debit and General Credit columns are general amount columns.

## Accuracy

Information recorded in a journal includes the debit and credit parts of each transaction recorded in one place. The information can be verified by comparing the data in the journal with the source document data to assure that all information is correct.

## Chronological record

Transactions are recorded in a journal by date in the order in which the transactions occur. All the information about each transaction is recorded in one place making the information for a specific transaction easier to locate.

## Double-entry accounting

Information for each transaction recorded in a journal is called an entry. The recording of debit and credit parts of a transaction is called double-entry accounting. In double-entry accounting, each transaction affects at least two accounts. Both the debit part and the credit part are recorded for each transaction. This procedure reflects the dual effect of each transaction on the business' records. For example, cash paid for advertising causes (1) a decrease in cash and (2) an increase in expenses. Double-entry accounting assures that debits equal credits.

# SOURCE DOCUMENTS

A business paper from which information is obtained for a journal entry is called a source document. Each transaction is described by a source document that proves that the transaction did occur. For example, Rugcare prepares a check stub for each cash payment made. The check stub describes information about the cash payment transaction for which the check is prepared. The accounting concept, *Objective Evidence*, is applied when a source document is prepared for each transaction. *(CONCEPT: Objective Evidence)*

A transaction should be recorded only if it actually occurs. The amounts recorded must be accurate and true. Nearly all transactions result in the preparation of a source document. One way to verify the accuracy of a specific journal entry is to compare the entry with the source document. Rugcare uses four source documents: checks, calculator tapes, receipts, and memorandums.

## Checks

A business form ordering a bank to pay cash from a bank account is called a check. The source document for cash payments is a check. Rugcare makes all cash payments by check. The checks are prenumbered to help Rugcare account for all checks. Rugcare's record of information on a check is the check stub prepared at the same time as the check. A check and check stub prepared by Rugcare are shown in Illustration 4-2.

Procedures for preparing checks and check stubs are described in Chapter 6.

Illustration 4-2
Check and check stub

## Calculator tapes

Rugcare collects cash at the time services are rendered to customers. At the end of each day, Rugcare uses a printing electronic calculator to total the amount of cash received from sales for that day. By totaling all the individual sales, a single source document is produced for the total sales of the day. Thus, time and space are saved by recording only one entry for all of a day's sales. The calculator tape is the source document for daily sales. *(CONCEPT: Objective Evidence)* A calculator tape used as a source document is shown in Illustration 4-3.

Illustration 4-3
Calculator tape used as a source document

Rugcare dates and numbers each calculator tape. For example, in Illustration 4-3, the number, *T12*, indicates that the tape is for the twelfth day of the month.

## Receipts

A business form giving written acknowledgement for cash received is called a receipt. When cash is received from sources other than sales, Rugcare prepares a receipt. The receipts are prenumbered to help account for all the receipts. A receipt is the source document for cash received from transactions other than sales. *(CONCEPT: Objective Evidence)* Rugcare's receipt is shown in Illustration 4-4.

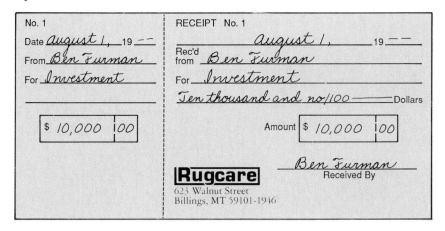

Illustration 4-4
Receipt used as a source document

## Memorandums

A form on which a brief message is written describing a transaction is called a memorandum. When no other source document is prepared for a transaction, or when additional explanation is needed about a transaction, Rugcare prepares a memorandum. *(CONCEPT: Objective Evidence)* Rugcare's memorandums are prenumbered to help account for all the memorandums. The memorandum used by Rugcare is shown in Illustration 4-5. A brief note is written on the memorandum to describe the transaction.

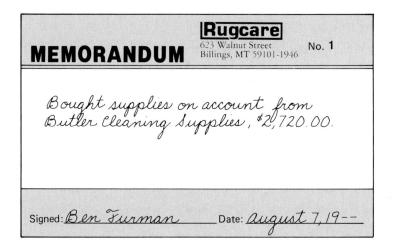

**MEMORANDUM**   **Rugcare**   No. 1
623 Walnut Street
Billings, MT 59101-1946

Bought supplies on account from Butler Cleaning Supplies, $2,720.00.

Signed: *Ben Furman*   Date: *August 7, 19--*

Illustration 4-5
Memorandum used as a
source document

# RECORDING TRANSACTIONS IN A FIVE-COLUMN JOURNAL

Information for each transaction recorded in a journal is known as an entry. An entry consists of four parts: (1) date, (2) debit, (3) credit, and (4) source document. Before a transaction is recorded in a journal, the transaction is analyzed into its debit and credit parts.

## Received cash from owner as an investment

*August 1, 19--.*
*Received cash from owner as an investment, $10,000.00. Receipt No. 1.*

The source document for this transaction is Receipt No. 1. *(CONCEPT: Objective Evidence)* The analysis of this transaction is shown in the T accounts.

All T account analysis in Chapter 4 is described in detail in Chapter 3.

The asset acount, Cash, is increased by a debit, $10,000.00. The owner's capital account, Ben Furman, Capital, is increased by a credit, $10,000.00. The journal entry for this transaction is shown in Illustration 4-6.

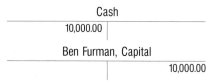

|  Cash  |  |
|---|---|
| 10,000.00 |  |

| Ben Furman, Capital |  |
|---|---|
|  | 10,000.00 |

| | | | | | | GENERAL | | SALES | CASH | | |
|---|---|---|---|---|---|---|---|---|---|---|---|
| DATE | | ACCOUNT TITLE | DOC. NO. | POST. REF. | | DEBIT | CREDIT | CREDIT | DEBIT | CREDIT | |
| 1 | Aug. 1 | Ben Furman, Capital | R1 | | | | 10 0 0 0 00 | | 10 0 0 0 00 | | 1 |

*JOURNAL*   PAGE *1*

Illustration 4-6
Journal entry to record
receiving cash from owner
as an investment

1 **Date.** Write the date, *19--, Aug. 1*, in the Date column.
This entry is the first one on this journal page. Therefore, the year and month are both written for this entry. Neither the year nor the month are written again on the same page.

2 **Debit.** The journal has a special amount column for debits to Cash. The title of the account is in the column heading. Therefore, the account title does not need to be written in the Account Title column. Write the debit amount, *$10,000.00*, in the Cash Debit column.

3 **Credit.** Write the title of the account credited, *Ben Furman, Capital*, in the Account Title column. There is no special amount column with the title of the account credited, Ben Furman, Capital, in its heading. Therefore, the credit amount is recorded in the General Credit column. Write the credit amount, *$10,000.00*, in the General Credit column.

　　All amounts recorded in the General Debit or General Credit amount columns must have an account title written in the Account Title column.

4 **Source document.** Write the source document number, *R1*, in the Doc. No. column. The source document number, *R1*, indicates that this is Receipt No. 1.

　　The source document number is a cross reference from the journal to the source document. If more details are needed about this transaction, a person can refer to Receipt No. 1.

### Paid cash for supplies

*August 3, 19--.*
*Paid cash for supplies, $1,577.00. Check No. 1.*

The source document for this transaction is Check No. 1. (*CONCEPT: Objective Evidence*) The analysis of this transaction is shown in the T accounts.

　　The asset account, Supplies, is increased by a debit, $1,577.00. The asset account, Cash, is decreased by a credit, $1,577.00. The journal entry for this transaction is shown in Illustration 4-7.

1 **Date.** Write the date, *3*, in the Date column. This is not the first entry on the journal page. Therefore, the year and month are not written for this entry.

| | DATE | ACCOUNT TITLE | DOC. NO. | POST. REF. | GENERAL DEBIT | GENERAL CREDIT | SALES CREDIT | CASH DEBIT | CASH CREDIT | |
|---|---|---|---|---|---|---|---|---|---|---|
| | | | | | 1 | 2 | 3 | 4 | 5 | |
| 2 | 3 | Supplies | C1 | | 1 5 7 7 00 | | | | 1 5 7 7 00 | 2 |

JOURNAL — PAGE *1*

**2** *Debit.* Write the title of the account debited, *Supplies*, in the Account Title column. There is no special amount column with the title of the account debited, Supplies, in its heading. Therefore, the debit amount is recorded in the General Debit column. Write the debit amount, *$1,577.00*, in the General Debit column.

*Illustration 4-7 Journal entry to record paying cash for supplies*

**3** *Credit.* The journal has a special amount column for credits to Cash. The title of the account is in the column heading. Therefore, the account title does not need to be written in the Account Title column. Write the credit amount, *$1,577.00*, in the Cash Credit column.

**4** *Source document.* Write the source document number, *C1*, in the Doc. No. column. The source document number, *C1*, indicates that this is Check No. 1.

## Paid cash for insurance

*August 4, 19--.*
*Paid cash for insurance, $1,200.00. Check No. 2.*

The source document for this transaction is Check No. 2. (CONCEPT: *Objective Evidence*) The analysis of this transaction is shown in the T accounts.

The asset account, Prepaid Insurance, is increased by a debit, $1,200.00. The asset account, Cash, is decreased by a credit, $1,200.00. The journal entry for this transaction is shown in Illustration 4-8.

Prepaid Insurance
1,200.00 |

Cash
| 1,200.00

| | DATE | ACCOUNT TITLE | DOC. NO. | POST. REF. | GENERAL DEBIT | GENERAL CREDIT | SALES CREDIT | CASH DEBIT | CASH CREDIT | |
|---|---|---|---|---|---|---|---|---|---|---|
| | | | | | 1 | 2 | 3 | 4 | 5 | |
| 3 | 4 | Prepaid Insurance | C2 | | 1 2 0 0 00 | | | | 1 2 0 0 00 | 3 |

JOURNAL — PAGE *1*

*Illustration 4-8 Journal entry to record paying cash for insurance*

**1** *Date.* Write the date, *4*, in the Date column.

2 *Debit.* Write the title of the account debited, *Prepaid Insurance*, in the Account Title column. There is no special amount column with the title of the account debited, Prepaid Insurance, in its heading. Therefore, the debit amount is recorded in the General Debit column. Write the debit amount, *$1,200.00,* in the General Debit column.

3 *Credit.* The journal has a special amount column for credits to Cash. The title of the account is in the column heading. Therefore, the account title does not need to be written in the Account Title column. Write the credit amount, *$1,200.00,* in the Cash Credit column.

4 *Source document.* Write the source document number, *C2,* in the Doc. No. column.

## Bought supplies on account

*August 7, 19--.*
*Bought supplies on account from Butler Cleaning Supplies, $2,720.00. Memorandum No. 1.*

Rugcare ordered these supplies by telephone. The supplies are received on August 7. Butler Cleaning Supplies has not yet sent Rugcare notice of the goods shipped. Rugcare wishes to record this transaction immediately. Therefore, Rugcare prepares a memorandum to describe the transaction.

| Supplies | |
|---|---|
| 2,720.00 | |

| Butler Cleaning Supplies | |
|---|---|
| | 2,720.00 |

The source document for this transaction is Memorandum No. 1. *(CONCEPT: Objective Evidence)* The analysis of this transaction is shown in the T accounts.

The asset account, Supplies, is increased by a debit, $2,720.00. The liability account, Butler Cleaning Supplies, is increased by a credit, $2,720.00. The journal entry for this transaction is shown in Illustration 4-9.

| | DATE | ACCOUNT TITLE | DOC. NO. | POST. REF. | GENERAL DEBIT | GENERAL CREDIT | SALES CREDIT | CASH DEBIT | CASH CREDIT | |
|---|---|---|---|---|---|---|---|---|---|---|
| 4 | 7 | *Supplies* | *M1* | | 2 7 2 0 00 | | | | | 4 |
| 5 | | *Butler Cleaning Supp.* | | | | 2 7 2 0 00 | | | | 5 |

JOURNAL — PAGE *1*

Illustration 4-9
Journal entry to record
buying supplies on account

1 *Date.* Write the date, *7,* in the Date column.

2 *Debit.* The journal does not have a special amount column for either debits to Supplies or credits to Butler Cleaning Supplies. Therefore, both account titles need to be written in the Account Title column. The debit and credit amounts are recorded in the General Debit and General Credit columns. Write the title of the account debited, *Supplies*, in the Account

Title column. Write the debit amount, *$2,720.00,* in the General Debit column.

3 ***Credit.*** On the next line, write the title of the account credited, *Butler Cleaning Supplies,* in the Account Title column. Write the credit amount, *$2,720.00,* in the General Credit column on the same line as the account title.

> This entry requires two lines in the journal because account titles for both the debit and credit amounts must be written in the Account Title column.

4 ***Source document.*** Write the source document number, *M1,* in the Doc. No. column on the first line of the entry.

## Paid cash on account

*August 11, 19--.*
*Paid cash on account to Butler Cleaning Supplies, $1,360.00. Check No. 3.*

The source document for this transaction is Check No. 3. *(CONCEPT: Objective Evidence)* The analysis of this transaction is shown in the T accounts.

The liability account, Butler Cleaning Supplies, is decreased by a debit, $1,360.00. The asset account, Cash, is decreased by a credit, $1,360.00. The journal entry for this transaction is shown in Illustration 4-10.

| Butler Cleaning Supplies | |
|---|---|
| 1,360.00 | |

| Cash | |
|---|---|
| | 1,360.00 |

| | JOURNAL | | | | | | | | PAGE *1* | | |
|---|---|---|---|---|---|---|---|---|---|---|---|
| | | | | | 1 | 2 | 3 | | 4 | 5 | |
| DATE | ACCOUNT TITLE | DOC. NO. | POST. REF. | | GENERAL | | SALES CREDIT | | CASH | | |
| | | | | | DEBIT | CREDIT | | | DEBIT | CREDIT | |
| 6 | 11 *Butler Cleaning Supp.* | C3 | | | 1 3 6 0 00 | | | | | 1 3 6 0 00 | 6 |

Illustration 4-10
Journal entry to record paying cash on account

1 ***Date.*** Write the date, *11,* in the Date column.

2 ***Debit.*** Write the title of the account debited, *Butler Cleaning Supplies,* in the Account Title column. There is no special amount column with the title of the account debited, Butler Cleaning Supplies, in its heading. Therefore, the debit amount is recorded in the General Debit column. Write the debit amount, *$1,360.00,* in the General Debit column.

3 ***Credit.*** The journal has a special amount column for credits to Cash. The title of the account is in the column heading. Therefore, the account title does not need to be written in the Account Title column. Write the credit amount, *$1,360.00,* in the Cash Credit column.

4 ***Source document.*** Write the source document number, *C3,* in the Doc. No. column.

## Received cash from sales

*August 12, 19--.*
*Received cash from sales, $525.00. Tape No. 12.*

The source document for this transaction is Calculator Tape No. 12. *(CONCEPT: Objective Evidence)* The analysis of this transaction is shown in the T accounts.

The asset account, Cash, is increased by a debit, $525.00. The revenue account, Sales, is increased by a credit, $525.00. The journal entry for this transaction is shown in Illustration 4-11.

| | | | | | | | | | | |
|---|---|---|---|---|---|---|---|---|---|---|
| | | | | | **JOURNAL** | | | | PAGE *1* | |
| | | | | 1 | 2 | 3 | 4 | 5 | | |
| DATE | ACCOUNT TITLE | DOC. NO. | POST. REF. | GENERAL | | SALES CREDIT | CASH | | | |
| | | | | DEBIT | CREDIT | | DEBIT | CREDIT | | |
| 12 √ | | T12 | √ | | | 525 00 | 525 00 | | | 7 |

Illustration 4-11
Journal entry to record
receiving cash from sales

1 *Date.* Write the date, *12,* in the Date column.

2 *Debit.* The journal has a special amount column for debits to Cash. The title of the account is in the column heading. Therefore, the account title does not need to be written in the Account Title column. Write the debit amount, *$525.00,* in the Cash Debit column.

3 *Credit.* The journal also has a special amount column for credits to Sales. The title of the account is in the column heading. Therefore, the account title does not need to be written in the Account Title column. Write the credit amount, *$525.00,* in the Sales Credit column.

> Because both amounts for this entry are recorded in special amount columns, no account titles are written in the Account Title column. Therefore, put a check mark in the Account Title column to show that no account titles need to be written for this transaction. A check mark is also placed in the Post. Ref. column to show that no separate amounts on this line are to be posted individually.
>
> Posting procedures are described in Chapter 5.

4 *Source document.* Write the source document number, *T12,* in the Doc. No. column.

## Paid cash for an expense

*August 12, 19--.*
*Paid cash for rent, $250.00. Check No. 4.*

The source document for this transaction is Check No. 4. *(CONCEPT: Objective Evidence)* The analysis of this transaction is shown in the T accounts.

The expense account, Rent Expense, is increased by a debit, $250.00. The asset account, Cash, is decreased by a credit, $250.00. The journal entry for this transaction is shown on line 8 in Illustration 4-12.

| Rent Expense | |
|---|---|
| 250.00 | |

| Cash | |
|---|---|
| | 250.00 |

JOURNAL     PAGE *1*

| | | DATE | ACCOUNT TITLE | DOC. NO. | POST. REF. | GENERAL DEBIT | GENERAL CREDIT | SALES CREDIT | CASH DEBIT | CASH CREDIT | |
|---|---|---|---|---|---|---|---|---|---|---|---|
| | | | | | | 1 | 2 | 3 | 4 | 5 | |
| 8 | | 12 | *Rent Expense* | *C4* | | *2 5 0 00* | | | | *2 5 0 00* | 8 |
| 9 | | 12 | *Utilities Expense* | *C5* | | *4 5 00* | | | | *4 5 00* | 9 |

1 **Date.** Write the date, *12,* in the Date column.

2 **Debit.** Write the title of the account debited, Rent Expense, in the Account Title column. There is no special amount column with the title of the account debited, Rent Expense, in its heading. Therefore, the debit amount is recorded in the General Debit column. Write the debit amount, *$250.00,* in the General Debit column.

3 **Credit.** The journal has a special amount column for credits to Cash. The title of the account is in the column heading. Therefore, the account title does not need to be written in the Account Title column. Write the credit amount, *$250.00,* in the Cash Credit column.

4 **Source document.** Write the source document number, *C4,* in the Doc. No. column.

Illustration 4-12
Journal entry to record paying cash for an expense

The journal entry shown in Illustration 4-12 includes a cash payment for another expense, Utilities Expense. This transaction is journalized in the same way as the cash payment for rent.

## Paid cash to owner for personal use

*August 12, 19--.*
*Paid cash to owner for personal use, $100.00. Check No. 6.*

The source document for this transaction is Check No. 6. *(CONCEPT: Objective Evidence)* The analysis of this transaction is shown in the T accounts.

The contra capital account, Ben Furman, Drawing, is increased by a debit, $100.00. The asset account, Cash, is decreased by a

| Ben Furman, Drawing | |
|---|---|
| 100.00 | |

| Cash | |
|---|---|
| | 100.00 |

credit, $100.00. The journal entry for this transaction is shown in Illustration 4-13.

| | | | | JOURNAL | | | | | PAGE 1 |
| | | | | | | | | | |

Illustration 4-13
Journal entry to record
paying cash to owner for
personal use

1 **Date.** Write the date, *12,* in the Date column.

2 **Debit.** Write the title of the account debited, *Ben Furman, Drawing*, in the Account Title column. There is no special amount column with the title of the account debited, Ben Furman, Drawing, in its heading. Therefore, the debit amount is recorded in the General Debit column. Write the debit amount, *$100.00,* in the General Debit column.

3 **Credit.** The journal has a special amount column for credits to Cash. The title of the account is in the column heading. Therefore, the account title does not need to be written in the Account Title column. Write the credit amount, *$100.00,* in the Cash Credit column.

4 **Source document.** Write the source document number, *C6,* in the Doc. No. column.

## PROVING AND RULING A JOURNAL

After Rugcare uses all but the last line on a journal page, columns are proved and ruled before totals are carried forward to the next page. At the end of each month, Rugcare also proves and rules the journal.

After all entries on August 20 are recorded, page 1 of Rugcare's journal is filled, as shown in Illustration 4-14.

Page 1 is proved and ruled before totals are carried forward to page 2.

### Proving a journal page

To prove a journal page, Rugcare verifies that the total debits on the page equal the total credits. Three steps are followed in proving a journal page.

1 *Add each of the amount columns.* Use a calculator if one is available. If a calculator is not available, total the columns on a sheet of paper.

2 *Add the debit column totals, and then add the credit column totals.* The figures from page 1 of Rugcare's journal are on the next page.

| Column | Debit Column Totals | Credit Column Totals |
|---|---|---|
| General | $ 7,920.00 | $12,920.00 |
| Sales | | 2,319.00 |
| Cash | 12,319.00 | 5,000.00 |
| Totals | $20,239.00 | $20,239.00 |

**3** *Verify that the total debits and total credits are equal.* The total debits and the total credits on page 1 of Rugcare's journal are $20,239.00. Because the total debits equal the total credits, page 1 of Rugcare's journal is proved.

If the total debits do not equal the total credits, the errors must be found and corrected before any more work is completed.

Illustration 4-14
Completed page 1 of a journal

| | DATE | | ACCOUNT TITLE | DOC. NO. | POST. REF. | GENERAL DEBIT | GENERAL CREDIT | SALES CREDIT | CASH DEBIT | CASH CREDIT | |
|---|---|---|---|---|---|---|---|---|---|---|---|
| 1 | Aug. 19-- | 1 | Ben Furman, Capital | R1 | | | 10 0 0 0 00 | | 10 0 0 0 00 | | 1 |
| 2 | | 3 | Supplies | C1 | | 1 5 7 7 00 | | | | 1 5 7 7 00 | 2 |
| 3 | | 4 | Prepaid Insurance | C2 | | 1 2 0 0 00 | | | | 1 2 0 0 00 | 3 |
| 4 | | 7 | Supplies | M1 | | 2 7 2 0 00 | | | | | 4 |
| 5 | | | Butler Cleaning Supp. | | | | 2 7 2 0 00 | | | | 5 |
| 6 | | 11 | Butler Cleaning Supp. | C3 | | 1 3 6 0 00 | | | | 1 3 6 0 00 | 6 |
| 7 | | 12 | √ | T12 | √ | | | 5 2 5 00 | 5 2 5 00 | | 7 |
| 8 | | 12 | Rent Expense | C4 | | 2 5 0 00 | | | | 2 5 0 00 | 8 |
| 9 | | 12 | Utilities Expense | C5 | | 4 5 00 | | | | 4 5 00 | 9 |
| 10 | | 12 | Ben Furman, Drawing | C6 | | 1 0 0 00 | | | | 1 0 0 00 | 10 |
| 11 | | 13 | Repair Expense | C7 | | 2 0 00 | | | | 2 0 00 | 11 |
| 12 | | 13 | Miscellaneous Expense | C8 | | 2 5 00 | | | | 2 5 00 | 12 |
| 13 | | 13 | √ | T13 | √ | | | 2 2 9 00 | 2 2 9 00 | | 13 |
| 14 | | 14 | Advertising Expense | C9 | | 6 8 00 | | | | 6 8 00 | 14 |
| 15 | | 14 | √ | T14 | √ | | | 3 6 0 00 | 3 6 0 00 | | 15 |
| 16 | | 17 | Petty Cash | C10 | | 2 0 0 00 | | | | 2 0 0 00 | 16 |
| 17 | | 17 | √ | T17 | √ | | | 3 5 0 00 | 3 5 0 00 | | 17 |
| 18 | | 18 | Miscellaneous Expense | C11 | | 7 0 00 | | | | 7 0 00 | 18 |
| 19 | | 18 | √ | T18 | √ | | | 3 2 0 00 | 3 2 0 00 | | 19 |
| 20 | | 19 | √ | T19 | √ | | | 2 9 0 00 | 2 9 0 00 | | 20 |
| 21 | | 20 | Repair Expense | C12 | | 8 5 00 | | | | 8 5 00 | 21 |
| 22 | | 20 | √ | T20 | √ | | | 2 4 5 00 | 2 4 5 00 | | 22 |
| 23 | | 20 | Supplies | M2 | | 2 0 0 00 | | | | | 23 |
| 24 | | | Dale Office Supplies | | | | 2 0 0 00 | | | | 24 |
| 25 | | 20 | Carried Forward | | √ | 7 9 2 0 00 | 12 9 2 0 00 | 2 3 1 9 00 | 12 3 1 9 00 | 5 0 0 0 00 | 25 |

JOURNAL    PAGE 1

## Ruling a journal page

After a journal page is proved, the page is ruled as shown in Illustration 4-14, page 63.

1 Rule a single line across all amount columns directly below the last entry to indicate that the columns are to be added.

2 On the next line, write the date, *20,* in the Date column.

3 Write the words, *Carried Forward,* in the Account Title column. A check mark is also placed in the Post. Ref. column to show that nothing on this line needs to be posted.

4 Write each column total below the single line.

5 Rule double lines below the column totals across all amount columns. The double lines mean that the totals have been verified as correct.

## Starting a new journal page

The column totals from the previous page are carried forward to a new page. The totals are recorded on the first line of the new page as shown in Illustration 4-15.

| | | | | | GENERAL | | SALES | CASH | |
| | DATE | ACCOUNT TITLE | DOC. NO. | POST. REF. | DEBIT | CREDIT | CREDIT | DEBIT | CREDIT |
|---|---|---|---|---|---|---|---|---|---|
| 1 | Aug. 20 | Brought Forward | | √ | 7 9 2 0 00 | 12 9 2 0 00 | 2 3 1 9 00 | 12 3 1 9 00 | 5 0 0 0 00 |
| 2 | | | | | | | | | |

JOURNAL — PAGE 2

Illustration 4-15
Starting a new journal page

1 Write the page number, *2,* at the top of the journal.

2 Write the date, *19--, Aug. 20,* in the Date column. Because this is the first time that a date is written on page 2, the year, month, and day are all written in the Date column.

3 Write the words, *Brought Forward,* in the Account Title column. A check mark is also placed in the Post. Ref. column to show that nothing on this line needs to be posted.

4 Record the column totals brought forward from the previous page.

## Completing a journal at the end of a month

Rugcare always proves and rules a journal at the end of each month even if the last page for the month is not full. Page 2 of Rugcare's journal on August 31 is shown in Illustration 4-16.

The entries on lines 10, 11, and 12, Illustration 4-16, are described in Chapter 6.

JOURNAL  PAGE 2

| | DATE | ACCOUNT TITLE | DOC. NO. | POST. REF. | GENERAL DEBIT | GENERAL CREDIT | SALES CREDIT | CASH DEBIT | CASH CREDIT | |
|---|---|---|---|---|---|---|---|---|---|---|
| 1 | Aug. 20 | Brought Forward | | √ | 7 9 2 0 00 | 12 9 2 0 00 | 2 3 1 9 00 | 12 3 1 9 00 | 5 0 0 0 00 | 1 |
| 2 | 21 √ | | T21 | √ | | | 2 7 0 00 | 2 7 0 00 | | 2 |
| 3 | 24 √ | | T24 | √ | | | 3 0 0 00 | 3 0 0 00 | | 3 |
| 4 | 25 √ | | T25 | √ | | | 3 1 0 00 | 3 1 0 00 | | 4 |
| 5 | 26 √ | | T26 | √ | | | 2 4 5 00 | 2 4 5 00 | | 5 |
| 6 | 27 | Utilities Expense | C13 | | 7 0 00 | | | | 7 0 00 | 6 |
| 7 | 27 √ | | T27 | √ | | | 2 9 0 00 | 2 9 0 00 | | 7 |
| 8 | 28 | Supplies | C14 | | 4 3 4 00 | | | | 4 3 4 00 | 8 |
| 9 | 28 √ | | T28 | √ | | | 2 6 7 00 | 2 6 7 00 | | 9 |
| 10 | 28 | Miscellaneous Expense | M3 | | | 3 00 | | | 3 00 | 10 |
| 11 | 31 | Miscellaneous Expense | C15 | | | 7 00 | | | 1 2 00 | 11 |
| 12 | | Repair Expense | | | | 5 00 | | | | 12 |
| 13 | 31 | Ben Furman, Drawing | C16 | | 5 0 0 00 | | | | 5 0 0 00 | 13 |
| 14 | 31 √ | | T31 | √ | | | 2 9 0 00 | 2 9 0 00 | | 14 |
| 15 | 31 | Totals | | | 8 9 3 9 00 | 12 9 2 0 00 | 4 2 9 1 00 | 14 2 9 1 00 | 6 0 1 9 00 | 15 |

**Proving page 2 of a journal.** The last page of a journal for a month is proved using the same steps previously described. Then, cash is proved and the journal is ruled. The proof of page 2 of Rugcare's journal is shown below.

Illustration 4-16
Ruling a journal at the end of a month

| Column | Debit Column Totals | Credit Column Totals |
|---|---|---|
| General | $ 8,939.00 | $12,920.00 |
| Sales | | 4,291.00 |
| Cash | 14,291.00 | 6,019.00 |
| Totals | $23,230.00 | $23,230.00 |

Page 2 of Rugcare's journal is proved because the total debits are equal to the total credits, $23,230.00.

**Proving cash.** Determining that the amount of cash agrees with the accounting records is called proving cash. Cash can be proved at any time Rugcare wishes to verify the accuracy of the cash records. However, Rugcare *always* proves cash at the end of the month when the journal is proved. Rugcare uses two steps to prove cash.

1  *Figure the cash balance.*

| | |
|---|---|
| Cash on hand at the beginning of the month . . . . . . . . . . . . | $    0.00 |

Rugcare began the month with no cash balance. Mr. Furman invested the initial cash on August 1.

| | |
|---|---|
| *Plus* total cash received during the month . . . . . . . . . . . . . . | +14,291.00 |

This amount is the total of the journal's Cash Debit column.

| | |
|---|---|
| *Equals* total. . . . . . . . . . . . . . . . . . . . . . . . . . . . . . . . . . . . . . . . | $14,291.00 |
| *Less* total cash paid during the month. . . . . . . . . . . . . . . . . . | − 6,019.00 |

This amount is the total of the journal's Cash Credit column.

| | |
|---|---|
| *Equals* cash balance at the end of the month. . . . . . . . . . . . . | $ 8,272.00 |
| Checkbook balance on the next unused check stub . . . . . . . | 8,272.00 |

2  *Verify that the cash balance equals the checkbook balance on the next unused check stub in the checkbook.* Because the cash balance figured from the journal and the checkbook balance are the same, *$8,272.00,* cash is proved.

**Ruling a journal at the end of a month.** A journal is ruled at the end of each month even if the last journal page is not full. Rugcare's journal is ruled as shown in Illustration 4-16, page 65.

The procedures for ruling a journal at the end of a month are similar to those for ruling a journal page to carry the totals forward.

Rugcare uses five steps in ruling a journal at the end of each month.

1  Rule a single line across all amount columns directly below the last entry to indicate that the columns are to be added.

2  On the next line, write the date, *31,* in the Date column.

3  Write the word, *Totals,* in the Account Title column.

Some of the column totals will be posted as described in Chapter 5. Therefore, a check mark is not placed in the Post. Ref. column for this line.

4  Write each column total below the single line.

5  Rule double lines below the column totals across all amount columns. The double lines mean that the totals have been verified as correct.

## GENERALLY ACCEPTED ACCOUNTING PRACTICES

In completing accounting work, Rugcare is guided by generally accepted accounting practices, including those shown in Illustration 4-17.

1. Errors are corrected in a way that does not cause doubts about what the correct information is. If an error is recorded, cancel the error by neatly

drawing a line through the incorrect item. Write the correct item immediately above the canceled item, as shown on line 17 of Illustration 4-17.

2. Sometimes an entire entry is incorrect and is discovered before the next entry is journalized. Draw neat lines through all parts of the incorrect entry. Journalize the entry correctly on the next blank line, as shown on lines 18 and 19, Illustration 4-17.

3. Sometimes several correct entries are recorded after an incorrect entry is made. The next blank lines are several entries later. Draw neat lines through all incorrect parts of the entry. Record the correct items on the same lines as the incorrect items, directly above the canceled parts. This procedure is shown on line 20 of Illustration 4-17.

4. Words in accounting records are written in full when space permits. Words may be abbreviated only when space is limited. All items are written legibly.

5. Dollars and cents signs and decimal points are not used when writing amounts on ruled accounting paper. Sometimes a color tint or a heavy vertical rule is used on printed accounting paper to separate the dollars and cents columns.

6. Two zeros are written in the cents column when an amount is in even dollars, such as $500.00. If the cents column is left blank, doubts may arise later about the correct amount.

7. A single line is ruled across amount columns to indicate addition or subtraction as shown on line 21, Illustration 4-17.

8. A double line is ruled across amount columns to indicate that the totals have been verified as correct.

9. Neatness is very important in accounting records so that there is never any doubt about what information has been recorded. A ruler is used to make single and double lines.

Illustration 4-17
Some generally accepted
accounting practices

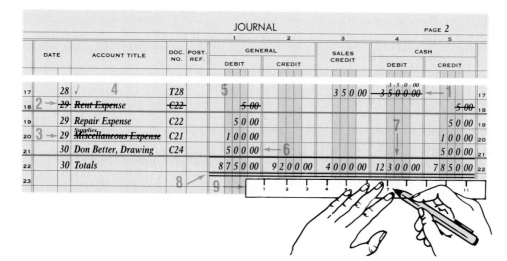

**1** Analyze transactions

a.   From source document
   information

| Receipts | | Calculator tapes |
| Checks | | Memorandums |

b.   Using T accounts

| Rent Expense | | Cash |
| --- | --- | --- |
| 50.00 | | | 50.00 |

c.   Verify for
   each entry that:

Debits ⟶ equal ⟶ Credits

**2** Record entries in a journal

| Transactions | Written in Account Title Column | Journal Amount Columns Used | | | | |
| --- | --- | --- | --- | --- | --- | --- |
| | | General | | Sales | Cash | |
| | | Debit | Credit | Credit | Debit | Credit |
| Received cash from owner as an investment | Capital Account Title | | √ | | √ | |
| Paid cash for supplies | Supplies | √ | | | | √ |
| Paid cash for insurance | Prepaid Insurance | √ | | | | √ |
| Bought supplies on account | Supplies Liability Account Title | √ | √ | | | |
| Paid cash on account | Liability Account Title | √ | | | | √ |
| Received cash from sales | √ | | | √ | √ | |
| Paid cash for an expense | Expense Account Title | √ | | | | √ |
| Paid cash to owner for personal use | Drawing Account Title | √ | | | | √ |

**3** Prove the journal

a.   Rule a single line across amount columns.

b.   Add amount columns.

c.   Add all debit totals and add all credit totals.

d.   Verify that total debits equal total credits.

**4** Prove cash

a.   Cash at beginning + Total cash received = Total
   Total − Total cash paid = Ending cash balance

b.   Verify that the cash balance is the same as the amount shown on
   the next unused check stub.

**5** Complete the journal by ruling double lines across all amount columns.

Illustration 4-18   Summary of journalizing transactions

# SUMMARY OF JOURNALIZING TRANSACTIONS

Rugcare's procedure for journalizing transactions is summarized in Illustration 4-18 on page 68.

## ACCOUNTING TERMS

What is the meaning of each of the following?

1. journal
2. journalizing
3. special amount column
4. general amount column

5. entry
6. double-entry accounting
7. source document
8. check

9. receipt
10. memorandum
11. proving cash

## QUESTIONS FOR INDIVIDUAL STUDY

1. What are the five amount columns in the journal used by Rugcare?
2. Which of the columns in Rugcare's journal are special amount columns?
3. What is the source document for a cash payment transaction?
4. What is the source document for a sales transaction?
5. What is the source document for cash received from transactions other than sales?
6. What is the source document for a transaction when no other source document is prepared or when additional explanation is needed?
7. What are the four parts of a journal entry?
8. What two journal amount columns are used to record cash received from the owner as an investment?
9. What two journal amount columns are

used to record cash paid for supplies?
10. What two journal amount columns are used to record cash paid for insurance?
11. What two journal amount columns are used to record supplies bought on account?
12. What two journal amount columns are used to record cash paid on account?
13. What two journal amount columns are used to record cash received from sales?
14. What two journal amount columns are used to record cash paid for an expense?
15. What two journal amount columns are used to record cash paid to the owner for personal use?
16. What is the procedure for proving a journal page?
17. What are the two steps that Rugcare uses in proving cash?

## CASES FOR MANAGEMENT DECISION

**CASE 1** During the summer, Willard Kelly does odd jobs to earn money. Mr. Kelly keeps all his money in a single checking account. He writes checks to pay for personal items and for business expenses. These payments include personal clothing, school supplies, gasoline for his car, and recreation. Mr. Kelly uses his check stubs as his accounting records. Are Mr. Kelly's accounting procedures and records correct? Explain your answer.

**CASE 2** In his business, Michael Rock uses a journal with the following columns: Date, Account Title, Check No., Cash Debit, and Cash Credit. Mr. Rock's wife, Jennifer, suggests that he needs three additional amount columns: General Debit, General Credit, and Sales Credit. Mr. Rock states that all his business transactions are for cash, and he never buys on account. Therefore, he does not see the need for more than the Cash Debit and Cash Credit special amount columns. Who is correct, Mr. or Mrs. Rock? Explain your answer.

## ▉ DRILLS FOR UNDERSTANDING

### DRILL 4-D1   Analyzing transactions

This drill provides continuing practice in analyzing transactions into debit and credit parts. Use Rugcare's chart of accounts, page 2.

*Transactions*
1. Paid cash for supplies, $100.00.
2. Bought supplies on account from Butler Cleaning Supplies, $500.00.
3. Paid cash to owner for personal use, $50.00.
4. Received cash from sales, $300.00.
5. Paid cash for rent, $200.00.
6. Paid cash for insurance, $250.00.
7. Received cash from owner as an investment, $1,000.00.
8. Paid cash for repairs, $25.00.
9. Paid cash for telephone bill, $30.00.
10. Paid cash for advertising, $40.00.
11. Paid cash on account to Butler Cleaning Supplies, $300.00.
12. Paid cash for miscellaneous expense, $3.00.

**Instructions: 1.** For each transaction, prepare two T accounts. On the T accounts, write the account titles affected by the transaction.

**2.** Write the debit or credit amount in each T account to show how the transaction affected that account. T accounts for Transaction 1 are given as an example.

### DRILL 4-D2   Analyzing transactions

This drill continues the practice in analyzing transactions. Mark Jacobs owns a service business called Jacobs Secretarial Services. Jacobs Secretarial Services uses the following accounts.

Cash
Supplies
Prepaid Insurance
Gable Supplies
Mark Jacobs, Capital
Mark Jacobs, Drawing

Sales
Advertising Expense
Miscellaneous Expense
Rent Expense
Repair Expense
Utilities Expense

Use a form similar to the following. Transaction 1 is given as an example.

| 1 | 2 | 3 | 4 | 5 | 6 | 7 |
|---|---|---|---|---|---|---|
| Trans. No. | Accounts Affected | Account Classification | How Is Account Affected? | | Entered in Account as a | |
| | | | (+) | (−) | Debit | Credit |
| 1. | Advertising Expense Cash | Expense Asset | ✓ | ✓ | ✓ | ✓ |

*Transactions*

1. Paid cash for advertising.
2. Paid cash for repairs.
3. Received cash from owner as an investment.
4. Paid cash for miscellaneous expense.
5. Bought supplies on account from Gable Supplies.
6. Paid cash on account to Gable Supplies.
7. Paid cash for water bill.
8. Paid cash for supplies.
9. Paid cash for rent.
10. Paid cash to owner for personal use.
11. Received cash from sales.
12. Paid cash for insurance.

**Instructions: 1.** In Column 2, write the titles of the accounts changed by each transaction.

**2.** For each account title, write the account classification in Column 3.

**3.** For each account title, place a check mark in either Column 4 or 5 to indicate if each account is increased (+) or decreased (−) by this transaction.

**4.** For each account title, place a check mark in either Column 6 or 7 to indicate if the amount is entered in the account as a debit or a credit.

## ■ APPLICATION PROBLEMS

### PROBLEM 4-1 **Journalizing transactions**

Dorothy Gilbert owns a service business called Lane Company. Lane Company uses the following accounts.

Cash
Supplies
Prepaid Insurance
Mertz Supplies
Dorothy Gilbert, Capital
Dorothy Gilbert, Drawing

Sales
Advertising Expense
Miscellaneous Expense
Rent Expense
Repair Expense
Utilities Expense

**Instructions: 1.** Journalize the following transactions completed during February of the current year. Use page 1 of a journal similar to the one described in this chapter for Rugcare. Source documents are abbreviated as follows: check, C; memorandum, M; receipt, R; calculator tape, T.

Feb.  1. Received cash from owner as an investment, $12,000.00. R1.
      3. Paid cash for rent, $600.00. C1.
      4. Paid cash for insurance, $1,200.00. C2.
      5. Bought supplies on account from Mertz Supplies, $1,500.00. M1.
      6. Paid cash for supplies, $1,000.00. C3.
      7. Paid cash on account to Mertz Supplies, $750.00. C4.
     10. Paid cash for miscellaneous expense, $5.00. C5.
     12. Received cash from sales, $500.00. T12.
     14. Received cash from sales, $450.00. T14.
     17. Paid cash for repairs, $75.00. C6.
     17. Received cash from sales, $300.00. T17.
     20. Received cash from sales, $370.00. T20.
     21. Received cash from sales, $470.00. T21.
     24. Received cash from sales, $400.00. T24.
     25. Paid cash for electric bill, $50.00. C7.
     25. Received cash from sales, $450.00. T25.
     26. Paid cash for advertising, $90.00. C8.
     26. Received cash from sales, $300.00. T26.
     27. Received cash from sales, $350.00. T27.
     28. Paid cash to owner for personal use, $250.00. C9.
     28. Received cash from sales, $500.00. T28.

**2.** Prove the journal. Rule a single line across all amount columns. Write the amount column totals below the single line.

**3.** Prove cash. The beginning cash balance on February 1 is zero. The ending cash balance on the next unused check stub is $12,070.00.

**4.** Rule the journal.

## PROBLEM 4-2   Journalizing transactions

Rona Dowling owns a service business called LawnCare. LawnCare uses the following accounts.

| | |
|---|---|
| Cash | Sales |
| Supplies | Advertising Expense |
| Prepaid Insurance | Miscellaneous Expense |
| Main Office Supplies | Rent Expense |
| Westley Supplies | Repair Expense |
| Rona Dowling, Capital | Utilities Expense |
| Rona Dowling, Drawing | |

**Instructions: 1.** Journalize the following transactions completed during April of the current year. Use page 1 of a journal similar to the one described in this chapter for Rugcare. Source documents are abbreviated as follows: check, C; memorandum, M; receipt, R; calculator tape, T.

Apr.  1. Received cash from owner as an investment, $10,000.00. R1.
      2. Paid cash for rent, $800.00. C1.
      3. Paid cash for insurance, $3,000.00. C2.
      6. Bought supplies on account from Westley Supplies, $2,000.00. M1.
      7. Paid cash for supplies, $700.00. C3.
      8. Paid cash on account to Westley Supplies, $1,000.00. C4.
      8. Received cash from sales, $500.00. T8.
      9. Paid cash for telephone bill, $60.00. C5.

9. Received cash from sales, $650.00. T9.
10. Paid cash for repairs, $85.00. C6.
10. Received cash from sales, $600.00. T10.
13. Paid cash for miscellaneous expense, $15.00. C7.
13. Received cash from sales, $700.00. T13.
14. Received cash from sales, $650.00. T14.
15. Paid cash to owner for personal use, $350.00. C8.
15. Received cash from sales, $500.00. T15.
16. Paid cash for supplies, $1,000.00. C9.
16. Received cash from sales, $600.00. T16.
17. Received cash from sales, $650.00. T17.
20. Bought supplies on account from Main Office Supplies, $500.00. M2.
20. Received cash from sales, $570.00. T20.
21. Received cash from sales, $670.00. T21.

**2.** Prove and rule page 1 of the journal. Carry the column totals forward to page 2 of the journal.
**3.** Use page 2 of the journal. Journalize the following transactions completed during April of the current year.

Apr. 22. Paid cash for electric bill, $55.00. C10.
22. Received cash from sales, $600.00. T22.
23. Bought supplies on account from Main Office Supplies, $50.00. M3.
23. Received cash from sales, $650.00. T23.
24. Paid cash for advertising, $100.00. C11.
24. Received cash from sales, $500.00. T24.
27. Received cash from sales, $550.00. T27.
28. Received cash from sales, $500.00. T28.
29. Paid cash for supplies, $150.00. C12.
29. Received cash from sales, $650.00. T29.
30. Paid cash to owner for personal use, $350.00. C13.
30. Received cash from sales, $500.00. T30.

**4.** Prove page 2 of the journal.
**5.** Prove cash. The beginning cash balance on April 1 is zero. The balance on the next unused check stub is $12,375.00.
**6.** Rule page 2 of the journal.

## ■ ENRICHMENT PROBLEMS

### MASTERY PROBLEM 4-M   Journalizing transactions

Rachel Frank owns a service business called Frank's Car Wash. Frank's Car Wash uses the following accounts.

| | |
|---|---|
| Cash | Sales |
| Supplies | Advertising Expense |
| Prepaid Insurance | Miscellaneous Expense |
| Delancy Supplies | Rent Expense |
| Long Supplies | Repair Expense |
| Rachel Frank, Capital | Utilities Expense |
| Rachel Frank, Drawing | |

**Instructions: 1.** Journalize the following transactions completed during June of the current year. Use page 1 of a journal similar to the one described in this chapter for Rugcare. Source documents are abbreviated as follows: check, C; memorandum, M; receipt, R; calculator tape, T.

June　1. Received cash from owner as an investment, $18,000.00. R1.
　　　2. Paid cash for rent, $900.00. C1.
　　　3. Paid cash for supplies, $1,500.00. C2.
　　　4. Bought supplies on account from Delancy Supplies, $3,000.00. M1.
　　　5. Paid cash for insurance, $4,500.00. C3.
　　　8. Paid cash on account to Delancy Supplies, $1,500.00. C4.
　　　8. Received cash from sales, $750.00. T8.
　　　9. Paid cash for electric bill, $75.00. C5.
　　　9. Received cash from sales, $700.00. T9.
　　10. Paid cash for miscellaneous expense, $7.00. C6.
　　10. Received cash from sales, $750.00. T10.
　　11. Paid cash for repairs, $100.00. C7.
　　11. Received cash from sales, $850.00. T11.
　　12. Received cash from sales, $700.00. T12.
　　15. Paid cash to owner for personal use, $350.00. C8.
　　15. Received cash from sales, $750.00. T15.
　　16. Paid cash for supplies, $1,500.00. C9.
　　16. Received cash from sales, $650.00. T16.
　　17. Bought supplies on account from Long Supplies, $750.00. M2.
　　17. Received cash from sales, $600.00. T17.
　　18. Received cash from sales, $800.00. T18.
　　19. Received cash from sales, $750.00. T19.

　　**2.** Prove and rule page 1 of the journal. Carry the column totals forward to page 2 of the journal.
　　**3.** Use page 2 of the journal. Journalize the following transactions completed during June of the current year.

June 22. Bought supplies on account from Long Supplies, $80.00. M3.
　　22. Received cash from sales, $700.00. T22.
　　23. Paid cash for advertising, $130.00. C10.
　　23. Received cash from sales, $650.00. T23.
　　24. Paid cash for telephone bill, $60.00. C11.
　　24. Received cash from sales, $600.00. T24.
　　25. Received cash from sales, $550.00. T25.
　　26. Paid cash for supplies, $70.00. C12.
　　26. Received cash from sales, $600.00. T26.
　　29. Received cash from sales, $750.00. T29.
　　30. Paid cash to owner for personal use, $375.00. C13.
　　30. Received cash from sales, $800.00. T30.

　　**4.** Prove page 2 of the journal.
　　**5.** Prove cash. The beginning cash balance on June 1 is zero. The balance on the next unused check stub is $18,883.00.
　　**6.** Rule page 2 of the journal.

## CHALLENGE PROBLEM 4-C  Journalizing transactions

Wilbur Moore owns a service business called Moore's Tailors. Moore's Tailors uses the following accounts.

| | |
|---|---|
| Cash | Sales |
| Supplies | Advertising Expense |
| Prepaid Insurance | Miscellaneous Expense |
| Marker Supplies | Rent Expense |
| O'Brien Supplies | Repair Expense |
| Wilbur Moore, Capital | Utilities Expense |
| Wilbur Moore, Drawing | |

**Instructions: 1.** Use page 1 of a journal similar to the following.

| Cash | | Date | Account Title | Doc. No. | Post. Ref. | General | | Sales Credit |
|---|---|---|---|---|---|---|---|---|
| Debit | Credit | | | | | Debit | Credit | |
| | | | | | | | | |

Journal    Page 1

Journalize the following transactions completed during June of the current year. Source documents are abbreviated as follows: check, C; memorandum, M; receipt, R; calculator tape, T.

June  1. Received cash from owner as an investment, $17,000.00. R1.
   2. Paid cash for supplies, $1,400.00. C1.
   3. Paid cash for rent, $800.00. C2.
   4. Paid cash for insurance, $3,000.00. C3.
   5. Bought supplies on account from Marker Supplies, $2,500.00. M1.
   7. Received cash from sales, $550.00. T7.
   9. Paid cash for telephone bill, $70.00. C4.
   9. Paid cash on account to Marker Supplies, $1,300.00. C5.
   10. Received cash from sales, $550.00. T10.
   11. Paid cash for miscellaneous expense, $6.00. C6.
   11. Received cash from sales, $550.00. T11.
   12. Paid cash for repairs, $90.00. C7.
   12. Received cash from sales, $600.00. T12.
   15. Paid cash for supplies, $1,300.00. C8.
   15. Received cash from sales, $540.00. T15.
   16. Paid cash to owner for personal use, $300.00. C9.
   16. Received cash from sales, $400.00. T16.
   17. Received cash from sales, $780.00. T17.
   18. Bought supplies on account from O'Brien Supplies, $900.00. M2.
   18. Received cash from sales, $600.00. T18.
   19. Paid cash for supplies, $85.00. C10.
   19. Received cash from sales, $850.00. T19.

**2.** Prove and rule page 1 of the journal. Carry the column totals forward to page 2 of the journal.
**3.** Use page 2 of the journal. Journalize the following transactions completed during June of the current year.

June 22. Received cash from sales, $700.00. T22.
      23. Bought supplies on account from Marker Supplies, $95.00. M3.
      23. Received cash from sales, $720.00. T23.
      24. Paid cash for advertising, $100.00. C11.
      24. Received cash from sales, $550.00. T24.
      25. Paid cash for water bill, $75.00. C12.
      25. Received cash from sales, $600.00. T25.
      26. Received cash from sales, $450.00. T26.
      29. Paid cash on account to O'Brien Supplies, $900.00. C13.
      29. Received cash from sales, $630.00. T29.
      30. Paid cash to owner for personal use, $450.00. C14.
      30. Received cash from sales, $360.00. T30.

**4.** Prove page 2 of the journal.

**5.** Prove cash. The cash balance on June 1 is zero. The balance on the next unused check stub is $16,554.00.

**6.** Rule page 2 of the journal.

# Posting to a General Ledger

## ENABLING PERFORMANCE TASKS

After studying Chapter 5, you will be able to:
a. Define accounting terms related to posting from a journal to a general ledger.
b. Identify accounting concepts and practices related to posting from a journal to a general ledger.
c. Prepare a chart of accounts for a service business organized as a proprietorship.
d. Post amounts from a journal to a general ledger.

Rugcare records transactions in a journal as described in Chapter 4. A journal is a permanent record of the debit and credit parts of each transaction with transactions recorded in chronological order. A journal does not show in one place all the changes in a single account. If only a journal is used, a business must search through all journal pages to find items affecting a single account balance. For this reason, a form is used to summarize in one place all the changes to a single account. A separate form is used for each account.

An account form is based on and includes the debit and credit sides of a T account as shown in Illustration 5-1.

Illustration 5-1
Relationship of a T account to an account form

In addition to debit and credit columns, space is provided in the account form for recording the transaction date and journal page number. This information can be used to trace a specific entry back to where a transaction is recorded in a journal.

The major disadvantage of the account form shown in Illustration 5-1 is that no current, up-to-date account balance is shown. If the form in Illustration 5-1 is used, an up-to-date balance must be figured each time the account is examined. Also, the balance is difficult and time consuming to figure when an account has a large number of entries. Therefore, a more commonly used account form has Debit and Credit Balance columns as shown in Illustration 5-2. Because the form has columns for the debit and credit balance, it is often referred to as the balance-ruled account form.

Illustration 5-2
Account form

| ACCOUNT | | | | | ACCOUNT NO. | |
|---|---|---|---|---|---|---|
| DATE | ITEM | POST. REF. | DEBIT | CREDIT | BALANCE | |
| | | | | | DEBIT | CREDIT |
| | | | | | | |
| | | | | | | |
| | | | | | | |
| | | | | | | |

Balance columns

The account balance is figured and recorded as each entry is recorded in the account. Recording information in an account is described later in this chapter. The T account is a useful device for analyzing transactions into debit and credit parts. However, the balance-ruled account form is more useful as a permanent record of changes to account balances than is the T account. Rugcare uses the balance-ruled account form.

# ARRANGING ACCOUNTS IN A GENERAL LEDGER

A group of accounts is called a ledger. A ledger that contains all accounts needed to prepare financial statements is called a general ledger. The name given to an account is known as an account title. The number assigned to an account is called an account number.

## Preparing a chart of accounts

A list of account titles and numbers showing the location of each account in a ledger is known as a chart of accounts. Rugcare's chart of accounts is shown in Illustration 5-3.

For ease of use while studying Part 1, Rugcare's chart of accounts is also shown on page 2.

---

**RUGCARE**
**Chart of Accounts**

Balance Sheet Accounts

**(100) ASSETS**

110 Cash
120 Petty Cash
130 Supplies
140 Prepaid Insurance

**(200) LIABILITIES**

210 Butler Cleaning Supplies
220 Dale Office Supplies

**(300) OWNER'S EQUITY**

310 Ben Furman, Capital
320 Ben Furman, Drawing
330 Income Summary

Income Statement Accounts

**(400) REVENUE**

410 Sales

**(500) EXPENSES**

510 Advertising Expense
520 Insurance Expense
530 Miscellaneous Expense
540 Rent Expense
550 Repair Expense
560 Supplies Expense
570 Utilities Expense

Illustration 5-3
Chart of accounts

---

Accounts in a general ledger are arranged in the same order as they appear on financial statements. Rugcare's chart of accounts, Illustration 5-3, shows five general ledger divisions. (1) Assets, (2) Liabilities, (3) Owner's Equity, (4) Revenue, and (5) Expenses.

## Numbering general ledger accounts

Rugcare assigns a three-digit account number to each account. For example, Supplies is assigned the number *130* as shown in Illustration 5-4.

1   3   0   **Supplies**

General ledger division    Location within general ledger division

Illustration 5-4
Account numbers

The first digit of each account number shows the general ledger division in which the account is located. For example, the asset division accounts are numbered in the 100s. Therefore, the number for the asset account, Supplies, begins with a *1*.

The second two digits indicate the location of each account within a general ledger division. The *1* in the account number 130, Supplies, indicates that the account is located in the asset division. The *30* in the account number for Supplies indicates that the account is located between account number 120 and account number 140.

Rugcare initially assigns account numbers by 10s so that new accounts can be added easily. Nine numbers are unused between each account on Rugcare's chart of accounts, Illustration 5-3. For example, numbers 111 to 119 are unused between accounts numbered 110 and 120. New numbers can be assigned between existing account numbers without renumbering all existing accounts. The procedure for arranging accounts in a general ledger, assigning account numbers, and keeping records current is called file maintenance.

Unused account numbers are assigned to new accounts. Rugcare records payments for gasoline in Miscellaneous Expense. If Mr. Furman found that the amount paid each month for gasoline had become a major expense, he might decide to use a separate account. The account might be titled Gasoline Expense. Rugcare arranges expense accounts in alphabetical order in its general ledger. Therefore, the new account would be inserted between Advertising Expense and Insurance Expense.

| | | |
|---|---|---|
| 510 | Advertising Expense | (Existing account) |
| | GASOLINE EXPENSE | (NEW ACCOUNT) |
| 520 | Insurance Expense | (Existing account) |

The number selected for the new account should leave some unused numbers on either side of it for other accounts that might need to be added. The middle, unused account number between existing numbers 510 and 520 is 515. Therefore, 515 is assigned as the account number for the new account.

| | | |
|---|---|---|
| 510 | Advertising Expense | (Existing account) |
| 515 | GASOLINE EXPENSE | (NEW ACCOUNT) |
| 520 | Insurance Expense | (Existing account) |

When an account is no longer needed, it is removed from the general ledger and the chart of accounts. For example, if Rugcare were to buy its own equipment and building, there would be no need for the rent expense account. The account numbered 540 would be removed, and that number would become unused and available to assign to another account if the need should arise.

When a new account is added at the end of a ledger division, the next number in a sequence of 10s is used. For example, suppose Rugcare needs to add another expense account, Water Expense, to show more detail about one of the utility expenses. The expense accounts are arranged in alphabetical order. Therefore, the new account would be added at the end of the expense section of the chart of accounts. The last used expense account number is 570, as shown on the chart of accounts, Illustration 5-3. The next number in the sequence of 10s is 580, which is assigned as the number of the new account.

| | | |
|---|---|---|
| 560 | Supplies Expense | (Existing account) |
| 570 | Utilities Expense | (Existing account) |
| 580 | WATER EXPENSE | (NEW ACCOUNT) |

Rugcare has relatively few general ledger accounts and does not antici-pate adding many new accounts in the future. Therefore, a three-digit ac-count number adequately provides for the few account numbers that might be added. However, as the number of general ledger accounts in-creases, a business may change to four or more digits.

Charts of accounts with more than three digits are described in later chapters.

## Opening general ledger accounts

Writing an account title and number on the heading of an account is called opening an account. A general ledger account is opened for each ac-count listed on a chart of accounts. Accounts are opened and arranged in a general ledger in the same order as on the chart of accounts.

Cash, account number 110, is the first account on Rugcare's chart of ac-counts. The cash account is opened as shown in Illustration 5-5.

| | | | | | | | |
|---|---|---|---|---|---|---|---|
| | | | | | | **BALANCE** | |
| DATE | ITEM | POST. REF. | DEBIT | CREDIT | DEBIT | CREDIT |
| ACCOUNT *Cash* | | | | | | ACCOUNT NO. *110* | |

Illustration 5-5
Opening an account in a general ledger

1  Write the account title, *Cash*, after the word *Account* in the heading.

2  Write the account number, *110*, after the words *Account No.* in the heading.

The same procedure is used to open all accounts listed on Rugcare's chart of accounts.

# POSTING FROM A JOURNAL TO A GENERAL LEDGER

Transferring information from a journal entry to a ledger account is called posting. Posting sorts journal entries so that all debits and credits affecting each account are brought together in one place. For example, all changes to Cash are brought together in the cash account.

Amounts in journal entries are recorded in either general amount columns or special amount columns. There are two rules for posting amounts from a journal. (1) Separate amounts in a journal's general amount columns are posted individually to the account written in the Account Title column. (2) Separate amounts in a journal's special amount columns are not posted individually. Instead, the special amount column totals are posted to the account named in the heading of the special amount column.

## Posting separate amounts

For most, but not all journal entries, at least one separate amount is posted individually to a general ledger account. When an entry in a journal includes an amount in a general amount column and an account title in the Account Title column, the amount is posted individually.

**Posting a separate amount from a General Debit column.** Each separate amount in the General Debit and General Credit columns of a journal is posted to the account written in the Account Title column. Posting an amount from the General Debit column is shown in Illustration 5-6.

Illustration 5-6
Posting an amount from a
General Debit column

1  Write the date, 19--, Aug. 3, in the Date column of the account, Supplies.

2  Write the journal page number, 1, in the Post. Ref. column of the account. Post. Ref. is an abbreviation for Posting Reference.

**3** Write the debit amount, *$1,577.00*, in the Debit amount column.

**4** Write the new account balance, *$1,577.00*, in the Balance Debit column. Because this entry is the first in the supplies account, the previous balance is zero. The new account balance is calculated as shown below.

| Previous Balance | + | Debit Column Amount | = | New Debit Balance |
|---|---|---|---|---|
| $0.00 | + | $1,577.00 | = | $1,577.00 |

**5** Return to the journal and write the account number, *130*, in the Post. Ref. column of the journal.

The numbers in the Post. Ref. columns of the general ledger account and the journal serve three purposes. (1) An entry in an account can be traced to its source in a journal. (2) An entry in a journal can be traced to where it was posted in an account. (3) If posting is interrupted, the accounting personnel can easily see which entries in the journal still need to be posted. A blank in the Post. Ref. column of the journal indicates that posting for that line still needs to be completed. *Therefore, the posting reference is always recorded in the journal as the last step in the posting procedure.*

A second amount is posted to the supplies account from Rugcare's journal, line 4, as shown in Illustration 5-7.

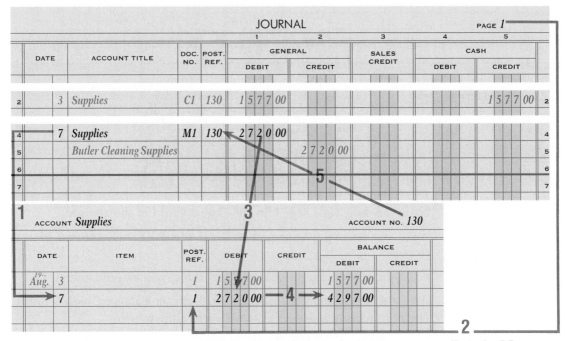

Illustration 5-7
Posting a second amount to an account

**1** Write the date, *7*, in the Date column of the account.

The month and year are written only once on a page of a ledger account unless the month or year changes.

**2** Write the journal page number, *1*, in the Post. Ref. column of the account.

**3** Write the debit amount, *$2,720.00*, in the Debit amount column.

**4** Write the new account balance, *$4,297.00*, in the Balance Debit column. The new account balance is calculated as shown below.

| Previous Debit Balance | + | Debit Column Amount | = | New Debit Balance |
|---|---|---|---|---|
| $1,577.00 | + | $2,720.00 | = | $4,297.00 |

**5** Return to the journal and write the account number, *130*, in the Post. Ref. column of the journal.

**Posting a separate amount from a General Credit column.** An amount in the General Credit column of a journal is posted as shown in Illustration 5-8.

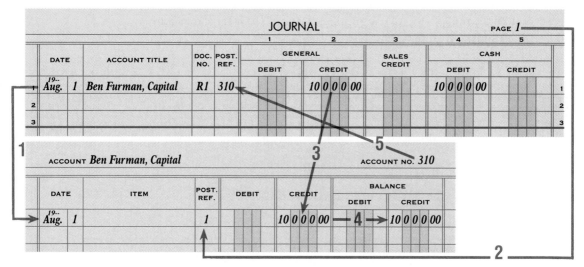

Illustration 5-8
Posting an amount from a
General Credit column

**1** Write the date, *19--, Aug. 1*, in the Date column of the account.

**2** Write the journal page number, *1*, in the Post. Ref. column of the account.

**3** Write the credit amount, *$10,000.00*, in the Credit amount column.

**4** Write the new account balance, *$10,000.00*, in the Balance Credit column. The new account balance is calculated as shown below.

| Previous Balance | + | Credit Column Amount | = | New Credit Balance |
|---|---|---|---|---|
| $0.00 | + | $10,000.00 | = | $10,000.00 |

**5** Return to the journal and write the account number, *310*, in the Post. Ref. column of the journal.

**Journal entries that are not posted individually.** Several lines in Rugcare's journal contain separate amounts that are not to be posted individually. These include forwarding totals and amounts recorded in special amount columns.

The totals brought forward from page 1 are shown on line 1 of the journal in Illustration 5-9. None of these separate total amounts on line 1 are posted individually to general ledger accounts. To assure that no postings are overlooked, no blank posting reference spaces should be left in the Post. Ref. column of the journal. Therefore, when the totals were forwarded to page 2 of the journal, a check mark was placed in the Post. Ref. column of line 1 to show that no separate amounts are posted individually.

| | DATE | ACCOUNT TITLE | DOC. NO. | POST. REF. | GENERAL DEBIT | GENERAL CREDIT | SALES CREDIT | CASH DEBIT | CASH CREDIT | |
|---|---|---|---|---|---|---|---|---|---|---|
| | | | | | 1 | 2 | 3 | 4 | 5 | |
| 1 | *Aug.* 19-- 20 | *Brought Forward* | | √ | 7 9 2 0 00 | 12 9 2 0 00 | 2 3 1 9 00 | 12 3 1 9 00 | 5 0 0 0 00 | 1 |
| 11 | 31 | *Miscellaneous Expense* | C15 | 530 | 7 00 | | | | 1 2 00 | 11 |
| 12 | | *Repair Expense* | | 550 | 5 00 | | | | | 12 |
| 13 | 31 | *Ben Furman, Drawing* | C16 | 320 | 5 0 0 00 | | | | 5 0 0 00 | 13 |
| 14 | 31 √ | | T31 | √ | | | 2 9 0 00 | 2 9 0 00 | | 14 |
| 15 | 31 | *Totals* | | | 8 9 3 9 00 | 12 9 2 0 00 | 4 2 9 1 00 | 14 2 9 1 00 | 6 0 1 9 00 | 15 |
| 16 | | | | | (√) | (√) | | | | 16 |
| 17 | | | | | | | | | | 17 |

**JOURNAL**                                                      PAGE *2*

Check mark indicates that amounts ARE NOT posted individually

Check marks indicate that general amount column totals ARE NOT posted

Separate amounts in the special amount columns, Sales Credit, Cash Debit, and Cash Credit, are not posted individually. For example, on line 14 of the journal, Illustration 5-9, two separate $290.00 amounts are recorded in two special amount columns, Sales Credit and Cash Debit.

A check mark was placed in the Post. Ref. column on line 14 when the entry was journalized. The check mark indicates that no separate amounts are posted individually from this line. Instead, the totals of the special amount columns are posted.

Illustration 5-9
Check marks show that amounts are not posted

## Posting the totals of amount columns

Separate amounts in special amount columns *are not* posted individually. The separate amounts are part of the special amount column totals. Only the totals of special amount columns *are* posted.

**Totals of General Debit and General Credit amount columns.** The General Debit and General Credit columns are not special amount columns because the column headings do not contain the name of an account. All of the separate amounts in the General Debit and General Credit amount columns are posted individually. Therefore, the column totals *are not* posted. A check mark in parentheses is placed below each general amount column total as shown in Illustration 5-9. The check mark indicates that the totals of the General Debit and General Credit columns are not posted.

A check mark in the Post. Ref. column indicates that amounts are not to be posted individually. On the totals line, the amounts in the special amount columns are posted. Therefore, a check mark is not placed in the Post. Ref. column for the totals line.

**Posting the totals of special amount columns.** Rugcare's journal has three special amount columns for which only totals are posted: Sales Credit, Cash Debit, and Cash Credit.

**Posting the total of the Sales Credit column.** The Sales Credit column of a journal is a special amount column with the account title Sales in the heading. Each separate amount in a special amount column could be posted individually. However, all of the separate amounts are debits or credits to the same account. Therefore, an advantage of a special amount column is that only the column total needs to be posted. For example, 14 separate sales transactions are recorded in the Sales Credit column of Rugcare's August journal. Instead of making 14 separate credit postings to Sales, only the column total is posted. As a result, only one posting is needed, which saves 13 postings. The smaller number of postings means 13 fewer opportunities to make a posting error. Posting special amount column totals saves time and results in greater accuracy.

The total of Rugcare's Sales Credit column is posted as shown in Illustration 5-10.

1  Write the date, *19--, Aug. 31*, in the Date column of the account, Sales.

2  Write the journal page number, *2*, in the Post. Ref. column of the account.

3  Write the column total, *$4,291.00*, in the Credit amount column.

4  Write the new account balance, *$4,291.00*, in the Balance Credit column. The new account balance is calculated as shown below.

| Previous Balance | + | Credit Column Amount | = | New Credit Balance |
|---|---|---|---|---|
| $0.00 | + | $4,291.00 | = | $4,291.00 |

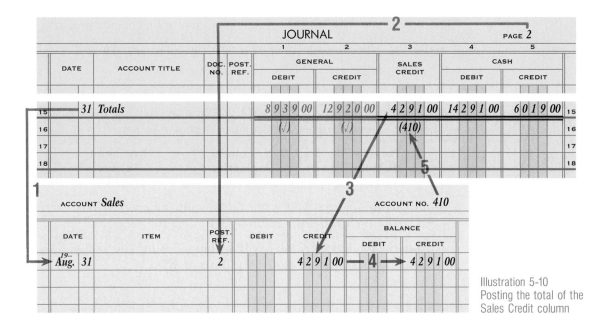

Illustration 5-10
Posting the total of the
Sales Credit column

**5** Return to the journal and write the account number in parentheses, *(410)*, below the Sales Credit column total.

**Posting the total of the Cash Debit column.** The Cash Debit column of a journal is posted as shown in Illustration 5-11.

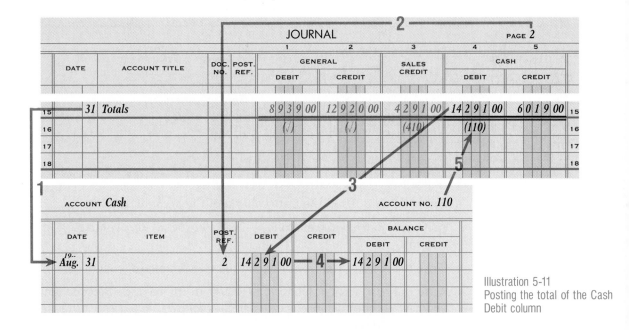

Illustration 5-11
Posting the total of the Cash
Debit column

1 Write the date, *19--, Aug. 31*, in the Date column of the account, Cash.

2 Write the journal page number, *2*, in the Post. Ref. column of the account.

3 Write the column total, *$14,291.00*, in the Debit amount column.

4 Write the new account balance, *$14,291.00*, in the Balance Debit column. The new account balance is calculated as shown below.

| Previous Balance | + | Debit Column Amount | = | New Debit Balance |
|---|---|---|---|---|
| $0.00 | + | $14,291.00 | = | $14,291.00 |

5 Return to the journal and write the account number in parentheses, *(110)*, below the Cash Debit column total.

**Posting the total of the Cash Credit column.** Posting the total of a journal's Cash Credit column is shown in Illustration 5-12.

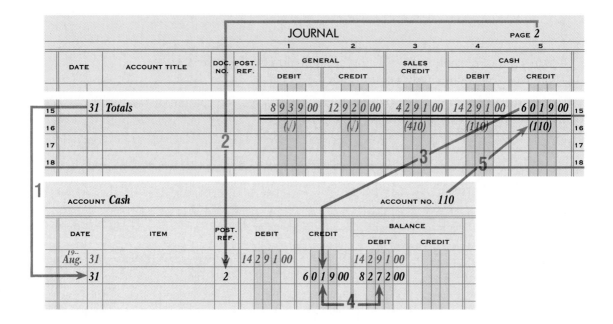

Illustration 5-12
Posting the total of the
Cash Credit column

1 Write the date, *31*, in the Date column of the account, Cash.

2 Write the journal page number, *2*, in the Post. Ref. column of the account.

3 Write the column total, *$6,019.00*, in the Credit amount column.

4 Write the new account balance, *$8,272.00*, in the Balance Debit column. The new account balance is calculated as follows.

| Previous Debit<br>Balance | − | Credit Column<br>Amount | = | New Debit<br>Balance |
|---|---|---|---|---|
| $14,291.00 | − | $6,019.00 | = | $8,272.00 |

Whenever the debits in an account exceed the credits, the account balance is a debit. Whenever the credits in an account exceed the debits, the account balance is a credit.

5 Return to the journal and write the account number in parentheses, *(110)*, below the Cash Credit column total.

## Journal page with posting completed

Page 2 of Rugcare's August journal, after all posting has been completed, is shown in Illustration 5-13.

JOURNAL                                                                        PAGE 2

|   | DATE | ACCOUNT TITLE | DOC. NO. | POST. REF. | GENERAL DEBIT | GENERAL CREDIT | SALES CREDIT | CASH DEBIT | CASH CREDIT |   |
|---|---|---|---|---|---|---|---|---|---|---|
| 1 | *19--*<br>*Aug.* 20 | *Brought Forward* |  | √ | 7 9 2 0 00 | 12 9 2 0 00 | 2 3 1 9 00 | 12 3 1 9 00 | 5 0 0 0 00 | 1 |
| 2 | 21 | √ | T21 | √ |  |  | 2 7 0 00 | 2 7 0 00 |  | 2 |
| 3 | 24 | √ | T24 | √ |  |  | 3 0 0 00 | 3 0 0 00 |  | 3 |
| 4 | 25 | √ | T25 | √ |  |  | 3 1 0 00 | 3 1 0 00 |  | 4 |
| 5 | 26 | √ | T26 | √ |  |  | 2 4 5 00 | 2 4 5 00 |  | 5 |
| 6 | 27 | *Utilities Expense* | C13 | 570 | 7 0 00 |  |  |  | 7 0 00 | 6 |
| 7 | 27 | √ | T27 | √ |  |  | 2 9 0 00 | 2 9 0 00 |  | 7 |
| 8 | 28 | *Supplies* | C14 | 130 | 4 3 4 00 |  |  |  | 4 3 4 00 | 8 |
| 9 | 28 | √ | T28 | √ |  |  | 2 6 7 00 | 2 6 7 00 |  | 9 |
| 10 | 28 | *Miscellaneous Expense* | M3 | 530 | 3 00 |  |  |  | 3 00 | 10 |
| 11 | 31 | *Miscellaneous Expense* | C15 | 530 | 7 00 |  |  |  | 1 2 00 | 11 |
| 12 |  | *Repair Expense* |  | 550 | 5 00 |  |  |  |  | 12 |
| 13 | 31 | *Ben Furman, Drawing* | C16 | 320 | 5 0 0 00 |  |  |  | 5 0 0 00 | 13 |
| 14 | 31 | √ | T31 | √ |  |  | 2 9 0 00 | 2 9 0 00 |  | 14 |
| 15 | 31 | *Totals* |  |  | 8 9 3 9 00 | 12 9 2 0 00 | 4 2 9 1 00 | 14 2 9 1 00 | 6 0 1 9 00 | 15 |
| 16 |  |  |  |  | (√) | (√) | (410) | (110) | (110) | 16 |
| 17 |  |  |  |  |  |  |  |  |  | 17 |

## General ledger with posting completed

Rugcare's general ledger, after all posting from the August journal is completed, is shown in Illustration 5-14.

The use of the accounts, Income Summary, Insurance Expense, and Supplies Expense, is described in Chapter 7.

Illustration 5-13
A journal page after posting has been completed

| ACCOUNT *Cash* | | | | | | ACCOUNT NO. *110* | |
|---|---|---|---|---|---|---|---|
| DATE | ITEM | POST. REF. | DEBIT | CREDIT | BALANCE | | |
| | | | | | DEBIT | CREDIT | |
| 19.. Aug. 31 | | 2 | 14 2 9 1 00 | | 14 2 9 1 00 | | |
| 31 | | 2 | | 6 0 1 9 00 | 8 2 7 2 00 | | |

| ACCOUNT *Petty Cash* | | | | | | ACCOUNT NO. *120* | |
|---|---|---|---|---|---|---|---|
| DATE | ITEM | POST. REF. | DEBIT | CREDIT | BALANCE | | |
| | | | | | DEBIT | CREDIT | |
| 19.. Aug. 17 | | 1 | 2 0 0 00 | | 2 0 0 00 | | |

| ACCOUNT *Supplies* | | | | | | ACCOUNT NO. *130* | |
|---|---|---|---|---|---|---|---|
| DATE | ITEM | POST. REF. | DEBIT | CREDIT | BALANCE | | |
| | | | | | DEBIT | CREDIT | |
| 19.. Aug. 3 | | 1 | 1 5 7 7 00 | | 1 5 7 7 00 | | |
| 7 | | 1 | 2 7 2 0 00 | | 4 2 9 7 00 | | |
| 20 | | 1 | 2 0 0 00 | | 4 4 9 7 00 | | |
| 28 | | 2 | 4 3 4 00 | | 4 9 3 1 00 | | |

| ACCOUNT *Prepaid Insurance* | | | | | | ACCOUNT NO. *140* | |
|---|---|---|---|---|---|---|---|
| DATE | ITEM | POST. REF. | DEBIT | CREDIT | BALANCE | | |
| | | | | | DEBIT | CREDIT | |
| 19.. Aug. 4 | | 1 | 1 2 0 0 00 | | 1 2 0 0 00 | | |

| ACCOUNT *Butler Cleaning Supplies* | | | | | | ACCOUNT NO. *210* | |
|---|---|---|---|---|---|---|---|
| DATE | ITEM | POST. REF. | DEBIT | CREDIT | BALANCE | | |
| | | | | | DEBIT | CREDIT | |
| 19.. Aug. 7 | | 1 | | 2 7 2 0 00 | | 2 7 2 0 00 | |
| 11 | | 1 | 1 3 6 0 00 | | | 1 3 6 0 00 | |

| ACCOUNT *Dale Office Supplies* | | | | | | ACCOUNT NO. *220* | |
|---|---|---|---|---|---|---|---|
| DATE | ITEM | POST. REF. | DEBIT | CREDIT | BALANCE | | |
| | | | | | DEBIT | CREDIT | |
| 19.. Aug. 20 | | 1 | | 2 0 0 00 | | 2 0 0 00 | |

Illustration 5-14
A general ledger after
posting has been
completed

Illustration 5-14
A general ledger after
posting has been
completed
(continued)

ACCOUNT *Ben Furman, Capital*                                    ACCOUNT NO. *310*

| DATE | | ITEM | POST. REF. | DEBIT | CREDIT | BALANCE | |
|---|---|---|---|---|---|---|---|
| | | | | | | DEBIT | CREDIT |
| 19--<br>Aug. | 1 | | 1 | | 10 0 0 0 00 | | 10 0 0 0 00 |

ACCOUNT *Ben Furman, Drawing*                                    ACCOUNT NO. *320*

| DATE | | ITEM | POST. REF. | DEBIT | CREDIT | BALANCE | |
|---|---|---|---|---|---|---|---|
| | | | | | | DEBIT | CREDIT |
| 19--<br>Aug. | 12 | | 1 | 1 0 0 00 | | 1 0 0 00 | |
| | 31 | | 2 | 5 0 0 00 | | 6 0 0 00 | |

ACCOUNT *Income Summary*                                    ACCOUNT NO. *330*

| DATE | ITEM | POST. REF. | DEBIT | CREDIT | BALANCE | |
|---|---|---|---|---|---|---|
| | | | | | DEBIT | CREDIT |
| | | | | | | |

ACCOUNT *Sales*                                    ACCOUNT NO. *410*

| DATE | | ITEM | POST. REF. | DEBIT | CREDIT | BALANCE | |
|---|---|---|---|---|---|---|---|
| | | | | | | DEBIT | CREDIT |
| 19--<br>Aug. | 31 | | 2 | | 4 2 9 1 00 | | 4 2 9 1 00 |

ACCOUNT *Advertising Expense*                                    ACCOUNT NO. *510*

| DATE | | ITEM | POST. REF. | DEBIT | CREDIT | BALANCE | |
|---|---|---|---|---|---|---|---|
| | | | | | | DEBIT | CREDIT |
| 19--<br>Aug. | 14 | | 1 | 6 8 00 | | 6 8 00 | |

ACCOUNT *Insurance Expense*                                    ACCOUNT NO. *520*

| DATE | ITEM | POST. REF. | DEBIT | CREDIT | BALANCE | |
|---|---|---|---|---|---|---|
| | | | | | DEBIT | CREDIT |
| | | | | | | |

# SUMMARY OF POSTING TO A GENERAL LEDGER

The procedures for posting from Rugcare's journal are summarized in
Illustration 5-15.

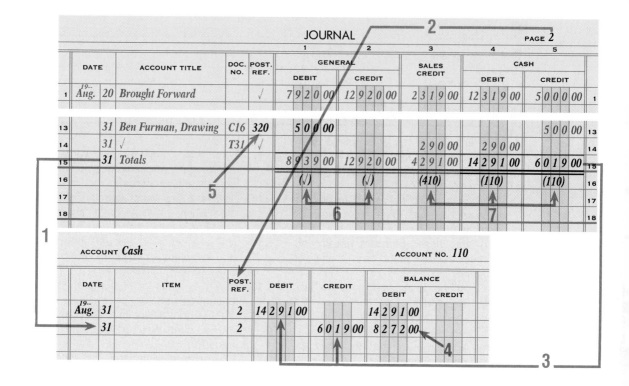

Seven steps are followed in posting an amount from a journal to a general ledger.

Illustration 5-15
Summary of posting to a general ledger

1 The date is written in the Date column of the account.

2 The journal page number is written in the Post. Ref. column of the account.

3 The amount is written in the Debit or Credit amount column of the account.

4 A new account balance is calculated and recorded in the Balance Debit or Balance Credit column of the account.

5 An account number is placed in the Post. Ref. column of the journal to show to which account a separate amount on that line has been posted. The account number is written in the journal *as the last step* in the posting procedure.

6 Check marks are placed in parentheses below general amount columns of a journal to show that the totals of these columns *are not* posted.

7 Account numbers are placed in parentheses below special amount column totals of a journal to show that these column totals have been posted.

## ACCOUNTING TERMS

What is the meaning of each of the following?
1. ledger
2. general ledger
3. account number
4. file maintenance
5. opening an account
6. posting

## QUESTIONS FOR INDIVIDUAL STUDY

1. Why are general ledger accounts used in an accounting system?
2. In what order are accounts arranged in a general ledger?
3. On Rugcare's chart of accounts, what is indicated by each digit in an account number?
4. Why are unused numbers usually left between account numbers on a chart of accounts?
5. What number is assigned to a new account inserted in a chart of accounts between accounts numbered 530 and 540?
6. What number is assigned to a new account added at the end of a division in which the last account is numbered 550?
7. What are the two steps in opening a new account?
8. Why are amounts posted from a journal to general ledger accounts?
9. What are the five steps in posting an amount from a journal to a general ledger account?
10. What three purposes are served by recording posting reference numbers in journals and accounts?
11. How is a new account balance calculated when the previous balance is a debit and a debit entry is posted?
12. Why are separate amounts in special amount columns of a journal not posted individually?
13. Why are totals of a journal's general amount columns not posted?
14. What is done to indicate that the general amount column totals are not posted?
15. What is done to indicate that a special amount column total in a journal has been posted?
16. How is a new account balance calculated when the previous balance is a debit, a credit entry is posted, and the previous debit balance is larger than the credit entry?

## CASES FOR MANAGEMENT DECISION

**CASE 1** Angela Desellio does not use a journal in her business records. She records the debits and credits for each transaction directly in the general ledger accounts. Is Ms. Desellio using the correct procedure? Explain your answer.

**CASE 2** Philip Westing does the accounting work for his business. When posting, he first transfers all of the information to the general ledger accounts. Then he returns to the journal and, all at one time, writes the account numbers in the Post. Ref. column of the journal. Diana Young also does the accounting work for her business. When posting, she writes all the account numbers in the Post. Ref. column of the journal before she transfers any information to the accounts. Is Mr. Westing or Miss Young following the correct procedure? Explain your answer.

## DRILLS FOR UNDERSTANDING

### DRILL 5-D1  Preparing a chart of accounts

The following account descriptions refer to the location of accounts in a chart of accounts similar to the one for Rugcare, page 2.

1. The first asset account
2. The first liability account
3. The first owner's equity account
4. The first revenue account
5. The first expense account

7. The fourth expense account
8. The owner's drawing account
9. The cash account
10. The sales account
11. The owner's capital account

6. The third asset account   Use a form similar to the following. Account description 1 is given as an example.

| 1 | 2 |
|---|---|
| **Account Description** | **Account Number** |
| 1. The first asset account | *110* |

**Instructions: 1.** In Column 1, write the account description.

**2.** In Column 2, write the account number. Account numbers are assigned by 10s.

**3.** Check your answers with Rugcare's chart of accounts, page 2. Determine if your answers are the same for each account as shown on the chart of accounts.

**4.** Cover your answers in Column 2. Practice rapidly recalling the account numbers for each account.

## DRILL 5-D2   Analyzing posting from a journal

**Instructions: 1.** Use completed page 2 of the journal shown in Illustration 5-13. For each of the following lines in that illustration, write the separate amount, if any, that is posted individually. Also, write the account title to which the amount is posted.

| | | |
|---|---|---|
| a. Line 6 | c. Line 10 | e. Line 12 |
| b. Line 9 | d. Line 11 | f. Line 13 |

**2.** Use the general ledger accounts shown in Illustration 5-14. Answer the following questions.

g. What item or transaction is represented by the amount in the cash account's Credit column?

h. What item or transaction is represented by the amount in the prepaid insurance account's Debit Balance column?

i. What item or transaction is represented by the amount in the sales account's Credit column?

j. Where in the journal is the information found about the item or transaction recorded in the advertising expense account's Debit column?

## ■ APPLICATION PROBLEMS

### PROBLEM 5-1   Preparing a chart of accounts

Marie Wilson owns a service business called Wilson's Services. Wilson's Services uses the following accounts.

Automobile Expense *510*
Bartel Supplies *210*
Cash *110*
Insurance Expense *520*
Marie Wilson, Capital *310*
Marie Wilson, Drawing *320*

Miscellaneous Expense *530*
Novack Office Supplies *220*
Prepaid Insurance *130*
Sales *410*
Supplies *120*
Supplies Expense *540*

**Instructions: 1.** Prepare a chart of accounts similar to the one described in this chapter. Arrange expense accounts in alphabetical order. Use 3-digit account numbers and number accounts within a division by 10s.

**2.** Two new accounts, Gasoline Expense and Utilities Expense, are to be added to the chart of accounts prepared in Instruction 1. Assign account numbers to the two new accounts.

### PROBLEM 5-2   Posting to a general ledger

Don Ley owns a service business called AquaCare. AquaCare's journal, which is needed to complete this problem, is in the working papers that accompany this textbook.

**Instructions: 1.** Open a general ledger account for each of the following accounts.

| Assets | | Revenue | |
|---|---|---|---|
| 110 | Cash | 410 | Sales |
| 120 | Supplies | | Expenses |
| 130 | Prepaid Insurance | 510 | Advertising Expense |
| | Liabilities | 520 | Miscellaneous Expense |
| 210 | Donard Supplies | 530 | Rent Expense |
| 220 | Fell Office Supplies | 540 | Utilities Expense |
| | Owner's Equity | | |
| 310 | Don Ley, Capital | | |
| 320 | Don Ley, Drawing | | |

**2.** Post the separate amounts on each line of the journal that need to be posted individually.

**3.** Post the journal special amount column totals.

## ◼ ENRICHMENT PROBLEMS

### MASTERY PROBLEM 5-M   Journalizing and posting to a general ledger

Al Hiatt owns a service business called Hiatt Cleaning. Hiatt Cleaning's general ledger accounts are given in the working papers that accompany this textbook.

**Instructions: 1.** Journalize the following transactions completed during November of the current year. Use page 1 of the journal. Source documents are abbreviated as follows: check, C; memorandum, M; receipt, R; calculator tape, T.

Nov.  1. Received cash from owner as an investment, $7,000.00. R1.
  3. Paid cash for rent, $300.00. C1.
  5. Paid cash for insurance, $200.00. C2.
  6. Received cash from sales, $750.00. T6.
  9. Paid cash for miscellaneous expense, $5.00. C3.
  11. Paid cash for supplies, $500.00. C4.
  13. Bought supplies on account from Major Supplies, $600.00. M1.
  13. Received cash from sales, $700.00. T13.
  16. Paid cash for electric bill, $40.00. C5.
  18. Paid cash on account to Major Supplies, $300.00. C6.
  20. Paid cash for advertising, $30.00. C7.
  20. Received cash from sales, $770.00. T20.
  25. Paid cash for supplies, $150.00. C8.
  27. Paid cash for supplies, $100.00. C9.
  27. Received cash from sales, $1,150.00. T27.

Nov. 30. Paid cash to owner for personal use, $300.00. C10.

30. Received cash from sales, $410.00. T30.

**2.** Prove the journal.

**3.** Prove cash. The beginning cash balance on November 1 is zero. The balance on the next unused check stub is $8,855.00.

**4.** Rule the journal.

**5.** Post from the journal to the general ledger.

## CHALLENGE PROBLEM 5-C   Journalizing and posting to a general ledger

Dee Worthy owns a service business called HouseCare. HouseCare's general ledger accounts are given in the working papers that accompany this textbook.

HouseCare uses the following journal.

**Journal**                                                                        **Page**

| | Debit | | Date | Account Title | Doc. No. | Post. Ref. | Credit | | |
|---|---|---|---|---|---|---|---|---|---|
| | Cash | General | | | | | General | Sales | Cash |
| 1 | | | | | | | | | |

**Instructions: 1.** Journalize the following transactions completed during March of the current year. Use page 5 of a journal. Source documents are abbreviated as follows: check, C; memorandum, M; receipt, R; calculator tape, T.

Mar.   1. Received cash from owner as an investment, $8,000.00. R1.

3. Paid cash for rent, $350.00. C1.

5. Paid cash for miscellaneous expense, $5.00. C2.

9. Paid cash for insurance, $250.00. C3.

11. Paid cash for supplies, $400.00. C4.

13. Received cash from sales, $450.00. T13.

16. Bought supplies on account from Hartwood Supplies, $700.00. M1.

18. Paid cash on account to Hartwood Supplies, $350.00. C5.

19. Paid cash for telephone bill, $60.00. C6.

20. Received cash from sales, $1,100.00. T20.

23. Paid cash for supplies, $150.00. C7.

23. Paid cash for advertising, $50.00. C8.

27. Paid cash for supplies, $150.00. C9.

27. Received cash from sales, $1,830.00. T27.

30. Paid cash to owner for personal use, $400.00. C10.

31. Received cash from sales, $410.00. T31.

**2.** Prove the journal.

**3.** Prove cash. The beginning cash balance on March 1 is zero. The balance on the next unused check stub is $9,625.00.

**4.** Rule the journal.

**5.** Post from the journal to the general ledger.

## CHAPTER

# 6

# Cash Control Systems

ENABLING PERFORMANCE TASKS

After studying Chapter 6, you will be able to:
a. Define accounting terms related to using a checking account and a petty cash fund.
b. Identify accounting concepts and practices related to using a checking account.
c. Prepare business papers related to using a checking account.
d. Reconcile a bank statement.
e. Establish and replenish a petty cash fund.
f. Record selected transactions related to using a checking account and a petty cash fund.

In accounting, money is usually referred to as cash. Most businesses make major cash payments by check. However, small cash payments for items such as postage and some supplies may be made from a cash fund kept at the place of business.

Because cash transactions occur more frequently than other types of transactions, more chances occur to make recording errors affecting cash. Cash can be transferred from one person to another without any question about ownership. Also, cash may be lost as it is moved from one place to another.

As a safety measure, Rugcare keeps most of its cash in a bank. Because all cash receipts are placed in a bank, Rugcare has written evidence to support its accounting records. Rugcare can compare its record of checks written with the bank's record of checks paid. Greater control of Rugcare's cash and greater accuracy of its cash records result from these procedures.

## CHECKING ACCOUNTS

A business form ordering a bank to pay cash from a bank account is known as a check. A bank account from which payments can be ordered by a depositor is called a checking account.

## Authorizing signatures

When a checking account is opened, the bank customer must provide a signature on a signature card for the bank records. If several persons are authorized to sign checks, each person's signature must be on the signature card. Checks should always be signed with the same signature as on the signature card. Only Ben Furman is authorized to sign checks for Rugcare.

## Depositing cash

A bank customer prepares a deposit slip each time cash or checks are placed in a bank account. Deposit slips may differ slightly from one bank to another. Each bank designs its own deposit slips to fit the bank's recording machines. However, all deposit slips contain the same basic information as the slip shown in Illustration 6-1.

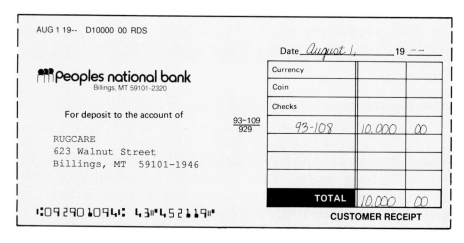

Illustration 6-1
Deposit slip

Checks are listed on a deposit slip according to the bank number on each check. For example, in Illustration 6-1, the number *93-108* identifies the bank on which the $10,000.00 check is written.

When a deposit is made, a bank gives the depositor a receipt. Many banks use a copy of the deposit slip with a printed or stamped verification as the receipt. The printed verification, *Aug 1 19-- D10000.00 RDS*, is shown along the top right edge of the deposit slip in Illustration 6-1. This printed verification means that a total of $10,000.00 was deposited on August 1. The initials *RDS* next to the amount are those of the bank employee who accepted the deposit.

Rugcare records the August 1 deposit on the next unused check stub, as shown in Illustration 6-2.

```
NO. 1          $ _____
Date _____ 19 ___
To _____
_____
For _____
_____

BAL. BRO'T. FOR'D. . . . . . . . . . . .        0 | 00
AMT. DEPOSITED. . . .  |8|1|--|  10,000 | 00
SUBTOTAL. . . . . . . . . . . Date        10,000 | 00
BANK CHARGES:
_____
_____

SUBTOTAL. . . . . . . . . . . . . . . . . .
AMT. THIS CHECK. . . . . . . . . . . . .
BAL. CAR'D. FOR'D. . . . . . . . . . . . .
```

Illustration 6-2
Deposit recorded on a
check stub

After the deposit is recorded on the check stub, a checkbook subtotal is figured. The balance brought forward on Check Stub No. 1 is zero. The previous balance, $0.00, *plus* the deposit, $10,000.00, *equals* the subtotal, $10,000.00.

Cash receipts are journalized at the time cash is received. Later, the cash receipts are deposited in the checking account. Therefore, no journal entry is needed for deposits because the cash receipts have already been journalized.

## Endorsing checks

Ownership of a check can be transferred. The name of the first owner is stated on a check following the words *Pay to the order of*. Therefore, the person to whom payment is to be made must indicate that ownership of the check is being transferred. One person transfers ownership to another person by signing on the back of a check. A signature or stamp on the back of a check transferring ownership is called an endorsement.

An endorsement should be signed exactly as the person's name appears on the front of the check. For example, a check made payable to B.E. Furman is endorsed on the back as *B.E. Furman*. Immediately below that endorsement, Mr. Furman writes his official signature, *Ben Furman*.

Ownership of a check might be transferred several times, resulting in several endorsements. Each endorser guarantees payment of the check. If a bank does not receive payment from the person who signed the check, each endorser is individually liable for payment.

Three types of endorsements are commonly used, each having a specific use in transferring ownership.

**Blank endorsement.** An endorsement consisting only of the endorser's signature is called a blank endorsement. A blank endorsement indicates that the subsequent owner is whoever has the check. A blank endorsement is shown in Illustration 6-3.

Federal regulations require that an endorsement be confined to a limited amount of space that is indicated on the back of a check.

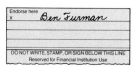

If a check with a blank endorsement is lost or stolen, the check can be cashed by anyone who has it. Ownership may be transferred without further endorsement. A blank endorsement should be used *only* when a person is at the bank ready to cash or deposit a check.

Illustration 6-3
Blank endorsement

**Special endorsement.** An endorsement indicating a new owner of a check is called a special endorsement. Special endorsements are sometimes known as endorsements in full. A special endorsement is shown in Illustration 6-4.

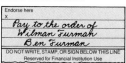

Special endorsements include the words *Pay to the order of* and the name of the new check owner. Only the person or business named in a special endorsement can cash, deposit, or further transfer ownership of the check.

Illustration 6-4
Special endorsement

**Restrictive endorsement.** An endorsement restricting further transfer of a check's ownership is called a restrictive endorsement. A restrictive endorsement limits use of the check to whatever purpose is stated in the endorsement. A restrictive endorsement is shown in Illustration 6-5.

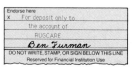

On all checks received, Rugcare stamps a restrictive endorsement which states that the check is for deposit only. This restrictive endorsement prevents unauthorized persons from cashing a check if it is lost or stolen.

Illustration 6-5
Restrictive endorsement

## Writing checks

Rugcare uses printed checks with check stubs attached. Consecutive numbers are preprinted on Rugcare's checks. Consecutive numbers on checks provide an easy way of identifying each check. Also, the numbers help keep track of all checks to assure that none are lost or misplaced.

**Preparing check stubs.** A check stub is a business' record of each check written for a cash payment transaction. *(CONCEPT: Objective Evidence)* To avoid forgetting to prepare a check stub, the check stub is prepared before the check is written. Rugcare's check stub and check are shown in Illustration 6-6.

Illustration 6-6
Completed check stub and check

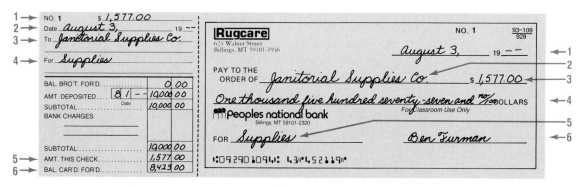

Six steps are used to complete Rugcare's Check Stub No. 1.

1 Write the amount of the check, *$1,577.00,* in the space after the dollar sign at the top of the stub.

2 Write the date of the check, *August 3, 19--,* on the Date line at the top of the stub.

3 Write to whom the check is to be paid, *Janitorial Supplies Co.,* on the To line at the top of the stub.

4 Record the purpose of the check, *Supplies,* on the For line.

5 Write the amount of the check, *$1,577.00,* in the amount column at the bottom of the stub on the line with the words "Amt. this Check."

6 Figure the new checking account balance, *$8,423.00,* and record the new balance in the amount column on the last line of the stub. The new balance is calculated as shown below.

| Subtotal | − | Amount of This Check | = | New Balance |
|---|---|---|---|---|
| $10,000.00 | − | $1,577.00 | = | $8,423.00 |

**Preparing checks.** After the check stub is completed, the check is written. The check shown in Illustration 6-6 is prepared as follows.

1 Write the date, *August 3, 19--,* in the space provided.

> The date should be the month, day, and year on which the check is issued. A check with a future date on it is called a postdated check. Most banks will not accept postdated checks because money cannot be withdrawn from a depositor's account until the date on the check.

2 Write to whom the check is to be paid, *Janitorial Supplies Co.,* following the words "Pay to the order of."

> If the person to whom a check is to be paid is a business, use the business' name rather than the owner's name. *(CONCEPT: Business Entity)* If the person to whom the check is to be paid is an individual, use that person's name.

3 Write the amount in figures, *$1,577.00,* following the dollar sign.

> Write the figures close to the printed dollar sign. This practice prevents anyone from writing another digit in front of the amount to change the amount of the check.

4 Write the amount in words, *One thousand five hundred seventy-seven and no/100,* on the line with the word "Dollars."

> This written amount verifies the amount written in figures after the dollar sign. Begin the words at the extreme left. Draw a line through the unused space up to the word "Dollars." This line prevents anyone from writing in additional words to change the amount.

If the amounts in words and in figures are not the same, a bank may pay only the amount in words. Often, when the amounts do not agree, a bank will refuse to pay the check.

**5** Write the purpose of the check, *Supplies*, on the line labeled "For."

On some checks this space is labeled "Memo." Some checks do not have a line for writing the purpose of the check.

**6** Sign the check.

A check should not be signed until each item on the check and its stub has been verified for accuracy.

**Voiding checks.** Banks usually refuse to accept altered checks. If any kind of error is made in preparing a check, a new check should be prepared. Because checks are prenumbered, all checks not used should be retained for the records. This practice helps account for all checks and assures that no checks have been lost or stolen.

A check that contains errors must be marked so that others will know that it is not to be used. The word *VOID* is written in large letters across both the check and its stub.

When Rugcare records a check in its journal, the check number is placed in the journal's Doc. No. column. If a check number is missing from the Doc. No. column, there is a question whether all checks have been journalized. To assure that all check numbers are listed in the journal, Rugcare records voided checks in the journal. The date is recorded in the journal's Date column. The word *VOID* is written in the Account Title column. The check number is recorded in the Doc. No. column. A dash is placed in the Cash Credit column.

# BANK STATEMENT

Banks keep separate records for each depositor. Information from deposit slips and checks are recorded daily in depositors' accounts. A report of deposits, withdrawals, and bank balance sent to a depositor by a bank is called a bank statement. Rugcare's bank statement for August 27 is shown in Illustration 6-7.

The balance for Rugcare's checking account on August 27, according to the bank's records, is $8,731.00.

When a bank receives checks, the amount of each check is deducted from the depositor's account. Then, the bank stamps the checks to indicate that the check is canceled and is not to be transferred further. Canceled checks are returned to a depositor with a bank statement. Outstanding checks are those checks issued by a depositor but not yet reported on a bank statement. Outstanding deposits are those deposits made at a bank but not yet shown on a bank statement. A bank may assess a charge for maintaining a checking account. Account service charges are also listed on a bank statement.

Banks may have different kinds of checking accounts to fit special needs of depositors. Each bank has its own regulations for its services, and fees are not charged for some checking accounts.

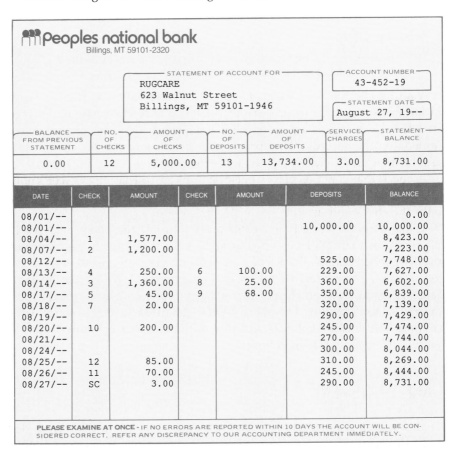

Illustration 6-7
Bank statement

## Verifying a bank statement

Although banks seldom make mistakes, occasionally a check or deposit might be recorded in a wrong account. When a bank statement is received, a depositor should verify its accuracy. If errors are discovered, the bank should be notified at once. However, a bank's records and a depositor's records may differ and still be correct. The difference may exist for several reasons.

1. A service charge may not have been recorded in the depositor's business records.
2. Outstanding deposits may be recorded in the depositor's records but not yet reported on a bank statement.

3. Outstanding checks may be recorded in the depositor's records but not yet reported on a bank statement.
4. A depositor may have made errors in doing arithmetic or in recording information in the business records. The most common mistakes made by depositors are arithmetic errors.
5. The bank may have made an error.

## Reconciling a bank statement

A bank statement is reconciled by verifying that information on a bank statement and a checkbook are in agreement. Rugcare reconciles a bank statement on the same day that the statement is received.

Rugcare's canceled checks are received with the bank statement. The returned checks are arranged in numerical order. For each canceled check, a check mark is placed on the corresponding check stub. A check stub with no check mark indicates an outstanding check.

On August 28 Rugcare receives a bank statement dated August 27. Rugcare uses a reconciliation form printed on the back of the bank statement. Rugcare's bank statement reconciliation is shown in Illustration 6-8.

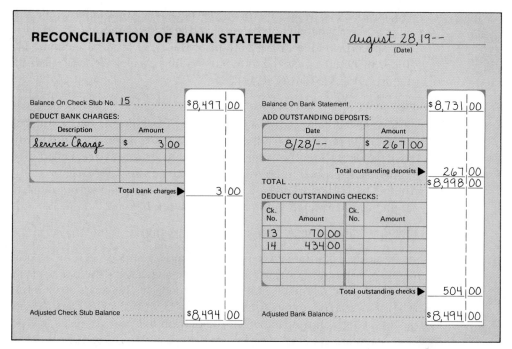

Rugcare uses three steps to reconcile a bank statement.

**1** Figure the adjusted check stub balance.

- Write the date on which the reconciliation is prepared, *August 28, 19--*.
- In the left amount column, list the balance brought forward on

Illustration 6-8
Bank statement
reconciliation

Check Stub No. 15, the next unused check stub, *$8,497.00*.
- In the space for bank charges, list any charges. The only such charge for Rugcare is the bank service charge, *$3.00*. The bank service charge is labeled *SC* on the bank statement.
- Write the adjusted checkbook balance, *$8,494.00*, in the space provided at the bottom of the left amount column. The balance on the check stub, $8,497.00, *minus* the bank's service charge, $3.00, *equals* the adjusted check stub balance, $8,494.00.

2 Figure the adjusted bank balance.
- Write the ending balance shown on the bank statement, *$8,731.00*, in the right amount column.
- Write the date, *8/28/--* and the amount, *$267.00*, of any outstanding deposits in the space provided. Add the outstanding deposits. Write the total outstanding deposits, *$267.00*, in the right amount column.
- Add the ending bank statement balance to the total outstanding deposits. Write the total, *$8,998.00*, in the space for the Total.
- List the outstanding checks, *Nos. 13 and 14*, and their amounts, *$70.00 and $434.00*, in the space provided. Add the amounts of the outstanding checks, and write the total, *$504.00*, in the right amount column.
- Figure the adjusted bank balance, and write the amount, *$8,494.00*, in the space provided at the bottom of the right amount column. The total, $8,998.00, *minus* the total outstanding checks, $504.00, *equals* the adjusted bank balance, $8,494.00.

3 Compare adjusted balances.
- The adjusted balances must be the same. The adjusted check stub balance is the same as the adjusted bank balance, *$8,494.00*. Because the two amounts are the same, the bank statement is reconciled. The completed reconciliation form is filed for future reference.
- If the two adjusted balances are not the same, the errors must be found and corrected before any more work is done.

## Recording a bank service charge on a check stub

The bank deducts the service charge from Rugcare's checking account each month. Although Rugcare did not write a check for the bank service charge, this cash payment must be recorded in Rugcare's accounting records as a cash payment. Rugcare makes a record of a bank service charge on a check stub as shown in Illustration 6-9.

Three steps are used to record a bank service charge on a check stub.

1 Write the words, *Service charge*, on the check stub under the heading Bank Charges.

2 Write the amount, *$3.00*, in the check stub's amount column.

3 Figure and record the new balance, *$8,494.00*, on the Subtotal line.

```
NO. 15              $ _____
Date _____ 19 ___
To _____

For _____

BAL. BRO'T. FOR'D. .............    8,230 00
AMT. DEPOSITED ....  8 28 - -       267 00
SUBTOTAL ...........    Date       8,497 00
BANK CHARGES:
        Service Charge               3 00

SUBTOTAL ...................        8,494 00
AMT. THIS CHECK ..............
BAL. CAR'D. FOR'D. .............
```

Illustration 6-9
Bank service charge
recorded on a check stub

## Journalizing a bank service charge

Because the bank service charge is a cash payment for which no check is written, Rugcare prepares a memorandum as the source document. Rugcare's bank service charges are relatively small and occur only once a month. Therefore, a separate ledger account for the expense is not used. Instead, Rugcare records the bank service charge as a miscellaneous expense.

*August 28, 19--.*
*Received bank statement showing August bank service charge, $3.00. Memorandum No. 3.*

A memorandum is the source document for a bank service charge transaction. *(CONCEPT: Objective Evidence)* The analysis of this transaction is shown in the T accounts.

Miscellaneous Expense is debited for $3.00 to show the increase in this expense account balance. Cash is credited for $3.00 to show the decrease in this asset account balance. The journal entry to record Rugcare's bank service charge is shown in Illustration 6-10.

```
      Miscellaneous Expense
          3.00      |

             Cash
                    |          3.00
```

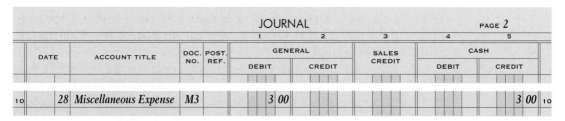

| | | | | GENERAL | | SALES | CASH | |
| DATE | ACCOUNT TITLE | DOC. NO. | POST. REF. | DEBIT | CREDIT | CREDIT | DEBIT | CREDIT |
|---|---|---|---|---|---|---|---|---|
| 28 | Miscellaneous Expense | M3 | | 3 00 | | | | 3 00 |

JOURNAL — PAGE 2

Illustration 6-10
Journal entry to record a
bank service charge

This entry is journalized using four steps.

1  *Date.* Write the date, *28*, in the Date column.

2  *Debit.* Write the title of the account to be debited, *Miscellaneous Expense*, in the Account Title column. Record the amount debited to Miscellaneous Expense, *$3.00*, in the General Debit column.

3 *Credit.* Record the amount credited to Cash, *$3.00,* in the Cash Credit column.

4 *Source document.* Write the source document number, *M3,* in the Doc. No. column.

> Rugcare reconciled its bank statement on August 28. The entry for the bank service charge is journalized on the same date. Rugcare continues to record entries in the journal until the end of the month as shown in Illustration 5-13, Chapter 5.

## DISHONORED CHECKS

A check that a bank refuses to pay is called a dishonored check. Banks may dishonor a check for a number of reasons. (1) The check appears to be altered. (2) The signature of the person who signed the check does not match the one on the signature card at the bank. (3) The amounts written in figures and in words do not agree. (4) The check is postdated. (5) The person who wrote the check has stopped payment on the check. (6) The account of the person who wrote the check has insufficient funds to pay the check.

Issuing a check on an account with insufficient funds is illegal in most states. Altering or forging a check is illegal in all states. A dishonored check may affect the credit rating of the person or business who issued the check. Checking accounts and records should be maintained in such a way that all checks will be honored when presented to the bank.

Sometimes money for a dishonored check can be collected directly from the person or business who wrote the check. Often, however, the value of a dishonored check cannot be recovered and becomes an expense to the business.

Most banks charge a fee for handling dishonored checks that have been previously accepted for deposit. This fee is an expense of the business receiving a dishonored check. Rugcare's bank charges a $5.00 fee for handling dishonored checks. Rugcare attempts to collect the $5.00 fee in addition to the amount of the dishonored check.

Rugcare records a check as a cash debit and deposits the check. When a check is dishonored, the bank deducts the amount of the check plus the fee, $5.00, from Rugcare's checking account. Therefore, Rugcare records a dishonored check in its journal as a cash payment transaction.

### Recording a dishonored check on a check stub

A dishonored check recorded on a check stub is shown in Illustration 6-11.

The words, *Dishonored check,* are written on the line below the words "Bank Charges." The total amount of the dishonored check plus the fee,

```
NO. 41          $ _____
Date _____  19 __
To _____
  _____
For _____
  _____

BAL. BRO'T. FOR'D. .............    6,128  00
AMT. DEPOSITED.... [  |  |  ]
                      Date
SUBTOTAL...................      6,128  00
BANK CHARGES:
     Service charge  3.00
     Dis. Check:  15.00
                                    18  00
SUBTOTAL...................      6,110  00
AMT. THIS CHECK..............
BAL. CAR'D. FOR'D.............
```

Illustration 6-11
Dishonored check recorded
on a check stub

*$15.00*, is written in the amount column on the same line. A new subtotal is figured by subtracting total bank charges, $18.00 ($3.00 service charge *plus* $15.00 dishonored check), from the balance brought forward, $6,128.00. The new subtotal, *$6,110.00*, is written on the Subtotal line. A new Balance Carried Forward is not figured until after Check No. 41 is written.

## Journalizing a dishonored check

During August, Rugcare received no checks that were subsequently dishonored. However, in November Rugcare did receive a check that was dishonored.

> November 29, 19--.
> Received notice from the bank of a dishonored check, $10.00, plus $5.00 fee; total, $15.00. Memorandum No. 6.

Because Rugcare did not write a check for this cash payment, a memorandum is prepared as the source document. *(CONCEPT: Objective Evidence)*

All checks received are deposited in Rugcare's checking account. The entry for each cash receipts transaction includes a debit to Cash. If a check is subsequently returned as dishonored, the previous cash debit for the amount of the check must be offset by a cash credit. The analysis of this transaction is shown in the T accounts.

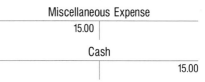

Miscellaneous Expense is debited for $15.00 to show the increase in this expense account balance. Cash is credited for $15.00 to show the decrease in this asset account balance. The journal entry to record this transaction is shown in Illustration 6-12.

This entry is journalized using four steps.

**1** *Date.* Write the date, *29*, in the Date column.

**2** *Debit.* Write the title of the account to be debited, *Miscellaneous Expense*, in the Account Title column. Record the amount debited to Miscellaneous Expense, *$15.00*, in the General Debit column.

| | | | JOURNAL | | | | | | PAGE **10** |
|---|---|---|---|---|---|---|---|---|---|
| | | | | 1 | 2 | 3 | 4 | 5 | |
| DATE | ACCOUNT TITLE | DOC. NO. | POST. REF. | GENERAL DEBIT | GENERAL CREDIT | SALES CREDIT | CASH DEBIT | CASH CREDIT | |
| 29 | *Miscellaneous Expense* | M6 | | 1 5 00 | | | | 1 5 00 | |

Illustration 6-12
Journal entry to record a
dishonored check

**3** *Credit.* Record the amount credited to Cash, *$15.00*, in the Cash Credit column.

**4** *Source document.* Write the source document number, *M6*, in the Doc. No. column.

## PETTY CASH

An amount of cash kept on hand and used for making small payments is called petty cash. Cash control is effective if all cash payments are made by check and cash receipts are deposited in the bank. However, a business usually has some small payments for which writing a check is not time or cost effective. Therefore, a business may maintain a separate cash fund for making small cash payments. The actual dollar amount considered to be a small payment differs from one business to another. Mr. Furman has set $5.00 as the maximum amount to be paid at any one time from the petty cash fund.

| Petty Cash | |
|---|---|
| Debit side NORMAL BALANCE Increases | Credit side Decreases |

The petty cash account is an asset with a normal debit balance. The balance of the petty cash account increases on the debit side and decreases on the credit side.

### Establishing a petty cash fund

On August 17 Mr. Furman decides that Rugcare needs a petty cash fund of $200.00. This amount should provide for the small cash payments anticipated during a month.

*August 17, 19--.*
*Paid cash to establish a petty cash fund, $200.00. Check No. 10.*

The source document for this transaction is Check No. 10. (CONCEPT: *Objective Evidence*) The analysis of this transaction is shown in the T accounts.

Petty Cash is debited for $200.00 to show the increase in this asset account balance. Cash is credited for $200.00 to show the decrease in this asset account balance. The journal entry to record this transaction is shown in Illustration 6-13. This entry is journalized using four steps.

| | | | | JOURNAL | | | | | | PAGE *1* | |
|---|---|---|---|---|---|---|---|---|---|---|---|

| | | | | | 1 | 2 | 3 | 4 | 5 | |
|---|---|---|---|---|---|---|---|---|---|---|
| | | | | | GENERAL | | SALES CREDIT | CASH | | |
| DATE | ACCOUNT TITLE | DOC. NO. | POST. REF. | | DEBIT | CREDIT | | DEBIT | CREDIT | |
| 17 | Petty Cash | C10 | | | 2 0 0 00 | | | | 2 0 0 00 | |

Illustration 6-13
Journal entry to record establishing a petty cash fund

1 *Date.* Write the date, *17*, in the Date column.

2 *Debit.* Write the title of the account to be debited, *Petty Cash*, in the Account Title column. Record the amount debited to Petty Cash, *$200.00*, in the General Debit column.

3 *Credit.* Record the amount credited to Cash, *$200.00*, in the Cash Credit column.

4 *Source document.* Write the source document number, *C10*, in the Doc. No. column.

Mr. Furman cashes the check and places the $200.00 in a locked petty cash box kept at Rugcare's place of business. Only Mr. Furman is authorized to make payments from the petty cash fund.

## Making payments from a petty cash fund

Each time a small payment is made from the petty cash fund, Mr. Furman prepares a form showing the purpose and amount of the payment. A form showing proof of a petty cash payment is called a petty cash slip.

A petty cash slip used by Rugcare is shown in Illustration 6-14.

**PETTY CASH SLIP**     **No. 1**

Date: *August 18, 19--*

Paid to: *Bernie's Repair Shop*

For: *Hose Repair*                    *$5.00*

Account: *Repair Expense*

Approved: *Ben Furman*

Illustration 6-14
Petty cash slip

A petty cash slip shows the following information. (1) Petty cash slip number. (2) Date of petty cash payment. (3) To whom paid. (4) Reason for the payment. (5) Amount paid. (6) Account in which amount is to be recorded. (7) Signature of person approving the petty cash payment.

The petty cash slips are kept in the petty cash box until the fund must be replenished. No entries are made in the journal for the individual petty cash payments.

## Replenishing a petty cash fund

As petty cash is paid out, the amount in the petty cash box decreases. Eventually, the petty cash fund must be replenished and the petty cash payments recorded. Rugcare replenishes its petty cash fund whenever the amount on hand is reduced to $75.00. Also, the petty cash fund is always replenished at the end of each month so that all of the expenses are recorded in the month they are incurred.

Rugcare completes four steps in replenishing the petty cash fund.

1 *Prove the petty cash fund.* On August 31 Mr. Furman proves petty cash as shown below.

Petty cash on hand . . . . . . . . . . . . . . . . . . . . . . . . . . . . . . . . . . . . . . . . . .   $188.00
*Count the cash remaining in the petty cash fund*
*Plus* total of petty cash slips . . . . . . . . . . . . . . . . . . . . . . . . . . . . . . . . . . .   + 12.00
*Add the amounts on the petty cash slips*
*Equals* petty cash fund . . . . . . . . . . . . . . . . . . . . . . . . . . . . . . . . . . . . . .   $200.00

The last line of the proof must show the same total as the original balance of the petty cash fund, $200.00. If petty cash does not prove, the errors must be found and corrected before any more work is done.

2 *Prepare a petty cash report.* At the end of August, Mr. Furman totals the petty cash slips and prepares a report. Rugcare's August petty cash report is shown in Illustration 6-15.

| PETTY CASH REPORT | Date: August 31, 19-- | |
|---|---|---|
| Explanation | Amounts | |
| Fund total | | 200 00 |
| Payments: | | |
| Miscellaneous Expense | 7 00 | |
| Repair Expense | 5 00 | |
| Less total payments | | 12 00 |
| Equals recorded amount on hand | | 188 00 |
| | | |
| Actual amount on hand | | 188 00 |

Illustration 6-15
Petty cash report

The report shows that a total of $12.00 has been paid out of petty cash for repairs and miscellaneous expenses. Thus, $12.00 needs to be added to the remaining $188.00 to bring the petty cash fund back to its normal size, $200.00.

3 *Write a check to replenish the petty cash fund.*

4 *Journalize the entry to replenish petty cash.*

*August 31, 19--.*
*Paid cash to replenish the petty cash fund, $12.00: miscellaneous expense, $7.00; repairs, $5.00. Check No. 15.*

The source document for this transaction is Check No. 15. *(CONCEPT: Objective Evidence)* The analysis of this transaction is shown in the T accounts.

Miscellaneous Expense is debited for $7.00 and Repair Expense is debited for $5.00 to show the increases in these expense account balances. Cash is credited for $12.00 to show a decrease in this asset account balance.

| Miscellaneous Expense | |
|---|---|
| 7.00 | |

| Repair Expense | |
|---|---|
| 5.00 | |

| Cash | |
|---|---|
| | 12.00 |

Unless the petty cash fund is permanently increased or decreased, the balance of the account is always the original amount of the fund. The check issued to replenish petty cash is a credit to Cash and does not affect Petty Cash. When the check is cashed, the money is placed in the petty cash box. The amount in the petty cash box changes as shown below.

| | |
|---|---|
| Amount in petty cash box before fund is replenished........... | $188.00 |
| Amount from check issued to replenish petty cash............. | + 12.00 |
| Amount in petty cash box after fund is replenished............ | $200.00 |

The total amount in the petty cash box, $200.00, is again the same as the balance of the petty cash account. The journal entry to record the transaction to replenish petty cash is shown in Illustration 6-16.

Illustration 6-16
Journal entry to record replenishing of petty cash

| | | | | | GENERAL | | SALES | CASH | |
|---|---|---|---|---|---|---|---|---|---|
| | DATE | ACCOUNT TITLE | DOC. NO. | POST. REF. | DEBIT | CREDIT | CREDIT | DEBIT | CREDIT |
| 11 | | 31 | Miscellaneous Expense | C15 | | 7 00 | | | | 12 00 | 11 |
| 12 | | | Repair Expense | | | 5 00 | | | | | 12 |

JOURNAL                         PAGE 2

This entry is journalized using four steps.

1  *Date.* Write the date, *31*, in the Date column.

2  *Debit.* Write the title of the first account to be debited, *Miscellaneous Expense*, in the Account Title column. Write the amount to be debited to Miscellaneous Expense, *$7.00*, in the General Debit column on the same line as the account title. Write the title of the second account to be debited, *Repair Expense*, on the next line in the Account Title column. Record the amount to be debited to Repair Expense, *$5.00*, in the General Debit column on the same line as the account title.

3  *Credit.* Record the amount to be credited to Cash, *$12.00*, in the Cash Credit column on the first line of this entry.

4  *Source document.* Write the source document number, *C15*, in the Doc. No. column.

The check is cashed, and the money is placed in the petty cash box. The amount in the petty cash box is now the original amount of the petty cash fund, $200.00. Petty cash on hand, $188.00, *plus* the cash to replenish, $12.00, *equals* the original amount of the petty cash fund, $200.00. The amount in the petty cash fund is now the same as the balance of the petty cash account, $200.00.

## SUMMARY OF CASH CONTROL SYSTEMS PROCEDURE

Illustration 6-17
Summary of checking
account procedures

A summary of procedures for using checking accounts is shown in Illustration 6-17.

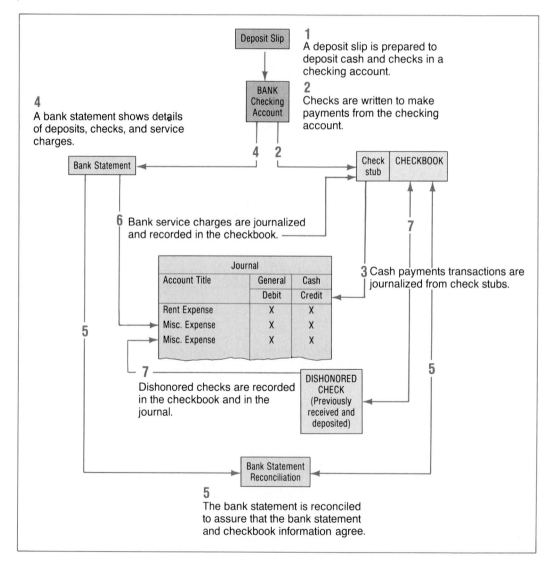

A summary of procedures for using a petty cash fund is shown in Illustration 6-18.

Illustration 6-18
Summary of petty cash
fund procedures

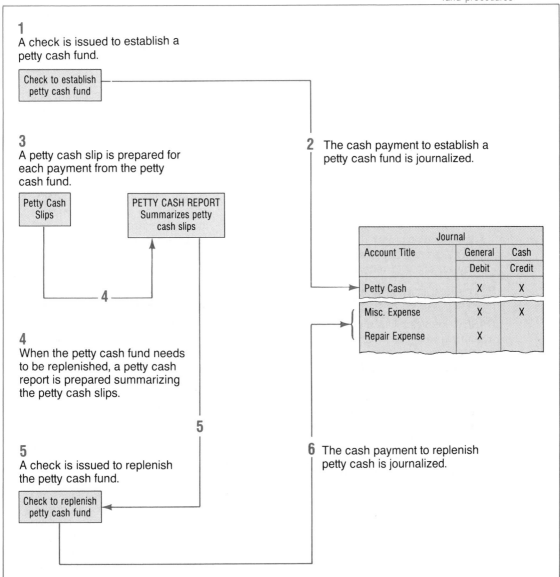

## ACCOUNTING TERMS

What is the meaning of each of the following?

1. checking account
2. endorsement
3. blank endorsement
4. special endorsement
5. restrictive endorsement
6. postdated check
7. bank statement
8. dishonored check
9. petty cash
10. petty cash slip

## QUESTIONS FOR INDIVIDUAL STUDY

1. What evidence does a depositor have that money has been deposited in a checking account?
2. Why is no journal entry made by a business for a deposit in a checking account?
3. Why is the amount written in both numbers and words on a check?
4. What is the most common way of voiding a check?
5. Under what circumstances can a depositor assume that a bank statement reconciliation is correct?
6. Which accounting concept is being applied when a memorandum is prepared for the service charges deducted from a checking account?
7. What accounts are affected, and how, by an entry to record a bank service

charge for a checking account?
8. What accounts are affected, and how, when Rugcare is notified that a deposited check has been dishonored?
9. What is the purpose of a petty cash fund?
10. What accounts are affected, and how, when a petty cash fund is established?
11. What is Rugcare's initial record of amounts that have been paid from the petty cash fund?
12. How is the petty cash fund proved?
13. What accounts are affected, and how, by an entry to replenish petty cash when the petty cash slips show payments for miscellaneous expense and repair expense?
14. When is a journal entry made to record payments from the petty cash fund?

## CASES FOR MANAGEMENT DECISION

**CASE 1** Iris Velez has a personal checking account in which she maintains a small balance. She receives a bank statement every three months. She files the statement and does not prepare a reconciliation. Sueanne Merker also has a personal checking account in which she maintains a balance of several hundred dollars. She receives bank statements once a month. She prepares a bank statement reconciliation for each bank statement received. Is Mrs. Velez or Ms. Merker following the better procedure? Explain your answer.

**CASE 2** Dorset Company decides to establish a petty cash fund. The owner, Edna Dorset, wants to establish a $100.00 petty cash fund and limit payments to $5.00 or less. The manager, Roy Evans, suggests a petty cash fund of $3,000.00 limited to pay-

ments of $50.00 or less. Mr. Evans claims this limit will help him avoid writing so many checks. Do you agree with Ms. Dorset or Mr. Evans? Explain your answer.

**CASE 3** Dot Lawn Care uses a petty cash fund. Denise Wong, the office manager, is authorized to make petty cash payments. When payments are made, she records them in a notebook on a form with the following column headings: Date, Purpose, To Whom, and Amount. She does not prepare a petty cash slip. When the petty cash fund needs replenishing, Mrs. Wong draws a single line under the last entry and summarizes the payments since petty cash was last replenished. This summary is used as the basis for writing a check to replenish petty cash. Do you agree with Mrs. Wong's petty cash procedures? Explain your answer.

## DRILLS FOR UNDERSTANDING

### DRILL 6-D1   Reconciling a bank statement

On July 29 of the current year, DeepClean received a bank statement dated July 28. The following information is obtained from the bank statement and from the records of the business.

| | | |
|---|---|---|
| Bank statement balance. . . . . . . . . . . . . . . . . . . . . . . . . . . . . . . . . . . . . . . . . . . . . . . . . . . . . | | $1,528.00 |
| Bank service charge . . . . . . . . . . . . . . . . . . . . . . . . . . . . . . . . . . . . . . . . . . . . . . . . . . . . . . . | | 2.00 |
| Outstanding deposit, July 28. . . . . . . . . . . . . . . . . . . . . . . . . . . . . . . . . . . . . . . . . . . . . . . | | 150.00 |
| Outstanding checks: | | |
| No. 103 . . . . . . . . . . . . . . . . . . . . . . . . . . . . . . . . . . . . . . . . . . . . . . . . . . . . . . . . . . . . | | 70.00 |
| No. 105 . . . . . . . . . . . . . . . . . . . . . . . . . . . . . . . . . . . . . . . . . . . . . . . . . . . . . . . . . . . . | | 35.00 |
| Checkbook balance on Check Stub No. 106 . . . . . . . . . . . . . . . . . . . . . . . . . . . . . . | | 1,575.00 |

**Instructions:** Prepare a bank statement reconciliation. Use July 29 of the current year as the date.

### DRILL 6-D2   Reconciling a bank statement

On September 30 of the current year, Ajax Service Co. received a bank statement dated September 29. The following information is obtained from the bank statement and from the records of the business.

| | | |
|---|---|---|
| Bank statement balance. . . . . . . . . . . . . . . . . . . . . . . . . . . . . . . . . . . . . . . . . . . . . . . . . . . . . | | $3,208.00 |
| Bank service charge . . . . . . . . . . . . . . . . . . . . . . . . . . . . . . . . . . . . . . . . . . . . . . . . . . . . . . . | | 5.00 |
| Outstanding deposits: | | |
| September 29 . . . . . . . . . . . . . . . . . . . . . . . . . . . . . . . . . . . . . . . . . . . . . . . . . . . . . . . | | 310.00 |
| September 30 . . . . . . . . . . . . . . . . . . . . . . . . . . . . . . . . . . . . . . . . . . . . . . . . . . . . . . . | | 330.00 |
| Outstanding checks: | | |
| No. 214 . . . . . . . . . . . . . . . . . . . . . . . . . . . . . . . . . . . . . . . . . . . . . . . . . . . . . . . . . . . . | | 90.00 |
| No. 215 . . . . . . . . . . . . . . . . . . . . . . . . . . . . . . . . . . . . . . . . . . . . . . . . . . . . . . . . . . . . | | 135.00 |
| No. 217 . . . . . . . . . . . . . . . . . . . . . . . . . . . . . . . . . . . . . . . . . . . . . . . . . . . . . . . . . . . . | | 50.00 |
| Checkbook balance on Check Stub No. 218 . . . . . . . . . . . . . . . . . . . . . . . . . . . . . . | | 3,578.00 |

**Instructions:** Prepare a bank statement reconciliation. Use September 30 of the current year as the date.

### DRILL 6-D3   Replenishing a petty cash fund

KeepClean replenished petty cash on the dates shown in Column 2 of the following table. The information in Columns 3 to 5 is obtained from the petty cash reports.

| 1 | 2 | 3 | 4 | 5 |
|---|---|---|---|---|
| | | **Summary of Petty Cash Slips** | | |
| **Trans.** | **Replenished on** | **Supplies** | **Advertising** | **Miscellaneous** |
| A | July 31 | 32.00 | 25.00 | |
| B | August 31 | 21.00 | 20.00 | 5.00 |
| C | September 30 | 40.00 | 20.00 | 15.00 |
| D | October 31 | 10.00 | | 20.00 |

**Instructions:** Prepare T accounts for Cash, Supplies, Advertising Expense, and Miscellaneous Expense. Use the T accounts to analyze each transaction given in the table. Label each amount in the T accounts with the corresponding transaction letter.

## ■ APPLICATION PROBLEMS

### PROBLEM 6-1   Endorsing checks

For each of the following situations, prepare the appropriate endorsement.

**Instructions: 1.** Write a blank endorsement. Use your own signature.

**2.** Write a special endorsement to transfer a check to Delbert Richardson. Use your own signature.

**3.** Write a restrictive endorsement to deposit a check in the account of OddJobs. Use your own signature.

### PROBLEM 6-2   Writing checks

You are authorized to sign checks for OddJobs.

**Instructions: 1.** Record the balance brought forward on Check Stub No. 50, $1,396.35.

**2.** Record a deposit of $390.00 made on October 30 of the current year on Check Stub No. 50.

**3.** Prepare check stubs and write the following checks. Use October 30 of the current year as the date.

Check No. 50. To Corner Garage for repairs, $138.00.
Check No. 51. To OfficeWorld for supplies, $50.00.
Check No. 52. To Dixon Papers for supplies, $15.00.

### PROBLEM 6-3   Reconciling a bank statement and recording a bank service charge

Use the bank statement, canceled checks, and check stubs given in the working papers accompanying this textbook.

**Instructions: 1.** Compare the canceled checks with the check stubs. For each canceled check, place a check mark next to the appropriate check stub number.

**2.** For each deposit shown on the bank statement, place a check mark next to the deposit amount on the appropriate check stub.

**3.** Prepare a bank statement reconciliation. Use August 29 of the current year as the date.

**4.** Record the following transactions on page 8 of a journal. The abbreviation for memorandum is M.

Sept. 1. Received bank statement showing August bank service charge, $5.00. M25.
     1. Received notice from the bank of a dishonored check, $170.00, plus $5.00 fee; total, $175.00. M26.

**5.** Record the bank service charge and dishonored check on Check Stub No. 165.

### PROBLEM 6-4   Establishing and replenishing a petty cash fund

SweepUp established a petty cash fund on August 3 of the current year. At the end of August, the business replenished the petty cash fund.

**Instructions:** Journalize the following transactions completed during August of the current year. Use page 10 of a journal. The abbreviation for check is C.

Aug.   3. Paid cash to establish a petty cash fund, $100.00. C57.
      31. Paid cash to replenish the petty cash fund, $78.00: supplies, $25.00; miscellaneous expense, $8.00; repairs, $45.00. C97.

ENRICHMENT PROBLEMS

**MASTERY PROBLEM 6-M**   **Reconciling a bank statement; journalizing a bank service charge, a dishonored check, and petty cash transactions**

Joseph Cruz owns a business called LawnMow. LawnMow completed the following transactions during August of the current year.

**Instructions: 1.** Journalize the following transactions completed during August of the current year. Use page 20 of a journal. Source documents are abbreviated as follows: check, C; memorandum, M.

Aug. 21. Paid cash to establish a petty cash fund, $100.00. C61.
   24. Paid cash for repairs, $135.00. C62.
   26. Paid cash for supplies, $40.00. C63.
   27. Received notice from the bank of a dishonored check, $35.00, plus $5.00 fee; total, $40.00. M22.
   28. Paid cash for miscellaneous expense, $12.00. C64.
   31. Paid cash to owner for personal use, $300.00. C65.
   31. Paid cash to replenish the petty cash fund, $55.00: supplies, $35.00; miscellaneous expense, $20.00. C66.

**2.** On August 31 of the current year, LawnMow received a bank statement dated August 30. Prepare a bank statement reconciliation. Use August 31 of the current year as the date. The following information is obtained from the August 30 bank statement and from the records of the business.

| | |
|---|---:|
| Bank statement balance | $1,521.00 |
| Bank service charge | 5.00 |
| Outstanding deposit, August 31 | 430.00 |
| Outstanding checks, Nos. 65 and 66. | |
| Checkbook balance on Check Stub No. 67 | 1,601.00 |

**3.** Continue using the journal and journalize the following transaction.

Aug. 31. Received bank statement showing August bank service charge, $5.00. M23.

**CHALLENGE PROBLEM 6-C**   **Reconciling a bank statement**

On November 30 of the current year, Johnson Company received a bank statement dated November 29. Miss Johnson placed a check mark beside the amount on each check stub for which a canceled check was received. She also placed a check mark on the check stub beside the amount of each deposit shown on the bank statement. She then prepared a bank statement reconciliation.

The last eight check stubs for the month of November and the bank statement reconciliation are given in the working papers accompanying this textbook. Both the check stubs and reconciliation contain errors.

**Instructions: 1.** Verify the amounts on the check stubs. Assume that the check amounts in the upper right corner of each stub are correct. Also assume that all deposits have been entered correctly on the check stubs.

**2.** Draw a line through all incorrect amounts on the check stubs. Write the correct amounts either above or below the incorrect amounts, depending on where space is available.

**3.** Prepare a correct bank statement reconciliation. Assume that the check marks written beside check and deposit amounts on the check stubs are correct. Therefore, the outstanding deposits and checks are those that are not checked.

# Reinforcement Activity 1, Part A

# An Accounting Cycle for a Proprietorship: Journalizing and Posting Transactions

Reinforcement activities strengthen the learning of accounting concepts and procedures. Reinforcement Activity 1 is a single problem divided into two parts. Part A includes learnings from Chapters 1 through 6. Part B includes learnings from Chapters 7 through 9. An accounting cycle is completed in Parts A and B for a single business—The Fitness Center.

## THE FITNESS CENTER

In May of the current year, Gail Davis starts a service business called The Fitness Center. The business provides exercise facilities for its clients. In addition, Miss Davis, a professional dietician, offers diet and exercise counseling for clients who request her assistance. The business rents the facilities with which it operates, pays the utilities, and is responsible for maintenance. The Fitness Center charges clients for each visit.

## CHART OF ACCOUNTS

The Fitness Center uses the following chart of accounts.

---

**THE FITNESS CENTER**
**Chart of Accounts**

| Balance Sheet Accounts | Income Statement Accounts |
|---|---|
| **(100) ASSETS** | **(400) REVENUE** |
| 110 Cash | 410 Sales |
| 120 Petty Cash | |
| 130 Supplies | **(500) EXPENSES** |
| 140 Prepaid Insurance | 510 Advertising Expense |
| | 520 Insurance Expense |
| **(200) LIABILITIES** | 530 Miscellaneous Expense |
| 210 Dunnel Supplies | 540 Rent Expense |
| 220 Morgan Office Supplies | 550 Repair Expense |
| | 560 Supplies Expense |
| **(300) OWNER'S EQUITY** | 570 Utilities Expense |
| 310 Gail Davis, Capital | |
| 320 Gail Davis, Drawing | |
| 330 Income Summary | |

---

# RECORDING TRANSACTIONS

**Instructions: 1.** Journalize the following transactions completed during May of the current year. Use page 1 of the journal. Source documents are abbreviated as follows: check stub, C; memorandum, M; receipt, R; calculator tape, T.

May ✓1. Received cash from owner as an investment, $15,000.00. R1.
　　✓1. Paid cash for rent, $1,000.00. C1.
　　✓2. Paid cash for electric bill, $45.00. C2.
　　✓4. Paid cash for supplies, $500.00. C3.
　　✓4. Paid cash for insurance, $960.00. C4.
　　✓7. Bought supplies on account from Dunnel Supplies, $800.00. M1.
　　✓11. Paid cash to establish a petty cash fund, $200.00. C5.
　　12. Received cash from sales, $550.00. T12.
　　13. Paid cash for repairs, $25.00. C6.
　　13. Paid cash for miscellaneous expense, $35.00. C7.
　　13. Received cash from sales, $185.00. T13.
　　14. Paid cash for advertising, $100.00. C8.
　　14. Received cash from sales, $335.00. T14.
　　15. Paid cash to owner for personal use, $250.00. C9.
　　15. Paid cash on account to Dunnel Supplies, $300.00. C10.
　　15. Received cash from sales, $325.00. T15.
　　18. Paid cash for miscellaneous expense, $100.00. C11.
　　18. Received cash from sales, $295.00. T18.
　　19. Received cash from sales, $155.00. T19.
　　20. Paid cash for repairs, $125.00. C12.
　　20. Bought supplies on account from Morgan Office Supplies, $150.00. M2.
　　20. Received cash from sales, $195.00. T20.

**2.** Prove and rule page 1 of the journal. Carry the column totals forward to page 2 of the journal.

**3.** Post the separate amounts on each line of page 1 of the journal that need to be posted individually.

**4.** Use page 2 of the journal. Journalize the following transactions.

May 21. Paid cash for water bill, $110.00. C13.
　　21. Received cash from sales, $235.00. T21.
　　25. Paid cash for supplies, $50.00. C14.
　　25. Received cash from sales, $295.00. T25.
　　26. Paid cash for miscellaneous expense, $25.00. C15.
　　26. Received cash from sales, $300.00. T26.
　　27. Received cash from sales, $195.00. T27.
　　28. Paid cash for telephone bill, $210.00. C16.
　　28. Received cash from sales, $275.00. T28.

**5.** The Fitness Center received a bank statement dated May 27. The following information is obtained from the bank statement and from the records of the business. Prepare a bank statement reconciliation. Use May 29 as the date.

| | |
|---|---:|
| Bank statement balance. . . . . . . . . . . . . . . . . . . . . . . . . . . . . . . . . . . . . . . . . . . . . . | $14,312.00 |
| Bank service charge . . . . . . . . . . . . . . . . . . . . . . . . . . . . . . . . . . . . . . . . . . . . . . . . | 3.00 |
| Outstanding deposit, May 28 . . . . . . . . . . . . . . . . . . . . . . . . . . . . . . . . . . . . . . . . | 275.00 |

Outstanding checks:
No. 14 . . . . . . . . . . . . . . . . . . . . . . . . . . . . . . . . . . . . . . . . . . . . . . . . . . . . . . . .   50.00
No. 15 . . . . . . . . . . . . . . . . . . . . . . . . . . . . . . . . . . . . . . . . . . . . . . . . . . . . . . . .   25.00
No. 16 . . . . . . . . . . . . . . . . . . . . . . . . . . . . . . . . . . . . . . . . . . . . . . . . . . . . . . . .   210.00
Checkbook balance on Check Stub No. 17 . . . . . . . . . . . . . . . . . . . . . . . . . . . . . . . .   14,305.00

**6.** Continue using page 2 of the journal, and journalize the following transactions.

May 29. Received bank statement showing May bank service charge, $3.00. M3.
    29. Paid cash for supplies, $60.00. C17.
    29. Received cash from sales, $240.00. T29.
    31. Paid cash to replenish the petty cash fund, $17.00: miscellaneous expense, $10.00; repairs, $7.00. C18.
    31. Paid cash to owner for personal use, $250.00. C19.
    31. Received cash from sales, $280.00. T31.

**7.** Prove page 2 of the journal.

**8.** Prove cash. The beginning cash balance on May 1 is zero. The balance on the next unused check stub is $14,495.00.

**9.** Rule page 2 of the journal.

**10.** Post the separate amounts on each line of page 2 of the journal that need to be posted individually.

**11.** Post the column totals on page 2 of the journal.

*The general ledger prepared in Reinforcement Activity 1, Part A, is needed to complete Reinforcement Activity 1, Part B.*

# Work Sheet for a Service Business

ENABLING PERFORMANCE TASKS

After studying Chapter 7, you will be able to:
a. Define accounting terms related to a work sheet for a service business organized as a proprietorship.
b. Identify accounting concepts and practices related to a work sheet for a service business organized as a proprietorship.
c. Plan adjustments for supplies and prepaid insurance.
d. Complete a work sheet for a service business organized as a proprietorship.
e. Identify selected procedures for finding and correcting errors in accounting records.

General ledger accounts contain information needed by managers and owners. Before the information can be used, however, it must be analyzed, summarized, and reported in a meaningful way. The accounting concept, *Consistent Reporting*, is applied when the same accounting procedures are followed in the same way in each accounting period. *(CONCEPT: Consistent Reporting)* For example, in one year a delivery business might report the number of deliveries made. The next year the same business reports the amount of revenue received for the deliveries made. The information for the two years cannot be compared because the business has not been consistent in reporting information about deliveries.

## FISCAL PERIODS

The length of time for which a business summarizes and reports financial information is called a fiscal period. A fiscal period is also known as an accounting period.  Businesses usually select a period of time, such as a month, six months, or a year, for which to summarize and report financial information.  The accounting concept, *Accounting Period Cycle*, is applied when changes in financial information are reported for a specific period of time in the form of financial statements.  *(CONCEPT: Accounting Period Cycle)*  Each business chooses a fiscal period length that meets its needs.  Because federal and state tax reports are based on one year, most businesses use a one-year fiscal period.  However, because Rugcare is a new business, Mr. Furman wishes to have financial information reported frequently to help him make decisions.  For this reason, Rugcare uses a one-month fiscal period.

A fiscal period can begin on any date.  However, most businesses begin their fiscal periods on the first day of a month.  Rugcare started business on August 1.  Therefore, Rugcare's monthly fiscal period is for the period from August 1 through August 31, inclusive.  Another business might use a one-year fiscal period from August 1 of one year through July 31 of the next year.  Many businesses use a calendar year starting on January 1 and ending on December 31.  Businesses often choose a one-year fiscal period that ends during a period of low business activity.  In this way, the end-of-year accounting work comes at a time when other business activities are the lightest.  For example, a store with a large volume of Christmas holiday sales might prefer to begin its fiscal period on February 1 or March 1.

> Most individuals use a one-year fiscal period that begins on January 1 and ends on December 31.  This fiscal period corresponds to the period for which they must file income tax returns for the federal and state governments.  However, individuals may use a different fiscal period if approved by the Internal Revenue Service.

Financial information may be analyzed, summarized, and reported on any date a business needs the information.  However, financial information is always summarized and reported at the end of a fiscal period.

## WORK SHEET

A columnar accounting form used to summarize the general ledger information needed to prepare financial statements is called a work sheet.

Accountants use a work sheet for four reasons.  (1) To summarize general ledger account balances to prove that debits equal credits.  (2) To plan needed changes to general ledger accounts to bring account balances up to date.  (3) To separate general ledger account balances according to the financial statements to be prepared.  (4) To figure the amount of net income or net loss for a fiscal period.

Journals and ledgers are permanent records of a business and are usually prepared in ink. However, a work sheet is a planning tool and is not considered a permanent accounting record. Therefore, a work sheet is prepared in pencil.

## Preparing the heading of a work sheet

The heading on a work sheet consists of three lines. (1) Name of the business. (2) Name of the report. (3) Date of the report. The heading for Rugcare's work sheet is shown in Illustration 7-1.

*Rugcare*

*Work Sheet*

*For Month Ended August 31, 19--*

Illustration 7-1
Heading on a work sheet

The date on Rugcare's work sheet indicates that the work sheet covers the 31 days from August 1 through and including August 31. If the work sheet were for a calendar year fiscal period, it might have a date stated as *For Year Ended December 31, 19--*. (CONCEPT: *Accounting Period Cycle*)

## Preparing a trial balance on a work sheet

The equality of debits and credits in the general ledger must be proved. The total of all debit account balances must equal the total of all credit account balances. A proof of the equality of debits and credits in a general ledger is called a trial balance. Rugcare prepares a trial balance on a work sheet. Rugcare's August 31 trial balance on a work sheet is shown in Illustration 7-2.

Information for the trial balance is taken from the general ledger. General ledger account titles are listed on a trial balance in the same order as listed on the chart of accounts. All the account titles are listed, even if some accounts do not have balances. The accounts that do not have balances in the Trial Balance columns will be needed in other parts of the work sheet.

Seven steps are used in preparing a trial balance on a work sheet.

1 Write the general ledger account titles in the work sheet's Account Title column.

2 Write the general ledger account debit balances in the Trial Balance Debit column. Write the general ledger account credit balances in the Trial Balance Credit column. If an account does not have a balance, the space in the Trial Balance columns is left blank.

Illustration 7-2
Trial balance on a work
sheet

| | ACCOUNT TITLE | TRIAL BALANCE | |
|---|---|---|---|
| | | DEBIT | CREDIT |
| 1 | Cash | 8 2 7 2 00 | |
| 2 | Petty Cash | 2 0 0 00 | |
| 3 | Supplies | 4 9 3 1 00 | |
| 4 | Prepaid Insurance | 1 2 0 0 00 | |
| 5 | Butler Cleaning Supplies | | 1 3 6 0 00 |
| 6 | Dale Office Supplies | | 2 0 0 00 |
| 7 | Ben Furman, Capital | | 10 0 0 0 00 |
| 8 | Ben Furman, Drawing | 6 0 0 00 | |
| 9 | Income Summary | | |
| 10 | Sales | | 4 2 9 1 00 |
| 11 | Advertising Expense | 6 8 00 | |
| 12 | Insurance Expense | | |
| 13 | Miscellaneous Expense | 1 0 5 00 | |
| 14 | Rent Expense | 2 5 0 00 | |
| 15 | Repair Expense | 1 1 0 00 | |
| 16 | Supplies Expense | | |
| 17 | Utilities Expense | 1 1 5 00 | |
| 18 | | 15 8 5 1 00 | 15 8 5 1 00 |
| 19 | | | |
| 20 | | | |
| 21 | | | |
| 22 | | | |
| 23 | | | |
| 24 | | | |
| 25 | | | |
| 26 | | | |

Rugcare

Work Sheet

For Month Ended August 31, 19--

3  Rule a single line across the two Trial Balance columns below the last
line on which an account title is written.  This single line shows that
the two columns are to be added.

4  Add both the Trial Balance Debit and Credit columns.  Use a calculator
if one is available.  For Rugcare's work sheet, the totals are Debit,
$15,851.00 and Credit, $15,851.00.

5  Check the equality of the two amount column totals.  If the two column
totals are the same, then debits equal credits in the general ledger ac-

counts. Because the totals, $15,851.00, are the same, the Trial Balance columns on Rugcare's work sheet are in balance.

If the two column totals are not the same and the trial balance is not in balance, recheck the Trial Balance columns to find the error. Other parts of a work sheet are not completed until the Trial Balance columns are proved. Suggestions for locating errors are described later in this chapter.

**6** Write each column's total, *$15,851.00*, below the single line.

**7** Rule double lines across both Trial Balance columns. The double lines mean that the Trial Balance column totals have been verified as correct.

## Planning adjustments on a work sheet

Sometimes a business will pay cash for an expense in one fiscal period, but the expense is not used until a later period. The expense should be reported in the same fiscal period that it is used to produce revenue. The accounting concept, *Matching Expenses with Revenue*, is applied when revenue from business activities and expenses associated with earning that revenue are recorded in the same accounting period. For example, Rugcare buys supplies in quantity in August, but some of the supplies are not used until September. Only the value of the supplies used in August should be reported as expenses in August. In this way, August revenue and the supplies expense associated with earning the August revenue are recorded in the same accounting period. *(CONCEPT: Matching Expenses with Revenue)*

In order to give accurate information on financial statements, some general ledger accounts must be brought up to date at the end of a fiscal period. For example, Rugcare debits an asset account, Supplies, each time supplies are bought. Supplies on hand are items of value owned by a business until the supplies are used. The value of supplies that are used becomes an expense to the business. However, recording an expense each time an individual supply, such as a pencil, is used would be impractical. Therefore, on August 31 the balance of the asset account, Supplies, is the value of all supplies bought rather than the value of only the supplies that have not been used. The amount of supplies that have been used must be deducted from the asset account, Supplies, and recorded in the expense account, Supplies Expense.

Likewise, the amount of insurance that has been used during the fiscal period is also an expense of the business. When the insurance premium for a year of insurance coverage is paid, the entire amount is debited to an asset account, Prepaid Insurance. Each day during August a portion of the insurance coverage is used. The value of the insurance used is an expense of the business. However, recording each day's amount of insurance used is impractical. Therefore, at the end of a fiscal period, the balance of Prepaid

Insurance is the value of all insurance coverage bought, rather than the value of only the insurance coverage that still remains. The amount of the insurance coverage used must be deducted from the asset account, Prepaid Insurance, and recorded in the expense account, Insurance Expense.

Changes recorded on a work sheet to update general ledger accounts at the end of a fiscal period are called adjustments. The assets of a business, such as supplies and prepaid insurance, are used to earn revenue. The portion of the assets consumed in order to earn revenue become expenses of the business. The portions consumed are no longer assets but are now expenses. Therefore, adjustments must be made to both the asset and expense accounts for supplies and insurance. After the adjustments are made, the expenses incurred to earn revenue are reported in the same fiscal period as the revenue is earned and reported. *(CONCEPT: Matching Expenses with Revenue)*

A work sheet is used to plan adjustments. Changes are not made in general ledger accounts until adjustments are journalized and posted. The accuracy of the planning for adjustments is checked on a work sheet before adjustments are actually journalized.

Procedures for journalizing Rugcare's adjustments are described in Chapter 9.

**Supplies adjustment.** On August 31, before adjustments, the balance of Supplies is $4,931.00, and the balance of Supplies Expense is zero, as shown in the T accounts.

BEFORE ADJUSTMENT

Supplies

Aug. 31 Bal.   4,931.00

Supplies Expense

On August 31 Mr. Furman counted the supplies on hand and found that the value of supplies still unused on that date was $2,284.00. The value of the supplies used is calculated as shown below.

| Supplies Account Balance, August 31 | − | Supplies On Hand, August 31 | = | Supplies Used During August |
|---|---|---|---|---|
| $4,931.00 | − | $2,284.00 | = | $2,647.00 |

Four questions are asked in analyzing the adjustment for the asset account, Supplies.

1. What is the balance of Supplies?.......................... $4,931.00
2. What should the balance be for this account? ............. $2,284.00
3. What must be done to correct the account balance? Decrease $2,647.00
4. What adjustment is made?
   Debit Supplies Expense ................................ $2,647.00
   Credit Supplies ...................................... $2,647.00

AFTER ADJUSTMENT

Supplies Expense

Adj. (a)   2,647.00

Supplies

Aug. 31 Bal.   4,931.00  | Adj. (a)   2,647.00
(New Bal.   2,284.00)

The effect of this adjustment is shown in the T accounts. The expense account, Supplies Expense, is increased by a debit, $2,647.00, the value of supplies used. The balance of Supplies Expense, $2,647.00, is the value of supplies used during the fiscal period from August 1 to August 31. *(CONCEPT: Matching Expenses with Revenue)*

The asset account, Supplies, is decreased by a credit, $2,647.00, the value of supplies used. The debit balance, $4,931.00, *less* the credit adjustment, $2,647.00, *equals* the new balance, $2,284.00. The new balance of Supplies is the same as the value of supplies on hand on August 31.

Rugcare's supplies adjustment is shown on lines 3 and 16 of the work sheet in Illustration 7-3.

Illustration 7-3
Supplies adjustment on a
work sheet

| | | 1 | 2 | 3 | 4 |
|---|---|---|---|---|---|
| | ACCOUNT TITLE | TRIAL BALANCE | | ADJUSTMENTS | |
| | | DEBIT | CREDIT | DEBIT | CREDIT |
| 3 | *Supplies* | 4 9 3 1 00 | | | (a)2 6 4 7 00 |
| 16 | *Supplies Expense* | | | (a)2 6 4 7 00 | |
| 17 | | | | | |

Three steps are used to record the supplies adjustment on the work sheet.

1 Write the debit amount, *$2,647.00,* in the work sheet's Adjustments Debit column on the line with the account title Supplies Expense (line 16).

2 Write the credit amount, *$2,647.00,* in the Adjustments Credit column on the line with the account title Supplies (line 3).

3 Label the two parts of this adjustment with a small letter *a* in parentheses *(a).* The letter *a* identifies the debit and credit amounts as part of the same adjustment.

**Prepaid insurance adjustment.** When Rugcare pays for insurance, the amount is debited to the asset account, Prepaid Insurance. However, to debit Insurance Expense daily for the amount of that day's insurance premium used is impractical. Therefore, at the end of a fiscal period, Rugcare's prepaid insurance account does not show the actual value of the remaining prepaid insurance.

On August 31, before adjustments, the balance of Prepaid Insurance is $1,200.00, and the balance of Insurance Expense is zero, as shown in the T accounts.

On August 31 Mr. Furman checked the insurance records and found that the value of insurance coverage remaining was $1,100.00. The value of insurance coverage used during the fiscal period is calculated as shown below.

BEFORE ADJUSTMENT
Insurance Expense

Prepaid Insurance

Aug. 31 Bal.   1,200.00

| Prepaid Insurance Balance, August 31 | – | Insurance Coverage Remaining Unused, August 31 | = | Insurance Coverage Used During August |
|---|---|---|---|---|
| $1,200.00 | – | $1,100.00 | = | $100.00 |

Four questions are asked in analyzing the adjustment for the asset account, Prepaid Insurance.

1. What is the balance of Prepaid Insurance . . . . . . . . . . . . . . . . . . . .   $1,200.00
2. What should the balance be for this account . . . . . . . . . . . . . .   $1,100.00
3. What must be done to correct the account balance? Decrease   $  100.00
4. What adjustment is made?
   Debit Insurance Expense . . . . . . . . . . . . . . . . . . . . . . . . . . . . . . . . .   $  100.00
   Credit Prepaid Insurance . . . . . . . . . . . . . . . . . . . . . . . . . . . . . . . .   $  100.00

AFTER ADJUSTMENT

Insurance Expense

| | |
|---|---|
| Adj. (b) | 100.00 |

Prepaid Insurance

| Aug. 31 | 1,200.00 | Adj. (b) | 100.00 |
|---|---|---|---|
| (New Bal. | 1,100.00) | | |

The effect of this adjustment is shown in the T accounts. The expense account, Insurance Expense, is increased by a debit, $100.00, the value of insurance used. The balance of Insurance Expense, $100.00, is the value of insurance coverage used from August 1 to August 31. (CONCEPT: Matching Expenses with Revenue)

The asset account, Prepaid Insurance, is decreased by a credit, $100.00, the value of insurance used. The debit balance, $1,200.00, less the credit adjustment, $100.00, equals the new balance, $1,100.00. The new balance of Prepaid Insurance is the same as the amount of insurance coverage unused on August 31.

Rugcare's prepaid insurance adjustment is shown on lines 4 and 12 of the work sheet in Illustration 7-4.

| | | 1 | 2 | 3 | 4 |
|---|---|---|---|---|---|
| | ACCOUNT TITLE | TRIAL BALANCE | | ADJUSTMENTS | |
| | | DEBIT | CREDIT | DEBIT | CREDIT |
| 1 | Cash | 8 2 7 2 00 | | | |
| 2 | Petty Cash | 2 0 0 00 | | | |
| 3 | Supplies | 4 9 3 1 00 | | | (a)2 6 4 7 00 |
| 4 | Prepaid Insurance | 1 2 0 0 00 | | | (b) 1 0 0 00 |
| 12 | Insurance Expense | | | (b) 1 0 0 00 | |
| 13 | Miscellaneous Expense | 1 0 5 00 | | | |
| 14 | Rent Expense | 2 5 0 00 | | | |
| 15 | Repair Expense | 1 1 0 00 | | | |
| 16 | Supplies Expense | | | (a)2 6 4 7 00 | |
| 17 | Utilities Expense | 1 1 5 00 | | | |
| 18 | | 15 8 5 1 00 | 15 8 5 1 00 | 2 7 4 7 00 | 2 7 4 7 00 |
| 19 | | | | | |

Illustration 7-4
Prepaid insurance adjustment on a work sheet

Three steps are used to record the prepaid insurance adjustment on a work sheet.

1 Write the debit amount, $100.00, in the work sheet's Adjustments Debit column on the line with the account title Insurance Expense (line 12).

**2** Write the credit amount, *$100.00*, in the Adjustments Credit column on the line with the account title Prepaid Insurance (line 4).

**3** Label the two parts of this adjustment with a small letter *b* in parentheses *(b)*. The letter *b* identifies the debit and credit amounts as part of the same adjustment.

**Proving the adjustments columns of a work sheet.** After all adjustments are recorded in a work sheet's Adjustments columns, the equality of debits and credits for the two columns is proved. Rugcare's completed Adjustments columns are shown in Illustration 7-4.

Three steps are used in proving a work sheet's Adjustments columns.

**1** Rule a single line across the two Adjustments columns on the same line as the single line for the Trial Balance columns.

**2** Add both the Adjustments Debit and Credit columns. If the two column totals are the same, then debits equal credits for these two columns, and the work sheet's Adjustments columns are in balance. On Rugcare's work sheet, the Adjustments Debit and Credit column totals are $2,747.00. Therefore, the Adjustments columns on Rugcare's work sheet are in balance. Write each column's total below the single line.

> If the two Adjustments column totals are not the same, the Adjustments columns are rechecked and errors corrected before completing the work sheet.

**3** Rule double lines across both Adjustments columns. The double lines mean that the totals have been verified as correct.

## Extending financial statement information on a work sheet

At the end of each fiscal period, Rugcare prepares two financial statements from information on a work sheet. *(CONCEPT: Accounting Period Cycle)* A financial statement that reports assets, liabilities, and owner's equity on a specific date is known as a balance sheet. A financial statement showing the revenue and expenses for a fiscal period is called an income statement. The up-to-date account balances on a work sheet are extended to columns for the two financial statements.

**Extending balance sheet account balances on a work sheet.** The balance sheet accounts are the asset, liability, and owner's equity accounts. Up-to-date balance sheet account balances are extended to the Balance Sheet Debit and Credit columns of the work sheet. The extension of Rugcare's balance sheet account balances is shown on lines 1 through 9 of the work sheet in Illustration 7-5.

Three steps are used in extending balance sheet items on a work sheet.

**1** Extend the up-to-date balance of each asset account.

**Rugcare**

**Work Sheet**

**For Month Ended August 31, 19--**

| | ACCOUNT TITLE | TRIAL BALANCE DEBIT | TRIAL BALANCE CREDIT | ADJUSTMENTS DEBIT | ADJUSTMENTS CREDIT | INCOME STATEMENT DEBIT | INCOME STATEMENT CREDIT | BALANCE SHEET DEBIT | BALANCE SHEET CREDIT | |
|---|---|---|---|---|---|---|---|---|---|---|
| 1 | Cash | 8272 00 | | | | | | 8272 00 | | 1 |
| 2 | Petty Cash | 200 00 | | | | | | 200 00 | | 2 |
| 3 | Supplies | 4931 00 | | | (a) 2647 00 | | | 2284 00 | | 3 |
| 4 | Prepaid Insurance | 1200 00 | | | (b) 100 00 | | | 1100 00 | | 4 |
| 5 | Butler Cleaning Supplies | | 1360 00 | | | | | | 1360 00 | 5 |
| 6 | Dale Office Supplies | | 200 00 | | | | | | 200 00 | 6 |
| 7 | Ben Furman, Capital | | 10000 00 | | | | | | 10000 00 | 7 |
| 8 | Ben Furman, Drawing | 600 00 | | | | | | 600 00 | | 8 |
| 9 | Income Summary | | | | | | | | | 9 |
| 10 | | | | | | | | | | 10 |

Illustration 7-5
Balance sheet account balances extended on a work sheet

- The balance of Cash in the Trial Balance Debit column is up to date because no adjustment affects this account. Extend the balance of Cash, *$8,272.00*, to the Balance Sheet Debit column. Balances of all asset accounts not affected by adjustments are extended in the same way.
- The balance of Supplies in the Trial Balance Debit column is not up to date because it is affected by an adjustment. Figure the up-to-date adjusted balance. The debit balance, $4,931.00, *minus* the credit adjustment, $2,647.00, *equals* the up-to-date adjusted balance, $2,284.00. Extend the up-to-date balance, *$2,284.00*, to the Balance Sheet Debit column. The same procedure is used to figure and extend the up-to-date adjusted balance of the other asset account affected by an adjustment, Prepaid Insurance.

2 Extend the up-to-date balance of each liability account.

- The balance of Butler Cleaning Supplies is the up-to-date balance because no adjustment affects this account. Extend the up-to-date balance, *$1,360.00*, to the Balance Sheet Credit column. The balance of the other liability account is extended in the same way.

3 Extend the up-to-date balances of the owner's equity accounts.

- The balance of Ben Furman, Capital in the Trial Balance Credit column is the up-to-date balance because no adjustment affects this account. Extend the balance, *$10,000.00*, to the Balance Sheet Credit column.
- The balance of Ben Furman, Drawing in the Trial Balance Debit column is the up-to-date balance because no adjustment affects this account. Extend the balance, *$600.00*, to the Balance Sheet Debit column.

• Income Summary has no balance in the Trial Balance columns. Therefore, no amount needs to be extended for this account.

**Extending income statement account balances on a work sheet.** Rugcare's income statement accounts are the revenue and expense accounts. The extension of income statement account balances is shown on lines 10 through 17 of the work sheet in Illustration 7-6.

*Rugcare*

*Work Sheet*

*For Month Ended August 31, 19--*

| | ACCOUNT TITLE | TRIAL BALANCE DEBIT | TRIAL BALANCE CREDIT | ADJUSTMENTS DEBIT | ADJUSTMENTS CREDIT | INCOME STATEMENT DEBIT | INCOME STATEMENT CREDIT | BALANCE SHEET DEBIT | BALANCE SHEET CREDIT | |
|---|---|---|---|---|---|---|---|---|---|---|
| | | 1 | 2 | 3 | 4 | 5 | 6 | 7 | 8 | |
| 10 | *Sales* | | 4 29 1 00 | | | | 4 29 1 00 | | | 10 |
| 11 | *Advertising Expense* | 6 8 00 | | | | 6 8 00 | | | | 11 |
| 12 | *Insurance Expense* | | | (b) 1 0 0 00 | | 1 0 0 00 | | | | 12 |
| 13 | *Miscellaneous Expense* | 1 0 5 00 | | | | 1 0 5 00 | | | | 13 |
| 14 | *Rent Expense* | 2 5 0 00 | | | | 2 5 0 00 | | | | 14 |
| 15 | *Repair Expense* | 1 1 0 00 | | | | 1 1 0 00 | | | | 15 |
| 16 | *Supplies Expense* | | | (a) 2 6 4 7 00 | | 2 6 4 7 00 | | | | 16 |
| 17 | *Utilities Expense* | 1 1 5 00 | | | | 1 1 5 00 | | | | 17 |
| 18 | | 15 85 1 00 | 15 85 1 00 | 2 74 7 00 | 2 74 7 00 | | | | | 18 |
| 19 | | | | | | | | | | 19 |

Two steps are used in extending income statement accounts on a work sheet.

*Illustration 7-6*
*Income statement account balances extended on a work sheet*

**1** Extend the up-to-date balance of the revenue account.

• The balance of Sales in the Trial Balance Credit column is the up-to-date balance because no adjustment affects this account. Extend the balance, $4,291.00, to the Income Statement Credit column.

**2** Extend the up-to-date balance of each expense account.

• The balance of Advertising Expense in the Trial Balance Debit column is the up-to-date balance because no adjustment affects this account. Extend the balance, $68.00, to the Income Statement Debit column. Balances of all expense accounts not affected by adjustments are extended in the same way.

• The balance of Insurance Expense in the Trial Balance columns is zero. This zero balance is not the up-to-date balance because this account is affected by an adjustment. Figure the up-to-date adjusted balance.

- The debit balance, $0.00, *plus* the debit adjustment, $100.00, *equals* the adjusted balance, $100.00. Extend the up-to-date adjusted debit balance, *$100.00*, to the Income Statement Debit column. The same procedure is used to figure and extend the up-to-date adjusted balance of each expense account affected by an adjustment.

**Figuring and recording net income on a work sheet.** The difference between total revenue and total expenses when total revenue is greater is called net income. Rugcare's August net income is shown on line 19 of the work sheet in Illustration 7-7.

Illustration 7-7
Completed work sheet

*Rugcare*

*Work Sheet*

*For Month Ended August 31, 19--*

| | ACCOUNT TITLE | TRIAL BALANCE DEBIT | TRIAL BALANCE CREDIT | ADJUSTMENTS DEBIT | ADJUSTMENTS CREDIT | INCOME STATEMENT DEBIT | INCOME STATEMENT CREDIT | BALANCE SHEET DEBIT | BALANCE SHEET CREDIT | |
|---|---|---|---|---|---|---|---|---|---|---|
| 1 | Cash | 8 2 7 2 00 | | | | | | 8 2 7 2 00 | | 1 |
| 2 | Petty Cash | 2 0 0 00 | | | | | | 2 0 0 00 | | 2 |
| 3 | Supplies | 4 9 3 1 00 | | | (a) 2 6 4 7 00 | | | 2 2 8 4 00 | | 3 |
| 4 | Prepaid Insurance | 1 2 0 0 00 | | | (b) 1 0 0 00 | | | 1 1 0 0 00 | | 4 |
| 5 | Butler Cleaning Supplies | | 1 3 6 0 00 | | | | | | 1 3 6 0 00 | 5 |
| 6 | Dale Office Supplies | | 2 0 0 00 | | | | | | 2 0 0 00 | 6 |
| 7 | Ben Furman, Capital | | 10 0 0 0 00 | | | | | | 10 0 0 0 00 | 7 |
| 8 | Ben Furman, Drawing | 6 0 0 00 | | | | | | 6 0 0 00 | | 8 |
| 9 | Income Summary | | | | | | | | | 9 |
| 10 | Sales | | 4 2 9 1 00 | | | | 4 2 9 1 00 | | | 10 |
| 11 | Advertising Expense | 6 8 00 | | | | 6 8 00 | | | | 11 |
| 12 | Insurance Expense | | | (b) 1 0 0 00 | | 1 0 0 00 | | | | 12 |
| 13 | Miscellaneous Expense | 1 0 5 00 | | | | 1 0 5 00 | | | | 13 |
| 14 | Rent Expense | 2 5 0 00 | | | | 2 5 0 00 | | | | 14 |
| 15 | Repair Expense | 1 1 0 00 | | | | 1 1 0 00 | | | | 15 |
| 16 | Supplies Expense | | | (a) 2 6 4 7 00 | | 2 6 4 7 00 | | | | 16 |
| 17 | Utilities Expense | 1 1 5 00 | | | | 1 1 5 00 | | | | 17 |
| 18 | | 15 8 5 1 00 | 15 8 5 1 00 | 2 7 4 7 00 | 2 7 4 7 00 | 3 3 9 5 00 | 4 2 9 1 00 | 12 4 5 6 00 | 11 5 6 0 00 | 18 |
| 19 | Net Income | | | | | 8 9 6 00 | | | 8 9 6 00 | 19 |
| 20 | | | | | | 4 2 9 1 00 | 4 2 9 1 00 | 12 4 5 6 00 | 12 4 5 6 00 | 20 |
| 21 | | | | | | | | | | 21 |

Five steps are used in figuring net income on a work sheet.

1 Rule a single line across the four Income Statement and Balance Sheet columns.

**2** Add both the Income Statement and Balance Sheet columns. Write the totals below the single line.

**3** Figure the net income. Rugcare's net income is calculated as shown below.

| Income Statement Credit Column Total | − | Income Statement Debit Column Total | = | Net Income |
|:---:|:---:|:---:|:---:|:---:|
| $4,291.00 | − | $3,395.00 | = | $896.00 |

Rugcare's August work sheet shows a net income because the Income Statement Credit column (revenue) exceeds the Income Statement Debit column (expenses).

**4** Write the amount of net income, *$896.00*, below the Income Statement Debit column total. Write the words, *Net Income*, on the same line in the Account Title column.

**5** Extend the amount of net income, *$896.00*, to the Balance Sheet Credit column on the same line as the words *Net Income*. The owner's equity account, Ben Furman, Capital, is increased by a credit. Therefore, the net income amount is extended to the Balance Sheet Credit column.

**Totaling and ruling a work sheet.** Four steps are used in totaling and ruling a work sheet.

**1** Rule a single line across the four Income Statement and Balance Sheet columns just below the net income amounts.

**2** Add the subtotal and net income amount for each column to get proving totals for the Income Statement and Balance Sheet columns. Write the proving totals below the single line. Proving totals are used to determine that the debits equal credits for each pair of column totals.

**3** Check the equality of the proving totals for each pair of columns.
   • As shown on line 20 of the work sheet in Illustration 7-7, the proving totals for the Income Statement columns, $4,291.00, are the same.
   • As shown on line 20 of the work sheet in Illustration 7-7, the proving totals for the Balance Sheet columns, $12,456.00, are the same.

A summary of preparing a work sheet is shown on the Work Sheet Overlay on pages 146A through 146C.

**4** Rule double lines across the Income Statement and Balance Sheet columns. The double lines mean that the totals have been verified as correct.

**Figuring and recording a net loss on a work sheet.** Rugcare's completed work sheet shows a net income. However, a business might have a net loss to report. The difference between total revenue and total expenses when total expenses is greater is called a net loss. A net loss on a work sheet is shown in Illustration 7-8.

| | ACCOUNT TITLE | | 5 | | 6 | | 7 | | 8 | |
|---|---|---|---|---|---|---|---|---|---|---|
| | | | INCOME STATEMENT | | | | BALANCE SHEET | | | |
| | | | DEBIT | | CREDIT | | DEBIT | | CREDIT | |
| 19 | | | 2 00 0 00 | | 1 90 0 00 | | 5 40 0 00 | | 5 50 0 00 | 19 |
| 20 | *Net Loss* | | | | 1 0 0 00 | | 1 0 0 00 | | | 20 |
| 21 | | | 2 00 0 00 | | 2 00 0 00 | | 5 50 0 00 | | | 21 |
| 22 | | | | | | | | | | 22 |
| 23 | | | | | | | | | | 23 |

Illustration 7-8
Net loss shown on a work
sheet

Six steps are used in completing a work sheet with a net loss.

1 Rule a single line across the four Income Statement and Balance Sheet columns.

2 Add both the Income Statement and Balance Sheet columns. Write the totals below the single line.

3 The net loss is calculated as shown below.

| Income Statement Debit Column Total | – | Income Statement Credit Column Total | = | Net Loss |
|---|---|---|---|---|
| $2,000.00 | – | $1,900.00 | = | $100.00 |

The Income Statement Debit column total (expenses) is greater than the Income Statement Credit column total (revenue). Therefore, because expenses exceed revenue, there is a net loss.

4 Write the amount of net loss, *$100.00*, below the Income Statement Credit column total. Write the words, *Net Loss*, on the same line in the Account Title column.

5 Extend the amount of net loss, *$100.00*, to the Balance Sheet Debit column on the same line as the words *Net Loss*. The owner's capital account is decreased by a debit. Therefore, a net loss is extended to the Balance Sheet Debit column.

6 Total and rule the work sheet using the same steps as when there is net income.

## FINDING AND CORRECTING ERRORS

Some errors in accounting records are not discovered until a work sheet is prepared. For example, a debit to the supplies account may not have been posted from a journal to the general ledger supplies account. The omission may not be discovered until the work sheet's trial balance does not balance. Also, information may be transferred incorrectly from general ledger accounts to the work sheet's trial balance. Additional errors may be made on a work sheet, such as recording adjustment information incorrectly or adding columns incorrectly.  In addition, errors may be made in extending amounts to the Income Statement and Balance Sheet columns.

Any errors found on a work sheet must be corrected before any further work is completed.  If an incorrect amount is found on a work sheet, erase the error and replace it with the correct amount.  If an amount is written in an incorrect column, erase the amount and record it in the correct column.  If column totals do not balance, add the columns again.

## Checking for typical arithmetic errors

When two column totals are not in balance, subtract the smaller total from the larger total to find the difference.  Check the difference between the two amounts against the following guides.

1 *The difference is 1, such as $.01, $.10, $1.00, or $10.00.*  For example, if the totals of the two columns are Debit, $12,542.00 and Credit, $12,543.00, the difference between the two columns is $1.00.  The error is most likely in addition.  Add the columns again.

2 *The difference can be divided evenly by 2.*  For example, the difference between two column totals is $48.00.  The difference, $48.00, *divided* by 2 *equals* $24.00 with no remainder.  Look for a $24.00 amount in the Trial Balance columns of the work sheet.  If the amount is found, check to make sure it has been recorded in the correct Trial Balance Debit or Credit column.  A $24.00 debit amount recorded in a credit column results in a difference between column totals of $48.00.  If the error is not found on the work sheet, check the general ledger accounts and journal entries.  An entry for $24.00 may have been recorded in an incorrect column in the journal or in an account.

3 *The difference can be divided evenly by 9.*  For example, the difference between two columns is $45.00.  The difference, $45.00, *divided* by 9 *equals* $5.00 with no remainder.  When the difference can be divided equally by 9, look for transposed numbers such as 54 written as 45 or 19 written as 91.  Also, check for a "slide."  A "slide" occurs when numbers are moved to the right or left in an amount column.  For example, $12.00 is recorded as $120.00 or $350.00 is recorded as $35.00.

4 *The difference is an omitted amount.*  Look for an amount equal to the difference.  If the difference is $50.00, look for an account balance of $50.00 that has not been extended.  Look for any $50.00 amount on the work sheet and determine if it has been handled correctly.  Look in the accounts and journals for a $50.00 amount, and check if that amount has been handled correctly.  Failure to record a $50.00 account balance will make a work sheet's Trial Balance column totals differ by $50.00.

## Checking for errors in the trial balance columns

1  Have all general ledger account balances been copied in the Trial Balance columns correctly?

2  Have all general ledger account balances been recorded in the correct Trial Balance column?

Correct any errors found and add the columns again.

## Checking for errors in the adjustments columns

1  Do the debits equal the credits for each adjustment?  Use the small letters that label each part of an adjustment to help check accuracy and equality of debits and credits.

2  Is the amount for each adjustment correct?

Correct any errors found and add the columns again.

## Checking for errors in the income statement and balance sheet columns

1  Has each amount been copied correctly when extended to the Income Statement or Balance Sheet column?

2  Has each account balance been extended to the correct Income Statement or Balance Sheet column?

3  Has the net income or net loss been figured correctly?

4  Has the net income or net loss been recorded in the correct Income Statement or Balance Sheet column?

Correct any errors found and add the columns again.

## Checking for errors in posting to general ledger accounts

Sometimes a pair of work sheet columns do not balance, and an error cannot be found on the work sheet.  If this is the situation, check the posting from the journal to the general ledger accounts.  As each item in an account or a journal entry is verified, a check mark should be placed next to it.  The check mark indicates that the item has been checked for accuracy.

1  Have all amounts that need to be posted actually been posted from the journal?

   • For an amount that has not been posted, complete the posting to the correct account.

   • In all cases where posting is corrected, refigure the account balance and correct it on the work sheet.

     When an omitted posting is recorded as described above, the dates in the general ledger accounts may be out of order.

**2** Have all amounts been posted to the correct accounts?

- For an amount posted to the wrong account, draw a line through the entire incorrect entry.  Refigure the account balance.
- Record the posting in the correct account.  Refigure the account balance, and correct the work sheet.  Make the correction in the general ledger accounts, as shown in Illustration 7-9.

Illustration 7-9
Correcting an error in posting to the wrong account

ACCOUNT **Supplies**                                      ACCOUNT NO. **130**

| DATE | | ITEM | POST. REF. | DEBIT | CREDIT | BALANCE DEBIT | BALANCE CREDIT |
|---|---|---|---|---|---|---|---|
| *Feb.* | *1* | | *1* | 4 0 0 00 | | 4 0 0 00 | |
| | *25* | | *2* | 9 0 00 | | 4 9 0 00 | |
| | *12* | | *1* | 5 0 00 | | 5 4 0 00 | |

ACCOUNT **Prepaid Insurance**                              ACCOUNT NO. **140**

| DATE | | ITEM | POST. REF. | DEBIT | CREDIT | BALANCE DEBIT | BALANCE CREDIT |
|---|---|---|---|---|---|---|---|
| *Feb.* | *9* | | *1* | 6 0 0 00 | | 6 0 0 00 | |
| | ~~*12*~~ | | ~~*1*~~ | ~~5 0 00~~ | | ~~6 5 0 00~~ | |

Errors in permanent records should *never* be erased.  Erasures in permanent records raise questions about whether important financial information has been altered.

**3** Have all amounts been written correctly?  Have all amounts been posted to the correct Debit or Credit columns of an account?

- If an amount has been written incorrectly, draw a line through the incorrect amount.  Write the correct amount just above the correction in the same space.  Refigure the account balance, and correct the account balance on the work sheet.  Correcting an error in writing an amount incorrectly is shown on the first line of the utilities expense account in Illustration 7-10.

• For an amount posted to the wrong amount column, draw a line through the incorrect item in the account. Record the posting in the correct amount column. Refigure the account balance, and correct the work sheet. Correcting an error in posting to a wrong amount column is shown on the second line of the utilities expense account in Illustration 7-10.

| ACCOUNT *Utilities Expense* | | | | | | ACCOUNT NO. *570* |
|---|---|---|---|---|---|---|

| DATE | | ITEM | POST. REF. | DEBIT | CREDIT | BALANCE | |
|---|---|---|---|---|---|---|---|
| | | | | | | DEBIT | CREDIT |
| *Sept.*¹⁹⁻⁻ | 8 | | 1 | 7 0 00 | | ~~7 0 0 00~~ 7 0 00 | |
| | 17 | | 1 | 2 7 00 | ~~2 7 00~~ | ~~6 7 3 00~~ 9 7 00 | |

Illustration 7-10
Correcting an amount written incorrectly and an error in posting to the wrong column of an account

## Checking for errors in journal entries

1 Do debits equal credits in each journal entry?

2 Is each journal entry amount recorded in the correct journal column?

3 Is information in the Account Title column correct for each journal entry?

4 Are all of the journal amount column totals correct?

5 Does the sum of debit column totals equal the sum of credit column totals in the journal?

6 Have all transactions been recorded?

Some suggestions for correcting errors in journal entries are described in Chapter 4.

## Preventing errors

The best way to prevent errors is to work carefully at all times. Check the work at each step in an accounting procedure. Most errors occur in doing the required arithmetic, especially in adding columns. When possible, use a calculator to add columns. When an error is discovered, do no more work until the cause of the error is found and corrections are made.

## ACCOUNTING TERMS

What is the meaning of each of the following?

**1.** fiscal period
**2.** work sheet
**3.** trial balance

**4.** adjustments
**5.** income statement

**6.** net income
**7.** net loss

## QUESTIONS FOR INDIVIDUAL STUDY

1. What are typical lengths of fiscal periods?
2. Which accounting concept is being applied when a business summarizes and reports financial information for a fiscal period?
3. What are four reasons for preparing a work sheet?
4. Why is a work sheet prepared in pencil?
5. What are the three lines of a work sheet heading?
6. How is the equality of debits and credits proved in a general ledger?
7. Why is an adjustment for supplies planned at the end of a fiscal period?
8. What four questions are asked in analyzing the supplies adjustment?
9. What accounts are affected, and how, by the adjustment for supplies?
10. After a supplies adjustment, what does the supplies account balance represent?
11. What accounts are affected, and how, by the adjustment for prepaid insurance?
12. Why are the Adjustments columns on a work sheet totaled?
13. What two financial statements are prepared from information on a work sheet?
14. What account balances are extended to the Balance Sheet columns on Rugcare's work sheet?
15. What account balances are extended to the Income Statement columns on Rugcare's work sheet?
16. If a work sheet shows a net income, in which two columns will the net income be recorded?
17. How are the amounts in the Income Statement and Balance Sheet columns of a work sheet proved?
18. If two work sheet column totals are not equal and the difference between the totals is one, what is the most likely error?
19. If two work sheet column totals are not equal and the difference between the totals is evenly divisible by nine, what is the most likely error?

## CASES FOR MANAGEMENT DECISION

**CASE 1** Peter Dowther owns a small business. At the end of a fiscal period, he does not make an adjustment for supplies. Are Mr. Dowther's accounting procedures correct? What effect will Mr. Dowther's procedures have on the business' financial reporting? Explain your answer.

**CASE 2** When posting amounts from a journal to general ledger accounts, a $10.00 debit to Miscellaneous Expense is mistakenly posted as a debit to Repair Expense. Will this error be discovered when the work sheet is prepared? Explain.

**CASE 3** When posting amounts from a journal to general ledger accounts, a $10.00 debit to Supplies is mistakenly posted as a credit to Utilities Expense. Will this error be discovered when the work sheet is prepared? Explain.

**CASE 4** When extending amounts on a work sheet, the debit balance for Advertising Expense is extended to the Balance Sheet Debit column. Will this error be discovered when the work sheet is prepared? Explain.

# ■ DRILLS FOR UNDERSTANDING

### DRILL 7-D1  **Extending account balances on a work sheet**

Use a form similar to the following.

| | 1 | 2 | | 5 | 6 | 7 | 8 |
|---|---|---|---|---|---|---|---|
| | Trial Balance | | | Income Statement | | Balance Sheet | |
| Account Title | Debit | Credit | | Debit | Credit | Debit | Credit |
| 1. *Advertising Expense* | ✓ | | | ✓ | | | |

**Instructions:** **1.** Write each of the following account titles in the Account Title column of the form.

1. Advertising Expense
2. Bell Supply
3. Cash
4. Miscellaneous Expense
5. Maria Dorn, Capital
6. Maria Dorn, Drawing
7. Prepaid Insurance
8. Rent Expense
9. Repair Expense
10. Sales
11. Supplies
12. Utilities Expense

**2.** Place a check mark in either Column 1 or 2 to indicate the Trial Balance column on a work sheet in which each account's balance will appear.

**3.** Place a check mark in Columns 5, 6, 7, or 8 to indicate the column to which each up-to-date account balance will be extended.

### DRILL 7-D2  **Figuring net income or net loss on a work sheet**

The following column totals are from the work sheets of five different businesses.

| Company | Income Statement | | Balance Sheet | |
|---|---|---|---|---|
| | Debit | Credit | Debit | Credit |
| A | $9,000 | $9,500 | $35,500 | $35,000 |
| B | 1,500 | 2,000 | 7,500 | 7,000 |
| C | 5,200 | 4,800 | 26,500 | 26,900 |
| D | 5,300 | 8,150 | 34,950 | 32,100 |
| E | 5,300 | 4,130 | 33,400 | 34,570 |

Use a form similar to the one on page 143. The amounts for Company A are given as an example.

**Instructions:** Complete the following for each company.

**1.** Write the Income Statement and Balance Sheet column totals on line 1.

**2.** Figure the amount of net income or net loss. Write the amount on line 2 in the correct columns. Label the amount as *Net Income* or *Net Loss*.

3. Add the amounts in each column.  Write the totals on line 3.
4. Verify the accuracy of your proving totals.

| | Income Statement | | Balance Sheet | |
|---|---|---|---|---|
| | Debit | Credit | Debit | Credit |
| Company A | | | | |
| 1. Column Totals | $9,000 | $9,500 | $35,500 | $35,000 |
| 2. *Net Income* | 500 | | | 500 |
| 3. Proving Totals | 9,500 | 9,500 | 35,500 | 35,500 |

 APPLICATION PROBLEMS

PROBLEM 7-1  **Completing a work sheet**

On September 30 of the current year, CleanLawn has the following general ledger accounts and balances.  The business uses a monthly fiscal period.

| | Account Balances | |
|---|---|---|
| **Account Titles** | **Debit** | **Credit** |
| Cash. . . . . . . . . . . . . . . . . . . . . . . . . . . . . . . . . . . . . . . . . . . | $3,000.00 | |
| Petty Cash . . . . . . . . . . . . . . . . . . . . . . . . . . . . . . . . . . . . | 100.00 | |
| Supplies . . . . . . . . . . . . . . . . . . . . . . . . . . . . . . . . . . . . . | 2,000.00 | |
| Prepaid Insurance. . . . . . . . . . . . . . . . . . . . . . . . . . . . . . | 900.00 | |
| Bix Supplies . . . . . . . . . . . . . . . . . . . . . . . . . . . . . . . . . . | | $  600.00 |
| OfficeWorld. . . . . . . . . . . . . . . . . . . . . . . . . . . . . . . . . . . | | 100.00 |
| Dorothy Daily, Capital . . . . . . . . . . . . . . . . . . . . . . . . . . | | 4,100.00 |
| Dorothy Daily, Drawing . . . . . . . . . . . . . . . . . . . . . . . . . | 200.00 | |
| Income Summary . . . . . . . . . . . . . . . . . . . . . . . . . . . . . . | — | — |
| Sales . . . . . . . . . . . . . . . . . . . . . . . . . . . . . . . . . . . . . . . . | | 2,505.00 |
| Advertising Expense. . . . . . . . . . . . . . . . . . . . . . . . . . . . | 75.00 | |
| Insurance Expense. . . . . . . . . . . . . . . . . . . . . . . . . . . . . | — | |
| Miscellaneous Expense . . . . . . . . . . . . . . . . . . . . . . . . . | 110.00 | |
| Rent Expense. . . . . . . . . . . . . . . . . . . . . . . . . . . . . . . . . | 600.00 | |
| Repair Expense. . . . . . . . . . . . . . . . . . . . . . . . . . . . . . . . | 180.00 | |
| Supplies Expense . . . . . . . . . . . . . . . . . . . . . . . . . . . . . . | — | |
| Utilities Expense . . . . . . . . . . . . . . . . . . . . . . . . . . . . . . . | 140.00 | |

**Instructions: 1.** Prepare the heading and trial balance on a work sheet.  Total and rule the Trial Balance columns.

　**2.** Analyze the following adjustment information into debit and credit parts.  Record the adjustments on the work sheet.

Adjustment Information, September 30

| | |
|---|---|
| Supplies on hand . . . . . . . . . . . . . . . . . . . . . . . . . . . . . . . . . . . . . . . . . . . | $1,100.00 |
| Value of prepaid insurance . . . . . . . . . . . . . . . . . . . . . . . . . . . . . . . . . | 600.00 |

**3.** Total and rule the Adjustments columns.
**4.** Extend the up-to-date balances to the Balance Sheet or Income Statement columns.

**5.** Rule a single line across the Income Statement and Balance Sheet columns. Total each column. Figure and record the net income or net loss. Label the amount in the Account Title column.

**6.** Total and rule the Income Statement and Balance Sheet columns.

## PROBLEM 7-2   Completing a work sheet

On October 31 of the current year, Village Service Co. has the following general ledger accounts and balances. The business uses a monthly fiscal period.

|  | Account Balances | |
| --- | --- | --- |
| **Account Titles** | **Debit** | **Credit** |
| Cash........................................... | $4,900.00 | |
| Petty Cash ..................................... | 300.00 | |
| Supplies ....................................... | 2,500.00 | |
| Prepaid Insurance............................... | 2,100.00 | |
| National Supplies .............................. | | $ 1,400.00 |
| Office Distributors.............................. | | 1,200.00 |
| Wensk Movies ................................. | | 800.00 |
| Susan Haile, Capital............................ | | 6,000.00 |
| Susan Haile, Drawing........................... | 1,200.00 | |
| Income Summary ............................... | — | — |
| Sales ......................................... | | 20,100.00 |
| Advertising Expense............................ | 4,200.00 | |
| Insurance Expense.............................. | — | |
| Miscellaneous Expense ......................... | 600.00 | |
| Rent Expense................................... | 8,000.00 | |
| Repair Expense................................. | 2,400.00 | |
| Supplies Expense ............................... | — | |
| Utilities Expense ............................... | 3,300.00 | |

**Instructions: 1.** Prepare the heading and trial balance on a work sheet. Total and rule the Trial Balance columns.

**2.** Analyze the following adjustment information into debit and credit parts. Record the adjustments on the work sheet.

### Adjustment Information, October 31

| | |
| --- | --- |
| Supplies on hand ............................................. | $1,500.00 |
| Value of prepaid insurance ...................................... | 900.00 |

**3.** Total and rule the Adjustments columns.

**4.** Extend the up-to-date balances to the Balance Sheet or Income Statement columns.

**5.** Rule a single line across the Income Statement and Balance Sheet columns. Total each column. Figure and record the net income or net loss. Label the amount in the Account Title column.

**6.** Total and rule the Income Statement and Balance Sheet columns.

## PROBLEM 7-3   Finding and correcting errors in accounting records

Paul Coty has completed the September monthly work sheet for his business, LeafyLift. The work sheet and general ledger accounts are given in the working papers accompanying this textbook.

Mr. Coty believes that he has made one or more errors in preparing the work sheet. He asks you to help him verify the work sheet.

**Instructions: 1.** Examine the work sheet and the general ledger accounts.  Make a list of the errors you find.

   **2.** Correct any errors you find in the general ledger accounts.

   **3.** Prepare a corrected work sheet.

## ◼ ENRICHMENT PROBLEMS

MASTERY PROBLEM 7-M   **Completing a work sheet**

On April 30 of the current year, FastGrow has the following general ledger accounts and balances.  The business uses a monthly fiscal period.

|                        | Account Balances |          |
| ---------------------- | ---------------- | -------- |
| **Account Titles**     | **Debit**        | **Credit** |
| Cash. . . . . . . . . . . . . . . . . . . . . . . . . . . . . . . . . . . . . . . . . | $5,800.00 |          |
| Petty Cash . . . . . . . . . . . . . . . . . . . . . . . . . . . . . . . . | 200.00    |          |
| Supplies . . . . . . . . . . . . . . . . . . . . . . . . . . . . . . . . . | 4,000.00  |          |
| Prepaid Insurance. . . . . . . . . . . . . . . . . . . . . . . . . . | 1,000.00  |          |
| Wheaton Supplies. . . . . . . . . . . . . . . . . . . . . . . . . . |           | $ 200.00 |
| Norton Company. . . . . . . . . . . . . . . . . . . . . . . . . . . |           | 115.00   |
| Roger Bently, Capital . . . . . . . . . . . . . . . . . . . . . . . . |           | 7,200.00 |
| Roger Bently, Drawing . . . . . . . . . . . . . . . . . . . . . . . | 400.00    |          |
| Income Summary . . . . . . . . . . . . . . . . . . . . . . . . . . . | —         |          |
| Sales . . . . . . . . . . . . . . . . . . . . . . . . . . . . . . . . . . . . |           | 5,300.00 |
| Advertising Expense. . . . . . . . . . . . . . . . . . . . . . . . . | 325.00    |          |
| Insurance Expense . . . . . . . . . . . . . . . . . . . . . . . . . . | —         |          |
| Miscellaneous Expense . . . . . . . . . . . . . . . . . . . . . . | 140.00    |          |
| Rent Expense. . . . . . . . . . . . . . . . . . . . . . . . . . . . . . | 500.00    |          |
| Supplies Expense . . . . . . . . . . . . . . . . . . . . . . . . . . | —         |          |
| Utilities Expense . . . . . . . . . . . . . . . . . . . . . . . . . . . | 450.00    |          |

**Instructions: 1.** Prepare the heading and trial balance on a work sheet.  Total and rule the Trial Balance columns.

   **2.** Analyze the following adjustment information into debit and credit parts.  Record the adjustments on the work sheet.

Adjustment Information, April 30

| Supplies on hand . . . . . . . . . . . . . . . . . . . . . . . . . . . . . . . . . . . . . . . . . . . | $2,050.00 |
| Value of prepaid insurance . . . . . . . . . . . . . . . . . . . . . . . . . . . . . . . . | 450.00 |

   **3.** Extend the up-to-date account balances to the Balance Sheet or Income Statement columns.

   **4.** Complete the work sheet.

CHALLENGE PROBLEM 7-C   **Completing a work sheet**

Clean and Mow had a small fire in its office. The fire destroyed some of the accounting records. On November 30 of the current year, the end of a monthly fiscal period, the following information was constructed from the remaining records and other sources.

**Remains of the general ledger:**

| Account Titles | Account Balances |
|---|---|
| Supplies . . . . . . . . . . . . . . . . . . . . . . . . . . . . | $1,800.00 |
| Donna Edwards, Drawing. . . . . . . . . . . . | 150.00 |
| Sales . . . . . . . . . . . . . . . . . . . . . . . . . . . . . | 4,000.00 |
| Advertising Expense . . . . . . . . . . . . . . . . | 420.00 |
| Rent Expense . . . . . . . . . . . . . . . . . . . . . . | 700.00 |
| Utilities Expense. . . . . . . . . . . . . . . . . . . . | 490.00 |

**Information from the business' checkbook:**

Cash balance on last unused check stub, $3,400.00
Total payments for miscellaneous expense, $60.00
Total payments for insurance, $325.00

**Information obtained through inquiries to other businesses:**

Owed to Outdoor Supplies, $2,000.00
Value of prepaid insurance, November 30, $250.00

**Information obtained by counting supplies on hand after the fire:**

Supplies on hand, $1,100.00

**Instructions: 1.** From the information given, prepare a heading and reconstruct a trial balance on a work sheet. The owner's capital account balance is the difference between the total of all debit account balances minus the total of all credit account balances.

    **2.** Complete the work sheet.

# SUMMARY OF PREPARATION OF A WORK SHEET FOR A SERVICE BUSINESS

The following overlay summarizes the preparation of a work sheet. Follow the directions below in using the overlay.

1. Before using the overlay, be sure the pages and transparent overlays are arranged correctly.  The correct arrangement is shown below.

2. Place your book in a horizontal position.  Study the steps on page C in preparing the work sheet.  You will be able to read the text through the transparent overlays.  When directed, carefully lift the transparent overlays and lay them over the work sheet as shown below.

# PREPARING A WORK SHEET

To correctly use the insert, read the steps below. Apply the transparent overlays when directed to do so in the steps.

**Rugcare**

**Work Sheet**

**For Month Ended August 31, 19--**

| ACCOUNT TITLE | TRIAL BALANCE DEBIT | TRIAL BALANCE CREDIT | ADJUSTMENTS DEBIT | ADJUSTMENTS CREDIT | INCOME STATEMENT DEBIT | INCOME STATEMENT CREDIT | BALANCE SHEET DEBIT | BALANCE SHEET CREDIT | |
|---|---|---|---|---|---|---|---|---|---|
| Cash | 8 2 7 2 00 | | | | | | | | 1 |
| Petty Cash | 2 0 0 00 | | | | | | | | 2 |
| Supplies | 4 9 3 1 00 | | | | | | | | 3 |
| Prepaid Insurance | 1 2 0 0 00 | | | | | | | | 4 |
| Butler Cleaning Supplies | | 1 3 6 0 00 | | | | | | | 5 |
| Dale Office Supplies | | 2 0 0 00 | | | | | | | 6 |
| Ben Furman, Capital | | 1 0 0 0 0 00 | | | | | | | 7 |
| Ben Furman, Drawing | 6 0 0 00 | | | | | | | | 8 |
| Income Summary | | | | | | | | | 9 |
| Sales | | 4 2 9 1 00 | | | | | | | 10 |
| Advertising Expense | 6 8 00 | | | | | | | | 11 |
| Insurance Expense | | | | | | | | | 12 |
| Miscellaneous Expense | 1 0 5 00 | | | | | | | | 13 |
| Rent Expense | 2 5 0 00 | | | | | | | | 14 |
| Repair Expense | 1 1 0 00 | | | | | | | | 15 |
| Supplies Expense | | | | | | | | | 16 |
| Utilities Expense | 1 1 5 00 | | | | | | | | 17 |
| | 15 8 5 1 00 | 15 8 5 1 00 | | | | | | | 18 |
| | | | | | | | | | 19 |
| | | | | | | | | | 20 |
| | | | | | | | | | 21 |
| | | | | | | | | | 22 |
| | | | | | | | | | 23 |
| | | | | | | | | | 24 |
| | | | | | | | | | 25 |

# PREPARING A WORK SHEET

1 Write the heading.

2 Record the trial balance.
- Write the general ledger account titles in the Account Title column.
- Write the account balances in either the Trial Balance Debit or Credit column.
- Rule a single line across the Trial Balance columns.
- Add the Trial Balance columns, and compare the totals.
- Rule double lines across both Trial Balance columns.
- *Carefully apply the first overlay.*

3 Record the supplies adjustment.
- Write the debit amount in the Adjustments Debit column on the line with the account title Supplies Expense.
- Write the credit amount in the Adjustments Credit column on the line with the account title Supplies.
- Label this adjustment (*a*).

4 Record the prepaid insurance adjustment.
- Write the debit amount in the Adjustments Debit column on the line with the account title Insurance Expense.
- Write the credit amount in the Adjustments Credit column on the line with the account title Prepaid Insurance.
- Label this adjustment (*b*).

5 Prove the Adjustments columns.
- Rule a single line across the Adjustments columns.
- Add the Adjustments columns, and compare the totals to assure that they are equal.
- Write the proving totals below the single line.
- Rule double lines across both Adjustments columns.
- *Carefully apply the second overlay.*

6 Extend all balance sheet account balances.
- Extend the up-to-date asset account balances to the Balance Sheet Debit column.
- Extend the up-to-date liability account balances to the Balance Sheet Credit column.
- Extend the owner's capital and drawing account balances to the Balance Sheet columns.

7 Extend all income statement account balances.
- Extend the up-to-date revenue account balance to the Income Statement Credit column.
- Extend the up-to-date expense account balances to the Income Statement Debit column.
- *Carefully apply the third overlay.*

8 Figure and record the net income (or net loss).
- Rule a single line across the Income Statement and Balance Sheet columns.
- Add the columns, and write the totals below the single line.
- Figure the net income or net loss amount.
- Write the amount of net income (or net loss) below the smaller of the two Income Statement column totals. Write the words *Net Income* or *Net Loss* in the Account Title column.
- Extend the amount of net income (or net loss) to the Balance Sheet columns. Write the amount under the smaller of the two column totals. Write the amount on the same line as the words *Net Income* (or *Net Loss*).

9 Total and rule the Income Statement and Balance Sheet columns.
- Rule a single line across the Income Statement and Balance Sheet columns immediately below the net income (or net loss) amounts.
- Add the net income (or net loss) to the previous column totals. Compare the column totals to assure that totals for each pair of columns are in balance.
- Write the proving totals for each column below the single line.
- Rule double lines across the Income Statement and Balance Sheet columns immediately below the proving totals.

# Financial Statements for a Proprietorship

## ENABLING PERFORMANCE TASKS

After studying Chapter 8, you will be able to:

a. Define the accounting term related to financial statements for a service business organized as a proprietorship.

b. Identify accounting concepts and practices related to preparation of financial statements for a service business organized as a proprietorship.

c. Prepare an income statement for a service business organized as a proprietorship.

d. Analyze an income statement using component percentages.

e. Prepare a balance sheet for a service business organized as a proprietorship.

The financial information needed by managers and owners to make good business decisions can be found in the general ledger accounts. However, the information in the general ledger is very detailed. Therefore, to make this general ledger information more usable, the information is summarized, organized, and reported to the owners and managers.

Also, *all* financial information *must* be reported if good business decisions are to be made. A financial statement with incomplete information is similar to a book with missing pages. The complete story is not told. If a business has both rent and utilities expenses but reports only the rent expense, managers will have incomplete information on which to base decisions. The accounting concept, *Adequate Disclosure*, is applied when financial statements contain all information necessary to understand a business' financial condition. *(CONCEPT: Adequate Disclosure)*

Rugcare prepares two financial statements: an income statement and a balance sheet. Rugcare always prepares financial statements at the end of each monthly fiscal period. *(CONCEPT: Accounting Period Cycle)* The time periods covered by Rugcare's financial statements are shown in Illustration 8-1.

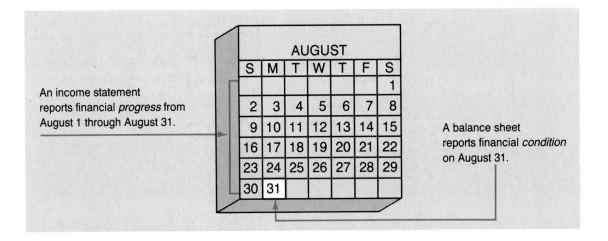

An income statement reports financial *progress* from August 1 through August 31.

A balance sheet reports financial *condition* on August 31.

An income statement reports financial information over a *specific period of time*, indicating the financial *progress* of a business in earning a net income or net loss.

A balance sheet reports financial information on a *specific date*, indicating the financial *condition* of a business. The financial condition of a business refers to its financial strength. If a business has adequate available assets and few liabilities, that business is financially strong. If the business' financial condition is not strong, adverse changes in the economy might cause the business to fail.

Illustration 8-1
Time periods for financial statements

## INCOME STATEMENT

Revenue is the earnings of a business from business activities. Expenses are the amounts a business pays to operate the business and earn the revenue. The revenue earned and the expenses incurred to earn that revenue are reported in the same fiscal period. *(CONCEPT: Matching Expenses with Revenue)*

Information needed to prepare financial statements could be obtained from the general ledger accounts. However, a work sheet is prepared to assist in planning the financial statements. Rugcare's income statement information on a work sheet is shown in Illustration 8-2, page 148.

Information needed to prepare Rugcare's income statement is obtained from two places on the work sheet. Account titles are obtained from the work sheet's Account Title column. Account balances are obtained from the work sheet's Income Statement columns.

The income statement for a service business has four sections: (1) heading, (2) revenue, (3) expenses, and (4) net income or net loss.

| ACCOUNT TITLE | | INCOME STATEMENT | | BALANCE SHEET | |
| --- | --- | --- | --- | --- | --- |
| | | DEBIT | CREDIT | DEBIT | CREDIT |
| 10 | Sales | | 4 2 9 1 00 | | |
| 11 | Advertising Expense | 6 8 00 | | | |
| 12 | Insurance Expense | 1 0 0 00 | | | |
| 13 | Miscellaneous Expense | 1 0 5 00 | | | |
| 14 | Rent Expense | 2 5 0 00 | | | |
| 15 | Repair Expense | 1 1 0 00 | | | |
| 16 | Supplies Expense | 2 6 4 7 00 | | | |
| 17 | Utilities Expense | 1 1 5 00 | | | |
| 18 | | 3 3 9 5 00 | 4 2 9 1 00 | | |
| 19 | Net Income | 8 9 6 00 | | | |
| 20 | | 4 2 9 1 00 | 4 2 9 1 00 | | |

Illustration 8-2
Income statement information on a work sheet

## Heading of an income statement

All financial statements have similar information in their three-line headings. (1) The name of the business. (2) The name of the statement. (3) The date of the statement. The three-line heading for Rugcare's income statement is shown in Illustration 8-3.

Illustration 8-3
Heading of an income statement

**Rugcare**
**Income Statement**
**For Month Ended August 31, 19--**

The income statement's date shows that this income statement reports information for the one-month fiscal period from August 1 through August 31.

## Revenue section of an income statement

Information from the work sheet's Account Title column and Income Statement Credit column is used to prepare the revenue section. The revenue section of an income statement is shown in Illustration 8-4.

Illustration 8-4
Revenue section of an income statement

| Revenue: | | | |
| --- | --- | --- | --- |
| Sales | | 4 2 9 1 00 | |

Write the name of this section, *Revenue:*, at the extreme left of the wide column on the first line. Write the title of the revenue account, *Sales*, on the next line indented about one centimeter. Record the balance of the account, *$4,291.00*, on the same line in the second amount column.

## Expenses section of an income statement

Information from the work sheet's Account Title column and Income Statement Debit column is used to prepare the expenses section. The expenses section of Rugcare's income statement is shown in Illustration 8-5.

| Expenses: | | |
|---|---|---|
| Advertising Expense | 6 8 00 | |
| Insurance Expense | 1 0 0 00 | |
| Miscellaneous Expense | 1 0 5 00 | |
| Rent Expense | 2 5 0 00 | |
| Repair Expense | 1 1 0 00 | |
| Supplies Expense | 2 6 4 7 00 | |
| Utilities Expense | 1 1 5 00 | |
| Total Expenses | | 3 3 9 5 00 |

Illustration 8-5
Expenses section of an income statement

Write the name of this section, *Expenses:*, at the extreme left of the wide column on the next blank line. Write the title of each expense account in the wide column indented about one centimeter. Record the balance of each expense account in the first amount column on the same line as the account title.

To indicate addition, rule a single line across the first amount column under the last expense account balance. Write the words, *Total Expenses*, on the next blank line in the wide column. Record the amount of total expenses, *$3,395.00*, on the same line in the second amount column.

## Net income section of an income statement

The amount of net income is calculated and verified using two steps.

1 The net income is calculated from information on the income statement as shown below.

> **Total Revenue − Total Expenses = Net Income**
> $4,291.00    −    $3,395.00   =   $896.00

2 The amount of net income, *$896.00*, is compared with the net income shown on the work sheet, Illustration 8-2. The net income calculated for

the income statement and the net income shown on the work sheet must be the same. The net income calculated for Rugcare's income statement, $896.00, is the same as that on the work sheet.

> If the net income calculated for the income statement is not the same as that shown on the work sheet, an error has been made. No more work on the income statement should be completed until the error is found and corrected.

A single line is drawn across the second amount column just below the amount of total expenses, as shown in Illustration 8-6.

| | | | % OF SALES |
|---|---:|---:|---:|
| **Rugcare** | | | |
| **Income Statement** | | | |
| **For Month Ended August 31, 19--** | | | |
| *Revenue:* | | | |
| Sales | | 4 2 9 1 00 | 100.0 |
| *Expenses:* | | | |
| Advertising Expense | 6 8 00 | | |
| Insurance Expense | 1 0 0 00 | | |
| Miscellaneous Expense | 1 0 5 00 | | |
| Rent Expense | 2 5 0 00 | | |
| Repair Expense | 1 1 0 00 | | |
| Supplies Expense | 2 6 4 7 00 | | |
| Utilities Expense | 1 1 5 00 | | |
| Total Expenses | | 3 3 9 5 00 | 79.1 |
| Net Income | | 8 9 6 00 | 20.9 |

Illustration 8-6
An income statement

Write the words, *Net Income,* on the next line at the extreme left of the wide column. On the same line, record the amount of net income, *$896.00,* in the second amount column. Rule double lines across both amount columns below the amount of net income to show that the amount has been verified as correct. Rugcare's completed income statement is shown in Illustration 8-6.

> If total expenses exceed total revenue, a net loss is reported on an income statement. When a net loss is reported, write the words, *Net Loss,* in the wide column. Subtract the total expenses from the revenue to calculate the net loss. Record the amount of net loss in the second amount column in parentheses. An amount written in parentheses on a financial statement indicates a negative amount.

## Component percentage analysis of an income statement

For a service business, the revenue reported on an income statement includes two components: (1) total expenses and (2) net income. To make decisions about future operations, Mr. Furman analyzes relationships between these two income statement components and the total sales. The percentage relationship between one financial statement item and the total that includes that item is called a component percentage. On an income statement, component percentages are calculated by dividing the amount of each component by the total amount of sales. Rugcare figures a component percentage for total expenses and net income. The relationship between each component and total sales is shown in a separate column on the income statement at the right of the amount columns.

**Acceptable component percentages.** For a component percentage to be useful, Mr. Furman needs to know what component percentages are acceptable for businesses similar to Rugcare. Various industry organizations publish average percentages for similar businesses. In the future Mr. Furman could also compare Rugcare's component percentages from one fiscal period with the percentages of previous fiscal periods.

**Total expenses component percentage.** The total expenses component percentage, based on information from the August income statement shown in Illustration 8-6, is calculated as shown below.

| Total Expenses ÷ Total Sales = | Total Expenses Component Percentage |
|---|---|
| $3,395.00 ÷ $4,291.00 = | 79.1% |

For businesses similar to Rugcare, an acceptable total expenses component percentage is not more than 80.0%. Therefore, Rugcare's percentage, 79.1%, is less than 80.0% and is acceptable.

**Net income component percentage.** The net income component percentage, based on information from the August income statement, is calculated as shown below.

| Net Income ÷ Total Sales = | Net Income Component Percentage |
|---|---|
| $896.00 ÷ $4,291.00 = | 20.9% |

For businesses similar to Rugcare, an acceptable net income component percentage is not less than 20.0%. Therefore, Rugcare's percentage, 20.9%, is greater than 20.0% and is acceptable. The net income component percentage will improve if Rugcare can reduce total expenses in future months. Also, the net income component percentage will improve if Rugcare can increase the amount of revenue in future months.

When there is a net loss, the component percentage for net loss is written in parentheses. A net loss is considered unacceptable.

## Income statement with two sources of revenue

Rugcare receives revenue from only one source, the sale of services for rug and carpet cleaning. Milton Lawn Service receives revenue from two sources, the sale of services to fertilize lawns and the sale of services to trim and care for trees. The business' owners want to know how much revenue is earned from each source. Therefore, the business uses two revenue accounts: Sales—Lawns and Sales—Tree Care.

When an income statement is prepared for Milton Lawn Service, both revenue accounts are listed, as shown in Illustration 8-7.

Illustration 8-7
Revenue section of an
income statement showing
two sources of revenue

| | | % OF SALES |
|---|---|---|
| *Milton Lawn Service* | | |
| *Income Statement* | | |
| *For Month Ended August 31, 19--* | | |
| *Revenue:* | | |
| Sales—Lawns | 3 3 6 0 00 | |
| Sales—Tree Care | 2 2 5 0 00 | |
| *Total Sales* | 5 6 1 0 00 | 100.0 |
| *Expenses:* | | |

Only the revenue section of Milton Lawn Service's income statement differs from the income statement prepared by Rugcare. Write the section heading, *Revenue:*, at the left of the wide column. Write the titles of both revenue accounts in the wide column indented about one centimeter. Record the balance of each account in the first amount column on the same line as the account title. Total the two revenue account balances. Write the total amount on the next line in the second amount column. Write the words, *Total Sales*, in the wide column indented about one centimeter on the same line as the total revenue amount.

# BALANCE SHEET

Information about assets, liabilities, and owner's equity might be obtained from the general ledger accounts or from a work sheet. However, the information is easier to use if reported in an organized manner such as on a balance sheet. Rugcare's balance sheet information on a work sheet is shown in Illustration 8-8.

| ACCOUNT TITLE | | 7 8 BALANCE SHEET | | |
|---|---|---|---|---|
| | | DEBIT | CREDIT | |
| 1 | Cash | 8 2 7 2 00 | | 1 |
| 2 | Petty Cash | 2 0 0 00 | | 2 |
| 3 | Supplies | 2 2 8 4 00 | | 3 |
| 4 | Prepaid Insurance | 1 1 0 0 00 | | 4 |
| 5 | Butler Cleaning Supplies | | 1 3 6 0 00 | 5 |
| 6 | Dale Office Supplies | | 2 0 0 00 | 6 |
| 7 | Ben Furman, Capital | | 10 0 0 0 00 | 7 |
| 8 | Ben Furman, Drawing | 6 0 0 00 | | 8 |
| 17 | | | | 17 |
| 18 | | 12 4 5 6 00 | 11 5 6 0 00 | 18 |
| 19 | Net Income | | 8 9 6 00 | 19 |
| 20 | | 12 4 5 6 00 | 12 4 5 6 00 | 20 |

Illustration 8-8
Balance sheet information
on a work sheet

Information needed to prepare Rugcare's balance sheet is obtained from two places on the work sheet. Account titles are obtained from the work sheet's Account Title column. Account balances are obtained from the work sheet's Balance Sheet columns.

A balance sheet has four sections: (1) heading, (2) assets, (3) liabilities, and (4) owner's equity.

## Heading of a balance sheet

The heading of a balance sheet consists of three lines. (1) The name of the business. (2) The name of the statement. (3) The date of the statement. Rugcare's balance sheet heading is shown in Illustration 8-9.

Illustration 8-9
Heading of a balance sheet

*Rugcare*

*Balance Sheet*

*August 31, 19--*

Assets, liabilities, and owner's equity are reported on Rugcare's balance sheet as of a specific date, August 31.

## Assets section of a balance sheet

A balance sheet reports information about the elements of the accounting equation.

$$Assets = Liabilities + Owner's\ Equity$$

The assets are on the LEFT side of the accounting equation and on the LEFT side of Rugcare's balance sheet.

The information needed to prepare the assets section is obtained from the work sheet's Account Title column and the Balance Sheet Debit column. The assets section of Rugcare's balance sheet is shown in Illustration 8-10.

| Assets | | |
|---|---:|---|
| Cash | 8 2 7 2 | 00 |
| Petty Cash | 2 0 0 | 00 |
| Supplies | 2 2 8 4 | 00 |
| Prepaid Insurance | 1 1 0 0 | 00 |
| | | |
| Total Assets | 11 8 5 6 | 00 |

Illustration 8-10
Assets section of a
balance sheet

Write the title of the section, *Assets*, in the middle of the left wide column. Under the heading write the titles of all asset accounts. Record the balance of each asset account in the left amount column on the same line as the account title.

## Equities section of a balance sheet

Two kinds of equities are reported on a balance sheet: (1) liabilities and (2) owner's equity. Liabilities and owner's equity are on the RIGHT side of the accounting equation and on the RIGHT side of Rugcare's balance sheet.

**Liabilities section of a balance sheet.** The information needed to prepare the liabilities section is obtained from the work sheet's Account Title column and the Balance Sheet Credit column. The liabilities are reported on a balance sheet as shown in Illustration 8-11.

| Liabilities | | |
|---|---:|---|
| Butler Cleaning Supplies | 1 3 6 0 | 00 |
| Dale Office Supplies | 2 0 0 | 00 |
| Total Liabilities | 1 5 6 0 | 00 |

Illustration 8-11
Liabilities section of a
balance sheet

Write the title of the section, *Liabilities,* in the middle of the right wide column. Under this heading write the titles of all liability accounts. Record the balance of each liability account in the right amount column on the same line as the account title. To indicate addition, rule a single line across the right amount column under the last amount. Write the words, *Total Liabilities,* in the right wide column on the next blank line. Record the total of all liabilities, *$1,560.00,* in the right amount column.

**Owner's equity section of a balance sheet.** Only the amount of current capital is reported on Rugcare's balance sheet. The amounts needed to calculate the current capital are found in the work sheet's Balance Sheet Debit and Credit columns. The amount of current capital is calculated as shown below.

| Capital Account Balance | + Net Income | – | Drawing Account Balance | = | Current Capital |
|---|---|---|---|---|---|
| $10,000.00 | + $896.00 | – | $600.00 | = | $10,296.00 |

The title of the owner's capital account is obtained from the work sheet's Account Title column. Owner's equity is reported on a balance sheet as shown in Illustration 8-12.

| Rugcare | | | | | |
|---|---|---|---|---|---|
| Balance Sheet | | | | | |
| August 31, 19-- | | | | | |
| **Assets** | | | **Liabilities** | | |
| Cash | 8 2 7 2 00 | | Butler Cleaning Supplies | 1 3 6 0 00 | |
| Petty Cash | 2 0 0 00 | | Dale Office Supplies | 2 0 0 00 | |
| Supplies | 2 2 8 4 00 | | Total Liabilities | 1 5 6 0 00 | |
| Prepaid Insurance | 1 1 0 0 00 | | **Owner's Equity** | | |
| | | | Ben Furman, Capital | 10 2 9 6 00 | |
| Total Assets | 11 8 5 6 00 | | Total Liab. and Owner's Eq. | 11 8 5 6 00 | |

Illustration 8-12
A balance sheet

Write the title of the section, *Owner's Equity,* in the middle of the right wide column on the next line. On the next line, write the title of the owner's capital account, *Ben Furman, Capital.* Record the current amount of owner's equity, *$10,296.00,* in the right amount column.

Rugcare's balance sheet prepared on August 31 is shown in Illustration 8-12. Rule a single line across both amount columns under the last amount in the amount column that is the longest. For Rugcare's balance sheet, the longest column is the right amount column. The line is ruled under the amount of Ben Furman's capital, $10,296.00. On the next line, in the right wide column, write the words, *Total Liab. and Owner's Eq.* Record the amount of total liabilities and owner's equity, *$11,856.00,* in the right amount column.

> The total assets amount is not recorded at the time the rest of the assets section is prepared. The placement of the total assets line is determined after the equities section is prepared so that the two final totals are on the same line.

Write the words, *Total Assets,* in the left wide column on the same line as the words *Total Liab. and Owner's Eq.* Record the amount of total assets, *$11,856.00,* in the left amount column.

Compare the totals of the two amount columns. Because the totals are the same on both sides of Rugcare's balance sheet, $11,856.00, the balance sheet is in balance. The accounting equation being reported is also in balance.

$$\text{Assets} = \text{Liabilities} + \text{Owner's Equity}$$
$$\$11,856.00 = \$1,560.00 + \$10,296.00$$

> If the total assets do not equal the total liabilities and owner's equity, the error or errors must be found and corrected before the balance sheet is completed.

Rule double lines across both the left and right amount columns just below the column totals to show that the totals have been verified as correct.

When a business has a net loss, current capital is calculated as shown below.

$$\begin{array}{ccccc} \text{Capital Account} & & \text{Drawing Account} & & \text{Current} \\ \text{Balance} & - \text{Net Loss} - & \text{Balance} & = & \text{Capital} \\ \$15,000.00 & - \$200.00 - & \$500.00 & = & \$14,300.00 \end{array}$$

The current capital, $14,300.00, is reported on the balance sheet in the same way as shown in Illustration 8-12.

## Owner's equity reported in detail on a balance sheet

Rugcare's balance sheet reports the current capital on August 31 but does not show how this amount was calculated. Rugcare is a small business with relatively few changes in owner's equity to report. Therefore, Ben Furman decided that the business does not need to report all the details in the owner's equity section. However, some businesses prefer to report the details about how owner's equity is calculated.

If Rugcare were to report details about owner's equity, the balance sheet would be prepared as shown in Illustration 8-13.

| | | | | |
|---|---|---|---|---|
| *Total Liabilities* | | | 1 5 6 0 00 | |
| | *Owner's Equity* | | | |
| *Ben Furman, Capital, August 1* | | *10,000.00* | | |
| *Net Income* | *896.00* | | | |
| *Less Ben Furman, Drawing* | *600.00* | *296.00* | | |
| *Ben Furman, Capital, August 31* | | | 10 2 9 6 00 | |
| *Total Liabilities and Owner's Equity* | | | 11 8 5 6 00 | |
| | | | | |
| | | | | |
| | | | | |

Illustration 8-13
Owner's equity reported in detail on a balance sheet

First, the owner's capital account balance, $10,000.00, is reported. Second, the balance of the drawing account, $600.00, is subtracted from the net income for the fiscal period, $896.00. The difference, $296.00, is added to the previous capital account balance. The current capital, $10,296.00, is recorded as the amount of Ben Furman, Capital on August 31.

# SUMMARY OF FINANCIAL STATEMENTS FOR A PROPRIETORSHIP

A summary of financial statements for a service business organized as a proprietorship is shown in Illustration 8-14, page 158.

1 An income statement is prepared using information from the Account Title column and Income Statement columns of a work sheet.

2 Component percentages for total expenses and net income are calculated as shown below.

Total Expenses ÷ Total Sales = Total Expenses Component Percentage
Net Income    ÷ Total Sales = Net Income Component Percentage

3 A balance sheet is prepared using information obtained from the work sheet's Account Title column and Balance Sheet columns. Current capital to be reported on the balance sheet is calculated as shown below.

$$\text{Capital Account Balance} + \text{Net Income} - \text{Drawing Account Balance} = \text{Current Capital}$$

Illustration 8-14     Summary of financial statements for a proprietorship

## ACCOUNTING TERM

What is the meaning of the following?

**1.** component percentage

## QUESTIONS FOR INDIVIDUAL STUDY

1. Which accounting concept is being applied when all the information about a business' financial condition is reported on financial statements?
2. Which accounting concept is being applied when financial statements are prepared at least once each year?
3. For what period of time does an income statement report financial progress of a business?
4. For what period of time does a balance sheet report financial condition of a business?
5. Which accounting concept is being applied when revenue earned and the expenses incurred to earn that revenue are recorded in the same fiscal period?
6. What does Rugcare do to assist in planning the preparation of financial statements?
7. Where does Rugcare obtain the information for preparing an income statement?
8. What are the four sections of an income statement?
9. What information is found in an income statement heading?
10. What are the two steps in figuring and verifying the net income on Rugcare's income statement?
11. How does Rugcare analyze its income statement?
12. What is the formula for calculating the total expenses component percentage?
13. What is the formula for calculating the net income component percentage?
14. How is revenue shown on an income statement when a business has two sources of revenue?
15. Where does Rugcare obtain the information for preparing a balance sheet?
16. What are the four sections of a balance sheet?
17. What information is found in a balance sheet heading?
18. What is the formula for calculating the amount of capital to report on a balance sheet?

## CASES FOR MANAGEMENT DECISION

**CASE 1** James Worth and Mary Derner each own small businesses. Mr. Worth prepares an income statement and balance sheet at the end of each day for his business. He claims that he needs the information to make business decisions. Mrs. Derner prepares an income statement and balance sheet for her business only at the end of each one-year fiscal period. She claims that she needs the information only at the end of the year when preparing tax reports. Which owner is using the better procedure? Explain your answer.

**CASE 2** Ralph Macy owns and manages a business that has produced an average annual net income of $21,600.00 for five years. George Wayne has offered to buy Mr. Macy's business and retain him as manager at a monthly salary of $2,000.00. What should Mr. Macy consider before selling his business and accepting the position as manager?

## DRILLS FOR UNDERSTANDING

DRILL 8-D1  **Classifying accounts**

Use a form similar to the following.

| 1 | 2 | 3 | 4 | 5 | 6 | 7 | 8 |
|---|---|---|---|---|---|---|---|
| | Account Classification | | | | | Financial Statement | |
| Account Title | Asset | Liab. | Owner's Equity | Revenue | Expense | Income Statement | Balance Sheet |
| 1. *Cash* | ✓ | | | | | | ✓ |

**Instructions: 1.** Write each of the following account titles in Column 1 of the form. The first account, Cash, is given as an example.

1. Cash
2. Alice Wayne, Capital
3. Alice Wayne, Drawing
4. Advertising Expense
5. Coen Office Supplies
6. Insurance Expense
7. Miscellaneous Expense
8. Mercer Supplies
9. Prepaid Insurance
10. Rent Expense
11. Sales
12. Supplies
13. Supplies Expense

**2.** Place a check mark in either Column 2, 3, 4, 5, or 6 to indicate the classification of each account.

**3.** Place a check mark in either Column 7 or 8 to indicate on which financial statement each account will be reported.

## DRILL 8-D2  Figuring net income or net loss and owner's current capital

The following information is given for several companies.

| | 1 | 2 | 3 | 4 | 5 | 6 |
|---|---|---|---|---|---|---|
| Company | Total Assets | Total Liabilities | Balance of | | Total Revenue | Total Expenses |
| | | | Capital | Drawing | | |
| A | $ 5,600 | $2,000 | $ 2,320 | $120 | $ 2,300 | $ 900 |
| B | 7,300 | 2,600 | 2,945 | 145 | 3,100 | 1,200 |
| C | 7,000 | 3,200 | 4,840 | 200 | 3,600 | 4,440 |
| D | 9,560 | 2,835 | 4,995 | 160 | 3,150 | 1,260 |
| E | 10,680 | 3,850 | 4,035 | 220 | 4,725 | 1,710 |
| F | 14,500 | 5,770 | 10,475 | 325 | 7,380 | 8,800 |
| G | 13,620 | 4,900 | 4,940 | 270 | 6,250 | 2,200 |
| H | 14,325 | 7,880 | 14,465 | 420 | 10,000 | 17,600 |

**Instructions:** Complete the following for each company.

**1.** Use the information in Columns 5 and 6. Figure the amount of net income or net loss for each company. For example, Company A: Revenue, $2,300, − expenses, $900, = net income, $1,400.

**2.** Figure the amount of current capital for each company using the net income or net loss from Instruction 1 and the information in Columns 3 and 4. For example, Company A: Capital account balance, $2,320, + net income, $1,400, − drawing, $120, = current capital, $3,600.

**3.** Use the accounting equation to check the accuracy of your answers in Instructions 1 and 2. For example, Company A: Assets, $5,600, = liabilities, $2,000, + owner's equity, $3,600. If the equation is not in balance, refigure and correct your answers to Instructions 1 and 2.

## ▮ APPLICATION PROBLEMS

### PROBLEM 8-1  Preparing an income statement

The following information is obtained from the work sheet of LawnMow for the month ended June 30 of the current year.

| | 5 | 6 | 7 | 8 | |
|---|---|---|---|---|---|
| ACCOUNT TITLE | INCOME STATEMENT | | BALANCE SHEET | | |
| | DEBIT | CREDIT | DEBIT | CREDIT | |
| 10  Sales | | 3 1 0 0 00 | | | 10 |
| 11  Advertising Expense | 3 0 00 | | | | 11 |
| 12  Insurance Expense | 1 4 0 00 | | | | 12 |
| 13  Miscellaneous Expense | 6 5 00 | | | | 13 |
| 14  Rent Expense | 8 0 0 00 | | | | 14 |
| 15  Supplies Expense | 4 0 0 00 | | | | 15 |
| 16  Utilities Expense | 7 5 00 | | | | 16 |
| 17 | 1 5 1 0 00 | 3 1 0 0 00 | | | 17 |
| 18  Net Income | 1 5 9 0 00 | | | | 18 |
| 19 | 3 1 0 0 00 | 3 1 0 0 00 | | | 19 |
| 20 | | | | | 20 |
| 21 | | | | | 21 |
| 22 | | | | | 22 |
| 23 | | | | | 23 |
| 24 | | | | | 24 |
| 25 | | | | | 25 |
| 26 | | | | | 26 |
| 27 | | | | | 27 |
| 28 | | | | | 28 |
| 29 | | | | | 29 |
| 30 | | | | | 30 |
| 31 | | | | | 31 |
| 32 | | | | | 32 |

**Instructions:** Prepare an income statement for the month ended June 30 of the current year. Figure and record the component percentages for total expenses and net income. Round percentage calculations to the nearest 0.1%.

## PROBLEM 8-2   Preparing a balance sheet

The following information is obtained from the work sheet of LawnMow for the month ended June 30 of the current year.

**Instructions:** Prepare a balance sheet for June 30 of the current year.

| | ACCOUNT TITLE | | BALANCE SHEET | | |
|---|---|---|---|---|---|
| | | | DEBIT | CREDIT | |
| 1 | Cash | | 7 5 3 0 00 | | 1 |
| 2 | Petty Cash | | 2 0 0 00 | | 2 |
| 3 | Supplies | | 6 8 6 0 00 | | 3 |
| 4 | Prepaid Insurance | | 2 5 0 0 00 | | 4 |
| 5 | Barker Supplies | | | 4 4 0 0 00 | 5 |
| 6 | Richmond Office Supplies | | | 1 3 0 0 00 | 6 |
| 7 | Clem Sutter, Capital | | | 11 0 0 0 00 | 7 |
| 8 | Clem Sutter, Drawing | | 1 2 0 0 00 | | 8 |
| 9 | Income Summary | | | | 9 |
| 16 | | | | | 16 |
| 17 | | | 18 2 9 0 00 | 16 7 0 0 00 | 17 |
| 18 | Net Income | | | 1 5 9 0 00 | 18 |
| 19 | | | 18 2 9 0 00 | 18 2 9 0 00 | 19 |
| 20 | | | | | 20 |
| 21 | | | | | 21 |
| 22 | | | | | 22 |
| 23 | | | | | 23 |
| 24 | | | | | 24 |
| 25 | | | | | 25 |
| 26 | | | | | 26 |
| 27 | | | | | 27 |
| 28 | | | | | 28 |
| 29 | | | | | 29 |
| 30 | | | | | 30 |
| 31 | | | | | 31 |
| 32 | | | | | 32 |
| 33 | | | | | 33 |
| 34 | | | | | 34 |
| 35 | | | | | 35 |
| 36 | | | | | 36 |
| 37 | | | | | 37 |
| 38 | | | | | 38 |

# ■ ENRICHMENT PROBLEMS

**Preparing financial statements**

The following information is obtained from the work sheet of Ace Delivery Service for the month ended July 31 of the current year.

**Instructions: 1.** Prepare an income statement for the month ended July 31 of the current year. Figure and record the component percentages for total expenses and net income. Round percentage calculations to the nearest 0.1%.
 **2.** Prepare a balance sheet for July 31 of the current year.

| | | | 5 | 6 | 7 | 8 | |
|---|---|---|---|---|---|---|---|
| | | | INCOME STATEMENT | | BALANCE SHEET | | |
| | ACCOUNT TITLE | | DEBIT | CREDIT | DEBIT | CREDIT | |
| 1 | Cash | | | | 7 50 0 00 | | 1 |
| 2 | Petty Cash | | | | 2 0 0 00 | | 2 |
| 3 | Supplies | | | | 7 80 0 00 | | 3 |
| 4 | Prepaid Insurance | | | | 2 60 0 00 | | 4 |
| 5 | Down Supplies | | | | | 4 70 0 00 | 5 |
| 6 | Melton Office Supplies | | | | | 1 20 0 00 | 6 |
| 7 | Clark Smith, Capital | | | | | 12 00 0 00 | 7 |
| 8 | Clark Smith, Drawing | | | | 1 40 0 00 | | 8 |
| 9 | Income Summary | | | | | | 9 |
| 10 | Sales | | | 5 67 0 00 | | | 10 |
| 11 | Advertising Expense | | 3 9 0 00 | | | | 11 |
| 12 | Insurance Expense | | 1 9 0 00 | | | | 12 |
| 13 | Miscellaneous Expense | | 1 5 0 00 | | | | 13 |
| 14 | Rent Expense | | 3 00 0 00 | | | | 14 |
| 15 | Supplies Expense | | 2 0 0 00 | | | | 15 |
| 16 | Utilities Expense | | 1 4 0 00 | | | | 16 |
| 17 | | | 4 07 0 00 | 5 67 0 00 | 19 50 0 00 | 17 90 0 00 | 17 |
| 18 | Net Income | | 1 60 0 00 | | | 1 60 0 00 | 18 |
| 19 | | | 5 67 0 00 | 5 67 0 00 | 19 50 0 00 | 19 50 0 00 | 19 |
| 20 | | | | | | | 20 |
| 21 | | | | | | | 21 |
| 22 | | | | | | | 22 |
| 23 | | | | | | | 23 |
| 24 | | | | | | | 24 |
| 25 | | | | | | | 25 |
| 26 | | | | | | | 26 |
| 27 | | | | | | | 27 |
| 28 | | | | | | | 28 |

CHALLENGE PROBLEM 8-C   **Preparing financial statements with two sources of revenue and a net loss**

The following information is obtained from the work sheet of Mercer Lawn Service for the month ended August 31 of the current year.

**Instructions: 1.** Prepare an income statement for the month ended August 31 of the current year. Figure and record the component percentages for total expenses and net loss. Place the percentage for net loss in parentheses to show that it is for a net loss. Round percentage calculations to the nearest 0.1%.

    **2.** Prepare a balance sheet for August 31 of the current year.

| | ACCOUNT TITLE | INCOME STATEMENT DEBIT | INCOME STATEMENT CREDIT | BALANCE SHEET DEBIT | BALANCE SHEET CREDIT | |
|---|---|---|---|---|---|---|
| 1 | Cash | | | 6 0 2 0 00 | | 1 |
| 2 | Petty Cash | | | 2 0 0 00 | | 2 |
| 3 | Supplies | | | 6 0 0 0 00 | | 3 |
| 4 | Prepaid Insurance | | | 2 5 0 0 00 | | 4 |
| 5 | Choice Supplies | | | | 3 0 0 00 | 5 |
| 6 | Poll Office Supplies | | | | 2 0 0 00 | 6 |
| 7 | Lydia Roland, Capital | | | | 13 0 0 0 00 | 7 |
| 8 | Lydia Roland, Drawing | | | 1 3 0 0 00 | | 8 |
| 9 | Income Summary | | | | | 9 |
| 10 | Sales—Lawn Care | | 4 7 0 0 00 | | | 10 |
| 11 | Sales—Shrub Care | | 2 6 0 0 00 | | | 11 |
| 12 | Advertising Expense | 3 9 0 00 | | | | 12 |
| 13 | Insurance Expense | 3 0 0 00 | | | | 13 |
| 14 | Miscellaneous Expense | 4 5 0 00 | | | | 14 |
| 15 | Rent Expense | 3 0 0 0 00 | | | | 15 |
| 16 | Supplies Expense | 3 1 0 0 00 | | | | 16 |
| 17 | Utilities Expense | 2 4 0 00 | | | | 17 |
| 18 | | 7 4 8 0 00 | 7 3 0 0 00 | 16 0 2 0 00 | 16 2 0 0 00 | 18 |
| 19 | Net Loss | | 1 8 0 00 | 1 8 0 00 | | 19 |
| 20 | | 7 4 8 0 00 | 7 4 8 0 00 | 16 2 0 0 00 | 16 2 0 0 00 | 20 |

# Recording Adjusting and Closing Entries for a Service Business

ENABLING PERFORMANCE TASKS

After studying Chapter 9, you will be able to:

a. Define accounting terms related to adjusting and closing entries for a service business organized as a proprietorship.
b. Identify accounting concepts and practices related to adjusting and closing entries for a service business organized as a proprietorship.
c. Record adjusting entries for a service business organized as a proprietorship.
d. Record closing entries for a service business organized as a proprietorship.
e. Prepare a post-closing trial balance for a service business organized as a proprietorship.

Rugcare prepares a work sheet at the end of each fiscal period to summarize the general ledger information needed to prepare financial statements. *(CONCEPT: Accounting Period Cycle)* Financial statements are prepared from information on the work sheet. *(CONCEPT: Adequate Disclosure)*

## RECORDING ADJUSTING ENTRIES

Rugcare's adjustments are analyzed and planned on a work sheet. However, these adjustments must be journalized so that they can be posted to the general ledger accounts. Journal entries recorded to update general ledger accounts at the end of a fiscal period are called adjusting entries.

Adjusting entries are recorded on the next journal page following the page on which the last daily transactions for the month are recorded. The adjusting entries are entered in the General Debit and General Credit columns of a journal.

Rugcare records two adjusting entries. (1) An adjusting entry to bring the supplies account up to date. (2) An adjusting entry to bring the prepaid insurance account up to date.

## Adjusting entry for supplies

The information needed to journalize the adjusting entry for supplies is obtained from lines 3 and 16 of Rugcare's work sheet. A partial work sheet and the adjusting entry for supplies are shown in Illustration 9-1.

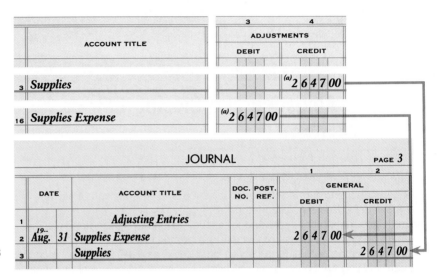

Illustration 9-1
Adjusting entry for supplies
recorded in a journal

The heading, *Adjusting Entries*, is written in the middle of the Account Title column of the journal. Because no source document is prepared for adjusting entries, the entries are identified with a heading in the journal. This heading explains all of the adjusting entries that follow. Therefore, the heading is written only once for all adjusting entries.

The date, *19--, Aug. 31*, is written in the Date column. The title of the account debited, *Supplies Expense*, is written in the Account Title column. The debit amount, *$2,647.00*, is recorded in the General Debit column on the same line as the account title. The title of the account credited, *Supplies*, is written on the next line. The credit amount, *$2,647.00*, is recorded in the General Credit column on the same line as the account title.

The effect of posting the adjusting entry for supplies to the general ledger accounts is shown in the T accounts.

Supplies Expense has an up-to-date balance of $2,647.00, which is the value of the supplies used during the fiscal period. Supplies has a new balance of $2,284.00, which is the value of the supplies on hand at the end of the fiscal period.

| Supplies Expense | |
|---|---|
| Adj. (a)   2,647.00 | |

| Supplies | |
|---|---|
| Bal.         4,931.00 | Adj. (a)        2,647.00 |
| (New Bal.   2,284.00) | |

## Adjusting entry for prepaid insurance

The information needed to journalize the adjusting entry for prepaid insurance is obtained from lines 4 and 12 of Rugcare's work sheet. A partial work sheet and the adjusting entry for prepaid insurance are shown in Illustration 9-2.

| | | 3 ADJUSTMENTS | 4 |
|---|---|---|---|
| ACCOUNT TITLE | | DEBIT | CREDIT |
| 4  *Prepaid Insurance* | | | (b)  1 0 0 00 |
| 12  *Insurance Expense* | | (b)  1 0 0 00 | |

**JOURNAL**  PAGE *3*

| | DATE | ACCOUNT TITLE | DOC. NO. | POST. REF. | 1 GENERAL DEBIT | 2 GENERAL CREDIT |
|---|---|---|---|---|---|---|
| 1 | | *Adjusting Entries* | | | | |
| 2 | *Aug.* 19.. *31* | *Supplies Expense* | | | 2 6 4 7 00 | |
| 3 | | *Supplies* | | | | 2 6 4 7 00 |
| 4 | *31* | *Insurance Expense* | | | 1 0 0 00 | |
| 5 | | *Prepaid Insurance* | | | | 1 0 0 00 |
| 6 | | | | | | |

Illustration 9-2
Adjusting entry for prepaid insurance recorded in a journal

The date, *31*, is written in the Date column. The title of the account debited, *Insurance Expense*, is written in the Account Title column. The debit amount, *$100.00*, is recorded in the General Debit column on the same line as the account title. The title of the account credited, *Prepaid Insurance*, is written on the next line in the Account Title column. The credit amount, *$100.00*, is recorded in the General Credit column on the same line as the account title.

The effect of posting the adjusting entry for insurance to the general ledger accounts is shown in the T accounts.

Insurance Expense has an up-to-date balance of $100.00, which is the value of insurance premiums used during the fiscal period. Prepaid Insurance has a new balance of $1,100.00, which is the value of insurance premiums that remain unused at the end of the fiscal period. (CONCEPT: *Matching Expenses with Revenue*)

| Insurance Expense | |
|---|---|
| Adj. (b)   100.00 | |

| Prepaid Insurance | |
|---|---|
| Bal.   1,200.00 | Adj. (b)   100.00 |
| *(New Bal.   1,100.00)* | |

## SUMMARY OF ADJUSTING ENTRIES FOR A SERVICE BUSINESS ORGANIZED AS A PROPRIETORSHIP

The two adjusting entries for a service business organized as a proprietorship are summarized in Illustration 9-3.

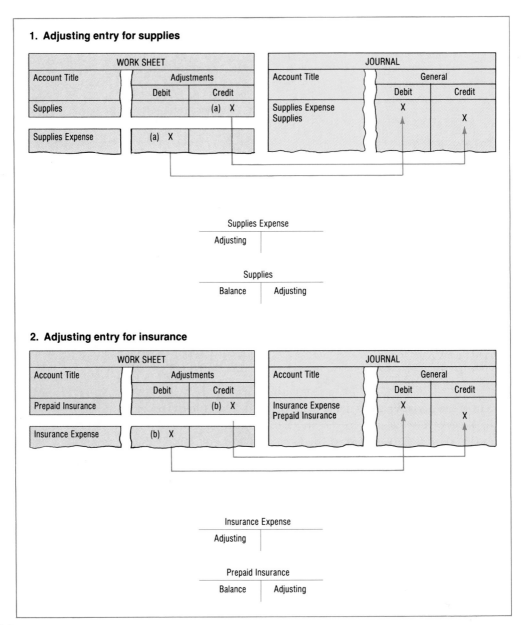

Illustration 9-3
Summary of adjusting
entries for a service
business organized as a
proprietorship

# RECORDING CLOSING ENTRIES

Accounts used to accumulate information from one fiscal period to the next are called permanent accounts. Permanent accounts are also referred to as real accounts. Permanent accounts include the asset and liability accounts and the owner's capital account. The ending account balances of permanent accounts for one fiscal period are the beginning account balances for the next fiscal period.

Accounts used to accumulate information until it is transferred to the owner's capital account are called temporary accounts. Temporary accounts are also referred to as nominal accounts. Temporary accounts include the revenue, expense, and owner's drawing accounts plus the income summary account. Temporary accounts show changes in the owner's capital for a single fiscal period. Therefore, at the end of a fiscal period, the balances of temporary accounts are summarized and transferred to the owner's capital account. The temporary accounts begin a new fiscal period with zero balances.

## Need for closing temporary accounts

Journal entries used to prepare temporary accounts for a new fiscal period are called closing entries. The temporary account balances must be reduced to zero at the end of each fiscal period. This procedure prepares the temporary accounts for recording information about the next fiscal period. Otherwise, the amounts for the next fiscal period would be added to amounts for previous fiscal periods. *(CONCEPT: Matching Expenses with Revenue)* The net income for the next fiscal period would be difficult to calculate because amounts from several fiscal periods remain in the accounts. Therefore, the temporary accounts must start each new fiscal period with zero balances.

To close a temporary account, an amount equal to its balance is recorded in the account on the side opposite to its balance. For example, if an account has a credit balance of $4,291.00, a debit of $4,291.00 is recorded to close the account.

## Need for the income summary account

Whenever a temporary account is closed, the closing entry must have equal debits and credits. If an account is debited for $3,000.00 to close the account, some other account must be credited for the same amount. A temporary account titled *Income Summary* is used to summarize the closing entries for the revenue and expense accounts.

The income summary account is unique because it does not have a normal balance side. The balance of this account is determined by the amounts posted to the account at the end of a fiscal period. When revenue is greater than total expenses, resulting in a net income, the income summary account has a credit balance, as shown in the T account.

| Income Summary | |
| --- | --- |
| Debit side | Credit side |
| Total expenses | Revenue (greater than expenses) |
| | (Credit balance is the net income.) |

When total expenses are greater than revenue, resulting in a net loss, the income summary account has a debit balance, as shown in the T account.

Income Summary

| Debit side | Credit side |
|---|---|
| Total expenses (greater than revenue) | Revenue |
| (Debit balance is the net loss.) | |

Thus, whether the balance of the income summary account is a debit or a credit depends upon whether the business earns a net income or incurs a net loss. Because Income Summary is a temporary account, the account is also closed at the end of a fiscal period when the net income or net loss is recorded.

Rugcare records four closing entries. (1) An entry to close income statement accounts with credit balances. (2) An entry to close income statement accounts with debit balances. (3) An entry to record net income or net loss and close Income Summary. (4) An entry to close the owner's drawing account.

Information needed to record the four closing entries is found in the Income Statement and Balance Sheet columns of the work sheet.

## Closing entry for an income statement account with a credit balance

Rugcare has one income statement account with a credit balance, Sales, as shown on the partial work sheet in Illustration 9-4. This credit balance

| | | 5 | 6 |
|---|---|---|---|
| | ACCOUNT TITLE | INCOME STATEMENT | |
| | | DEBIT | CREDIT |
| 10 | *Sales* | | 4 2 9 1 00 — (Debit to close) |

| | | JOURNAL | | | PAGE 3 | |
|---|---|---|---|---|---|---|
| | | | | | 1 | 2 |
| | DATE | ACCOUNT TITLE | DOC. NO. | POST. REF. | GENERAL | |
| | | | | | DEBIT | CREDIT |
| 6 | | *Closing Entries* | | | | |
| 7 | *31* | *Sales* | | | 4 2 9 1 00 | |
| 8 | | *Income Summary* | | | | 4 2 9 1 00 |
| 9 | | | | | | |
| 10 | | | | | | |
| 11 | | | | | | |
| 12 | | | | | | |

Illustration 9-4
Closing entry for an income statement account with a credit balance

must be reduced to zero to prepare the account for the next fiscal period. To reduce the balance to zero, Sales is debited for the amount of the balance. Because debits must equal credits for each journal entry, some other account must be credited. The account used for the credit part of this closing entry is Income Summary. The closing entry for Sales is journalized as shown in Illustration 9-4.

No source document is used for closing entries. Therefore, the heading, *Closing Entries*, is written in the Account Title column of the journal. For Rugcare, this heading is placed in the journal on the first blank line after the last adjusting entry.

The date, *31*, is written on the next line in the Date column. The title of the account debited, *Sales*, is written in the Account Title column. The debit amount, *$4,291.00*, is recorded in the General Debit column on the same line as the account title. The title of the account credited, *Income Summary*, is written in the Account Title column on the next journal line. The credit amount, *$4,291.00*, is recorded in the General Credit amount column on the same line as the account title.

The effect of this closing entry on the general ledger accounts is shown in the T accounts.

The balance of Sales is now zero, and the account is ready for the next fiscal period. The credit balance of Sales is transferred to Income Summary.

| Sales | | | |
|---|---|---|---|
| Closing | 4,291.00 | Bal. | 4,291.00 |
| | | *(New Bal. zero)* | |

| Income Summary | |
|---|---|
| | Closing (revenue) |
| | 4,291.00 |

## Closing entry for income statement accounts with debit balances

Rugcare has several income statement accounts with debit balances. The seven expense accounts have normal debit balances at the end of a fiscal period, as shown on the partial work sheet in Illustration 9-5 on page 172. The balances of the expense accounts must be reduced to zero to prepare the accounts for the next fiscal period. Each expense account is credited for an amount equal to its balance, and Income Summary is debited for the total of all the expense account balances. The closing entry for the expense accounts is journalized as shown in Illustration 9-5.

The heading for closing entries is written only once. Therefore, the closing entry for expenses starts on the next blank line in the journal.

The date, *31*, is written in the Date column. The title of the account debited, *Income Summary*, is written in the Account Title column. The amount debited to Income Summary is not entered in the amount column until all expenses have been journalized and the total amount calculated. The account title and balance of each expense account is recorded in the Account Title and General Credit columns. After all expense accounts and their balances have been written in the journal, the credit amounts for this entry are added. The total of all expenses, *$3,395.00*, is recorded in the General Debit column on the same line as the account title, Income Summary.

The effect of the closing entry for Rugcare's expense accounts is shown in the T accounts.

**Income Summary**

| Closing (expenses) | 3,395.00 | Closing (revenue) | 4,291.00 |
| | | (New Bal. | 896.00) |

**Advertising Expense**

| Bal. | 68.00 | Closing | 68.00 |
| (New Bal. zero) | | | |

**Insurance Expense**

| Bal. | 100.00 | Closing | 100.00 |
| (New Bal. zero) | | | |

**Miscellaneous Expense**

| Bal. | 105.00 | Closing | 105.00 |
| (New Bal. zero) | | | |

**Rent Expense**

| Bal. | 250.00 | Closing | 250.00 |
| (New Bal. zero) | | | |

**Repair Expense**

| Bal. | 110.00 | Closing | 110.00 |
| (New Bal. zero) | | | |

**Supplies Expense**

| Bal. | 2,647.00 | Closing | 2,647.00 |
| (New Bal. zero) | | | |

**Utilities Expense**

| Bal. | 115.00 | Closing | 115.00 |
| (New Bal. zero) | | | |

The balance of each expense account is returned to zero, and the accounts are ready for the next fiscal period. The debit balances of the expense accounts are recorded in Income Summary as one debit amount. The balance of Income Summary is the net income for the fiscal period, $896.00.

## Closing entry to record net income or loss and close the income summary account

Rugcare's net income is on the partial work sheet shown in Illustration 9-6. The amount of net income increases the owner's capital and, therefore, must be credited to the owner's capital account. The balance of the temporary account, Income Summary, must be reduced to zero to prepare the account for the next fiscal period. The closing entry to record net income and close the income summary account is journalized as shown in Illustration 9-6.

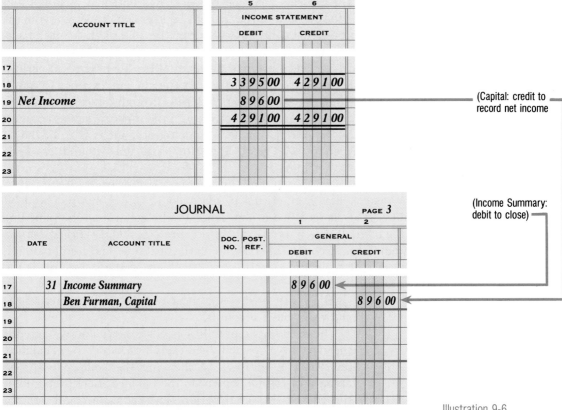

Illustration 9-6
Closing entry to record net income and close the income summary account

The date, *31*, is written in the Date column. The title of the account debited, *Income Summary*, is written in the Account Title column. The debit amount, *$896.00,* is recorded in the General Debit column on the same line as the account title. The title of the account credited, *Ben Furman, Capital,* is written in the Account Title column on the next line. The credit amount, *$896.00,* is recorded in the General Credit column on the same line as the account title.

The effect of this closing entry on the general ledger accounts is shown in the T accounts.

The debit to the income summary account, $896.00, reduces the account balance to zero and prepares the account for the next fiscal period. The credit, $896.00, increases the balance of the owner's capital account, Ben Furman, Capital.

If the business incurs a net loss, the closing entry is a debit to the owner's capital account and a credit to the income summary account.

**Income Summary**

| Closing (expenses) 3,395.00 | Closing (revenue) 4,291.00 |
|---|---|
| Closing          896.00 | *(New Bal. zero)* |

**Ben Furman, Capital**

| | Bal.          10,000.00 |
|---|---|
| | Closing (net income) 896.00 |
| | *(New Bal.    10,896.00)* |

## Closing entry for the owner's drawing account

Withdrawals are assets that the owner takes out of a business and which decrease the amount of the owner's equity. The drawing account is a temporary account that accumulates information separately for each fiscal period. Therefore, the drawing account balance is reduced to zero at the end of one fiscal period to prepare the account for the next fiscal period.

The drawing account is neither a revenue nor an expense account. Therefore, the drawing account is not closed through Income Summary. The drawing account balance is closed directly to the owner's capital account.

The closing entry for the owner's drawing account is journalized as shown in Illustration 9-7. The closing entry is on lines 19 and 20 of the journal.

The date, *31,* is written in the Date column. The title of the account debited, *Ben Furman, Capital,* is written in the Account Title column. The debit amount, *$600.00,* is recorded in the General Debit column on the same line with the account title. The title of the account credited, *Ben Furman, Drawing,* is written in the Account Title column on the next line. The credit amount, *$600.00,* is written in the General Credit column on the same line as the account title.

**Ben Furman, Capital**

| Closing          600.00 | Bal.          10,000.00 |
|---|---|
| | Net Income      896.00 |
| | *(New Bal.    10,296.00)* |

**Ben Furman, Drawing**

| Bal.          600.00 | Closing          600.00 |
|---|---|
| *(New Bal. zero)* | |

The effect of the entry to close the drawing account is shown in the T accounts.

The drawing account has a zero balance and is ready for the next fiscal period. The capital account's new balance, $10,296.00, is verified by checking the balance with the amount of capital shown on the balance sheet prepared at the end of the fiscal period. The capital account balance shown on Rugcare's balance sheet in Chapter 8, Illustration 8-12, is $10,296.00. The two amounts are the same, and the capital account balance is verified.

| ACCOUNT TITLE | | 7 BALANCE SHEET DEBIT | 8 CREDIT | |
|---|---|---|---|---|
| 7 | Ben Furman, Capital | | 10 00 00 | 7 |
| 8 | Ben Furman, Drawing | 6 00 00 | | 8 |

(Credit to close)

| JOURNAL | | | | | | PAGE 3 | |
|---|---|---|---|---|---|---|---|

| | DATE | ACCOUNT TITLE | DOC. NO. | POST. REF. | 1 GENERAL DEBIT | 2 CREDIT | |
|---|---|---|---|---|---|---|---|
| 6 | | *Closing Entries* | | | | | |
| 7 | 31 | Sales | | | 4 29 1 00 | | |
| 8 | | Income Summary | | | | 4 29 1 00 | |
| 9 | 31 | Income Summary | | | 3 39 5 00 | | |
| 10 | | Advertising Expense | | | | 6 8 00 | |
| 11 | | Insurance Expense | | | | 1 00 00 | |
| 12 | | Miscellaneous Expense | | | | 1 05 00 | |
| 13 | | Rent Expense | | | | 2 50 00 | |
| 14 | | Repair Expense | | | | 1 10 00 | |
| 15 | | Supplies Expense | | | | 2 64 7 00 | |
| 16 | | Utilities Expense | | | | 1 15 00 | |
| 17 | 31 | Income Summary | | | 8 96 00 | | |
| 18 | | Ben Furman, Capital | | | | 8 96 00 | |
| 19 | 31 | Ben Furman, Capital | | | 6 00 00 | | |
| 20 | | Ben Furman, Drawing | | | | 6 00 00 | |
| 21 | | | | | | | |
| 22 | | | | | | | |
| 23 | | | | | | | |
| 24 | | | | | | | |
| 25 | | | | | | | |
| 26 | | | | | | | |

Illustration 9-7
Closing entry for the drawing account recorded in a journal

# SUMMARY OF CLOSING ENTRIES FOR A SERVICE BUSINESS ORGANIZED AS A PROPRIETORSHIP

Closing entries are journalized and posted to prepare temporary accounts for the next fiscal period. The income summary account is used to summarize all revenue and expense accounts before recording net income or net loss in the owner's capital account. A summary of closing entries is shown in Illustration 9-8.

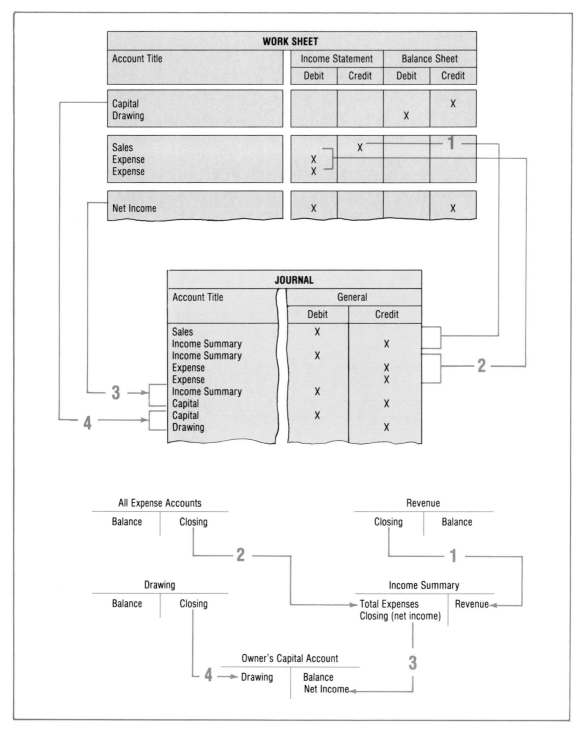

Illustration 9-8    Summary of closing entries for a service business organized as a proprietorship

To complete a fiscal period, Rugcare records four journal entries to close temporary accounts.

1  Close income statement accounts with credit balances. *(revenue)*

2  Close income statement accounts with debit balances. *(expenses)*

3  Record the net income or net loss in the owner's capital account and close Income Summary.

4  Close the owner's drawing account.

# GENERAL LEDGER AFTER
# ADJUSTING AND CLOSING ENTRIES ARE POSTED

Rugcare's general ledger after the adjusting and closing entries are posted is shown in Illustration 9-9. When an account has a zero balance, lines are drawn in both the Balance Debit and Balance Credit columns. The lines assure a reader that a balance has not been omitted.

ACCOUNT *Cash*                                                     ACCOUNT NO. *110*

| DATE | ITEM | POST. REF. | DEBIT | CREDIT | BALANCE DEBIT | BALANCE CREDIT |
|---|---|---|---|---|---|---|
| 19-- Aug. 31 | | 2 | 14 2 9 1 00 | | 14 2 9 1 00 | |
| 31 | | 2 | | 6 0 1 9 00 | 8 2 7 2 00 | |

ACCOUNT *Petty Cash*                                              ACCOUNT NO. *120*

| DATE | ITEM | POST. REF. | DEBIT | CREDIT | BALANCE DEBIT | BALANCE CREDIT |
|---|---|---|---|---|---|---|
| 19-- Aug. 17 | | 1 | 2 0 0 00 | | 2 0 0 00 | |

ACCOUNT *Supplies*                                               ACCOUNT NO. *130*

| DATE | ITEM | POST. REF. | DEBIT | CREDIT | BALANCE DEBIT | BALANCE CREDIT |
|---|---|---|---|---|---|---|
| 19-- Aug. 3 | | 1 | 1 5 7 7 00 | | 1 5 7 7 00 | |
| 7 | | 1 | 2 7 2 0 00 | | 4 2 9 7 00 | |
| 20 | | 1 | 2 0 0 00 | | 4 4 9 7 00 | |
| 28 | | 2 | 4 3 4 00 | | 4 9 3 1 00 | |
| 31 | | 3 | | 2 6 4 7 00 | 2 2 8 4 00 | |

Illustration 9-9
General ledger accounts after adjusting and closing entries are posted

ACCOUNT **Prepaid Insurance**                                              ACCOUNT NO. *140*

| DATE | | ITEM | POST. REF. | DEBIT | CREDIT | BALANCE | |
|---|---|---|---|---|---|---|---|
| | | | | | | DEBIT | CREDIT |
| *19--* Aug. | 4 | | 1 | 1 2 0 0 00 | | 1 2 0 0 00 | |
| | 31 | | 3 | | 1 0 0 00 | 1 1 0 0 00 | |

ACCOUNT **Butler Cleaning Supplies**                                       ACCOUNT NO. *210*

| DATE | | ITEM | POST. REF. | DEBIT | CREDIT | BALANCE | |
|---|---|---|---|---|---|---|---|
| | | | | | | DEBIT | CREDIT |
| *19--* Aug. | 7 | | 1 | | 2 7 2 0 00 | | 2 7 2 0 00 |
| | 11 | | 1 | 1 3 6 0 00 | | | 1 3 6 0 00 |

ACCOUNT **Dale Office Supplies**                                           ACCOUNT NO. *220*

| DATE | | ITEM | POST. REF. | DEBIT | CREDIT | BALANCE | |
|---|---|---|---|---|---|---|---|
| | | | | | | DEBIT | CREDIT |
| *19--* Aug. | 20 | | 1 | | 2 0 0 00 | | 2 0 0 00 |

ACCOUNT **Ben Furman, Capital**                                            ACCOUNT NO. *310*

| DATE | | ITEM | POST. REF. | DEBIT | CREDIT | BALANCE | |
|---|---|---|---|---|---|---|---|
| | | | | | | DEBIT | CREDIT |
| *19--* Aug. | 1 | | 1 | | 10 0 0 0 00 | | 10 0 0 0 00 |
| | 31 | | 3 | | 8 9 6 00 | | 10 8 9 6 00 |
| | 31 | | 3 | 6 0 0 00 | | | 10 2 9 6 00 |

ACCOUNT **Ben Furman, Drawing**                                            ACCOUNT NO. *320*

| DATE | | ITEM | POST. REF. | DEBIT | CREDIT | BALANCE | |
|---|---|---|---|---|---|---|---|
| | | | | | | DEBIT | CREDIT |
| *19--* Aug. | 12 | | 1 | 1 0 0 00 | | 1 0 0 00 | |
| | 31 | | 2 | 5 0 0 00 | | 6 0 0 00 | |
| | 31 | | 3 | | 6 0 0 00 | —— | —— |

Illustration 9-9
General ledger accounts
after adjusting and closing
entries are posted
(continued)

Illustration 9-9
General ledger accounts
after adjusting and closing
entries are posted
(continued)

ACCOUNT *Income Summary*          ACCOUNT NO. *330*

| DATE | | ITEM | POST. REF. | DEBIT | CREDIT | BALANCE DEBIT | BALANCE CREDIT |
|---|---|---|---|---|---|---|---|
| 19-- Aug. | 31 | | 3 | | 4 2 9 1 00 | | 4 2 9 1 00 |
| | 31 | | 3 | 3 3 9 5 00 | | | 8 9 6 00 |
| | 31 | | 3 | 8 9 6 00 | | —— | —— |

ACCOUNT *Sales*          ACCOUNT NO. *410*

| DATE | | ITEM | POST. REF. | DEBIT | CREDIT | BALANCE DEBIT | BALANCE CREDIT |
|---|---|---|---|---|---|---|---|
| 19-- Aug. | 31 | | 2 | | 4 2 9 1 00 | | 4 2 9 1 00 |
| | 31 | | 3 | 4 2 9 1 00 | | —— | —— |

ACCOUNT *Advertising Expense*          ACCOUNT NO. *510*

| DATE | | ITEM | POST. REF. | DEBIT | CREDIT | BALANCE DEBIT | BALANCE CREDIT |
|---|---|---|---|---|---|---|---|
| 19-- Aug. | 14 | | 1 | 6 8 00 | | 6 8 00 | |
| | 31 | | 3 | | 6 8 00 | —— | —— |

ACCOUNT *Insurance Expense*          ACCOUNT NO. *520*

| DATE | | ITEM | POST. REF. | DEBIT | CREDIT | BALANCE DEBIT | BALANCE CREDIT |
|---|---|---|---|---|---|---|---|
| 19-- Aug. | 31 | | 3 | 1 0 0 00 | | 1 0 0 00 | |
| | 31 | | 3 | | 1 0 0 00 | —— | —— |

ACCOUNT *Miscellaneous Expense*          ACCOUNT NO. *530*

| DATE | | ITEM | POST. REF. | DEBIT | CREDIT | BALANCE DEBIT | BALANCE CREDIT |
|---|---|---|---|---|---|---|---|
| 19-- Aug. | 13 | | 1 | 2 5 00 | | 2 5 00 | |
| | 18 | | 1 | 7 0 00 | | 9 5 00 | |
| | 28 | | 2 | 3 00 | | 9 8 00 | |
| | 31 | | 2 | 7 00 | | 1 0 5 00 | |
| | 31 | | 3 | | 1 0 5 00 | —— | —— |

Illustration 9-9
General ledger accounts
after adjusting and closing
entries are posted
(concluded)

# POST-CLOSING TRIAL BALANCE

After the closing entries are posted, Rugcare verifies that debits equal credits in the general ledger accounts by preparing a trial balance. A trial balance prepared after the closing entries are posted is called a post-closing trial balance.

Only general ledger accounts with balances are included on a post-closing trial balance. The permanent accounts (assets, liabilities, and owner's capital) have balances and do appear on a post-closing trial balance. Because the temporary accounts (income summary, revenue, expense, and drawing) are closed and have zero balances, they do not appear on a post-closing trial balance. Rugcare's post-closing trial balance is shown in Illustration 9-10.

| Rugcare | | |
|---|---|---|
| Post-Closing Trial Balance | | |
| August 31, 19-- | | |
| ACCOUNT TITLE | DEBIT | CREDIT |
| Cash | 8 2 7 2 00 | |
| Petty Cash | 2 0 0 00 | |
| Supplies | 2 2 8 4 00 | |
| Prepaid Insurance | 1 1 0 0 00 | |
| Butler Cleaning Supplies | | 1 3 6 0 00 |
| Dale Office Supplies | | 2 0 0 00 |
| Ben Furman, Capital | | 10 2 9 6 00 |
| Totals | 11 8 5 6 00 | 11 8 5 6 00 |

Illustration 9-10
Post-closing trial balance

Rugcare uses eight steps to prepare a post-closing trial balance.

1 Write the heading on three lines.

2 Write the titles of all general ledger accounts with balances in the Account Title column.

3 On the same line with each account title, write each account's balance in either the Debit or Credit column.

4 Rule a single line across both amount columns below the last amount, and add each amount column.

5 Compare the two column totals. The two column totals must be the same. The total of all debits must equal the total of all credits in a general ledger. The totals of both columns on Rugcare's post-closing trial balance are the same, $11,856.00. Rugcare's post-closing trial balance shows that the general ledger account balances are in balance and ready for the new fiscal period. If the two column totals are not the same, the errors must be found and corrected before any more work is completed.

6 Write the word, *Totals*, on the line below the last account title.

7 Write the column totals, *$11,856.00*, below the single line.

8 Rule double lines across both amount columns to show that the totals have been verified as correct.

## SUMMARY OF AN ACCOUNTING CYCLE FOR A SERVICE BUSINESS

Chapters 1 through 9 describe Rugcare's accounting activities for a one-month fiscal period. The series of accounting activities included in recording financial information for a fiscal period is called an accounting cycle. *(CONCEPT: Accounting Period Cycle)* Rugcare's accounting cycle is summarized in Illustration 9-11.

For the next fiscal period, the cycle begins again at Step 1.

Illustration 9-11
Summary of an accounting cycle for a service business

## ACCOUNTING TERMS

What is the meaning of each of the following?

**1.** adjusting entries
**2.** permanent accounts
**3.** temporary accounts
**4.** closing entries
**5.** post-closing trial balance
**6.** accounting cycle

## QUESTIONS FOR INDIVIDUAL STUDY

**1.** Which accounting concept is being applied when information in a general ledger is summarized on a work sheet at the end of each fiscal period?

**2.** Why are adjusting entries journalized and posted at the end of a fiscal period?

**3.** How are adjusting entries identified in a journal?

**4.** What accounts are affected, and how, by the adjusting entry for supplies?

**5.** What accounts are affected, and how, by the adjusting entry for prepaid insurance?

**6.** Why are closing entries journalized and posted at the end of a fiscal period?

**7.** How is the income summary account used?

**8.** Why is the income summary account considered unique?

**9.** What kind of balance will the income

**10.** What kind of balance will the income summary account have if a business has a net loss?

**11.** What four closing entries are recorded by Rugcare?

**12.** What effect do withdrawals have on the owner's equity?

**13.** After the closing entries are posted, how is the balance of the capital account verified?

**14.** Why is a post-closing trial balance prepared after the closing entries have been posted?

**15.** What accounts appear on a post-closing trial balance?

**16.** What are the eight steps of an accounting cycle?

## CASES FOR MANAGEMENT DECISION

**CASE 1** Thomas Westcott forgot to journalize and post the adjusting entry for prepaid insurance at the end of the June fiscal period. What effect will this omission have on the records of Mr. Westcott's business as of June 30? Explain your answer.

**CASE 2** Jason Fields states that his business is so small that he just records supplies and insurance as expenses when he pays for them. Thus, at the end of a fiscal period, Mr. Fields does not record adjusting and closing entries for his business. Do you agree with his accounting procedures? Explain your answer.

**CASE 3** On July 31 Iris Medina's work sheet shows a capital account balance of $9,000.00. Miss Medina's post-closing trial balance shows a capital account balance of $8,955.00. What could have caused the change in the capital account's balance?

**CASE 4** Sueanne Worth owns a business that uses only twelve general ledger accounts. She carefully checks each journal entry to assure that debits equal credits for the entry. Before preparing financial statements, she checks carefully to assure that debits equal credits in each pair of columns on the work sheet. She checks to assure that debits equal credits in each of the adjusting and closing entries. Because of these careful checks during a fiscal period, she believes that her records are accurate, and she does not need to prepare a post-closing trial balance. Do you agree with Ms. Worth? Explain your answer.

## ▇ DRILL FOR UNDERSTANDING

### DRILL 9-D1   Determining accounts affected by adjusting and closing entries

Rapid Service Company uses the following general ledger accounts.

1. Advertising Expense
2. Baer Supplies
3. Cash
4. Gates Office Supplies
5. Irma Downs, Capital
6. Irma Downs, Drawing
7. Income Summary
8. Insurance Expense

9. Miscellaneous Expense
10. Prepaid Insurance
11. Rent Expense
12. Sales
13. Supplies
14. Supplies Expense
15. Utilities Expense

Use a form similar to the following.

| 1 | 2 | 3 | 4 | 5 | 6 | 7 |
|---|---|---|---|---|---|---|
| | Account Is Affected by an Adjusting Entry | | Account Is Affected by a Closing Entry | | After Closing Entries Are Posted, Account Has a Balance | |
| Account Title | Yes | No | Yes | No | Yes | No |
| 1. *Advertising Expense* | | ✓ | ✓ | | | ✓ |

**Instructions: 1.** List the account titles in Column 1. The first account, Advertising Expense, is given as an example.

**2.** For each account title, place a check mark in either Column 2 or 3 to indicate whether the account is affected by an adjusting entry.

**3.** For each account title, place a check mark in either Column 4 or 5 to indicate whether the account is affected by a closing entry.

**4.** For each account title, place a check mark in either Column 6 or 7 to indicate whether the account has a balance after the closing entries are posted.

## ▇ APPLICATION PROBLEM

### PROBLEM 9-1   Journalizing and posting adjusting and closing entries; preparing a post-closing trial balance

Eiler Company's partial work sheet for the month ended October 31 of the current year is given on the next page. The general ledger accounts are given in the working papers that accompany this textbook. (The general ledger accounts do not show all details for the fiscal period. The "Balance" shown in each account is the account's balance before adjusting and closing entries are posted.)

**Instructions: 1.** Use page 3 of a journal. Journalize and post the adjusting entries.

**2.** Continue to use page 3 of the journal. Journalize and post the closing entries.

**3.** Prepare a post-closing trial balance.

| | 3 | 4 | 5 | 6 | 7 | 8 | |
|---|---|---|---|---|---|---|---|
| **ACCOUNT TITLE** | ADJUSTMENTS | | INCOME STATEMENT | | BALANCE SHEET | | |
| | DEBIT | CREDIT | DEBIT | CREDIT | DEBIT | CREDIT | |
| 1 Cash | | | | | 2 6 0 0 00 | | 1 |
| 2 Supplies | | (a) 1 4 5 00 | | | 5 6 0 00 | | 2 |
| 3 Prepaid Insurance | | (b) 1 9 0 00 | | | 2 1 0 00 | | 3 |
| 4 Kurtz Supplies | | | | | | 3 0 0 00 | 4 |
| 5 Wiley Supplies | | | | | | 9 0 00 | 5 |
| 6 Norma Delk, Capital | | | | | | 2 8 5 0 00 | 6 |
| 7 Norma Delk, Drawing | | | | | 2 5 0 00 | | 7 |
| 8 Income Summary | | | | | | | 8 |
| 9 Sales | | | | 1 1 0 0 00 | | | 9 |
| 10 Insurance Expense | (b) 1 9 0 00 | | 1 9 0 00 | | | | 10 |
| 11 Miscellaneous Expense | | | 6 5 00 | | | | 11 |
| 12 Rent Expense | | | 3 2 0 00 | | | | 12 |
| 13 Supplies Expense | (a) 1 4 5 00 | | 1 4 5 00 | | | | 13 |
| 14 | 3 3 5 00 | 3 3 5 00 | 7 2 0 00 | 1 1 0 0 00 | 3 6 2 0 00 | 3 2 4 0 00 | 14 |
| 15 Net Income | | | 3 8 0 00 | | | 3 8 0 00 | 15 |
| 16 | | | 1 1 0 0 00 | 1 1 0 0 00 | 3 6 2 0 00 | 3 6 2 0 00 | 16 |
| 17 | | | | | | | 17 |
| 18 | | | | | | | 18 |
| 19 | | | | | | | 19 |
| 20 | | | | | | | 20 |
| 21 | | | | | | | 21 |
| 22 | | | | | | | 22 |
| 23 | | | | | | | 23 |
| 24 | | | | | | | 24 |
| 25 | | | | | | | 25 |

# ENRICHMENT PROBLEMS

**MASTERY PROBLEM 9-M**  **Journalizing and posting adjusting and closing entries; preparing a post-closing trial balance**

Kellerman Services' partial work sheet for the month ended November 30 of the current year is given on the next page. The general ledger accounts are given in the working papers that accompany this textbook. (The general ledger accounts do not show all details for the fiscal period. The "Balance" shown in each account is the account's balance before adjusting and closing entries are posted.)

**Instructions: 1.** Use page 3 of a journal. Journalize and post the adjusting entries.
   **2.** Continue to use page 3 of the journal. Journalize and post the closing entries.
   **3.** Prepare a post-closing trial balance.

| | | 3 | 4 | 5 | 6 | 7 | 8 | |
|---|---|---|---|---|---|---|---|---|
| | ACCOUNT TITLE | ADJUSTMENTS | | INCOME STATEMENT | | BALANCE SHEET | | |
| | | DEBIT | CREDIT | DEBIT | CREDIT | DEBIT | CREDIT | |
| 1 | Cash | | | | | 3 5 0 0 00 | | 1 |
| 2 | Supplies | | (a) 1 9 5 00 | | | 7 5 0 00 | | 2 |
| 3 | Prepaid Insurance | | (b) 2 6 0 00 | | | 2 8 0 00 | | 3 |
| 4 | Kern Supplies | | | | | | 5 0 0 00 | 4 |
| 5 | Waite Supplies | | | | | | 1 2 0 00 | 5 |
| 6 | A. Kellerman, Capital | | | | | | 3 7 2 5 00 | 6 |
| 7 | A. Kellerman, Drawing | | | | | 3 5 0 00 | | 7 |
| 8 | Income Summary | | | | | | | 8 |
| 9 | Sales | | | | 1 5 0 0 00 | | | 9 |
| 10 | Insurance Expense | (b) 2 6 0 00 | | 2 6 0 00 | | | | 10 |
| 11 | Miscellaneous Expense | | | 8 5 00 | | | | 11 |
| 12 | Rent Expense | | | 4 2 5 00 | | | | 12 |
| 13 | Supplies Expense | (a) 1 9 5 00 | | 1 9 5 00 | | | | 13 |
| 14 | | 4 5 5 00 | 4 5 5 00 | 9 6 5 00 | 1 5 0 0 00 | 4 8 8 0 00 | 4 3 4 5 00 | 14 |
| 15 | Net Income | | | 5 3 5 00 | | | 5 3 5 00 | 15 |
| 16 | | | | 1 5 0 0 00 | 1 5 0 0 00 | 4 8 8 0 00 | 4 8 8 0 00 | 16 |

## CHALLENGE PROBLEM 9-C   Preparing a work sheet; journalizing adjusting and closing entries

A trial balance on a work sheet for Reed Company is given in the working papers that accompany this textbook.

**Instructions: 1.** Complete the work sheet. Use December 31 of the current year as the date.

### Adjustment Information, December 31

| | |
|---|---|
| Supplies on hand . . . . . . . . . . . . . . . . . . . . . . . . . . . . . . . . . . . . . . . . . . . . . . . | $980.00 |
| Value of prepaid insurance . . . . . . . . . . . . . . . . . . . . . . . . . . . . . . . . . . . . . . . | 700.00 |

**2.** Use page 3 of a journal. Journalize the adjusting entries.
**3.** Continue to use page 3 of the journal. Journalize the closing entries.

# Reinforcement Activity 1, Part B

# An Accounting Cycle for a Proprietorship: End-of-Fiscal-Period Work

*The general ledger prepared in Reinforcement Activity 1, Part A, is needed to complete Reinforcement Activity 1, Part B.*

Reinforcement Activity 1, Part B, includes end-of-fiscal-period activities studied in Chapters 7 through 9.

## WORK SHEET

**Instructions: 12.** Prepare a trial balance on a work sheet. Use a one-month fiscal period ended May 31 of the current year.
**13.** Analyze the following adjustment information into debit and credit parts. Record the adjustments on the work sheet.

Adjustment Information, May 31

Supplies on hand . . . . . . . . . . . . . . . . . . . . . . . . . . . . . . . . . . . . . . . . . . . . . . . . . . . . . .  $515.00
Value of prepaid insurance . . . . . . . . . . . . . . . . . . . . . . . . . . . . . . . . . . . . . . . . . . . . .  800.00

**14.** Total and rule the Adjustments columns.
**15.** Extend the up-to-date account balances to the Balance Sheet and Income Statement columns.
**16.** Complete the work sheet.

## FINANCIAL STATEMENTS

**17.** Prepare an income statement. Figure and record the component percentages for sales, total expenses, and net income. Round percentage calculations to the nearest 0.1%.
**18.** Prepare a balance sheet.

## ADJUSTING ENTRIES

**19.** Use page 3 of the journal. Journalize and post the adjusting entries.

## CLOSING ENTRIES

**20.** Continue using page 3 of the journal. Journalize and post the closing entries.

## POST-CLOSING TRIAL BALANCE

**21.** Prepare a post-closing trial balance.

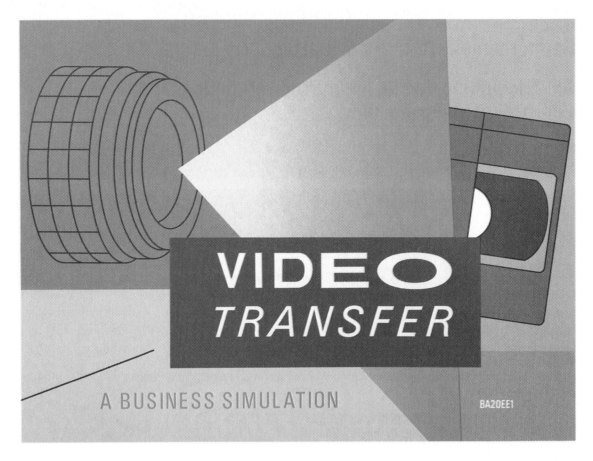

VIDEO
TRANSFER

A BUSINESS SIMULATION                    BA20EE1

This simulation covers the transactions completed by Video Transfer, a service business organized as a proprietorship. Video Transfer begins business on September 1 of the current year. The business produces personal videos for such events as weddings and family reunions. In addition, the business also transfers home movies and slides to video tape.

The activities included in the accounting cycle for Video Transfer are listed below. The company uses a journal and a general ledger similar to those described for Rugcare in Part 1. The books of account needed to complete this simulation are available from the publisher.

The following activities are included in this simulation.

1. Journalizing transactions in a journal.
2. Forwarding column totals to a new journal page.
3. Preparing a bank statement reconciliation and recording a bank service charge.
4. Proving cash.
5. Proving and ruling a journal.
6. Posting from a journal to a general ledger.
7. Preparing a trial balance on a work sheet.
8. Recording adjustments on a work sheet.
9. Completing a work sheet.
10. Preparing financial statements (income statement and balance sheet).
11. Journalizing and posting adjusting entries.
12. Journalizing and posting closing entries.
13. Preparing a post-closing trial balance.

# Video Transfer

# A Business Simulation

This simulation covers the transactions completed by Video Transfer, a service business organized as a proprietorship. Video Transfer begins business on September 1 of the current year. The business produces personal videos for such events as weddings and family reunions. In addition, the business also transfers home movies and slides to video tape.

## ACCOUNTING CYCLE

Video Transfer uses a one-month fiscal period. The fiscal period for this simulation begins on September 1 and ends on September 30 of the current year.

## ACCOUNTING RECORDS

Video Transfer uses accounting records similar to the following.

| Accounting Forms and Records | Chapter | Illustration Number |
|---|---|---|
| Journal | 4 | 4-14 |
| General ledger | 5 | 5-14 |
| Bank statement reconciliation | 6 | 6-8 |
| Trial balance and work sheet | 7 | 7-7 |
| Income statement | 8 | 8-6 |
| Balance sheet | 8 | 8-12 |
| Adjusting entries | 9 | 9-2 |
| Closing entries | 9 | 9-7 |

## SOURCE DOCUMENTS

Video Transfer uses the following source documents. *(CONCEPT: Objective Evidence)*

| Source Documents | Abbreviations | For Transactions |
|---|---|---|
| Calculator tapes | T | Cash received from sales |
| Receipts | R | Cash received from other than sales |
| Check stubs | C | Cash payments |
| Memorandums | M | Transactions not covered by the first three source documents |

## CHART OF ACCOUNTS

Video Transfer uses the following chart of accounts.

**VIDEO TRANSFER**
**Chart of Accounts**

| Balance Sheet Accounts | | Income Statement Accounts | |
|---|---|---|---|
| **(100) ASSETS** | | **(400) REVENUE** | |
| 110 | Cash | 410 | Sales |
| 120 | Petty Cash | | |
| 130 | Supplies | **(500) EXPENSES** | |
| 140 | Prepaid Insurance | 510 | Advertising Expense |
| | | 520 | Insurance Expense |
| **(200) LIABILITIES** | | 530 | Miscellaneous Expense |
| 210 | Dorn Supplies | 540 | Rent Expense |
| 220 | Setter Office Supplies | 550 | Repair Expense |
| 230 | Video Distributors | 560 | Supplies Expense |
| | | 570 | Utilities Expense |
| **(300) OWNER'S EQUITY** | | | |
| 310 | Martha Day, Capital | | |
| 320 | Martha Day, Drawing | | |
| 330 | Income Summary | | |

## RECORDING TRANSACTIONS

**Instructions: 1.** Use page 1 of the journal. Journalize the following transactions completed during September of the current year.

*Trans.*
*No.*

| | | |
|---|---|---|
| 1 | Sept. | 1. Received cash from owner as an investment, $16,000.00. R1. |
| 2 | | 2. Paid cash for supplies, $800.00. C1. |
| 3 | | 3. Paid cash for insurance, $400.00. C2. |
| 4 | | 3. Paid cash to establish a petty cash fund, $200.00. C3. |
| 5 | | 3. Bought supplies on account from Video Distributors, $450.00. M1. |
| 6 | | 4. Paid cash for rent, $1,400.00. C4. |
| 7 | | 6. Paid cash for electric bill, $50.00. C5. |
| 8 | | 7. Received cash from sales, $475.00. T7. |
| 9 | | 8. Paid cash for advertising, $100.00. C6. |
| 10 | | 8. Received cash from sales, $110.00. T8. |
| 11 | | 9. Paid cash on account to Video Distributors, $200.00. C7. |
| 12 | | 9. Paid cash to owner for personal use, $200.00. C8. |
| 13 | | 9. Received cash from sales, $280.00. T9. |
| 14 | | 10. Paid cash for miscellaneous expense, $35.00. C9. |
| 15 | | 10. Received cash from sales, $225.00. T10. |
| 16 | | 11. Paid cash for miscellaneous expense, $50.00. C10. |
| 17 | | 11. Received cash from sales, $300.00. T11. |
| 18 | | 12. Paid cash for repairs, $60.00. C11. |

*Trans.*
*No.*

| | |
|---|---|
| 19 | Sept. 12. Received cash from sales, $200.00. T12. |
| 20 | 13. Paid cash for supplies, $300.00. C12. |
| 21 | 13. Bought supplies on account from Setter Office Supplies, $150.00. M2. |
| 22 | 13. Received cash from sales, $175.00. T13. |

**2.** Prove and rule page 1 of the journal. Carry the column totals forward to page 2 of the journal.

**3.** Prepare a report using information from page 1 of the journal. Use a form similar to the following. Give the report to your instructor.

Name _____
Today's date _____
Column totals from page _____ of the journal:

| Column | Debit | Credit |
|---|---|---|
| General . . . . . . . . . . . . . . | $_____ | $_____ |
| Sales . . . . . . . . . . . . . . | | _____ |
| Cash . . . . . . . . . . . . . . | _____ | _____ |
| Totals. . . . . . . . . . . . . . | $_____ | $_____ |

**4.** Post the separate amounts on each line of the journal that need to be posted individually.

**5.** Use page 2 of the journal. Journalize the following transactions.

*Trans.*
*No.*

| | |
|---|---|
| 23 | Sept. 14. Paid cash for miscellaneous expense, $30.00. C13. |
| 24 | 14. Bought supplies on account from Video Distributors, $140.00. M3. |
| 25 | 14. Received cash from sales, $380.00. T14. |
| 26 | 15. Paid cash for repairs, $30.00. C14. |
| 27 | 15. Paid cash for miscellaneous expense, $40.00. C15. |
| 28 | 15. Received cash from sales, $100.00. T15. |
| 29 | 16. Paid cash for miscellaneous expense, $35.00. C16. |
| 30 | 16. Paid cash for advertising, $110.00. C17. |
| 31 | 16. Paid cash to owner for personal use, $200.00. C18. |
| 32 | 16. Received cash from sales, $285.00. T16. |
| 33 | 17. Paid cash for water bill, $65.00. C19. |
| 34 | 17. Paid cash for supplies, $110.00. C20. |
| 35 | 17. Received cash from sales, $265.00. T17. |
| 36 | 18. Paid cash for miscellaneous expense, $10.00. C21. |
| 37 | 18. Received cash from sales, $310.00. T18. |
| 38 | 19. Paid cash for miscellaneous expense, $10.00. C22. |
| 39 | 19. Received cash from sales, $250.00. T19. |
| 40 | 20. Paid cash for supplies, $125.00. C23. |
| 41 | 20. Bought supplies on account from Setter Office Supplies, $160.00. M4. |
| 42 | 20. Received cash from sales, $180.00. T20. |
| 43 | 21. Received cash from sales, $120.00. T21. |

**6.** Prove and rule page 2 of the journal. Carry the column totals forward to page 3 of the journal.

**7.** Prepare a report using information from page 2 of the journal. Use a form similar to the one shown in Instruction 3. Give the report to your instructor.

**8.** Post the separate amounts on each line of the journal that need to be posted individually.

**9.** Use page 3 of the journal. Journalize the following transactions.

*Trans.*
*No.*

| | | |
|---|---|---|
| 44 | Sept. 22. | Bought supplies on account from Dorn Supplies, $600.00. M5. |
| 45 | 22. | Received cash from sales, $225.00. T22. |
| 46 | 23. | Paid cash for repairs, $8.00. C24. |
| 47 | 23. | Paid cash to owner for personal use, $200.00. C25. |
| 48 | 23. | Received cash from sales, $230.00. T23. |
| 49 | 24. | Paid cash for miscellaneous expense, $60.00. C26. |
| 50 | 24. | Received cash from sales, $170.00. T24. |
| 51 | 25. | Paid cash for telephone bill, $105.00. C27. |
| 52 | 25. | Received cash from sales, $185.00. T25. |
| 53 | 26. | Received cash from sales, $165.00. T26. |
| 54 | 27. | Paid cash for supplies, $100.00. C28. |
| 55 | 27. | Paid cash on account to Dorn Supplies, $400.00. C29. |
| 56 | 27. | Received cash from sales, $190.00. T27. |

**10.** On September 27 Video Transfer received a bank statement dated September 26. The following information is obtained from the bank statement and from the records of the business. Prepare a bank statement reconciliation.

| | |
|---|---|
| Bank statement balance . . . . . . . . . . . . . . . . . . . . . . . . . . . . . . . . . . . . | $15,700.00 |
| Outstanding deposits: | |
| September 26 . . . . . . . . . . . . . . . . . . . . . . . . . . . . . . . . . . . . . . . . . | 165.00 |
| September 27 . . . . . . . . . . . . . . . . . . . . . . . . . . . . . . . . . . . . . . . . . | 190.00 |
| Outstanding checks: | |
| Nos. 24, 26, 27, 28, and 29 | |
| Bank service charge . . . . . . . . . . . . . . . . . . . . . . . . . . . . . . . . . . . . | 5.00 |
| Checkbook balance on the next unused check stub . . . . . . . . . . . . . | 15,387.00 |

**11.** Continue using page 3 of the journal, and journalize the following transactions.

*Trans.*
*No.*

| | | |
|---|---|---|
| 57 | Sept. 27. | Received bank statement showing September bank service charge, $5.00. M6. |
| 58 | 28. | Received cash from sales, $265.00. T28. |
| 59 | 29. | Received cash from sales, $250.00. T29. |
| 60 | 30. | Paid cash to replenish the petty cash fund, $55.00: miscellaneous expense, $30.00; repairs, $25.00. C30. |
| 61 | 30. | Paid cash to owner for personal use, $200.00. C31. |
| 62 | 30. | Received cash from sales, $265.00. T30. |

**12.** Prove page 3 of the journal.

**13.** Prove cash. The beginning cash balance on September 1 is zero. The balance on the next unused check stub is $15,907.00.

**14.** Rule page 3 of the journal.

**15.** Prepare a report using information from page 3 of the journal. Use a form similar to the one shown in Instruction 3. Give the report to your instructor.

**16.** Post the separate amounts on each line of the journal that need to be posted individually.

**17.** Post the column totals of the journal.

# END-OF-FISCAL-PERIOD WORK

**Instructions: 18.** Prepare a trial balance on a work sheet. Use a one-month fiscal period ended September 30 of the current year.

**19.** Analyze the following adjustment information into debit and credit parts. Record the adjustments on the work sheet. Total and rule the Adjustments columns.

### Adjustment Information, September 30

| | |
|---|---|
| Supplies on hand . . . . . . . . . . . . . . . . . . . . . . . . . . . . . . . . . . . . . . . . . . . . . . . . . . . . . . . . . . | $890.00 |
| Value of prepaid insurance . . . . . . . . . . . . . . . . . . . . . . . . . . . . . . . . . . . . . . . . . . . . . . . . . | 300.00 |

**20.** Extend the up-to-date account balances to the Balance Sheet and Income Statement columns.

**21.** Complete the work sheet.

**22.** Prepare an income statement. Figure and record the component percentages for sales, total expenses, and net income. Round percentage calculations to the nearest 0.1%.

**23.** Prepare a balance sheet.

**24.** Use page 4 of the journal. Journalize and post the adjusting entries.

**25.** Continue to use page 4 of the journal. Journalize and post the closing entries.

**26.** Prepare a post-closing trial balance.

**27.** Assemble all forms and records in the following order. Be sure your name is on *each* sheet. Present your completed simulation to your instructor.

> Journal pages
> General ledger
> Bank reconciliation
> Work sheet
> Income statement
> Balance sheet
> Post-closing trial balance

# Automated Accounting for a Service Business

**2**

## GENERAL BEHAVIORAL GOALS

1. Know accounting terminology related to an automated accounting system for a service business organized as a proprietorship.
2. Understand accounting concepts and practices related to an automated accounting system for a service business organized as a proprietorship.
3. Demonstrate accounting procedures used in an automated accounting system for a service business organized as a proprietorship.

# PETLODGE
## Chart of Accounts

### Balance Sheet Accounts

#### (100) ASSETS

| | |
|---|---|
| 110 | Cash |
| 120 | Petty Cash |
| 130 | Supplies—Office |
| 140 | Supplies—Pet |
| 150 | Prepaid Insurance |

#### (200) LIABILITIES

| | |
|---|---|
| 210 | Marino Kennel Supply |
| 220 | Vega Office Supply |

#### (300) OWNER'S EQUITY

| | |
|---|---|
| 310 | Victoria Peak, Capital |
| 320 | Victoria Peak, Drawing |
| 330 | Income Summary |

### Income Statement Accounts

#### (400) REVENUE

| | |
|---|---|
| 410 | Boarding Fees |

#### (500) EXPENSES

| | |
|---|---|
| 510 | Advertising Expense |
| 520 | Insurance Expense |
| 530 | Miscellaneous Expense |
| 540 | Rent Expense |
| 550 | Supplies Expense—Office |
| 560 | Supplies Expense—Pet |
| 570 | Utilities Expense |

The chart of accounts for Petlodge is
illustrated above for ready reference as you
study Part 2 of this textbook.

# 10

# Starting an Automated Accounting System

## ENABLING PERFORMANCE TASKS

After studying Chapter 10, you will be able to:
a. Define accounting terms related to starting an automated accounting system.
b. Identify accounting concepts and practices related to starting an automated accounting system.
c. Prepare a general ledger file maintenance input form for a chart of accounts.
d. Prepare a general ledger input form for opening balances.

Business owners and managers depend on accounting records and reports to provide the information needed for effective decision making. These records and reports must contain current, accurate, and complete information that can be reported in useful and timely financial statements. Complete information must include the recording and reporting of all details or facts about the financial condition and progress of the business. Details or facts are called data. Although procedures used to record and report financial data may vary among businesses, the accounting concepts are the same.

Financial data may be recorded and reported by hand or by machine. An accounting system in which data are recorded and reported mostly by hand is called manual accounting. Some businesses use automated machines to speed the recording and reporting process. An accounting system in which data are recorded and reported mostly by using automated machines is called automated accounting. Even in automated accounting, some procedures are done by hand.

## AUTOMATED ACCOUNTING

Victoria Peak operates a small service business known as Petlodge. *(CONCEPT: Business Entity)* Petlodge provides hourly, daily, and weekly boarding services for pets. Petlodge rents the building in which it is located as well as the furnishings needed to operate the business. Ms. Peak expects the business to make money and to continue indefinitely. *(CONCEPT: Going Concern)*

Petlodge has been using a manual accounting system. The business wants to improve the accounting system by doing the work faster and less expensively. Petlodge is considering using an automated accounting system.

## Using computers in automated accounting

Automated accounting uses a variety of machines. A machine that accepts data, applies procedures, and produces results according to stored instructions is called a computer. Both large and small businesses make use of computers to record and report accounting data. Using a computer does not change accounting concepts. Only the methods change. Regardless of the accounting system used, financial data are reported for a specified period of time. *(CONCEPT: Accounting Period Cycle)* A computer performs the routine and repetitive operations. Different types of computers are used to record and process accounting data.

## Types of computers

Automated accounting systems were initially used only by larger businesses. The high cost of computers made it impractical for smaller businesses to go beyond manual systems. Today, however, computers are available for use by all businesses regardless of size. The computer cost is based on the amount of data that can be processed and the processing speed. Currently, three types of computers are used for recording and reporting accounting data: (1) mainframe computers, (2) minicomputers, and (3) microcomputers.

**Mainframe computers.** A large-sized computer with the greatest computing speed, largest storage capacity, and the most powerful processing capability is called a mainframe computer. A mainframe computer was the first type of computer developed to process business data. A mainframe computer is the most expensive of all types of computers. A mainframe computer is used primarily by businesses that need to process large amounts of data at very fast processing speeds.

**Minicomputers.** A medium-sized computer with intermediate computing speed, storage capacity, and processing capability is called a minicomputer. A minicomputer was the second type of computer developed to process business data. A minicomputer is less expensive than a mainframe computer. Minicomputers are used primarily by businesses with less data to be processed and less need for processing speed than businesses using mainframe computers.

**Microcomputers.** A small-sized computer with the slowest computing speed, smallest storage capacity, and the least processing capability is called a microcomputer. A microcomputer is often referred to as a personal or desktop computer. The most recent development in the computer field, the microcomputer is also the least expensive of all computers. Technological advancements have made the microcomputer very popular for business use because of increases in storage capacity and processing capability and attractive prices. A microcomputer is used primarily when data to be processed requires a processing speed greater than can be achieved with manual methods.

After gathering facts about the various types of computers, Petlodge decided to rent a microcomputer and begin using an automated accounting system. Petlodge found that an automated accounting system would reduce processing time and be less expensive than the current manual accounting system.

# PLANNING FOR AUTOMATED ACCOUNTING

Planning for automated accounting is similar to planning for manual accounting. Planning any accounting system consists of two steps. (1) Setting goals—deciding what is to be recorded and reported. (2) Establishing procedures—deciding what steps to follow in carrying out the goals.

Accuracy is equally important in both manual and automated accounting. Results in any accounting system can only be as accurate as the data put into the system. For example, if $175.30 is recorded as $715.80, data on financial statements for any accounting system will be incorrect.

## Phases of automated accounting

The four phases of automated accounting are (1) input, (2) processing, (3) storage, and (4) output.

Data put into a computer are called input. Input may be data on receipts, checks, and other business forms. Working with data according to precise instructions is called processing. Posting transaction data to general ledger accounts is an example of the processing phase. Filing or holding data until it is needed is called storage. Keeping data in general ledger accounts until it is needed is an example of the storage phase. Information produced by a computer is called output. Examples of output are facts about assets, liabilities, owner's equity, revenue, and expenses reported on financial statements. Output can also be printed on forms such as checks.

## Computer instructions

Step-by-step instructions for completing each job must be prepared before any data can be processed by a computer. A set of instructions followed by a computer to process data is called a computer program. The term "program" may also describe a set of step-by-step instructions for processing data by manual means. Several computer programs are needed for automated accounting. Programs used to direct the operations of a computer are called software.

A person who prepares a computer program is called a computer programmer. A person needs special training to be a computer programmer. Understanding accounting concepts and procedures is helpful to a computer programmer. Just as important, an accountant needs to know basic computer concepts and procedures in order to assist a computer programmer and to use a computer.

## COMPUTER UNITS

A computer is divided into four separate units. (1) Central processing unit. (2) Input unit. (3) Output unit. (4) Secondary storage unit. Each unit serves a special function. Computer units are called hardware. Illustration 10-1 shows a block diagram of the four computer units as well as the people action required before and after processing data.

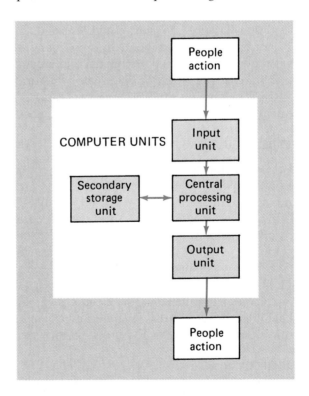

Illustration 10-1
Computer units

Four types of people action are necessary before data can be processed by a computer. (1) Describe output type and form. (2) Write instructions for the computer. (3) Arrange data to be processed (input) according to specific procedures. (4) Key-enter input into the computer.

Three types of people action are necessary after data have been processed by a computer. (1) Check output for accuracy. (2) Interpret output for decision making. (3) File output for future reference.

## Central processing unit

A central processing unit (CPU) performs three distinct functions. (1) Controls all computer units. (2) Stores computer instructions and data currently being processed. (3) Processes stored data.

Illustration 10-2 shows a microcomputer with the four computer units.

Illustration 10-2
Microcomputer

## Input unit

Before data can be processed by a computer, data must be converted to machine-readable form. A computer unit that converts data from human-readable to machine-readable form is referred to as an input unit. An input unit is linked to and controlled by a CPU.

A common input unit is a computer keyboard. A computer keyboard looks much like a typewriter keyboard. Operation of a computer keyboard is also similar to operation of a typewriter keyboard. After each character has been key-entered, the character is displayed on a television-like screen often referred to as a computer monitor.

The terms "key-enter," "key-entered," and "key-entering" are used in this textbook to indicate keying information using the keyboard and then pressing the Enter key. The Enter key is called "Return" on some keyboards.

## Output unit

The end result of processing data by a computer is the output. A computer unit that converts data from machine-readable to human-readable form is referred to as an output unit. An output unit is linked to and controlled by a CPU. Different kinds of output units, such as monitors and printers, may be used by computers.

**Computer monitor.** A computer monitor is used to display data entered from a keyboard as well as data that has been processed.

**Computer printer.** An output unit that produces a printed, human-readable copy of processed data is known as a printer. Computer output in printed, human-readable form is called a printout. Petlodge's microcomputer uses a printer to produce printed output.

## Secondary storage unit

A CPU has limited space for internal data storage. A computer's storage capacity can be expanded by using secondary storage units. Secondary storage units are sometimes known as auxiliary or external storage. Data are transferred from secondary storage to a CPU as needed during processing.

Magnetic disks are the most widely used secondary storage for microcomputers. Petlodge's microcomputer uses a disk for secondary storage. Illustration 10-3 shows a microcomputer with a disk being inserted.

Illustration 10-3
Microcomputer with a disk
being inserted

# AUTOMATED GENERAL LEDGER ACCOUNTING

Petlodge's automated accounting system is based on the same accounting concepts as a manual accounting system. Only equipment and procedures differ. Software to process accounting data is included with the microcomputer that Petlodge rents.

## Building a chart of accounts

Chart of accounts numbering systems are similar for both automated and manual accounting. Petlodge uses the same three-digit numbering system described for Rugcare in Chapter 5. Petlodge also uses the same procedures for making changes to its chart of accounts as described for Rugcare. The procedures for arranging accounts in a general ledger, assigning account numbers, and keeping records current is known as file maintenance.

The chart of accounts, page 196, shows all balance sheet and income statement divisions. The chart also lists all accounts within a division. The accounts are listed in the order that they appear on financial statements.

Before data from a chart of accounts are key-entered into a computer, a general ledger file maintenance input form (FORM GL-1) is prepared. Petlodge's general ledger file maintenance input form is shown in Illustration 10-4.

RUN    DATE  **09 01 , --**
　　　　　　  MM DD YY

### GENERAL LEDGER
### FILE MAINTENANCE
Input Form

FORM GL-1

| | ACCOUNT NUMBER | ACCOUNT TITLE | |
|---|---|---|---|
| 1 | 110 | Cash | 1 |
| 2 | 120 | Petty Cash | 2 |
| 3 | 130 | Supplies - Office | 3 |
| 4 | 140 | Supplies - Pet | 4 |
| 5 | 150 | Prepaid Insurance | 5 |
| 6 | 210 | Marino Kennel Supply | 6 |
| 7 | 220 | Vega Office Supply | 7 |
| 8 | 310 | Victoria Peak, Capital | 8 |
| 9 | 320 | Victoria Peak, Drawing | 9 |
| 10 | 330 | Income Summary | 10 |
| 11 | 410 | Boarding Fees | 11 |
| 12 | 510 | Advertising Expense | 12 |
| 13 | 520 | Insurance Expense | 13 |
| 14 | 530 | Miscellaneous Expense | 14 |
| 15 | 540 | Rent Expense | 15 |
| 16 | 550 | Supplies Expense - Office | 16 |
| 17 | 560 | Supplies Expense - Pet | 17 |
| 18 | 570 | Utilities Expense | 18 |

Illustration 10-4
General ledger file
maintenance input form

The input form shows the account numbers and account titles. The computer software requires that chart of accounts data be key-entered into the computer sequentially—account number first followed by account title. Therefore, the file maintenance input form used by Petlodge arranges the chart of accounts data in the same order as data are entered on the computer keyboard. The computer software also specifies the maximum number of spaces that can be used for account numbers and account titles. Any account titles that contain more characters than the software will accept must be abbreviated when recorded on the file maintenance input form (FORM GL-1).

> The general ledger file maintenance input form has marks in the Account Title column to indicate how many characters the software will accept for an account title. All of Petlodge's account titles fit the 25-character space allowed, so none have to be abbreviated.

Three steps are followed in preparing each line of Petlodge's general ledger file maintenance input form for the chart of accounts.

1  Write the run date, *09/01/--*, in the space provided at the top of the form. After all accounts have been recorded on the input form, the chart of accounts data are key-entered into the computer. The date to be printed on reports prepared by a computer is called the run date. Petlodge changed from manual to automated accounting on September 1. Therefore, the run date, 09/01/--, indicates that the chart of accounts data entered on the file maintenance input form are effective as of 09/01/--.

2  Write each account number in the Account Number column.

3  Write each account title in the Account Title column just as it will appear on the output.

> The account numbers and account titles are obtained from the chart of accounts, page 196. Petlodge's revenue account is titled *Boarding Fees* to describe the type of revenue received for boarding services.

## Processing a chart of accounts

In manual accounting data for each account are kept on separate ledger forms. A ledger represents the storage phase of manual accounting. In Petlodge's automated accounting system, data about each account are stored on a disk. The disk serves the same purpose in automated accounting as the ledger in manual accounting. The disk represents the automated accounting storage phase.

In an automated accounting system, the activities are arranged so that each activity may be selected using a keyboard or some other input device. A list of options from which an activity may be selected is called a menu. Petlodge's software has a General Ledger Main Menu. An entry selected using the keyboard displays the General Ledger Main Menu shown in Illustration 10-5.

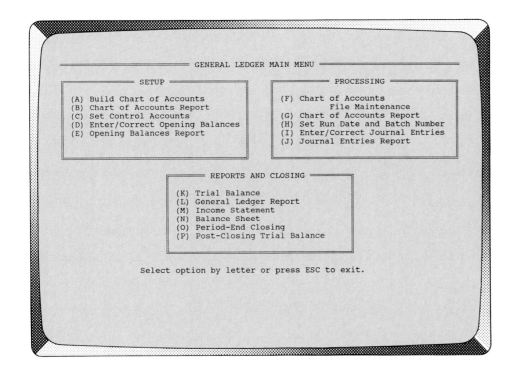

```
========================= GENERAL LEDGER MAIN MENU =========================

======= SETUP =======                          ======= PROCESSING =======
  (A)  Build Chart of Accounts                    (F)  Chart of Accounts
  (B)  Chart of Accounts Report                          File Maintenance
  (C)  Set Control Accounts                        (G)  Chart of Accounts Report
  (D)  Enter/Correct Opening Balances             (H)  Set Run Date and Batch Number
  (E)  Opening Balances Report                    (I)  Enter/Correct Journal Entries
                                                  (J)  Journal Entries Report

                       ======= REPORTS AND CLOSING =======
                         (K)  Trial Balance
                         (L)  General Ledger Report
                         (M)  Income Statement
                         (N)  Balance Sheet
                         (O)  Period-End Closing
                         (P)  Post-Closing Trial Balance

                 Select option by letter or press ESC to exit.
```

The activities listed in the *Setup* section of the menu are described in this chapter. The activities listed in the *Processing* and *Reports and Closing* sections are described in Chapter 11.

Illustration 10-5
General ledger main menu displayed on a computer monitor

Option A is selected to build a chart of accounts. Spaces for entering general ledger chart of accounts data are displayed on the computer monitor. Chart of accounts data are then key-entered, as shown for the cash account in Illustration 10-6, page 206.

After all accounts have been key-entered, Option B is selected from the General Ledger Main Menu, Illustration 10-5. This option directs the computer to prepare a chart of accounts report. Petlodge's chart of accounts report is shown in Illustration 10-7, page 206.

The report is checked for accuracy by comparing it with the data recorded on the file maintenance input form. After the accuracy check, the report is filed for future reference.

## Setting control accounts

Computer software is generally written for use by many different types of businesses. Therefore, general ledger account numbers may not be the same from one business to the next. For this reason, most computer software requires that selected general ledger accounts be identified for special handling by the software. General ledger accounts that must be

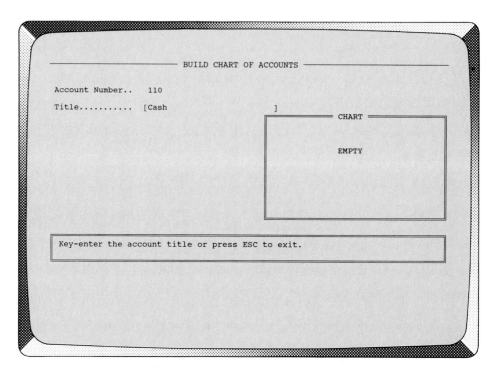

Illustration 10-6      Computer monitor display for chart of accounts data

```
  RUN DATE: 09/01/--                        PETLODGE
                                        CHART OF ACCOUNTS

  -------------------
  ACCOUNT     ACCOUNT
  NUMBER      TITLE
  -------------------
  110         Cash
  120         Petty Cash
  130         Supplies--Office
  140         Supplies--Pet
  150         Prepaid Insurance
  210         Marino Kennel Supply
  220         Vega Office Supply
  310         Victoria Peak, Capital
  320         Victoria Peak, Drawing
  330         Income Summary
  410         Boarding Fees
  510         Advertising Expense
  520         Insurance Expense
  530         Miscellaneous Expense
  540         Rent Expense
  550         Supplies Expense--Office
  560         Supplies Expense--Pet
  570         Utilities Expense
```

Illustration 10-7      Chart of accounts report

identified for special handling by computer software are called control accounts. The software used by Petlodge requires that control accounts be identified from the chart of accounts report. Option C is selected from the General Ledger Main Menu to set the control accounts. The computer monitor displays the control accounts needed and spaces for recording the account numbers from the chart of accounts report. The computer monitor display with the control accounts set is shown in Illustration 10-8.

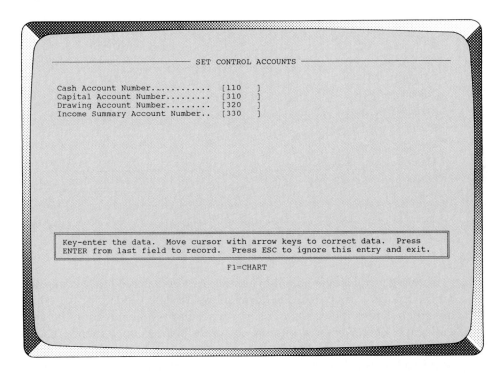

```
─────────────────── SET CONTROL ACCOUNTS ───────────────────


    Cash Account Number............  [110  ]
    Capital Account Number.........  [310  ]
    Drawing Account Number.........  [320  ]
    Income Summary Account Number..  [330  ]









    ┌─────────────────────────────────────────────────────────────┐
    │ Key-enter the data.  Move cursor with arrow keys to correct data.  Press │
    │ ENTER from last field to record.  Press ESC to ignore this entry and exit. │
    └─────────────────────────────────────────────────────────────┘

                          F1=CHART
```

The cash account number is needed to allow the computer to keep track of all entries to the cash account. This feature makes it easy to do a cash proof at any time during a fiscal period.

Illustration 10-8
Computer monitor display
with control accounts set

The capital, drawing, and income summary account numbers are needed for end-of-fiscal-period work.

## Journalizing opening balances

The books for Petlodge's manual accounting system are closed on August 31. Petlodge changes to an automated accounting system on September 1. Data from the August 31 manually prepared post-closing trial balance are used to journalize the account balances for the new automated accounting system. A memorandum is used as the source document for the account balances. *(CONCEPT: Objective Evidence)* A copy of the post-closing trial balance is stapled to the memorandum to avoid having to copy the data to the memorandum. Petlodge's August 31 post-closing trial balance is shown in Illustration 10-9.

| ACCOUNT TITLE | DEBIT | CREDIT |
|---|---|---|
| Cash | 12 5 0 0 00 | |
| Petty Cash | 3 0 0 00 | |
| Supplies—Office | 1 2 6 0 00 | |
| Supplies—Pet | 1 5 1 5 00 | |
| Prepaid Insurance | 7 6 5 00 | |
| Marino Kennel Supply | | 9 4 3 00 |
| Vega Office Supply | | 3 8 7 00 |
| Victoria Peak, Capital | | 15 0 1 0 00 |
| Totals | 16 3 4 0 00 | 16 3 4 0 00 |

*Petlodge*
*Post-Closing Trial Balance*
*August 31, 19--*

Illustration 10-9
Post-closing trial balance

Before general ledger account balances are key-entered into a computer, an input form is prepared. The form shows all data needed for recording account balances. The computer software requires that entries to the general ledger be key-entered into the computer in a certain sequence. Therefore, the input form used by Petlodge arranges the data in the same order as data are entered on the computer keyboard. By having data arranged in the correct sequence, key-entering the data is faster. Petlodge uses a general ledger input form (FORM GL-2) to journalize general ledger account balances. The input form resembles a journal used in manual accounting. However, there is one major difference between the type of data journalized on an input form and on a journal used in manual accounting. In manual accounting account titles are used to identify the accounts affected by each journal entry. In automated accounting account numbers are used because computers work more efficiently with numbers than with alphabetic characters. Account titles are stored on secondary storage during the processing of the chart of accounts. The computer obtains the account titles from secondary storage when the account titles are needed for financial reports. Petlodge's completed general ledger input form for the account balances from the post-closing trial balance is shown in Illustration 10-10.

| RUN DATE 09/01/-- | | GENERAL LEDGER | | FORM GL-2 |
| --- | --- | --- | --- | --- |
| MM DD YY | | Input Form | | |
| BATCH NO. 1 | | | | |

| | 1 | 2 | 3 | 4 | 5 | |
| --- | --- | --- | --- | --- | --- | --- |
| | DAY | DOC. NO. | ACCOUNT NUMBER | DEBIT AMOUNT | CREDIT AMOUNT | |
| 1 | 01 | M1 | 110 | 12500 00 | | 1 |
| 2 | | | 120 | 300 00 | | 2 |
| 3 | | | 130 | 1260 00 | | 3 |
| 4 | | | 140 | 1515 00 | | 4 |
| 5 | | | 150 | 765 00 | | 5 |
| 6 | | | 210 | | 943 00 | 6 |
| 7 | | | 220 | | 387 00 | 7 |
| 8 | | | 310 | | 15010 00 | 8 |
| 25 | | | | | | 25 |
| | | | BATCH TOTALS | 16340 00 | 16340 00 | |

Illustration 10-10
General ledger input form
for account balances

Eight steps are followed in journalizing account balances on Petlodge's general ledger input form.

1 Write the run date, *09/01/--*, in the space provided at the top of the form. The run date is the date Petlodge starts its automated accounting system.

2 Write the batch number, *1*, in the space provided at the top of the form. Each group of journal entries to be processed by a computer, regardless of the number of entries, is identified by a number. The number assigned to a group of journal entries is called a batch number. As the opening balances entry is the first group of journal entries, batch number 1 is automatically assigned by the computer.

3 Write the day, *01*, on line 1 in the Day column. Enter the day only on line 1 because the day is the same for all lines.

4 Write the document number, *M1*, on the same line in the Doc. No. column. Enter the document number only on line 1 because the document number is the same for all lines.

5 Write the account number in the Account Number column for each general ledger account with a balance. These accounts are listed on the post-closing trial balance, Illustration 10-9. The account numbers are listed on the chart of accounts report, Illustration 10-7.

6 Write the account balance in either the Debit Amount or Credit Amount column. The account balances are given on the post-closing trial balance, Illustration 10-9.

7 After all account balances have been journalized, total the Debit Amount and Credit Amount columns. Enter the totals on the Batch Totals line provided at the bottom of the form.

8 Compare the two totals to be sure that debits equal credits. Also compare the batch totals with the totals on the trial balance to be sure that amounts were recorded correctly.

## Processing account balances

In manual accounting account balances are journalized in a journal and posted to accounts stored in a ledger. In Petlodge's automated accounting system, account balances are journalized and posted to accounts stored on a disk.

Option D is selected from the General Ledger Main Menu to enter the opening account balances. Spaces for key-entering each account balance are displayed on the computer monitor. Data for entering the account balance for the first line of the general ledger input form are shown in Illustration 10-11.

Illustration 10-11
Computer monitor display
with an account balance
entered

```
————————————— ENTER/CORRECT OPENING BALANCES BATCH 1 —————————————


    Journal Entry Number      1
    Day of Month........  [01]
    Document Number.....  [M1     ]
    Acct.#  Debit Amt. Credit Amt.
    [110   ][12500      ][          ]
    [      ][           ][          ]
    [      ][           ][          ]
    [      ][           ][          ]
    [      ][           ][          ]
    [      ][           ][          ]
    [      ][           ][          ]
    [      ][           ][          ]

    Proof Total:
             .00

    Note:  Press END key to move cursor to the last data field.
    ┌───────────────────────────────────────────────────────────────┐
    │ Key-enter the data.  Move cursor with arrow keys to correct data.  Press │
    │ ENTER from last field to record.  Press ESC to ignore this entry and exit. │
    └───────────────────────────────────────────────────────────────┘

              F1=CHART    F2=JOURNAL ENTRIES    F3=CORRECTIONS
```

 The computer automatically assigns a sequential number to each journal entry, beginning with the number *1*. This procedure allows an entry needing correction at a later date to be easily retrieved from computer storage by referencing the journal entry number.

After all account balances have been key-entered and posted, Option E is selected from the General Ledger Main Menu. This option directs the computer to prepare an opening balances report. Petlodge's opening balances report is shown in Illustration 10-12.

```
RUN DATE: 09/01/--                     PETLODGE
                              OPENING BALANCES BATCH 1

-------------------------------------------------------------------------------
JE#    DATE      ACCOUNT NUMBER & TITLE            DEBIT AMOUNT   CREDIT AMOUNT
-------------------------------------------------------------------------------
0001  09/01/--  110   Cash                          12500.00
                120   Petty Cash                       300.00
                130   Supplies--Office                1260.00
                140   Supplies--Pet                   1515.00
                150   Prepaid Insurance                765.00
                210      Marino Kennel Supply                         943.00
                220      Vega Office Supply                           387.00
                310      Victoria Peak, Capital                     15010.00
                      DOCUMENT: M1


                      TOTALS                        16340.00       16340.00

                      IN BALANCE
```

The opening balances report is checked for accuracy by comparing the totals on the report with the batch totals on the input form. If the totals are the same, the opening balances report is assumed to be correct. The opening balances report is filed for future reference.

Illustration 10-12
Opening balances report

# SUMMARY OF STARTING AN AUTOMATED ACCOUNTING SYSTEM

The steps followed by Petlodge to start an automated general ledger accounting system are summarized in Illustration 10-13.

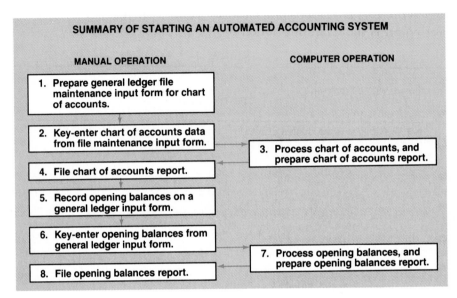

Illustration 10-13
Summary of steps for
starting an automated
general ledger accounting
system

## ACCOUNTING TERMS

What is the meaning of each of the following?

1. data
2. manual accounting
3. automated accounting
4. computer
5. mainframe computer
6. minicomputer
7. microcomputer

8. input
9. processing
10. storage
11. output
12. computer program
13. software
14. computer programmer

15. hardware
16. printout
17. run date
18. menu
19. control accounts
20. batch number

## QUESTIONS FOR INDIVIDUAL STUDY

1. What type of information do owners and managers depend on for effective decision making?
2. Which accounting concept is being applied when a business expects to make money and continue indefinitely?
3. Does using a computer change accounting concepts? Why?

4. Which accounting concept is being applied when financial data are reported for a specified period of time?
5. What are the three types of computers used for recording and reporting accounting data?
6. What are the two steps necessary for planning an accounting system?

7. What are the four phases of automated accounting?
8. What does an accountant need to know in order to assist a computer programmer and to use a computer?
9. What three types of people action are necessary after data have been processed by a computer?
10. What is the most widely used secondary storage for microcomputers?
11. Why does Petlodge use a special form to enter the general ledger chart of accounts?
12. How is a chart of accounts report checked for accuracy?
13. Which accounting concept is being applied when a memorandum is used as the source document for opening balances?
14. Why does Petlodge use a special form to journalize opening balances?

## ■ CASES FOR MANAGEMENT DECISION

**CASE 1** Floyd Ulicki owns and operates a service business. The business uses a manual accounting system. Mr. Ulicki does the accounting himself; however, operating the business has been taking more and more of his time. Consequently, he has been having difficulty finding time to run an efficient accounting system. Mr. Ulicki is considering hiring an accountant or renting a computer to improve his accounting system. What factors should he consider in making the decision to either hire an accountant or rent a computer and automate his accounting system?

**CASE 2** Susan Lane owns and operates a physical fitness center. She has been using a manual accounting system. She wants to improve her accounting system by having work done faster and less expensively. After gathering facts about the various types of accounting systems, she decides to rent a microcomputer and begin using automated accounting. Mrs. Lane is concerned, however, about not knowing how to program a computer. She is considering either learning how to write computer programs or hiring a computer programmer. What would you recommend?

## ■ DRILLS FOR UNDERSTANDING

**DRILL 10-D1**  **Preparing a chart of accounts for automated accounting**

The following account descriptions refer to the location of accounts in a chart of accounts similar to the one for Petlodge.

1. The first asset account.
2. The first liability account.
3. The first owner's equity account.
4. The first revenue account.
5. The first expense account.
6. The second asset account.
7. The second liability account.
8. The second owner's equity account.
9. The second expense account.
10. The third expense account.

Use a form similar to the following.

| 1 | 2 |
|---|---|
| **Account Descriptions** | **Account Number** |
| 1. *The first asset account.* | *110* |

**Instructions: 1.** In Column 1 write the account description. Account description 1 is given as an example.

    **2.** In Column 2 write the account number. Account numbers are assigned by 10s.

    **3.** Check your answers with Petlodge's chart of accounts, page 196.

### DRILL 10-D2   Analyzing steps for starting an automated accounting system

**Instructions:** Refer to Illustration 10-13, page 212, and answer the following questions.

1. What form is prepared to build the chart of accounts?
2. Is key-entering the chart of accounts into the computer a manual or computer operation?
3. In which step is the chart of accounts processed by the computer?
4. Is the preparation of a chart of accounts report a manual or computer operation?
5. What form is prepared for the opening balances?
6. In which step are the opening balances key-entered into the computer?
7. In which step is an opening balances report prepared?
8. Is the preparation of an opening balances report a manual or computer operation?

## ■ APPLICATION PROBLEMS

### PROBLEM 10-1   Preparing a general ledger file maintenance input form

E-Z Rest Motel has the following general ledger chart of accounts.

| Balance Sheet Accounts | | Income Statement Accounts | |
|---|---|---|---|
| **(100) ASSETS** | | **(400) REVENUE** | |
| 110 | Cash | 410 | Room Rentals |
| 120 | Petty Cash | | |
| 130 | Supplies—Cleaning | **(500) EXPENSES** | |
| 140 | Supplies—Office | | |
| 150 | Prepaid Insurance | 510 | Advertising Expense |
| | | 520 | Insurance Expense |
| **(200) LIABILITIES** | | 530 | Miscellaneous Expense |
| | | 540 | Rent Expense |
| 210 | Gentec Enterprises | 550 | Supplies Expense—Cleaning |
| 220 | Superior Office Supply | 560 | Supplies Expense—Office |
| | | 570 | Utilities Expense |
| **(300) OWNER'S EQUITY** | | | |
| 310 | Darrell King, Capital | | |
| 320 | Darrell King, Drawing | | |
| 330 | Income Summary | | |

**Instructions:** Prepare a general ledger file maintenance input form (FORM GL-1) for the general ledger chart of accounts. Use December 1 of the current year as the run date.

### PROBLEM 10-2   Journalizing opening balances in an automated accounting system

E-Z Rest Motel has the following post-closing trial balance on November 30 of the current year.

|  | | | | | | |
|---|---|---|---|---|---|---|
| *E-Z Rest Motel* | | | | | | |
| *Post-Closing Trial Balance* | | | | | | |
| *November 30, 19--* | | | | | | |

| ACCOUNT TITLE | DEBIT | CREDIT |
|---|---|---|
| *Cash* | 14 6 4 0 00 | |
| *Petty Cash* | 3 0 0 00 | |
| *Supplies—Cleaning* | 1 4 8 0 00 | |
| *Supplies—Office* | 1 1 6 0 00 | |
| *Prepaid Insurance* | 1 8 4 0 00 | |
| *Gentec Enterprises* | | 1 2 2 5 00 |
| *Superior Office Supply* | | 7 4 3 00 |
| *Darrell King, Capital* | | 17 4 5 2 00 |
| *Totals* | 19 4 2 0 00 | 19 4 2 0 00 |

**Instructions: 1.** Journalize the opening balances for E-Z Rest Motel on a general ledger input form (FORM GL-2). Use December 1 of the current year as the run date and the date of the opening balances. Use account numbers from the chart of accounts given in Problem 10-1. Batch No. 1; Memorandum No. 1.

 **2.** Total and prove the Debit Amount and Credit Amount columns. Record the batch totals.

# ■ ENRICHMENT PROBLEMS

MASTERY PROBLEM 10-M   **Preparing a general ledger file maintenance input form and journalizing opening balances**

AAA Secretarial Service has the following general ledger chart of accounts and post-closing trial balance on June 30 of the current year.

| Balance Sheet Accounts | | Income Statement Accounts | |
|---|---|---|---|
| **(100) ASSETS** | | **(400) REVENUE** | |
| 110 | Cash | 410 | Secretarial Fees |
| 120 | Petty Cash | | |
| 130 | Supplies | **(500) EXPENSES** | |
| 140 | Prepaid Insurance | | |
| | | 510 | Advertising Expense |
| **(200) LIABILITIES** | | 520 | Insurance Expense |
| | | 530 | Miscellaneous Expense |
| 210 | Armeda Office Products | 540 | Rent Expense |
| 220 | Perez Office Supply | 550 | Supplies Expense |
| | | 560 | Utilities Expense |
| **(300) OWNER'S EQUITY** | | | |
| 310 | Kay Dewitt, Capital | | |
| 320 | Kay Dewitt, Drawing | | |
| 330 | Income Summary | | |

*AAA Secretarial Service*

*Post-Closing Trial Balance*

*June 30, 19--*

| ACCOUNT TITLE | DEBIT | CREDIT |
|---|---|---|
| Cash | 13 9 2 0 00 | |
| Petty Cash | 3 0 0 00 | |
| Supplies | 3 9 1 0 00 | |
| Prepaid Insurance | 2 0 7 0 00 | |
| Armeda Office Products | | 1 4 6 5 00 |
| Perez Office Supply | | 6 3 5 00 |
| Kay Dewitt, Capital | | 18 1 0 0 00 |
| Totals | 20 2 0 0 00 | 20 2 0 0 00 |

**Instructions: 1.** Prepare a general ledger file maintenance input form (FORM GL-1) for the general ledger chart of accounts. Use July 1 of the current year as the run date.

**2.** Journalize the opening balances for AAA Secretarial Service on a general ledger input form (FORM GL-2). Use July 1 of the current year as the run date and the date of the opening balances. Batch No. 1; Memorandum No. 1.

**3.** Total and prove the Debit Amount and Credit Amount columns. Record the batch totals.

CHALLENGE PROBLEM 10-C  **Preparing a general ledger file maintenance input form and journalizing opening balances**

Sutton Auto Towing has the following general ledger chart of accounts and post-closing trial balance on May 31 of the current year.

| Balance Sheet Accounts | | Income Statement Accounts | |
|---|---|---|---|
| | **(100) ASSETS** | | **(400) REVENUE** |
| 110 | Cash | 410 | Towing Fees |
| 120 | Petty Cash | | |
| 130 | Supplies | | **(500) EXPENSES** |
| 140 | Prepaid Insurance | | |
| | | 510 | Advertising Expense |
| | **(200) LIABILITIES** | 520 | Gasoline Expense |
| | | 530 | Insurance Expense |
| 210 | Beck Office Supplies | 540 | Miscellaneous Expense |
| 220 | Sandel Service Station | 550 | Rent Expense—Building |
| | | 560 | Rent Expense—Truck |
| | **(300) OWNER'S EQUITY** | 570 | Supplies Expense |
| | | 580 | Utilities Expense |
| 310 | Dale Irvin, Capital | | |
| 320 | Dale Irvin, Drawing | | |
| 330 | Income Summary | | |

| Sutton Auto Towing | | | | |
| :--- | :---: | :---: | :---: | :---: |
| Post-Closing Trial Balance | | | | |
| May 31, 19-- | | | | |
| ACCOUNT TITLE | | DEBIT | | CREDIT |
| Cash | | 10 2 5 0 00 | | |
| Petty Cash | | 3 0 0 00 | | |
| Supplies | | 1 1 4 5 00 | | |
| Prepaid Insurance | | 5 2 5 00 | | |
| Beck Office Supply | | | | 2 8 5 00 |
| Sandel Service Station | | | | 8 4 0 00 |
| Dale Irvin, Capital | | | | 11 0 9 5 00 |
| Totals | | 12 2 2 0 00 | | 12 2 2 0 00 |

**Instructions: 1.** Prepare a general ledger file maintenance input form (FORM GL-1) for the general ledger chart of accounts. Use June 1 of the current year as the run date.

**2.** Journalize the opening balances for Sutton Auto Towing on a general ledger input form (FORM GL-2). Use June 1 of the current year as the run date and the date of the opening balances. Batch No. 1; Memorandum No. 1.

**3.** Total and prove the Debit Amount and Credit Amount columns. Record the batch totals.

*The solution to Challenge Problem 10-C is needed to complete Computer Application 1.*

# Safety and Health Considerations
# When Using Microcomputers

## ELECTRICAL EQUIPMENT

The following rules protect the operator of the equipment, other persons in the environment, and the equipment itself.

1. Do not unplug equipment by pulling on the electrical cord. Instead, grasp the plug at the outlet and remove it.
2. Do not stretch electrical cords across an aisle where someone might trip over them.
3. Avoid food and beverages near equipment where a spill might result in an electrical short.
4. Do not attempt to remove the cover of equipment for any reason while the power is turned on.
5. Do not attempt to repair equipment while it is plugged in. To avoid damage most repairs should be done by an authorized service technician.
6. Always turn the power off when finished using equipment.
7. Do not overload extension cords.
8. Follow manufacturer recommendations for safe use.
9. Replace frayed electrical cords immediately.

## MICROCOMPUTERS

1. To avoid damage to the drives, do not insert pencils or other implements in floppy disk drives.
2. To prevent overheating, avoid blocking air vents.
3. Position keyboards to prevent bumping or dropping them off the work surface.

## MONITORS

1. Most manufacturers advise repair by authorized service technicians only.

2. Adjust brightness and focus for comfortable viewing.
3. Avoid glare on the monitor screen.
4. Do not leave fingerprints on the screen. Keep the screen clear of dust. Only use a soft cloth for cleaning the screen.

## PRINTERS

1. Do not let jewelry, ties, scarves, loose sleeves, or other clothing get caught in the machinery. This could result in damage to the machinery and could cause personal injury.
2. Exercise caution when using toxic chemicals such as toner in order to avoid spills.

## DISKETTES

1. Put write/protect tabs on all program software to avoid accidental erasure.
2. Do not bend or fold diskettes.
3. Do not write on a diskette with a hard or sharp-pointed pen or pencil; use a felt-tip marker.
4. Do not touch exposed surfaces of diskettes.
5. Be sure the disk drive is not running when you insert or remove a diskette.
6. Keep diskettes away from extreme hot or cold temperatures. Do not leave diskettes in a car during very hot or cold weather.
7. Keep diskettes away from magnetic fields such as transformers and magnets.
8. Store diskettes in the storage envelopes.
9. Keep diskettes away from smoke, ashes, and dust, including chalk dust.
10. Do not leave diskettes in the disk drive for prolonged periods, such as overnight.

# Computer Application 1
# Starting an Automated Accounting System

The general ledger file maintenance input form and the general ledger input form completed in Challenge Problem 10-C, Chapter 10, are needed to complete Computer Application 1.

Sutton Auto Towing completed the required input forms for starting an automated accounting system. Chapter 10 describes the required manual and computer operations. Computer Application 1 provides an opportunity to process the data from the completed forms using a microcomputer.

Computer Application 1 is designed to be used with the *Automated Accounting for the Microcomputer*, 3d edition, software. The software provides the option of either displaying or printing reports. If a printer is available, select the *Print* option when given the choice of displaying or printing reports. If a printer is not available, select the *Display* option. Selecting the *Display* option causes the report to be displayed on the computer monitor.

## ■ COMPUTER APPLICATION PROBLEM

COMPUTER APPLICATION PROBLEM 1   **Starting an automated accounting system**

**Instructions: 1.** Load the *Automated Accounting for the Microcomputer* software. Select Computer Application 1 (CA-1) from the CENTURY 21 ACCOUNTING Template Disk. The accounting system setup data and company name have been entered and are stored on the Template Disk.

**2.** Key-enter the chart of accounts data from the completed general ledger input form prepared in Challenge Problem 10-C.

**3.** Display/Print the chart of accounts report. Check the report for accuracy.

**4.** Key-enter the control account numbers.

**5.** Key-enter the opening balances from the completed general ledger input form prepared in Challenge Problem 10-C.

**6.** Display/Print the opening balances report. Check the report for accuracy by comparing the report totals with the batch totals on the general ledger input form.

# CHAPTER
# 11

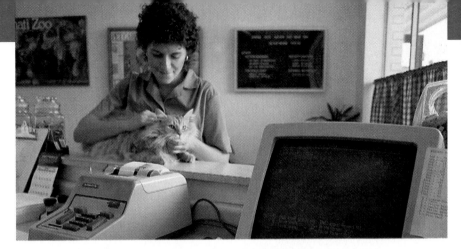

# Using an Automated Accounting System

ENABLING PERFORMANCE TASKS

After studying Chapter 11, you will be able to:
a. Define accounting terms related to using an automated accounting system.
b. Identify accounting concepts and practices related to using an automated accounting system.
c. Perform file maintenance activities.
d. Journalize transactions on a general ledger input form.
e. Journalize adjusting entries on a general ledger input form.

A business should study immediate and future accounting needs before deciding to change from a manual to an automated accounting system. The cost of changing accounting systems must also be considered. Petlodge determined that an automated accounting system would reduce processing time and be less expensive than the manual accounting system. Chapter 10 describes accounting procedures used by Petlodge to start an automated accounting system. Chapter 11 describes procedures followed by Petlodge to use an automated accounting system for daily accounting activities and end-of-fiscal-period work.

## FILE MAINTENANCE

In manual accounting file maintenance activities for a general ledger chart of accounts require working with individual ledger accounts. (1) An account is deleted by removing the account from the file. (2) An account title or number is changed by preparing a new ledger account. (3) An account is added by preparing a new ledger form and inserting the account in the proper order within the file. In automated accounting a general ledger chart of accounts is stored on secondary computer storage. File maintenance activities include recording deletions and additions on a general ledger file maintenance input form. The deletions and additions are key-entered into the computer to change the file on secondary storage.

## Deleting an account

Petlodge has limited advertising expense. Therefore, a decision is made to delete this account from the general ledger and record advertising as a miscellaneous expense. The entry on a general ledger file maintenance input form to delete Advertising Expense is shown on line 1 of Illustration 11-1.

| | ACCOUNT NUMBER | ACCOUNT TITLE | |
|---|---|---|---|
| 1 | 510 | (Delete) | 1 |
| 2 | 540 | Rent Expense—Building | 2 |
| 3 | 545 | Rent Expense—Computer | 3 |

GENERAL LEDGER
FILE MAINTENANCE
Input Form

RUN   DATE   *09 01 --*
MM DD YY

FORM GL-1

Illustration 11-1
Entries for file maintenance

Three steps are followed to complete a general ledger file maintenance input form to delete an account.

1  Write the run date, *09/01/--*, in the space provided at the top of the form. This run date indicates the effective date of the file maintenance data.

2  Write the account number of the account to be deleted, *510*, in the Account Number column. Obtain the account number from the chart of accounts report, Illustration 10-7, page 206.

3  Write the word, *(Delete)*, on the same line in the Account Title column. A word that is not to be key-entered into the computer is placed in parentheses. Placing the word *Delete* in parentheses indicates that the word is not an account title and is not to be key-entered into the computer.

## Adding an account

Petlodge decides to keep a separate record of the rent paid for the microcomputer and software. Petlodge records the payment of the monthly rent on the building in the rent expense account. Petlodge decides to use a second rent expense account for the computer rental. Because renting the computer represents a major expense, Petlodge wants to be able to record and report the exact amount of this expense. *(CONCEPT: Adequate Disclosure)*

**Changing an account title.** Because a second rent expense account is being added, Petlodge wishes to clearly identify each type of rent expense. Therefore, the current account titled *Rent Expense* is changed to *Rent Expense—Building*. The entry to change an account title is shown on line 2 of Illustration 11-1.

Two steps are followed to complete a general ledger file maintenance input form to change an account title.

1 Write the account number of the account to be changed, *540*, on the next blank line in the Account Number column. Obtain the account number from the chart of accounts report.

2 Write the new account title, *Rent Expense—Building*, on the same line in the Account Title column.

**Adding a new account.** A new account number is determined using procedures described in Chapter 5. The account number assigned must place the account in the proper order within the expenses division in the chart of accounts. Expense accounts are listed in alphabetical order. Petlodge assigns accounts by 10s within each general ledger division. Using the unused middle number, the new account number for Rent Expense—Computer is assigned as follows.

| | | |
|---|---|---|
| 540 | Rent Expense—Building | (New account title of existing account) |
| 545 | RENT EXPENSE—COMPUTER | (NEW ACCOUNT) |
| 550 | Supplies Expense—Office | (Existing account) |

If no exact middle number is available, the nearest *even whole number* is used. For example, the middle number between 545 and 550 is 547.5. The number 547.5 contains four digits and cannot be assigned in a three-digit numbering system. Therefore, 548, the nearest *even whole number* would be used.

New accounts that are added after the last account in a division are assigned the next number in the sequence of 10s. For example, an account added as the last account in a division ending with the number 550 would be assigned the number 560.

Two steps are followed to complete a general ledger file maintenance input form to add an account, as shown on line 3 of Illustration 11-1.

1 Write the account number of the new account to be added, *545*, on the next blank line in the Account Number column.

2 Write the new account title, *Rent Expense—Computer*, on the same line in the Account Title column.

## Processing file maintenance data

The General Ledger Main Menu is shown in Illustration 11-2.

Option F is selected to perform file maintenance. Spaces for entering file maintenance data are displayed on the computer monitor.

Data on each line of the input form are then key-entered. After all changes have been key-entered and processed, Option G is selected from the General Ledger Main Menu. This option directs the computer to prepare a revised chart of accounts report. The report reflects all changes

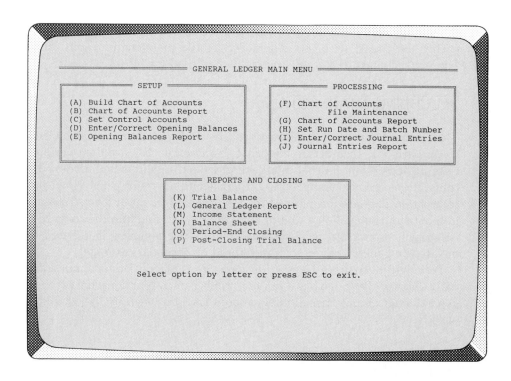

GENERAL LEDGER MAIN MENU

SETUP

(A) Build Chart of Accounts
(B) Chart of Accounts Report
(C) Set Control Accounts
(D) Enter/Correct Opening Balances
(E) Opening Balances Report

PROCESSING

(F) Chart of Accounts
        File Maintenance
(G) Chart of Accounts Report
(H) Set Run Date and Batch Number
(I) Enter/Correct Journal Entries
(J) Journal Entries Report

REPORTS AND CLOSING

(K) Trial Balance
(L) General Ledger Report
(M) Income Statement
(N) Balance Sheet
(O) Period-End Closing
(P) Post-Closing Trial Balance

Select option by letter or press ESC to exit.

made to the chart of accounts. The revised chart of accounts report is shown in Illustration 11-3.

Illustration 11-2
General ledger main menu

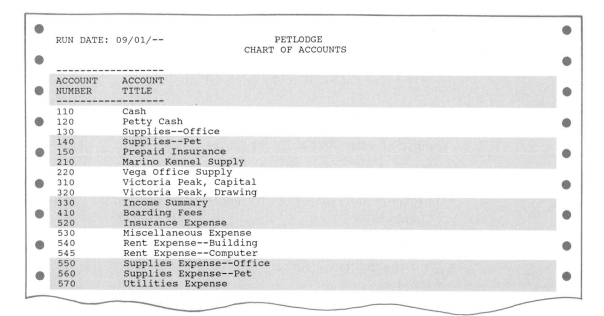

```
RUN DATE: 09/01/--                    PETLODGE
                                  CHART OF ACCOUNTS

      ------------------
      ACCOUNT     ACCOUNT
      NUMBER      TITLE
      ------------------
      110         Cash
      120         Petty Cash
      130         Supplies--Office
      140         Supplies--Pet
      150         Prepaid Insurance
      210         Marino Kennel Supply
      220         Vega Office Supply
      310         Victoria Peak, Capital
      320         Victoria Peak, Drawing
      330         Income Summary
      410         Boarding Fees
      520         Insurance Expense
      530         Miscellaneous Expense
      540         Rent Expense--Building
      545         Rent Expense--Computer
      550         Supplies Expense--Office
      560         Supplies Expense--Pet
      570         Utilities Expense
```

Illustration 11-3    Revised chart of accounts report

Petlodge checks the accuracy of the revised chart of accounts by comparing the report with the general ledger file maintenance input form. The revised chart of accounts report is then filed for future reference.

# RECORDING TRANSACTIONS

In manual accounting transactions are analyzed into their debit and credit parts and recorded in a journal. Transaction data are then periodically posted from a journal to a general ledger. In automated accounting transactions are also analyzed into their debit and credit parts. However, transaction data are journalized on a general ledger input form. Transaction data journalized on an input form are key-entered into the computer. After each transaction has been key-entered, the computer is directed to post to the general ledger accounts stored on secondary storage.

Petlodge journalizes transaction data on a general ledger input form daily. Because Petlodge has a limited number of transactions, data from a general ledger input form are key-entered and processed on the computer weekly.

## Cash payment of an expense

*September 1, 19--.*
*Paid cash for building rental, $1,200.00. Check No. 245.*

The source document for this transaction is Check No. 245. *(CONCEPT: Objective Evidence)* The analysis of this kind of transaction is described in Chapter 3. Rent Expense—Building is debited and Cash is credited for $1,200.00. The general ledger input form entry to record this transaction is shown on lines 1 and 2 of Illustration 11-4.

Eight steps are followed to journalize transactions on a general ledger input form.

1 Write the run date, *09/05/--*, in the space provided at the top of the form. The run date indicates that the transaction data entered on the input form are for the week ended September 5.

2 Write the batch number, 2, in the space provided at the top of the form. Batch number 1 was assigned to the opening balances, Illustration 10-10, Chapter 10. Therefore, batch number 2 is assigned to the first group of transactions.

3 Write the day, *01*, on line 1 in the Day column.

4 Write the document number, *C245*, on the same line in the Doc. No. column.

5 Write the account number, *540*, of the account debited, *Rent Expense—Building*, on the same line in the Account Number column.

| RUN DATE 09 05 , -- | | GENERAL LEDGER | | FORM GL-2 |
|---|---|---|---|---|

| | DAY | DOC. NO. | ACCOUNT NUMBER | DEBIT AMOUNT | CREDIT AMOUNT | |
|---|---|---|---|---|---|---|
| 1 | 01 | C245 | 540 | 1200 00 | | 1 |
| 2 | | | 110 | | 1200 00 | 2 |
| 3 | 01 | C246 | 545 | 875 00 | | 3 |
| 4 | | | 110 | | 875 00 | 4 |
| 5 | 02 | C247 | 530 | 85 00 | | 5 |
| 6 | | | 110 | | 85 00 | 6 |
| 7 | 02 | C248 | 320 | 600 00 | | 7 |
| 8 | | | 110 | | 600 00 | 8 |
| 9 | 03 | C249 | 210 | 250 00 | | 9 |
| 10 | | | 110 | | 250 00 | 10 |
| 11 | 03 | C250 | 130 | 63 00 | | 11 |
| 12 | | | 110 | | 63 00 | 12 |
| 13 | 04 | C251 | 130 | 87 00 | | 13 |
| 14 | | | 140 | 46 00 | | 14 |
| 15 | | | 530 | 69 00 | | 15 |
| 16 | | | 110 | | 202 00 | 16 |
| 17 | 04 | R12 | 110 | 1000 00 | | 17 |
| 18 | | | 310 | | 1000 00 | 18 |
| 19 | 05 | T5 | 110 | 935 00 | | 19 |
| 20 | | | 410 | | 935 00 | 20 |

BATCH NO. 2

GENERAL LEDGER
Input Form

| | | | | |
|---|---|---|---|---|
| 1 | 2 | 3 | 4 | 5 |

BATCH TOTALS     5210 00     5210 00

Illustration 11-4
General ledger input form
with transactions recorded

6   Write the debit amount, *$1,200.00*, on the same line in the Debit Amount column.

7   On the second line, write the account number, *110*, of the account credited, Cash, in the Account Number column. The Day and Doc. No. columns are left blank on the second line of an entry. The date and document number are recorded only once for each transaction.

8   Write the credit amount, *$1,200.00*, on the same line in the Credit Amount column.

These same procedures are used to record all cash payment transactions.

## Cash payment to owner as a withdrawal

Assets taken out of a business for an owner's personal use are known as withdrawals. Petlodge's general ledger has an account titled *Victoria Peak, Drawing* for recording withdrawals. A drawing account balance decreases an owner's capital account balance. Therefore, a drawing account has a normal debit balance.

> September 2, 19--.
> *Paid cash to owner for personal use, $600.00. Check No. 248.*

The source document for this transaction is Check No. 248. *(CONCEPT: Objective Evidence)* The analysis of this kind of transaction is described in Chapter 3. Victoria Peak, Drawing is debited and Cash is credited for $600.00. The general ledger input form entry to record this transaction is shown on lines 7 and 8 of Illustration 11-4. Petlodge follows the same procedures to complete lines 7 and 8 as described for lines 1 and 2.

## Cash payment of a liability

> September 3, 19--.
> *Paid cash on account to Marino Kennel Supply, $250.00. Check No. 249.*

The source document for this transaction is Check No. 249. *(CONCEPT: Objective Evidence)* The analysis of this kind of transaction is described in Chapter 3. Marino Kennel Supply is debited and Cash is credited for $250.00. The general ledger input form entry to record this transaction is shown on lines 9 and 10 of Illustration 11-4.

## Cash payment for supplies

> September 3, 19--.
> *Paid cash for office supplies, $63.00. Check No. 250.*

The source document for this transaction is Check No. 250. *(CONCEPT: Objective Evidence)* The analysis of this kind of transaction is described in Chapter 3. Supplies—Office is debited and Cash is credited for $63.00. The general ledger input form entry to record this transaction is shown on lines 11 and 12 of Illustration 11-4.

## Cash payment to replenish petty cash

Petlodge deposits all cash in a bank. However, some cash is kept in a petty cash fund for making change at the cash register and for making small cash payments. Petlodge has a petty cash fund of $300.00 that is replenished whenever the fund drops below $100.00.

> September 4, 19--.
> *Paid cash to replenish the petty cash fund, $202.00: office supplies, $87.00; pet supplies, $46.00; miscellaneous, $69.00. Check No. 251.*

The source document for this transaction is Check No. 251. *(CONCEPT: Objective Evidence)* The analysis of this kind of transaction is described in Chapter 6. Supplies—Office is debited for $87.00, and Supplies—Pet is debited for $46.00. Miscellaneous Expense is debited for $69.00. Cash is credited for $202.00, the total amount needed to replenish the petty cash fund. The general ledger input form entry to record this transaction is shown on lines 13 through 16 of Illustration 11-4.

## Cash receipt from owner as an investment

From time to time, Victoria Peak invests cash in Petlodge. When cash is invested, both the cash account balance and the capital account balance are increased.

*September 4, 19--.*
*Received cash from owner as an investment, $1,000.00. Receipt No. 12.*

The source document for this transaction is Receipt No. 12. *(CONCEPT: Objective Evidence)* The analysis of this kind of transaction is described in Chapter 3. Cash is debited and Victoria Peak, Capital is credited for $1,000.00. The general ledger input form entry to record this transaction is shown on lines 17 and 18 of Illustration 11-4.

## Cash receipt from boarding fees

Petlodge receives a fee for boarding pets. Cash is collected and recorded when the boarding is finished.

*September 5, 19--.*
*Received cash from boarding fees, $935.00. Cash Register Tape No. 5.*

The source document for this transaction is Cash Register Tape No. 5. *(CONCEPT: Objective Evidence)* Petlodge uses a cash register to record all boarding fees collected. The cash register prints each transaction on a paper tape inside the machine. A printed receipt is also provided for each customer. Amounts on the cash register tape may be totaled daily or weekly. Petlodge records the total boarding fees collected weekly. The tape is marked with the letter *T* and the day of the month it is removed from the cash register.

The analysis of this kind of transaction is described in Chapter 3. Cash is debited and Boarding Fees is credited for $935.00. The general ledger input form entry to record this transaction is shown on lines 19 and 20 of Illustration 11-4.

## Completing a general ledger input form

After all transactions have been recorded, Petlodge totals the Debit Amount and Credit Amount columns. The totals are recorded on the Batch Totals line provided at the bottom of the input form. If more than one general ledger input form is required to record transactions, the amount columns for all pages are totaled. A journal entry should not be split on two different general ledger input forms. Therefore, if a complete journal entry cannot be entered on an input form, a new input form is started. The totals for all pages are then entered *only* on the last page on the Batch Totals line. The two totals are compared to assure that debits equal credits. Because the two totals are the same, *$5,210.00*, the entries on this input form are assumed to be correct.

## Processing journal entries

Option H is selected from the General Ledger Main Menu, to set the run date, 09/05/--, and the batch number, 2, as shown in Illustration 11-5.

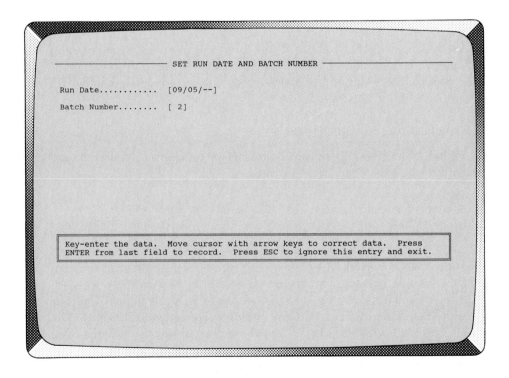

```
───────────────── SET RUN DATE AND BATCH NUMBER ─────────────────


    Run Date...........  [09/05/--]

    Batch Number........  [ 2]
```

```
    ┌────────────────────────────────────────────────────────────────┐
    │ Key-enter the data.  Move cursor with arrow keys to correct data.  Press │
    │ ENTER from last field to record.   Press ESC to ignore this entry and exit. │
    └────────────────────────────────────────────────────────────────┘
```

Illustration 11-5
Computer monitor display
with run date and batch
number recorded

Option I is selected from the General Ledger Main Menu to key-enter journal entries. Spaces for entering the data are displayed on the computer monitor. Petlodge key-enters the transaction data from the general ledger input form one line at a time. Lines 1 and 2 are shown entered in Illustration 11-6.

After all lines on the input form have been entered and posted, Option J is selected from the General Ledger Main Menu. This option directs the

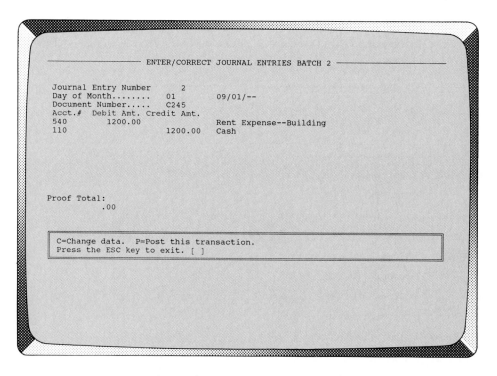

```
──────────────── ENTER/CORRECT JOURNAL ENTRIES BATCH 2 ────────────────

    Journal Entry Number      2
    Day of Month........    01      09/01/--
    Document Number.....   C245
    Acct.#  Debit Amt. Credit Amt.
    540        1200.00              Rent Expense--Building
    110                  1200.00    Cash




    Proof Total:
              .00


    ┌─────────────────────────────────────────────────────────────┐
    │ C=Change data.   P=Post this transaction.                    │
    │ Press the ESC key to exit. [ ]                               │
    └─────────────────────────────────────────────────────────────┘
```

computer to prepare a journal entries report. The journal entries report for batch number 2 is shown in Illustration 11-7, page 230.

Illustration 11-6
Computer monitor display
of a journal entry

Petlodge checks the journal entries report for accuracy by comparing the report totals, *$5,210.00*, with the batch totals on the general ledger input form, *$5,210.00*. Because the totals are the same, the journal entries report is assumed to be correct. The journal entries report is then filed for future reference.

## Proving cash

Petlodge also proves cash after each journal entries report involving cash transactions is prepared. The computer keeps track of cash receipts and cash payments. The total cash receipts and cash payments are listed on the journal entries report, Illustration 11-7, to aid in proving cash. Petlodge proves cash on September 5 as shown below.

| | |
|---|---|
| Cash on hand at the beginning of the month . . . . . . . . . . . . . . . | $12,500.00 |
| (Opening balances report, Illustration 10-12) | |
| *Plus* total cash receipts . . . . . . . . . . . . . . . . . . . . . . . . . . . . . . . . . . | + 1,935.00 |
| (Journal entries report, Illustration 11-7) | |
| *Equals* total. . . . . . . . . . . . . . . . . . . . . . . . . . . . . . . . . . . . . . . . . . | $14,435.00 |
| *Less* total cash payments . . . . . . . . . . . . . . . . . . . . . . . . . . . . . . . | − 3,275.00 |
| (Journal entries report, Illustration 11-7) | |
| *Equals* cash on hand, September 5 . . . . . . . . . . . . . . . . . . . . . . . . | $11,160.00 |

The checkbook balance on the next unused check stub is $11,160.00. The checkbook balance and the cash balance on hand are the same. Therefore, cash is proved.

```
RUN DATE: 09/05/--                          PETLODGE
                                   JOURNAL ENTRIES BATCH# 2

-----------------------------------------------------------------------------
JE#    DATE     ACCOUNT NUMBER & TITLE          DEBIT AMOUNT  CREDIT AMOUNT
-----------------------------------------------------------------------------
0002  09/01/-- 540    Rent Expense--Building        1200.00
               110       Cash                                      1200.00
                       DOCUMENT: C245

0003  09/01/-- 545    Rent Expense--Computer          875.00
               110       Cash                                       875.00
                       DOCUMENT: C246

0004  09/02/-- 530    Miscellaneous Expense            85.00
               110       Cash                                        85.00
                       DOCUMENT: C247

0005  09/02/-- 320    Victoria Peak, Drawing          600.00
               110       Cash                                       600.00
                       DOCUMENT: C248

0006  09/03/-- 210    Marino Kennel Supply            250.00
               110       Cash                                       250.00
                       DOCUMENT: C249

0007  09/03/-- 130    Supplies--Office                 63.00
               110       Cash                                        63.00
                       DOCUMENT: C250

0008  09/04/-- 130    Supplies--Office                 87.00
               140    Supplies--Pet                    46.00
               530    Miscellaneous Expense            69.00
               110       Cash                                       202.00
                       DOCUMENT: C251

0009  09/04/-- 110    Cash                           1000.00
               310       Victoria Peak, Capital                    1000.00
                       DOCUMENT: R12

0010  09/05/-- 110    Cash                            935.00
               410       Boarding Fees                              935.00
                       DOCUMENT: T5

                                                  ---------------  ---------------
               TOTALS                                   5210.00         5210.00
                                                  ===============  ===============
               IN BALANCE

Cash Receipts         1935.00
Cash Payments         3275.00
```

Illustration 11-7
Journal entries report

# COMPLETING END-OF-FISCAL-PERIOD WORK

In manual accounting a trial balance is prepared on a work sheet to prove the equality of debits and credits in a general ledger. Adjustments are then planned and the work sheet is completed as described in Part 1 for Rugcare. Financial statements are then manually prepared from data on a completed work sheet. Adjusting and closing entries are entered in a journal and manually posted to general ledger accounts. A post-closing trial balance is prepared manually from general ledger accounts to prove equality of debits and credits after posting adjusting and closing entries.

In automated accounting end-of-fiscal-period reports are printed by a computer according to instructions in the computer software. The run date used for all end-of-fiscal-period reports is the ending date of the accounting period. Petlodge prepares financial statements at the end of each monthly fiscal period. *(CONCEPT: Accounting Period Cycle)* Two financial statements are prepared. (1) Income statement. (2) Balance sheet. Before printing financial statements, Option K is selected from the General Ledger Main Menu to direct the computer to prepare a trial balance. The trial balance is prepared to prove equality of general ledger debits and credits. The trial balance is also used to plan adjustments to general ledger accounts. Petlodge's trial balance is shown in Illustration 11-8.

```
RUN DATE: 09/30/--                    PETLODGE
                                   TRIAL BALANCE
---------------------------------------------------------------------
ACCOUNT       ACCOUNT
NUMBER        TITLE                      DEBIT AMOUNT      CREDIT AMOUNT
---------------------------------------------------------------------
  110         Cash                         14393.00
  120         Petty Cash                     300.00
  130         Supplies--Office              1410.00
  140         Supplies--Pet                 2136.00
  150         Prepaid Insurance              765.00
  210         Marino Kennel Supply                           1323.00
  220         Vega Office Supply                               195.00
  310         Victoria Peak, Capital                         16010.00
  320         Victoria Peak, Drawing        1200.00
  410         Boarding Fees                                   5455.00
  530         Miscellaneous Expense          439.00
  540         Rent Expense--Building        1200.00
  545         Rent Expense--Computer         875.00
  570         Utilities Expense              265.00
                                         --------------    --------------
              TOTALS                        22983.00          22983.00
                                         ==============    ==============
```

Illustration 11-8
Trial balance

## Planning adjusting entries

At the end of an accounting period, certain general ledger accounts need to be brought up to date. *(CONCEPT: Matching Expenses with Revenue)*

**Supplies adjustments.** Petlodge has two accounts for supplies, Supplies—Office and Supplies—Pet. Two accounts are used in adjusting each supplies account—an asset account and an expense account. Petlodge's two adjustments for the supplies accounts are similar to those described for Rugcare in Part 1.

The value of office supplies used, *$295.00*, is debited to Supplies Expense—Office. Supplies—Office is credited for the same amount. The value of pet supplies used, *$530.00*, is debited to Supplies Expense—Pet. Supplies—Pet is credited for the same amount.

**Prepaid insurance adjustment.** Insurance premiums, when paid, are debited to the asset account Prepaid Insurance. Insurance expense, however, must be recorded for the month in which the insurance coverage is actually used. *(CONCEPT: Matching Expenses with Revenue)* Prepaid Insurance and Insurance Expense are, therefore, adjusted at the end of each fiscal period. Petlodge's prepaid insurance adjustment is the same as the one described in Part 1. The value of insurance used, *$85.00*, is debited to Insurance Expense. The same amount is credited to Prepaid Insurance.

Petlodge's adjusting entries are recorded on a general ledger input form, as shown in Illustration 11-9.

| RUN DATE 09 30 / -- | | GENERAL LEDGER | | FORM GL-2 |
|---|---|---|---|---|
| MM DD YY | | Input Form | | |
| BATCH NO. 7 | | | | |

| | DAY | DOC. NO. | ACCOUNT NUMBER | DEBIT AMOUNT | CREDIT AMOUNT | |
|---|---|---|---|---|---|---|
| 1 | 30 | Adj. Ent. | 550 | 295 00 | | 1 |
| 2 | | | 130 | | 295 00 | 2 |
| 3 | 30 | Adj. Ent. | 560 | 530 00 | | 3 |
| 4 | | | 140 | | 530 00 | 4 |
| 5 | 30 | Adj. Ent. | 520 | 85 00 | | 5 |
| 6 | | | 150 | | 85 00 | 6 |

| | | | BATCH TOTALS | 910 00 | 910 00 |
|---|---|---|---|---|---|

Illustration 11-9
General ledger input form with adjusting entries recorded

The run date, *09/30/--*, is used to indicate that the adjusting entries are for the month ended 09/30/--. The batch number, *7*, is used as the next sequential number for all batches recorded during the month of September. Batch numbers 3 through 6 were used for the four remaining weekly transaction batches journalized during the month. The day, *30*, is written in the Day Column for each entry. The abbreviation for adjusting entries, *Adj.Ent.*, is written in the Doc. No. column for each entry.

## Processing adjusting entries

Option H is selected from the General Ledger Main Menu to record a new run date and batch number. Option I is selected from the General

Ledger Main Menu to enter the adjusting entries. Spaces are displayed on the computer monitor for entering the adjusting entries. Petlodge key-enters the adjusting entries from the input form one line at a time. After all lines on the input form have been key-entered and posted, Option J is selected from the General Ledger Main Menu. This option directs the computer to prepare a journal entries report for the adjusting entries. The journal entries report for the adjusting entries is shown in Illustration 11-10.

```
RUN DATE: 09/30/--                    PETLODGE
                            JOURNAL ENTRIES BATCH# 7

   ---------------------------------------------------------------------
   JE#    DATE     ACCOUNT NUMBER & TITLE         DEBIT AMOUNT  CREDIT AMOUNT
   ---------------------------------------------------------------------
   0038  09/30/-- 550    Supplies Expense--Office     295.00
                  130      Supplies--Office                         295.00
                         DOCUMENT: Adj.Ent.

   0039  09/30/-- 560    Supplies Expense--Pet        530.00
                  140      Supplies--Pet                            530.00
                         DOCUMENT: Adj.Ent.

   0040  09/30/-- 520    Insurance Expense             85.00
                  150      Prepaid Insurance                         85.00
                         DOCUMENT: Adj.Ent.

                                                   ---------------  ---------------
                  TOTALS                                910.00          910.00
                                                   ===============  ===============
                  IN BALANCE
```

Petlodge checks the journal entries report for accuracy by comparing the report with the input form. The journal entries report is then filed for future reference.

Illustration 11-10
Journal entries report for adjusting entries

## General ledger report

If individual accounts from the general ledger need to be examined, a general ledger report may be prepared. This report shows all entries to general ledger accounts during the fiscal period. Option L is selected from the General Ledger Main Menu to direct the computer to prepare a general ledger report. A partial general ledger report showing all entries posted to Supplies—Office is shown in Illustration 11-11.

Illustration 11-11
Partial general ledger report

```
RUN DATE: 09/30/--                    PETLODGE
                             GENERAL LEDGER

   ---------------------------------------------------------------------
   ACCOUNT          J.E.   BATCH           DOCUMENT
   NUMBER  TITLE    NO.    NUMBER  DATE    NUMBER   DEBIT AMOUNT  CREDIT AMOUNT
   ---------------------------------------------------------------------
   130     Supplies--Office
                    0001    01    09/01/-- M1         1260.00
                    0007    02    09/03/-- C250         63.00
                    0008    02    09/04/-- C251         87.00
                    0038    07    09/30/-- Adj.Ent.                   295.00
                                          End.Bal.    1115.00
```

## Processing an income statement

After the general ledger report has been prepared, Option M is selected from the General Ledger Main Menu. This option directs the computer to prepare an income statement. Petlodge's income statement is shown in Illustration 11-12.

```
                              PETLODGE
                           INCOME STATEMENT
                       FOR PERIOD ENDED 09/30/--
                                                            % OF NET
    R E V E N U E                                           REVENUE
    -------------                                           --------
    Boarding Fees                       5455.00              100.00
                                   ----------------
    NET REVENUE                                  5455.00     100.00


    E X P E N S E S
    ---------------
    Insurance Expense                     85.00                1.56
    Miscellaneous Expense                439.00                8.05
    Rent Expense--Building              1200.00               22.00
    Rent Expense--Computer               875.00               16.04
    Supplies Expense--Office             295.00                5.41
    Supplies Expense--Pet                530.00                9.72
    Utilities Expense                    265.00                4.86
                                   ----------------
    TOTAL EXPENSES                               3689.00      67.63
                                          ----------------
    NET INCOME                                   1766.00      32.37
                                          ================
```

Illustration 11-12
Income statement

## Income statement analysis

The percentage relationship between one financial statement item and the total that includes that item is known as a component percentage. Petlodge's software computes a component percentage for each expense, total expenses, and net income. The relationship between each component and sales is shown in a separate column of the income statement.

Ms. Peak first analyzes the total expenses and net income components to determine if the percentages are acceptable. Acceptable component percentages are determined by comparing the component percentages with percentages published by industry organizations or similar businesses. Ms. Peak also compares the component percentages with the percentages reported on prior income statements. If the total expenses percentage is not acceptable, each individual expense is analyzed to determine causes for an unacceptable component percentage for total expenses.

**Total expenses component percentage.** For businesses similar to Petlodge, an acceptable total expenses percentage is not more than 70.00%. Therefore, Petlodge's component percentage, 67.63%, is acceptable.

**Net income component percentage.** For businesses similar to Petlodge, an acceptable net income component percentage is not less than 30.00%.

Therefore, Petlodge's net income component percentage, 32.37%, is acceptable. Reducing the total expenses component percentage in future fiscal periods will result in an improvement in the net income component percentage.

## Processing a balance sheet

Option N is selected from the General Ledger Main Menu to direct the computer to prepare a balance sheet. Petlodge's balance sheet is shown in Illustration 11-13.

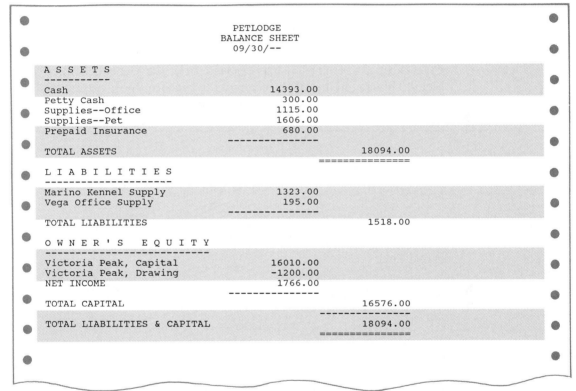

```
                            PETLODGE
                          BALANCE SHEET
                           09/30/--

    A S S E T S
    -----------
    Cash                          14393.00
    Petty Cash                      300.00
    Supplies--Office               1115.00
    Supplies--Pet                  1606.00
    Prepaid Insurance               680.00
                                 ---------------
    TOTAL ASSETS                                    18094.00
                                              ================

    L I A B I L I T I E S
    ---------------------
    Marino Kennel Supply           1323.00
    Vega Office Supply              195.00
                                 ---------------
    TOTAL LIABILITIES                                1518.00

    O W N E R ' S   E Q U I T Y
    ---------------------------
    Victoria Peak, Capital         16010.00
    Victoria Peak, Drawing         -1200.00
    NET INCOME                      1766.00
                                 ---------------
    TOTAL CAPITAL                                   16576.00
                                              ---------------
    TOTAL LIABILITIES & CAPITAL                     18094.00
                                              ================
```

Illustration 11-13
Balance sheet

A balance sheet may be prepared in one of two forms: (1) account form or (2) report form. A balance sheet listing assets on the left and equities on the right is called an account form of balance sheet. The account form of balance sheet, used by Rugcare, is described in Part 1. A balance sheet listing the assets, liabilities, and owner's equity vertically is called a report form of balance sheet. Petlodge's computer prints the report form of balance sheet, as shown in Illustration 11-13.

After the income statement and balance sheet have been reviewed and analyzed, the statements are filed for future reference.

## Closing temporary accounts

In manual accounting closing entries for all temporary accounts are manually entered in a journal and posted to general ledger accounts. *(CONCEPT: Matching Expenses with Revenue)* In Petlodge's automated accounting system, the computer software contains instructions for closing temporary accounts. When Petlodge wants to close temporary accounts, Option O is selected from the General Ledger Main Menu. This option directs the computer to post closing entries to general ledger accounts. Because no journal entries need to be entered on the keyboard, no general ledger input form or journal entries report is prepared.

## Processing a post-closing trial balance

After the financial statements have been prepared and closing entries have been posted, Option P is selected from the General Ledger Main Menu. This option directs the computer to prepare a post-closing trial balance. Petlodge's post-closing trial balance is shown in Illustration 11-14.

```
RUN DATE: 09/30/--                     PETLODGE
                              POST-CLOSING TRIAL BALANCE

    ----------------------------------------------------------------------
    ACCOUNT        ACCOUNT
    NUMBER         TITLE                    DEBIT AMOUNT      CREDIT AMOUNT
    ----------------------------------------------------------------------
      110          Cash                        14393.00
      120          Petty Cash                    300.00
      130          Supplies--Office             1115.00
      140          Supplies--Pet                1606.00
      150          Prepaid Insurance             680.00
      210          Marino Kennel Supply                          1323.00
      220          Vega Office Supply                             195.00
      310          Victoria Peak, Capital                       16576.00
                                            -------------      -------------
                   TOTALS                      18094.00          18094.00
                                            =============      =============
```

Illustration 11-14
Post-closing trial balance

After the post-closing trial balance has been checked for equality of debits and credits, the trial balance is filed for future reference.

# ELECTRONIC SPREADSHEETS

Accountants regularly use paper with columns and rows to analyze financial data. This paper is frequently referred to as analysis paper. Work sheets are prepared manually on analysis paper. Sometimes a work sheet completed on analysis paper is referred to as a spreadsheet. Analysis paper is often used to answer "what if" questions about business operations. An example of "What if?" analysis is figuring the result on net income if revenue is increased by various percentages. When changes are made manually, amounts must be erased and new amounts must be entered. Also, totals must be recalculated, which increases the possibility of errors. If a number of "What if?" questions are needed, a new version must be manually prepared for each set of data. Therefore, preparing a number of versions manually is time consuming.

Computers have made analyzing financial data much easier by increasing the speed and accuracy of calculations. Computers can automatically perform calculations and display and print the results in rows and columns similar to an accountant's analysis paper. A form generated by computer software and consisting of multiple rows and columns in which data can be entered and analyzed is called an electronic spreadsheet. Electronic spreadsheets eliminate the need to manually erase data and recalculate totals when a change is made. Electronic spreadsheets are regularly used by accountants to perform "What if?" financial analysis.

## SUMMARY OF USING AN AUTOMATED GENERAL LEDGER ACCOUNTING SYSTEM

Petlodge's automated general ledger accounting system is summarized in Illustration 11-15 below and on page 238. Steps 1 through 8 were described in Chapter 10. Steps 9 through 23 are presented in this chapter.

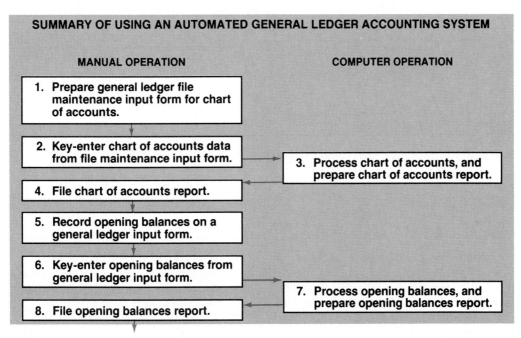

Illustration 11-15     Summary of using an automated general ledger accounting system

SUMMARY OF USING AN AUTOMATED GENERAL LEDGER ACCOUNTING SYSTEM

**MANUAL OPERATION**             **COMPUTER OPERATION**

9. Journalize transaction data on general ledger input form.

10. Key-enter journal entries from input form.

11. Process journal entries, and prepare journal entries report.

12. Prove cash.

13. File journal entries report.

14. Prepare trial balance at end of fiscal period.

15. Journalize adjusting entries on general ledger input form.

16. File trial balance.

17. Key-enter adjusting entries from input form.

18. Process adjusting entries, and prepare journal entries report.

19. File journal entries report.

20. Prepare income statement and balance sheet.

21. File income statement and balance sheet.

22. Process closing entries and prepare post-closing trial balance.

23. File post-closing trial balance.

Illustration 11-15     Summary of using an automated general ledger accounting system (concluded)

## ◼ ACCOUNTING TERMS

What is the meaning of each of the following?

1. account form of balance sheet
2. report form of balance sheet
3. electronic spreadsheet

## ◼ QUESTIONS FOR INDIVIDUAL STUDY

1. What items should be considered before deciding to change from a manual to an automated accounting system?
2. What form is used to enter deletions from and additions to a general ledger chart of accounts?

3. Why is a word which is not to be entered into a computer written in parentheses in the Account Title column of a file maintenance input form?
4. Which accounting concept is being applied when Petlodge decides to add a

second rent expense account?

5. How does Petlodge assign account numbers within each general ledger division?

6. Where is transaction data recorded before being entered into a computer?

7. In automated accounting, how are transaction data posted to general ledger accounts?

8. Why does Petlodge enter transaction data into the computer weekly instead of daily?

9. Why does Petlodge keep some money in a petty cash fund?

10. After a journal entries report is prepared, how does Petlodge check the report for accuracy?

11. How often does Petlodge prove cash?

12. Why is a computer generated trial balance prepared at the end of a fiscal period?

13. How does Petlodge determine acceptable component percentages?

14. Why does Petlodge's automated accounting system not require manual recording of closing entries?

15. Why do accountants use electronic spreadsheets?

## ▆ CASES FOR MANAGEMENT DECISION

**CASE 1** Irma Angulo is starting a new business called Quality Tailor Services. She has rented a microcomputer and software for an automated general ledger accounting system. In building her general ledger chart of accounts, she plans to use a two-digit general ledger account number. What problems, if any, will a two-digit general ledger account number create?

**CASE 2** Bruce Miller owns and operates a chain of five health clubs. One club is located in the downtown business area. Four clubs are located in suburban areas. A computer system is installed in the downtown club. All five clubs use a general ledger input form to record daily transactions for computer processing. Each morning a general ledger input form is prepared for the previous day's business. The completed forms are delivered to the downtown club to be processed by the computer. The automated accounting procedures do not provide a way to distinguish in which club transactions occurred. Data are processed as if only one club were involved. A need exists to be able to analyze business activity by club. What changes might be made so that transactions could be identified by club?

## ▆ DRILLS FOR UNDERSTANDING

### DRILL 11-D1  Adding new general ledger account numbers

This drill provides practice in assigning account numbers to new accounts being added to a general ledger chart of accounts. Use the following partial chart of accounts and list of new accounts to be added to the chart of accounts.

| Account No. | Account Title | New Accounts to Be added |
|---|---|---|
| 110 | Cash | Petty Cash |
| 120 | Supplies—Office | Supplies—Store |
| 130 | Prepaid Insurance | Draper Enterprises |
| 210 | Adkins Supply Company | Equipment Repair Expense |
| 510 | Advertising Expense | Insurance Expense |
| 520 | Miscellaneous Expense | Rent Expense—Computer |
| 530 | Rent Expense—Store | Supplies Expense—Store |
| 540 | Supplies Expense—Office | Utilities Expense |

Use a form similar to the following.

| 1 | 2 |
|---|---|
| **New General Ledger Account Title** | **Account Number Assigned** |
| *Petty Cash* | *115* |

**Instructions: 1.** In Column 1 write the account titles of the new accounts to be added to the general ledger chart of accounts.

**2.** In Column 2 write the account number assigned to each new account title. Use the unused middle number method of assigning new account numbers. The account number assigned to Petty Cash is given as an example.

### DRILL 11-D2   Analyzing steps completed in an automated accounting system

**Instructions:** Refer to Illustration 11-15, pages 237–238, and answer the following questions.

1. What form is used to journalize transactions?
2. Is proving cash a manual or computer operation?
3. What form is used to journalize adjusting entries?
4. Does the printing of a trial balance at the end of a fiscal period precede or follow the planning of adjusting entries?
5. Is the processing of adjusting entries a manual or computer operation?
6. Is the preparation of an income statement and a balance sheet a manual or computer operation?
7. Is the processing of closing entries a manual or computer operation?
8. Is the preparation of a post-closing trial balance a manual or computer operation?

## ▊ APPLICATION PROBLEMS

### PROBLEM 11-1   Performing file maintenance activities

Kortage Small Engine Repair performed the following file maintenance activities.

| Accounts Deleted | | Accounts Added | |
|---|---|---|---|
| 220 | Lapham Services Co. | 135 | Supplies—Parts |
| 560 | Utilities Expense | 550 | Supplies Expense—Parts |

**Instructions:** Prepare a general ledger file maintenance input form (FORM GL-1). Use November 1 of the current year as the run date.

### PROBLEM 11-2   Journalizing transactions on a general ledger input form

Sowle Travel Agency has the following general ledger chart of accounts.

| Account No. | Account Title | Account No. | Account Title |
|---|---|---|---|
| 110 | Cash | 410 | Fees |
| 120 | Petty Cash | 510 | Advertising Expense |
| 130 | Supplies—Computer | 530 | Miscellaneous Expense |
| 140 | Supplies—Office | 540 | Rent Expense—Computer |
| 210 | Grant Computer Products | 550 | Rent Expense—Office |
| 220 | Poyer Office Supply | 580 | Utilities Expense |
| 310 | Hazel Sowle, Capital | | |
| 320 | Hazel Sowle, Drawing | | |

**Instructions: 1.** Journalize the following transactions on a general ledger input form (FORM GL-2). Use June 6 of the current year as the run date. Batch No. 2. Source documents are abbreviated as follows: check, C; receipt, R; cash register tape, T.

*Transactions*

June  1. Paid cash for office rent, $950.00. C145.
1. Paid cash for computer rent, $825.00. C146.
1. Paid cash to owner for personal use, $600.00. C147.
2. Paid cash for office supplies, $263.00. C148.
2. Paid cash on account to Grant Computer Products, $360.00. C149.
3. Paid cash for advertising, $85.00. C150.
3. Paid cash for computer supplies, $135.00. C151.
4. Paid cash for miscellaneous expense, $45.00. C152.
4. Received cash from owner as an investment, $3,500.00. R23.
5. Paid cash on account to Poyer Office Supply, $265.00. C153.
5. Paid cash for electric bill, $145.00. C154.
6. Paid cash to replenish the petty cash fund, $201.00: computer supplies, $76.00; office supplies, $72.00; miscellaneous, $53.00. C155.
6. Received cash from fees, $1,986.00. T6.

**2.** Total and prove the Debit Amount and Credit Amount columns. Record the batch totals.

## PROBLEM 11-3  Journalizing adjusting entries on a general ledger input form

Velo Accounting Service has the following general ledger accounts that need adjustment at the end of the fiscal period.

| Account No. | Account Title | Account Balance |
|---|---|---|
| 130 | Supplies—Computer.................. | $1,220.00 |
| 140 | Supplies—Office ...................... | 1,740.00 |
| 150 | Prepaid Insurance ..................... | 1,280.00 |
| 530 | Insurance Expense ..................... | — |
| 560 | Supplies Expense—Computer .......... | — |
| 570 | Supplies Expense—Office.............. | — |

**Adjustment Information, August 31**

| | |
|---|---|
| Value of computer supplies on hand.................... | $ 865.00 |
| Value of office supplies on hand ...................... | 1,380.00 |
| Value of prepaid insurance ........................... | 1,120.00 |

**Instructions: 1.** Journalize the adjusting entries on a general ledger input form (FORM GL-2). Use August 31 of the current year as the run date. Batch No. 7.

    **2.** Total and prove the Debit Amount and Credit Amount columns. Record the batch totals.

## ■ ENRICHMENT PROBLEMS

**MASTERY PROBLEM 11-M**    **Preparing input forms for an automated accounting system**

Arthur's Bowling Lanes has the following general ledger chart of accounts.

| Balance Sheet Accounts | | Income Statement Accounts | |
|---|---|---|---|
| **(100) ASSETS** | | **(400) REVENUE** | |
| 110 | Cash | 410 | Sales |
| 120 | Supplies—Bowling | | |
| 130 | Supplies—Office | | **(500) EXPENSES** |
| 140 | Prepaid Insurance | | |
| | | 510 | Advertising Expense |
| **(200) LIABILITIES** | | 520 | Insurance Expense |
| | | 530 | Miscellaneous Expense |
| 210 | Costello Bowling Supplies | 540 | Rent Expense |
| 220 | Hayes Office Supply | 550 | Supplies Expense—Bowling |
| 230 | Top-Line Bowling Supplies | 560 | Supplies Expense—Office |
| **(300) OWNER'S EQUITY** | | | |
| 310 | Clyde Arthur, Capital | | |
| 320 | Clyde Arthur, Drawing | | |
| 330 | Income Summary | | |

Arthur's Bowling Lanes performed the following file maintenance activities.

| **Account Deleted** | **Account Title Change** | **Accounts Added** |
|---|---|---|
| Advertising Expense | Rent Expense | Petty Cash |
| | TO | Rent Expense — Computer |
| | Rent Expense — Building | Utilities Expense |

**Instructions: 1.** Assign account numbers to the new accounts using the unused middle number method.

**2.** Prepare a general ledger file maintenance input form (FORM GL-1). Use December 1 of the current year as the run date.

**3.** Journalize the following transactions on a general ledger input form (FORM GL-2). Use December 31 of the current year as the run date. Batch No. 6. Source documents are abbreviated as follows: check, C; receipt, R; cash register tape, T.

*Transactions*

Dec. 27. Paid cash for miscellaneous expense, $125.00. C235.
　27. Paid cash for bowling supplies, $185.00. C236.
　28. Paid cash for office supplies, $143.00. C237.
　29. Paid cash on account to Costello Bowling Supplies, $438.00. C238.
　29. Received cash from owner as an investment, $4,000.00. R12.
　30. Paid cash for miscellaneous expense, $95.00. C239.
　30. Paid cash to replenish the petty cash fund, $103.00: bowling supplies, $42.00; office supplies, $36.00; miscellaneous, $25.00. C240.
　30. Paid cash for telephone bill, $116.00. C241.
　31. Paid cash for computer rent, $835.00. C242.
　31. Paid cash to owner for personal use, $850.00. C243.
　31. Received cash from sales, $1,980.00. T31.

**4.** Total and prove the Debit Amount and Credit Amount columns. Record the batch totals.

**5.** The following accounts need adjustment at the end of the fiscal period. Journalize the adjusting entries on a general ledger input form (FORM GL-2). Use December 31 of the current year as the run date. Batch No. 7.

| Account Title | Account Balance |
|---|---|
| Supplies — Bowling . . . . . . . . . . . . . . . . . . . . . . . . . . . . . . . . . . . | $2,110.00 |
| Supplies — Office . . . . . . . . . . . . . . . . . . . . . . . . . . . . . . . . . . . . | 1,427.00 |
| Prepaid Insurance . . . . . . . . . . . . . . . . . . . . . . . . . . . . . . . . . . | 1,890.00 |

**Adjustment Information, December 31**

| | |
|---|---|
| Value of bowling supplies on hand . . . . . . . . . . . . . . . . . . . . . | $1,480.00 |
| Value of office supplies on hand . . . . . . . . . . . . . . . . . . . . . . | 940.00 |
| Value of prepaid insurance . . . . . . . . . . . . . . . . . . . . . . . . . . . | 1,680.00 |

**6.** Total and prove the Debit Amount and Credit Amount columns. Record the batch totals.

**CHALLENGE PROBLEM 11-C   Preparing input forms for an automated accounting system**

ShurFit Tailors has the following general ledger chart of accounts.

|                    |                              |
|--------------------|------------------------------|
| <u>Balance Sheet Accounts</u> | <u>Income Statement Accounts</u> |

**(100) ASSETS**

| 110 | Cash |
| 120 | Petty Cash |
| 130 | Supplies—Fabric |
| 140 | Supplies—Office |
| 150 | Prepaid Insurance |

**(200) LIABILITIES**

| 210 | Empire Fabrics |
| 220 | Ganto Office Supply |
| 230 | Palm Fabrics |

**(300) OWNER'S EQUITY**

| 310 | Linda Kline, Capital |
| 320 | Linda Kline, Drawing |
| 330 | Income Summary |

**(400) REVENUE**

| 410 | Tailoring Fees |

**(500) EXPENSES**

| 510 | Advertising Expense |
| 520 | Insurance Expense |
| 530 | Miscellaneous Expense |
| 540 | Rent Expense |
| 550 | Supplies Expense—Fabric |
| 560 | Supplies Expense—Office |

ShurFit Tailors performed the following file maintenance activities.

| **Account Deleted** | **Account Title Change** | **Accounts Added** |
|---------------------|--------------------------|--------------------|
| Empire Fabrics | Rent Expense | Regarus Textiles |
|  | TO | Rent Expense—Computer |
|  | Rent Expense—Building | Utilities Expense |

**Instructions: 1.** Assign account numbers to the new accounts using the unused middle number method.

**2.** Prepare a general ledger file maintenance input form (FORM GL-1). Use July 1 of the current year as the run date.

**3.** Journalize the following transactions on a general ledger input form (FORM GL-2). Use July 31 of the current year as the run date. Batch No. 6. Source documents are abbreviated as follows: check, C; receipt, R; cash register tape, T.

*Transactions*

July 27. Paid cash for fabric supplies, $255.00. C335.
  27. Paid cash for advertising, $130.00. C336.
  28. Paid cash for office supplies, $93.00. C337.
  29. Paid cash on account to Palm Fabrics, $387.00. C338.
  29. Received cash from owner as an investment, $3,000.00. R15.
  30. Paid cash for miscellaneous expense, $45.00. C339.
  30. Paid cash to replenish the petty cash fund, $205.00: fabric supplies, $102.00; office supplies, $57.00; miscellaneous, $46.00. C340.

July 30. Paid cash for electric bill, $146.00. C341.
   31. Paid cash for computer rent, $780.00. C342.
   31. Paid cash to owner for personal use, $750.00. C343.
   31. Received cash from tailoring fees, $1,740.00. T31.

**4.** Total and prove the Debit Amount and Credit Amount columns. Record the batch totals.

**5.** The following accounts need adjustment at the end of the fiscal period. Journalize the adjusting entries on a general ledger input form (FORM GL-2). Use July 31 of the current year as the run date. Batch No. 7.

| Account Title | Account Balance |
|---|---|
| Supplies—Fabric...................................... | $1,930.00 |
| Supplies—Office...................................... | 1,480.00 |
| Prepaid Insurance.................................... | 1,520.00 |

| Adjustment Information, July 31 | |
|---|---|
| Value of fabric supplies on hand ...................... | $1,360.00 |
| Value of office supplies on hand ...................... | 1,233.00 |
| Value of prepaid insurance ........................... | 1,330.00 |

**6.** Total and prove the Debit Amount and Credit Amount columns. Record the batch totals.

*The solution to Challenge Problem 11-C is needed to complete Computer Application 2.*

# Computer Application 2
# Using an Automated Accounting System

The general ledger file maintenance input form and the general ledger input forms completed in Challenge Problem 11-C, Chapter 11, are needed to complete Computer Application 2.

ShurFit Tailors completed the input forms for using an automated accounting system. The manual and computer operations required are described in Chapter 11. Computer Application 2 provides an opportunity to process the data from the completed forms using a microcomputer.

Computer Application 2 is designed to be used with the *Automated Accounting for the Microcomputer*, 3d edition, software. The software provides the option of either displaying or printing reports. If a printer is available, select the *Print* option when given the choice of displaying or printing reports. If a printer is not available, select the *Display* option. Selecting the *Display* option causes the report to be displayed on the computer monitor.

## ■ COMPUTER APPLICATION PROBLEM

**COMPUTER APPLICATION PROBLEM 2**  **Using an automated accounting system**

**Instructions: 1.** Load the *Automated Accounting for the Microcomputer* software. Select Computer Application 2 (CA-2) from the CENTURY 21 ACCOUNTING Template Disk. The accounting system data, chart of accounts, opening balances, and company name have been entered and are stored on the Template Disk.

**2.** Key-enter the file maintenance data from the completed general ledger file maintenance input form prepared in Challenge Problem 11-C.

**3.** Display/Print the revised chart of accounts report. Check the report for accuracy.

**4.** Key-enter the transactions from the completed general ledger input form prepared in Challenge Problem 11-C.

**5.** Display/Print the journal entries report. Check the report for accuracy by comparing the report totals with the batch totals on the general ledger input form.

**6.** Prove cash. The beginning cash balance was $10,850.00. The balance on the next unused check stub is $12,799.00.

**7.** Display/Print the trial balance.

**8.** Key-enter the adjusting entries from the completed general ledger input form prepared in Challenge Problem 11-C.

**9.** Display/Print the journal entries report. Check the report for accuracy by comparing the report totals with the totals on the general ledger input form.

**10.** Display/Print the income statement.

**11.** Display/Print the balance sheet.

**12.** Close the ledger.

**13.** Display/Print the post-closing trial balance.

# Partnership Accounting for a Merchandising Business

# 3

**GENERAL BEHAVIORAL GOALS**

1. Know accounting terminology related to an accounting system for a merchandising business organized as a partnership.
2. Understand accounting concepts and practices related to an accounting system for a merchandising business organized as a partnership.
3. Demonstrate accounting procedures used in an accounting system for a merchandising business organized as a partnership.

# CARLAND
## Chart of Accounts
### General Ledger

| Balance Sheet Accounts | Income Statement Accounts |
|---|---|

## (1000) ASSETS

1110  Cash
1120  Petty Cash
1130  Accounts Receivable
1140  Merchandise Inventory
1145  Supplies—Office
1150  Supplies—Store
1160  Prepaid Insurance

## (2000) LIABILITIES

2110  Accounts Payable
2120  Employee Income Tax Payable
2130  FICA Tax Payable
2140  Sales Tax Payable
2150  Unemployment Tax Payable—Federal
2160  Unemployment Tax Payable—State
2170  Health Insurance Premiums Payable
2180  U.S. Savings Bonds Payable
2190  United Way Donations Payable

## (3000) OWNERS' EQUITY

3110  Amy Kramer, Capital
3120  Amy Kramer, Drawing
3130  Dario Mesa, Capital
3140  Dario Mesa, Drawing
3150  Income Summary

## (4000) OPERATING REVENUE

4110  Sales

## (5000) COST OF MERCHANDISE

5110  Purchases

## (6000) OPERATING EXPENSES

6110  Advertising Expense
6120  Credit Card Fee Expense
6130  Insurance Expense
6140  Miscellaneous Expense
6150  Payroll Taxes Expense
6160  Rent Expense
6170  Salary Expense
6175  Supplies Expense—Office
6180  Supplies Expense—Store
6190  Utilities Expense

---

## Subsidiary Ledgers

| Accounts Receivable Ledger | Accounts Payable Ledger |
|---|---|
| 110  Ashley Delivery | 210  Antelo Supply |
| 120  Autohaus Service | 220  Bell Office Products |
| 130  Friendly Auto Service | 230  Filtrex Tires |
| 140  Keystone Delivery | 240  Nilon Motor Parts |
| 150  Powell Rent-A-Car | 250  Q-Ban Distributors |
| 160  Wood Sales & Service | 260  Veloz Automotive |

The charts of accounts for CarLand are illustrated above for
ready reference as you study Part 3 of this textbook.

# Journalizing Purchases and Cash Payments

## ENABLING PERFORMANCE TASKS

After studying Chapter 12, you will be able to:

a. Define accounting terms related to purchases and cash payments for a merchandising business.

b. Identify accounting concepts and practices related to purchases and cash payments for a merchandising business.

c. Analyze purchases and cash payments transactions for a merchandising business.

d. Journalize purchases and cash payments transactions for a merchandising business.

Rugcare, the business described in Part 1, is owned by one person. Petlodge, described in Part 2, is also owned by one person. A business owned by one person is known as a proprietorship.

Many businesses require the skills of more than one person. Many businesses also need more capital than one owner can provide. Therefore, many businesses are owned by two or more persons. A business in which two or more persons combine their assets and skills is called a partnership. Each member of a partnership is called a partner. Partners must agree on how each partner will share the business' profit or loss. As in proprietorships, reports and financial records of the business are kept separate from the personal records of the partners. (CONCEPT: Business Entity)

Both Rugcare and Petlodge, the businesses described in Parts 1 and 2, sell services for a fee. A business that sells a service for a fee is known as a service business. However, many other businesses purchase goods to sell. A business that purchases and sells goods is called a merchandising business. Goods that a merchandising business purchases to sell are called merchandise. The selling of merchandise rather than a service is what makes the activities of a merchandising business different from those of a service business.

CarLand, the business described in this part, is a merchandising business organized as a partnership. The business is owned by Amy Kramer and Dario Mesa. The business purchases and sells automotive supplies. CarLand rents the building in which the business is located as well as the equipment used for operation. CarLand expects to make money and continue in business indefinitely. *(CONCEPT: Going Concern)*

# USING AN EXPANDED JOURNAL

A service business generally has a large number of cash transactions and a limited number of noncash transactions. Noncash transactions are those that do not involve either the receipt or payment of cash. Rugcare uses a 5-column journal, described in Part 1, to record all cash and noncash transactions.

## Need for expanded journal

CarLand, a merchandising business, has many noncash and other frequently occurring transactions that affect single accounts. CarLand could use the same journal as the one used by Rugcare. However, without adding more special amount columns to the journal, the large number of transactions would require many entries in the General Debit and Credit columns.

## Form of expanded journal

To save time and space in journalizing transactions, CarLand uses an 11-column journal. The journal includes additional special amount columns for recording frequently occurring transactions that affect single accounts. A journal expanded to provide for the recording of frequently occurring transactions that affect single accounts is shown in Illustration 12-1.

Illustration 12-1
Amount columns of an
expanded journal

An expanded journal is commonly used by small merchandising businesses in which only one person records transactions. Amy Kramer records all transactions for CarLand.

CarLand's journal, Illustration 12-1, has special amount columns for the recording of frequently occurring transactions related to the purchasing and selling of merchandise. The columns are arranged to make accurate journalizing and posting easier. Debit and credit columns for Cash, Accounts Receivable, and Accounts Payable are arranged in pairs. This arrangement helps avoid errors in recording amounts in the wrong columns. All columns are placed to the right of the Account Title column. The General Debit and Credit amount columns are placed first so that amounts in these columns will be close to the titles in the Account Title column.

> The number and arrangement of columns in a journal is determined by the type and frequency of transactions. CarLand determined that the journal described above would best meet the needs of the business.

## JOURNALIZING PURCHASES OF MERCHANDISE

The price a business pays for goods it purchases to sell is called cost of merchandise. The selling price of merchandise must be greater than the cost of merchandise for a business to make a profit. The amount added to the cost of merchandise to establish the selling price is called markup. Revenue earned from the sale of merchandise includes both the cost of merchandise and markup. Only the markup increases capital. Accounts for the cost of merchandise are kept in a separate division of the general ledger. The cost of merchandise division is shown in CarLand's chart of accounts, page 250.

In addition to purchasing merchandise to sell, a merchandising business also buys supplies and other assets for use in the business. A business from which merchandise is purchased or supplies or other assets are bought is called a vendor.

The account used for recording the cost of merchandise purchased to sell is titled Purchases. Purchases is classified as a cost account because it is in the cost of merchandise division in the chart of accounts. The cost account Purchases is a temporary account. Because the cost of merchandise purchased for resale reduces capital when the merchandise is sold, the cost account Purchases has a normal debit balance. Therefore, the purchases account is increased by a debit and decreased by a credit, as shown in the T account.

| Purchases | |
| --- | --- |
| Debit side<br>Normal balance<br>Increase | Credit side<br><br>Decrease |

The cost account, Purchases, is used only to record the value of merchandise purchased. Therefore, only purchases of merchandise are recorded in the Purchases Debit column of the journal. All other items bought, such as supplies, are recorded in the General Debit column of the journal. Merchandise and other items bought are recorded and reported at the price agreed upon at the time the transactions occur. The price agreed upon at the time the transaction occurs may be lower than the given price. The accounting concept, *Historical Cost*, is applied when the actual amount paid for merchandise or other items bought is recorded. *(CONCEPT: Historical Cost)*

## Purchase of merchandise for cash

CarLand pays cash for some purchases. All cash payments are made by check.

November 2, 19--.
Purchased merchandise for cash, $483.00. Check No. 259.

The source document for a cash purchase is the check issued. *(CONCEPT: Objective Evidence)*

A cash purchase transaction increases the purchases account balance and decreases the cash account balance. The analysis of the cash purchase transaction is shown in the T accounts.

Because the purchases account has a normal debit balance, Purchases is debited for $483.00 to show the increase in this cost account. The cash account also has a normal debit balance. Therefore, Cash is credited for $483.00 to show the decrease in this asset account.

The journal entry to record this transaction is shown in Illustration 12-2.

```
            Purchases
   483.00   |

              Cash
            |   483.00
```

Illustration 12-2
Journal entry to record a
purchase of merchandise
for cash

| | DATE | | ACCOUNT TITLE | DOC. NO. | POST. REF. | | PURCHASES DEBIT | CASH DEBIT | CASH CREDIT | |
|---|---|---|---|---|---|---|---|---|---|---|
| | | | PAGE 21 | | | | 9 | 10 | 11 | |
| 1 | 19-- Nov. | 2 | √ | C259 | √ | | 4 8 3 00 | | 4 8 3 00 | 1 |

The date, *19--, Nov. 2*, is recorded in the Date column. Both the debit and credit amounts will be recorded in special amount columns. Therefore, a check mark is placed in the Account Title column to show that no account title needs to be written. The check number, *C259*, is recorded in the Doc. No. column. Both the debit and credit amounts will be posted as part of special amount column totals. Therefore, a check mark is placed in the Post. Ref. column to show that amounts on this line are not to be posted individually. The debit to Purchases, *$483.00*, is entered in the Purchases Debit column. The credit to Cash, *$483.00*, is entered in the Cash Credit column.

## Purchase of merchandise on account

A transaction in which the merchandise purchased is to be paid for later is called a purchase on account. Some businesses that purchase on account from only a few vendors keep a separate general ledger account for each vendor to whom money is owed. Businesses that purchase on account from many vendors will have many accounts for vendors. To avoid a bulky general ledger, the total amount owed to all vendors can be summarized in a single general ledger account. A liability account that summarizes the amounts owed to all vendors is titled Accounts Payable. CarLand uses an accounts payable account.

The liability account, Accounts Payable, has a normal credit balance. Therefore, the accounts payable account is increased by a credit and decreased by a debit, as shown in the T account.

| Accounts Payable | |
|---|---|
| Debit side | Credit side |
| | Normal balance |
| Decrease | Increase |

When a vendor sells merchandise to a buyer, the vendor prepares a form showing what has been sold. A form describing the goods sold, the quantity, and the price is called an invoice. An invoice used as a source document for recording a purchase on account transaction is called a purchase invoice. (CONCEPT: Objective Evidence) A purchase invoice received by CarLand is shown in Illustration 12-3.

| | | | REC'D 11/02/-- P74 |
|---|---|---|---|

veloz automotive
2611 Industrial
Fremont, NH 03044-2672

TO: CarLand
1374 Parklane
Rockville, RI 02873-4121

DATE:  10/26/--
INV. NO.:  2768
TERMS:  30 days
ACCT. NO.:  260

| QUANTITY | CAT. NO. | DESCRIPTION | UNIT PRICE | TOTAL |
|---|---|---|---|---|
| 8 | 4422 | All-season tires | 73.00 | 584.00✓ |
| 6 | 4424 | All-season tires | 73.00 | 438.00✓ |
| 12 | 6620 | Floor mats | 16.00 | 192.00✓ |
| 12 | 7715 | Seat covers | 45.00 | 540.00✓ |
| | | Total | | 1,754.00 |

Illustration 12-3
Purchase invoice

A purchase invoice lists the quantity, the description, the price of each item, and the total amount of the invoice. A purchase invoice provides the information needed for recording a purchase on account.

When CarLand receives a purchase invoice, a date and a number are stamped in the upper right-hand corner. The date stamped is the date the invoice is received. CarLand received the invoice in Illustration 12-3 on 11/02/--. This date should not be confused with the vendor's date on the invoice, 10/26/--. CarLand assigns numbers in sequence to easily identify all purchase invoices. The number stamped on the invoice, *P74*, is the number assigned by CarLand to this purchase invoice. This number should not be confused with the invoice number, 2768, assigned by the vendor. Each vendor uses a different numbering system. Therefore, vendor invoice numbers could not be recorded in sequence, which would make it impossible to detect a missing invoice.

A buyer needs to know that all items ordered have been received and that the prices are correct. The check marks on the invoice show that the items have been received and that amounts have been checked and are correct. The initials near the total are those of the person at CarLand who checked the invoice.

An agreement between a buyer and a seller about payment for merchandise is called the terms of sale. The terms of sale on the invoice, Illustration 12-3, are 30 days. These terms mean that payment is due within 30 days from the date of the invoice. The invoice is dated October 26. Therefore, payment must be made by November 25.

*November 2, 19--.*
*Purchased merchandise on account from Veloz Automotive, $1,754.00. Purchase Invoice No. 74.*

The source document for a purchase on account is the purchase invoice received with the merchandise. *(CONCEPT: Objective Evidence)*

A purchase on account transaction increases the amount owed to a vendor. This transaction increases the purchases account balance and increases the accounts payable account balance. The analysis of this purchase on account transaction is shown in the T accounts.

Because the purchases account has a normal debit balance, Purchases is debited for $1,754.00 to show the increase in this cost account. The accounts payable account has a normal credit balance. Therefore, Accounts Payable is credited for $1,754.00 to show the increase in this liability account.

Illustration 12-4
Journal entry to record a
purchase of merchandise
on account

The journal entry to record this purchase on account transaction is shown in Illustration 12-4.

| PAGE *21* | | | | JOURNAL | | | ACCOUNTS PAYABLE | | PURCHASES DEBIT |
|---|---|---|---|---|---|---|---|---|---|
| | DATE | ACCOUNT TITLE | DOC. NO. | POST. REF. | | 7 | 8 | 9 | |
| | | | | | | DEBIT | CREDIT | | |
| 2 | 2 | *Veloz Automotive* | *P74* | | | | 1 7 5 4 00 | 1 7 5 4 00 | |

The date, 2, is written in the Date column. No special amount column is provided for Veloz Automotive. Therefore, the vendor's name, *Veloz Automotive*, is recorded in the Account Title column. CarLand's purchase invoice number, *P74*, is entered in the Doc. No. column. The credit to Accounts Payable, *$1,754.00*, is recorded in the Accounts Payable Credit column. The debit to Purchases, *$1,754.00*, is recorded in the Purchases Debit column.

The debit to Purchases and the credit to Accounts Payable are recorded in special amount columns. Therefore, writing the titles of either general ledger account in the Account Title column is not necessary. However, the name of the vendor is written in the Account Title column to show to whom the amount is owed. The way CarLand keeps records of the amount owed to each vendor is described in Chapter 14.

## JOURNALIZING BUYING SUPPLIES

CarLand buys supplies for use in the business. Supplies are not recorded in the purchases account because supplies are not intended for sale. Cash register tapes and price tags are examples of supplies used in a merchandising business.

### Buying supplies for cash

CarLand buys most of its supplies for cash.

*November 5, 19--.*
*Paid cash for office supplies, $87.00. Check No. 261.*

The source document for buying supplies for cash is the check issued in payment. *(CONCEPT: Objective Evidence)*

This transaction increases the office supplies account balance and decreases the cash account balance. The analysis of the buying supplies for cash transaction is shown in the T accounts.

Because the office supplies account has a normal debit balance, Supplies—Office is debited for $87.00 to show the increase in this asset account. The cash account also has a normal debit balance. Therefore, Cash is credited for $87.00 to show the decrease in this asset account.

The journal entry to record this buying supplies for cash transaction is shown in Illustration 12-5, page 258.

The date, 5, is recorded in the Date column. No special amount column is provided for Supplies—Office. Therefore, the account title, *Supplies—Office*, is written in the Account Title column. The check number, *C261*, is entered in the Doc. No. column. The debit to Supplies—Office, *$87.00*, is recorded in the General Debit column. The credit to Cash, *$87.00*, is recorded in the Cash Credit column.

| | PAGE 21 | | JOURNAL | | | | | | | | PAGE 21 | | |
|---|---|---|---|---|---|---|---|---|---|---|---|---|---|
| | | | | | | 1 | 2 | | | 10 | 11 | | |
| | DATE | ACCOUNT TITLE | DOC. NO. | POST. REF. | GENERAL | | | | CASH | | | |
| | | | | | DEBIT | CREDIT | | | DEBIT | CREDIT | | |
| 6 | 5 | Supplies—Office | C261 | | 8 7 00 | | | | | 8 7 00 | | 6 |
| 7 | | | | | | | | | | | | 7 |
| 8 | | | | | | | | | | | | 8 |

Illustration 12-5
Journal entry to record
buying supplies for cash

## Buying supplies on account

CarLand usually buys supplies for cash. Occasionally, however, Car-Land buys some supplies on account.

*November 6, 19--.*
*Bought store supplies on account from Antelo Supply, $160.00. Memorandum No. 43.*

When CarLand buys supplies on account, an invoice is received from the vendor. This invoice is similar to the purchase invoice received when merchandise is purchased. To assure that no mistake is made, a memorandum is attached to the invoice noting that the invoice is for supplies and not for purchases. Memorandum 43 is shown in Illustration 12-6.

**CARLAND**    **MEMORANDUM**

NO.  43
DATE November 6, 19--

Attached invoice is for store
supplies bought on account.

Illustration 12-6
Memorandum for buying
supplies on account

The source document for buying supplies on account is the memorandum with its attached invoice. (CONCEPT: *Objective Evidence*)

| Supplies—Store | |
|---|---|
| 160.00 | |

| Accounts Payable | |
|---|---|
| | 160.00 |

This transaction increases the store supplies account balance and increases the accounts payable account balance. The analysis of the buying supplies on account transaction is shown in the T accounts.

Because the store supplies account has a normal debit balance, Supplies—Store is debited for $160.00 to show the increase in this asset account. The accounts payable account has a normal credit balance. Therefore, Accounts Payable is credited for $160.00 to show the increase in this liability account.

The journal entry to record this buying supplies on account transaction is shown in Illustration 12-7.

Illustration 12-7
Journal entry to record
buying supplies on account

| | | | | | GENERAL | | | ACCOUNTS PAYABLE | |
| | | | | | 1 | 2 | | 7 | 8 |
| PAGE *21* | JOURNAL | | | | | | | | |
| DATE | ACCOUNT TITLE | DOC. NO. | POST. REF. | DEBIT | CREDIT | | DEBIT | CREDIT |
|---|---|---|---|---|---|---|---|---|---|
| 9 | 6 | *Supplies—Store* | *M43* | | *1 6 0 00* | | | | |
| 10 | | *Antelo Supply* | | | | | | | *1 6 0 00* |

The date, 6, is written in the Date column. No special amount column is provided for Supplies—Store. Therefore, the account title, *Supplies—Store*, is recorded in the Account Title column. The memorandum number, *M43*, is entered in the Doc. No. column. The debit to Supplies—Store, *$160.00*, is written in the General Debit column on the same line. An account title is also required for the credit part of the entry. Therefore, the vendor name, *Antelo Supply*, is recorded in the Account Title column on the next line. The credit to Accounts Payable, *$160.00*, is entered in the Accounts Payable Credit column on the same line.

# JOURNALIZING CASH PAYMENTS

Most of CarLand's cash payments are to vendors or for expenses. Payment to vendors is made according to the terms of sale on the purchase invoices. Payment for an expense is usually made at the time the expense occurs.

## Cash payment on account

CarLand pays by check for all cash purchases and for payments on account.

*November 7, 19--.*
*Paid cash on account to Filtrex Tires, $970.00, covering Purchase Invoice No. 72. Check No. 263.*

The source document for a cash payment on account is the check issued in payment. (CONCEPT: *Objective Evidence*)

This cash payment on account transaction decreases the amount owed to vendors. This transaction decreases the accounts payable account balance and decreases the cash account balance. The analysis of the cash payment on account transaction is shown in the T accounts.

Because the accounts payable account has a normal credit balance, Accounts Payable is debited for $970.00 to show the decrease in this liability account. The cash account has a normal debit balance. Therefore, Cash is credited for $970.00 to show the decrease in this asset account.

The journal entry to record this cash payment on account transaction is shown in Illustration 12-8.

| | DATE | ACCOUNT TITLE | DOC. NO. | POST. REF. | ACCOUNTS PAYABLE DEBIT | ACCOUNTS PAYABLE CREDIT | CASH DEBIT | CASH CREDIT | |
|---|---|---|---|---|---|---|---|---|---|
| 13 | 7 | *Filtrex Tires* | C263 | | 970 00 | | | 970 00 | 13 |
| 14 | | | | | | | | | 14 |
| 15 | | | | | | | | | 15 |
| 16 | | | | | | | | | 16 |

PAGE *21*   JOURNAL   PAGE *21*

*Illustration 12-8*
*Journal entry to record a cash payment on account*

The date, 7, is written in the Date column. No special amount column is provided for Filtrex Tires. Therefore, the vendor name, *Filtrex Tires*, is recorded in the Account Title column. The check number, *C263*, is entered in the Doc. No. column. The debit to Accounts Payable, *$970.00*, is written in the Accounts Payable Debit column. The credit to Cash, *$970.00*, is written in the Cash Credit column.

## Cash payment of an expense

CarLand usually pays for an expense at the time the transaction occurs.

*November 9, 19--.*
*Paid cash for advertising, $125.00. Check No. 265.*

The source document for a cash payment of an expense is the check issued in payment. *(CONCEPT: Objective Evidence)*

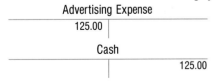

This cash payment increases the advertising expense account balance and decreases the cash account balance. The analysis of the cash payment of an expense transaction is shown in the T accounts.

Because the advertising expense account has a normal debit balance, Advertising Expense is debited for $125.00 to show the increase in this expense account. The cash account also has a normal debit balance. Therefore, Cash is credited for $125.00 to show the decrease in this asset account.

The journal entry to record this cash payment of an expense transaction is shown in Illustration 12-9.

| PAGE *21* | JOURNAL | | | | | | 1 | | 2 | | | | 10 | | PAGE *21* 11 | |
|---|---|---|---|---|---|---|---|---|---|---|---|---|---|---|---|---|
| | | | | DOC. NO. | POST. REF. | | GENERAL | | | | | | | CASH | | |
| DATE | ACCOUNT TITLE | | | | | | DEBIT | | CREDIT | | | | DEBIT | | CREDIT | |
| 17 | *9* | *Advertising Expense* | | *C265* | | | *1 2 5 00* | | | | | | | | *1 2 5 00* | 17 |
| 18 | | | | | | | | | | | | | | | | 18 |
| 19 | | | | | | | | | | | | | | | | 19 |

The date, *9,* is written in the Date column. No special amount column is provided for Advertising Expense. Therefore, the account title, *Advertising Expense,* is recorded in the Account Title column. The check number, *C265,* is entered in the Doc. No. column. The debit to Advertising Expense, *$125.00,* is written in the General Debit column. The credit to Cash, *$125.00,* is written in the Cash Credit column.

*Illustration 12-9*
*Journal entry to record a cash payment of an expense*

## Cash payment to replenish petty cash

CarLand deposits all cash in a bank. Some cash, however, is kept in a petty cash fund for making change at the cash register and for making small cash payments. CarLand has a petty cash fund of $500.00, which is replenished whenever the petty cash on hand drops below $200.00.

*November 9, 19--.*
*Paid cash to replenish the petty cash fund, $301.00: office supplies, $58.00; store supplies, $65.00; advertising, $92.00; miscellaneous, $86.00. Check No. 266.*

The source document for a cash payment to replenish petty cash is the check issued. *(CONCEPT: Objective Evidence)*

This cash payment increases the balances of the supplies accounts and several expense accounts and decreases the cash account balance. The analysis of the cash payment transaction to replenish petty cash is shown in the T accounts.

The supplies accounts have normal debit balances. Therefore, Supplies—Office is debited for $58.00 and Supplies—Store is debited for $65.00 to show the increases in these two asset accounts. The expense accounts also have normal debit balances. Therefore, Advertising Expense is debited for $92.00 and Miscellaneous Expense is debited for $86.00 to show the increases in these expense accounts. The cash account has a normal debit balance. Therefore, Cash is credited for $301.00, the total amount needed to replenish the petty cash fund, to show the decrease in this asset account.

| Supplies—Office | |
|---|---|
| 58.00 | |

| Supplies—Store | |
|---|---|
| 65.00 | |

| Advertising Expense | |
|---|---|
| 92.00 | |

| Miscellaneous Expense | |
|---|---|
| 86.00 | |

| Cash | |
|---|---|
| | 301.00 |

The journal entry to record this cash payment to replenish petty cash transaction is shown in Illustration 12-10, page 262.

| PAGE *21* | JOURNAL | | | | | | | PAGE *21* | |
|---|---|---|---|---|---|---|---|---|---|
| | | | | 1 | 2 | | | 10 | 11 |
| DATE | ACCOUNT TITLE | DOC. NO. | POST. REF. | GENERAL | | | | CASH | |
| | | | | DEBIT | CREDIT | | | DEBIT | CREDIT |
| 18    9 | *Supplies—Office* | C266 | | 5 8 00 | | | | | 3 0 1 00   18 |
| 19 | *Supplies—Store* | | | 6 5 00 | | | | | 19 |
| 20 | *Advertising Expense* | | | 9 2 00 | | | | | 20 |
| 21 | *Miscellaneous Expense* | | | 8 6 00 | | | | | 21 |

Illustration 12-10
Journal entry to record a
cash payment to replenish
petty cash

The date, *9*, is written once in the Date column, line 18. No special amount columns are provided for any of the accounts for which the petty cash fund was used. Therefore, the account titles are recorded in the Account Title column. The check number, *C266*, is entered once in the Doc. No. column, line 18. The debit amounts are written in the General Debit column. The credit amount is recorded in the Cash Credit column.

## JOURNALIZING OTHER TRANSACTIONS

Most transactions of merchandising businesses are related to purchasing and selling merchandise. A merchandising business, however, has other transactions that must be recorded. CarLand records these other transactions in its journal.

### Withdrawals by partners

| Amy Kramer, Drawing | |
|---|---|
| Debit side | Credit side |
| Normal balance | |
| Increase | Decrease |

| Dario Mesa, Drawing | |
|---|---|
| Debit side | Credit side |
| Normal balance | |
| Increase | Decrease |

Assets taken out of a business for the personal use of an owner are known as withdrawals. The two assets generally taken out of a merchandising business are cash and merchandise. Withdrawals reduce the amount of a business' capital. The account titles of the partners' drawing accounts are Amy Kramer, Drawing and Dario Mesa, Drawing. The drawing accounts are classified as contra capital accounts. Since capital accounts have credit balances, partners' drawing accounts have normal debit balances. Therefore, the drawing accounts are increased by a debit and decreased by a credit, as shown in the T accounts.

Withdrawals could be recorded as debits directly to the partners' capital accounts. However, withdrawals are normally recorded in separate accounts so that the total amounts are easily determined for each accounting period.

**Cash withdrawal.** When either Amy Kramer or Dario Mesa withdraws cash from CarLand, a check is written for the payment.

*November 10, 19--.*
*Dario Mesa, partner, withdrew cash for personal use, $1,500.00. Check No. 267.*

The source document for a cash withdrawal is the check issued. *(CONCEPT: Objective Evidence)*

This cash withdrawal increases Dario Mesa's drawing account balance and decreases the cash account balance. The analysis of the cash withdrawal transaction is shown in the T accounts.

| Dario Mesa, Drawing | |
|---|---|
| 1,500.00 | |

| Cash | |
|---|---|
| | 1,500.00 |

Because the drawing account has a normal debit balance, Dario Mesa, Drawing is debited for $1,500.00 to show the increase in this contra capital account. The cash account also has a normal debit balance. Therefore, Cash is credited for $1,500.00 to show the decrease in this asset account.

The journal entry to record this cash withdrawal is shown in Illustration 12-11.

| PAGE *21* | | | | | JOURNAL | | | | PAGE *21* |
|---|---|---|---|---|---|---|---|---|---|
| | | | | | 1 | 2 | | 10 | 11 |
| | DATE | ACCOUNT TITLE | DOC. NO. | POST. REF. | GENERAL DEBIT | GENERAL CREDIT | | CASH DEBIT | CASH CREDIT |
| 22 | 10 | *Dario Mesa, Drawing* | C267 | | 1 5 0 0 00 | | | | 1 5 0 0 00 |

Illustration 12-11
Journal entry to record a cash withdrawal by a partner

The date, *10*, is written in the Date column. No special amount column is provided for Dario Mesa, Drawing. Therefore, the contra capital account title, *Dario Mesa, Drawing*, is recorded in the Account Title column. The check number, *C267*, is entered in the Doc. No. column. The debit to Dario Mesa, Drawing, *$1,500.00*, is written in the General Debit column. The credit to Cash, *$1,500.00*, is written in the Cash Credit column.

**Merchandise withdrawal.** A partner may also withdraw merchandise for personal use.

*November 12, 19--.*
*Dario Mesa, partner, withdrew merchandise for personal use, $200.00. Memorandum No. 44.*

The source document for a withdrawal of merchandise is the memorandum prepared by the partner withdrawing the merchandise. *(CONCEPT: Objective Evidence)*

This merchandise withdrawal increases Dario Mesa's drawing account balance and decreases the purchases account balance. The analysis of the merchandise withdrawal transaction is shown in the T accounts.

| Dario Mesa, Drawing |
|---|
| 200.00 |

| Purchases |
|---|
| 200.00 |

Because the drawing account has a normal debit balance, Dario Mesa, Drawing is debited for $200.00 to show the increase in this contra capital account. The purchases account also has a normal debit balance. Therefore, Purchases is credited for $200.00 to show the decrease in this cost account.

The journal entry to record this merchandise withdrawal is shown in Illustration 12-12.

**Illustration 12-12**
Journal entry to record a merchandise withdrawal by a partner

| PAGE *21* | JOURNAL | | | | | |
|---|---|---|---|---|---|---|
| | | | | | 1 | 2 |
| DATE | ACCOUNT TITLE | DOC. NO. | POST. REF. | GENERAL | | |
| | | | | DEBIT | CREDIT | |
| 26 | *12* | *Dario Mesa, Drawing* | M44 | | 2 0 0 00 | |
| 27 | | *Purchases* | | | | 2 0 0 00 |

The date, *12*, is written in the Date column. Neither a Drawing Debit nor a Purchases Credit column is provided in the journal because merchandise withdrawals do not occur frequently. Therefore, the account title, *Dario Mesa, Drawing*, is recorded in the Account Title column. The memorandum number, *M44*, is entered in the Doc. No. column. The debit to Dario Mesa, Drawing, *$200.00*, is written in the General Debit column. The account title, *Purchases*, is recorded in the Account Title column on the next line. The credit to Purchases, *$200.00*, is entered in the General Credit column.

## Correcting entry

Errors may be made even though care is taken in recording transactions. Simple errors may be corrected by ruling through the incorrect item, as described in Chapter 4. However, a transaction may have been improperly journalized and posted to the ledger. When an error in a journal entry has already been posted, the incorrect journal entry should be corrected with an additional journal entry. A journal entry made to correct an error in the ledger is called a correcting entry.

*November 13, 19--.*
*Discovered that a payment of cash for advertising in October was journalized and posted in error as a debit to* Miscellaneous Expense *instead of* Advertising Expense, *$120.00. Memorandum No. 45.*

If an accounting error is discovered, a memorandum is prepared describing the correction to be made. The source document for a correcting entry is the memorandum prepared. *(CONCEPT: Objective Evidence)* A memorandum for this correcting entry is shown in Illustration 12-13.

To correct the error, an entry is made to add $120.00 to the advertising expense account. The entry must also deduct $120.00 from the miscellaneous expense account. The correcting entry increases the advertising expense account balance and decreases the miscellaneous expense account balance. The analysis of the correcting entry is shown in the T accounts.

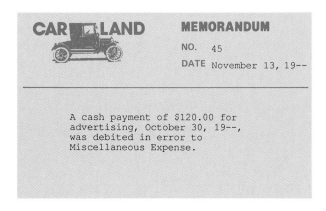

Illustration 12-13
Memorandum for a
correcting entry

Because the advertising expense account has a normal debit balance, Advertising Expense is debited for $120.00 to show the increase in this expense account. The miscellaneous expense account also has a normal debit balance. Therefore, Miscellaneous Expense is credited for $120.00 to show the decrease in this expense account.

Advertising Expense

| 120.00 | |

Miscellaneous Expense

| | 120.00 |

The journal entry to record this correcting entry is shown in Illustration 12-14.

| | DATE | ACCOUNT TITLE | DOC. NO. | POST. REF. | GENERAL DEBIT | GENERAL CREDIT |
|---|---|---|---|---|---|---|
| 28 | 13 | *Advertising Expense* | M45 | | 1 2 0 00 | |
| 29 | | *Miscellaneous Expense* | | | | 1 2 0 00 |

PAGE *21*   JOURNAL

Illustration 12-14
Journal entry to record a
correcting entry

The date, *13*, is written in the Date column. The account title, *Advertising Expense*, is recorded in the Account Title column. The memorandum number, *M45*, is entered in the Doc. No. column. The debit to Advertising Expense, *$120.00*, is entered in the General Debit column. The account title, *Miscellaneous Expense*, is written in the Account Title column on the next line. The credit to Miscellaneous Expense, *$120.00*, is recorded in the General Credit column.

# SUMMARY OF JOURNALIZING PURCHASES, CASH PAYMENTS, AND OTHER TRANSACTIONS

The chart shown in Illustration 12-15 summarizes the entries for purchases, cash payments, and other transactions in an expanded journal.

| TRANSACTION | JOURNAL | | | | | | | | | | |
| --- | --- | --- | --- | --- | --- | --- | --- | --- | --- | --- | --- |
| | 1 | 2 | 3 | 4 | 5 | 6 | 7 | 8 | 9 | 10 | 11 |
| | GENERAL | | ACCOUNTS RECEIVABLE | | SALES CREDIT | SALES TAX PAYABLE CREDIT | ACCOUNTS PAYABLE | | PURCHASES DEBIT | CASH | |
| | DEBIT | CREDIT | DEBIT | CREDIT | | | DEBIT | CREDIT | | DEBIT | CREDIT |
| Purchase merchandise for cash | | | | | | | | | X | | X |
| Purchase merchandise on account | | | | | | | | X | X | | |
| Buying supplies for cash | X | | | | | | | | | | X |
| Buying supplies on account | X | | | | | | | X | | | |
| Cash payment on account | | | | | | | X | | | | X |
| Cash payment of an expense | X | | | | | | | | | | X |
| Cash payment to replenish petty cash | X | | | | | | | | | | X |
| Cash withdrawal | X | | | | | | | | | | X |
| Merchandise withdrawal | X | X | | | | | | | | | |

Illustration 12-15    Summary of entries for purchases, cash payments, and other transactions in an expanded journal

## ■ ACCOUNTING TERMS

What is the meaning of each of the following?

1. partnership
2. partner
3. merchandising business
4. merchandise
5. cost of merchandise
6. markup
7. vendor
8. purchase on account
9. invoice
10. purchase invoice
11. terms of sale
12. correcting entry

## ■ QUESTIONS FOR INDIVIDUAL STUDY

1. Why would two or more persons want to own a single business?
2. What makes the activities of a merchandising business different from those of a service business?
3. What are noncash transactions?
4. Why does CarLand use an 11-column journal rather than a 5-column journal like the one used by Rugcare?
5. What is the title of the account that shows the cost of merchandise purchased for sale?
6. What is the account classification of Purchases?
7. Which accounting concept is being applied when merchandise and other items bought are recorded and reported at the price agreed upon at the time the transactions occur?
8. What accounts are affected, and how, when merchandise is purchased for cash?
9. Why is a check mark placed in the Account Title column of an expanded journal for a cash purchase transaction?
10. Why would a business use a single general ledger account to summarize the amount owed to all vendors?
11. What is the name of the liability account that summarizes the amounts owed to all vendors?
12. Why does CarLand use its own set of sequential purchase invoice numbers rather than using the numbers assigned by vendors?

13. What accounts are affected, and how, when merchandise is purchased on account?
14. Why are the account titles (Purchases and Accounts Payable) for a purchase on account entry not written in the Account Title column?
15. Why are supplies bought recorded in a separate supplies account rather than in the purchases account?
16. What accounts are affected, and how, when store supplies are bought on account?

17. What accounts are affected, and how, when a cash payment on account is made?
18. How does CarLand use a petty cash fund?
19. What accounts are affected, and how, when a withdrawal of merchandise is made?
20. When should a journal entry be made to correct errors in recording transactions?

## ◼ CASES FOR MANAGEMENT DECISION

**CASE 1** Deborah Butler owns and operates a gift shop in a downtown shopping area. Because of a shopping mall that has opened in one of the suburbs, the gift shop's business has been declining. Ms. Butler has an opportunity to move the business to the shopping mall. Additional capital, however, is required to move and operate the business in a new location. The local bank has agreed to lend the money needed. The business hours would be extended at the new location. The business would also be open seven days a week. The extended hours plus the expected increase in business would require the hiring of one additional employee. Ms. Butler has been contacted by Fred Chaney, a person with similar merchandising experience, who would like to become a partner. As an alternative to borrowing cash, Mr. Chaney would provide the capital necessary to move the business to the new location. For the capital provided, Mr. Chaney would share equally in the net income or loss of the business. Mr. Chaney would also share equally in the operation of the business. Should Ms. Butler (1) borrow the money from the bank, or (2) bring in a partner? Explain your answer.

**CASE 2** Daryl Hodges is a high school student who works part-time in a local clothing store. As part of his duties, he records daily transactions in a journal. One day he asks the owner: "You use the purchase invoice as your source document for recording purchases of merchandise on account. You use a memorandum as your source document for recording the entry when supplies are bought on account. Why don't you use the invoice for both entries?" How would you respond to this question?

## ◼ DRILLS FOR UNDERSTANDING

### DRILL 12-D1 **Analyzing transactions into debit and credit parts**

**Instructions:** Prepare two T accounts for each of the following transactions. Use the T accounts to analyze each transaction. Use account titles similar to CarLand's, as shown in the chart of accounts, page 250. The partners' names are Irma Gilbert and Alex Jensen. The first transaction is given as an example.

| Purchases | | Cash | |
|---|---|---|---|
| 200.00 | | | 200.00 |

*Transactions*

1. Purchased merchandise for cash, $200.00.
2. Purchased merchandise on account from Klein Co., $900.00.
3. Paid cash for office supplies, $75.00.
4. Bought store supplies on account from Central Supply, $240.00.
5. Bought office supplies on account from Cratin Supply, $125.00.
6. Purchased merchandise for cash, $175.00.
7. Paid cash for office supplies, $70.00.
8. Paid cash on account to Matson Company, $750.00.
9. Purchased merchandise on account from Garber Company, $1,200.00.
10. Paid cash for advertising, $85.00.
11. Irma Gilbert, partner, withdrew cash for personal use, $1,000.00.
12. Alex Jensen, partner, withdrew cash for personal use, $1,000.00.
13. Irma Gilbert, partner, withdrew merchandise for personal use, $130.00.
14. Paid cash on account to Butler Enterprises, $360.00.
15. Discovered that a transaction for office supplies bought last month was journalized and posted in error as a debit to Prepaid Insurance instead of Supplies—Office, $60.00.
16. Alex Jensen, partner, withdrew merchandise for personal use, $95.00.

*The solution to Drill 12-D1 is needed to complete Drill 12-D2.*

## DRILL 12-D2   Analyzing journal entries

*The solution to Drill 12-D1 is needed to complete Drill 12-D2.*

**Instructions:** Use a form similar to the following. Based on the answers in Drill 12-D1, write the amounts in the amount columns to be used to journalize each transaction. Transaction 1 is given as an example.

| Transaction | General | | Accounts Payable | | Purchases | Cash | |
|---|---|---|---|---|---|---|---|
| | Debit | Credit | Debit | Credit | Debit | Debit | Credit |
| 1. Debit amount | | | | | $200.00 | | |
| Credit amount | | | | | | | $200.00 |

## ■ APPLICATION PROBLEM

## PROBLEM 12-1   Journalizing purchases, cash payments, and other transactions

Mary Demski and Eileen Ivan, partners, own a gift shop.

**Instructions:** Journalize the following transactions completed during September of the current year. Use page 21 of a journal similar to the one described in this chapter for CarLand. Source documents are abbreviated as follows: check, C; memorandum, M; purchase invoice, P.

Sept.  1. Purchased merchandise for cash, $150.00. C220.
1. Purchased merchandise on account from Kemp Fashions, $1,350.00. P60.
2. Paid cash for office supplies, $75.00. C221.
2. Purchased merchandise on account from Bonner & Co., $740.00. P61.
3. Purchased merchandise on account from Burton Fabrics, $585.00. P62.

Sept.  4. Paid cash for office supplies, $55.00. C222.
7. Bought store supplies on account from Pulver Supply, $135.00. M42.
7. Purchased merchandise for cash, $120.00. C223.
8. Paid cash for telephone bill, $120.00. C224.
9. Bought office supplies on account from Lorand Supply, $85.00. M43.
11. Purchased merchandise for cash, $110.00. C225.
12. Paid cash for store supplies, $60.00. C226.
14. Mary Demski, partner, withdrew cash for personal use, $1,200.00. C227.
14. Eileen Ivan, partner, withdrew cash for personal use, $1,200.00. C228.
18. Paid cash on account to Kemp Fashions, $1,350.00, covering P60. C229.
21. Paid cash for advertising, $87.00. C230.
22. Paid cash on account to Bonner & Co., $740.00, covering P61. C231.
24. Mary Demski, partner, withdrew merchandise for personal use, $160.00. M44.
25. Discovered that a transaction for office supplies bought in August was journalized and posted in error as a debit to Purchases instead of Supplies—Office, $88.00. M45.
26. Paid cash on account to Burton Fabrics, $585.00, covering P62. C232.
29. Eileen Ivan, partner, withdrew merchandise for personal use, $120.00. M46.
30. Paid cash to replenish the petty cash fund, $305.00: office supplies, $63.00; store supplies, $51.00; advertising, $88.00; miscellaneous, $103.00. C233.
30. Paid cash on account to Pulver Supply, $135.00, covering M42. C234.

## ■ ENRICHMENT PROBLEMS

MASTERY PROBLEM 12-M   **Journalizing purchases, cash payments, and other transactions**

Sylvia Prior and Julia Steger, partners, own a bookstore.

**Instructions:** Journalize the following transactions completed during November of the current year. Use page 23 of a journal similar to the one described in this chapter for CarLand. Source documents are abbreviated as follows: check, C; memorandum, M; purchase invoice, P.

Nov.  2. Paid cash for rent, $1,250.00. C261.
2. Sylvia Prior, partner, withdrew cash for personal use, $1,500.00. C262.
2. Julia Steger, partner, withdrew cash for personal use, $1,500.00. C263.
3. Purchased merchandise for cash, $130.00. C264.
4. Paid cash on account to BFL Publishing, $920.00, covering P71. C265.
4. Purchased merchandise on account from Quality Books, $1,450.00. P74.
5. Paid cash for office supplies, $48.00. C266.
7. Julia Steger, partner, withdrew merchandise for personal use, $42.00. M32.
9. Paid cash for electric bill, $154.00. C267.
9. Paid cash on account to Quality Books, $1,235.00, covering P72. C268.
10. Bought store supplies on account from Carson Supply Co., $106.00. M33.
11. Paid cash on account to Matson Book Service, $975.00, covering P73. C269.
14. Purchased merchandise on account from Falk Book Co., $1,525.00. P75.
16. Paid cash for store supplies, $62.00. C270.
16. Sylvia Prior, partner, withdrew merchandise for personal use, $64.00. M34.
17. Bought store supplies on account from Gray Supplies, $214.00. M35.
18. Purchased merchandise for cash, $145.00. C271.
18. Paid cash to replenish the petty cash fund, $302.00: office supplies, $73.00; store supplies, $47.00; advertising, $92.00; miscellaneous, $90.00. C272.
19. Paid cash on account to Quality Books, $1,450.00, covering P74. C273.

Nov. 21. Purchased merchandise on account from Voss Publishing, $925.00. P76.
   24. Paid cash on account to Falk Book Co., $1,525.00, covering P75. C274.
   26. Discovered that a transaction for office supplies bought in October was journalized and posted in error as a debit to Purchases instead of Supplies—Office, $94.00. M36.
   28. Bought store supplies on account from Carson Supply, $118.00. M37.
   30. Purchased merchandise for cash, $68.00. C275.

## CHALLENGE PROBLEM 12-C   Journalizing correcting entries

A review of Meir Decorating's accounting records for last month revealed the following errors.

**Instructions:** Journalize the needed correcting entries on page 8 of a journal similar to the one described in this chapter for CarLand. Use December 2 of the current year.

Dec. 2. Discovered that a withdrawal of merchandise by Alice Reyes, partner, was journalized and posted in error as a credit to Cash instead of Purchases, $116.00. M35.
   2. Discovered that a transaction for office supplies bought for cash was journalized and posted in error as a debit to Purchases instead of Supplies—Office, $95.00. M36.
   2. Discovered that a payment for advertising was journalized and posted in error as a debit to Miscellaneous Expense instead of Advertising Expense, $125.00. M37.
   2. Discovered that a transaction for store supplies bought on account was journalized and posted in error as a debit to Utilities Expense instead of Supplies—Store, $52.00. M38.
   2. Discovered that a purchase of merchandise on account was journalized and posted in error as a debit to Supplies—Office instead of Purchases, $850.00. M39.
   2. Discovered that a payment for rent was journalized and posted in error as a debit to Salary Expense instead of Rent Expense, $1,200.00. M40.
   2. Discovered that a withdrawal of cash by Harold Atkins, partner, was journalized and posted in error as a credit to Purchases instead of Cash, $200.00. M41.
   2. Discovered that a payment for a miscellaneous expense was journalized and posted in error as a debit to Supplies Expense—Store instead of Miscellaneous Expense, $89.00. M42.
   2. Discovered that a transaction for office supplies bought for cash was journalized and posted in error as a debit to Prepaid Insurance instead of Supplies—Office, $160.00. M43.
   2. Discovered that a payment for store supplies was journalized and posted in error as a debit to Supplies—Office instead of Supplies—Store, $151.00. M44.

# Journalizing Sales and Cash Receipts

## ENABLING PERFORMANCE TASKS

After studying Chapter 13, you will be able to:
a. Define accounting terms related to sales and cash receipts for a merchandising business.
b. Identify accounting concepts and practices related to sales and cash receipts for a merchandising business.
c. Analyze sales and cash receipts transactions for a merchandising business.
d. Journalize sales and cash receipts transactions for a merchandising business.
e. Prove and rule a journal.

Purchases and sales of merchandise are the two major activities of a merchandising business. A person or business to whom merchandise or services are sold is called a customer. Rugcare, described in Part 1, sells services. CarLand, described in this part, sells merchandise. Other businesses may sell both services and merchandise.

## SALES TAX

Laws of most states and some cities require that a tax be collected from customers for each sale made. A tax on a sale of merchandise or services is called a sales tax. Sales tax rates are usually stated as a percentage of sales. Regardless of the tax rates used, accounting procedures are the same.

Every business collecting a sales tax needs accurate records of the amount of tax collected. Businesses must file reports with the proper government unit and pay the amount of sales tax collected. Records need to show (1) total

| Sales Tax Payable | |
|---|---|
| Debit side | Credit side |
| | Normal balance |
| Decrease | Increase |

sales and (2) total sales tax. The amount of sales tax collected by CarLand is a business liability until paid to the state government. Therefore, the sales tax amount is recorded in a separate liability account titled *Sales Tax Payable*. The liability account, Sales Tax Payable, has a normal credit balance. This account is increased by a credit and decreased by a debit, as shown in the T account.

CarLand operates in a state with a 6% sales tax rate. A customer must pay for the price of the goods plus the sales tax. The total amount of a sale of merchandise priced at $200.00 is calculated as shown below.

| Price of Goods | × | Sales Tax Rate | = | Sales Tax |
|---|---|---|---|---|
| $200.00 | × | 6% | = | $12.00 |
| Price of Goods | + | Sales Tax | = | Total Amount Received |
| $200.00 | + | $12.00 | = | $212.00 |

A customer must pay $212.00 for the merchandise ($200.00 for the goods plus $12.00 for the sales tax). CarLand records the price of goods sold, the sales tax, and the total amount received.

# JOURNALIZING SALES AND CASH RECEIPTS FOR SALES

A sale of merchandise may be (1) for cash or (2) on account. A sale of merchandise increases the revenue of a business. Regardless of when payment is made, the revenue should be recorded at the time of a sale, not on the date cash is received. For example, on June 15 CarLand sells merchandise on account to a customer. The customer pays CarLand for the merchandise on July 12. CarLand records the revenue on June 15, the date of the sale. The accounting concept, *Realization of Revenue*, is applied when revenue is recorded at the time goods or services are sold. *(CONCEPT: Realization of Revenue)*

## Cash and credit card sales

CarLand sells most of its merchandise for cash. A sale in which cash is received for the total amount of the sale at the time of the transaction is called a cash sale. CarLand also sells merchandise to customers who have a bank approved credit card. A sale in which a credit card is used for the total amount of the sale at the time of the transaction is called a credit card sale. Major bank approved credit cards include VISA, MasterCard, Discover Card, and Carte Blanche. CarLand accepts all major bank approved credit cards from customers. A customer who uses a credit card promises to pay the amount due on the credit card transaction to the bank issuing the credit card.

CarLand prepares a credit card slip for each credit card sale. At the end of each week, these credit card slips are included with CarLand's bank deposit. CarLand's bank accepts the credit card slips the same way it accepts checks and cash for deposit. The bank increases CarLand's bank account by the total amount of the credit card sales deposited. If a credit card was issued by another bank, CarLand's bank sends the credit card slips to the issuing bank. The bank that issues the credit card then bills the customer and collects the amount owed. The bank that accepts and processes the credit card slips for a business charges a fee for this service. This fee is included on CarLand's monthly bank statement.

Cash and credit card sales are both revenue items that increase the revenue account, Sales. Because the bank accepts credit card slips the same way it accepts cash, CarLand's bank account increases after each deposit as though cash had been deposited. Therefore, CarLand combines all sales for cash and credit cards and records the two revenue items as a single cash sales transaction.

> *November 7, 19--.*
> *Recorded cash and credit card sales, $6,450.00, plus sales tax, $387.00; total, $6,837.00. Cash Register Tape No. 7.*

CarLand uses a cash register to list all cash and credit card sales. When a transaction is entered on the cash register, a paper tape is printed as a receipt for the customer. The cash register also internally accumulates data about total cash and credit card sales.

At the end of each week, a cash register tape is printed showing total cash and credit card sales. The tape is removed from the cash register and marked with a *T* and the date (T7). The cash register tape is used by CarLand as the source document for weekly cash and credit card sales transactions. *(CONCEPT: Objective Evidence)*

A cash and credit card sales transaction increases the balances of the cash account, the sales account, and the sales tax payable account. The analysis of this transaction is shown in the T accounts.

Because the asset account, Cash, has a normal debit balance, Cash is debited for the total sales and sales tax, $6,837.00, to show the increase in this asset account. The sales account has a normal credit balance. Therefore, Sales is credited for the total price of all goods sold, $6,450.00, to show the increase in this revenue account. The sales tax payable account also has a normal credit balance. Therefore, Sales Tax Payable is credited for the total sales tax, $387.00, to show the increase in this liability account.

The journal entry to record this cash and credit card sales transaction is shown in Illustration 13-1.

| Cash | |
|---|---|
| 6,837.00 | |

| Sales | |
|---|---|
| | 6,450.00 |

| Sales Tax Payable | |
|---|---|
| | 387.00 |

Illustration 13-1
Journal entry to record
cash and credit card sales

| PAGE 21 | | JOURNAL | | | | | | | |
|---|---|---|---|---|---|---|---|---|---|
| | | | | | 5 | 6 | 10 | 11 | |
| DATE | ACCOUNT TITLE | DOC. NO. | POST. REF. | | SALES CREDIT | SALES TAX PAYABLE CREDIT | CASH DEBIT | CASH CREDIT | |
| 14 | 7 √ | | T7 √ | | 6 4 5 0 00 | 3 8 7 00 | 6 8 3 7 00 | | 14 |

The date, *7*, is written in the Date column. Special amount columns are provided for all accounts in this transaction. Therefore, a check mark is placed in the Account Title column to show that no account title needs to be written. The cash register tape number, *T7*, is recorded in the Doc. No. column. A check mark is also placed in the Post. Ref. column to show that amounts on this line do not need to be posted individually. The credit to Sales, *$6,450.00*, is written in the Sales Credit column. The credit to Sales Tax Payable, *$387.00*, is recorded in the Sales Tax Payable Credit column. The debit to Cash, *$6,837.00*, is entered in the Cash Debit column.

## Sales on account

A sale for which cash will be received at a later date is called a sale on account. A sale on account is also known as a charge sale. CarLand sells on account only to businesses. Other customers must either pay cash or use a credit card.

| Accounts Receivable ||
|---|---|
| Debit side | Credit side |
| Normal balance | |
| Increase | Decrease |

CarLand summarizes the total due from all charge customers in a general ledger account titled *Accounts Receivable*. Accounts Receivable is an asset account with a normal debit balance. Therefore, the accounts receivable account is increased by a debit and decreased by a credit, as shown in the T account.

When merchandise is sold on account, the seller prepares a form showing what has been sold. A form describing the goods sold, the quantity, and the price is known as an invoice. An invoice used as a source document for recording a sale on account is called a sales invoice. (*CONCEPT: Objective Evidence*) A sales invoice is also known as a sales ticket or a sales slip. The sales invoice used by CarLand is shown in Illustration 13-2.

| CAR⬛LAND | | Sold to: | Friendly Auto Service | | No. | 72 |
|---|---|---|---|---|---|---|
| 1374 Parklane Rockville, RI 02873-4121 | | | 430 Main Street | | Date | 11/3/-- |
| | | | Alton, RI 02803-1163 | | Terms | 30 days |
| | | Cust. No. | 130 | | | |

| Stock No. | Description | Quantity | Unit Price | Amount |
|---|---|---|---|---|
| 4422 | All-season tires | 2 | 110.00 | 220.00 |
| 7710 | Seat covers | 8 | 57.50 | 460.00 |
| | | | | |
| | | | | |
| | | | | |
| | | | Subtotal | 680.00 |
| Customer's Signature | | Salesclerk | Sales Tax | 40.80 |
| *Jean Friendly* | | *a.j.* | Total | 720.80 |

Illustration 13-2
Sales invoice

The seller considers an invoice for a sale on account to be a sales invoice. The same invoice is considered by the customer to be a purchase invoice.

A sales invoice is prepared in duplicate. The original copy is given to the customer. The carbon copy is used as the source document for the sale on account transaction. *(CONCEPT: Objective Evidence)* Sales invoices are numbered in sequence. The number 72 is the number of the sales invoice issued to Friendly Auto Service.

*November 3, 19--.*
*Sold merchandise on account to Friendly Auto Service, $680.00, plus sales tax, $40.80; total, $720.80. Sales Invoice No. 72.*

A sale on account transaction increases the amount to be collected later from a customer. Payment for this sale will be received at a later date. However, the sale is recorded at the time the sale is made because the sale has taken place and payment is due to CarLand. *(CONCEPT: Realization of Revenue)* The analysis of the sale on account transaction is shown in the T accounts.

Because the accounts receivable account has a normal debit balance, Accounts Receivable is debited for the total sales and sales tax, $720.80, to show the increase in this asset account. The sales account has a normal credit balance. Therefore, Sales is credited for the price of the goods, $680.00, to show the increase in this revenue account. The sales tax payable account also has a normal credit balance. Therefore, Sales Tax Payable is credited for the total sales tax, $40.80, to show the increase in this liability account.

The journal entry to record this sale on account transaction is shown in Illustration 13-3.

| PAGE 21 | | | | | JOURNAL | | | | |
|---|---|---|---|---|---|---|---|---|---|
| | | | | | **3** | **4** | **5** | **6** | |
| | | | | | ACCOUNTS RECEIVABLE | | SALES CREDIT | SALES TAX PAYABLE CREDIT | |
| | DATE | ACCOUNT TITLE | DOC. NO. | POST. REF. | DEBIT | CREDIT | | | |
| 4 | 3 | *Friendly Auto Service* | S72 | | 7 2 0 80 | | 6 8 0 00 | 4 0 80 | |
| 5 | | | | | | | | | |

The date, *3*, is written in the Date column. The customer name, *Friendly Auto Service*, is recorded in the Account Title column. The sales invoice number, *S72*, is entered in the Doc. No. column. The debit to Accounts Receivable, *$720.80*, is written in the Accounts Receivable Debit column. The credit to Sales, *$680.00*, is recorded in the Sales Credit column. The credit to Sales Tax Payable, *$40.80*, is entered in the Sales Tax Payable Credit column.

Illustration 13-3
Journal entry to record a sale on account

The debit and credit amounts are recorded in special amount columns. Therefore, writing the titles of the ledger accounts in the Account Title column is not necessary. However, the name of the customer is written in the Account Title column to show from whom the amount is due. Car-Land's procedures for keeping records of the amounts to be collected from each customer are described in Chapter 14.

## Cash receipts on account

When cash is received on account from a customer, CarLand prepares a receipt. The receipts are prenumbered so that all receipts can be accounted for. Receipts are prepared in duplicate. The original copy of the receipt is given to the customer. The carbon copy of the receipt is used as the source document for the cash receipt on account transaction. *(CONCEPT: Objective Evidence)*

*November 6, 19--.*
*Received cash on account from Autohaus Service, $1,802.00, covering S65.*
*Receipt No. 86.*

A cash receipt on account transaction decreases the amount to be collected from a customer. This transaction increases the cash account balance and decreases the accounts receivable account balance. The analysis of the cash receipt on account transaction is shown in the T accounts.

Because the cash account has a normal debit balance, Cash is debited for the amount of cash received, $1,802.00, to show the increase in this asset account. The accounts receivable account also has a normal debit balance. Therefore, Accounts Receivable is credited for $1,802.00 to show the decrease in this asset account.

Illustration 13-4
Journal entry to record a cash receipt on account

The journal entry to record this cash receipt on account transaction is shown in Illustration 13-4.

| | PAGE 21 | JOURNAL | | | ACCOUNTS RECEIVABLE | | CASH | | PAGE 21 |
|---|---|---|---|---|---|---|---|---|---|
| | DATE | ACCOUNT TITLE | DOC. NO. | POST. REF. | DEBIT | CREDIT | DEBIT | CREDIT | |
| 11 | 6 | Autohans Service | R86 | | | 1 8 0 2 00 | 1 8 0 2 00 | | 11 |
| 12 | | | | | | | | | 12 |

The date, *6*, is written in the Date column. The customer name, *Autohaus Service*, is recorded in the Account Title column. The receipt number, *R86*, is entered in the Doc. No. column. The credit to Accounts Receivable, *$1,802.00*, is written in the Accounts Receivable Credit column. The debit to Cash, *$1,802.00*, is recorded in the Cash Debit column.

# PROVING AND RULING AN EXPANDED JOURNAL

A journal is proved and ruled whenever a journal page is filled and always at the end of a month.

## Totaling and proving an expanded journal page

After all November 14 entries are recorded, page 21 of CarLand's journal is filled. Page 21 is totaled and proved before column totals are forwarded to page 22. To prove a journal page, CarLand uses a calculator to verify that the total debit amounts equal the total credit amounts. CarLand's debit totals equal the credit totals on page 21 of the journal. Therefore, the equality of debits and credits has been proved.

## Ruling an expanded journal page to carry totals forward

After a journal page has been proved, the journal must be prepared for forwarding. CarLand's journal column totals prepared for forwarding are shown on line 34, Illustration 13-5 on pages 278 and 279.

Five steps are followed to rule CarLand's journal.

1   Rule a single line across all amount columns directly below the last entry to indicate that the columns are to be added.

2   On the next line write the date, *14*, in the Date column.

3   Write the words, *Carried Forward*, in the Account Title column. A check mark is also placed in the Post. Ref. column to show that nothing on this line needs to be posted.

4   Write each column total below the single line.

5   Rule double lines below the column totals across all amount columns to show that the totals have been verified as correct.

## Starting a new expanded journal page

The totals from the previous journal page are carried forward to the next journal page. The totals are recorded on the first line of the new page. Column totals brought forward to a new page are shown on line 1, Illustration 13-6 on pages 278 and 279.

Four steps are followed for forwarding totals.

1   Write the page number, *22*, at the top of the journal.

2   Write the date, *19--, Nov. 14*, in the Date column.

3   Write the words, *Brought Forward*, in the Account Title column. A check mark is also placed in the Post. Ref. column to show that nothing on this line needs to be posted.

4   Record the column totals brought forward from page 21 of the journal.

PAGE *21*                                           JOURNAL

| | DATE | | ACCOUNT TITLE | DOC. NO. | POST. REF. | GENERAL DEBIT | GENERAL CREDIT | ACCOUNTS RECEIVABLE DEBIT | ACCOUNTS RECEIVABLE CREDIT | |
|---|---|---|---|---|---|---|---|---|---|---|
| 1 | *Nov.* | *2* | √ | *C259* | √ | | | | | 1 |
| 2 | | *2* | *Veloz Automotive* | *P74* | | | | | | 2 |
| 32 | | *14* | *Powell Rent-A-Car* | *R89* | | | | | 3 1 8 00 | 32 |
| 33 | | *14* | √ | *T14* | √ | | | | | 33 |
| 34 | | *14* | *Carried Forward* | | √ | 4 2 9 3 00 | 3 2 0 00 | 3 3 9 2 00 | 3 9 7 5 00 | 34 |

Illustration 13-5    Journal prepared for forwarding (left page)

PAGE *22*                                           JOURNAL

| | DATE | | ACCOUNT TITLE | DOC. NO. | POST. REF. | GENERAL DEBIT | GENERAL CREDIT | ACCOUNTS RECEIVABLE DEBIT | ACCOUNTS RECEIVABLE CREDIT | |
|---|---|---|---|---|---|---|---|---|---|---|
| 1 | *Nov.* | *14* | *Brought Forward* | | √ | 4 2 9 3 00 | 3 2 0 00 | 3 3 9 2 00 | 3 9 7 5 00 | 1 |

Illustration 13-6    Journal totals brought forward to a new page (left page)

## Proving an expanded journal at the end of a month

Equality of debits and credits in a journal is proved at the end of each month. All columns are totaled using a calculator. A journal is proved when the debit totals equal the credit totals. The proof for CarLand's journal, Illustration 13-7, pages 280 and 281, is calculated as shown below.

| Col. No. | Column Title | Debit Totals | Credit Totals |
|---|---|---|---|
| 1 | General Debit ........................ | $15,686.22 | |
| 2 | General Credit ....................... | | $ 2,029.02 |
| 3 | Accounts Receivable Debit .............. | 9,222.00 | |
| 4 | Accounts Receivable Credit ............ | | 7,950.00 |
| 5 | Sales Credit .......................... | | 31,600.00 |
| 6 | Sales Tax Payable Credit............... | | 1,896.00 |
| 7 | Accounts Payable Debit................ | 10,820.00 | |
| 8 | Accounts Payable Credit............... | | 15,870.00 |
| 9 | Purchases Debit ...................... | 14,773.00 | |
| 10 | Cash Debit .......................... | 32,224.00 | |
| 11 | Cash Credit .......................... | | 23,380.20 |
| | Totals............................... | $82,725.22 | $82,725.22 |

The two totals, *$82,725.22*, are equal. Equality of debits and credits in CarLand's journal for November is proved.

| | | | | | | | | PAGE *21* | |
|---|---|---|---|---|---|---|---|---|---|
| 5 | 6 | 7 | 8 | 9 | 10 | 11 | | | |
| SALES CREDIT | SALES TAX PAYABLE CREDIT | ACCOUNTS PAYABLE | | PURCHASES DEBIT | CASH | | | | |
| | | DEBIT | CREDIT | | DEBIT | CREDIT | | | |
| | | | | 4 8 3 00 | | 4 8 3 00 | | | 1 |
| | | | 1 7 5 4 00 | 1 7 5 4 00 | | | | | 2 |
| | | | | | 3 1 8 00 | | | | 32 |
| 5 1 0 0 00 | 3 0 6 00 | | | | 5 4 0 6 00 | | | | 33 |
| 14 7 5 0 00 | 8 8 5 00 | 5 3 6 0 00 | 11 6 9 0 00 | 12 0 1 3 00 | 16 2 1 8 00 | 9 6 5 6 00 | | | 34 |

Illustration 13-5    Journal prepared for forwarding (right page)

| | | | | | | | PAGE *22* | |
|---|---|---|---|---|---|---|---|---|
| 5 | 6 | 7 | 8 | 9 | 10 | 11 | | |
| SALES CREDIT | SALES TAX PAYABLE CREDIT | ACCOUNTS PAYABLE | | PURCHASES DEBIT | CASH | | | |
| | | DEBIT | CREDIT | | DEBIT | CREDIT | | |
| 14 7 5 0 00 | 8 8 5 00 | 5 3 6 0 00 | 11 6 9 0 00 | 12 0 1 3 00 | 16 2 1 8 00 | 9 6 5 6 00 | | 1 |

Illustration 13-6    Journal totals brought forward to a new page (right page)

## Proving cash at the end of a month

CarLand's cash proof at the end of November is calculated as shown below.

| | |
|---|---|
| Cash on hand at the beginning of the month . . . . . . . . . . . . . . . | $14,706.20 |
| (November 1 balance of cash account in general ledger) | |
| *Plus* total cash received during the month . . . . . . . . . . . . . . . . . | 32,224.00 |
| (Cash Debit column total, line 16, Illustration 13-7) | |
| *Equals* total. . . . . . . . . . . . . . . . . . . . . . . . . . . . . . . . . . . . . . . . | $46,930.20 |
| *Less* total cash paid during the month. . . . . . . . . . . . . . . . . . . . | 23,380.20 |
| (Cash Credit column total, line 16, Illustration 13-7) | |
| *Equals* cash balance on hand at end of the month. . . . . . . . . . . | $23,550.00 |

The last check written in November is Check No. 276. The balance on the next unused check stub is $23,550.00. Since the balance on the next unused check stub is the same as the cash proof, cash is proved.

## Ruling an expanded journal at the end of a month

CarLand's journal is ruled at the end of each month. CarLand's expanded journal totaled and ruled at the end of November is shown on line 16, Illustration 13-7. Five steps are followed to rule a journal.

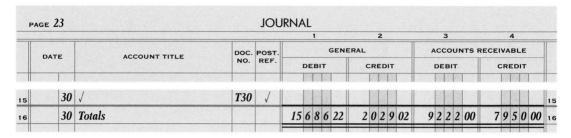

1 Rule a single line across all amount columns directly below the last entry to indicate that the columns are to be added.

2 On the next line write the date, *30*, in the Date column.

3 Write the word, *Totals*, in the Account Title column.

4 Write each column total below the single line.

5 Rule double lines across all amount columns to show that the totals have been verified as correct.

> Some of the column totals will be posted as described in Chapter 14. Therefore, a check mark is not placed in the Post. Ref. column for this line.

Illustration 13-8
Summary of entries for sales and cash receipts transactions in an expanded journal

## SUMMARY OF JOURNALIZING SALES AND CASH RECEIPTS

The chart shown in Illustration 13-8 summarizes the entries for sales and cash receipts transactions in an expanded journal.

| TRANSACTION | JOURNAL | | | | | | | | | | |
|---|---|---|---|---|---|---|---|---|---|---|---|
| | 1 | 2 | 3 | 4 | 5 | 6 | 7 | 8 | 9 | 10 | 11 |
| | GENERAL | | ACCOUNTS RECEIVABLE | | SALES CREDIT | SALES TAX PAYABLE CREDIT | ACCOUNTS PAYABLE | | PURCHASES DEBIT | CASH | |
| | DEBIT | CREDIT | DEBIT | CREDIT | | | DEBIT | CREDIT | | DEBIT | CREDIT |
| Cash and credit card sale | | | | | X | X | | | | X | |
| Sale on account | | | X | | X | X | | | | | |
| Cash receipt on account | | | | X | | | | | | X | |

## ■ ACCOUNTING TERMS

What is the meaning of each of the following?

**1.** customer
**2.** sales tax
**3.** cash sale
**4.** credit card sale
**5.** sale on account
**6.** sales invoice

| | | | | | | PAGE *23* | | |
| --- | --- | --- | --- | --- | --- | --- | --- | --- |
| 5 | 6 | 7 | 8 | 9 | 10 | 11 | | |
| SALES CREDIT | SALES TAX PAYABLE CREDIT | ACCOUNTS PAYABLE | | PURCHASES DEBIT | CASH | | | |
| | | DEBIT | CREDIT | | DEBIT | CREDIT | | |
| 15 | 1 1 5 0 00 | | 6 9 00 | | | | 1 2 1 9 00 | | | 15 |
| 16 | 31 6 0 0 00 | 1 8 9 6 00 | 10 8 2 0 00 | 15 8 7 0 00 | 14 7 7 3 00 | 32 2 2 4 00 | 23 3 8 0 20 | 16 |

Illustration 13-7    Journal page totaled and ruled at the end of a month (right page)

# ■ QUESTIONS FOR INDIVIDUAL STUDY

1. What are the two major activities of a merchandising business?
2. How are sales tax rates usually stated?
3. Why must every business that collects a sales tax keep accurate records of the amount of tax collected?
4. What two amounts must sales tax records show?
5. Why is sales tax collected considered a liability?
6. What is the normal balance of the sales tax payable account, and how is the account increased and decreased?
7. Which accounting concept is being applied when revenue is recorded at the time a sale is made, regardless of when payment is made?
8. Which accounting concept is being applied when a cash register tape is used as the source document for cash and credit card sales?
9. How often does CarLand journalize cash sales?
10. What accounts are affected, and how, for a cash and credit card sales

transaction?
11. Why is a check mark placed in the Account Title column of an expanded journal when journalizing cash and credit card sales?
12. What is another name used for a sale on account?
13. What is the title of the general ledger account used to summarize the total amount due from all charge customers?
14. What is the source document for a sale on account transaction?
15. What are other names used for a sales invoice?
16. What accounts are affected, and how, for a sale on account transaction?
17. Which amount columns in a journal are used to record a sale on account transaction?
18. What accounts are affected, and how, for a cash receipt on account transaction?
19. How often is the equality of debits and credits in a journal proved?
20. How often is a journal page ruled?

# ■ CASES FOR MANAGEMENT DECISION

**CASE 1** Carrie and Karl Lott, partners, operate a shoe store. A 5-column journal similar to the one described in Chapter 4 is used to record all transactions. The business sells merchandise for cash and on account. The business also purchases most of its merchandise on account. Mrs. Lott asked an accountant to check the accounting system

and recommend changes. The accountant suggests that an expanded journal similar to the one described in Chapters 12 and 13 be used. Which journal would be better? Why?

**CASE 2** Amy Pryor, an accountant for a sporting goods store, has noted a major increase in overdue amounts from charge customers. All invoice amounts from sales on account are due within 30 days. The amounts due have reduced the amount of cash available for the day-to-day operation of the business. Miss Pryor recommends that the business (1) stop all sales on account and (2) begin accepting bank credit cards. The owner is reluctant to accept the recom-

mendations because the business might lose some reliable customers who do not have credit cards. Also, the business will have increased expenses because of the credit card fee. How would you respond to Miss Pryor's recommendations? What alternatives might the owner consider?

# ▮ DRILLS FOR UNDERSTANDING

### DRILL 13-D1   Analyzing transactions into debit and credit parts

**Instructions:** Prepare T accounts for each of the following transactions. Use the T accounts to analyze each transaction. A 5% sales tax has been added to each sale. The first transaction is given as an example.

| Cash | Sales | Sales Tax Payable |
|---|---|---|
| 1,575.00 | 1,500.00 | 75.00 |

*Transactions*

1. Recorded cash and credit card sales, $1,500.00, plus sales tax, $75.00; total, $1,575.00.
2. Sold merchandise on account to Steven Kramer, $300.00, plus sales tax, $15.00; total, $315.00.
3. Sold merchandise on account to Mark Fields, $360.00, plus sales tax, $18.00; total, $378.00.
4. Received cash on account from Jackson White, $157.50.
5. Received cash on account from Gloria Burton, $68.25.
6. Recorded cash and credit card sales, $1,750.00, plus sales tax, $87.50; total, $1,837.50.

*The solution to Drill 13-D1 is needed to complete Drill 13-D3.*

### DRILL 13-D2   Analyzing the effect of sales transactions on accounts

**Instructions: 1.** Prepare a T account for each of the following accounts: Cash, Accounts Receivable, Sales, and Sales Tax Payable.

**2.** Using the T accounts, show which accounts are debited and credited for the following transactions. Add a 6% sales tax to each sale. Write the transaction number in parentheses to the left of each amount. The first transaction is given as an example.

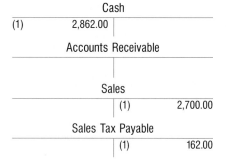

| Cash | |
|---|---|
| (1) 2,862.00 | |

| Accounts Receivable | |
|---|---|
| | |

| Sales | |
|---|---|
| | (1) 2,700.00 |

| Sales Tax Payable | |
|---|---|
| | (1) 162.00 |

*Transactions*

1. Recorded cash and credit card sales, $2,700.00.
2. Sold merchandise on account to Melissa Bedo, $180.00.
3. Sold merchandise on account to Kim Lea, $170.00.
4. Received cash on account from Maria Jones, $148.40.
5. Received cash on account from Jack Mumford, $79.50.
6. Recorded cash and credit card sales, $2,375.00.

DRILL 13-D3  **Analyzing journal entries**

*The solution to Drill 13-D1 is needed to complete Drill 13-D3.*

**Instructions:** Use a form similar to the following. Based on the answers in Drill 13-D1, write the amounts in the amount columns to be used to journalize each transaction. Transaction 1 is given as an example.

| Transaction | Accounts Rec. Debit | Accounts Rec. Credit | Sales Credit | Sales Tax Payable Credit | Cash Debit | Cash Credit |
|---|---|---|---|---|---|---|
| 1. Debit amount | | | | | $1,575.00 | |
| Credit amount | | | $1,500.00 | | | |
| Credit amount | | | | $75.00 | | |

# APPLICATION PROBLEM

PROBLEM 13-1  **Journalizing sales and cash receipts**

Mark Butler and Betty Rivers, partners, own a tennis equipment and clothing store.

**Instructions: 1.** Journalize the following transactions completed during September of the current year. Use page 16 of a journal similar to the one described in this chapter. A 4% sales tax has been added to each sale. Source documents are abbreviated as follows: receipt, R; sales invoice, S; cash register tape, T.

Sept.  1. Sold merchandise on account to Valerie Seeley, $50.00, plus sales tax, $2.00; total, $52.00. S66.
    2. Sold merchandise on account to Jill Folker, $125.00, plus sales tax, $5.00; total, $130.00. S67.
    4. Sold merchandise on account to Jerome Hodges, $85.00, plus sales tax, $3.40; total, $88.40. S68.
    5. Received cash on account from Rita Picken, $140.40, covering S62. R93.
    5. Recorded cash and credit card sales, $2,360.00, plus sales tax, $94.40; total, $2,454.40. T5.
    7. Received cash on account from Karla Doyle, $182.00, covering S63. R94.
    9. Sold merchandise on account to Anthony Zolte, $115.00, plus sales tax, $4.60; total, $119.60. S69.
    12. Recorded cash and credit card sales, $2,890.00, plus sales tax, $115.60; total, $3,005.60. T12.
    12. Received cash on account from Jonathan Ames, $50.40, covering S64. R95.
    14. Received cash on account from Robert Hall, $67.60, covering S65. R96.
    15. Sold merchandise on account to Beth Klein, $115.00, plus sales tax, $4.60; total, $119.60. S70.
    17. Received cash on account from Valerie Seeley, $52.00, covering S66. R97.
    19. Recorded cash and credit card sales, $2,810.00, plus sales tax, $112.40; total, $2,922.40. T19.
    25. Received cash on account from Jill Folker, $130.00, covering S67. R98.
    26. Sold merchandise on account to Jill Folker, $75.00, plus sales tax, $3.00; total, $78.00. S71.

Sept. 26. Recorded cash and credit card sales, $2,650.00, plus sales tax, $106.00; total, $2,756.00. T26.
   28. Received cash on account from Jerome Hodges, $88.40, covering S68. R99.
   29. Sold merchandise on account to Karla Doyle, $95.00, plus sales tax, $3.80; total, $98.80. S72.
   30. Recorded cash and credit card sales, $1,540.00, plus sales tax, $61.60; total, $1,601.60. T30.

   **2.** Total the journal. Prove the equality of debits and credits.
   **3.** Rule the journal.

# ■ ENRICHMENT PROBLEMS

### MASTERY PROBLEM 13-M   **Journalizing transactions**

Kevin Sykes and David Webb, partners, own a bicycle and motorcycle store.

**Instructions: 1.** Journalize the following transactions completed during November of the current year. Use page 18 of a journal similar to the one described in this chapter. A 6% sales tax has been added to each sale. Source documents are abbreviated as follows: check, C; memorandum, M; purchase invoice, P; receipt, R; sales invoice, S; cash register tape, T.

Nov.  2. Paid cash for rent, $1,250.00. C244.
   2. Kevin Sykes, partner, withdrew cash for personal use, $600.00. C245.
   2. David Webb, partner, withdrew cash for personal use, $600.00. C246.
   3. Paid cash for electric bill, $130.00. C247.
   3. Purchased merchandise on account from Vista Cycle Co., $2,275.00. P58.
   4. Paid cash on account to Daley Motorcycles, $1,360.00, covering P56. C248.
   5. Sold merchandise on account to Loree Adams, $1,130.00, plus sales tax, $67.80; total, $1,197.80. S61.
   5. Paid cash for office supplies, $62.00. C249.
   6. Purchased merchandise for cash, $165.00. C250.
   7. Recorded cash and credit card sales, $5,850.00, plus sales tax, $351.00; total, $6,201.00. T7.
   9. Sold merchandise on account to Victor Droste, $358.00, plus sales tax, $21.48; total, $379.48. S62.
   9. Received cash on account from Wayne Ivory, $1,775.50, covering S57. R112.
   11. Bought office supplies on account from Walden Supply, $68.00. M43.
   12. Purchased merchandise for cash, $180.00. C251.
   12. Received cash on account from Robert Melvin, $996.40, covering S58. R113.
   13. Paid cash on account to Action Cycles, $1,365.00, covering P57. C252.
   14. David Webb, partner, withdrew merchandise for personal use, $385.00. M44.
   14. Recorded cash and credit card sales, $2,680.00, plus sales tax, $160.80; total, $2,840.80. T14.
   16. Kevin Sykes, partner, withdrew cash for personal use, $600.00. C253.
   16. David Webb, partner, withdrew cash for personal use, $600.00. C254.
   17. Purchased merchandise on account from United Bicycle Co., $825.00. P59.
   18. Purchased merchandise for cash, $196.00. C255.
   18. Bought store supplies on account from Baker Supply, $92.00. M45.
   19. Paid cash on account to Walden Supply, $68.00, covering M43. C256.
   21. Recorded cash and credit card sales, $2,430.00, plus sales tax, $145.80; total, $2,575.80. T21.

Nov. 23. Discovered that a payment of cash for advertising in October was journalized and posted in error as a debit to Miscellaneous Expense instead of Advertising Expense, $125.00. M46.

23. Paid cash for office supplies, $44.00. C257.

**2.** Prepare page 18 of the journal for forwarding. Total the amount columns. Prove the equality of debits and credits, and record the totals to be carried forward on line 32.

**3.** Record the totals brought forward on line 1 of page 19 of the journal. Prove the equality of debits and credits again.

**4.** Journalize the following transactions on page 19 of the journal.

Nov. 23. Received cash on account from Esther Lorand, $630.70, covering S59. R114.

24. Sold merchandise on account to Celia Sotelo, $325.00, plus sales tax, $19.50; total, $344.50. S63.

27. Purchased merchandise on account from Cycle World, $1,240.00. P60.

27. Paid cash for advertising, $85.00. C258.

28. Recorded cash and credit card sales, $2,680.00, plus sales tax, $160.80; total, $2,840.80. T28.

28. Received cash on account from Leonard Kane, $1,147.00, covering S60. R115.

30. Sold merchandise on account to Jonathan Hunt, $45.00, plus sales tax, $2.70; total, $47.70. S64.

30. Paid cash to replenish the petty cash fund, $301.00: office supplies, $62.00; store supplies, $71.00; advertising, $88.00; miscellaneous, $80.00. C259.

30. Recorded cash and credit card sales, $640.00, plus sales tax, $38.40; total, $678.40. T30.

**5.** Total page 19 of the journal. Prove the equality of debits and credits.

**6.** Prove cash. The November 1 cash account balance in the general ledger was $9,431.00. On November 30 the balance on the next unused check stub was $21,511.40.

**7.** Rule page 19 of the journal.

## CHALLENGE PROBLEM 13-C  Journalizing transactions

The columns of a journal may be arranged in different ways. For example, the journal used in this chapter is referred to as an expanded journal. All of the amount columns are to the right of the Account Title column. However, another arrangement is to have the amount columns divided by the Account Title column. Some of the amount columns are to the left and some are to the right of the Account Title column.

**Instructions: 1.** Use a journal with the columns arranged as follows.

| Cash | | Date | Account Title | Doc. No. | Post. Ref. | General | | Accts. Rec. | | Sales Cr. | Sales Tax Pay. Cr. | Accts. Payable | | Purchases Dr. |
|---|---|---|---|---|---|---|---|---|---|---|---|---|---|---|
| Dr. | Cr. | | | | | Dr. | Cr. | Dr. | Cr. | | | Dr. | Cr. | |
| | | | | | | | | | | | | | | |

**2.** Use the transactions and instructions for Mastery Problem 13-M. Complete all of the instructions using the journal above.

# CHAPTER
# 14

# Posting to General and Subsidiary Ledgers

## ENABLING PERFORMANCE TASKS

After studying Chapter 14, you will be able to:
a. Define accounting terms related to posting to ledgers.
b. Identify accounting practices related to posting to ledgers.
c. Post to a general ledger from a journal.
d. Open accounts in ledgers.
e. Post to subsidiary ledgers from a journal.
f. Prepare subsidiary schedules.

A journal provides a permanent record of transactions listed in chronological order. Journal entries are sorted and summarized by transferring information to ledger accounts. Transferring information from journal entries to ledger accounts is known as posting. Posting information from a journal to ledger accounts summarizes in one place transactions affecting each account.

## LEDGERS AND CONTROLLING ACCOUNTS

A business' size, number of transactions, and type of transactions determine the number of ledgers used in an accounting system.

### General ledger

A ledger that contains all accounts needed to prepare financial statements is known as a general ledger. A general ledger sorts and summarizes all information affecting income statement and balance sheet accounts. A business with transactions involving mostly the receipt and payment of cash may use only a general ledger. Rugcare, described in Part 1, uses only a general ledger. CarLand also uses a general ledger. CarLand's general ledger chart of accounts is on page 250. However, because of the business' size and the number and type of transactions, CarLand also uses additional ledgers in its accounting system.

## Subsidiary ledgers

A business needs to know the amount owed each vendor as well as the amount to be collected from each charge customer. Therefore, a separate account is needed for each vendor and each customer. A general ledger could contain an account for each vendor and for each customer. However, a business with many vendors and customers would have a bulky general ledger and a long trial balance. CarLand eliminates these problems by keeping a separate ledger for vendors and a separate ledger for customers. Each separate ledger is summarized in a single general ledger account. A ledger that is summarized in a single general ledger account is called a subsidiary ledger. A subsidiary ledger containing only accounts for vendors from whom items are purchased or bought on account is called an accounts payable ledger. A subsidiary ledger containing only accounts for charge customers is called an accounts receivable ledger.

## Controlling accounts

The total amount owed to all vendors is summarized in a single general ledger account, Accounts Payable. The total amount to be collected from all charge customers is summarized in a single general ledger account, Accounts Receivable.

An account in a general ledger that summarizes all accounts in a subsidiary ledger is called a controlling account. The balance of a controlling account equals the total of all account balances in its related subsidiary ledger. Thus, the balance of the controlling account, Accounts Payable, equals the total of all vendor account balances in the accounts payable subsidiary ledger. The balance of the controlling account, Accounts Receivable, equals the total of all charge customer account balances in the accounts receivable subsidiary ledger.

# POSTING TO A GENERAL LEDGER

Daily general ledger account balances are usually not necessary. Balances of general ledger accounts are needed only when financial statements are prepared. Posting from a journal to a general ledger can be done periodically throughout a month. The number of transactions determines how often to post to a general ledger. A business with many transactions would normally post more often than a business with few transactions. Posting often helps keep the work load evenly distributed throughout a month. However, posting must always be done at the end of a month. CarLand uses the same 4-column general ledger account form and posting procedures as described for Rugcare in Chapter 5.

## Posting a journal's general amount columns

Amounts recorded in a journal's general amount columns are amounts for which no special amount columns are provided. Therefore, separate amounts in a journal's General Debit and General Credit columns *ARE* posted individually to the accounts written in the journal's Account Title column. The posting of the General Debit entry on line 6 of CarLand's journal is shown in Illustration 14-1.

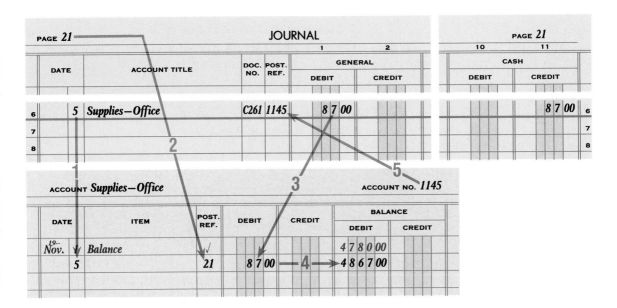

Illustration 14-1
Posting from a journal's
General Debit column

Five steps are followed to post the debit entry to the general ledger.

1 Write the date, *5*, in the Date column of the account.

2 Write the journal page number, *21*, in the Post. Ref. column of the account.

3 Write the debit amount, *$87.00*, in the account's Debit amount column.

4 Add the amount in the Debit amount column to the previous balance in the Balance Debit column ($4,780.00 + $87.00 = $4,867.00). Write the new account balance, *$4,867.00*, in the Balance Debit column.

5 Write the general ledger account number, *1145*, in the Post. Ref. column of the journal.

## Posting a journal's special amount columns

CarLand's journal has nine special amount columns. Separate amounts written in these special amount columns *ARE NOT* posted individually to the general ledger. Separate amounts in a special amount column all affect the same general ledger account. Therefore, only the totals of special amount columns *ARE* posted to the general ledger. Each special amount column total is posted to the general ledger account listed in the column heading. Posting of the Cash Credit amount column total is shown in Illustration 14-2.

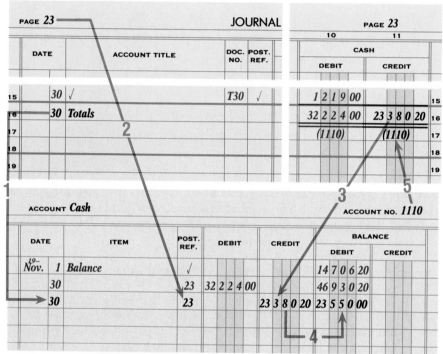

Illustration 14-2
Posting the Cash Credit
column total

Five steps are followed to post the Cash Credit column total.

1  Write the date, *30,* in the Date column of the account.

2  Write the journal page number, *23,* in the Post. Ref. column of the account.

3  Write the Cash Credit column total, *$23,380.20,* in the account's Credit amount column.

4  Subtract the amount in the Credit amount column from the previous balance in the Balance Debit column ($46,930.20 − $23,380.20 = $23,550.00). Write the new account balance, *$23,550.00,* in the Balance Debit column.

5  Return to the journal and write the general ledger account number, *1110,* in parentheses below the Cash Credit column total.

## Rules for posting a journal's column totals

Rules for posting a journal's column totals are shown in Illustration 14-3.

| PAGE 23 | | | | | | | JOURNAL | | | |
|---|---|---|---|---|---|---|---|---|---|---|
| | | | | | | 1 | 2 | 3 | 4 | |
| | DATE | ACCOUNT TITLE | DOC. NO. | POST. REF. | GENERAL | | ACCOUNTS RECEIVABLE | | | |
| | | | | | DEBIT | CREDIT | DEBIT | CREDIT | | |
| 16 | 30 | Totals | | | 15 6 8 6 22 | 2 0 2 9 02 | 9 2 2 2 00 | 7 9 5 0 00 | 16 |
| 17 | | | | | (√) | (√) | (1130) | (1130) | 17 |
| 18 | | | | | | | | | 18 |
| 19 | | | | | | | | | 19 |

Illustration 14-3
Rules for posting a
journal's column totals

General amount
column totals
ARE NOT posted

Special amount
column totals
ARE posted

A check mark is placed in parentheses below the General Debit and General Credit column totals to indicate that the two amount column totals *ARE NOT* posted. The general ledger account number of the account listed in the column heading is written in parentheses below the special amount column totals to show that the totals *ARE* posted.

## Opening a new page for an account in a general ledger

The number of entries that may be recorded on each general ledger account form depends on the number of lines provided. When all lines have been used, a new page is prepared. The account name, account number, and account balance are recorded on the new page.

On November 1 CarLand prepared a new page for Cash in the general ledger because the existing page was full. On that day, the account balance was $14,706.20. The new page for Cash in the general ledger is shown in Illustration 14-4.

| ACCOUNT Cash | | | | | | ACCOUNT NO. 1110 | | |
|---|---|---|---|---|---|---|---|---|
| DATE | ITEM | POST. REF. | DEBIT | CREDIT | BALANCE | | | |
| | | | | | DEBIT | CREDIT | | |
| Nov. 1 | Balance | √ | | | 14 7 0 6 20 | | | |
| | | | | | | | | |
| | | | | | | | | |
| | | | | | | | | |

Illustration 14-4
Opening a new page for an
account in a general ledger

The account title and account number are written on the heading at the top of the new page. The date, *19--, Nov. 1*, is recorded in the Date column. The word *Balance* is written in the Item column. A check mark is placed in the Post. Ref. column to show that the entry has been carried forward from a previous page rather than posted from a journal. The account balance, *$14,706.20*, is written in the Balance Debit column.

# ASSIGNING ACCOUNT NUMBERS
# TO SUBSIDIARY LEDGER ACCOUNTS

CarLand assigns a vendor number to each account in the accounts payable ledger. A customer number is also assigned to each account in the accounts receivable ledger. A three-digit number is used. The first digit identifies the division in which the controlling account appears in the general ledger. The second two digits show each account's location within a subsidiary ledger. Accounts are assigned by 10s beginning with the second digit. Accounts in the subsidiary ledgers can be located by either number or name.

The vendor number for Antelo Supply is 210. The first digit, 2, shows that the controlling account is a liability, Accounts Payable. The second and third digits, *10*, show the vendor number assigned to Antelo Supply.

The customer number for Ashley Delivery is 110. The first digit, *1*, shows that the controlling account is an asset, Accounts Receivable. The second and third digits, *10*, show the customer number assigned to Ashley Delivery.

The procedure for adding new accounts to subsidiary ledgers is the same as described for Rugcare's general ledger in Chapter 5. Accounts are arranged in alphabetic order within the subsidiary ledgers. New accounts are assigned the unused middle number. If the proper alphabetic order places a new account as the last account, the next number in the sequence of 10s is assigned. CarLand's chart of accounts for the subsidiary ledgers is on page 250.

# POSTING TO AN ACCOUNTS PAYABLE LEDGER

When the balance of a vendor account in an accounts payable ledger is changed, the balance of the controlling account, Accounts Payable, is also changed. The total of all vendor account balances in the accounts payable ledger equals the balance of the controlling account, Accounts Payable. The relationship between the accounts payable ledger and the general ledger controlling account, Accounts Payable, is shown in Illustration 14-5.

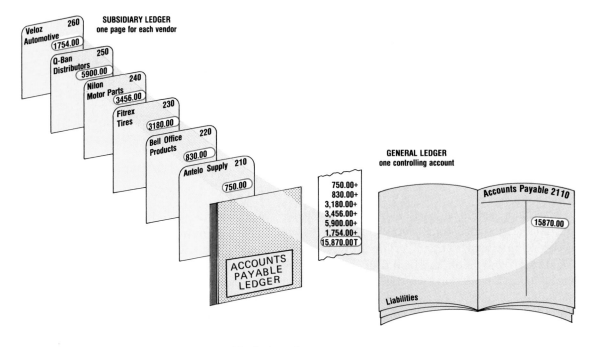

Illustration 14-5
Relationship of accounts
payable ledger and general
ledger controlling account

## Accounts payable ledger form

CarLand uses the 3-column accounts payable subsidiary account form shown in Illustration 14-6.

Illustration 14-6
Three-column account
form used in an accounts
payable ledger

| VENDOR *Veloz Automotive* | | | | | | VENDOR NO. *260* |
|---|---|---|---|---|---|---|
| DATE | ITEM | POST. REF. | DEBIT | CREDIT | CREDIT BALANCE | |

Information to be recorded in the accounts payable ledger is essentially the same as that recorded in the 4-column general ledger account. The information includes the date, posting reference, debit or credit amount, and new account balance. Accounts payable are liabilities, and liabilities have normal credit balances. Therefore, the Debit Balance column is usually not needed for the accounts payable ledger accounts. The accounts payable account form is the same as the general ledger account form except that there is no Debit Balance column.

Accounts in CarLand's accounts payable ledger are arranged in alphabetic order and kept in a loose-leaf binder. Periodically, accounts for new vendors are added and accounts no longer used are removed from the accounts payable ledger.

If the number of accounts becomes large enough to make a loose-leaf binder inappropriate, ledger pages may be kept in a file cabinet.

## Opening vendor accounts

Each new account is opened by writing the vendor name and vendor number on the heading of the ledger account. The account opened for Veloz Automotive is shown in Illustration 14-6.

The vendor name is obtained from the first purchase invoice received. The vendor number is assigned using the three-digit numbering system described on page 291. The correct alphabetic order for Veloz Automotive places the account as the sixth account in the accounts payable subsidiary ledger. Vendor number 260 is assigned to Veloz Automotive.

> Some businesses record both the vendor name and vendor address on the ledger form. However, the address information is usually kept in a separate name and address file. This practice eliminates having to record the vendor address on the ledger form each time a new ledger page is opened or the address changes.

## Posting from a journal to an accounts payable ledger

Each entry in the Accounts Payable columns of a journal affects the vendor named in the Account Title column. CarLand posts each amount in these two columns often. Posting often keeps each vendor account balance up to date. Totals of Accounts Payable special amount columns are posted to the general ledger at the end of each month.

**Posting a credit to an accounts payable ledger.** Posting a credit for a purchase on account from the journal to the accounts payable ledger is shown in Illustration 14-7.

Illustration 14-7
Posting a credit to an accounts payable ledger

Five steps are followed to post the entry on line 2 of the journal to the accounts payable ledger.

1 Write the date, *19--, Nov. 2*, in the Date column of the account.

2 Write the journal page number, *21*, in the Post. Ref. column of the account.

3 Write the credit amount, *$1,754.00*, in the Credit amount column of the account for Veloz Automotive.

4 Add the amount in the Credit amount column to the previous balance in the Credit Balance column. (Veloz Automotive has no previous balance; therefore, $0 + $1,754.00 = $1,754.00.) Write the new account balance, *$1,754.00*, in the Credit Balance column.

5 Write the vendor number, *260*, in the Post. Ref. column of the journal. The vendor number shows that the posting for this entry is completed.

The controlling account in the general ledger, Accounts Payable, is also increased by this entry. At the end of the month, the journal's Accounts Payable Credit column total is posted to the controlling account, Accounts Payable.

**Posting a debit to an accounts payable ledger.** The same steps are followed to post a debit to a vendor account as are used to post a credit. However, the debit amount is entered in the Debit amount column of the vendor account. The debit amount is subtracted from the previous credit balance. Posting a cash payment on account from the journal to the accounts payable ledger is shown in Illustration 14-8.

Illustration 14-8
Posting a debit to an
accounts payable ledger

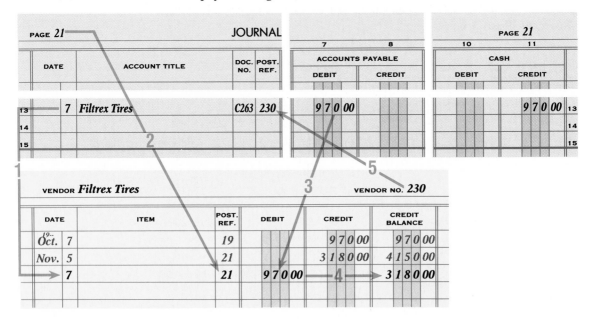

The controlling account in the general ledger, Accounts Payable, is decreased by this entry. At the end of the month, the journal's Accounts Payable Debit column total is posted to the controlling account, Accounts Payable.

## Opening a new page for a vendor in an accounts payable ledger

The number of entries that may be recorded on each account form depends on the number of lines provided. When all lines have been used, a new page is prepared. The vendor name, vendor number, and account balance are recorded on the new page.

On November 1 CarLand prepared a new page for Nilon Motor Parts in the accounts payable ledger because the existing page was full. On that day, the account balance was $4,840.00. The new page for Nilon Motor Parts in the accounts payable ledger is shown in Illustration 14-9.

| | DATE | ITEM | POST. REF. | DEBIT | CREDIT | CREDIT BALANCE |
|---|---|---|---|---|---|---|
| VENDOR *Nilon Motor Parts* | | | | | VENDOR NO. *240* | |
| | 19--<br>Nov. 1 | *Balance* | ✓ | | | 4 8 4 0 00 |
| | | | | | | |

Illustration 14-9
Opening a new page for a vendor in the accounts payable ledger

The vendor name and vendor number are written at the top of the account page. The date, *19--, Nov. 1*, is recorded in the Date column. The word *Balance* is written in the Item column. A check mark is placed in the Post. Ref. column to show that the amount has been carried forward from a previous page rather than posted from a journal. The account balance, *$4,840.00*, is written in the Credit Balance column.

## Completed accounts payable ledger

CarLand's accounts payable ledger after all posting has been completed is shown in Illustration 14-10.

| | DATE | ITEM | POST. REF. | DEBIT | CREDIT | CREDIT BALANCE |
|---|---|---|---|---|---|---|
| VENDOR *Antelo Supply* | | | | | VENDOR NO. *210* | |
| | 19--<br>Oct. 12 | | 19 | | 4 3 0 00 | 4 3 0 00 |
| | Nov. 6 | | 21 | | 1 6 0 00 | 5 9 0 00 |
| | 12 | | 21 | 4 3 0 00 | | 1 6 0 00 |
| | 23 | | 22 | | 5 9 0 00 | 7 5 0 00 |
| | | | | | | |
| | | | | | | |

Illustration 14-10
Accounts payable ledger after posting has been completed

**VENDOR** *Bell Office Products*                                          **VENDOR NO.** *220*

| DATE | | ITEM | POST. REF. | DEBIT | CREDIT | CREDIT BALANCE |
|---|---|---|---|---|---|---|
| *Oct.* | 23 | | 20 | | 6 2 0 00 | 6 2 0 00 |
| *Nov.* | 23 | | 22 | 6 2 0 00 | | |
| | 24 | | 22 | | 8 3 0 00 | 8 3 0 00 |

**VENDOR** *Filtrex Tires*                                          **VENDOR NO.** *230*

| DATE | | ITEM | POST. REF. | DEBIT | CREDIT | CREDIT BALANCE |
|---|---|---|---|---|---|---|
| *Oct.* | 7 | | 19 | | 9 7 0 00 | 9 7 0 00 |
| *Nov.* | 5 | | 21 | | 3 1 8 0 00 | 4 1 5 0 00 |
| | 7 | | 21 | 9 7 0 00 | | 3 1 8 0 00 |

**VENDOR** *Nilon Motor Parts*                                          **VENDOR NO.** *240*

| DATE | | ITEM | POST. REF. | DEBIT | CREDIT | CREDIT BALANCE |
|---|---|---|---|---|---|---|
| *Nov.* | 1 | Balance | √ | | | 4 8 4 0 00 |
| | 4 | | 21 | | 3 4 5 6 00 | 8 2 9 6 00 |
| | 20 | | 22 | 4 8 4 0 00 | | 3 4 5 6 00 |

**VENDOR** *Q-Ban Distributors*                                          **VENDOR NO.** *250*

| DATE | | ITEM | POST. REF. | DEBIT | CREDIT | CREDIT BALANCE |
|---|---|---|---|---|---|---|
| *Nov.* | 1 | Balance | √ | | | 3 9 6 0 00 |
| | 6 | | 21 | 3 9 6 0 00 | | |
| | 13 | | 21 | | 3 1 4 0 00 | 3 1 4 0 00 |
| | 20 | | 22 | | 2 7 6 0 00 | 5 9 0 0 00 |

**VENDOR** *Veloz Automotive*                                          **VENDOR NO.** *260*

| DATE | | ITEM | POST. REF. | DEBIT | CREDIT | CREDIT BALANCE |
|---|---|---|---|---|---|---|
| *Nov.* | 2 | | 21 | | 1 7 5 4 00 | 1 7 5 4 00 |

Illustration 14-10
Accounts payable ledger
after posting has been
completed
(concluded)

# POSTING TO AN ACCOUNTS RECEIVABLE LEDGER

When the balance of a customer account in an accounts receivable ledger is changed, the balance of the controlling account, Accounts Receivable, is also changed. The total of all customer account balances in the accounts receivable ledger equals the balance of the controlling account, Accounts Receivable. The relationship between the accounts receivable ledger and the general ledger controlling account, Accounts Receivable, is shown in Illustration 14-11.

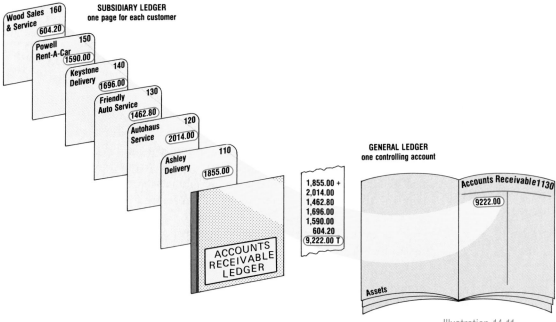

Illustration 14-11
Relationship of accounts receivable ledger and general ledger controlling account

## Accounts receivable ledger form

CarLand uses the 3-column accounts receivable subsidiary account form shown in Illustration 14-12.

| CUSTOMER *Friendly Auto Service* | | | | | CUSTOMER NO. *130* | |
|---|---|---|---|---|---|---|
| DATE | ITEM | POST. REF. | DEBIT | CREDIT | DEBIT BALANCE | |
| | | | | | | |
| | | | | | | |
| | | | | | | |
| | | | | | | |
| | | | | | | |
| | | | | | | |

Illustration 14-12
Three-column account form used in an accounts receivable ledger

The accounts receivable account form is similar to the one used for the accounts payable ledger. Accounts receivable are assets, and assets have normal debit balances. Therefore, the form used in the accounts receivable ledger has a Debit Balance column instead of a Credit Balance column.

Accounts in CarLand's accounts receivable ledger are arranged in alphabetic order and kept in a loose-leaf binder. Periodically, accounts for new customers are added and accounts no longer used are removed from the accounts receivable ledger. The customer number 130 had been assigned to a former customer. That account, however, had been removed from the ledger. Therefore, customer number 130 is available for assignment to Friendly Auto Service.

Some businesses record both the customer name and customer address on the ledger form. However, the address information is usually kept in a separate name and address file. This practice eliminates having to record the customer address on the ledger form each time a new ledger page is opened or the address changes.

## Opening customer accounts

Procedures for opening customer accounts are similar to those used for opening vendor accounts. The customer name is obtained from the first sales invoice prepared for a customer. The customer number is assigned using the three-digit numbering system described on page 291. The customer name and customer number are written on the heading of the ledger account. The account opened for Friendly Auto Service is shown in Illustration 14-12.

## Posting from a journal to an accounts receivable ledger

Each entry in the Accounts Receivable columns of a journal affects the customer named in the Account Title column. Each amount listed in these two columns is posted to a customer account in the accounts receivable ledger often. Posting often keeps each customer account balance up to date. Totals of Accounts Receivable special amount columns are posted to the general ledger at the end of each month.

**Posting a debit to an accounts receivable ledger.** Posting a debit for a sale on account from the journal to the accounts receivable ledger is shown in Illustration 14-13.

Five steps are followed to post the entry on line 4 of the journal to the accounts receivable ledger.

1 Write the date, *3*, in the Date column of the account.

2 Write the journal page number, *21*, in the Post. Ref. column of the account.

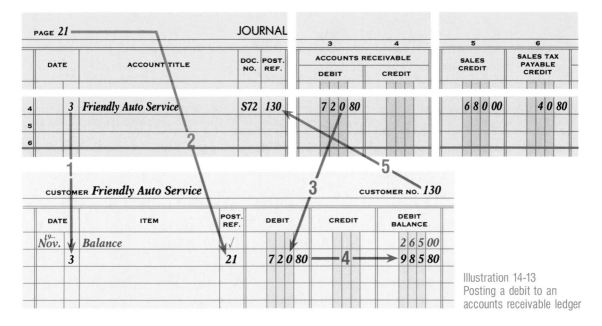

Illustration 14-13
Posting a debit to an
accounts receivable ledger

**3** Write the debit amount, *$720.80*, in the Debit amount column of the account for Friendly Auto Service.

**4** Add the amount in the Debit amount column to the previous balance in the Debit Balance column ($265.00 + $720.80 = $985.80). Write the new account balance, *$985.80*, in the Debit Balance column.

**5** Write the customer number, *130*, in the Post. Ref. column of the journal. The customer number shows that the posting for this entry is completed.

The controlling account in the general ledger, Accounts Receivable, is also increased by this entry. At the end of the month, the journal's Accounts Receivable Debit column total is posted to the controlling account, Accounts Receivable.

**Posting a credit to an accounts receivable ledger.** The same steps are followed to post a credit to a customer account as are used to post a debit. However, the credit amount is written in the Credit amount column of the customer account. The credit amount is subtracted from the previous debit balance. Posting a cash receipt on account from the journal to the accounts receivable ledger is shown in Illustration 14-14 on page 300.

The controlling account in the general ledger, Accounts Receivable, is decreased by this entry. However, the amount is not posted individually to the accounts receivable account. At the end of the month, the amount, *$318.00*, is posted as part of the special amount column total to Accounts Receivable.

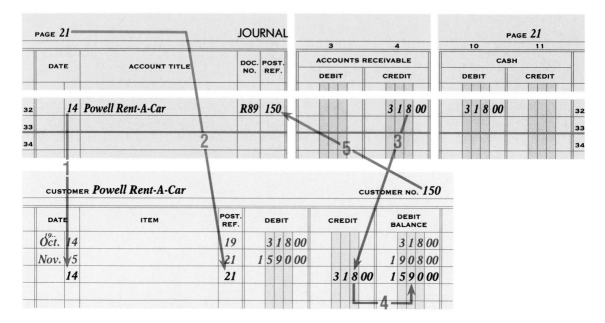

Illustration 14-14
Posting a credit to an
accounts receivable ledger

## Opening a new page for a customer in an accounts receivable ledger

Procedures for opening a new page in an accounts receivable ledger are similar to those for an accounts payable ledger. The customer name and customer number are written at the top of the new account page. The date is recorded in the Date column. The word *Balance* is written in the Item column. A check mark is placed in the Post. Ref. column to show that the amount has been carried forward from a previous page rather than posted from a journal. The account balance is recorded in the Debit Balance column.

## Completed accounts receivable ledger

CarLand's accounts receivable ledger after all posting has been completed is shown in Illustration 14-15.

CUSTOMER *Ashley Delivery*                                    CUSTOMER NO. *110*

| DATE | | ITEM | POST. REF. | DEBIT | CREDIT | DEBIT BALANCE |
|---|---|---|---|---|---|---|
| Nov.^19.. | 1 | Balance | ✓ | | | 2 4 9 1 00 |
| | 9 | | 21 | 4 7 7 00 | | 2 9 6 8 00 |
| | 16 | | 22 | 1 3 7 8 00 | | 4 3 4 6 00 |
| | 17 | | 22 | | 2 4 9 1 00 | 1 8 5 5 00 |

Illustration 14-15
Accounts receivable ledger
after posting has been
completed

Illustration 14-15
Accounts receivable ledger
after posting has been
completed
(concluded)

CUSTOMER *Autohaus Service*                                            CUSTOMER NO. *120*

| DATE | | ITEM | POST. REF. | DEBIT | CREDIT | DEBIT BALANCE |
|---|---|---|---|---|---|---|
| Nov. | 1 | Balance | ✓ | | | 1 8 0 2 00 |
| | 6 | | 21 | | 1 8 0 2 00 | |
| | 18 | | 22 | 2 0 1 4 00 | | 2 0 1 4 00 |

CUSTOMER *Friendly Auto Service*                                       CUSTOMER NO. *130*

| DATE | | ITEM | POST. REF. | DEBIT | CREDIT | DEBIT BALANCE |
|---|---|---|---|---|---|---|
| Nov. | 1 | Balance | ✓ | | | 2 6 5 00 |
| | 3 | | 21 | 7 2 0 80 | | 9 8 5 80 |
| | 24 | | 22 | 7 4 2 00 | | 1 7 2 7 80 |
| | 25 | | 22 | | 2 6 5 00 | 1 4 6 2 80 |

CUSTOMER *Keystone Delivery*                                           CUSTOMER NO. *140*

| DATE | | ITEM | POST. REF. | DEBIT | CREDIT | DEBIT BALANCE |
|---|---|---|---|---|---|---|
| Oct. | 10 | | 19 | 9 5 4 00 | | 9 5 4 00 |
| Nov. | 10 | | 21 | | 9 5 4 00 | |
| | 24 | | 22 | 3 1 8 00 | | 3 1 8 00 |
| | 29 | | 22 | 1 3 7 8 00 | | 1 6 9 6 00 |

CUSTOMER *Powell Rent-A-Car*                                           CUSTOMER NO. *150*

| DATE | | ITEM | POST. REF. | DEBIT | CREDIT | DEBIT BALANCE |
|---|---|---|---|---|---|---|
| Oct. | 14 | | 19 | 3 1 8 00 | | 3 1 8 00 |
| Nov. | 5 | | 21 | 1 5 9 0 00 | | 1 9 0 8 00 |
| | 14 | | 21 | | 3 1 8 00 | 1 5 9 0 00 |

CUSTOMER *Wood Sales & Service*                                        CUSTOMER NO. *160*

| DATE | | ITEM | POST. REF. | DEBIT | CREDIT | DEBIT BALANCE |
|---|---|---|---|---|---|---|
| Nov. | 1 | Balance | ✓ | | | 2 1 2 0 00 |
| | 11 | | 21 | 6 0 4 20 | | 2 7 2 4 20 |
| | 13 | | 21 | | 9 0 1 00 | 1 8 2 3 20 |
| | 20 | | 22 | | 1 2 1 9 00 | 6 0 4 20 |

# PROVING THE ACCURACY OF POSTING

A single error in posting to a ledger account may cause the trial balance to be out of balance. An error in posting may cause the cash account balance to disagree with the actual cash on hand. An error in posting may also cause the income to be understated or overstated on an income statement. An error in posting may also cause a business to overpay or underpay its vendors. Posting must be accurate to assure correct account balances. Therefore, to prove the accuracy of posting, three things are done. (1) Cash is proved. (2) Subsidiary schedules are prepared to prove that the total of the balances in the subsidiary ledgers equals the balance of the controlling account in the general ledger. (3) A trial balance is prepared to prove that debits equal credits in the general ledger.

Preparation of a trial balance is described in Chapter 17.

## Proving cash

The method used to prove cash is described in Chapter 13. The cash proof total is compared with the balance on the next unused check stub in the checkbook.

## Proving the subsidiary ledgers

A controlling account balance in a general ledger must equal the sum of all account balances in a subsidiary ledger. CarLand proves the accounts payable and accounts receivable subsidiary ledgers at the end of each month.

**Proving accounts payable.** A listing of vendor accounts, account balances, and total amount due all vendors is called a schedule of accounts payable. A schedule of accounts payable is prepared after all entries in a journal are posted. CarLand's schedule of accounts payable, prepared on November 30, is shown in Illustration 14-16.

| CarLand | |
|---|---|
| *Schedule of Accounts Payable* | |
| *November 30, 19--* | |
| *Antelo Supply* | 7 5 0 00 |
| *Bell Office Products* | 8 3 0 00 |
| *Filtrex Tires* | 3 1 8 0 00 |
| *Nilon Motor Parts* | 3 4 5 6 00 |
| *Q-Ban Distributors* | 5 9 0 0 00 |
| *Veloz Automotive* | 1 7 5 4 00 |
| *Total Accounts Payable* | 15 8 7 0 00 |

Illustration 14-16
Schedule of accounts
payable

The balance of Accounts Payable in the general ledger is $15,870.00. The total of the schedule of accounts payable is $15,870.00. Because the two amounts are the same, the accounts payable ledger is proved.

**Proving accounts receivable.** A listing of customer accounts, account balances, and total amount due from all customers is called a schedule of accounts receivable. A schedule of accounts receivable is prepared after all entries in a journal are posted. CarLand's schedule of accounts receivable, prepared on November 30, is shown in Illustration 14-17.

| CarLand | |
|---|---|
| **Schedule of Accounts Receivable** | |
| **November 30, 19--** | |
| *Ashley Delivery* | 1 8 5 5 00 |
| *Autohaus Service* | 2 0 1 4 00 |
| *Friendly Auto Service* | 1 4 6 2 80 |
| *Keystone Delivery* | 1 6 9 6 00 |
| *Powell Rent-A-Car* | 1 5 9 0 00 |
| *Wood Sales & Service* | 6 0 4 20 |
| *Total Accounts Receivable* | 9 2 2 2 00 |

Illustration 14-17
Schedule of accounts
receivable

The balance of Accounts Receivable in the general ledger is $9,222.00. The total of the schedule of accounts receivable is $9,222.00. Because the two amounts are the same, the accounts receivable ledger is proved.

# SUMMARY OF POSTING TO GENERAL AND SUBSIDIARY LEDGERS

A summary of the posting steps from Rugcare's journal is in Chapter 5. The steps described for Rugcare also apply to posting from an expanded journal. However, special amount columns and controlling accounts require an additional set of posting steps.

## Posting from a journal's general columns

As shown in Illustration 14-18 on page 304, separate amounts in General columns *ARE* posted individually. Totals of General Debit and Credit columns *ARE NOT* posted.

Illustration 14-18
Summary of posting from
a journal's general columns

## Posting from a journal's special columns

As shown in Illustration 14-19, totals of special amount columns *ARE* posted to the account named in the column heading. The column total shown *IS* posted as a credit to the named account. Separate amounts in special columns *ARE NOT* posted individually unless the columns affect a controlling account.

Illustration 14-19
Summary of posting from
a journal's special columns

## Posting from a journal's special columns for controlling accounts

As shown in Illustration 14-20, separate amounts and total amounts are posted from special columns for controlling accounts. Separate amounts in the Accounts Receivable Debit and Credit columns *ARE* posted individually to customer accounts. These accounts are found in the accounts receivable ledger. As the last posting step, a customer number is written in the Post. Ref. column of the journal. The customer number shows that posting of a separate amount to a customer account has been completed.

Totals of special columns *ARE* posted to the controlling accounts named in the column headings. The total of an Accounts Receivable Debit column is posted as a debit to Accounts Receivable in the general ledger. The total of an Accounts Receivable Credit column is posted as a credit to Accounts Receivable in the general ledger. As a last posting step, an account number is placed in parentheses under the total of a special amount column. The number shows the general ledger account to which the total was posted.

Illustration 14-20
Summary of posting from special columns for controlling accounts

The same principles used for Accounts Receivable amount columns also apply to Accounts Payable amount columns in a journal.

## ■ ACCOUNTING TERMS

What is the meaning of each of the following?

**1.** subsidiary ledger
**2.** accounts payable ledger
**3.** accounts receivable ledger

**4.** controlling account
**5.** schedule of accounts payable

**6.** schedule of accounts receivable

## ■ QUESTIONS FOR INDIVIDUAL STUDY

**1.** How is journal entry information sorted and summarized?

**2.** What determines the number of ledgers used in an accounting system?

**3.** What ledger contains all accounts needed to prepare an income statement and a balance sheet?

**4.** What type of business would generally use a single ledger?

**5.** Why would a business keep a separate account for each vendor and each customer?

**6.** Why would a business keep a separate ledger for vendors and a separate ledger for customers?

**7.** What is the title of the general ledger controlling account for vendors?

**8.** What is the title of the general ledger controlling account for customers?

**9.** Why is posting to a general ledger done only periodically throughout the month?

**10.** What determines the frequency of posting to a general ledger?

**11.** Why are amounts recorded in a journal's general amount columns posted individually?

**12.** Why are separate amounts in special amount columns not posted individually to the general ledger?

**13.** Why is a check mark placed in parentheses below the General Debit and General Credit column totals?

**14.** What does the first digit in a vendor or customer number identify?

**15.** Why does the 3-column account form used in an accounts payable ledger have a Credit Balance column?

**16.** Why is posting of separate amounts in the Accounts Payable columns done often?

**17.** How often are the totals of the Accounts Payable columns of a journal posted?

**18.** Why is a check mark entered in the Post. Ref. column when a new page is opened for a vendor?

**19.** Why does the 3-column account form used in an accounts receivable ledger have a Debit Balance column?

**20.** How are subsidiary ledgers proved at the end of a month?

## ▮ CASES FOR MANAGEMENT DECISION

**CASE 1** Edna Doyle, an accountant, is asked to evaluate the accounting system of Dotson's Department Store. The general ledger includes individual accounts for each vendor and customer. When checking the records and accounting procedures, Ms. Doyle notes the bulky general ledger and long trial balance. Dotson's Department Store uses a 5-column journal to record all transactions. A general ledger is used to maintain all income statement, balance sheet, vendor, and customer accounts. Transactions affecting vendor or customer accounts are recorded in the General Debit or General Credit columns of the journal. Separate vendor and customer entries are then posted individually to accounts in the general ledger. What recommendations should Ms. Doyle make concerning the handling of vendor and customer accounts?

**CASE 2** Automart purchased merchandise on account six weeks ago for $400.00 from Belview Supply. A check for $400.00 was sent three weeks ago in payment of the account. Although no additional purchases have been made, Automart recently received a bill from Belview Supply that listed the balance due as $800.00. What probably caused this error? When would the error probably be discovered?

**CASE 3** Leon Reyes observes his accountant at work and says, "You post each individual accounts receivable entry in the journal. Then you post the totals of the Accounts Receivable columns. You are posting these entries twice, which will make the records wrong." The accountant does not agree that the posting procedure is incorrect. Is Mr. Reyes or his accountant correct? Why?

## ▮ DRILLS FOR UNDERSTANDING

### DRILL 14-D1   Analyzing transactions of a merchandising business

**Instructions:** Prepare T accounts for each of the following transactions. Use the T accounts to analyze each transaction. A 6% sales tax has been added to each sale. The first transaction is given as an example.

| Accounts Receivable | | Sales | | Sales Tax Payable | |
|---|---|---|---|---|---|
| 127.20 | | | 120.00 | | 7.20 |

*Transactions*

1. Sold merchandise on account to Sarah Burke, $120.00, plus sales tax, $7.20; total, $127.20.
2. Paid cash on account to Casa Enterprises, $950.00.
3. Paid cash for rent, $1,250.00.
4. Discovered that a payment for advertising was journalized and posted in error as a debit to Miscellaneous Expense instead of Advertising Expense, $125.00.
5. Paid cash for office supplies, $80.00.
6. Recorded cash and credit card sales, $1,850.00, plus sales tax, $111.00; total, $1,961.00.
7. Joyce Berling, partner, withdrew merchandise for personal use, $90.00.
8. Purchased merchandise on account from Irvine Products, $1,640.00.
9. Received cash on account from Carl Downing, $227.90.
10. Purchased merchandise for cash, $130.00.
11. Michael Zolty, partner, withdrew cash for personal use, $700.00.
12. Bought store supplies on account from Carter Supply, $315.00.

*The solution to Drill 14-D1 is needed to complete Drill 14-D2.*

## DRILL 14-D2   Analyzing, journalizing, and posting transactions of a merchandising business

*The solution to Drill 14-D1 is needed to complete Drill 14-D2.*

**Instructions: 1.** Use a form similar to the following. Based on the answers in Drill 14-D1, place a check mark in the amount columns to be used to journalize each transaction. Transaction 1 is given as an example.

| Transaction | Amount columns in the journal | | | | | | | | | | |
|---|---|---|---|---|---|---|---|---|---|---|---|
| | General | | Accts. Rec. | | Sales Credit | Sales Tax Pay. Credit | Accts. Payable | | Purch. Debit | Cash | |
| | Debit | Credit | Debit | Credit | | | Debit | Credit | | Debit | Credit |
| 1. Debit amount | | | ✓ | | | | | | | | |
| Credit amount | | | | | ✓ | | | | | | |
| Credit amount | | | | | | ✓ | | | | | |

**2.** Use a form similar to the following. Based on the answers to Instruction 1, place a check mark in the proper column to indicate whether the amount will or will not be posted individually to the ledgers. Transaction 1 is given as an example.

| Transaction | Posted individually to | | | Not posted individually to any ledger |
|---|---|---|---|---|
| | General Ledger | Accts. Receivable Ledger | Accts. Payable Ledger | |
| 1. Debit amount | | ✓ | | |
| Credit amount | | | | ✓ |
| Credit amount | | | | ✓ |

■ APPLICATION PROBLEM
_____

**PROBLEM 14-1**   **Opening accounts and posting to ledgers from a journal**

The journal for Carpet Magic is given in the working papers accompanying this textbook.

**Instructions: 1.** Open new pages for the following accounts in the general ledger. Record the balances as of September 1 of the current year.

| Account No. | Account Title | Account Balance |
|---|---|---|
| 1110 | Cash ................................................... | $ 18,300.00 |
| 1130 | Accounts Receivable .................................. | 8,470.00 |
| 1150 | Supplies—Office ...................................... | 3,680.00 |
| 1160 | Supplies—Store ...................................... | 4,260.00 |
| 1170 | Prepaid Insurance .................................... | 1,560.00 |
| 2110 | Accounts Payable ..................................... | 10,555.00 |
| 2120 | Sales Tax Payable .................................... | 1,235.00 |
| 3120 | Diane Engler, Drawing ................................ | 8,000.00 |
| 3140 | Paul Sisco, Drawing .................................. | 8,340.00 |
| 4110 | Sales ................................................ | 172,420.00 |
| 5110 | Purchases ............................................ | 96,500.00 |
| 6110 | Advertising Expense .................................. | 1,860.00 |
| 6140 | Miscellaneous Expense ................................ | 1,310.00 |
| 6160 | Rent Expense ......................................... | 8,000.00 |

**2.** Open new pages for the following vendor accounts in the accounts payable ledger. Record the balances as of September 1 of the current year.

| Vendor No. | Vendor Name | Purchase No. | Account Balance |
|---|---|---|---|
| 210 | Crown Carpet Co. ............................ | 52 | $2,575.00 |
| 220 | Marlow Industries ............................ | 53 | 4,220.00 |
| 230 | Superior Carpeting ........................... | — | — |
| 240 | V & P Carpet Co. ............................. | 51 | 3,760.00 |

**3.** Open new pages for the following customer accounts in the accounts receivable ledger. Record the balances as of September 1 of the current year.

| Customer No. | Customer Name | Sales No. | Account Balance |
|---|---|---|---|
| 110 | Cameo Shoe Store ............................ | 44 | $3,680.00 |
| 120 | Paula Hughs ................................. | 42 | 1,850.00 |
| 130 | Elsa Leyba .................................. | 43 | 2,940.00 |
| 140 | Scott Ward .................................. | — | — |

**4.** Post the separate items recorded in the following columns of the journal. (a) General Debit and Credit. (b) Accounts Receivable Debit and Credit. (c) Accounts Payable Debit and Credit.

**5.** Post the totals of the special columns of the journal.

**6.** Prepare a schedule of accounts payable. Compare the total of the schedule with the balance of the controlling account, Accounts Payable, in the general ledger. If the totals are not the same, find and correct the errors.

**7.** Prepare a schedule of accounts receivable. Compare the total of the schedule with the balance of the controlling account, Accounts Receivable, in the general ledger. If the totals are not the same, find and correct the errors.

# ■ ENRICHMENT PROBLEMS

MASTERY PROBLEM 14-M **Posting to ledgers from a journal**

The journal and ledgers for Anton Leather Goods are given in the working papers accompanying this textbook.

**Instructions: 1.** Post the separate items recorded in the following columns of the journal. (a) General Debit and Credit. (b) Accounts Receivable Debit and Credit. (c) Accounts Payable Debit and Credit.

**2.** Post the totals of the special columns of the journal.

**3.** Prepare a schedule of accounts payable and a schedule of accounts receivable. Prove the accuracy of the subsidiary ledgers by comparing the schedule totals with the balances of the controlling accounts in the general ledger. If the totals are not the same, find and correct the errors.

CHALLENGE PROBLEM 14-C **Journalizing and posting business transactions**

The general ledger, accounts payable, and accounts receivable accounts for Par Golf Products are given in the working papers accompanying this textbook. The balances are recorded as of November 1 of the current year.

## PARTIAL GENERAL LEDGER

| Account No. | Account Title | Account Balance |
|---|---|---|
| 1110 | Cash | $ 16,850.00 |
| 1130 | Accounts Receivable | 2,867.30 |
| 1150 | Supplies—Office | 2,635.00 |
| 1160 | Supplies—Store | 2,160.00 |
| 2110 | Accounts Payable | 8,023.00 |
| 2120 | Sales Tax Payable | 1,312.00 |
| 3120 | Maria Adolfo, Drawing | 12,800.00 |
| 3140 | Lawrence Phipps, Drawing | 12,540.00 |
| 4110 | Sales | 218,749.00 |
| 5110 | Purchases | 112,500.00 |
| 6110 | Advertising Expense | 2,940.00 |
| 6140 | Miscellaneous Expense | 1,410.00 |
| 6160 | Rent Expense | 9,500.00 |
| 6190 | Utilities Expense | 1,785.00 |

## ACCOUNTS PAYABLE LEDGER

| Vendor No. | Vendor Name | Purchase No. | Account Balance |
|---|---|---|---|
| 210 | Artex Golf Products | P74 | $2,430.00 |
| 220 | Ecola Golf Equipment | P72 | 1,965.00 |
| 230 | Garcia Supply | — | — |
| 240 | Patton Golf Co. | P75 | 948.00 |
| 250 | Valiant Golf Co. | P73 | 2,680.00 |

## ACCOUNTS RECEIVABLE LEDGER

| Customer No. | Customer Name | Sales No. | Account Balance |
|---|---|---|---|
| 110 | William Backus | S52 | $ 795.00 |
| 120 | Linda Boge | S50 | 678.40 |
| 130 | Jonathan Dunbar | — | — |
| 140 | James Patco | S53 | 1,160.70 |
| 150 | Bertha Welsh | S51 | 233.20 |

**Instructions: 1.** Journalize the following transactions completed during November of the current year. Use page 18 of a journal similar to the one described in this chapter. Add a 6% sales tax to all sales transactions. Source documents are abbreviated as follows: check, C; memorandum, M; purchase invoice, P; receipt, R; sales invoice, S; cash register tape, T.

Nov. 2. Paid cash for rent, $950.00. C275.
3. Purchased merchandise on account from Valiant Golf Co., $1,625.00. P76.
4. Purchased merchandise for cash, $119.00. C276.
5. Received cash on account from Linda Boge, $678.40, covering S50. R45.
7. Paid cash on account to Ecola Golf Equipment, $1,965.00, covering P72. C277.
7. Recorded cash and credit card sales, $4,730.00. T7.
  *Posting.* Post the items that are to be posted individually.
9. Maria Adolfo, partner, withdrew merchandise for personal use, $165.00. M35.
11. Sold merchandise on account to James Patco, $255.00. S54.
12. Discovered that store supplies bought for cash was journalized and posted in error as a debit to Advertising Expense instead of Supplies—Store, $93.00. M36.
14. Bought store supplies on account from Garcia Supply, $215.00. M37.
14. Recorded cash and credit card sales, $4,840.00. T14.
  *Posting.* Post the items that are to be posted individually.
16. Maria Adolfo, partner, withdrew cash for personal use, $1,200.00. C278.
16. Lawrence Phipps, partner, withdrew cash for personal use, $1,200.00. C279.
17. Paid cash for electric bill, $183.50. C280.
20. Paid cash on account to Valiant Golf Co., $2,680.00, covering P73. C281.
21. Recorded cash and credit card sales, $4,480.00. T21.
  *Posting.* Post the items that are to be posted individually.
23. Paid cash on account to Artex Golf Products, $2,430.00, covering P74. C282.
24. Sold merchandise on account to Jonathan Dunbar, $1,095.00. S55.
26. Received cash on account from Bertha Welsh, $233.20, covering S51. R46.
26. Purchased merchandise on account from Patton Golf Co., $1,285.00. P77.
27. Received cash on account from William Backus, $795.00, covering S52. R47.
28. Purchased merchandise on account from Artex Golf Products, $2,325.00. P78.
28. Sold merchandise on account to Bertha Welsh, $1,095.00. S56.
28. Recorded cash and credit card sales, $4,630.00. T28.
  *Posting.* Post the items that are to be posted individually.
30. Paid cash to replenish the petty cash fund, $302.00: office supplies, $48.00; store supplies, $62.00; advertising, $74.00; miscellaneous, $118.00. C283.
30. Recorded cash and credit card sales, $840.00. T30.
  *Posting.* Post the items that are to be posted individually.

**2.** Total the journal. Prove the equality of debits and credits.
**3.** Prove cash. The balance on the next unused check stub is $28,218.30.
**4.** Rule the journal.
**5.** Post the totals of the special columns of the journal.
**6.** Prepare a schedule of accounts payable and a schedule of accounts receivable. Prove the accuracy of the subsidiary ledgers by comparing the schedule totals with the balances of the controlling accounts in the general ledger. If the totals are not the same, find and correct the errors.

# Computer Application 3
# Automated Accounting Cycle for a
# Partnership: Journalizing and
# Posting Transactions

A business' financial information may be recorded, summarized, and reported using either a manual or an automated accounting system. Petlodge, the service business described in Part 2, uses an automated accounting system. CarLand, the merchandising business described in Part 3, uses a manual accounting system. CarLand's manual journalizing procedures for purchases, cash payments, sales, and cash receipts are described in Chapters 12 and 13. Manual posting procedures are described in Chapter 14. Computer Application 3 describes procedures for using a microcomputer to journalize and post CarLand's business transactions. Computer Application Problem 3 contains instructions for using a microcomputer to solve Challenge Problem 14-C, Chapter 14.

## AUTOMATED ACCOUNTING PROCEDURES FOR CARLAND

CarLand uses six forms to arrange its data for automated accounting.

1. General ledger file maintenance input form (FORM GL-1)—for building or changing a general ledger chart of accounts.
2. Accounts payable file maintenance input form (FORM AP-1)—for building or changing an accounts payable chart of accounts.
3. Accounts receivable file maintenance input form (FORM AR-1)—for building or changing an accounts receivable chart of accounts.
4. General ledger input form (FORM GL-2)—for recording general ledger opening account balances and for recording journal entries not affecting either accounts payable or accounts receivable.
5. Accounts payable input form (FORM AP-2)—for recording vendor

opening account balances and for recording purchases on account, buying supplies on account, and cash payments on account.

6. Accounts receivable input form (FORM AR-2)—for recording customer opening account balances and for recording sales on account and cash receipts on account.

# BUILDING A CHART OF ACCOUNTS

CarLand's chart of accounts for the general and subsidiary ledgers is on page 250.

## Building a general ledger chart of accounts

The same procedures described for Petlodge in Part 2 are used to build CarLand's general ledger chart of accounts. A general ledger file maintenance input form (FORM GL-1) is used to describe the general ledger chart of accounts for computer processing. The cash account is entered as shown in Illustration C3-1. All general ledger account numbers and titles are entered on the input form in the same way.

GENERAL LEDGER
FILE MAINTENANCE
Input Form

RUN   DATE  11 01 / --
          MM  DD  YY

FORM GL-1

| | ACCOUNT NUMBER | ACCOUNT TITLE | |
|---|---|---|---|
| 1 | 1110 | Cash | 1 |
| 2 | | | 2 |
| 3 | | | 3 |
| 4 | | | 4 |
| 5 | | | 5 |

Illustration C3-1
General ledger file
maintenance input form for
chart of accounts

The General Ledger Main Menu is shown in Illustration C3-2.

Option A is selected from the General Ledger Main Menu to display spaces for key-entering the general ledger chart of accounts data into the computer. After all chart of accounts data are entered, Option B is selected from the General Ledger Main Menu. This option directs the computer to prepare a chart of accounts report.

## Building an accounts payable chart of accounts

An accounts payable file maintenance input form (FORM AP-1) is used to describe CarLand's accounts payable chart of accounts for computer processing. The vendor account of Antelo Supply is shown recorded on

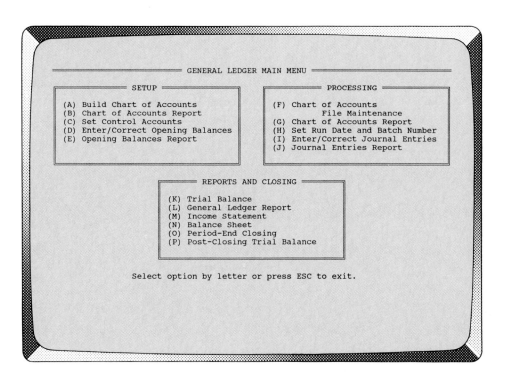

```
========== GENERAL LEDGER MAIN MENU ==========

====== SETUP ======              ====== PROCESSING ======
(A) Build Chart of Accounts       (F) Chart of Accounts
(B) Chart of Accounts Report              File Maintenance
(C) Set Control Accounts          (G) Chart of Accounts Report
(D) Enter/Correct Opening Balances (H) Set Run Date and Batch Number
(E) Opening Balances Report       (I) Enter/Correct Journal Entries
                                  (J) Journal Entries Report

            ====== REPORTS AND CLOSING ======
            (K) Trial Balance
            (L) General Ledger Report
            (M) Income Statement
            (N) Balance Sheet
            (O) Period-End Closing
            (P) Post-Closing Trial Balance

        Select option by letter or press ESC to exit.
```

line 1 in Illustration C3-3. All vendor numbers and names are entered on the input form in the same way.

Illustration C3-2
General ledger main menu

| | | ACCOUNTS PAYABLE FILE MAINTENANCE Input Form | FORM AP-1 |
|---|---|---|---|

RUN DATE 11/01/-- MM DD YY

| | VENDOR NUMBER | VENDOR NAME | |
|---|---|---|---|
| 1 | 210 | Antelo Supply | 1 |
| 2 | 220 | Bell Office Products | 2 |
| 3 | 230 | Filtrex Tires | 3 |
| 4 | 240 | Nilon Motor Parts | 4 |
| 5 | 250 | Q-Ban Distributors | 5 |
| 6 | 260 | Veloz Automotive | 6 |

Illustration C3-3
Accounts payable file
maintenance input form for
chart of accounts

The Accounts Payable Main Menu is shown in Illustration C3-4.

Option A is selected from the Accounts Payable Main Menu to display spaces for key-entering the accounts payable chart of accounts data. After all vendor accounts have been key-entered, Option B is selected from the Accounts Payable Main Menu. This option directs the computer to prepare a vendor list.

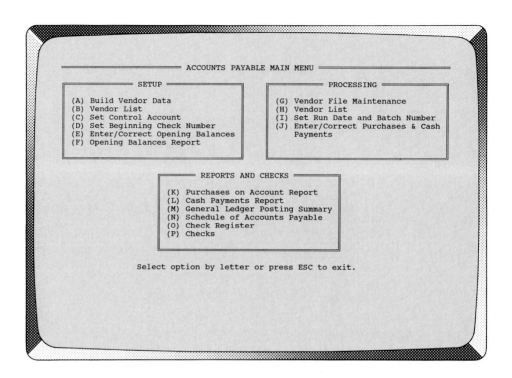

Illustration C3-4
Accounts payable main
menu

## Building an accounts receivable chart of accounts

An accounts receivable file maintenance input form (FORM AR-1) is used to describe CarLand's accounts receivable chart of accounts for computer processing. The customer account of Ashley Delivery is shown recorded on line 1 in Illustration C3-5. All customer numbers and names are entered on the input form in the same way.

ACCOUNTS RECEIVABLE
FILE MAINTENANCE
Input Form

RUN  DATE  **11** / **01** / **--**
                MM  DD  YY

FORM AR-1

| | CUSTOMER NUMBER | CUSTOMER NAME | |
|---|---|---|---|
| 1 | 110 | A s h l e y   D e l i v e r y | 1 |
| 2 | 120 | A u t o h a u s   S e r v i c e | 2 |
| 3 | 130 | F r i e n d l y   A u t o   S e r v i c e | 3 |
| 4 | 140 | K e y s t o n e   D e l i v e r y | 4 |
| 5 | 150 | P o w e l l   R e n t - A - C a r | 5 |
| 6 | 160 | W o o d   S a l e s   &   S e r v i c e | 6 |
| 7 | | | 7 |

Illustration C3-5
Accounts receivable file
maintenance input form for
chart of accounts

The Accounts Receivable Main Menu is shown in Illustration C3-6.

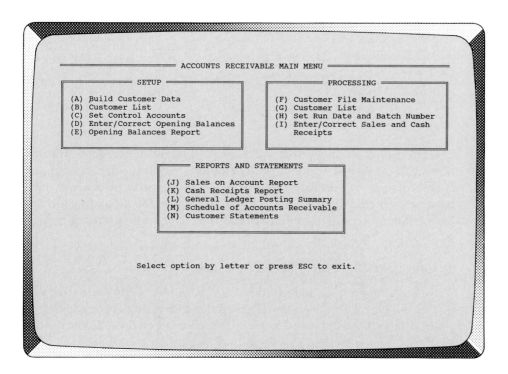

```
══════════════════ ACCOUNTS RECEIVABLE MAIN MENU ══════════════════
┌─══════ SETUP ══════─┐         ┌─══════ PROCESSING ══════─┐
│ (A) Build Customer Data        │  (F) Customer File Maintenance │
│ (B) Customer List              │  (G) Customer List            │
│ (C) Set Control Accounts       │  (H) Set Run Date and Batch Number │
│ (D) Enter/Correct Opening Balances │  (I) Enter/Correct Sales and Cash │
│ (E) Opening Balances Report    │      Receipts                 │
└────────────────────┘         └────────────────────┘

      ┌─══════ REPORTS AND STATEMENTS ══════─┐
      │ (J) Sales on Account Report          │
      │ (K) Cash Receipts Report             │
      │ (L) General Ledger Posting Summary   │
      │ (M) Schedule of Accounts Receivable  │
      │ (N) Customer Statements              │
      └──────────────────────────────────────┘


        Select option by letter or press ESC to exit.
```

Option A is selected from the Accounts Receivable Main Menu to display spaces for key-entering the accounts receivable chart of accounts data. After all customer accounts have been key-entered, Option B is selected from the Accounts Receivable Main Menu. This option directs the computer to prepare a customer list.

Illustration C3-6
Accounts receivable main menu

# RECORDING OPENING ACCOUNT BALANCES

In an automated accounting system, opening account balances for the general and subsidiary ledgers are recorded on input forms.

## Recording general ledger opening account balances

A general ledger input form (FORM GL-2) is used to journalize general ledger opening account balances. The same procedures described for Petlodge, Chapter 10, are followed by CarLand to journalize general ledger opening account balances. The opening account balance for CarLand's cash account is shown in Illustration C3-7. All general ledger opening account balances are journalized in the same way.

Illustration C3-7
General ledger input form
for opening account
balances

Option D is selected from the General Ledger Main Menu, Illustration C3-2, to display spaces for key-entering general ledger opening account balances. After all general ledger opening account balances have been key-entered and posted, Option E is selected from the General Ledger Main Menu. This option directs the computer to prepare an opening balances report.

## Recording vendor opening account balances

An accounts payable input form (FORM AP-2) is used to journalize vendor opening account balances for computer processing. The opening account balance for Q-Ban Distributors is shown recorded on line 1 in Illustration C3-8.

Illustration C3-8
Accounts payable input
form for vendor opening
account balances

Nine steps are followed to journalize the opening account balance for Q-Ban Distributors on an accounts payable input form.

1 Enter the run date, *11/01/--*, in the space provided at the top of the form. The run date is the date CarLand starts its automated accounting system.

2 Enter the batch number, *1*, in the space provided at the top of the form. The number assigned to a group of journal entries is known as a batch number. Since the vendor opening account balances represent the first entries to the accounts payable ledger, batch number 1 is assigned.

3 Enter the purchase invoice number, *P71*, in the Purch. Invoice No. column. The purchase invoice number is the source document number for merchandise purchased on account still owed by CarLand. *(CONCEPT: Objective Evidence)*

4 Enter the vendor number, *250*, in the Vend. No. column. The vendor number is obtained from the vendor list.

5 Enter the date, *10/06/--*, in the Purchases Date column. This date is the date of Purchase Invoice No. 71.

6 Enter the general ledger account number for Purchases, *5110*, in the Gen. Ledger Acct. No. column.

7 Enter the amount, *$3,960.00*, in the Invoice Amount column.

8 Enter the disposition code, *A*, in the Disp. Code column. A disposition code indicates the action to be performed on the entry. Entering an *A* in this column indicates that the entry is a purchase of merchandise on account or a supplies bought on account transaction. This action is similar to recording a debit to Purchases and a credit to Accounts Payable in a journal. Entering an *M* in this column indicates that a previously recorded entry to Accounts Payable is to be paid with a check prepared manually. This action is similar to recording a debit to Accounts Payable and a credit to Cash in a journal.

9 After all vendor opening account balances have been journalized, the Invoice Amount column is totaled. The total is entered on the Batch Total line provided at the bottom of the form. If more than one accounts payable input form is required to journalize vendor opening account balances, the Invoice Amount column for all pages is totaled. The total for all pages is then entered *only* on the last page on the Batch Total line.

All vendor opening account balances are journalized in the same way. Some vendor account opening balances, however, are for supplies bought on account rather than purchases of merchandise on account. The entry for Antelo Supply on line 3 of the accounts payable input form in Illustration C3-8 is for supplies bought on account. The source document number recorded in the Purch. Invoice No. column is *M35*, the memorandum prepared when the supplies were bought on account. The general ledger account number recorded in the Gen. Ledger Acct. No. column is *1150*, the account number for Supplies—Store. This has the effect of recording a debit to Supplies—Store and a credit to Accounts Payable.

Option E is selected from the Accounts Payable Main Menu, Illustration C3-4, to display spaces for key-entering each vendor account balance. After all vendor opening account balances have been key-entered and posted, Option F is selected from the Accounts Payable Main Menu. This option directs the computer to prepare an opening balances report. The vendor opening balances report is checked for accuracy by comparing the report total with the batch total on the accounts payable input form. If the totals are not the same, the errors must be found and corrected. If the totals are the same, the vendor opening balances report is assumed to be correct.

## Recording customer opening account balances

An accounts receivable input form (FORM AR-2) is used to journalize customer opening account balances for computer processing. The opening account balance for Autohaus Service is shown recorded on line 1 in Illustration C3-9. All customer opening account balances are journalized in the same way.

| | SALES INVOICE NO. | CUST. NO. | MO. | DAY | YR. | GEN. LEDGER ACCT. NO. | INVOICE AMOUNT | SALES TAX % | MO. | DAY | YR. | DOC. NO. | CASH RECEIVED | |
|---|---|---|---|---|---|---|---|---|---|---|---|---|---|---|
| 1 | S65 | 120 | 10 | 06 | -- | 4110 | 1700 00 | 6 | | | | | | 1 |
| 2 | S66 | 140 | 10 | 10 | -- | 4110 | 900 00 | 6 | | | | | | 2 |
| 3 | S67 | 160 | 10 | 13 | -- | 4110 | 850 00 | 6 | | | | | | 3 |
| 4 | S68 | 150 | 10 | 14 | -- | 4110 | 300 00 | 6 | | | | | | 4 |
| 5 | S69 | 110 | 10 | 17 | -- | 4110 | 2350 00 | 6 | | | | | | 5 |
| 6 | S70 | 160 | 10 | 20 | -- | 4110 | 1150 00 | 6 | | | | | | 6 |
| 7 | S71 | 130 | 10 | 25 | -- | 4110 | 250 00 | 6 | | | | | | 7 |
| 8 | | | | | | | | | | | | | | 8 |
| 24 | | | | | | | | | | | | | | 24 |
| 25 | | | | | | | | | | | | | | 25 |

RUN DATE 11/01/--  MM DD YY

BATCH NO. 1

ACCOUNTS RECEIVABLE Input Form

FORM AR-2

SALES — CASH RECEIPTS

BATCH TOTALS  7500 00

Illustration C3-9
Accounts receivable input form for customer opening account balances

Nine steps are followed to journalize the opening account balance for Autohaus Service on an accounts receivable input form.

1 Enter the run date, *11/01/--*, in the space provided at the top of the form. The run date is the date CarLand starts its automated accounting system.

2 Enter the batch number, *1*, in the space provided at the top of the form. Since the customer opening account balances represent the first entries to the accounts receivable ledger, batch number 1 is assigned.

3 Enter the sales invoice number, *S65*, in the Sales Invoice No. column. This sales invoice number is the source document number for a sale of merchandise on account still due CarLand. *(CONCEPT: Objective Evidence)*

4 Enter the customer number, *120*, in the Cust. No. column. The customer number is obtained from the customer list.

5 Enter the date, *10/06/--*, in the Sales Date column. This date is the date CarLand issued Sales Invoice No. 65.

6 Enter the general ledger account number for Sales, *4110*, in the Gen. Ledger Acct. No. column.

7 Enter the amount, *$1,700.00*, in the Invoice Amount column.

8 Enter the sales tax percent, *6*, in the Sales Tax % column. The computer figures the sales tax amount based on the sales tax rate entered in the Sales Tax % column. CarLand operates in a state with a 6% sales tax rate.

9 After all customer opening account balances have been journalized, the Invoice Amount column is totaled. The total is recorded on the Batch Totals line provided at the bottom of the form. If more than one accounts receivable input form is required to record opening account balances, the Invoice Amount column for all pages is totaled. The total for all pages is then recorded *only* on the last page on the Batch Totals line.

Option D is selected from the Accounts Receivable Main Menu, Illustration C3-6, to display spaces for key-entering each customer account balance. After all customer opening account balances have been key-entered and posted, Option E is selected from the Accounts Receivable Main Menu. This option directs the computer to prepare an opening balances report. The customer opening balances report is checked for accuracy by comparing the report total with the batch total on the accounts receivable input form. If the totals are not the same, the errors must be found and corrected. If the totals are the same, the customer opening balances report is assumed to be correct.

# RECORDING TRANSACTIONS
# NOT AFFECTING SUBSIDIARY LEDGERS

CarLand records all transactions that affect vendor and customer accounts on accounts payable and accounts receivable input forms. All other transactions are recorded on a general ledger input form.

## Purchase of merchandise for cash

*November 2, 19--.*
*Purchased merchandise for cash, $483.00. Check No. 259.*

The entry to journalize this transaction is on lines 1 and 2 of the general ledger input form shown in Illustration C3-10. Purchases is debited and Cash is credited for $483.00.

The run date, *11/30/--*, is written in the space provided at the top of the form. The run date indicates that the transaction data entered on the input form are for November 1 through 30. The batch number, 2, is written in the space provided at the top of the form. Since batch number 1 was assigned to the general ledger opening account balances, batch number 2 is used for the group of journal entries for November 1 through 30.

On line 1, the day, *02*, is written in the Day column. The document number, *C259*, is entered in the Doc. No. column. The purchases account number, *5110*, is written in the Account Number column. The amount debited to Purchases, *$483.00*, is entered in the Debit Amount column.

On line 2, the cash account number, *1110*, is written in the Account Number column. The Day and Doc. No. columns are left blank starting with the second line of an entry. The date and document number are entered only once for each complete transaction. The amount credited to Cash, *$483.00*, is written in the Credit Amount column.

The same procedures are used to journalize any transactions that do not affect either the accounts payable or accounts receivable subsidiary ledgers.

## Buying supplies for cash

*November 5, 19--.*
*Paid cash for office supplies, $87.00. Check No. 261.*

The entry to journalize this transaction is on lines 5 and 6 of Illustration C3-10. Supplies—Office is debited and Cash is credited for $87.00.

## Cash and credit card sales

*November 7, 19--.*
*Recorded cash and credit card sales, $6,450.00, plus sales tax, $387.00; total, $6,837.00. Cash Register Tape No. 7.*

The entry to journalize this transaction is on lines 7 through 9 of Illustration C3-10. Cash is debited for $6,837.00. Sales Tax Payable is credited for $387.00. Sales is credited for $6,450.00.

RUN DATE <u>11 30 / --</u>
    MM  DD  YY

BATCH NO. [ 2 ]

**GENERAL LEDGER**
Input Form

[ FORM GL-2 ]

| | 1 | 2 | 3 | 4 | 5 | |
|---|---|---|---|---|---|---|
| | DAY | DOC. NO. | ACCOUNT NUMBER | DEBIT AMOUNT | CREDIT AMOUNT | |
| 1 | 02 | C259 | 5110 | 483 00 | | 1 |
| 2 | | | 1110 | | 483 00 | 2 |
| 3 | 02 | C260 | 6160 | 1500 00 | | 3 |
| 4 | | | 1110 | | 1500 00 | 4 |
| 5 | 05 | C261 | 1145 | 87 00 | | 5 |
| 6 | | | 1110 | | 87 00 | 6 |
| 7 | 07 | T7 | 1110 | 6837 00 | | 7 |
| 8 | | | 2140 | | 387 00 | 8 |
| 9 | | | 4110 | | 6450 00 | 9 |
| 10 | 09 | C264 | 6190 | 300 00 | | 10 |
| 11 | | | 1110 | | 300 00 | 11 |
| 12 | 09 | C265 | 6110 | 125 00 | | 12 |
| 13 | | | 1110 | | 125 00 | 13 |
| 14 | 09 | C266 | 1145 | 58 00 | | 14 |
| 15 | | | 1150 | 65 00 | | 15 |
| 16 | | | 6110 | 92 00 | | 16 |
| 17 | | | 6140 | 86 00 | | 17 |
| 18 | | | 1110 | | 301 00 | 18 |
| 19 | 10 | C267 | 3140 | 1500 00 | | 19 |
| 20 | | | 1110 | | 1500 00 | 20 |
| 21 | 12 | M44 | 3140 | 200 00 | | 21 |
| 22 | | | 5110 | | 200 00 | 22 |
| 23 | 13 | M45 | 6110 | 120 00 | | 23 |
| 24 | | | 6140 | | 120 00 | 24 |
| 25 | | | | | | 25 |
| 22 | 30 | T30 | 1110 | 1219 00 | | 22 |
| 23 | | | 2140 | | 69 00 | 23 |
| 24 | | | 4110 | | 1150 00 | 24 |
| 25 | | | | | | 25 |
| | | | BATCH TOTALS | 38863 22 | 38863 22 | |

Illustration C3-10
General ledger input form
with transactions entered

## Cash payment of an expense

*November 9, 19--.*
*Paid cash for advertising, $125.00. Check No. 265.*

The entry to journalize this transaction is on lines 12 and 13 of Illustration C3-10. Advertising Expense is debited and Cash is credited for $125.00.

## Cash payment to replenish petty cash

*November 9, 19--.*
*Paid cash to replenish the petty cash fund, $301.00: office supplies, $58.00; store supplies, $65.00; advertising, $92.00; miscellaneous, $86.00. Check No. 266.*

The entry to journalize this transaction is on lines 14 through 18 of Illustration C3-10. Supplies—Office is debited for $58.00, and Supplies—Store is debited for $65.00. Advertising Expense is debited for $92.00, and Miscellaneous Expense is debited for $86.00. Cash is credited for $301.00, the total amount needed to replenish the petty cash fund.

## Changes in capital

*November 10, 19--.*
*Dario Mesa, partner, withdrew cash for personal use, $1,500.00. Check No. 267.*

The entry to journalize this transaction is on lines 19 and 20 of Illustration C3-10. Dario Mesa, Drawing is debited and Cash is credited for $1,500.00.

*November 12, 19--.*
*Dario Mesa, partner, withdrew merchandise for personal use, $200.00. Memorandum No. 44.*

The entry to journalize this transaction is on lines 21 and 22 of Illustration C3-10. Dario Mesa, Drawing is debited and Purchases is credited for $200.00.

## Correcting entry

*November 13, 19--.*
*Discovered that a payment of cash for advertising in October was journalized and posted in error as a debit to Miscellaneous Expense instead of Advertising Expense, $120.00. Memorandum No. 45.*

The entry to journalize this transaction is on lines 23 and 24 of Illustration C3-10. Advertising Expense is debited and Miscellaneous Expense is credited for $120.00.

Carland's general ledger input form has 25 lines. After the correcting entry is recorded on lines 23 and 24, only one line remains on the form. The debit and credit parts of a transaction should always be recorded on the same page of an input form. Therefore, the next transaction is recorded on the second page of a general ledger input form.

CarLand's general ledger entries required three pages of general ledger input forms. The last four lines of the third page are shown at the bottom of Illustration C3-10.

After all transactions have been journalized, the Debit Amount and Credit Amount columns are totaled. The totals are entered on the Batch

Totals line provided at the bottom of the last page of general ledger input forms. The amount columns for all pages are totaled. The totals for all pages are then entered *only* on the last page on the Batch Totals line. The two totals are compared to assure that debits equal credits. As the two totals are the same, $38,863.22, the entries on the general ledger input form are assumed to be correct.

## Processing transactions not affecting subsidiary ledgers

Option H is selected from the General Ledger Main Menu, Illustration C3-2, to set the run date, *11/30/--*, and the batch number, 2. Option I is selected from the General Ledger Main Menu to display spaces for entering the journal entries. After all lines on the input forms for batch number 2 have been entered and posted, Option J is selected from the General Ledger Main Menu. This option directs the computer to prepare a journal entries report. CarLand's journal entries report is shown in Illustration C3-11 on page 324.

Each journal entries report is checked for accuracy by comparing the report totals with the totals on the general ledger input form. As the totals are the same, $38,863.22, the journal entries report is assumed to be correct and is filed for future reference. If the totals are not the same, the errors must be found and corrected.

# RECORDING ACCOUNTS PAYABLE TRANSACTIONS

Three types of transactions affect CarLand's accounts payable. (1) Purchases of merchandise on account. (2) Buying supplies on account. (3) Cash payments on account. An accounts payable input form (FORM AP-2) is used to journalize all transactions affecting accounts payable.

## Purchase of merchandise on account

*November 2, 19--.*
*Purchased merchandise on account from Veloz Automotive, $1,754.00. Purchase Invoice No. 74.*

The entry to journalize this transaction is on line 1 of Illustration C3-12 on page 325.

The run date, *11/30/--*, is written in the space provided at the top of the form. The run date indicates that the transaction data journalized on the input form are for the month ended November 30. The batch number, 2, is written in the space provided at the top of the form. Batch number 1 was assigned to the accounts payable opening balances. The purchase invoice number, *P74*, is entered in the Purch. Invoice No. column. The vendor number, *260*, is recorded in the Vend. No. column. The day, *11/02/--*, is written in the Purchases Date columns. The purchases account number, *5110*, is entered in the Gen. Ledger Acct. No. column. The invoice amount,

```
RUN DATE: 11/30/--                    CARLAND
                             JOURNAL ENTRIES BATCH# 2

------------------------------------------------------------------------
JE#   DATE      ACCOUNT NUMBER & TITLE          DEBIT AMOUNT  CREDIT AMOUNT
------------------------------------------------------------------------
0005  11/02/--  5110   Purchases                   483.00
                1110      Cash                                    483.00
                DOCUMENT: C259

0006  11/02/--  6160   Rent Expense               1500.00
                1110      Cash                                   1500.00
                DOCUMENT: C260

0007  11/05/--  1145   Supplies--Office             87.00
                1110      Cash                                     87.00
                DOCUMENT: C261

0008  11/07/--  1110   Cash                       6837.00
                2140      Sales Tax Payable                       387.00
                4110      Sales                                  6450.00
                DOCUMENT: T7

0009  11/09/--  6190   Utilities Expense           300.00
                1110      Cash                                    300.00
                DOCUMENT: C264

0010  11/09/--  6110   Advertising Expense         125.00
                1110      Cash                                    125.00
                DOCUMENT: C265

0011  11/09/--  1145   Supplies--Office             58.00
                1150   Supplies--Store              65.00
                6110   Advertising Expense          92.00
                6140   Miscellaneous Expense        86.00
                1110      Cash                                    301.00
                DOCUMENT: C266

0012  11/10/--  3140   Dario Mesa, Drawing        1500.00
                1110      Cash                                   1500.00
                DOCUMENT: C267

0013  11/12/--  3140   Dario Mesa, Drawing         200.00
                5110      Purchases                               200.00
                DOCUMENT: M44

0014  11/13/--  6110   Advertising Expense         120.00
                6140      Miscellaneous Expense                   120.00
                DOCUMENT: M45

0026  11/30/--  1110   Cash                       1219.00
                2140      Sales Tax Payable                        69.00
                4110      Sales                                  1150.00
                DOCUMENT: T30

                                                 ---------------  ---------------
                TOTALS                              38863.22         38863.22
                                                 ===============  ===============
                IN BALANCE

Cash Receipts        24274.00
Cash Payments        12560.20
```

Illustration C3-11    Journal entries report

*$1,754.00*, is written in the Invoice Amount column. The disposition code, *A*, is entered in the Disp. Code column. Entering an *A* in this column indicates that the entry is on account.

## Buying supplies on account

*November 6, 19--.*
*Bought store supplies on account from Antelo Supply, $160.00. Memorandum No. 43.*

The entry to journalize this transaction is on line 4 of Illustration C3-12. The procedures for journalizing this entry are the same as for a purchase of merchandise on account except for the entries in the Purch. Invoice No. and Gen. Ledger Acct. No. columns. The memorandum number, *M43*, is written in the Purch. Invoice No. column. The store supplies account number, *1150*, is entered in the Gen. Ledger Acct. No. column.

RUN DATE 11 30 /-- (MM DD YY)  BATCH NO. 2

**ACCOUNTS PAYABLE** Input Form — FORM AP-2

| | PURCH. INVOICE NO. | VEND. NO. | MO. | DAY | YR. | GEN. LEDGER ACCT. NO. | INVOICE AMOUNT | MO. | DAY | YR. | DISP. CODE | MANUAL CHECK NO. | |
|---|---|---|---|---|---|---|---|---|---|---|---|---|---|
| 1 | P74 | 260 | 11 | 02 | -- | 5110 | 1754 00 | | | | A | | 1 |
| 2 | P75 | 240 | 11 | 04 | -- | 5110 | 3456 00 | | | | A | | 2 |
| 3 | P76 | 230 | 11 | 05 | -- | 5110 | 3180 00 | | | | A | | 3 |
| 4 | M43 | 210 | 11 | 06 | -- | 1150 | 160 00 | | | | A | | 4 |
| 5 | P71 | | | | | | | 11 | 06 | -- | M | 262 | 5 |
| 6 | P72 | | | | | | | 11 | 07 | -- | M | 263 | 6 |
| 7 | M35 | | | | | | | 11 | 12 | -- | M | 268 | 7 |
| 8 | P77 | 250 | 11 | 13 | -- | 5110 | 3140 00 | | | | A | | 8 |
| 9 | P78 | 250 | 11 | 20 | -- | 5110 | 2760 00 | | | | A | | 9 |
| 10 | P73 | | | | | | | 11 | 20 | -- | M | 273 | 10 |
| 11 | M47 | 210 | 11 | 23 | -- | 1150 | 590 00 | | | | A | | 11 |
| 12 | M39 | | | | | | | 11 | 23 | -- | M | 274 | 12 |
| 13 | M48 | 220 | 11 | 24 | -- | 1145 | 830 00 | | | | A | | 13 |
| 14 | | | | | | | | | | | | | 14 |
| 24 | | | | | | | | | | | | | 24 |
| 25 | | | | | | | | | | | | | 25 |

BATCH TOTAL 15870 00

DISPOSITION CODE:
A = ON ACCOUNT
M = MANUAL CHECK

Illustration C3-12
Accounts payable input form with transactions entered

## Cash payment on account

*November 7, 19--.*
*Paid cash on account to Filtrex Tires, $970.00, covering Purchase Invoice*
*No. 72. Check No. 263.*

The entry to journalize this transaction is on line 6 of Illustration C3-12. The purchase invoice number to be paid, *P72*, is entered in the Purch. Invoice No. column. The Purchases columns are left blank for a cash payment on account transaction. These data were stored on secondary storage when the initial purchase of merchandise on account was journalized and posted. The date, *11/07/--*, is entered in the Cash Payments Date columns. The disposition code, *M*, is written in the Disp. Code column. Writing an *M* in the Disp. Code column indicates that a check is to be manually prepared. The manual check number, *263*, is entered in the Manual Check No. column.

After all accounts payable transactions have been journalized, the Invoice Amount column is totaled. The total is entered on the Batch Total line provided at the bottom of the accounts payable input form, as shown in Illustration C3-12. If more than one accounts payable input form is required to journalize accounts payable transactions, the Invoice Amount column for all pages is totaled. The total for all pages is then entered *only* on the last page on the Batch Total line.

## Processing accounts payable transactions

Option I is selected from the Accounts Payable Main Menu, Illustration C3-4, to set the run date, *11/30/--*, and the batch number, 2. Option J is selected from the Accounts Payable Main Menu to display spaces for entering purchases and cash payments. After all lines on the input form have been entered and posted, Option K is selected from the Accounts Payable Main Menu. This option directs the computer to prepare a purchases on account report. CarLand's purchases on account report is shown in Illustration C3-13.

Illustration C3-13
Purchases on account
report

```
 RUN DATE: 11/30/--                    CARLAND
                         PURCHASES ON ACCOUNT BATCH# 2

      -------------------------------------------------------------
      VENDOR                    PURCH.          G.L.
      NO. NAME                  INV.   DATE   ACCOUNT    AMOUNT
      -------------------------------------------------------------
      260 Veloz Automotive      P74  11/02/-- 5110      1754.00
      240 Nilon Motor Parts     P75  11/04/-- 5110      3456.00
      230 Filtrex Tires         P76  11/05/-- 5110      3180.00
      210 Antelo Supply         M43  11/06/-- 1150       160.00
      250 Q-Ban Distributors    P77  11/13/-- 5110      3140.00
      250 Q-Ban Distributors    P78  11/20/-- 5110      2760.00
      210 Antelo Supply         M47  11/23/-- 1150       590.00
      220 Bell Office Products  M48  11/24/-- 1145       830.00
                                                       ----------
          TOTALS                                       15870.00
                                                       ==========
```

The purchases on account report is checked for accuracy by comparing the report total with the batch total of the accounts payable input form. As the total is the same, $15,870.00, the purchases on account report is assumed to be correct. The accounts payable input form and purchases on account report are filed for future reference.

Option L is selected from the Accounts Payable Main Menu to direct the computer to prepare a cash payments report. CarLand's cash payments report is shown in Illustration C3-14.

```
RUN DATE: 11/30/--                    CARLAND
                              CASH PAYMENTS BATCH# 2
     ------------------------------------------------------------------
     VENDOR                    INVOICE                              MAN.
     NO. NAME                  NO.  DATE      AMOUNT   TYPE        CHK.
     ------------------------------------------------------------------
     250 Q-Ban Distributors    P71 11/06/--  3960.00  Payment      262
     230 Filtrex Tires         P72 11/07/--   970.00  Payment      263
     210 Antelo Supply         M35 11/12/--   430.00  Payment      268
     240 Nilon Motor Parts     P73 11/20/--  4840.00  Payment      273
     220 Bell Office Products   M39 11/23/--   620.00  Payment      274

        TOTAL CASH PAYMENTS  10820.00
```

Illustration C3-14
Cash payments report

Option M is selected from the Accounts Payable Main Menu to direct the computer to prepare a general ledger posting summary. This summary lists all entries posted by the computer to the general ledger resulting from processing the accounts payable transactions. The general ledger posting summary for accounts payable transactions is shown in Illustration C3-15.

```
RUN DATE: 11/30/--                    CARLAND
                     GENERAL LEDGER POSTING SUMMARY BATCH# 2
     --------------------------------------------------------------
     ACCOUNT  ACCOUNT
     NUMBER   TITLE                        DEBIT        CREDIT
     --------------------------------------------------------------
     1110     Cash                                     10820.00
     1145     Supplies--Office            830.00
     1150     Supplies--Store             750.00
     2110     Accounts Payable          10820.00
     2110     Accounts Payable                         15870.00
     5110     Purchases                 14290.00
                                        ----------   ----------
              TOTALS                    26690.00     26690.00
                                        ==========   ==========
```

Illustration C3-15
General ledger posting
summary for accounts
payable transactions

Option N is selected from the Accounts Payable Main Menu to prepare a schedule of accounts payable. CarLand's schedule of accounts payable on November 30 is shown in Illustration C3-16.

```
RUN DATE: 11/30/--                    CARLAND
                            SCHEDULE OF ACCOUNTS PAYABLE

------------------------------------
VENDOR NUMBER AND NAME
        INVOICE    DATE      AMOUNT
------------------------------------
210   Antelo Supply
            M43    11/06/--    160.00
            M47    11/23/--    590.00
        VENDOR TOTAL           750.00

220   Bell Office Products
            M48    11/24/--    830.00
        VENDOR TOTAL           830.00

230   Filtrex Tires
            P76    11/05/--   3180.00
        VENDOR TOTAL          3180.00

240   Nilon Motor Parts
            P75    11/04/--   3456.00
        VENDOR TOTAL          3456.00

250   Q-Ban Distributors
            P77    11/13/--   3140.00
            P78    11/20/--   2760.00
        VENDOR TOTAL          5900.00

260   Veloz Automotive
            P74    11/02/--   1754.00
        VENDOR TOTAL          1754.00

                            ------------
    FINAL TOTAL               15870.00
                            ============
```

Illustration C3-16
Schedule of accounts
payable

# RECORDING ACCOUNTS RECEIVABLE TRANSACTIONS

Two types of transactions affect CarLand's accounts receivable. (1) Sales on account. (2) Cash receipts on account. An accounts receivable input form (FORM AR-2) is used to journalize all transactions affecting accounts receivable.

## Sale on account

*November 3, 19--.*
*Sold merchandise on account to Friendly Auto Service, $680.00, plus sales tax, $40.80; total, $720.80. Sales Invoice No. 72.*

The entry to journalize this transaction is shown recorded on line 1 of Illustration C3-17.

The run date, *11/30/--*, is written in the space provided at the top of the form. The run date indicates that the transaction data entered on the input form are for the month ended November 30. The batch number, 2, is written in the space provided at the top of the form. Batch number 1 was assigned to the opening accounts receivable balances. The sales invoice number, *S72*, is entered in the Sales Invoice No. column. The customer number is entered in the Cust. No. column. The date, *11/03/--*, is entered in the Sales Date columns. The sales account number, *4110*, is written in the Gen. Ledger Acct. No. column. The invoice amount, *$680.00*, is entered in the Invoice Amount column. The sales tax rate, *6*, is written in the Sales Tax % column. The Cash Receipts columns are left blank for a sale on account entry. These columns are used only to enter a cash receipt on account entry.

RUN DATE __11/30/--__
MM DD YY

BATCH NO. __2__

ACCOUNTS RECEIVABLE
Input Form

FORM AR-2

| | SALES INVOICE NO. | CUST. NO. | DATE MO. | DAY | YR. | GEN. LEDGER ACCT. NO. | INVOICE AMOUNT | SALES TAX % | DATE MO. | DAY | YR. | DOC. NO. | CASH RECEIVED | |
|---|---|---|---|---|---|---|---|---|---|---|---|---|---|---|
| 1 | S72 | 130 | 11 | 03 | -- | 4110 | 680 00 | 6 | | | | | | 1 |
| 2 | S73 | 150 | 11 | 05 | -- | 4110 | 1500 00 | 6 | | | | | | 2 |
| 3 | S65 | | | | | | | | 11 | 06 | -- | R86 | 1802 00 | 3 |
| 4 | S74 | 110 | 11 | 09 | -- | 4110 | 450 00 | 6 | | | | | | 4 |
| 5 | S66 | | | | | | | | 11 | 10 | -- | R87 | 954 00 | 5 |
| 6 | S75 | 160 | 11 | 11 | -- | 4110 | 570 00 | 6 | | | | | | 6 |
| 7 | S67 | | | | | | | | 11 | 13 | -- | R88 | 901 00 | 7 |
| 8 | S68 | | | | | | | | 11 | 14 | -- | R89 | 318 00 | 8 |
| 9 | S76 | 110 | 11 | 16 | -- | 4110 | 1300 00 | 6 | | | | | | 9 |
| 10 | S69 | | | | | | | | 11 | 17 | -- | R90 | 2491 00 | 10 |
| 11 | S77 | 120 | 11 | 18 | -- | 4110 | 1900 00 | 6 | | | | | | 11 |
| 12 | S70 | | | | | | | | 11 | 20 | -- | R91 | 1219 00 | 12 |
| 13 | S78 | 130 | 11 | 24 | -- | 4110 | 700 00 | 6 | | | | | | 13 |
| 14 | S79 | 140 | 11 | 24 | -- | 4110 | 300 00 | 6 | | | | | | 14 |
| 15 | S71 | | | | | | | | 11 | 25 | -- | R92 | 265 00 | 15 |
| 16 | S80 | 140 | 11 | 29 | -- | 4110 | 1300 00 | 6 | | | | | | 16 |
| 17 | | | | | | | | | | | | | | 17 |
| 24 | | | | | | | | | | | | | | 24 |
| 25 | | | | | | | | | | | | | | 25 |

BATCH TOTALS __8700 00__ __7950 00__

Illustration C3-17
Accounts receivable input form with transactions entered

## Cash receipt on account

*November 6, 19--.*
*Received cash on account from Autohaus Service, $1,802.00, covering S65.*
*Receipt No. 86.*

The entry to journalize this transaction is on line 3 of Illustration C3-17.

The sales invoice number for the cash received, *S65*, is written in the Sales Invoice No. column. The Sales columns are left blank for a cash receipt on account transaction. These data were stored on secondary storage when the initial sale on account transaction was journalized and posted. The date, *11/06/--*, is written in the Cash Receipts Date columns. The source document number, *R86*, is entered in the Doc. No. column. The amount of cash received, *$1,802.00*, is written in the Cash Received column.

After all accounts receivable transactions have been journalized, the Invoice Amount and Cash Received columns are totaled. The totals are entered on the Batch Totals line provided at the bottom of the form. If more than one accounts receivable input form is required to journalize accounts receivable transactions, the amount columns for all pages are totaled. The totals for all pages are then entered *only* on the last page on the Batch Totals line.

## Processing accounts receivable transactions

Option H is selected from the Accounts Receivable Main Menu, Illustration C3-6, to set the run date, *11/30/--*, and the batch number, 2. Option I is selected from the Accounts Receivable Main Menu to display spaces for entering sales and cash receipts. After all lines on the input form have been entered and posted, Option J is selected from the Accounts Receivable Main Menu. This option directs the computer to prepare a sales on account report. CarLand's sales on account report is shown in Illustration C3-18.

Illustration C3-18
Sales on account report

```
  RUN DATE: 11/30/--                    CARLAND
                             SALES ON ACCOUNT BATCH# 2

       ------------------------------------------------------------
       CUSTOMER                 INVOICE           G.L.    INVOICE     SALES
       NO. NAME                 NO.     DATE    ACCOUNT   AMOUNT       TAX
       ------------------------------------------------------------
       130 Friendly Auto Service  S72   11/03/--  4110     680.00      40.80
       150 Powell Rent-A-Car       S73   11/05/--  4110    1500.00      90.00
       110 Ashley Delivery         S74   11/09/--  4110     450.00      27.00
       160 Wood Sales & Service    S75   11/11/--  4110     570.00      34.20
       110 Ashley Delivery         S76   11/16/--  4110    1300.00      78.00
       120 Autohaus Service        S77   11/18/--  4110    1900.00     114.00
       130 Friendly Auto Service   S78   11/24/--  4110     700.00      42.00
       140 Keystone Delivery       S79   11/24/--  4110     300.00      18.00
       140 Keystone Delivery       S80   11/29/--  4110    1300.00      78.00
                                                        ---------   ---------
       TOTALS                                            8700.00      522.00
                                                        =========   =========
```

The sales on account report is checked for accuracy by comparing the report total with the input form batch total of the Invoice Amount column. As the total is the same, $8,700.00, the sales on account total is assumed to be correct.

Option K is selected from the Accounts Receivable Main Menu to direct the computer to prepare a cash receipts report. CarLand's cash receipts report is shown in Illustration C3-19.

```
RUN DATE: 11/30/--                   CARLAND
                           CASH RECEIPTS BATCH# 2

     ----------------------------------------------------------------
     CUSTOMER                   INVOICE         DOC.
     NO. NAME                   NO.    DATE     NO.    AMOUNT TYPE
     ----------------------------------------------------------------
     120 Autohaus Service       S65    11/06/-- R86    1802.00 Receipt
     140 Keystone Delivery      S66    11/10/-- R87     954.00 Receipt
     160 Wood Sales & Service   S67    11/13/-- R88     901.00 Receipt
     150 Powell Rent-A-Car      S68    11/14/-- R89     318.00 Receipt
     110 Ashley Delivery        S69    11/17/-- R90    2491.00 Receipt
     160 Wood Sales & Service   S70    11/20/-- R91    1219.00 Receipt
     130 Friendly Auto Service  S71    11/25/-- R92     265.00 Receipt
                                                     ----------
        TOTALS                                          7950.00
                                                     ==========
```

Illustration C3-19
Cash receipts report

The cash receipts report is checked for accuracy by comparing the report total with the input form batch total of the Cash Received column. As the totals are the same, $7,950.00, the cash received amount is assumed to be correct. The accounts receivable input form and the sales on account and cash receipts reports are then filed for future reference.

Option L is selected from the Accounts Receivable Main Menu to direct the computer to prepare a general ledger posting summary. This summary lists all entries posted by the computer to the general ledger resulting from processing the accounts receivable transactions. CarLand's general ledger posting summary for accounts receivable transactions is shown in Illustration C3-20.

Illustration C3-20
General ledger posting summary for accounts receivable transactions

```
RUN DATE: 11/30/--                   CARLAND
                     GENERAL LEDGER POSTING SUMMARY BATCH# 2

     ----------------------------------------------------------------
     ACCOUNT  ACCOUNT
     NUMBER   TITLE                         DEBIT       CREDIT
     ----------------------------------------------------------------
     1110     Cash                         7950.00
     1130     Accounts Receivable          9222.00
     1130     Accounts Receivable                      7950.00
     2140     Sales Tax Payable                         522.00
     4110     Sales                                    8700.00
                                         ----------- -----------
              TOTALS                       17172.00    17172.00
                                         =========== ===========
```

Option M is selected from the Accounts Receivable Main Menu to direct the computer to prepare a schedule of accounts receivable. CarLand's schedule of accounts receivable on November 30 is shown in Illustration C3-21.

Illustration C3-21
Schedule of accounts
receivable

```
RUN DATE: 11/30/--                      CARLAND
                          SCHEDULE OF ACCOUNTS RECEIVABLE

------------------------------------------------------------
CUSTOMER                        INVOICE
NO. NAME                        NO.     DATE        AMOUNT
------------------------------------------------------------
110 Ashley Delivery             S74   11/09/--      477.00
110 Ashley Delivery             S76   11/16/--     1378.00
    CUSTOMER TOTAL                                 1855.00

120 Autohaus Service            S77   11/18/--     2014.00
    CUSTOMER TOTAL                                 2014.00

130 Friendly Auto Service       S72   11/03/--      720.80
130 Friendly Auto Service       S78   11/24/--      742.00
    CUSTOMER TOTAL                                 1462.80

140 Keystone Delivery           S79   11/24/--      318.00
140 Keystone Delivery           S80   11/29/--     1378.00
    CUSTOMER TOTAL                                 1696.00

150 Powell Rent-A-Car           S73   11/05/--     1590.00
    CUSTOMER TOTAL                                 1590.00

160 Wood Sales & Service        S75   11/11/--      604.20
    CUSTOMER TOTAL                                  604.20

                                              -----------
    FINAL TOTAL                                    9222.00
                                              ===========
```

## COMPUTER APPLICATION PROBLEM

COMPUTER APPLICATION PROBLEM 3    **Journalizing and posting transactions**

**Instructions: 1.** Journalize transactions from Challenge Problem 14-C, Chapter 14, on appropriate computer input forms.

a. Journalize entries *NOT* affecting either accounts payable or accounts receivable on a general ledger input form (FORM GL-2). Use November 30 of the current year as the run date. Batch No. 2.

b. Journalize purchases on account, supplies bought on account, and cash payments on account on an accounts payable input form (FORM AP-2). Use November 30 of the current year as the run date. Batch No. 2.

c. Journalize sales on account and cash received on account on an accounts receivable input form (FORM AR-2). Use November 30 of the current year as the run date. Batch No. 2.

**2.** Load the *Automated Accounting for the Microcomputer* software. Select Computer Application 3 (CA-3) from the CENTURY 21 ACCOUNTING Template Disk. The accounting system data, chart of accounts, opening balances, and company name have been entered and are stored on the Template Disk.

**3.** Key-enter data from the completed general ledger input form.

**4.** Display/Print the journal entries report.

**5.** Key-enter data from the completed accounts payable input form.

**6.** Display/Print the purchases on account report.

**7.** Display/Print the cash payments report.

**8.** Display/Print the general ledger posting summary.

**9.** Display/Print the schedule of accounts payable.

**10.** Key-enter data from the completed accounts receivable input form.

**11.** Display/Print the sales on account report.

**12.** Display/Print the cash receipts report.

**13.** Display/Print the general ledger posting summary.

**14.** Display/Print the schedule of accounts receivable.

# CHAPTER
# 15

# Preparing Payroll Records

ENABLING PERFORMANCE TASKS

After studying Chapter 15, you will be able to:
a.  Define accounting terms related to payroll records.
b.  Identify accounting practices related to payroll records.
c.  Figure employee earnings and deductions.
d.  Complete payroll records.
e.  Prepare payroll checks.

CarLand employs several people to work in the business. These employees record the time they work for CarLand each day. Periodically CarLand pays its employees for the number of hours each employee has worked. The money paid for employee services is called a salary. The period covered by a salary payment is called a pay period. A business may decide to pay employee salaries every week, every two weeks, twice a month, or once a month. CarLand uses a semimonthly pay period. Employees are paid twice a month, on the 15th and last day of each month.

The total amount earned by all employees for a pay period is called a payroll. The payroll is reduced by state and federal taxes and other deductions, such as health insurance, to determine the amount paid to all employees. Special payroll records support the recording of payroll transactions in a journal. The business also uses these records to inform employees of their annual earnings and to prepare payroll reports for the government.

## PAYROLL TIME CARDS

A payroll system must include an accurate record of the time each employee has worked. Several methods are used for keeping time records. Employee time records are frequently kept on time cards. Time cards are used as the basic source of information to prepare a payroll.

Some time cards only require employees to record the total hours worked each day. Employees who record the total hours worked each day usually complete time cards by hand.

A business may use a time card that requires employees to record their arrival and departure times. CarLand uses a time clock to record the daily arrival and departure times of its employees. The time card for Patrick S. Turner for the pay period December 1-15 is shown in Illustration 15-1.

| EMPLOYEE NO. | 4 | | | | | | |

NAME   Patrick S. Turner

PERIOD ENDING   December 15, 19--

| MORNING | | AFTERNOON | | OVERTIME | | HOURS | |
| --- | --- | --- | --- | --- | --- | --- | --- |
| IN | OUT | IN | OUT | IN | OUT | REG | OT |
| 758 | 1202 | 1259 | 506 | | | 8 | |
| 759 | 1200 | 1257 | 501 | | | 8 | |
| 755 | 1201 | 1256 | 502 | 701 | 933 | 8 | 2½ |
| 756 | 1203 | | | | | 8 | |
| 754 | 1204 | 1259 | 501 | | | 8 | |
| 755 | 1200 | 1258 | 501 | 628 | 831 | 8 | 2 |

| | HOURS | RATE | AMOUNT |
| --- | --- | --- | --- |
| REGULAR | 88 | 8.00 | 704.00 |
| OVERTIME | 4½ | 12.00 | 54.00 |
| TOTAL HOURS | 92½ | TOTAL EARNINGS | 758.00 |

Illustration 15-1
Payroll time card

## Analyzing a payroll time card

Mr. Turner's employee number is at the top of the card. Below the employee number are the employee name and the ending date of the pay period.

CarLand's time cards have three sections, Morning, Afternoon, and Overtime, with In and Out columns under each section. When Mr. Turner reported for work on December 1, he inserted the card in the time clock. The clock recorded his time of arrival, 7:58, on the first line of the time card. The other entries on this line indicate that he left for lunch at 12:02. He returned at 12:59 and left for the day at 5:06. On December 3 he worked overtime, starting at 7:01 and leaving at 9:33.

CarLand figures overtime pay for each employee who works more than 8 hours in one day. No employee works more than 5 days in any one week.

## Figuring hours worked

The first task in preparing a payroll is to figure the number of hours worked by each employee. Four steps are followed to figure employee hours worked.

1 Figure the number of regular hours for each day and enter the amounts in the Hours Reg column.

Mr. Turner works 8 hours during a normal day. The hours worked on December 3, the third line of the time card, are figured using the arrival and departure times imprinted on the time card. Times are rounded to the nearest quarter hour to figure the hours worked.

|  | Departure Time | − | Arrival Time | = | Hours Worked |
|---|---|---|---|---|---|
| Morning: |  |  |  |  |  |
| Time card | 12:01 |  | 7:55 |  |  |
| Nearest quarter hour | 12:00 | − | 8:00 | = | 4:00 |
| Afternoon: |  |  |  |  |  |
| Time card | 5:02 |  | 12:56 |  |  |
| Nearest quarter hour | 5:00 | − | 1:00 | = | 4:00 |
| Total regular hours worked on December 3 |  |  |  |  | 8:00 |

The hours worked in the morning and afternoon are figured separately. The morning departure time of 12:01 is rounded to the nearest quarter hour, 12:00. The rounded arrival time, 8:00, *subtracted* from the departure time, 12:00, *equals* the morning hours worked. Hours worked of 4:00 means that Mr. Turner worked 4 hours and no (00) minutes. The total regular hours worked, *8*, is recorded in the Hours Reg column on line 3 of the time card.

2 Figure the number of overtime hours for each day and enter the amounts in the Hours OT column.

Overtime hours for December 3 are figured using the same procedure as for regular hours.

|  | Departure Time | − | Arrival Time | = | Hours Worked |
|---|---|---|---|---|---|
| Time card | 9:33 |  | 7:01 |  |  |
| Nearest quarter hour | 9:30 | − | 7:00 | = | 2:30 |

The hours worked of 2:30 means that Mr. Turner worked 2 hours and 30 minutes (1/2 hour) of overtime. Therefore, *2 1/2* is recorded in the Hours OT column.

3 Add the hours worked in the Hours Reg and OT columns. Enter the totals in the spaces provided at the bottom of the time card.

Mr. Turner worked 88 regular hours (8 hours × 11 days) and 4 1/2 overtime hours during the semimonthly pay period. Therefore, *88* is recorded in the Regular Hours space at the bottom of the card and *4 1/2* is recorded in the Overtime Hours space.

4 Add the Hours column to figure the total hours. Enter the total in the Hours column at the bottom of the time card.

Mr. Turner worked 88 regular hours and 4 1/2 overtime hours for a total of 92 1/2 hours. Total hours, *92 1/2*, are entered in the Total Hours space.

## Figuring employee total earnings

Once the total regular and overtime hours are determined, employee earnings can be calculated. The total pay due for a pay period before deductions is called total earnings. Total earnings are sometimes referred to as gross pay or gross earnings. Four steps are followed to figure employee total earnings.

**1** Enter the rate for regular time in the Rate column. Figure the regular earnings by multiplying regular hours times the regular rate.

Mr. Turner's regular hourly rate, *$8.00*, is entered in the Regular Rate space. The regular earnings are calculated as shown below.

| Regular Hours | × | Regular Rate | = | Regular Earnings |
|---|---|---|---|---|
| 88 | × | $8.00 | | $704.00 |

The amount of regular earnings, *$704.00*, is entered in the Regular Amount space.

**2** Enter the rate for overtime in the Rate column.

Mr. Turner is paid 1 1/2 times his regular rate for overtime work. The overtime rate for Mr. Turner is calculated as shown below.

| Regular Rate | × | 1 1/2 | = | Overtime Rate |
|---|---|---|---|---|
| $8.00 | × | 1 1/2 | = | $12.00 |

The overtime rate, *$12.00*, is entered in the Overtime Rate space.

**3** Figure the overtime earnings by multiplying overtime hours times the overtime rate.

The overtime earnings for Mr. Turner are calculated as shown below.

| Overtime Hours | × | Overtime Rate | = | Overtime Earnings |
|---|---|---|---|---|
| 4 1/2 | × | $12.00 | = | $54.00 |

The amount of overtime earnings, *$54.00*, is entered in the Overtime Amount space.

**4** Add the Amount column to figure the total earnings.

The total earnings for Mr. Turner are calculated as shown below.

| Regular Earnings | + | Overtime Earnings | = | Total Earnings |
|---|---|---|---|---|
| $704.00 | + | $54.00 | = | $758.00 |

The amount of total earnings, *$758.00*, is entered in the Total Earnings space.

CarLand owes Mr. Turner $758.00 for his work during the pay period ending December 15. However, taxes and other deductions must be subtracted from total earnings to determine the actual amount CarLand will pay Mr. Turner. Therefore, CarLand will not pay Mr. Turner the entire $758.00.

# PAYROLL TAXES

Taxes based on the payroll of a business are called payroll taxes. A business is required by law to withhold certain payroll taxes from employee salaries. A business is also required to pay additional payroll taxes. All payroll taxes are based on employee total earnings. Therefore, accurate and detailed payroll records must be maintained. Errors in payroll records could cause incorrect payroll tax payments. Federal and state governments may charge a business a penalty for failure to pay correct payroll taxes on time.

Payroll taxes withheld represent a liability for the employer until payment is made. Federal payroll taxes may be paid to a Federal Reserve Bank. The taxes may also be paid to a bank authorized to receive such funds for the government. Local and state governments that assess payroll taxes also designate how, when, and where a business will pay the liability for employee taxes withheld.

## Employee income tax

A business must withhold federal income taxes from employee total earnings. Federal income taxes withheld must be forwarded periodically to the federal government. Federal income tax is withheld from employee earnings in all 50 states. Employers in many states also are required to withhold state, city, or county income taxes from employee earnings.

The information used to determine the amount of income tax withheld is identified on Form W-4, Employee's Withholding Allowance Certificate. The completed Form W-4 for Mr. Turner is shown in Illustration 15-2.

Information from the completed Form W-4 is used when a business figures the amount of federal income taxes to be withheld. Employers are required to have on file a current Form W-4 for all employees. The amount of income tax withheld is based on employee marital status and withholding allowances.

**Marital status**. Employees identify on Form W-4 whether they are married or single. A married employee will have less income tax withheld than a single employee with the same total earnings.

Mr. Turner checked the married box for item 3 of the Form W-4 shown in Illustration 15-2.

| Form **W-4** | **Employee's Withholding Allowance Certificate** | OMB No. 1545-0010 |
|---|---|---|
| Department of the Treasury<br>Internal Revenue Service | ▶ **For Privacy Act and Paperwork Reduction Act Notice, see reverse.** | |

| **1** Type or print your first name and middle initial<br>Patrick S. Turner | Last name | **2** Your social security number<br>450-70-6432 |
|---|---|---|

Home address (number and street or rural route)
1625 Northland Drive

City or town, state, and ZIP code
Rockville, RI   02873

**3** Marital Status

☐ Single   ☒ Married
☐ Married, but withhold at higher Single rate.
**Note:** *If married, but legally separated, or spouse is a nonresident alien, check the Single box.*

**4** Total number of allowances you are claiming (from line G above or from the Worksheets on back if they apply) . . . . **4** | 4

**5** Additional amount, if any, you want deducted from each pay . . . . . . . . . . . . . . . . **5** $ —0—

**6** I claim exemption from withholding and I certify that I meet **ALL** of the following conditions for exemption:
- Last year I had a right to a refund of **ALL** Federal income tax withheld because I had **NO** tax liability; **AND**
- This year I expect a refund of **ALL** Federal income tax withheld because I expect to have **NO** tax liability; **AND**
- This year if my income exceeds $500 and includes nonwage income, another person cannot claim me as a dependent.

If you meet all of the above conditions, enter the year effective and "EXEMPT" here . . . . . ▶ **6** | 19

**7** Are you a full-time student? (**Note:** *Full-time students are not automatically exempt.*) . . . . . . . . . . **7** ☐ Yes ☐ No

Under penalties of perjury, I certify that I am entitled to the number of withholding allowances claimed on this certificate or entitled to claim exempt status.

Employee's signature ▶ *Patrick S. Turner*   Date▶ *June 27*   19 --

**8** Employer's name and address (**Employer:** Complete 8 and 10 **only if sending to IRS**) | **9** Office code (optional) | **10** Employer identification number

Illustration 15-2
Form W-4, Employee's
Withholding Allowance
Certificate

**Withholding allowance.** A deduction from total earnings for each person legally supported by a taxpayer is called a withholding allowance. The larger the number of the withholding allowances claimed, the smaller the income tax withheld from employee salaries.

Mr. Turner claimed four withholding allowances, one each for himself, his wife, and his two children. The number of withholding allowances was recorded in item 4 of the Form W-4.

Most employees are required to have federal income taxes withheld from their salaries. An exemption from withholding is available for certain low-income and part-time employees. The employee must meet the requirements listed in the instructions which accompany Form W-4. The requirements are very restrictive. Most students with part-time jobs who live with their parents do *not* qualify for the exemption. Students who earn over $500 in salary or any interest from a savings or checking account are not eligible to claim the exemption.

The federal government occasionally changes the way income taxes are withheld from employee total earnings. The Form W-4 shown in Illustration 15-2 was the form in use when the materials for this textbook were prepared. Employers must be aware of changes in tax laws and forms. If Form W-4 is changed, an employer must obtain a new W-4 from each employee.

## Employee and employer social security tax

The federal social security law includes three programs.

1. Old-age, survivors, and disability insurance benefits for qualified employees and their spouses, widows or widowers, dependent children, and parents.

2. Payments to senior citizens for the cost of certain hospital and related services. The federal health insurance program for people who have reached retirement age is called Medicare.

3. Grants to states that provide benefits for persons temporarily unemployed and for certain relief and welfare purposes.

Each employee must have a social security number. Most employees will have received their social security number as a child. Employees without social security numbers can apply for a number at the nearest Social Security office.

**FICA tax.** A federal tax paid by employees and employers for old-age, survivors, disability, and hospitalization insurance is called FICA tax. FICA is the abbreviation for the Federal Insurance Contributions Act. FICA tax is based on the total earnings of the employees. Employers are required to withhold FICA tax from a specified amount of employee salary paid in a calendar year. In addition, employers must pay the same amount of FICA tax as withheld from employee salaries.

**Federal unemployment tax.** A federal tax used for state and federal administrative expenses of the unemployment program is called federal unemployment tax. This tax is paid entirely by employers.

**State unemployment tax.** A state tax used to pay benefits to unemployed workers is called state unemployment tax. This tax is usually paid by employers. The Social Security Act specifies certain standards for unemployment compensation laws. Therefore, a high degree of uniformity exists in state unemployment laws. However, details of state unemployment laws do differ. Because of these differences, employers must know the requirements of the states in which they operate.

**Retention of records.** Employers are required to retain all payroll records showing payments and deductions. Some records must be retained longer than others. Records pertaining to social security tax payments and deductions must be retained for four years. The length of time state unemployment tax payment records must be retained varies from state to state.

## PAYROLL REGISTER

A business form used to record payroll information is called a payroll register. A payroll register summarizes the total earnings and payroll withholdings of all employees. CarLand's payroll register for the semimonthly period ended December 15 is shown in Illustration 15-3.

Regular, overtime, and total earnings are recorded in a payroll register from information on time cards. Amounts deducted for payroll taxes, health insurance, and charitable contributions are calculated and recorded in a payroll register. Also, the total amount to be paid to each employee and the check number of each payroll check are recorded in a payroll register.

| SEMIMONTHLY PERIOD ENDED *December 15, 19--* | | | PAYROLL REGISTER | | | | | | | | | DATE OF PAYMENT *December 15, 19--* | |

| | EMPL. NO. | EMPLOYEE NAME | MARITAL STATUS | NO. OF ALLOWANCES | EARNINGS | | | DEDUCTIONS | | | | | NET PAY | CHECK. NO. | |
|---|---|---|---|---|---|---|---|---|---|---|---|---|---|---|---|
| | | | | | REGULAR | OVERTIME | TOTAL | FEDERAL INCOME TAX | FICA TAX | HEALTH INSURANCE | OTHER | TOTAL | | | |
| 1 | 2 | *Bauch, Mary R.* | M | 2 | 660 00 | | 660 00 | 57 00 | 52 80 | 38 00 | B 5 00 | 152 80 | 507 20 | 419 | 1 |
| 2 | 5 | *Clay, Richard P.* | S | 1 | 80 00 | | 80 00 | 00 | 6 40 | | | 6 40 | 73 60 | 420 | 2 |
| 3 | 1 | *Javorski, Adam B.* | M | 2 | 384 00 | 18 00 | 402 00 | 17 00 | 32 16 | 38 00 | | 87 16 | 314 84 | 421 | 3 |
| 4 | 6 | *Maggio, Brenda A.* | S | 1 | 40 00 | | 40 00 | 00 | 3 20 | | | 3 20 | 36 80 | 422 | 4 |
| 5 | 4 | *Turner, Patrick S.* | M | 4 | 704 00 | 54 00 | 758 00 | 45 00 | 60 64 | 50 00 | B 10 00 / uw 10 00 | 175 64 | 582 36 | 423 | 5 |
| 6 | 3 | *Wilkes, Samuel R.* | S | 1 | 616 00 | | 616 00 | 73 00 | 49 28 | 32 00 | | 154 28 | 461 72 | 424 | 6 |
| 7 | | | | | 2484 00 | 72 00 | 2556 00 | 192 00 | 204 48 | 158 00 | B 15 00 / uw 10 00 | 579 48 | 1976 52 | | 7 |
| 8 | | | | | | | | | | | | | | | 8 |

The two partners of CarLand, Amy Kramer and Dario Mesa, are not listed on the payroll register. Owners of partnerships are not employees of the company. Cash payments to partners are recorded as withdrawals rather than as salaries.

Illustration 15-3
Payroll register

## Recording earnings in a payroll register

The employee number, name, marital status, and withholding allowances are listed in a payroll register. Employee earnings for a pay period are written in the appropriate columns of a payroll register.

Recorded on line 5 of the payroll register are Mr. Turner's employee number, 4, and name, *Turner, Patrick S.* Also recorded are Mr. Turner's marital status, *M* for married; the number of withholding allowances, 4; regular earnings, $704.00; overtime earnings, $54.00; and total earnings, $758.00. This information is obtained from Mr. Turner's Form W-4 and time card.

## Recording deductions in a payroll register

The deductions section of a payroll register is used to record the payroll taxes and other deductions withheld from employee earnings. Also, some companies deduct amounts for retirement plans. These deductions will vary from one company to another depending on policies established between management and employees.

Five steps are followed to figure and record deductions.

1   The Federal Income Tax column is used to record the amount of federal income tax withheld from employee earnings. This amount is determined from tables furnished by the federal government. Portions of the tables showing the tax to be withheld are shown in Illustration 15-4 on pages 342 and 343.

**SEMIMONTHLY PAYROLL PERIOD — MARRIED PERSONS**

| And the wages are– | | And the number of withholding allowances claimed is– | | | | | | | | | | |
|---|---|---|---|---|---|---|---|---|---|---|---|---|
| At least | But less than | 0 | 1 | 2 | 3 | 4 | 5 | 6 | 7 | 8 | 9 | 10 |
| | | The amount of income tax to be withheld shall be– | | | | | | | | | | |
| $0 | $130 | | | | | | | | | | | |
| 130 | 135 | 1 | | | | | | | | | | |
| 135 | 140 | 2 | | | | | | | | | | |
| 140 | 145 | 2 | | | | | | | | | | |
| 145 | 150 | 3 | | | | | | | | | | |
| 400 | 410 | 42 | 30 | 17 | 5 | | | | | | | |
| 410 | 420 | 43 | 31 | 19 | 7 | | | | | | | |
| 420 | 430 | 45 | 33 | 20 | 8 | | | | | | | |
| 430 | 440 | 46 | 34 | 22 | 10 | | | | | | | |
| 440 | 450 | 48 | 36 | 23 | 11 | | | | | | | |
| 450 | 460 | 49 | 37 | 25 | 13 | | | | | | | |
| 460 | 470 | 51 | 39 | 26 | 14 | 2 | | | | | | |
| 470 | 480 | 52 | 40 | 28 | 16 | 3 | | | | | | |
| 480 | 490 | 54 | 42 | 29 | 17 | 5 | | | | | | |
| 490 | 500 | 55 | 43 | 31 | 19 | 6 | | | | | | |
| 500 | 520 | 57 | 45 | 33 | 21 | 9 | | | | | | |
| 520 | 540 | 60 | 48 | 36 | 24 | 12 | | | | | | |
| 540 | 560 | 63 | 51 | 39 | 27 | 15 | 3 | | | | | |
| 560 | 580 | 66 | 54 | 42 | 30 | 18 | 6 | | | | | |
| 580 | 600 | 69 | 57 | 45 | 33 | 21 | 9 | | | | | |
| 600 | 620 | 72 | 60 | 48 | 36 | 24 | 12 | | | | | |
| 620 | 640 | 75 | 63 | 51 | 39 | 27 | 15 | 2 | | | | |
| 640 | 660 | 78 | 66 | 54 | 42 | 30 | 18 | 5 | | | | |
| 660 | 680 | 81 | 69 | 57 | 45 | 33 | 21 | 8 | | | | |
| 680 | 700 | 84 | 72 | 60 | 48 | 36 | 24 | 11 | | | | |
| 700 | 720 | 87 | 75 | 63 | 51 | 39 | 27 | 14 | 2 | | | |
| 720 | 740 | 90 | 78 | 66 | 54 | 42 | 30 | 17 | 5 | | | |
| 740 | 760 | 93 | 81 | 69 | 57 | 45 | 33 | 20 | 8 | | | |
| 760 | 780 | 96 | 84 | 72 | 60 | 48 | 36 | 23 | 11 | | | |
| 780 | 800 | 99 | 87 | 75 | 63 | 51 | 39 | 26 | 14 | 2 | | |
| 800 | 820 | 102 | 90 | 78 | 66 | 54 | 42 | 29 | 17 | 5 | | |
| 820 | 840 | 105 | 93 | 81 | 69 | 57 | 45 | 32 | 20 | 8 | | |
| 840 | 860 | 108 | 96 | 84 | 72 | 60 | 48 | 35 | 23 | 11 | | |
| 860 | 880 | 111 | 99 | 87 | 75 | 63 | 51 | 38 | 26 | 14 | 2 | |
| 880 | 900 | 114 | 102 | 90 | 78 | 66 | 54 | 41 | 29 | 17 | 5 | |
| 900 | 920 | 117 | 105 | 93 | 81 | 69 | 57 | 44 | 32 | 20 | 8 | |
| 920 | 940 | 120 | 108 | 96 | 84 | 72 | 60 | 47 | 35 | 23 | 11 | |
| 940 | 960 | 123 | 111 | 99 | 87 | 75 | 63 | 50 | 38 | 26 | 14 | 2 |
| 960 | 980 | 126 | 114 | 102 | 90 | 78 | 66 | 53 | 41 | 29 | 17 | 5 |
| 980 | 1,000 | 129 | 117 | 105 | 93 | 81 | 69 | 56 | 44 | 32 | 20 | 8 |
| 1,000 | 1,020 | 132 | 120 | 108 | 96 | 84 | 72 | 59 | 47 | 35 | 23 | 11 |
| 1,020 | 1,040 | 135 | 123 | 111 | 99 | 87 | 75 | 62 | 50 | 38 | 26 | 14 |
| 1,040 | 1,060 | 138 | 126 | 114 | 102 | 90 | 78 | 65 | 53 | 41 | 29 | 17 |
| 1,060 | 1,080 | 141 | 129 | 117 | 105 | 93 | 81 | 68 | 56 | 44 | 32 | 20 |
| 1,080 | 1,100 | 144 | 132 | 120 | 108 | 96 | 84 | 71 | 59 | 47 | 35 | 23 |
| 1,100 | 1,120 | 147 | 135 | 123 | 111 | 99 | 87 | 74 | 62 | 50 | 38 | 26 |
| 1,120 | 1,140 | 150 | 138 | 126 | 114 | 102 | 90 | 77 | 65 | 53 | 41 | 29 |
| 1,140 | 1,160 | 153 | 141 | 129 | 117 | 105 | 93 | 80 | 68 | 56 | 44 | 32 |
| 1,160 | 1,180 | 156 | 144 | 132 | 120 | 108 | 96 | 83 | 71 | 59 | 47 | 35 |
| 1,180 | 1,200 | 159 | 147 | 135 | 123 | 111 | 99 | 86 | 74 | 62 | 50 | 38 |
| 1,200 | 1,220 | 162 | 150 | 138 | 126 | 114 | 102 | 89 | 77 | 65 | 53 | 41 |
| 1,220 | 1,240 | 165 | 153 | 141 | 129 | 117 | 105 | 92 | 80 | 68 | 56 | 44 |
| 1,240 | 1,260 | 168 | 156 | 144 | 132 | 120 | 108 | 95 | 83 | 71 | 59 | 47 |
| 1,260 | 1,280 | 171 | 159 | 147 | 135 | 123 | 111 | 98 | 86 | 74 | 62 | 50 |
| 1,280 | 1,300 | 174 | 162 | 150 | 138 | 126 | 114 | 101 | 89 | 77 | 65 | 53 |
| 1,300 | 1,320 | 177 | 165 | 153 | 141 | 129 | 117 | 104 | 92 | 80 | 68 | 56 |
| 1,320 | 1,340 | 180 | 168 | 156 | 144 | 132 | 120 | 107 | 95 | 83 | 71 | 59 |
| 1,340 | 1,360 | 183 | 171 | 159 | 147 | 135 | 123 | 110 | 98 | 86 | 74 | 62 |
| 1,360 | 1,380 | 187 | 174 | 162 | 150 | 138 | 126 | 113 | 101 | 89 | 77 | 65 |
| 1,380 | 1,400 | 192 | 177 | 165 | 153 | 141 | 129 | 116 | 104 | 92 | 80 | 68 |

(boxed label within table: **SEMIMONTHLY MARRIED PERSONS**)

Illustration 15-4
Section of income tax withholding tables for semimonthly pay period

Mr. Turner's federal income tax on total earnings of $758.00 is found in the table for married persons. Since CarLand pays its payroll twice a month, the table for a semimonthly pay period is used. The proper wage bracket is from $740.00 to $760.00. The income tax to be withheld is the amount shown on this line under the column for four allowances, $45.00.

No federal income tax was withheld from the earnings of Richard Clay and Brenda Maggio. Although they are students who work part-time, they are not exempt from federal income tax withholding. They did not, however, have enough total earnings *in this pay period* to require any income tax to be withheld. Federal income tax withholding tables are also available for daily, weekly, biweekly, and monthly pay periods. The tables in Illustration 15-4 are those available when materials for this textbook were prepared.

## SEMIMONTHLY PAYROLL PERIOD — SINGLE PERSONS

| And the wages are— | | And the number of withholding allowances claimed is— | | | | | | | | | | |
|---|---|---|---|---|---|---|---|---|---|---|---|---|
| At least | But less than | 0 | 1 | 2 | 3 | 4 | 5 | 6 | 7 | 8 | 9 | 10 |
| | | The amount of income tax to be withheld shall be— | | | | | | | | | | |
| $0 | $45 | | | | | | | | | | | |
| 45 | 50 | 1 | | | | | | | | | | |
| 50 | 55 | 1 | | | | | | | | | | |
| 55 | 60 | 2 | | | | | | | | | | |
| 60 | 65 | 3 | | | | | | | | | | |
| 65 | 70 | 4 | | | | | | | | | | |
| 70 | 75 | 4 | | | | | | | | | | |
| 75 | 80 | 5 | | | | | | | | | | |
| 80 | 85 | 6 | | | | | | | | | | |
| 85 | 90 | 7 | | | | | | | | | | |
| 380 | 390 | 51 | 39 | 27 | 15 | 2 | | | | | | |
| 390 | 400 | 53 | 41 | 28 | 16 | 4 | | | | | | |
| 400 | 410 | 54 | 42 | 30 | 18 | 5 | | | | | | |
| 410 | 420 | 56 | 44 | 31 | 19 | 7 | | | | | | |
| 420 | 430 | 57 | 45 | 33 | 21 | 8 | | | | | | |
| 430 | 440 | 59 | 47 | 34 | 22 | 10 | | | | | | |
| 440 | 450 | 60 | 48 | 36 | 24 | 11 | | | | | | |
| 450 | 460 | 62 | 50 | 37 | 25 | 13 | 1 | | | | | |
| 460 | 470 | 63 | 51 | 39 | 27 | 14 | 2 | | | | | |
| 470 | 480 | 65 | 53 | 40 | 28 | 16 | 4 | | | | | |
| 480 | 490 | 66 | 54 | 42 | 30 | 17 | 5 | | | | | |
| 490 | 500 | 68 | 56 | 43 | 31 | 19 | 7 | | | | | |
| 500 | 520 | 70 | 58 | 46 | 33 | 21 | 9 | | | | | |
| 520 | 540 | 73 | 61 | 49 | 36 | 24 | 12 | | | | | |
| 540 | 560 | 76 | 64 | 52 | 39 | 27 | 15 | 3 | | | | |
| 560 | 580 | 79 | 67 | 55 | 42 | 30 | 18 | 6 | | | | |
| 580 | 600 | 82 | 70 | 58 | 45 | 33 | 21 | 9 | | | | |
| 600 | 620 | 85 | 73 | 61 | 48 | 36 | 24 | 12 | | | | |
| 620 | 640 | 88 | 76 | 64 | 51 | 39 | 27 | 15 | 3 | | | |
| 640 | 660 | 91 | 79 | 67 | 54 | 42 | 30 | 18 | 6 | | | |
| 660 | 680 | 94 | 82 | 70 | 57 | 45 | 33 | 21 | 9 | | | |
| 680 | 700 | 97 | 85 | 73 | 60 | 48 | 36 | 24 | 12 | | | |
| 700 | 720 | 100 | 88 | 76 | 63 | 51 | 39 | 27 | 15 | 2 | | |
| 720 | 740 | 103 | 91 | 79 | 66 | 54 | 42 | 30 | 18 | 5 | | |
| 740 | 760 | 106 | 94 | 82 | 69 | 57 | 45 | 33 | 21 | 8 | | |
| 760 | 780 | 109 | 97 | 85 | 72 | 60 | 48 | 36 | 24 | 11 | | |
| 780 | 800 | 112 | 100 | 88 | 75 | 63 | 51 | 39 | 27 | 14 | 2 | |
| 800 | 820 | 118 | 103 | 91 | 78 | 66 | 54 | 42 | 30 | 17 | 5 | |
| 820 | 840 | 123 | 106 | 94 | 81 | 69 | 57 | 45 | 33 | 20 | 8 | |
| 840 | 860 | 129 | 109 | 97 | 84 | 72 | 60 | 48 | 36 | 23 | 11 | |
| 860 | 880 | 135 | 112 | 100 | 87 | 75 | 63 | 51 | 39 | 26 | 14 | 2 |
| 880 | 900 | 140 | 118 | 103 | 90 | 78 | 66 | 54 | 42 | 29 | 17 | 5 |
| 900 | 920 | 146 | 123 | 106 | 93 | 81 | 69 | 57 | 45 | 32 | 20 | 8 |
| 920 | 940 | 151 | 129 | 109 | 96 | 84 | 72 | 60 | 48 | 35 | 23 | 11 |
| 940 | 960 | 157 | 134 | 112 | 99 | 87 | 75 | 63 | 51 | 38 | 26 | 14 |
| 960 | 980 | 163 | 140 | 117 | 102 | 90 | 78 | 66 | 54 | 41 | 29 | 17 |
| 980 | 1,000 | 168 | 146 | 123 | 105 | 93 | 81 | 69 | 57 | 44 | 32 | 20 |
| 1,000 | 1,020 | 174 | 151 | 128 | 108 | 96 | 84 | 72 | 60 | 47 | 35 | 23 |
| 1,020 | 1,040 | 179 | 157 | 134 | 111 | 99 | 87 | 75 | 63 | 50 | 38 | 26 |
| 1,040 | 1,060 | 185 | 162 | 140 | 117 | 102 | 90 | 78 | 66 | 53 | 41 | 29 |
| 1,060 | 1,080 | 191 | 168 | 145 | 122 | 105 | 93 | 81 | 69 | 56 | 44 | 32 |
| 1,080 | 1,100 | 196 | 174 | 151 | 128 | 108 | 96 | 84 | 72 | 59 | 47 | 35 |
| 1,100 | 1,120 | 202 | 179 | 156 | 134 | 111 | 99 | 87 | 75 | 62 | 50 | 38 |
| 1,120 | 1,140 | 207 | 185 | 162 | 139 | 116 | 102 | 90 | 78 | 65 | 53 | 41 |
| 1,140 | 1,160 | 213 | 190 | 168 | 145 | 122 | 105 | 93 | 81 | 68 | 56 | 44 |
| 1,160 | 1,180 | 219 | 196 | 173 | 150 | 128 | 108 | 96 | 84 | 71 | 59 | 47 |
| 1,180 | 1,200 | 224 | 202 | 179 | 156 | 133 | 111 | 99 | 87 | 74 | 62 | 50 |
| 1,200 | 1,220 | 230 | 207 | 184 | 162 | 139 | 116 | 102 | 90 | 77 | 65 | 53 |
| 1,220 | 1,240 | 235 | 213 | 190 | 167 | 144 | 122 | 105 | 93 | 80 | 68 | 56 |
| 1,240 | 1,260 | 241 | 218 | 196 | 173 | 150 | 127 | 108 | 96 | 83 | 71 | 59 |

**SEMIMONTHLY SINGLE PERSONS**

Illustration 15-4
Section of income tax withholding tables for semimonthly pay period

2  The FICA Tax column is used to record the amount deducted for social security tax. FICA tax is calculated by multiplying total earnings by the tax rate. From time to time, Congress changes the tax rate used to figure FICA taxes. A FICA tax rate of 8% is used to illustrate the FICA tax calculations in this textbook. The FICA tax for Mr. Turner is calculated as shown below.

| Total Earnings | × | FICA Tax Rate | = | FICA Tax Deduction |
|---|---|---|---|---|
| $758.00 | × | 8% | = | $60.64 |

Congress has limited the amount of FICA tax that each individual must pay. The FICA tax is not calculated on total earnings over a specified amount. The maximum amount of earnings on which a tax is calculated is called a tax base. A tax base of $50,000.00 is used for the FICA tax calculations in this textbook.

Before recording Mr. Turner's $60.64 FICA tax in the payroll register, his accumulated earnings are compared to the tax base. Between January 1 and December 1, Mr. Turner has earned $16,794.00. Since his earnings are less than the tax base, the FICA tax is recorded in the payroll register. If Mr. Turner had accumulated earnings over $50,000.00, no FICA tax would be owed and no amount would have been recorded in the payroll register.

3 The Health Insurance column is used to record health insurance premiums. Full-time employees of CarLand participate in a group health insurance plan to take advantage of lower group rates.

Mr. Turner's semimonthly health insurance premium is $50.00. Premiums are set by the insurance company and are usually based on the employee marital status and whether coverage is for an individual or a family. Some health insurance premiums may be based on the number of individuals covered.

4 The Other column is used to record voluntary deductions requested by an employee. Entries are identified by code letters. CarLand uses the letter *B* to identify amounts withheld for buying U.S. Savings Bonds. *UW* is used to identify amounts withheld for employee contributions to United Way.

Mr. Turner has authorized CarLand to withhold $10.00 each pay period to buy U.S. Savings Bonds for him. Mr. Turner has also authorized that $10.00 be withheld as a contribution to the United Way.

5 The Total column is used to record total deductions. All deductions on a line for each employee are added. The total deductions for Mr. Turner are calculated as shown below.

| Federal Income Tax | + | FICA Tax | + | Health Insurance | + | Other | = | Total Deductions |
|---|---|---|---|---|---|---|---|---|
| $45.00 | + | $60.64 | + | $50.00 | + | $20.00 | = | $175.64 |

## Figuring net pay in a payroll register

The total earnings paid to an employee after payroll taxes and other deductions is called net pay. Net pay is figured by subtracting total deductions from total earnings. The Net Pay column is used to record the amount. The net pay for Mr. Turner is calculated as shown below.

| Total Earnings | − | Total Deductions | = | Net Pay |
|---|---|---|---|---|
| $758.00 | − | $175.64 | = | $582.36 |

## Completing a payroll register

After the net pay has been recorded for each employee, each amount column is totaled. A separate total is shown for each different type of deduction in the Other column. Accuracy of these totals is verified by subtracting the Total Deductions column total from the Total Earnings column total as shown below.

| Total Earnings | – | Total Deductions | = | Net Pay |
|---|---|---|---|---|
| $2,556.00 | – | $579.48 | = | $1,976.52 |

The net pay calculated above, $1,976.52, is compared to the total of the Net Pay column. The payroll register is proved because these amounts are equal. If the amounts are not equal, the errors must be found and corrected. After the payroll register is proved, a double rule is drawn below the totals across all amount columns. When the payroll register is completed and proved, the register is given to a partner of the company for approval.

Before checks are written for employee net pay, the payroll calculations are checked for accuracy. A partner approves the payroll after the accuracy is verified. After each check is written, the check number is recorded in the Ck. No. column.

# PAYROLL CHECKS

CarLand pays its employees with checks written on a special payroll checking account. A check for the total net pay is written on CarLand's general checking account. The check is deposited in the payroll checking account. Illustration 15-5 shows the check written for the December 1-15 pay period. The check amount, $1,976.52, is the total of the Net Pay column of the payroll register in Illustration 15-3.

Illustration 15-5
Check for total net pay

The information used to prepare payroll checks is taken from a payroll register. The payroll check for Mr. Turner is shown in Illustration 15-6. A special payroll check form is used that has a detachable stub for recording earnings and amounts deducted. Employees keep the stubs for a record of deductions and cash received.

| Check No. **423** | | |
|---|---|---|
| PERIOD ENDING | 12 15 -- | |
| EARNINGS | $ 758 00 | |
| REG. | $ 704.00 | |
| O.T. | $ 54.00 | |
| DEDUCTIONS | $ 175 64 | |
| INC. TAX | $ 45.00 | |
| FICA TAX | $ 60.64 | |
| HEALTH INS. | $ 50.00 | |
| OTHER | $ 10.00 | |
| NET PAY | $ 582 36 | |

PAYROLL ACCOUNT

December 15, 19 --

No. **423**

57–63
115

Pay to the order of *Patrick S. Turner*          $ 582.36

*Five hundred eighty-two and 36/100* ———— Dollars

FOR CLASSROOM USE ONLY

FIRST SECURITY BANK OF ROCKVILLE

CARLAND

*Dario Mesa*

⑆0 11500638⑆ 005972165⑈

Illustration 15-6
Payroll check with detachable stub

A separate checking account for payroll checks helps to protect and control payroll payments. The exact amount needed to pay the payroll is deposited in the special payroll account. If amounts on checks are altered or unauthorized payroll checks are prepared, the amount in the special payroll account would be insufficient to cover all the checks. Thus, the bank and CarLand would be alerted quickly to an unauthorized payroll check. Also, since payroll checks are drawn on the separate account, any balance in this account will correspond to the sum of outstanding payroll checks.

Some businesses deposit employee net pay directly to each employee bank account by using electronic funds transfer (EFT). When EFT is used, the bank's computer deducts the amount of net pay from the business' bank account and adds the amount to each employee bank account. The payroll must still be figured, but individual checks are not written and do not have to be distributed. Under this system, each employee receives a statement of earnings and deductions similar to the detachable stub on a payroll check.

## EMPLOYEE EARNINGS RECORDS

A business form used to record details affecting payments made to an employee is called an employee earnings record. This information is recorded each pay period. The record includes earnings, deductions, net pay, and accumulated earnings for the calendar year. Employee earnings records enable the company to complete required tax forms at the end of the year.

## Recording information in an employee earnings record

CarLand keeps all employee earnings records on cards. One card for each employee is used for each quarter in the calendar year. After a payroll register has been prepared, the payroll data for each employee are recorded in each employee earnings record. The December 15 payroll register data for Patrick S. Turner are recorded in his fourth quarter employee earnings record shown in Illustration 15-7.

EARNINGS RECORD FOR QUARTER ENDED *September 30, 19--*

EMPLOYEE NO. 4   Turner   Patrick   S.   MARITAL STATUS M   WITHHOLDING ALLOWANCES 4
LAST NAME   FIRST   MIDDLE INITIAL

EARNINGS RECORD FOR QUARTER ENDED *December 31, 19--*

EMPLOYEE NO. 4   Turner   Patrick   S.   MARITAL STATUS M   WITHHOLDING ALLOWANCES 4
LAST NAME   FIRST   MIDDLE INITIAL

RATE OF PAY $8.00 PER HR.   SOCIAL SECURITY NO. 450-70-6432   POSITION Sales Clerk

| PAY PERIOD | | EARNINGS | | | DEDUCTIONS | | | | | NET PAY | ACCUMULATED EARNINGS |
|---|---|---|---|---|---|---|---|---|---|---|---|
| NO. | ENDED | REGULAR | OVERTIME | TOTAL | FEDERAL INCOME TAX | FICA TAX | HEALTH INSURANCE | OTHER | TOTAL | | |
| 1 | 10/15 | 640 00 | 60 00 | 700 00 | 39 00 | 56 00 | 50 00 | B 10 00 / UW 10 00 | 165 00 | 535 00 | 14618 00 |
| 2 | 10/31 | 768 00 | | 768 00 | 48 00 | 61 44 | 50 00 | B 10 00 / UW 10 00 | 179 44 | 588 56 | 15386 00 |
| 3 | 11/15 | 704 00 | | 704 00 | 39 00 | 56 32 | 50 00 | B 10 00 / UW 10 00 | 165 32 | 538 68 | 16090 00 |
| 4 | 11/30 | 704 00 | | 704 00 | 39 00 | 56 32 | 50 00 | B 10 00 / UW 10 00 | 165 32 | 538 68 | 16794 00 |
| 5 | 12/15 | 704 00 | 54 00 | 758 00 | 45 00 | 60 64 | 50 00 | B 10 00 / UW 10 00 | 175 64 | 582 36 | 17552 00 |
| 6 | 12/31 | 640 00 | | 640 00 | 30 00 | 51 20 | 50 00 | B 10 00 / UW 10 00 | 151 20 | 488 80 | 18192 00 |
| 7 | | | | | | | | | | | |
| QUARTERLY TOTALS | | 4160 00 | 114 00 | 4274 00 | 240 00 | 341 92 | 300 00 | B 60 00 / UW 60 00 | 1001 92 | 3272 08 | |

Accumulated Earnings (prior quarter card): 9376 00 · 10190 00 · 10874 00 · 11692 00 · 12456 00 · 13814 00 · 13918 00

OTHER DEDUCTIONS: B—U.S. SAVINGS BONDS; UW—UNITED WAY

Quarterly totals are used in the preparation of payroll reports required by the government. The accumulated earnings are also used to determine if the employee has earned more than the FICA tax base.

Illustration 15-7
Employee earnings record

## Analyzing an employee earnings record

Mr. Turner's name, employee number, social security number, and other payroll data are entered at the top of his fourth quarter employee earnings record.

Amount columns of an employee earnings record are the same as amount columns of a payroll register. Amounts opposite an employee name in a payroll register are recorded in the corresponding columns of the employee earnings record. The pay period ending December 15 is the fifth pay period in the fourth quarter. Therefore, Mr. Turner's earnings and deductions for that pay period are entered on line 5 of his employee earnings record.

The earnings record also has an Accumulated Earnings column. The first entry in this column is the accumulated earnings at the end of the previous quarter. Accumulated earnings of $13,918.00 were carried forward from the third quarter earnings record to the fourth quarter earnings record, as shown in Illustration 15-7.

Total earnings for a pay period are added to the accumulated earnings in the previous line to figure the new total accumulated earnings. Accumulated earnings are sometimes referred to as year-to-date earnings. Mr. Turner's accumulated earnings as of December 15 are calculated as shown below.

| Accumulated Earnings as of December 1 | + | Total Earnings for Pay Period Ended December 15 | = | Accumulated Earnings as of December 15 |
|---|---|---|---|---|
| $16,794.00 | + | $758.00 | = | $17,552.00 |

The Accumulated Earnings column shows the total earnings for Mr. Turner since the first of the year. The amounts in the Accumulated Earnings column supply an up-to-date reference for an employee's year-to-date earnings. When employee earnings reach the tax base, certain payroll taxes do not apply. For example, employers pay state and federal unemployment taxes only on a specified amount of each employee earnings. Also, the FICA taxes are paid only on the first $50,000 of total earnings.

Quarterly totals will be calculated on Mr. Turner's employee earnings record after the payroll for the pay period ended December 31 is recorded. The Quarterly Totals line provides space for the totals for the quarter. The accuracy of the quarterly totals is verified with the same steps used to verify payroll register totals. The Total Deductions column total is subtracted from the Total Earnings column total as shown below.

| Total Earnings | – | Total Deductions | = | Net Pay |
|---|---|---|---|---|
| $4,274.00 | – | $1,001.92 | = | $3,272.08 |

The net pay calculated above, $3,272.08, is compared to the total of the Net Pay column. The earnings record is proved because these amounts are equal. These totals are needed to prepare required government reports.

## PROCESSING A PAYROLL USING A PEGBOARD

Preparing a payroll requires figuring, recording, and reporting payroll information. Each business selects a system for processing the payroll that results in adequate control for the least amount of cost.

A special device used to write the same information at one time on several forms is called a pegboard. One type of pegboard is shown in Illustration 15-8.

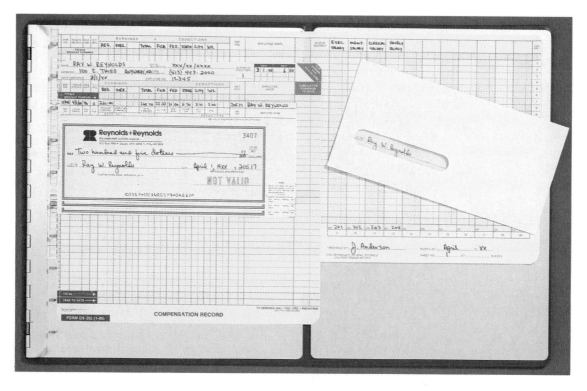

Illustration 15-8
A pegboard

The name pegboard comes from the pegs along one side of the board. The forms used with this device have holes punched along one side. Each of the forms is placed on the pegs. Thus, the line on each form on which information is to be written is aligned one below the other.

When a payroll is recorded, a page of the payroll register is attached to the pegboard. Next, the employee earnings record is properly positioned on top of the payroll register page. Then the check is positioned on top of both of these sheets. As the check stub is written, the carbonless paper imprints the same information on the employee earnings record and the payroll register. The information is written only once. However, the information is recorded on three different records at the same time. Recording information on several forms with one writing is referred to as the write-it-once principle.

The pegboard has two major purposes. First, the pegboard provides a solid writing base for writing on the forms by hand. Second, information is recorded on several forms with one writing, thus saving time and reducing the chance of error.

## SUMMARY OF PREPARING PAYROLL RECORDS

The steps required to prepare payroll records are summarized in Illustration 15-9.

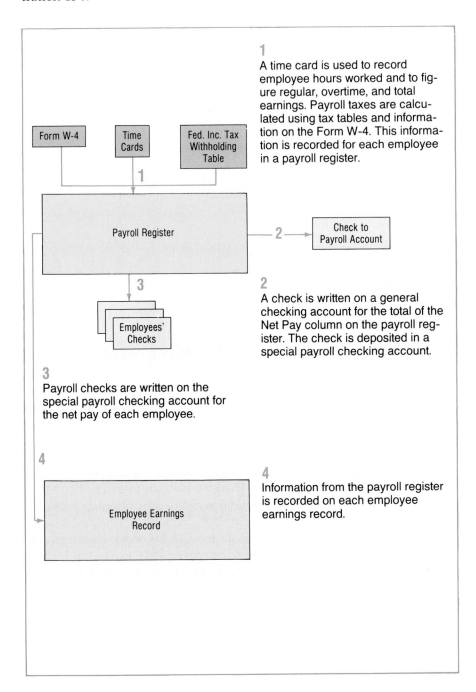

**1**

A time card is used to record employee hours worked and to figure regular, overtime, and total earnings. Payroll taxes are calculated using tax tables and information on the Form W-4. This information is recorded for each employee in a payroll register.

**2**

A check is written on a general checking account for the total of the Net Pay column on the payroll register. The check is deposited in a special payroll checking account.

**3**

Payroll checks are written on the special payroll checking account for the net pay of each employee.

**4**

Information from the payroll register is recorded on each employee earnings record.

Illustration 15-9
Summary of preparing
payroll records

## ■ ACCOUNTING TERMS

What is the meaning of each of the following?

1. salary
2. pay period
3. payroll
4. total earnings
5. payroll taxes

6. withholding allowance
7. Medicare
8. FICA tax
9. federal unemployment tax
10. state unemployment tax

11. payroll register
12. tax base
13. net pay
14. employee earnings record
15. pegboard

## ■ QUESTIONS FOR INDIVIDUAL STUDY

1. How often may a business decide to pay its employees?
2. What information is presented at the top of a time card?
3. To compute hours worked to the nearest quarter hour, how would an arrival time of 7:54 be rounded?
4. On what amount are employee payroll taxes based?
5. What factors determine the amount of federal income tax withheld from an employee?
6. How does the number of withholding allowances affect the amount of federal income tax withheld?
7. Who pays FICA tax?
8. How long must records pertaining to social security tax payments and deductions be retained?
9. What is the source of the earnings amounts reported in a payroll register?
10. Why are partners of a company not listed in the company's payroll register?
11. How is the amount of federal income tax withheld from employee salaries determined?
12. Under what circumstances can an employee who is not exempt from federal income tax withholding have no tax withheld on a payroll register?
13. What must an employer know to be able to figure the amount of FICA tax to be withheld from the salary of an employee?
14. How is a payroll register proved?
15. What amount is deposited into a payroll checking account?
16. Where is the information obtained to prepare a payroll check?
17. What is the major purpose of the Accumulated Earnings column of an employee earnings record?
18. What are two major purposes for using a pegboard for processing a payroll?

## ■ CASES FOR MANAGEMENT DECISION

**CASE 1** Kilton Hardware currently requires each employee to inform the accounting clerk of the total hours worked each day during the pay period. The total number of hours worked by all employees has been steadily increasing during the prior pay periods. The new store manager has suggested that a time clock be installed to record arrival and departure times. The accounting clerk believes the current system is satisfactory. Do you agree with the new manager or the accounting clerk? Explain your response.

**CASE 2** A banker has recommended that Tillman Construction Company open a second checking account. The company would write payroll checks against the new checking account. The company's 50 employees are currently paid with checks written against its general checking account. Do you agree with the banker's recommendation? Explain the reason for your decision.

## ■ DRILLS FOR UNDERSTANDING

### DRILL 15-D1   Figuring employee earnings

The following information is taken from the time card of each employee.

| Employee Number | Hours Worked | | Regular Rate |
|---|---|---|---|
| | Regular | Overtime | |
| 1 | 40 | 1 | $6.00 |
| 2 | 40 | 5 | 9.00 |
| 3 | 30 | 0 | 6.50 |
| 4 | 25 | 0 | 7.75 |
| 5 | 40 | 4 | 8.50 |
| 6 | 35 | 0 | 7.00 |

**Instructions:** For each employee, figure the amount of regular, overtime, and total earnings. Overtime hours are paid at one and one-half times the regular rate.

### DRILL 15-D2   Determining payroll tax withholdings

The following information is taken from the semimonthly payroll register.

| Employee | | Marital Status | No. of Allowances | Total Earnings |
|---|---|---|---|---|
| No. | Name | | | |
| 2 | Adams, Winston | M | 2 | $870.00 |
| 6 | Forte, Peter | M | 3 | 780.00 |
| 3 | Gable, Joanne | S | 1 | 670.00 |
| 1 | Jenkins, Mary | M | 5 | 760.00 |
| 8 | Little, Edward | S | 1 | 650.00 |
| 7 | Nelson, Janice | S | 2 | 710.00 |
| 4 | Pate, Kim | S | 1 | 640.00 |
| 5 | Sanders, Michael | M | 3 | 890.00 |

**Instructions: 1.** Determine the federal income tax that must be withheld for each of the eight employees. Use the tax withholding tables shown in Illustration 15-4.

**2.** Calculate the amount of FICA tax that must be withheld for each employee using an 8% tax rate. None of the eight employees has accumulated earnings greater than the tax base.

## ■ APPLICATION PROBLEMS

### PROBLEM 15-1   Completing payroll time cards

Employee time cards are given in the working papers accompanying this textbook.

**Instructions: 1.** Figure the regular, overtime, and total hours worked by each employee. Any hours over the regular 8-hour day are considered overtime. Record the hours on the time cards.

**2.** Determine the regular, overtime, and total earnings for each employee. The overtime rate is 1 1/2 times the regular rate. Complete the time cards.

## PROBLEM 15-2   Preparing a semimonthly payroll

The following information is for the semimonthly pay period April 1-15 of the current year.

| No. | Name | Marital Status | No. of Allowances | Regular | Overtime | Health Insurance | Savings Bonds |
|-----|------|----------------|-------------------|---------|----------|------------------|---------------|
| 2 | Agne, Roberta | S | 1 | $704.00 | 36.00 | $28.00 | $10.00 |
| 10 | Beville, Michael | M | 3 | 424.00 | | 45.00 | |
| 9 | Day, Mellisa | M | 2 | 739.20 | 63.00 | 36.00 | 5.00 |
| 3 | Finley, Lisa | M | 2 | 560.00 | | 36.00 | 5.00 |
| 6 | Gunter, Jill | S | 1 | 484.00 | 33.00 | | |
| 11 | Locke, Alan | S | 1 | 589.60 | | | |
| 1 | O'Neal, Barton | S | 2 | 756.80 | 64.50 | 28.00 | |
| 5 | Soehn, Lucille | M | 4 | 809.60 | | 45.00 | 25.00 |
| 4 | Webb, Ronald | M | 3 | 686.40 | 23.40 | 45.00 | |
| 7 | Wyatt, Pamela | S | 1 | 809.40 | 41.40 | | 10.00 |
| 8 | Yang, Kim | M | 2 | 598.40 | | 28.00 | |
| 12 | Zucconi, Robert | S | 1 | 572.00 | 19.50 | | 5.00 |

*(Table headers: Employee [No., Name]; Marital Status; No. of Allowances; Earnings [Regular, Overtime]; Deductions [Health Insurance, Savings Bonds])*

**Instructions: 1.** Prepare a payroll register. The date of payment is April 15. Use the federal income tax withholding tables in Illustration 15-4 to find the income tax withholding for each employee. Calculate FICA tax withholding using an 8% tax rate. None of the employee accumulated earnings has exceeded the FICA tax base.

**2.** Prepare a check for the total amount of the net pay. Make the check payable to Payroll Account, and sign your name as partner of City Hardware Company. The beginning check stub balance is $8,365.79.

**3.** Prepare payroll checks for Jill Gunter, Check No. 765, and Ronald Webb, Check No. 769. Sign your name as a partner of City Hardware Company. Record the two payroll check numbers in the payroll register.

## PROBLEM 15-3   Preparing an employee earnings record

Derrick Hammond had the following earnings for the six semimonthly pay periods in April, May, and June of the current year.

| Pay Period Ended | Regular | Overtime | Total |
|------------------|---------|----------|-------|
| 4/15 | $1,232.00 | $105.00 | $1,337.00 |
| 4/30 | 1,120.00 | 63.00 | 1,183.00 |
| 5/15 | 1,232.00 | — | 1,232.00 |
| 5/31 | 952.00 | — | 952.00 |
| 6/15 | 1,232.00 | 147.00 | 1,379.00 |
| 6/30 | 1,120.00 | — | 1,120.00 |

*(Table headers: Pay Period Ended; Earnings [Regular, Overtime, Total])*

The following additional data about Derrick Hammond are needed to complete the employee earnings record.

1. Employee number: 32
2. Marital status: married
3. Withholding Allowances: 2
4. Rate of pay: regular, $14.00
5. Social security number: 218-78-2164
6. Position: service manager
7. Accumulated earnings for the first quarter: $7,928.00
8. Deductions from total earnings:
   a. Health insurance: $40.00 each semimonthly pay period
   b. U. S. Savings Bonds: $10.00 each semimonthly pay period
   c. Federal income tax: determined each pay period by using the withholding tables in Illustration 15-4
   d. FICA taxes: 8% of total earnings each pay period

**Instructions: 1.** Prepare an employee earnings record for Derrick Hammond for the second quarter of the year.

**2.** Verify the accuracy of the completed employee earnings record. The Quarter Total for Regular and Overtime Earnings should equal the Quarter Total for Net Pay plus Total Deductions. The Quarter Total for Total Earnings should equal the end-of-quarter Accumulated Earnings minus the beginning-of-quarter Accumulated Earnings.

## ■ ENRICHMENT PROBLEMS

### MASTERY PROBLEM 15-M   Preparing a semimonthly payroll

The following information is for the semimonthly pay period May 16-31 of the current year.

| Employee | | | | Earnings | | Deductions | |
|---|---|---|---|---|---|---|---|
| No. | Name | Marital Status | No. of Allow- ances | Regular | Overtime | Health Insurance | Savings Bonds |
| 3 | Abney, Patricia | M | 2 | $512.00 | $12.80 | $30.00 | $10.00 |
| 6 | Blanks, Wilma | S | 1 | 576.00 | 21.60 | | |
| 8 | Fitts, Deborah | M | 3 | 624.00 | 11.70 | 38.00 | 5.00 |
| 1 | Greer, Daniel | M | 2 | 399.00 | 34.20 | 30.00 | 5.00 |
| 5 | Habig, Vincent | S | 1 | 672.00 | | | |
| 9 | Jones, Phyllis | M | 2 | 608.00 | 79.80 | 30.00 | 10.00 |
| 10 | Malloy, Timothy | S | 2 | 544.00 | 10.20 | 30.00 | 10.00 |
| 2 | Paxton, Alice | M | 4 | 496.00 | | 44.00 | |
| 4 | Tait, Michelle | S | 1 | 640.00 | 36.00 | | |
| 7 | Walzak, Thomas | S | 1 | 472.00 | | | 15.00 |

**Instructions: 1.** Prepare a payroll register. The date of payment is May 31. Use the income tax withholding tables in Illustration 15-4 to find the income tax withholding for each employee. Calculate FICA tax withholding using an 8% tax rate. None of the employee accumulated earnings has exceeded the FICA tax base.

**2.** Prepare a check for the total amount of the net pay. Make the check payable to Payroll Account, and sign your name as a partner of Mercer Company. The beginning check stub balance is $10,287.20.

**3.** Prepare payroll checks for Daniel Greer, Check No. 426, and Michelle Tait, Check No. 431. Sign your name as a partner of Mercer Company. Record the two payroll check numbers in the payroll register.

## CHALLENGE PROBLEM 15-C   Figuring piecework wages

Production workers in factories are frequently paid on the basis of the number of units they produce. This payroll method is referred to as the piecework incentive wage plan. Most piecework incentive wage plans include a guaranteed hourly rate to employees regardless of the number of units they produce. This guaranteed hourly rate is referred to as the base rate.

Time and motion study engineers usually determine the standard time required for producing a single unit. Assume, for example, that time studies determine that one-third of an hour is the standard time required to produce a unit. Then the standard rate for an 8-hour day would be 24 units (8 hours divided by 1/3 hour = 24 units per day). If a worker's daily base pay is $66.00, the incentive rate per unit is $2.75 ($66.00 divided by 24 units = $2.75 per unit). Therefore, the worker who produces 24 or fewer units per day is paid the base pay, $66.00. However, each worker is paid an additional $2.75 for each unit over 24 produced each day.

Southern Woodworks Company has eight employees in production departments that are paid on a piecework incentive wage plan. The following standard and incentive wage rates are listed by department.

| Department | Standard Production per Employee | Incentive Rate per Unit |
|---|---|---|
| Cutting | 30 units per day | $2.30 |
| Assembly | 20 units per day | $4.10 |
| Finishing | 40 units per day | $1.80 |

Each employee worked eight hours a day during the semimonthly pay period, August 1-15. Payroll records for August 1-15 are summarized in the following table.

| Employee | | Marital Status | No. of Allow- ances | Guaranteed Daily Rate | Units Produced per Day | | | | | | | | | |
|---|---|---|---|---|---|---|---|---|---|---|---|---|---|---|
| | | | | | Pay Period August 1–15 | | | | | | | | | |
| No. | Name | | | | 2 | 3 | 4 | 5 | 6 | 9 | 10 | 11 | 12 | 13 |
| | Cutting Department | | | | | | | | | | | | | |
| C2 | Simpson, Alan | S | 1 | $69.00 | 29 | 32 | 31 | 34 | 28 | 27 | 30 | 32 | 36 | 26 |
| C4 | Creek, Janice | M | 1 | $69.00 | 32 | 31 | 28 | 29 | 27 | 29 | 31 | 32 | 27 | 28 |
| C8 | Pate, Marie | M | 2 | $69.00 | 31 | 28 | 27 | 24 | 31 | 33 | 32 | 29 | 30 | 29 |
| | Assembly Department | | | | | | | | | | | | | |
| A1 | Meese, Frank | S | 1 | $82.00 | 20 | 21 | 19 | 19 | 18 | 18 | 19 | 21 | 20 | 21 |
| A6 | Harris, Kevin | M | 3 | $82.00 | 25 | 21 | 17 | 18 | 19 | 21 | 20 | 20 | 21 | 18 |
| A7 | Martin, Angela | S | 1 | $82.00 | 22 | 24 | 25 | 21 | 20 | 19 | 23 | 21 | 18 | 17 |
| | Finishing Department | | | | | | | | | | | | | |
| F5 | Quinn, Karen | M | 2 | $72.00 | 41 | 40 | 38 | 39 | 42 | 43 | 41 | 40 | 38 | 37 |
| F3 | Raines, Jon | M | 2 | $72.00 | 37 | 37 | 38 | 38 | 39 | 38 | 40 | 41 | 41 | 42 |

**Instructions:** Prepare a payroll register. The earnings column headed Incentive is used instead of Overtime. The date of payment is August 16. Use the income tax withholding tables in Illustration 15-4. Calculate the employee FICA tax withholding using an 8% tax rate. None of the employees has health insurance or other deductions.

# Payroll Accounting, Taxes, and Reports

ENABLING PERFORMANCE TASKS

After studying Chapter 16, you will be able to:
a. Identify accounting concepts and practices related to payroll accounts, taxes, and reports.
b. Analyze payroll transactions.
c. Journalize and post payroll transactions.
d. Prepare selected payroll tax reports.

Payroll information for each pay period is recorded in a payroll register. Each pay period the payroll information for each employee is also recorded on each employee earnings record. Separate payroll accounts for each employee are not kept in the general ledger. Instead, accounts are kept in the general ledger to summarize total earnings and deductions for all employees.

The payroll register and employee earnings records provide all the payroll information needed to prepare a payroll and payroll tax reports. Journal entries are made to record the payment of the payroll and the employer payroll taxes. In addition, various quarterly and annual payroll tax reports are required to report the payment of payroll taxes.

## RECORDING A PAYROLL

The payroll register for CarLand's semimonthly pay period ended December 15 is shown in Illustration 16-1.

### Analyzing payment of a payroll

The column totals of a payroll register provide the debit and credit amounts needed to journalize a payroll. CarLand's December 15 payroll is summarized in the following T accounts.

**Salary Expense**

| | |
|---|---|
| Dec. 15 | 2,556.00 |

=

**Employee Income Tax Payable**

| | |
|---|---|
| Dec. 15 | 192.00 |

**FICA Tax Payable**

| | |
|---|---|
| Dec. 15 | 204.48 |

**Health Insurance Premiums Payable**

| | |
|---|---|
| Dec. 15 | 158.00 |

**U.S. Savings Bonds Payable**

| | |
|---|---|
| Dec. 15 | 15.00 |

**United Way Donations Payable**

| | |
|---|---|
| Dec. 15 | 10.00 |

**Cash**

| | |
|---|---|
| Dec. 15 | 1,976.52 |

SEMIMONTHLY PERIOD ENDED *December 15, 19--*   PAYROLL REGISTER   DATE OF PAYMENT *December 15, 19--*

| | EMPL. NO. | EMPLOYEE NAME | MARITAL STATUS | NO. OF ALLOWANCES | EARNINGS REGULAR | OVERTIME | TOTAL | DEDUCTIONS FEDERAL INCOME TAX | FICA TAX | HEALTH INSURANCE | OTHER | TOTAL | NET PAY | CHECK. NO. | |
|---|---|---|---|---|---|---|---|---|---|---|---|---|---|---|---|
| 1 | 2 | Bauch, Mary R. | M | 2 | 660 00 | | 660 00 | 57 00 | 52 80 | 38 00 | B 5 00 | 152 80 | 507 20 | 419 | 1 |
| 2 | 5 | Clay, Richard P. | S | 1 | 80 00 | | 80 00 | 00 | 6 40 | | | 6 40 | 73 60 | 420 | 2 |
| 3 | 1 | Javorski, Adam B. | M | 2 | 384 00 | 18 00 | 402 00 | 17 00 | 32 16 | 38 00 | | 87 16 | 314 84 | 421 | 3 |
| 4 | 6 | Maggio, Brenda A. | S | 1 | 40 00 | | 40 00 | 00 | 3 20 | | | 3 20 | 36 80 | 422 | 4 |
| 5 | 4 | Turner, Patrick S. | M | 4 | 704 00 | 54 00 | 758 00 | 45 00 | 60 64 | 50 00 | B 10 00 / uw 10 00 | 175 64 | 582 36 | 423 | 5 |
| 6 | 3 | Wilkes, Samuel R. | S | 1 | 616 00 | | 616 00 | 73 00 | 49 28 | 32 00 | | 154 28 | 461 72 | 424 | 6 |
| 7 | | | | | 2484 00 | 72 00 | 2556 00 | 192 00 | 204 48 | 158 00 | B 15 00 / uw 10 00 | 579 48 | 1976 52 | | 7 |

The Total Earnings column total, $2,556.00, is the salary expense for the period. Salary Expense is debited for this amount.

Illustration 16-1
Payroll register

The Federal Income Tax column total, $192.00, is the amount withheld from employee salaries for federal income tax. The amount withheld is a liability of the business until the taxes are sent to the federal government. Employee Income Tax Payable is credited for $192.00 to record this liability.

The FICA Tax column total, $204.48, is the amount withheld from salaries of all employees for FICA tax. The amount withheld is a liability of the business until the tax is paid to the government. FICA Tax Payable is credited for $204.48.

The Health Insurance column total, $158.00, is the amount withheld from salaries for health insurance premiums. The amount withheld is a liability of the business until the premiums are paid to the insurance company. Health Insurance Premiums Payable is credited for $158.00 to record this liability.

The Other column of the deductions section may contain more than one total. Two types of *Other* deductions are recorded in CarLand's payroll register. The $15.00 Other column total identified with the letter *B* is withheld to buy savings bonds for employees. The $10.00 total identified with the letters *UW* is withheld for employee United Way pledges. Until these amounts have been paid by the employer, they are liabilities of the business. U.S. Savings Bonds Payable is credited for $15.00. United Way Donations Payable is credited for $10.00.

The Net Pay column total, $1,976.52, is the net amount paid to employees. Cash is credited for $1,976.52. A check for the total net pay amount, $1,976.52, is written on CarLand's general checking account. This amount is deposited in a special payroll checking account used only for employee payroll checks. Individual payroll checks are then written on the special payroll checking account.

## Journalizing payment of a payroll

*December 15, 19--.*
*Paid cash for semimonthly payroll, $1,976.52 (total payroll, $2,556.00, less deductions: employee income tax, $192.00; FICA tax, $204.48; health insurance premiums, $158.00; U.S. Savings Bonds, $15.00; United Way donations, $10.00). Check No. 287.*

The source document for payment of a payroll is the check written for the total net pay. *(CONCEPT: Objective Evidence)* The journal entry to record payment of CarLand's December 15 payroll is shown in Illustration 16-2.

| | | | | | GENERAL | | | CASH | |
| PAGE 24 | | | | | JOURNAL | | PAGE 24 | | |
| | | | | | 1 | 2 | | 10 | 11 |
| DATE | ACCOUNT TITLE | DOC. NO. | POST. REF. | | DEBIT | CREDIT | | DEBIT | CREDIT |
|---|---|---|---|---|---|---|---|---|---|
| 21 | 15 | Salary Expense | C287 | | 2 5 5 6 00 | | | | 1 9 7 6 52 | 21 |
| 22 | | Employee Income Tax Pay. | | | | 1 9 2 00 | | | | 22 |
| 23 | | FICA Tax Payable | | | | 2 0 4 48 | | | | 23 |
| 24 | | Health Insurance Premiums Pay. | | | | 1 5 8 00 | | | | 24 |
| 25 | | U.S. Savings Bonds Payable | | | | 1 5 00 | | | | 25 |
| 26 | | United Way Donations Payable | | | | 1 0 00 | | | | 26 |

Illustration 16-2
Journal entry to record
a payroll

The date, *15*, is written in the Date column. The title of the account debited, *Salary Expense*, is recorded in the Account Title column. The check number, *C287*, is entered in the Doc. No. column. The amount debited to Salary Expense, *$2,556.00*, is written in the General Debit column. On the same line, the net amount paid to employees, *$1,976.52*, is written in the Cash Credit column. Five liability accounts are credited for the amounts deducted from employee salaries. The five account titles are written in the Account Title column. The five credit amounts are written in the General Credit column.

## Posting the journal entry for payment of a payroll

Amounts recorded in the General columns of a journal are posted individually to general ledger accounts. After the December 15 payroll entry is posted, the liability and salary expense accounts appear as shown in Illustration 16-3.

Illustration 16-3
General ledger accounts
after journal entry for
payment of a payroll
is posted

| ACCOUNT *United Way Donations Payable* | | | | | ACCOUNT NO. *2190* | |
|---|---|---|---|---|---|---|
| DATE | ITEM | POST. REF. | DEBIT | CREDIT | BALANCE DEBIT | BALANCE CREDIT |
| Dec. 1 | Balance | √ | | | | 4 0 00 |
| 15 | | 24 | | 1 0 00 | | 5 0 00 |

| ACCOUNT *Salary Expense* | | | | | ACCOUNT NO. *6170* | |
|---|---|---|---|---|---|---|
| DATE | ITEM | POST. REF. | DEBIT | CREDIT | BALANCE DEBIT | BALANCE CREDIT |
| Dec. 1 | Balance | √ | | | 54 9 5 2 00 | |
| 15 | | 24 | 2 5 5 6 00 | | 57 5 0 8 00 | |

Illustration 16-3
General ledger accounts after journal entry for payment of a payroll is posted (concluded)

The credit to Cash, $1,976.52, is not posted separately to the cash account. The amount is included in the journal's Cash Credit column total that is posted at the end of the month.

# RECORDING EMPLOYER PAYROLL TAXES

Employers must pay to the government the taxes withheld from employee earnings. CarLand has withheld federal income tax and FICA tax from employee salaries. The amounts withheld are liabilities to the business until they are actually paid to the government. In addition, employers must pay several of their own payroll taxes. Employer payroll taxes are business expenses.

## Calculating employer payroll taxes

Most employers must pay three separate payroll taxes. These taxes are (1) employer FICA tax, (2) federal unemployment tax, and (3) state unemployment tax. Employer payroll taxes expense is based on a percentage of employee earnings.

**Employer FICA tax.** CarLand withheld $204.48 in FICA tax from employee wages for the pay period ended December 15. CarLand owes the same amount of FICA taxes as the amount withheld from employees.

Therefore, CarLand's FICA tax for the pay period ended December 15 is also $204.48.

Congress sets the FICA tax rate for employees and employers. Periodically, Congress may change the tax rate and tax base. The employer FICA tax rate is the same as the employee FICA tax rate. A tax rate of 8% and a tax base of $50,000.00 are used in this textbook.

The FICA tax is the only payroll tax paid by *both* the employees and the employer. Employees pay 8% of their total earnings up to the $50,000.00 tax base as a FICA tax. Employers also pay 8% of each employee's total earnings up to the $50,000.00 tax base as a FICA tax.

**Federal unemployment tax.** Federal unemployment insurance laws require that employers pay taxes for unemployment compensation. These tax funds are used to pay workers benefits for limited periods of unemployment and to administer the unemployment compensation program. All of the federal unemployment tax is paid by the employer.

The federal unemployment tax for most businesses is 0.8% of total earnings of each employee up to a tax base of $7,000.00 during a calendar year. The total earnings of CarLand's December 1-15 pay period subject to the federal unemployment tax is referred to as unemployment taxable earnings. The amount of unemployment taxable earnings is figured as shown in Illustration 16-4.

| CarLand Taxable Earnings for December 15, 19-- Pay Period | | |
|---|---|---|
| Accumulated Earnings as of Nov. 30, 19-- | Total Earnings for Dec. 15, 19-- Pay Period | Unemployment Taxable Earnings |
| Bauch, Mary R.......  $14,520.00 | $660.00 | $    — |
| Clay, Richard P. ......  2,160.00 | 80.00 | 80.00 |
| Javorski, Adam B.....  5,792.50 | 402.00 | 402.00 |
| Maggio, Brenda A.....  1,680.00 | 40.00 | 40.00 |
| Turner, Patrick S......  16,794.00 | 758.00 | — |
| Wilkes, Samuel R. ....  4,976.50 | 616.00 | 616.00 |
|  |  | $1,138.00 |

Illustration 16-4
Total earnings subject to
federal unemployment tax

Accumulated earnings are figured on each employee earnings record. Patrick S. Turner's accumulated earnings as of November 30, *$16,794.00*, are recorded in the first column. Total earnings for Mr. Turner for the December 15 pay period, *$758.00*, are recorded in the second column. Since the accumulated earnings for Mr. Turner are greater than $7,000.00, none of his current earnings are subject to federal unemployment tax. Thus, the amount of unemployment taxable earnings recorded in the third column is zero.

The accumulated earnings for Samuel R. Wilkes, $4,976.50, are less than $7,000.00. Therefore, his total earnings for the December 15 pay period are subject to federal unemployment tax. Total earnings for Mr. Wilkes for the December 15 pay period, *$616.00*, are recorded in the Unemployment Taxable Earnings column.

The total earnings for the pay period are entered in the Unemployment Taxable Earnings column for employees whose accumulated earnings are less than $7,000.00. The sum of the Unemployment Taxable Earnings Column, $1,138.00, is the amount used to calculate federal unemployment tax.

CarLand's federal unemployment tax is calculated as shown below.

| Unemployment Taxable Earnings | × | Federal Unemployment Tax Rate | = | Federal Unemployment Tax |
|---|---|---|---|---|
| $1,138.00 | × | .8% | = | $9.10 |

**State unemployment tax.** Most states require that employers pay unemployment tax of 5.4% on the first $7,000.00 earned by each employee. The unemployment taxable earnings used to calculate the federal unemployment tax are also used to calculate the state unemployment tax. The unemployment taxable earnings subject to the state unemployment tax are figured in Illustration 16-4. Thus, the state employment tax to be paid by CarLand is calculated as shown below.

| Unemployment Taxable Earnings | × | State Unemployment Tax Rate | = | State Unemployment Tax |
|---|---|---|---|---|
| $1,138.00 | × | 5.4% | = | $61.45 |

## Journalizing employer payroll taxes

Employer payroll taxes are paid to the government at a later date. However, the transaction to record employer payroll taxes expense is journalized on the same date the payroll is journalized. The salary expense and the employer payroll taxes expense are, therefore, both recorded in the same accounting period.

*December 15, 19--.*
*Recorded employer payroll taxes expense, $275.03, for the semimonthly pay period ended December 15. Taxes owed are: FICA tax, $204.48; federal unemployment tax, $9.10; state unemployment tax, $61.45. Memorandum No. 54.*

The source document for journalizing employer payroll taxes is a memorandum. *(CONCEPT: Objective Evidence)* The entry to record employer payroll taxes is analyzed in the T accounts.

Payroll Taxes Expense is debited for $275.03 to show the increase in the balance of this expense account. Three liability accounts are credited to show the increase in payroll tax liabilities. FICA Tax Payable is credited for $204.48. Unemployment Tax Payable—Federal is credited for $9.10. Unemployment Tax Payable—State is credited for $61.45.

CarLand's journal entry to record the employer payroll taxes expense is shown in Illustration 16-5.

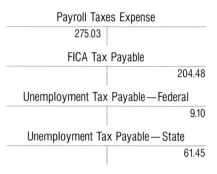

| | Payroll Taxes Expense | |
|---|---|---|
| 275.03 | | |

| | FICA Tax Payable | |
|---|---|---|
| | | 204.48 |

| | Unemployment Tax Payable—Federal | |
|---|---|---|
| | | 9.10 |

| | Unemployment Tax Payable—State | |
|---|---|---|
| | | 61.45 |

**JOURNAL**

PAGE *24* / PAGE *24*

| | DATE | ACCOUNT TITLE | DOC. NO. | POST. REF. | GENERAL DEBIT | GENERAL CREDIT | CASH DEBIT | CASH CREDIT | |
|---|---|---|---|---|---|---|---|---|---|
| 27 | 15 | *Payroll Taxes Expense* | M54 | | 275 03 | | | | 27 |
| 28 | | *FICA Tax Payable* | | | | 204 48 | | | 28 |
| 29 | | *Unemployment Tax Pay.—Federal* | | | | 9 10 | | | 29 |
| 30 | | *Unemployment Tax Pay.—State* | | | | 61 45 | | | 30 |
| 31 | | | | | | | | | 31 |

The date, *15*, is written in the Date column. The title of the account debited, *Payroll Taxes Expense*, is written in the Account Title column. The memorandum number, *M54*, is entered in the Doc. No. column. The debit amount, *$275.03*, is entered in the General Debit column. The titles of the liability accounts are entered in the Account Title column. The amounts credited to the liability accounts are entered in the General Credit column.

Illustration 16-5
Journal entry to record employer payroll taxes

## Posting an employer payroll taxes entry

After the entry for the employer payroll taxes is posted, the accounts involved appear as shown in Illustration 16-6.

ACCOUNT *FICA Tax Payable*          ACCOUNT NO. *2130*

| | DATE | ITEM | POST. REF. | DEBIT | CREDIT | BALANCE DEBIT | BALANCE CREDIT | |
|---|---|---|---|---|---|---|---|---|
| | 15 | | 24 | | 204 48 | | 204 48 | |
| | 15 | | 24 | | 204 48 | | 408 96 | |

Illustration 16-6
General ledger accounts after journal entry for employer payroll taxes expense is posted

ACCOUNT *Unemployment Tax Payable—Federal*   ACCOUNT NO. *2150*

| DATE | | ITEM | POST. REF. | DEBIT | CREDIT | BALANCE DEBIT | BALANCE CREDIT |
|---|---|---|---|---|---|---|---|
| Dec. | 1 | Balance | √ | | | | 4 0 48 |
| | 15 | | 24 | | 9 10 | | 4 9 58 |

ACCOUNT *Unemployment Tax Payable—State*   ACCOUNT NO. *2160*

| DATE | | ITEM | POST. REF. | DEBIT | CREDIT | BALANCE DEBIT | BALANCE CREDIT |
|---|---|---|---|---|---|---|---|
| Dec. | 1 | Balance | √ | | | | 2 7 3 22 |
| | 15 | | 24 | | 6 1 45 | | 3 3 4 67 |

ACCOUNT *Payroll Taxes Expense*   ACCOUNT NO. *6150*

| DATE | | ITEM | POST. REF. | DEBIT | CREDIT | BALANCE DEBIT | BALANCE CREDIT |
|---|---|---|---|---|---|---|---|
| Dec. | 1 | Balance | √ | | | 6 7 3 8 96 | |
| | 15 | | 24 | 2 7 5 03 | | 7 0 1 3 99 | |

Illustration 16-6
General ledger accounts after journal entry for employer payroll taxes expense is posted (concluded)

The FICA Tax Payable account has two credits. The first credit, $204.48, is the FICA tax withheld from *employee* wages for the semimonthly period ended December 15. This amount was posted from the journal entry that recorded payment of the payroll, Illustration 16-2. The second credit, $204.48, is the *employer* liability for FICA tax. This amount was posted from the journal entry that recorded the employer payroll taxes, Illustration 16-5.

## Summary of amounts posted to the general ledger

Both the employees and employer owe payroll taxes. Federal income tax and FICA tax are withheld from employee salaries. An equal amount of FICA tax is owed by the employer. The employer must also record federal and state unemployment taxes. The payroll taxes resulting from Car-Land's December 1-15 pay period are summarized below.

| | **Employees** | **Employer** |
|---|---|---|
| Federal Income Tax | $192.00 | — |
| FICA Tax | 204.48 | $204.48 |
| Federal Unemployment Tax | — | 9.10 |
| State Unemployment Tax | — | 61.45 |
| Total | $396.48 | $275.03 |

Only the employer payroll taxes, $275.03, are recorded as payroll taxes expense in CarLand's general ledger accounts. The payroll taxes of both the employees and the employer create liabilities to the business which must be paid at times specified by the government.

# REPORTING WITHHOLDING AND PAYROLL TAXES

Each employer is required by law to periodically report the payroll taxes withheld from employee salaries and the employer payroll taxes due the government. Some reports are submitted quarterly and others are submitted annually.

## Employer quarterly federal tax return

Each employer must file a quarterly federal tax return showing the federal income tax and FICA taxes due the government. This information is submitted every three months on Form 941, Employer's Quarterly Federal Tax Return. Form 941 is filed before the last day of the month following the end of a calendar quarter. CarLand's Form 941 for the calendar quarter ended December 31 is shown in Illustration 16-7, page 366. The information needed to prepare Form 941 is obtained from employee earnings records.

Total earnings, $15,192.90, are recorded on line 2 of Form 941. This amount is the sum of the fourth quarter total earnings of all CarLand employees. The amount of total earnings, $15,192.90, is also recorded on the line to the left of line 6. The income tax withheld, $1,168.00, is recorded on line 3 of Form 941. The amount is the total of the fourth quarter federal income tax withheld from CarLand's employees.

The social security (FICA) taxes due are calculated as shown below.

| Total Earnings | × | FICA Tax Rate | = | Social Security (FICA) Tax |
|---|---|---|---|---|
| $15,192.90 | × | 16% | = | $2,430.86 |

The 16% tax rate is the sum of the *employee* 8% FICA tax rate and the *employer* 8% FICA tax rate. The FICA tax amount, $2,430.86, is recorded on line 6 of Form 941.

CarLand is required to pay the federal government the sum of the FICA tax and federal income tax withheld. The amount of the payment is figured as shown below.

| Federal Income Tax Withheld | + | FICA Tax | = | Total Payment |
|---|---|---|---|---|
| $1,168.00 | + | $2,430.86 | = | $3,598.86 |

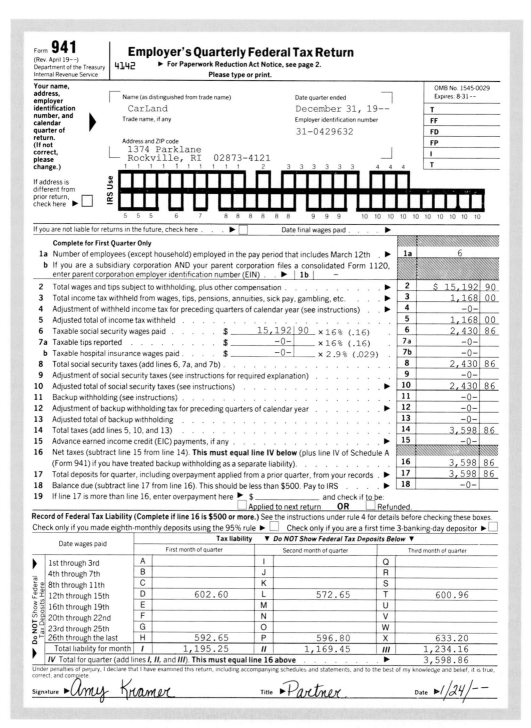

Illustration 16-7      Form 941, Employer's Quarterly Federal Tax Return

The total payment owed to the federal government, *$3,598.86*, is recorded on line 14 of Form 941.

The lower section of Form 941 lists the amounts and dates when payroll taxes were withheld from employees and are due from the employer. For the pay period ended December 15, the amount of taxes owed is figured as shown below.

| Federal Income Tax Withheld | | Employee FICA Tax | | Employer FICA Tax | | Federal Tax Liability |
|---|---|---|---|---|---|---|
| $192.00 | + | $204.48 | + | $204.48 | = | $600.96 |

The federal tax liability for the December 15 pay period, *$600.96*, is recorded on line T of Form 941. The December 15 pay period ended in the third month of the quarter between the 12th and 15th of the month. The December 15 pay period is, therefore, recorded on line T.

## Employer annual report to employees of taxes withheld

Each employer who withholds income tax and FICA tax from employee earnings must furnish each employee with an annual report of these withholdings. The report shows total year's earnings and the amounts withheld for taxes for an employee. These amounts are obtained from the employee earnings records. The report is prepared on the Internal Revenue Service Form W-2, Wage and Tax Statement.

Employers are required to furnish Form W-2 to each employee by January 31 of the next year. If an employee ends employment before December 31, Form W-2 must be furnished within 30 days of the last date of employment.

The Form W-2 prepared by CarLand for Patrick S. Turner is shown in Illustration 16-8, on page 368.

Four copies (A to D) of Form W-2 are prepared for each employee. Copies B and C are given to the employee. The employee attaches Copy B to a personal federal income tax return and keeps Copy C for a personal record. The employer sends Copy A to the Social Security Administration and keeps Copy D for the business' records.

> Businesses in states with state income tax must prepare additional copies of Form W-2. The employee attaches the additional copy to the personal state income tax return.

## Employer annual reporting of payroll taxes

Form W-3, Transmittal of Income and Tax Statements, is sent to the Social Security Administration by February 28 each year. Form W-3 reports the previous year's earnings and payroll taxes withheld for all employees. Attached to Form W-3 is Copy A of each employee Form W-2. A Form W-3 prepared by CarLand is shown in Illustration 16-9.

| 1 Control number | 22222 | OMB No. 1545-0008 | | | | | |
|---|---|---|---|---|---|---|---|

| 2 Employer's name, address, and ZIP code | 6 Statutory employee ☐  Deceased ☐  Pension plan ☐  Legal rep. ☐  942 emp. ☐  Subtotal ☐  Deferred compensation ☐  Void ☐ |
|---|---|

CarLand
1374 Parklane
Rockville, RI 02873-4121

| 7 Allocated tips | 8 Advance EIC payment |
|---|---|
| 9 Federal income tax withheld  1,032.00 | 10 Wages, tips, other compensation  18,192.00 |

| 3 Employer's identification number  31-0429632 | 4 Employer's state I.D. number | 11 Social security tax withheld  1,455.36 | 12 Social security wages  18,192.00 |
|---|---|---|---|

| 5 Employee's social security number  450-70-6432 | 13 Social security tips | 14 Nonqualified plans |
|---|---|---|

| 19 Employee's name, address and ZIP code | 15 Dependent care benefits | 16 Fringe benefits incl. in Box 10 |
|---|---|---|

Patrick S. Turner
1625 Northland Drive
Rockville, RI 02873-5073

| 17 | 18 Other |
|---|---|

| 20 | 21 | 22 | 23 |
|---|---|---|---|
| 24 State income tax | 25 State wages, tips, etc. | 26 Name of state | 27 Local income tax | 28 Local wages, tips, etc. | 29 Name of locality |

**Copy A For Social Security Administration**                         Dept. of the Treasury—Internal Revenue Service

Form **W-2 Wage and Tax Statement  19 --**

Illustration 16-8
Form W-2, Wage and Tax
Statement

| 1 Control number | 33333 | OMB No. 1545-0008 | |
|---|---|---|---|

| Kind of Payer ▶ | 2 941/941E ☒  Military ☐  943 ☐ | 3 Employer's state I.D. number | 5 Total number of statements |
| | CT-1 ☐  942 ☐  Medicare gov't. emp. ☐ | 4 | 6 |

| 6 Establishment number | 7 Allocated tips | 8 Advance EIC payments |
|---|---|---|

| 9 Federal income tax withheld  4,612.00 | 10 Wages, tips, and other compensation  60,153.00 | 11 Social security tax withheld  4,812.24 |
|---|---|---|

| 12 Social security wages  60,153.00 | 13 Social security tips | 14 Nonqualified plans |
|---|---|---|

| 15 Dependent care benefits | 16 Adjusted total social security wages and tips | 17 Deferred compensation |
|---|---|---|

| 18 Employer's identification number  31 — 0429632 | 19 Other EIN used this year |
|---|---|

| 20 Employer's name  CarLand

1374 Parklane
Rockville, RI 02873-4121

22 Employer's address and ZIP code | 21 Gross annuity, pension, etc. (Form W-2P) |
| 23 Taxable amount (Form W-2P) |
| 24 Income tax withheld by third-party payer |

Under penalties of perjury, I declare that I have examined this return and accompanying documents, and to the best of my knowledge and belief, they are true, correct, and complete.

Signature ▶ *Amy Kramer*   Title ▶ *Partner*   Date ▶ 2/27/--

Telephone number (optional)

Form **W-3 Transmittal of Income and Tax Statements  19 --**                Department of the Treasury
Internal Revenue Service

Illustration 16-9
Form W-3, Transmittal of
Income and Tax
Statements

At the end of a calendar year, employers must also report to the federal and state governments a summary of all earnings paid to employees during the twelve months.

Employers with more than 250 employees have different procedures for reporting withholding tax information. The information is sent to the Internal Revenue Service in computer files rather than the actual Forms W-2 and W-3.

# PAYING WITHHOLDING AND PAYROLL TAXES

At least quarterly, employers must pay to the federal government the federal income taxes and FICA taxes withheld from employee salaries. The payment also includes the amount of employer FICA taxes.

## Paying the liability for employee income tax and FICA tax

Employee withheld income tax, employee FICA tax, and employer FICA tax are paid periodically in a combined payment. Tax payments are made to banks authorized by the Internal Revenue Service to accept these payments or to a Federal Reserve bank. The timing of these tax payments is based on the amount of taxes owed. A payment is accompanied by a Form 8109, Federal Tax Deposit Coupon, which shows the amount and purpose of the payment.

In December, CarLand withheld $402.00 from employee salaries for federal income taxes. The liability for FICA tax for December is $832.16. This amount includes both the employer share and the amounts withheld from employees. CarLand's federal tax payment is sent January 15 to an authorized bank with Form 8109 as shown in Illustration 16-10.

Illustration 16-10
Form 8109, Federal Tax Deposit Coupon for withheld income tax and FICA taxes

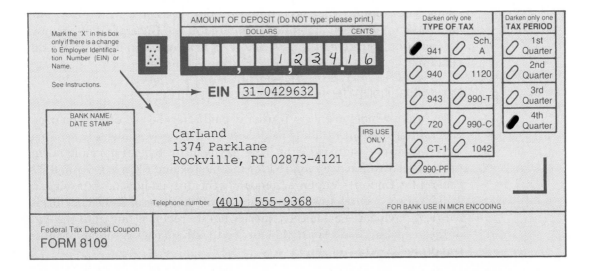

The type of tax, federal income and FICA taxes, is identified by marking the 941 circle. These taxes are reported to the government using Form 941. The calendar quarter is identified on the right side of the form.

*January 15, 19--.*
*Paid cash for liability for employee income tax, $402.00, and for FICA tax, $832.16; total, $1,234.16. Check No. 305.*

The source document for this transaction is the check written to pay the payroll taxes liability. *(CONCEPT: Objective Evidence)* This transaction is analyzed in the T accounts.

The balances of the liability accounts are reduced by this transaction. Therefore, Employee Income Tax Payable is debited for $402.00. FICA Tax Payable is debited for $832.16. The balance of the Cash account is decreased by a credit for the total payment, $1,234.16.

The journal entry to record payment of these liabilities is shown in Illustration 16-11.

| PAGE 27 | | JOURNAL | | | 1 | 2 | | 10 | 11 PAGE 27 |
|---|---|---|---|---|---|---|---|---|---|
| DATE | ACCOUNT TITLE | | DOC. NO. | POST. REF. | GENERAL DEBIT | GENERAL CREDIT | | CASH DEBIT | CASH CREDIT |
| 25 | 15 | *Employee Income Tax Payable* | C305 | | 4 0 2 00 | | | | | 25 |
| 26 | | *FICA Tax Payable* | | | 8 3 2 16 | | | | | 26 |
| 27 | | | | | | | | | | 27 |

*Note: Cash Credit 1 2 3 4 16 on line 25*

Illustration 16-11
Journal entry to record payment of liability for employee income tax and FICA tax

The date, *15*, is written in the Date column. The titles of the two accounts debited, *Employee Income Tax Payable* and *FICA Tax Payable*, are written in the Account Title column. The check number, *C305*, is entered in the Doc. No. column. The two debit amounts are entered in the General Debit column. The amount of the credit to Cash, *$1,234.16*, is recorded in the Cash Credit column.

## Paying the liability for federal unemployment tax

Federal unemployment tax is usually paid after the end of each quarter. Federal unemployment tax is paid to the federal government by sending the check to a designated bank. The payment for federal unemployment tax is similar to the one required for income tax and FICA tax. Form 8109, Federal Tax Deposit Coupon, accompanies the unemployment tax payment.

CarLand's federal unemployment tax at the end of December 31 is $59.15. A payment is made each quarter but no report is due until the end of the year. CarLand's Form 8109 for the fourth quarter is shown in Illustration 16-12.

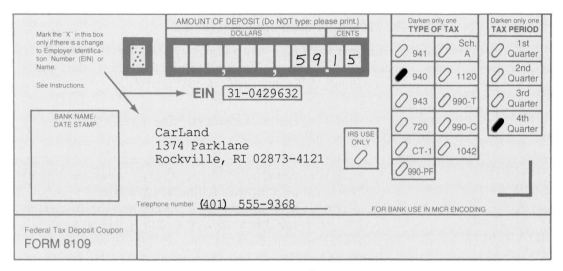

Federal Tax Deposit Coupon
FORM 8109

The type of tax, federal unemployment tax, is identified by marking the 940 circle since this tax is reported to the government using Form 940. The calendar quarter is identified on the right side of the form.

*Illustration 16-12*
*Form 8109, Federal Tax Deposit Coupon for federal unemployment tax*

*January 31, 19--.*
*Paid cash for federal unemployment tax liability for quarter ended December 31, $59.15. Check No. 318.*

The source document for this transaction is the check written to pay the payroll tax liability. *(CONCEPT: Objective Evidence)* This transaction is analyzed in the T accounts.

The balance of the liability account is reduced by this transaction. Therefore, Unemployment Tax Payable—Federal is debited for $59.15. The balance of the asset account, Cash, is decreased by a credit for the payment, $59.15.

The journal entry to record payment of the liability for federal unemployment taxes is shown in Illustration 16-13.

Unemployment Tax Payable—Federal

| 59.15 | |
|---|---|

Cash

| | 59.15 |
|---|---|

| PAGE *28* | JOURNAL | | | | | | PAGE *28* | |
|---|---|---|---|---|---|---|---|---|

The date, *31*, is written in the Date column. The title of the account debited, *Unemployment Tax Payable—Federal*, is written in the Account Title column. The check number, *C318*, is entered in the Doc. No. column. The check amount, *$59.15*, is entered in the General Debit and Cash Credit columns.

*Illustration 16-13*
*Journal entry to record payment of liability for federal unemployment tax*

## Paying the liability for state unemployment tax

State requirements for reporting and paying state unemployment taxes vary. In general, employers are required to pay the state unemployment tax during the month following each calendar quarter.

*January 31, 19--.*
*Paid cash for state unemployment tax liability for quarter ended December 31, $399.26. Check No. 319.*

The source document for this transaction is the check written to pay the liability. *(CONCEPT: Objective Evidence)* This transaction is analyzed in the T accounts.

The liability account is reduced by this transaction. Therefore, Unemployment Tax Payable—State is debited for $399.26. The balance of the asset account, Cash, is decreased by a credit, $399.26.

The journal entry to record payment of the liability for state unemployment tax is shown in Illustration 16-14.

| PAGE 28 | | | | JOURNAL | | | | | PAGE 28 | |
|---|---|---|---|---|---|---|---|---|---|---|
| | | | | | 1 | 2 | | 10 | 11 | |
| | DATE | ACCOUNT TITLE | DOC. NO. | POST. REF. | GENERAL DEBIT | GENERAL CREDIT | | CASH DEBIT | CASH CREDIT | |
| 28 | 31 | Unemployment Tax Pay.—State | C319 | | 3 9 9 26 | | | | 3 9 9 26 | 28 |
| 29 | | | | | | | | | | 29 |
| 30 | | | | | | | | | | 30 |
| 31 | | | | | | | | | | 31 |

Illustration 16-14
Journal entry to record payment of liability for state unemployment tax

The date, *31*, is written in the Date column. The title of the account debited, *Unemployment Tax Payable—State*, is written in the Account Title column. The check number, *C319*, is entered in the Doc. No. column. The check amount, *$399.26*, is entered in the General Debit and Cash Credit columns.

# SUMMARY OF PAYROLL ACCOUNTING, TAXES, AND REPORTS

The payroll register provides the amounts required to journalize the payroll. Employer payroll taxes are calculated and recorded in the journal. Later, the employee and employer payroll taxes are paid to the federal and state governments. The entries to journalize a payroll and payroll taxes are summarized in Illustration 16-15.

| ACCOUNT TITLE | 1 | 2 | 10 | 11 |
|---|---|---|---|---|
| | GENERAL | | CASH | |
| | DEBIT | CREDIT | DEBIT | CREDIT |
| Pay the Payroll: | | | | |
| Salary Expense | X | | | X |
| Employee Income Tax Payable | | X | | |
| FICA Tax Payable | | X | | |
| Health Insurance Premiums Payable | | X | | |
| U.S. Savings Bonds Payable | | X | | |
| United Way Donations Payable | | X | | |
| Record Employer Payroll Taxes: | | | | |
| Payroll Taxes Expense | X | | | |
| FICA Tax Payable | | X | | |
| Unemployment Tax Payable—Federal | | X | | |
| Unemployment Tax Payable—State | | X | | |
| Pay Employee and Employer Taxes: | | | | |
| Employee Income Tax Payable | X | | | X |
| FICA Tax Payable | X | | | |
| Unemployment Tax Payable—Federal | X | | | X |
| Unemployment Tax Payable—State | X | | | X |

Illustration 16-15
Summary of payroll journal entries

The chart in Illustration 16-16 summarizes the types of payroll taxes and who pays each tax.

| Tax | Who Pays the Tax | |
|---|---|---|
| | Employee | Employer |
| Federal Income Tax | X | |
| FICA Tax | X | X |
| Federal Unemployment Tax | | X |
| State Unemployment Tax | | X |

Illustration 16-16
Summary of payroll taxes

## QUESTIONS FOR INDIVIDUAL STUDY

1. Why does a business need to keep payroll information about individual employees?
2. What two business forms provide the payroll information needed about individual employees?
3. What accounts are affected, and how, by an entry to record a payroll?
4. Where is the amount obtained which is used to write a payroll check?
5. What is the source document for journalizing payment of a payroll?
6. What are the three payroll taxes paid by most employers?
7. What is the only payroll tax paid by both the employee and the employer?
8. What amount is used to calculate federal unemployment tax?
9. When is the transaction to record employer payroll taxes expense journalized?
10. Which accounting concept is being applied when a memorandum is used as the source document for journalizing employer payroll taxes?
11. What accounts are affected, and how, by an entry to record employer payroll taxes?
12. Where is the information obtained that is needed to prepare a quarterly federal tax return, Form 941?
13. How is the 16% FICA tax rate used on Form 941 figured?
14. What amounts are used to figure the tax liability for a pay period as reported on the quarterly federal tax return, Form 941?
15. What information is reported on a Form W-2, Wage and Tax Statement?
16. Who receives a completed Form W-2, Wage and Tax Statement?
17. What should an employee do with Copies B and C of Form W-2, Wage and Tax Statement, received from an employer?
18. What is the purpose of Form W-3, Transmittal of Income and Tax Statements?
19. What payroll taxes are deposited using Form 8109, Federal Tax Deposit Coupon?
20. What accounts are affected, and how, by an entry to record payment of an employer liability for federal unemployment tax?

## CASES FOR MANAGEMENT DECISION

**CASE 1** The partners of Smith and Tyson have decided to hire a sales manager. They agree that the business can only afford to pay the manager a salary of $30,000.00. The accounting clerk informs the partners that hiring the manager will cost the business more than the $30,000.00 salary. Do you agree with the accounting clerk? Explain your response.

**CASE 2** Miller Manufacturing had total salary expense for the month of November of $40,000.00. Sandra Peterson, accounting clerk, figured the November employer FICA tax as $3,200.00 ($40,000.00 × 8%). Samuel Grissom, accountant, stated that the FICA taxes withheld from employee earnings were $2,850.00. What is the most likely reason for the difference between Ms. Peterson's and Mr. Grissom's figures for FICA taxes? Explain.

## DRILLS FOR UNDERSTANDING

### DRILL 16-D1   Analyzing payroll transactions

**Instructions: 1.** Prepare the following T accounts for four different businesses: Cash, Employee Income Tax Payable, FICA Tax Payable, Unemployment Tax Payable — Federal, Unemployment Tax Payable — State, Payroll Taxes Expense, and Salary Expense.

| Busi-ness | Total Earnings | Federal Income Tax Withheld | Employee FICA Tax | Employer FICA Tax | Federal Unemployment Tax | State Unemployment Tax |
|---|---|---|---|---|---|---|
| A | $ 9,000.00 | $1,350.00 | $ 720.00 | $ 720.00 | $ 72.00 | $486.00 |
| B | 4,200.00 | 590.00 | 336.00 | 336.00 | 33.60 | 226.80 |
| C | 12,600.00 | 2,016.00 | 1,008.00 | 1,008.00 | 100.80 | 680.40 |
| D | 7,800.00 | 1,140.00 | 624.00 | 624.00 | 62.40 | 421.20 |

**2.** Use T accounts to analyze the following payroll entries for each business. (a) Entry to record payment of a payroll. (b) Entry to record employer payroll taxes.

### DRILL 16-D2   Calculating employer payroll taxes

The following payroll information is taken from a payroll register and employee earnings records.

| Employee Name | Accumulated Earnings, April 30 | Total Earnings for May 1–15 Pay Period |
|---|---|---|
| Blette, Kathryn | $ 4,689.00 | $ 586.00 |
| Easton, Phillip | 3,882.50 | 427.00 |
| Goodpaster, Sandra | 8,450.00 | 1,045.00 |
| Lake, Margaret | 5,725.90 | 827.75 |
| Raymond, Peter | 7,329.00 | 945.60 |
| Saenz, Raul | 10,426.00 | 1,236.00 |
| Williams, Patricia | 4,107.25 | 518.50 |

**Instructions: 1.** Calculate the amount of earnings subject to unemployment taxes. Unemployment taxes are owed on the first $7,000.00 of earnings for each employee.

**2.** Calculate the amount of employer payroll taxes owed for the May 1-15 pay period. Employer payroll tax rates are as follows: FICA, 8%; federal unemployment, 0.8%; state unemployment, 5.4%.

##  APPLICATION PROBLEMS

### PROBLEM 16-1   Journalizing and posting payment of semimonthly payrolls

Lambert's payroll register has the following totals for two semimonthly pay periods, August 1-15 and August 16-31 of the current year.

| Period | Total Earnings | Deductions | | | | Net Pay |
|---|---|---|---|---|---|---|
| | | Federal Income Tax | FICA Tax | Other | Total | |
| Aug. 1–15 ............... | $3,670.00 | $514.00 | $293.60 | B $90.00 | $897.60 | $2,772.40 |
| Aug. 16–31 ............... | $3,180.00 | $437.00 | $254.40 | B $75.00 | $766.40 | $2,413.60 |
| Other Deductions: B—U.S. Savings Bonds | | | | | | |

**Instructions: 1.** Journalize payment of the two payrolls on page 17 of a journal. The first payroll was paid by Check No. 756 on August 15 of the current year. The second payroll was paid by Check No. 768 on August 31 of the current year.

**2.** Post the items that are to be posted individually. The balances in the general ledger are recorded as of August 1 of the current year.

| Account No. | Account Title | August 1 Balance |
|---|---|---|
| 2120 | Employee Income Tax Payable | $  — |
| 2130 | FICA Tax Payable | — |
| 2150 | Unemployment Tax Payable—Federal | — |
| 2160 | Unemployment Tax Payable—State | — |
| 2180 | U.S. Savings Bonds Payable | — |
| 6150 | Payroll Taxes Expense | 4,939.23 |
| 6170 | Salary Expense | 38,609.00 |

*The general ledger accounts used in Problem 16-1 are needed to complete Problem 16-2.*

## PROBLEM 16-2   Calculating, journalizing, and posting employer payroll taxes

*The general ledger accounts used in Problem 16-1 are needed to complete Problem 16-2.*

Lambert's semimonthly payroll register totals are shown in Problem 16-1. Employer payroll tax rates are as follows: FICA, 8%; federal unemployment, 0.8%; state unemployment, 5.4%. Unemployment taxes are owed on the first $7,000.00 of earnings for each employee.

Use the following information about accumulated earnings and total earnings for the August 1-15 pay period.

| Employee Name | Accumulated Earnings, July 31 | Total Earnings for August 1–15 Pay Period | Total Earnings for August 16–31 Pay Period |
|---|---|---|---|
| Carson, Michael | $  4,634.00 | $767.50 | $634.50 |
| Franks, Janice | 5,623.50 | 430.00 | 324.50 |
| Hester, Mary | 12,230.00 | 924.00 | 874.00 |
| Marchese, Thomas | 2,346.50 | 213.00 | 138.00 |
| Pait, Kim | 3,243.00 | 624.50 | 573.00 |
| Toler, Troy | 10,532.00 | 711.00 | 636.00 |

**Instructions: 1.** Figure the amount of earnings subject to unemployment taxes for the August 1-15 pay period.

**2.** Calculate the employer payroll tax amounts for the August 1-15 pay period.

**3.** Journalize the employer payroll taxes on page 18 of a journal. Use the date of August 15 of the current year. The source document is Memorandum No. 75.

**4.** Post the items that are to be posted individually.

**5.** Total earnings for the August 16-31 pay period are as follows.

| | |
|---|---|
| Carson, Michael | $634.50 |
| Franks, Janice | 324.50 |
| Hester, Mary | 874.00 |
| Marchese, Thomas | 138.00 |
| Pait, Kim | 573.00 |
| Toler, Troy | 636.00 |

Calculate the employer payroll taxes for the August 16-31 pay period. Figure August 15 accumulated earnings by adding total earnings for the August 1-15 pay period to the July 31 accumulated earnings.

**6.** Journalize the employer payroll taxes on page 18 of a journal. Use the date of August 31 of the current year. The source document is Memorandum No. 82.

**7.** Post the items that are to be posted individually.

## PROBLEM 16-3   Reporting employer quarterly withholding and payroll taxes

The following payroll data is for Jenson Clothing Company for the second quarter of the current year.

| Date Paid | Total Earnings | Federal Income Tax Withheld | Employee FICA Tax Withheld |
|---|---|---|---|
| April 15 | $2,825.00 | $416.00 | $226.00 |
| April 30 | 2,987.00 | 438.00 | 238.96 |
| May 15 | 3,142.00 | 468.00 | 251.36 |
| May 31 | 2,936.00 | 428.00 | 234.88 |
| June 15 | 3,212.00 | 489.00 | 256.96 |
| June 30 | 2,849.00 | 422.00 | 227.92 |

**Additional data.**
1. Company address: 669 Eagle Street, Warrenville, IL 62325-4600
2. Employer identification number: 60-8909267
3. Number of employees: 5
4. Federal tax payments have been made on May 15, June 15, and July 15.

**Instructions:** Prepare a Form 941, Employer's Quarterly Federal Tax Return, for Jenson Clothing Company. The return is for the second quarter of the current year. Use the date July 21. Sign your name as a partner of the company.

## PROBLEM 16-4   Calculating and journalizing withholding and payroll taxes

The following payroll data is for Hawbecker Company for the first quarter of the current year.

| Period | Total Earnings | Federal Income Tax Withheld |
|---|---|---|
| March | $12,537.00 | $2,138.00 |
| First Quarter | 37,293.00 | — |

In addition, total earnings are subject to 8% employee and 8% employer FICA tax. The federal unemployment tax rate is 0.8% and the state unemployment tax rate is 5.4% of total earnings. No total earnings have exceeded the tax base for calculating unemployment taxes.

**Instructions: 1.** Calculate the appropriate liability amount of FICA tax for March. Journalize the payment of the federal income tax and FICA tax liabilities on page 7 of a journal. The taxes were paid by Check No. 785 on April 3 of the current year.

**2.** Calculate the appropriate federal unemployment tax liability for the first quarter. Journalize payment of this liability in the journal. The tax was paid by Check No. 802 on April 30 of the current year.

**3.** Calculate the appropriate state unemployment tax liability for the first quarter. Journalize payment of this liability in the journal. The tax was paid by Check No. 803 on April 30 of the current year.

# ENRICHMENT PROBLEMS

### MASTERY PROBLEM 16-M   Journalizing and posting payroll transactions

Star Equipment completed payroll transactions during the period April 1 to May 15 of the current year. Payroll tax rates are as follows: FICA, 8%; federal unemployment, 0.8%; state unemployment, 5.4%. The company buys savings bonds for employees as accumulated withholdings reach the necessary amount to purchase a bond. No total earnings have exceeded the tax base for calculating unemployment taxes.

The balances in the general ledger are recorded as of April 1 of the current year.

| Account No. | Account Title | April 1 Balance |
|---|---|---|
| 2120 | Employee Income Tax Payable | $    945.00 |
| 2130 | FICA Tax Payable | 984.99 |
| 2150 | Unemployment Tax Payable — Federal | 147.75 |
| 2160 | Unemployment Tax Payable — State | 997.30 |
| 2180 | U.S. Savings Bonds Payable | 200.00 |
| 6150 | Payroll Taxes Expense | 2,622.53 |
| 6170 | Salary Expense | 18,468.50 |

**Instructions: 1.** Journalize the following transactions on page 14 of a journal. Source documents are abbreviated as follows: check, C, and memorandum, M.

Apr. 15. Paid cash for liability for employee income tax, $945.00, and for FICA tax, $984.99; total, $1,929.99. C356.

   15. Paid cash for semimonthly payroll, $2,463.52 (total payroll, $3,256.00, less deductions: employee income tax, $482.00; FICA tax, $260.48; U.S. Savings Bonds, $50.00). C357.

   15. Recorded employer payroll taxes expense. M25.

   15. Paid cash for U.S. Savings Bonds for employees, $250.00. C358.

   30. Paid cash for semimonthly payroll, $2,527.36, (total payroll, $3,358.00, less deductions: employee income tax, $512.00; FICA tax, $268.64; U.S. Savings Bonds, $50.00). C376.

   30. Recorded employer payroll taxes expense. M29.

   30. Paid cash for federal unemployment tax liability for quarter ended March 31, $147.75. C377.

   30. Paid cash for state unemployment tax liability for quarter ended March 31, $997.30. C378.

   *Posting.* Post the items that are to be posted individually.

May 15. Paid cash for liability for employee income tax, $994.00, and for FICA tax, $1,058.24; total, $2,052.24. C405.

   15. Paid cash for semimonthly payroll, $2,373.40 (total payroll, $3,145.00, less deductions: employee income tax, $470.00; FICA tax, $251.60; U.S. Savings Bonds, $50.00). C406.

   15. Recorded employer payroll taxes expense. M36.

   *Posting.* Post the items that are to be posted individually.

   **2.** Prove and rule the journal.

## CHALLENGE PROBLEM 16-C  Journalizing and posting payroll transactions

Danner Hardware completed payroll transactions during the period January 1 to April 30 of the current year. Payroll tax rates are as follows: FICA, 8%; federal unemployment, 0.8%; and state unemployment, 5.4%. The company buys savings bonds for employees as the accumulated withholdings reach the necessary amount to purchase a bond. No total earnings have exceeded the tax base for calculating unemployment taxes.

The balances in the general ledger are recorded as of January 1 of the current year.

| Account No. | Account Title | January 1 Balance |
|---|---|---|
| 2120 | Employee Income Tax Payable | $1,215.00 |
| 2130 | FICA Tax Payable | 1,342.68 |
| 2150 | Unemployment Tax Payable—Federal | 83.62 |
| 2160 | Unemployment Tax Payable—State | 564.45 |
| 2180 | U.S. Savings Bonds Payable | 300.00 |
| 6150 | Payroll Taxes Expense | — |
| 6170 | Salary Expense | — |

**Instructions: 1.** Journalize the following transactions on page 1 of a journal. Source documents are abbreviated as follows: check, C, and memorandum, M.

Jan.  2. Paid cash for 12 U.S. Savings Bonds at $25.00 each for employees. C143.
     15. Paid cash for December liability for employee income tax and for FICA tax. C152.
     31. Paid cash for federal unemployment tax liability for quarter ended December 31. C158.
     31. Paid cash for state unemployment tax liability for quarter ended December 31. C159.
     31. Paid cash for monthly payroll, $6,283.04 (total payroll, $8,487.00, less deductions: employee income tax, $1,425.00; FICA tax, $678.96; U.S. Savings Bonds, $100.00). C164.
     31. Recorded employer payroll taxes expense. M95.
         *Posting.* Post the items that are to be posted individually.
Feb. 15. Paid cash for January liability for employee income tax and for FICA tax. C170.
     28. Paid cash for monthly payroll, $6,348.16 (total payroll, $8,598.00, less deductions: employee income tax, $1,462.00; FICA tax, $687.84; U.S. Savings Bonds, $100.00). C180.
     28. Recorded employer payroll taxes expense. M104.
         *Posting.* Post the items that are to be posted individually.
Mar. 15. Paid cash for February liability for employee income tax and for FICA tax. C195.
     31. Paid cash for monthly payroll, $6,660.76 (total payroll, $9,028.00, less deductions: employee income tax, $1,545.00; FICA tax, $722.24; U.S. Savings Bonds, $100.00). C206.
     31. Recorded employer payroll taxes expense. M113.
         *Posting.* Post the items that are to be posted individually.
Apr.  1. Paid cash for 12 U.S. Savings Bonds at $25.00 each for employees. C207.
     15. Paid cash for March liability for employee income tax and for FICA tax. C218.
     30. Paid cash for federal unemployment tax liability for quarter ended March 31. C224.
     30. Paid cash for state unemployment tax liability for quarter ended March 31. C225.
         *Posting.* Post the items that are to be posted individually.

**2.** Prove and rule the journal.

# Reinforcement Activity 2, Part A

# An Accounting Cycle for a Partnership: Journalizing and Posting Transactions

Reinforcement Activity 2 reinforces learnings from Part 3, Chapters 12 through 19. Activities cover a complete accounting cycle for a merchandising business organized as a partnership. Reinforcement Activity 2 is a single problem divided into two parts. Part A includes learnings from Chapters 12 through 16. Part B includes learnings from Chapters 17 through 19.

The accounting work of a single merchandising business for the last month of a yearly fiscal period is used in this reinforcement activity. The records kept and reports prepared, however, illustrate the application of accounting concepts for all merchandising businesses.

## CLEARVIEW OPTICAL

Tara Bruski and James Myler, partners, own and operate ClearView Optical, a merchandising business. The business sells a complete line of fashion, sun, and sport eyewear. ClearView is located in a downtown shopping area and is open for business Monday through Saturday. A monthly rent is paid for the building and fixtures. ClearView accepts credit cards from customers.

## CHART OF ACCOUNTS

ClearView Optical uses the chart of accounts shown on the next page.

## JOURNAL AND LEDGERS

The journal and ledgers used by ClearView Optical are listed in the following chart. Models of the journal and ledgers are shown in the textbook illustrations given in the chart.

| Journal and Ledgers | Chapter | Illustration Number |
|---|---|---|
| Expanded journal...................................... | 13 | 13–5 |
| Accounts payable ledger ............................. | 14 | 14–10 |
| Accounts receivable ledger ........................... | 14 | 14–15 |
| General ledger....................................... | 17 | 17–1 |

## RECORDING TRANSACTIONS

The December 1 account balances for the general and subsidiary ledgers are given in the working papers accompanying this textbook.

**Instructions: 1.** Journalize the transactions beginning on the bottom of page 382 on page 23 of a journal. A 6% sales tax has been added to each sale. Source documents are abbreviated as follows: check, C; memorandum, M; purchase invoice, P; receipt, R; sales invoice, S; cash register tape, T.

## CLEARVIEW OPTICAL
## Chart of Accounts

| Balance Sheet Accounts | Income Statement Accounts |
|---|---|

**(1000) ASSETS**
1110 Cash
1120 Petty Cash
1130 Accounts Receivable
1140 Merchandise Inventory
1145 Supplies—Office
1150 Supplies—Store
1160 Prepaid Insurance

**(2000) LIABILITIES**
2110 Accounts Payable
2120 Employee Income Tax Payable
2130 FICA Tax Payable
2140 Sales Tax Payable
2150 Unemployment Tax Payable—Federal
2160 Unemployment Tax Payable—State
2170 Health Insurance Premiums Payable
2180 U.S. Savings Bonds Payable
2190 United Way Donations Payable

**(3000) OWNERS' EQUITY**
3110 Tara Bruski, Capital
3120 Tara Bruski, Drawing
3130 James Myler, Capital
3140 James Myler, Drawing
3150 Income Summary

**(4000) OPERATING REVENUE**
4110 Sales

**(5000) COST OF MERCHANDISE**
5110 Purchases

**(6000) OPERATING EXPENSES**
6110 Advertising Expense
6120 Credit Card Fee Expense
6130 Insurance Expense
6140 Miscellaneous Expense
6150 Payroll Taxes Expense
6160 Rent Expense
6170 Salary Expense
6175 Supplies Expense—Office
6180 Supplies Expense—Store
6190 Utilities Expense

## Subsidiary Ledgers

| Accounts Receivable Ledger | Accounts Payable Ledger |
|---|---|
| 110 Theresa Abbey | 210 A & B Optical Co. |
| 120 Nancy Bonner | 220 Central Office Supply |
| 130 Jonathan Doran | 230 Kosh Optical Lab |
| 140 Irma Iznaga | 240 Optical Imports |
| 150 Brian Patco | 250 Trend Optics Co. |
| 160 Norman Witte | 260 Weaver Supply |

Dec. 1. Paid cash for rent, $1,000.00. C272.
    1. Tara Bruski, partner, withdrew cash for personal use, $1,200.00. C273.
    1. James Myler, partner, withdrew cash for personal use, $1,200.00. C274.
    2. Paid cash for electric bill, $288.50. C275.
    2. Received cash on account from Nancy Bonner, $344.50, covering S64. R82.
    3. Paid cash for miscellaneous expense, $60.00. C276.

Dec.  3. Paid cash on account to Trend Optics Co., $483.80, covering P73. C277.
      4. Sold merchandise on account to Theresa Abbey, $375.00, plus sales tax, $22.50; total, $397.50. S67.
      5. Recorded cash and credit card sales, $4,830.00, plus sales tax, $289.80; total, $5,119.80. T5.
         *Posting.* Post the items that are to be posted individually.
      7. Sold merchandise on account to Jonathan Doran, $385.00, plus sales tax, $23.10; total, $408.10. S68.
      7. Received cash on account from Norman Witte, $360.40, covering S65. R83.
      8. Bought office supplies on account from Central Office Supply, $293.00. M43.
      9. Purchased merchandise on account from Optical Imports, $1,125.00. P77.
      9. Bought store supplies on account from Weaver Supply, $275.00. M44.
     10. Tara Bruski, partner, withdrew merchandise for personal use, $250.00. M45.
     10. Paid cash for office supplies, $145.00. C278.
     10. Discovered that a payment of cash for advertising in November was journalized and posted in error as a debit to Miscellaneous Expense instead of Advertising Expense, $125.00. M46.
     11. Paid cash on account to Kosh Optical Lab, $975.80, covering P74. C279.
     11. Purchased merchandise on account from Trend Optics Co., $860.00. P78.
     12. Paid cash for store supplies, $220.00. C280.
     12. Recorded cash and credit card sales, $5,940.00, plus sales tax, 356.40; total, $6,296.40. T12.
         *Posting.* Post the items that are to be posted individually.
     14. James Myler, partner, withdrew merchandise for personal use, $325.00. M47.
     14. Purchased merchandise on account from Kosh Optical Lab, $2,730.00. P79.
     14. Sold merchandise on account to Brian Patco, $140.00, plus sales tax, $8.40; total, $148.40. S69.
     14. Paid cash for advertising, $345.00. C281.
     15. Paid cash on account to A & B Optical Co., $1,060.40, covering P75. C282.
     15. Received cash on account from Irma Iznaga, $683.70, covering S66. R84.
     15. Sold merchandise on account to Nancy Bonner, $410.00, plus sales tax, $24.60; total, $434.60. S70.
         *Posting.* Post the items that are to be posted individually.

   **2.** Prove and rule page 23 of the journal.
   **3.** Carry the column totals forward to page 24 of the journal.
   **4.** Journalize the following transactions on page 24 of the journal.

Dec. 15. Paid cash for semimonthly payroll, $1,751.80 (total payroll, $2,315.00, less deductions: employee income tax, $181.00; FICA tax, $185.20; health insurance, $142.00; U.S. Savings Bonds, $25.00; United Way donations, $30.00). C283.
     15. Recorded employer payroll taxes, $250.30, for the semimonthly pay period ended December 15. Taxes owed are: FICA tax, $185.20; federal unemployment tax, $8.40; and state unemployment tax, $56.70. M48.
     19. Recorded cash and credit card sales, $5,760.00, plus sales tax, $345.60; total, $6,105.60. T19.
     23. Paid cash on account to Optical Imports, $1,840.00, covering P76. C284.
     26. Recorded cash and credit card sales, $5,820.00, plus sales tax, $349.20; total, $6,169.20. T26.
         *Posting.* Post the items that are to be posted individually.

ClearView Optical's bank charges a fee for handling the collection of credit card sales deposited during the month. The credit card fee is deducted from ClearView Optical's bank account. The amount is then shown on the bank statement. The credit card fee is recorded in the journal as a reduction in cash.

Dec. 28. Recorded credit card fee expense, $285.20. M49. (Debit Credit Card Fee Expense; credit Cash.)

    30. Purchased merchandise on account from A & B Optical Co., $1,620.00. P80.

    31. Paid cash to replenish the petty cash fund, $304.00: office supplies, $62.00; store supplies, $59.00; advertising, $87.00; miscellaneous, $96.00. C285.

    31. Paid cash for semimonthly payroll, $1,882.00 (total payroll, $2,460.00, less deductions: employee income tax, $184.20; FICA tax, $196.80; health insurance, $142.00; U.S. Savings Bonds, $25.00; United Way donations, $30.00). C286.

    31. Recorded employer payroll taxes, $263.92, for the semimonthly pay period ended December 31. Taxes owed are: FICA tax, $196.80; federal unemployment tax, $8.66; and state unemployment tax, $58.46. M50.

    31. Received bank statement showing December bank service charge, $4.50. M51.

    31. Recorded cash and credit card sales, $3,240.00, plus sales tax, $194.40; total, $3,434.40. T31.

        *Posting.* Post the items that are to be posted individually.

**5.** Total page 24 of the journal. Prove the equality of debits and credits.

**6.** Prove cash. The balance on the next unused check stub was $34,918.00.

**7.** Rule the journal.

**8.** Post the totals of the special columns of the journal.

**9.** Prepare a schedule of accounts payable and a schedule of accounts receivable. Prove the accuracy of the subsidiary ledgers by comparing the schedule totals with the balances of the controlling accounts in the general ledger. If the totals are not the same, find and correct the errors.

*The ledgers used in Reinforcement Activity 2, Part A, are needed to complete Reinforcement Activity 2, Part B.*

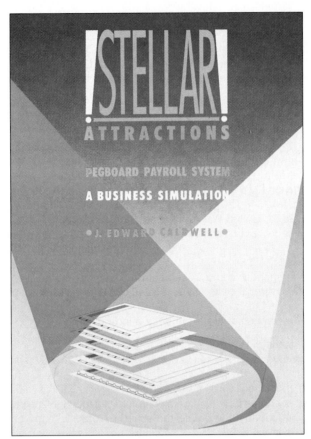

*Stellar Attractions Pegboard Payroll System* provides experience in preparing records using a pegboard and no-carbon-required forms. When data are entered on the statement of earnings and deductions stub on the check, the employee earnings record and the payroll register are simultaneously prepared. Posting is eliminated. The following activities are included in the accounting cycle for Stellar Attractions. This business simulation is available from the publisher.

## Activities in Stellar Attractions

1. Preparing necessary forms for new employees.
2. Completing time cards by entering summary data.
3. Assembling forms on a pegboard: checks with earnings and deductions stubs, employee earnings records, and payroll register. All records are completed with one writing.
4. Recording time card summary data on the statement of earnings and deductions stubs of checks on the pegboard.
5. Determining appropriate deductions using tax tables and figuring net pay.
6. Recording deductions and net pay on the statement of earnings and deductions stubs.
7. Totaling, proving, ruling, and filing the payroll register. Filing employee earnings records.
8. Separating, writing, and signing payroll checks.
9. Totaling and proving employee earnings records for the end of the quarter and year to date.
10. Preparing quarterly and annual reports.

# Work Sheet for a Merchandising Business

ENABLING PERFORMANCE TASKS

After studying Chapter 17, you will be able to:
a. Define accounting terms related to a work sheet for a merchandising business.
b. Identify accounting concepts and practices related to a work sheet for a merchandising business.
c. Plan adjustments on a work sheet for a merchandising business.
d. Complete a work sheet for a merchandising business.

Management decisions about future business operations are often based on financial information. Financial information shows whether a profit is being made or a loss is being incurred. Profit or loss information helps an owner or manager determine future changes. Financial information is also needed to prepare required tax reports. A business summarizes financial information at least once each fiscal period. CarLand uses a one-year fiscal period that begins on January 1 and ends on December 31. Therefore, CarLand summarizes its financial information on December 31 of each year.

## GENERAL LEDGER WITH POSTING COMPLETED

CarLand's completed general ledger on December 31, after all transactions have been posted, is shown in Illustration 17-1. No entries have been posted in the following accounts: Income Summary, Insurance Expense, Supplies Expense—Office, and Supplies Expense—Store. Transactions during the year did not affect these accounts.

ACCOUNT *Cash*                                                                    ACCOUNT NO. *1110*

| DATE | | ITEM | POST. REF. | DEBIT | CREDIT | BALANCE | |
|---|---|---|---|---|---|---|---|
| | | | | | | DEBIT | CREDIT |
| Dec. | 1 | Balance | √ | | | 23 5 5 0 00 | |
| | 31 | | 25 | 30 9 8 4 00 | | 54 5 3 4 00 | |
| | 31 | | 25 | | 30 3 0 0 43 | 24 2 3 3 57 | |

ACCOUNT *Petty Cash*                                                              ACCOUNT NO. *1120*

| DATE | | ITEM | POST. REF. | DEBIT | CREDIT | BALANCE | |
|---|---|---|---|---|---|---|---|
| | | | | | | DEBIT | CREDIT |
| Jan. | 1 | Balance | √ | | | 5 0 0 00 | |

ACCOUNT *Accounts Receivable*                                                     ACCOUNT NO. *1130*

| DATE | | ITEM | POST. REF. | DEBIT | CREDIT | BALANCE | |
|---|---|---|---|---|---|---|---|
| | | | | | | DEBIT | CREDIT |
| Dec. | 1 | Balance | √ | | | 9 2 2 2 00 | |
| | 31 | | 25 | 8 6 9 2 00 | | 17 9 1 4 00 | |
| | 31 | | 25 | | 8 5 8 2 00 | 9 3 3 2 00 | |

ACCOUNT *Merchandise Inventory*                                                   ACCOUNT NO. *1140*

| DATE | | ITEM | POST. REF. | DEBIT | CREDIT | BALANCE | |
|---|---|---|---|---|---|---|---|
| | | | | | | DEBIT | CREDIT |
| Jan. | 1 | Balance | √ | | | 225 4 0 0 00 | |

ACCOUNT *Supplies—Office*                                                         ACCOUNT NO. *1145*

| DATE | | ITEM | POST. REF. | DEBIT | CREDIT | BALANCE | |
|---|---|---|---|---|---|---|---|
| | | | | | | DEBIT | CREDIT |
| Dec. | 1 | Balance | √ | | | 4 9 8 0 00 | |
| | 3 | | 24 | 1 6 0 00 | | 5 1 4 0 00 | |
| | 9 | | 24 | 8 6 00 | | 5 2 2 6 00 | |
| | 18 | | 25 | 1 2 4 00 | | 5 3 5 0 00 | |
| | 31 | | 25 | 5 0 00 | | 5 4 0 0 00 | |

Illustration 17-1
General ledger with posting
completed

Illustration 17-1
General ledger with posting
completed (continued)

ACCOUNT *Supplies—Store*                                    ACCOUNT NO. *1150*

| DATE | | ITEM | POST. REF. | DEBIT | CREDIT | BALANCE | |
|---|---|---|---|---|---|---|---|
| | | | | | | DEBIT | CREDIT |
| *Dec.*¹⁹⁻⁻ | 1 | Balance | √ | | | 5 1 3 0 00 | |
| | 7 | | 24 | 2 3 0 00 | | 5 3 6 0 00 | |
| | 31 | | 25 | 7 3 00 | | 5 4 3 3 00 | |
| | 31 | | 25 | 3 4 7 00 | | 5 7 8 0 00 | |

ACCOUNT *Prepaid Insurance*                                 ACCOUNT NO. *1160*

| DATE | | ITEM | POST. REF. | DEBIT | CREDIT | BALANCE | |
|---|---|---|---|---|---|---|---|
| | | | | | | DEBIT | CREDIT |
| *Dec.*¹⁹⁻⁻ | 1 | Balance | √ | | | 4 8 4 0 00 | |

ACCOUNT *Accounts Payable*                                  ACCOUNT NO. *2110*

| DATE | | ITEM | POST. REF. | DEBIT | CREDIT | BALANCE | |
|---|---|---|---|---|---|---|---|
| | | | | | | DEBIT | CREDIT |
| *Dec.*¹⁹⁻⁻ | 1 | Balance | √ | | | | 15 8 7 0 00 |
| | 31 | | 25 | 15 5 4 5 59 | | | 3 2 4 41 |
| | 31 | | 25 | | 10 1 2 7 49 | | 10 4 5 1 90 |

ACCOUNT *Employee Income Tax Payable*                       ACCOUNT NO. *2120*

| DATE | | ITEM | POST. REF. | DEBIT | CREDIT | BALANCE | |
|---|---|---|---|---|---|---|---|
| | | | | | | DEBIT | CREDIT |
| *Dec.*¹⁹⁻⁻ | 1 | Balance | √ | | | | 3 8 4 00 |
| | 15 | | 24 | 3 8 4 00 | | — | — |
| | 15 | | 24 | | 1 9 2 00 | | 1 9 2 00 |
| | 31 | | 25 | | 2 1 0 00 | | 4 0 2 00 |

ACCOUNT **FICA Tax Payable**                    ACCOUNT NO. *2130*

| DATE | ITEM | POST. REF. | DEBIT | CREDIT | BALANCE DEBIT | BALANCE CREDIT |
|---|---|---|---|---|---|---|
| Dec. 1 | Balance | √ | | | | 8 17 92 |
| 15 | | 24 | 8 17 92 | | ——— | |
| 15 | | 24 | | 2 04 48 | | 2 04 48 |
| 15 | | 24 | | 2 04 48 | | 4 08 96 |
| 31 | | 25 | | 2 11 60 | | 6 20 56 |
| 31 | | 25 | | 2 11 60 | | 8 32 16 |

ACCOUNT **Sales Tax Payable**                    ACCOUNT NO. *2140*

| DATE | ITEM | POST. REF. | DEBIT | CREDIT | BALANCE DEBIT | BALANCE CREDIT |
|---|---|---|---|---|---|---|
| Dec. 1 | Balance | √ | | | | 1 89 6 00 |
| 15 | | 24 | 1 89 6 00 | | ——— | |
| 31 | | 25 | | 1 76 0 00 | | 1 76 0 00 |

ACCOUNT **Unemployment Tax Payable—Federal**           ACCOUNT NO. *2150*

| DATE | ITEM | POST. REF. | DEBIT | CREDIT | BALANCE DEBIT | BALANCE CREDIT |
|---|---|---|---|---|---|---|
| Dec. 1 | Balance | √ | | | | 40 48 |
| 15 | | 24 | | 9 10 | | 49 58 |
| 31 | | 25 | | 9 57 | | 59 15 |

ACCOUNT **Unemployment Tax Payable—State**           ACCOUNT NO. *2160*

| DATE | ITEM | POST. REF. | DEBIT | CREDIT | BALANCE DEBIT | BALANCE CREDIT |
|---|---|---|---|---|---|---|
| Dec. 1 | Balance | √ | | | | 2 73 22 |
| 15 | | 24 | | 6 1 45 | | 3 34 67 |
| 31 | | 25 | | 6 4 59 | | 3 99 26 |

Illustration 17-1
General ledger with posting completed (continued)

Illustration 17-1
General ledger with posting
completed (continued)

ACCOUNT *Health Insurance Premiums Payable*                     ACCOUNT NO. *2170*

| DATE | | ITEM | POST. REF. | DEBIT | CREDIT | BALANCE DEBIT | BALANCE CREDIT |
|---|---|---|---|---|---|---|---|
| Dec.<sup>19--</sup> | 1 | Balance | ✓ | | | | 5 2 4 00 |
| | 15 | | 24 | | 1 5 8 00 | | 6 8 2 00 |
| | 31 | | 25 | | 1 5 8 00 | | 8 4 0 00 |

ACCOUNT *U.S. Savings Bonds Payable*                     ACCOUNT NO. *2180*

| DATE | | ITEM | POST. REF. | DEBIT | CREDIT | BALANCE DEBIT | BALANCE CREDIT |
|---|---|---|---|---|---|---|---|
| Dec.<sup>19--</sup> | 1 | Balance | ✓ | | | | 1 0 00 |
| | 15 | | 24 | | 1 5 00 | | 2 5 00 |
| | 31 | | 25 | | 1 5 00 | | 4 0 00 |

ACCOUNT *United Way Donations Payable*                     ACCOUNT NO. *2190*

| DATE | | ITEM | POST. REF. | DEBIT | CREDIT | BALANCE DEBIT | BALANCE CREDIT |
|---|---|---|---|---|---|---|---|
| Dec.<sup>19--</sup> | 1 | Balance | ✓ | | | | 4 0 00 |
| | 15 | | 24 | | 1 0 00 | | 5 0 00 |
| | 31 | | 25 | | 1 0 00 | | 6 0 00 |

ACCOUNT *Amy Kramer, Capital*                     ACCOUNT NO. *3110*

| DATE | | ITEM | POST. REF. | DEBIT | CREDIT | BALANCE DEBIT | BALANCE CREDIT |
|---|---|---|---|---|---|---|---|
| Jan.<sup>19--</sup> | 1 | Balance | ✓ | | | | 101 1 1 8 00 |

ACCOUNT *Amy Kramer, Drawing*                     ACCOUNT NO. *3120*

| DATE | | ITEM | POST. REF. | DEBIT | CREDIT | BALANCE DEBIT | BALANCE CREDIT |
|---|---|---|---|---|---|---|---|
| Dec.<sup>19--</sup> | 1 | Balance | ✓ | | | 16 7 0 0 00 | |
| | 15 | | 24 | 1 5 0 0 00 | | 18 2 0 0 00 | |

ACCOUNT *Dario Mesa, Capital*                                    ACCOUNT NO. *3130*

| DATE | ITEM | POST. REF. | DEBIT | CREDIT | BALANCE DEBIT | BALANCE CREDIT |
|------|------|-----------|-------|--------|-------|--------|
| 19.. Jan. 1 | Balance | √ | | | | 101 2 2 8 00 |

ACCOUNT *Dario Mesa, Drawing*                                    ACCOUNT NO. *3140*

| DATE | ITEM | POST. REF. | DEBIT | CREDIT | BALANCE DEBIT | BALANCE CREDIT |
|------|------|-----------|-------|--------|-------|--------|
| 19.. Dec. 1 | Balance | √ | | | 17 1 0 0 00 | |
| 15 | | 24 | 1 5 0 0 00 | | 18 6 0 0 00 | |

ACCOUNT *Income Summary*                                         ACCOUNT NO. *3150*

| DATE | ITEM | POST. REF. | DEBIT | CREDIT | BALANCE DEBIT | BALANCE CREDIT |
|------|------|-----------|-------|--------|-------|--------|
| | | | | | | |

ACCOUNT *Sales*                                                  ACCOUNT NO. *4110*

| DATE | ITEM | POST. REF. | DEBIT | CREDIT | BALANCE DEBIT | BALANCE CREDIT |
|------|------|-----------|-------|--------|-------|--------|
| 19.. Dec. 1 | Balance | √ | | | | 323 2 6 6 00 |
| 31 | | 25 | | 29 3 3 4 00 | | 352 6 0 0 00 |

ACCOUNT *Purchases*                                              ACCOUNT NO. *5110*

| DATE | ITEM | POST. REF. | DEBIT | CREDIT | BALANCE DEBIT | BALANCE CREDIT |
|------|------|-----------|-------|--------|-------|--------|
| 19.. Dec. 1 | Balance | √ | | | 148 1 7 2 51 | |
| 31 | | 25 | 10 1 2 7 49 | | 158 3 0 0 00 | |

ACCOUNT *Advertising Expense*                                    ACCOUNT NO. *6110*

| DATE | ITEM | POST. REF. | DEBIT | CREDIT | BALANCE DEBIT | BALANCE CREDIT |
|------|------|-----------|-------|--------|-------|--------|
| 19.. Dec. 1 | Balance | √ | | | 4 8 6 0 00 | |
| 4 | | 24 | 1 6 5 00 | | 5 0 2 5 00 | |
| 16 | | 25 | 8 3 00 | | 5 1 0 8 00 | |
| 22 | | 25 | 3 9 2 00 | | 5 5 0 0 00 | |

Illustration 17-1
General ledger with posting
completed (continued)

Illustration 17-1
General ledger with posting
completed (continued)

ACCOUNT *Credit Card Fee Expense*  ACCOUNT NO. *6120*

| DATE | | ITEM | POST. REF. | DEBIT | CREDIT | BALANCE | |
|---|---|---|---|---|---|---|---|
| | | | | | | DEBIT | CREDIT |
| Dec. | 1 | Balance | √ | | | 2 1 7 5 00 | |
| | 28 | | 25 | 7 1 5 00 | | 2 8 9 0 00 | |

ACCOUNT *Insurance Expense*  ACCOUNT NO. *6130*

| DATE | ITEM | POST. REF. | DEBIT | CREDIT | BALANCE | |
|---|---|---|---|---|---|---|
| | | | | | DEBIT | CREDIT |

ACCOUNT *Miscellaneous Expense*  ACCOUNT NO. *6140*

| DATE | | ITEM | POST. REF. | DEBIT | CREDIT | BALANCE | |
|---|---|---|---|---|---|---|---|
| | | | | | | DEBIT | CREDIT |
| Dec. | 1 | Balance | √ | | | 1 7 3 2 15 | |
| | 9 | | 24 | 3 9 00 | | 1 7 7 1 15 | |
| | 17 | | 25 | 1 6 3 00 | | 1 9 3 4 15 | |
| | 22 | | 25 | 1 0 6 00 | | 2 0 4 0 15 | |
| | 31 | | 25 | 1 4 2 00 | | 2 1 8 2 15 | |

ACCOUNT *Payroll Taxes Expense*  ACCOUNT NO. *6150*

| DATE | | ITEM | POST. REF. | DEBIT | CREDIT | BALANCE | |
|---|---|---|---|---|---|---|---|
| | | | | | | DEBIT | CREDIT |
| Dec. | 1 | Balance | √ | | | 6 7 3 8 96 | |
| | 15 | | 24 | 2 7 5 03 | | 7 0 1 3 99 | |
| | 31 | | 25 | 2 8 5 76 | | 7 2 9 9 75 | |

ACCOUNT *Rent Expense*  ACCOUNT NO. *6160*

| DATE | | ITEM | POST. REF. | DEBIT | CREDIT | BALANCE | |
|---|---|---|---|---|---|---|---|
| | | | | | | DEBIT | CREDIT |
| Dec. | 1 | Balance | √ | | | 16 5 0 0 00 | |
| | 1 | | 24 | 1 5 0 0 00 | | 18 0 0 0 00 | |

| ACCOUNT *Salary Expense* | | | | | ACCOUNT NO. *6170* | |
|---|---|---|---|---|---|---|
| DATE | ITEM | POST. REF. | DEBIT | CREDIT | BALANCE DEBIT | BALANCE CREDIT |
| Dec. 1 | Balance | √ | | | 54 9 5 2 00 | |
| 15 | | 24 | 2 5 5 6 00 | | 57 5 0 8 00 | |
| 31 | | 25 | 2 6 4 5 00 | | 60 1 5 3 00 | |

| ACCOUNT *Supplies Expense—Office* | | | | | ACCOUNT NO. *6175* | |
|---|---|---|---|---|---|---|
| DATE | ITEM | POST. REF. | DEBIT | CREDIT | BALANCE DEBIT | BALANCE CREDIT |

| ACCOUNT *Supplies Expense—Store* | | | | | ACCOUNT NO. *6180* | |
|---|---|---|---|---|---|---|
| DATE | ITEM | POST. REF. | DEBIT | CREDIT | BALANCE DEBIT | BALANCE CREDIT |

| ACCOUNT *Utilities Expense* | | | | | ACCOUNT NO. *6190* | |
|---|---|---|---|---|---|---|
| DATE | ITEM | POST. REF. | DEBIT | CREDIT | BALANCE DEBIT | BALANCE CREDIT |
| Dec. 1 | Balance | √ | | | 2 9 1 5 00 | |
| 3 | | 24 | 1 8 0 00 | | 3 0 9 5 00 | |
| 9 | | 24 | 8 5 00 | | 3 1 8 0 00 | |

Illustration 17-1
General ledger with posting completed (concluded)

## AN 8-COLUMN WORK SHEET
## FOR A MERCHANDISING BUSINESS

A columnar accounting form on which the financial information needed to prepare financial statements is summarized is known as a work sheet. A work sheet is used to plan adjustments and sort financial statement information. A work sheet may be prepared whenever a business wishes to summarize and report financial information. A work sheet is always prepared at the end of each fiscal period because financial statements are prepared at the end of each fiscal period. *(CONCEPT: Accounting Period Cycle)* CarLand prepares a work sheet and financial statements annually.

Work sheets for service and merchandising businesses are similar.

CarLand's work sheet is similar to the one used by Rugcare described in Chapter 7. CarLand's work sheet, however, also includes accounts for accounts receivable, merchandise inventory, accounts payable, sales tax, and purchases.

# RECORDING A TRIAL BALANCE ON A WORK SHEET

To prove the equality of debits and credits in the general ledger, a trial balance is prepared. CarLand prepares a trial balance in the Trial Balance columns of a work sheet. CarLand's trial balance on December 31 is shown in Illustration 17-2, page 394.

General ledger accounts are listed in the work sheet's Account Title column in the same order in which they appear in the general ledger. All accounts are listed regardless of whether there is a balance or not. Listing all accounts reduces the possibility of overlooking an account that needs to be brought up to date.

# PLANNING ADJUSTMENTS ON A WORK SHEET

After posting is completed at the end of a fiscal period, some general ledger accounts, such as the two supplies accounts and the prepaid insurance account, are not up to date. Adjustments for supplies and prepaid insurance are described in Chapter 7. In addition to supplies and prepaid insurance, CarLand needs to adjust the merchandise inventory account. Changes recorded on a work sheet to update general ledger accounts at the end of a fiscal period are known as adjustments.

Adjustments are planned in the Adjustments columns of a work sheet. Adjustments recorded on a work sheet are for planning purposes only. The general ledger account balances are not changed until journal entries are recorded and posted. Journal entries made to bring general ledger accounts up to date are known as adjusting entries.

## Merchandise inventory adjustment

The amount of goods on hand is called an inventory. The amount of goods on hand for sale to customers is called merchandise inventory. The general ledger account in which merchandise inventory is recorded is titled *Merchandise Inventory*. Merchandise Inventory is an asset account with a normal debit balance, as shown in the T account.

| Merchandise Inventory | |
|---|---|
| Debit side<br>Normal balance<br>Increase | Credit side<br><br>Decrease |

**Analyzing a merchandise inventory adjustment.** CarLand's merchandise inventory account on January 1, the beginning of the fiscal year, has a debit balance of $225,400.00, as shown in the T account.

|  | ACCOUNT TITLE | TRIAL BALANCE | |
|---|---|---|---|
|  |  | DEBIT | CREDIT |
| 1 | Cash | 24 2 3 3 57 |  |
| 2 | Petty Cash | 5 0 0 00 |  |
| 3 | Accounts Receivable | 9 3 3 2 00 |  |
| 4 | Merchandise Inventory | 225 4 0 0 00 |  |
| 5 | Supplies—Office | 5 4 0 0 00 |  |
| 6 | Supplies—Store | 5 7 8 0 00 |  |
| 7 | Prepaid Insurance | 4 8 4 0 00 |  |
| 8 | Accounts Payable |  | 10 4 5 1 90 |
| 9 | Employee Income Tax Payable |  | 4 0 2 00 |
| 10 | FICA Tax Payable |  | 8 3 2 16 |
| 11 | Sales Tax Payable |  | 1 7 6 0 00 |
| 12 | Unemploy. Tax Payable—Fed. |  | 5 9 15 |
| 13 | Unemploy. Tax Payable—State |  | 3 9 9 26 |
| 14 | Health Ins. Premiums Pay. |  | 8 4 0 00 |
| 15 | U.S. Savings Bonds Payable |  | 4 0 00 |
| 16 | United Way Donations Payable |  | 6 0 00 |
| 17 | Amy Kramer, Capital |  | 101 1 1 8 00 |
| 18 | Amy Kramer, Drawing | 18 2 0 0 00 |  |
| 19 | Dario Mesa, Capital |  | 101 2 2 8 00 |
| 20 | Dario Mesa, Drawing | 18 6 0 0 00 |  |
| 21 | Income Summary |  |  |
| 22 | Sales |  | 352 6 0 0 00 |
| 23 | Purchases | 158 3 0 0 00 |  |
| 24 | Advertising Expense | 5 5 0 0 00 |  |
| 25 | Credit Card Fee Expense | 2 8 9 0 00 |  |
| 26 | Insurance Expense |  |  |
| 27 | Miscellaneous Expense | 2 1 8 2 15 |  |
| 28 | Payroll Taxes Expense | 7 2 9 9 75 |  |
| 29 | Rent Expense | 18 0 0 0 00 |  |
| 30 | Salary Expense | 60 1 5 3 00 |  |
| 31 | Supplies Expense—Office |  |  |
| 32 | Supplies Expense—Store |  |  |
| 33 | Utilities Expense | 3 1 8 0 00 |  |
| 34 |  | 569 7 9 0 47 | 569 7 9 0 47 |
| 35 |  |  |  |

CarLand

Work Sheet

For Year Ended December 31, 19--

Illustration 17-2    Trial balance on a work sheet

The balance of the merchandise inventory account on December 31, the end of the fiscal year, is the same amount, $225,400.00. The January 1 and December 31 balances are the same because no entries have been made in the account during the fiscal year. The changes in inventory resulting from purchases and sales transactions have not been recorded in the merchandise inventory account.

| Merchandise Inventory | |
| --- | --- |
| Jan. 1 Bal.  225,400.00 | |

Each purchase transaction increases the amount of merchandise on hand. However, all purchases are recorded in the purchases account. Each sales transaction decreases the amount of merchandise on hand. However, all sales are recorded in the sales account. This procedure makes it easier to determine quickly the total purchases and sales during a fiscal period. During a fiscal period, the amount of merchandise on hand increases each time merchandise is purchased. The amount of merchandise on hand also decreases each time merchandise is sold. The merchandise inventory account balance, therefore, must be adjusted to reflect the changes resulting from purchases and sales during a fiscal period.

The two accounts used to adjust the merchandise inventory are Merchandise Inventory and Income Summary. The T accounts show the merchandise inventory and income summary accounts before the merchandise inventory adjustment is made.

BEFORE ADJUSTMENT

| Income Summary | |
| --- | --- |
| | |

| Merchandise Inventory | |
| --- | --- |
| Jan. 1 Bal.  225,400.00 | |

Before the adjustment, the merchandise inventory account has a January 1 debit balance of $225,400.00. The merchandise inventory account balance, however, is not up to date. The actual count of merchandise on December 31 shows that the inventory is valued at $212,200.00. Therefore, the merchandise inventory account balance must be adjusted to show the current value of merchandise on hand.

Most accounts needing adjustment at the end of a fiscal period have a related temporary account. For example, when the account Supplies is adjusted, Supplies Expense is the related expense account, a temporary account. Merchandise Inventory, however, does not have a related expense account. Therefore, Income Summary, a temporary account, is used to adjust the merchandise inventory account at the end of a fiscal period.

Four questions are asked in analyzing the adjustment for merchandise inventory.

| | |
| --- | --- |
| 1. What is the balance of Merchandise Inventory?.. | $225,400.00 |
| 2. What should the balance be for this account? | $212,200.00 |
| 3. What must be done to correct the account balance? Decrease......................... | $ 13,200.00 |
| 4. What adjustment is made? | |
| Debit Income Summary ................... | $ 13,200.00 |
| Credit Merchandise Inventory.............. | $ 13,200.00 |

The merchandise inventory adjustment is shown in the T accounts.

AFTER ADJUSTMENT

**Income Summary**

| Adj. (a) | 13,200.00 | |
|---|---|---|

**Merchandise Inventory**

| Jan. 1 Bal. | 225,400.00 | Adj. (a) | 13,200.00 |
|---|---|---|---|
| *(New Bal.* | *212,200.00)* | | |

Income Summary is debited and Merchandise Inventory is credited for $13,200.00. The beginning debit balance of Merchandise Inventory, $225,400.00, *minus* the adjustment credit amount, $13,200.00, *equals* the ending debit balance of Merchandise Inventory, $212,200.00.

**Recording a merchandise inventory adjustment on a work sheet.** The merchandise inventory adjustment is shown on lines 4 and 21 in the work sheet's Adjustments columns in Illustration 17-3.

Illustration 17-3
Merchandise inventory
adjustment on a
work sheet

| | | | 1 | 2 | 3 | 4 |
|---|---|---|---|---|---|---|
| | ACCOUNT TITLE | | TRIAL BALANCE | | ADJUSTMENTS | |
| | | | DEBIT | CREDIT | DEBIT | CREDIT |
| 4 | *Merchandise Inventory* | | 225 4 0 0 00 | | **3** → | (a)13 2 0 0 00 |
| 21 | *Income Summary* | | | | (a)13 2 0 0 00 | |
| 22 | | | | | **1** | **2** |

Three steps are used to record CarLand's adjustment for merchandise inventory on a work sheet.

**1** Write the debit amount, *$13,200.00*, in the Adjustments Debit column on the line with the account title Income Summary (line 21).

**2** Write the credit amount, *$13,200.00*, in the Adjustments Credit column on the line with the account title Merchandise Inventory (line 4).

**3** Label the two parts of this adjustment with the small letter *a* in parentheses, *(a)*.

AFTER ADJUSTMENT

**Merchandise Inventory**

| Jan. 1 Bal. | 245,600.00 | |
|---|---|---|
| Adj. (a) | 5,200.00 | |
| *(New Bal.* | *250,800.00)* | |

**Income Summary**

| | Adj. (a) | 5,200.00 |
|---|---|---|

If the amount of merchandise inventory on hand is greater than the balance of Merchandise Inventory, opposite entries would be made—debit Merchandise Inventory and credit Income Summary. For example, Kobrin Company's merchandise inventory account on January 1 has a debit balance of $245,600.00. The count of merchandise on December 31 shows that the inventory is valued at $250,800.00. The merchandise on hand is $5,200.00 *greater* than the balance of Merchandise Inventory. This merchandise inventory adjustment is shown in the T accounts.

Merchandise Inventory is debited and Income Summary is credited for $5,200.00.

## Supplies adjustments

CarLand uses office and store supplies in the daily operation of the business. The amount of supplies *not used* during a fiscal period represents an asset. The amount of supplies *used* during a fiscal period represents an expense. Accurate financial reporting includes recording expenses in the fiscal period in which the expenses contribute to earning revenue. *(CONCEPT: Matching Expenses with Revenue)*

**Analyzing an office supplies inventory adjustment.** CarLand's office supplies account on December 31, the end of the fiscal period, has a debit balance of $5,400.00, as shown in the T account.

| Supplies — Office | |
| --- | --- |
| Dec. 31 Bal.  5,400.00 | |

The account balance for Supplies—Office, $5,400.00, includes two items. (1) The account balance on January 1. (2) The cost of office supplies bought during the year. The account balance does not reflect the value of any office supplies *used* during the year (an expense). Therefore, the office supplies account balance must be adjusted to show the value of office supplies on hand on December 31. The amount of supplies on hand on December 31 is determined by counting the supplies on hand and calculating their value.

The two accounts used to adjust office supplies are Supplies—Office and Supplies Expense—Office. The T accounts show the two accounts before the adjustment is made.

BEFORE ADJUSTMENT

| Supplies Expense — Office | |
| --- | --- |
| | |

| Supplies — Office | |
| --- | --- |
| Dec. 31 Bal.  5,400.00 | |

Before the adjustment, the office supplies account has a December 31 debit balance of $5,400.00. However, office supplies have been used throughout the fiscal period. These changes in office supplies were not recorded in the office supplies account. Therefore, the office supplies account balance is not up to date. The actual count of office supplies on December 31 shows that the value of the office supplies inventory is $1,460.00. The office supplies account balance must be adjusted to show the current value of the office supplies inventory.

Four questions are asked in analyzing the adjustment for office supplies inventory.

1. What is the balance of Supplies—Office ......... $5,400.00
2. What should the balance be for this account? . $1,460.00
3. What must be done to correct the account
   balance? Decrease......................... $3,940.00
4. What adjustment is made?
   Debit Supplies Expense—Office.............. $3,940.00
   Credit Supplies—Office.................... $3,940.00

The office supplies inventory adjustment is shown in the T accounts.

Supplies Expense—Office is debited and Supplies—Office is credited for $3,940.00. The beginning debit balance of Supplies—Office, $5,400.00, *minus* the adjustment credit amount, $3,940.00, *equals* the ending debit balance of Supplies—Office, $1,460.00.

AFTER ADJUSTMENT

| Supplies Expense — Office | |
| --- | --- |
| Adj. (b)     3,940.00 | |

| Supplies — Office | |
| --- | --- |
| Dec. 31 Bal.   5,400.00 | Adj. (b)     3,940.00 |
| *(New Bal.     1,460.00)* | |

**Recording supplies inventory adjustments on a work sheet.** CarLand makes a similar adjustment for store supplies. The steps in recording the *two* supplies inventory adjustments are the same as those described for Rugcare in Chapter 7. The *two* supplies inventory adjustments are shown in the Adjustments columns of the work sheet in Illustration 17-4. The adjustment for Supplies—Office is labeled *(b)* and is shown on lines 5 and 31. The adjustment for Supplies—Store is labeled *(c)* and is shown on lines 6 and 32.

| | | 1 | 2 | 3 | 4 |
|---|---|---|---|---|---|
| | ACCOUNT TITLE | TRIAL BALANCE | | ADJUSTMENTS | |
| | | DEBIT | CREDIT | DEBIT | CREDIT |
| 5 | *Supplies—Office* | 5 4 0 0 00 | | | *(b)*3 9 4 0 00 |
| 6 | *Supplies—Store* | 5 7 8 0 00 | | | *(c)*3 2 6 0 00 |
| 31 | *Supplies Expense—Office* | | | *(b)*3 9 4 0 00 | |
| 32 | *Supplies Expense—Store* | | | *(c)*3 2 6 0 00 | |
| 33 | | | | | |

Illustration 17-4
Supplies inventory
adjustments on a
work sheet

## Prepaid insurance adjustment

Payment for insurance protection is paid in advance. The value of prepaid insurance *not expired* during a fiscal period is an asset. The value of prepaid insurance *expired* during a fiscal period is an expense.

Prepaid Insurance

Dec. 31 Bal.   4,840.00

**Analyzing a prepaid insurance adjustment.** CarLand's prepaid insurance account on December 31, the end of the fiscal period, has a debit balance of $4,840.00, as shown in the T account.

The account balance for Prepaid Insurance, $4,840.00, includes two items. (1) The account balance on January 1. (2) The cost of insurance premiums paid during the year. The account balance does not reflect the value of the insurance *expired* during the year (an expense). Therefore, the prepaid insurance account balance must be adjusted to bring the balance up to date. *(CONCEPT: Matching Expenses with Revenue)*

BEFORE ADJUSTMENT

Insurance Expense

Prepaid Insurance

Dec. 31 Bal.   4,840.00

The two accounts used to adjust the prepaid insurance account are Prepaid Insurance and Insurance Expense. The T accounts show the two accounts before the adjustment is made.

Before the adjustment, the prepaid insurance account has a December 31 debit balance of $4,840.00. The account balance, however, is not up to date. The value of the prepaid insurance *not expired* is determined to be $2,200.00. The prepaid insurance account balance must be adjusted to show its current value.

Four questions are asked in analyzing the adjustment for prepaid insurance.

1. What is the balance of Prepaid Insurance?........ $4,840.00
2. What should the balance be for this account? . $2,200.00
3. What must be done to correct the account
   balance? Decrease........................... $2,640.00
4. What adjustment is made?
   Debit Insurance Expense..................... $2,640.00
   Credit Prepaid Insurance ................... $2,640.00

The prepaid insurance adjustment is shown in the T accounts.

Insurance Expense is debited and Prepaid Insurance is credited for $2,640.00. The beginning debit balance of Prepaid Insurance, $4,840.00, *minus* the adjustment credit amount, $2,640.00, *equals* the ending debit balance of Prepaid Insurance, $2,200.00.

AFTER ADJUSTMENT

| Insurance Expense | | |
|---|---|---|
| Adj. (d) | 2,640.00 | |

| Prepaid Insurance | | |
|---|---|---|
| Dec. 31 Bal. | 4,840.00 | Adj. (d)    2,640.00 |
| (New Bal. | 2,200.00) | |

**Recording a prepaid insurance adjustment on a work sheet.** The steps in recording the prepaid insurance adjustment on a work sheet are the same as those followed by Rugcare in Chapter 7. The adjustment for Prepaid Insurance is labeled *(d)* and is shown in the Adjustments columns on lines 7 and 26 of the work sheet in Illustration 17-5.

| | | 1 | 2 | 3 | 4 |
|---|---|---|---|---|---|
| | ACCOUNT TITLE | TRIAL BALANCE | | ADJUSTMENTS | |
| | | DEBIT | CREDIT | DEBIT | CREDIT |
| 7 | *Prepaid Insurance* | 4 8 4 0 00 | | | (d)2 6 4 0 00 |
| 26 | *Insurance Expense* | | | (d)2 6 4 0 00 | |

Illustration 17-5
Prepaid insurance adjustment on a work sheet

# COMPLETING A WORK SHEET

CarLand follows the same procedures for completing a work sheet as described for Rugcare in Chapter 7 with the exception of the income summary account. Rugcare sells a service, not merchandise. Therefore, Rugcare has no amount recorded in the income summary account, a related account used to adjust Merchandise Inventory. CarLand sells merchandise. Therefore, the income summary account is used as the related account to adjust Merchandise Inventory. The merchandise inventory adjustment reflects the increases and decreases in the amount of goods on hand resulting from sales and purchases. Therefore, the amount recorded in Income Summary is extended to the work sheet's Income Statement Debit or Credit column. An Income Summary debit amount is extended to the Income Statement Debit column. An Income Summary credit amount is extended to the Income Statement Credit column. CarLand's completed work sheet is shown in Illustration 17-6 on pages 400 and 401.

## CarLand
### Work Sheet
#### For Year Ended December 31, 19--

| | TRIAL BALANCE | | ADJUSTMENTS | | INCOME STATEMENT | | BALANCE SHEET | |
| ACCOUNT TITLE | DEBIT | CREDIT | DEBIT | CREDIT | DEBIT | CREDIT | DEBIT | CREDIT |
|---|---|---|---|---|---|---|---|---|
| 1 Cash | 24 23 3 57 | | | | | | 24 23 3 57 | |
| 2 Petty Cash | 50 0 00 | | | | | | 50 0 00 | |
| 3 Accounts Receivable | 9 33 2 00 | | | | | | 9 33 2 00 | |
| 4 Merchandise Inventory | 225 4 0 0 00 | | | (a) 13 2 0 0 00 | | | 212 2 0 0 00 | |
| 5 Supplies—Office | 5 40 0 00 | | | (b) 3 9 4 00 | | | 1 4 6 00 | |
| 6 Supplies—Store | 5 78 0 00 | | | (c) 3 2 6 00 | | | 2 5 2 00 | |
| 7 Prepaid Insurance | 4 84 0 00 | | | (d) 2 6 4 00 | | | 2 2 0 00 | |
| 8 Accounts Payable | | 10 4 5 1 90 | | | | | | 10 4 5 1 90 |
| 9 Employee Income Tax Pay. | | 4 0 2 00 | | | | | | 4 0 2 00 |
| 10 FICA Tax Payable | | 8 3 2 16 | | | | | | 8 3 2 16 |
| 11 Sales Tax Payable | | 1 76 0 00 | | | | | | 1 76 0 00 |
| 12 Unemploy. Tax Pay.—Federal | | 5 9 15 | | | | | | 5 9 15 |
| 13 Unemploy. Tax Pay.—State | | 3 9 9 26 | | | | | | 3 9 9 26 |
| 14 Health Ins. Premiums Pay. | | 8 4 0 00 | | | | | | 8 4 0 00 |
| 15 U.S. Savings Bonds Payable | | 4 0 00 | | | | | | 4 0 00 |
| 16 United Way Donations Payable | | 6 0 00 | | | | | | 6 0 00 |
| 17 Amy Kramer, Capital | | 101 11 8 00 | | | | | | 101 11 8 00 |
| 18 Amy Kramer, Drawing | 18 2 0 0 00 | | | | | | 18 2 0 0 00 | |
| 19 Dario Mesa, Capital | | 101 2 2 8 00 | | | | | | 101 2 2 8 00 |
| 20 Dario Mesa, Drawing | 18 6 0 0 00 | | | | | | 18 6 0 0 00 | |

| # | Account Title | Trial Balance Dr. | Trial Balance Cr. | Adjustments Dr. | Adjustments Cr. | Income Statement Dr. | Income Statement Cr. | Balance Sheet Dr. | Balance Sheet Cr. |
|---|---|---|---|---|---|---|---|---|---|
| 21 | *Income Summary* | | | (a) 13 2 0 0 00 | | 13 2 0 0 00 | | | |
| 22 | *Sales* | | 352 6 0 0 00 | | | | 352 6 0 0 00 | | |
| 23 | *Purchases* | 158 3 0 0 00 | | | | 158 3 0 0 00 | | | |
| 24 | *Advertising Expense* | 5 5 0 0 00 | | | | 5 5 0 0 00 | | | |
| 25 | *Credit Card Fee Expense* | 2 8 9 0 00 | | | | 2 8 9 0 00 | | | |
| 26 | *Insurance Expense* | | | (a) 2 6 4 0 00 | | 2 6 4 0 00 | | | |
| 27 | *Miscellaneous Expense* | 2 1 8 2 15 | | | | 2 1 8 2 15 | | | |
| 28 | *Payroll Taxes Expense* | 7 2 9 9 75 | | | | 7 2 9 9 75 | | | |
| 29 | *Rent Expense* | 18 0 0 0 00 | | | | 18 0 0 0 00 | | | |
| 30 | *Salary Expense* | 60 1 5 3 00 | | | | 60 1 5 3 00 | | | |
| 31 | *Supplies Expense—Office* | | | (b) 3 9 4 0 00 | | 3 9 4 0 00 | | | |
| 32 | *Supplies Expense—Store* | | | (c) 3 2 6 0 00 | | 3 2 6 0 00 | | | |
| 33 | *Utilities Expense* | 3 1 8 0 00 | | | | 3 1 8 0 00 | | | |
| 34 | | 569 7 9 0 47 | 569 7 9 0 47 | 23 0 4 0 00 | 23 0 4 0 00 | 280 5 4 4 90 | 352 6 0 0 00 | 289 2 4 5 57 | 217 1 9 0 47 |
| 35 | *Net Income* | | | | | 72 0 5 5 10 | | | 72 0 5 5 10 |
| 36 | | | | | | 352 6 0 0 00 | 352 6 0 0 00 | 289 2 4 5 57 | 289 2 4 5 57 |
| 37 | | | | | | | | | |
| 38 | | | | | | | | | |

Illustration 17-6
Completed work sheet for
a merchandising business

# SUMMARY OF COMPLETING AN 8-COLUMN WORK SHEET FOR A MERCHANDISING BUSINESS

Illustration 17-7
Summary of an 8-column
work sheet for a
merchandising business

Illustration 17-7 summarizes the steps followed in completing an 8-column work sheet for a merchandising business.

| | ACCOUNT TITLE | TRIAL BALANCE DEBIT | TRIAL BALANCE CREDIT | ADJUSTMENTS DEBIT | ADJUSTMENTS CREDIT | INCOME STATEMENT DEBIT | INCOME STATEMENT CREDIT | BALANCE SHEET DEBIT | BALANCE SHEET CREDIT | |
|---|---|---|---|---|---|---|---|---|---|---|
| 1 | Cash | 24 2 3 3 57 | | | | | | 24 2 3 3 57 | | 1 |
| 2 | Petty Cash | 5 0 0 00 | | | | | | 5 0 0 00 | | 2 |
| 4 | Merchandise Inventory | 225 4 0 0 00 | | | (a) 13 2 0 0 00 | | | 212 2 0 0 00 | | 4 |
| 5 | Supplies—Office | 5 4 0 0 00 | | | (b) 3 9 4 0 00 | | | 1 4 6 0 00 | | 5 |
| 8 | Accounts Payable | | 10 4 5 1 90 | | | | | | 10 4 5 1 90 | 8 |
| 19 | Dario Mesa, Capital | | 101 2 2 8 00 | | | | | | 101 2 2 8 00 | 19 |
| 20 | Dario Mesa, Drawing | 18 6 0 0 00 | | | | | | 18 6 0 0 00 | | 20 |
| 21 | Income Summary | | | (a) 13 2 0 0 00 | | 13 2 0 0 00 | | | | 21 |
| 22 | Sales | | 352 6 0 0 00 | | | | 352 6 0 0 00 | | | 22 |
| 23 | Purchases | 158 3 0 0 00 | | | | 158 3 0 0 00 | | | | 23 |
| 32 | Supplies Expense—Store | | | (c) 3 2 6 0 00 | | 3 2 6 0 00 | | | | 32 |
| 33 | Utilities Expense | 3 1 8 0 00 | | | | 3 1 8 0 00 | | | | 33 |
| 34 | | 569 7 9 0 47 | 569 7 9 0 47 | 23 0 4 0 00 | 23 0 4 0 00 | 280 5 4 4 90 | 352 6 0 0 00 | 289 2 4 5 57 | 217 1 9 0 47 | 34 |
| 35 | Net Income | | | | | 72 0 5 5 10 | | | 72 0 5 5 10 | 35 |
| 36 | | | | | | 352 6 0 0 00 | 352 6 0 0 00 | 289 2 4 5 57 | 289 2 4 5 57 | 36 |
| 37 | | | | | | | | | | 37 |

1  Prepare a trial balance in the Trial Balance columns.

2  Analyze and record adjustments in the Adjustments columns.

3  Extend balance sheet items to the work sheet's Balance Sheet columns.

4  Extend income statement items, including Income Summary, to the work sheet's Income Statement columns.

5  Total the Income Statement and Balance Sheet columns.

6  Figure the net income or net loss. If the Income Statement Credit column total (revenue) is larger than the Debit column total (costs and

expenses), a net income has occurred. If the Income Statement Debit column total (costs and expenses) is larger than the Credit column total (revenue), a net loss has occurred. CarLand's net income is calculated as shown below.

| Income Statement Credit Column Total | − | Income Statement Debit Column Total | = | Net Income |
|---|---|---|---|---|
| $352,600.00 | − | $280,544.90 | = | $72,055.10 |

7  Extend the amount of net income or net loss to the Balance Sheet Debit or Credit column. When a net income occurs, the net income amount is extended to the Balance Sheet Credit amount column, as shown for CarLand on line 35. When a net loss occurs, the net loss amount is extended to the Balance Sheet Debit amount column.

8  Total the four Income Statement and Balance Sheet amount columns.

9  Check that the totals for each pair of columns are in balance. As shown on CarLand's work sheet on line 36, the totals for the Income Statement columns, $352,600.00, are the same. The totals for the Balance Sheet columns, $289,245.57, are also the same. CarLand's work sheet is in balance.

# A 10-COLUMN WORK SHEET FOR A MERCHANDISING BUSINESS

Some large merchandising businesses *with many accounts to be adjusted* at the end of a fiscal period may use a 10-column work sheet. A 10-column work sheet includes an additional pair of amount columns titled *Adjusted Trial Balance*, as shown in the 10-column work sheet in Illustration 17-8.

After adjustments have been recorded, the balance for each account listed in the Trial Balance columns is extended to the Adjusted Trial Balance columns. The Adjusted Trial Balance columns are then totaled to prove equality of debits and credits after adjustments. Following proof of debits and credits, amounts in the Adjusted Trial Balance columns are extended to the Balance Sheet and Income Statement columns. The Income Statement and Balance Sheet columns are totaled and ruled the same way as on an 8-column work sheet.

Any business with adjustments to make at the end of a fiscal period could use either an 8-column or a 10-column work sheet. However, completing two extra amount columns when most of the account balances *are not* adjusted requires extra time and work. Account balances not adjusted must be extended from the Trial Balance columns to the Adjusted Trial Balance columns. Whereas, with an 8-column work sheet, account balances *not* adjusted are extended directly to the Balance Sheet or Income Statement columns. CarLand prefers to use an 8-column work sheet because only four adjustments are needed at the end of each fiscal period.

| | ACCOUNT TITLE | TRIAL BALANCE | | ADJUSTMENTS | |
| --- | --- | --- | --- | --- | --- |
| | | DEBIT | CREDIT | DEBIT | CREDIT |
| 1 | Cash | 24 2 3 3 57 | | | | 1 |
| 2 | Petty Cash | 5 0 0 00 | | | | 2 |
| 3 | Accounts Receivable | 9 3 3 2 00 | | | | 3 |
| 4 | Merchandise Inventory | 225 4 0 0 00 | | | (a)13 2 0 0 00 | 4 |
| 5 | Supplies—Office | 5 4 0 0 00 | | | (b) 3 9 4 0 00 | 5 |
| 6 | Supplies—Store | 5 7 8 0 00 | | | (c) 3 2 6 0 00 | 6 |
| 7 | Prepaid Insurance | 4 8 4 0 00 | | | (d) 2 6 4 0 00 | 7 |
| 8 | Accounts Payable | | 10 4 5 1 90 | | | 8 |
| 9 | Employee Income Tax Payable | | 4 0 2 00 | | | 9 |
| 10 | FICA Tax Payable | | 8 3 2 16 | | | 10 |
| 11 | Sales Tax Payable | | 1 7 6 0 00 | | | 11 |
| 29 | Rent Expense | 18 0 0 0 00 | | | | 29 |
| 30 | Salary Expense | 60 1 5 3 00 | | | | 30 |
| 31 | Supplies Expense—Office | | | (b) 3 9 4 0 00 | | 31 |
| 32 | Supplies Expense—Store | | | (c) 3 2 6 0 00 | | 32 |
| 33 | Utilities Expense | 3 1 8 0 00 | | | | 33 |
| 34 | | 569 7 9 0 47 | 569 7 9 0 47 | 23 0 4 0 00 | 23 0 4 0 00 | 34 |
| 35 | Net Income | | | | | 35 |
| 36 | | | | | | 36 |

**CarLand**

**Work Sheet**

**For Year Ended December 31, 19--**

Illustration 17-8      Ten-column work sheet (left page)

## ■ ACCOUNTING TERMS

What is the meaning of each of the following?

**1.** inventory          **2.** merchandise inventory

## ■ QUESTIONS FOR INDIVIDUAL STUDY

**1.** Why do some general ledger accounts not have any entries posted and, therefore, zero balances at the end of a fiscal period?

**2.** Why is a work sheet used at the end of a fiscal period?

**3.** Which accounting concept is being applied when a work sheet is prepared at the end of each fiscal period?

**4.** Why are all general ledger accounts listed on the Trial Balance columns of a work sheet?

**5.** Which of CarLand's general ledger accounts need to be brought up to date at the end of a fiscal period?

**6.** What type of account is Merchandise Inventory, and what is its normal balance?

| | 5 | 6 | 7 | 8 | 9 | 10 | |
|---|---|---|---|---|---|---|---|
| | ADJUSTED TRIAL BALANCE | | INCOME STATEMENT | | BALANCE SHEET | | |
| | DEBIT | CREDIT | DEBIT | CREDIT | DEBIT | CREDIT | |
| 1 | 24 2 3 3 57 | | | | 24 2 3 3 57 | | 1 |
| 2 | 5 0 0 00 | | | | 5 0 0 00 | | 2 |
| 3 | 9 3 3 2 00 | | | | 9 3 3 2 00 | | 3 |
| 4 | 212 2 0 0 00 | | | | 212 2 0 0 00 | | 4 |
| 5 | 1 4 6 0 00 | | | | 1 4 6 0 00 | | 5 |
| 6 | 2 5 2 0 00 | | | | 2 5 2 0 00 | | 6 |
| 7 | 2 2 0 0 00 | | | | 2 2 0 0 00 | | 7 |
| 8 | | 10 4 5 1 90 | | | | 10 4 5 1 90 | 8 |
| 9 | | 4 0 2 00 | | | | 4 0 2 00 | 9 |
| 10 | | 8 3 2 16 | | | | 8 3 2 16 | 10 |
| 11 | | 1 7 6 0 00 | | | | 1 7 6 0 00 | 11 |
| 29 | 18 0 0 0 00 | | 18 0 0 0 00 | | | | 29 |
| 30 | 60 1 5 3 00 | | 60 1 5 3 00 | | | | 30 |
| 31 | 3 9 4 0 00 | | 3 9 4 0 00 | | | | 31 |
| 32 | 3 2 6 0 00 | | 3 2 6 0 00 | | | | 32 |
| 33 | 3 1 8 0 00 | | 3 1 8 0 00 | | | | 33 |
| 34 | 592 8 3 0 47 | 592 8 3 0 47 | 280 5 4 4 90 | 352 6 0 0 00 | 289 2 4 5 57 | 217 1 9 0 47 | 34 |
| 35 | | | 72 0 5 5 10 | | | 72 0 5 5 10 | 35 |
| 36 | | | 352 6 0 0 00 | 352 6 0 0 00 | 289 2 4 5 57 | 289 2 4 5 57 | 36 |

Illustration 17-8     Ten-column work sheet (right page)

7. Why are the beginning and ending balances of the merchandise inventory account before adjustments the same?

8. What accounts are affected, and how, by the adjustment for merchandise inventory?

9. What does the amount of supplies not used during a fiscal period represent to a business?

10. Which accounting concept is being applied when expenses are recorded in the same accounting period in which the expenses contribute to earning revenue?

11. What two items are included in Car-Land's office supplies account balance before adjustment?

12. What accounts are affected, and how, by the adjustment for office supplies inventory?

13. What two items are included in Car-Land's prepaid insurance account balance before adjustment?

14. What accounts are affected, and how, by a prepaid insurance adjustment?

15. What type of merchandising business might use a 10-column work sheet?

16. What two additional amount columns are found on a 10-column work sheet?

## ■ CASES FOR MANAGEMENT DECISION

**CASE 1** After completing a work sheet, Kramer Merchandising Outlet finds that through an oversight, paper bags still in boxes were overlooked in figuring the supplies inventory. The value of the paper bags overlooked is $50.00. Joseph Kramer suggests that the accountant not worry about such a small amount because the oversight does not have any effect on balancing the Income Statement and Balance Sheet columns of the work sheet. Mr. Kramer further indicates that the oversight will be corrected anyway when the store supplies are counted at the end of the next fiscal period.

The accountant recommends that the work sheet be redone to reflect the refigured supplies inventory. Do you agree with Mr. Kramer or the accountant? Explain your answer.

**CASE 2** Quality Shoes paid $1,440.00 for a one-year fire insurance policy. The company prepares an income statement and balance sheet every three months. However, the accountant prepares a prepaid insurance adjustment only at the end of the year. Rachel Delfield, one of the partners in the business, thinks the prepaid insurance should be adjusted every three months. Who is correct? Why?

## ■ DRILLS FOR UNDERSTANDING

### DRILL 17-D1   Analyzing adjusting entries

The following chart contains adjustment information related to the preparation of work sheets for three businesses.

| Business | Account Title and Balance | | End-of-Fiscal-Period Information | |
|---|---|---|---|---|
| A | Merchandise Inventory... | $148,000.00 | Merchandise inventory .. | $134,000.00 |
| | Supplies—Office ....... | 5,750.00 | Office supp. inventory ... | 4,200.00 |
| | Supplies—Store ........ | 4,920.00 | Store supp. inventory.... | 3,840.00 |
| | Prepaid Insurance ...... | 1,860.00 | Value of prepaid insurance | 1,240.00 |
| B | Merchandise Inventory... | $182,000.00 | Merchandise inventory .. | $166,000.00 |
| | Supplies—Office ....... | 4,680.00 | Office supp. inventory ... | 3,460.00 |
| | Supplies—Store ........ | 5,930.00 | Store supp. inventory.... | 4,320.00 |
| | Prepaid Insurance ...... | 2,520.00 | Value of prepaid insurance | 1,260.00 |
| C | Merchandise Inventory... | $166,500.00 | Merchandise inventory .. | $178,000.00 |
| | Supplies—Office ....... | 5,460.00 | Office supp. inventory ... | 4,520.00 |
| | Supplies—Store ........ | 6,480.00 | Store supp. inventory.... | 4,960.00 |
| | Prepaid Insurance ...... | 2,160.00 | Value of prepaid insurance | 1,080.00 |

Use a form similar to the following.

| 1 | 2 | 3 | 4 | 5 |
|---|---|---|---|---|
| | | | **Adjustment Column** | |
| **Business** | **Adjustment Number** | **Accounts Affected** | **Debit** | **Credit** |
| A | 1. | *Income Summary* | *$14,000.00* | |
| | | *Merchandise Inventory* | | *$14,000.00* |

**Instructions:** For each business list the accounts affected and the amounts for each of the following adjustments. List the account titles in Column 3 and the amounts in either Column 4 or 5. Adjustment 1 for Business A is given as an example.

*Adjustments*

1. Merchandise inventory adjustment.
2. Office supplies inventory adjustment.
3. Store supplies inventory adjustment.
4. Prepaid insurance adjustment.

**DRILL 17-D2   Extending balance sheet and income statement items**

Madison Enterprise's work sheet has the following Trial Balance and Adjustments columns.

| | | | | | | |
|---|---|---|---|---|---|---|
| | | | | 1 | 2 | 3 | 4 |

<table>
<tr><td colspan="7" align="center">*Madison Enterprises*</td></tr>
<tr><td colspan="7" align="center">*Work Sheet*</td></tr>
<tr><td colspan="7" align="center">*For Year Ended December 31, 19--*</td></tr>
<tr><td rowspan="2">ACCOUNT TITLE</td><td colspan="2">TRIAL BALANCE</td><td colspan="2">ADJUSTMENTS</td></tr>
<tr><td>DEBIT</td><td>CREDIT</td><td>DEBIT</td><td>CREDIT</td></tr>
<tr><td>1 *Cash*</td><td>21 770 00</td><td></td><td></td><td></td></tr>
<tr><td>2 *Petty Cash*</td><td>500 00</td><td></td><td></td><td></td></tr>
<tr><td>3 *Accounts Receivable*</td><td>8 911 00</td><td></td><td></td><td></td></tr>
<tr><td>4 *Merchandise Inventory*</td><td>211 870 00</td><td></td><td></td><td>(a)12 408 00</td></tr>
<tr><td>5 *Supplies—Office*</td><td>5 076 00</td><td></td><td></td><td>(b) 3 704 00</td></tr>
<tr><td>6 *Supplies—Store*</td><td>5 430 00</td><td></td><td></td><td>(c) 3 065 00</td></tr>
<tr><td>7 *Prepaid Insurance*</td><td>4 620 00</td><td></td><td></td><td>(d) 2 520 00</td></tr>
<tr><td>8 *Accounts Payable*</td><td></td><td>8 950 00</td><td></td><td></td></tr>
<tr><td>9 *Sales Tax Payable*</td><td></td><td>1 654 00</td><td></td><td></td></tr>
<tr><td>10 *Diane Casey, Capital*</td><td></td><td>98 230 00</td><td></td><td></td></tr>
<tr><td>11 *Diane Casey, Drawing*</td><td>17 108 00</td><td></td><td></td><td></td></tr>
<tr><td>12 *Julia Gibbs, Capital*</td><td></td><td>98 764 00</td><td></td><td></td></tr>
<tr><td>13 *Julia Gibbs, Drawing*</td><td>17 482 00</td><td></td><td></td><td></td></tr>
<tr><td>14 *Income Summary*</td><td></td><td></td><td>(a)12 408 00</td><td></td></tr>
<tr><td>15 *Sales*</td><td></td><td>263 700 00</td><td></td><td></td></tr>
<tr><td>16 *Purchases*</td><td>148 800 00</td><td></td><td></td><td></td></tr>
<tr><td>17 *Advertising Expense*</td><td>5 170 00</td><td></td><td></td><td></td></tr>
<tr><td>18 *Credit Card Fee Expense*</td><td>2 720 00</td><td></td><td></td><td></td></tr>
<tr><td>19 *Insurance Expense*</td><td></td><td></td><td>(d) 2 520 00</td><td></td></tr>
<tr><td>20 *Miscellaneous Expense*</td><td>2 051 00</td><td></td><td></td><td></td></tr>
<tr><td>21 *Rent Expense*</td><td>16 800 00</td><td></td><td></td><td></td></tr>
<tr><td>22 *Supplies Expense—Office*</td><td></td><td></td><td>(b) 3 704 00</td><td></td></tr>
<tr><td>23 *Supplies Expense—Store*</td><td></td><td></td><td>(c) 3 065 00</td><td></td></tr>
<tr><td>24 *Utilities Expense*</td><td>2 990 00</td><td></td><td></td><td></td></tr>
<tr><td>25</td><td>471 298 00</td><td>471 298 00</td><td>21 697 00</td><td>21 697 00</td></tr>
</table>

**Instructions: 1.** Extend the balance sheet items to the Balance Sheet columns of the work sheet.
   **2.** Extend the income statement items to the Income Statement columns of the work sheet.
   **3.** Complete the work sheet.
a. Total the Income Statement and Balance Sheet columns.
b. Figure and record the net income or net loss.
c. Total and rule the Income Statement and Balance Sheet columns.

# ■ APPLICATION PROBLEMS

PROBLEM 17-1   **Completing a work sheet**

On December 31 of the current year, Eastside Supply has the following general ledger accounts and balances. The trial balance is recorded on the work sheet in the working papers accompanying this textbook.

| Account Title | Balance |
|---|---|
| Cash | $ 22,460.00 |
| Petty Cash | 500.00 |
| Accounts Receivable | 9,195.00 |
| Merchandise Inventory | 218,600.00 |
| Supplies—Office | 5,230.00 |
| Supplies—Store | 5,610.00 |
| Prepaid Insurance | 4,515.00 |
| Accounts Payable | 9,235.00 |
| Sales Tax Payable | 1,145.00 |
| Pablo Sanchez, Capital | 81,236.00 |
| Pablo Sanchez, Drawing | 14,640.00 |
| Carmen Zapata, Capital | 81,778.00 |
| Carman Zapata, Drawing | 14,820.00 |
| Income Summary | — |
| Sales | 274,900.00 |
| Purchases | 123,705.00 |
| Advertising Expense | 5,335.00 |
| Credit Card Fee Expense | 2,810.00 |
| Insurance Expense | — |
| Miscellaneous Expense | 2,134.00 |
| Rent Expense | 15,600.00 |
| Supplies Expense—Office | — |
| Supplies Expense—Store | — |
| Utilities Expense | 3,140.00 |

**Instructions: 1.** Analyze the following adjustment information, and record the adjustments on the work sheet.

| Adjustment Information, December 31 | |
|---|---|
| Merchandise inventory | $196,610.00 |
| Office supplies inventory | 1,410.00 |
| Store supplies inventory | 2,450.00 |
| Value of prepaid insurance | 1,935.00 |

   **2.** Figure and record the net income or net loss.
   **3.** Complete the work sheet.

## PROBLEM 17-2  Completing a work sheet

On December 31 of the current year, Jomar has the following general ledger accounts and balances. The trial balance is recorded on the work sheet in the working papers accompanying this textbook.

| Account Title | Balance |
|---|---|
| Cash . . . . . . . . . . . . . . . . . . . . . . . . . . . . . . . . . . . . . . . . . . . . . . . . . . . . . . . | $ 22,100.00 |
| Petty Cash . . . . . . . . . . . . . . . . . . . . . . . . . . . . . . . . . . . . . . . . . . . . . . . . . . . | 300.00 |
| Accounts Receivable . . . . . . . . . . . . . . . . . . . . . . . . . . . . . . . . . . . . . . . . . . . . | 9,620.00 |
| Merchandise Inventory . . . . . . . . . . . . . . . . . . . . . . . . . . . . . . . . . . . . . . . . . | 243,600.00 |
| Supplies—Office. . . . . . . . . . . . . . . . . . . . . . . . . . . . . . . . . . . . . . . . . . . . . . . | 5,730.00 |
| Supplies—Store . . . . . . . . . . . . . . . . . . . . . . . . . . . . . . . . . . . . . . . . . . . . . . . | 5,380.00 |
| Prepaid Insurance. . . . . . . . . . . . . . . . . . . . . . . . . . . . . . . . . . . . . . . . . . . . . . | 5,060.00 |
| Accounts Payable. . . . . . . . . . . . . . . . . . . . . . . . . . . . . . . . . . . . . . . . . . . . . . | 9,864.00 |
| Sales Tax Payable . . . . . . . . . . . . . . . . . . . . . . . . . . . . . . . . . . . . . . . . . . . . . | 916.00 |
| Lidia Jomar, Capital. . . . . . . . . . . . . . . . . . . . . . . . . . . . . . . . . . . . . . . . . . . . . | 151,850.00 |
| Lidia Jomar, Drawing . . . . . . . . . . . . . . . . . . . . . . . . . . . . . . . . . . . . . . . . . . . | 12,860.00 |
| Philip Jomar, Capital . . . . . . . . . . . . . . . . . . . . . . . . . . . . . . . . . . . . . . . . . . . | 150,894.00 |
| Philip Jomar, Drawing . . . . . . . . . . . . . . . . . . . . . . . . . . . . . . . . . . . . . . . . . . | 12,674.00 |
| Income Summary . . . . . . . . . . . . . . . . . . . . . . . . . . . . . . . . . . . . . . . . . . . . . . | — |
| Sales . . . . . . . . . . . . . . . . . . . . . . . . . . . . . . . . . . . . . . . . . . . . . . . . . . . . . . . . | 183,110.00 |
| Purchases . . . . . . . . . . . . . . . . . . . . . . . . . . . . . . . . . . . . . . . . . . . . . . . . . . . | 147,150.00 |
| Advertising Expense . . . . . . . . . . . . . . . . . . . . . . . . . . . . . . . . . . . . . . . . . . . | 5,820.00 |
| Credit Card Fee Expense . . . . . . . . . . . . . . . . . . . . . . . . . . . . . . . . . . . . . . . . | 1,615.00 |
| Insurance Expense. . . . . . . . . . . . . . . . . . . . . . . . . . . . . . . . . . . . . . . . . . . . . | — |
| Miscellaneous Expense. . . . . . . . . . . . . . . . . . . . . . . . . . . . . . . . . . . . . . . . . | 2,285.00 |
| Rent Expense . . . . . . . . . . . . . . . . . . . . . . . . . . . . . . . . . . . . . . . . . . . . . . . . | 19,200.00 |
| Supplies Expense—Office . . . . . . . . . . . . . . . . . . . . . . . . . . . . . . . . . . . . . . | — |
| Supplies Expense—Store. . . . . . . . . . . . . . . . . . . . . . . . . . . . . . . . . . . . . . . | — |
| Utilities Expense. . . . . . . . . . . . . . . . . . . . . . . . . . . . . . . . . . . . . . . . . . . . . . | 3,240.00 |

**Instructions: 1.** Analyze the following adjustment information, and record the adjustments on the work sheet.

### Adjustment Information, December 31

| | |
|---|---|
| Merchandise inventory . . . . . . . . . . . . . . . . . . . . . . . . . . . . . . . . . . . . . . . . . | $246,600.00 |
| Office supplies inventory. . . . . . . . . . . . . . . . . . . . . . . . . . . . . . . . . . . . . . . . | 1,790.00 |
| Store supplies inventory . . . . . . . . . . . . . . . . . . . . . . . . . . . . . . . . . . . . . . . . | 1,510.00 |
| Value of prepaid insurance . . . . . . . . . . . . . . . . . . . . . . . . . . . . . . . . . . . . . . | 2,300.00 |

**2.** Figure and record the net income or net loss.
**3.** Complete the work sheet.

 ## ENRICHMENT PROBLEMS

## MASTERY PROBLEM 17-M  Completing a work sheet

On December 31 of the current year, Marine Supply has the following general ledger accounts and balances. The trial balance is recorded on the work sheet in the working papers accompanying this textbook.

| Account Title | Balance |
|---|---|
| Cash . . . . . . . . . . . . . . . . . . . . . . . . . . . . . . . . . . . . . . . . . . . . . . . . . . . . . . . . | $ 23,740.00 |
| Petty Cash . . . . . . . . . . . . . . . . . . . . . . . . . . . . . . . . . . . . . . . . . . . . . . . . . . . | 500.00 |

| | |
|---|---:|
| Accounts Receivable | 10,200.00 |
| Merchandise Inventory | 185,300.00 |
| Supplies—Office | 5,585.00 |
| Supplies—Store | 5,735.00 |
| Prepaid Insurance | 4,275.00 |
| Accounts Payable | 9,680.00 |
| Sales Tax Payable | 1,376.00 |
| Mark Edwards, Capital | 88,740.00 |
| Mark Edwards, Drawing | 18,380.00 |
| David Parker, Capital | 89,459.00 |
| David Parker, Drawing | 18,610.00 |
| Income Summary | — |
| Sales | 275,300.00 |
| Purchases | 161,290.00 |
| Advertising Expense | 5,920.00 |
| Credit Card Fee Expense | 2,735.00 |
| Insurance Expense | — |
| Miscellaneous Expense | 2,365.00 |
| Rent Expense | 16,800.00 |
| Supplies Expense—Office | — |
| Supplies Expense—Store | — |
| Utilities Expense | 3,120.00 |

**Instructions:** Use the following adjustment information. Complete the work sheet.

### Adjustment Information, December 31

| | |
|---|---:|
| Merchandise inventory | $208,600.00 |
| Office supplies inventory | 1,855.00 |
| Store supplies inventory | 2,355.00 |
| Value of prepaid insurance | 1,575.00 |

## CHALLENGE PROBLEM 17-C   Completing a 10-column work sheet

On December 31 of the current year, Ultimate Fashion has the following general ledger accounts and balances. The trial balance is recorded on the work sheet in the working papers accompanying this textbook.

| Account Title | Balance |
|---|---:|
| Cash | $ 25,340.00 |
| Petty Cash | 500.00 |
| Accounts Receivable | 9,485.00 |
| Merchandise Inventory | 215,870.00 |
| Supplies—Office | 5,130.00 |
| Supplies—Store | 5,335.00 |
| Prepaid Insurance | 3,960.00 |
| Accounts Payable | 10,320.00 |
| Sales Tax Payable | 810.00 |
| Debra Brown, Capital | 109,635.00 |
| Debra Brown, Drawing | 18,340.00 |
| Richard Leyba, Capital | 108,845.00 |
| Richard Leyba, Drawing | 18,560.00 |
| Income Summary | — |
| Sales | 192,380.00 |
| Purchases | 86,570.00 |
| Advertising Expense | 6,140.00 |

| | | |
|---|---|---|
| Credit Card Fee Expense . . . . . . . . . . . . . . . . . . . . . . . . . . . . . . . . . . . . . . . . | 2,385.00 |
| Insurance Expense. . . . . . . . . . . . . . . . . . . . . . . . . . . . . . . . . . . . . . . . . . . . . | — |
| Miscellaneous Expense. . . . . . . . . . . . . . . . . . . . . . . . . . . . . . . . . . . . . . . . . | 2,530.00 |
| Rent Expense . . . . . . . . . . . . . . . . . . . . . . . . . . . . . . . . . . . . . . . . . . . . . . . . | 18,600.00 |
| Supplies Expense—Office . . . . . . . . . . . . . . . . . . . . . . . . . . . . . . . . . . . . . | — |
| Supplies Expense—Store. . . . . . . . . . . . . . . . . . . . . . . . . . . . . . . . . . . . . . . | — |
| Utilities Expense. . . . . . . . . . . . . . . . . . . . . . . . . . . . . . . . . . . . . . . . . . . . . . | 3,245.00 |

**Instructions:** Use the following adjustment information. Complete the 10-column work sheet.

### Adjustment Information, December 31

| | |
|---|---|
| Merchandise inventory . . . . . . . . . . . . . . . . . . . . . . . . . . . . . . . . . . . . . . . . . | $205,370.00 |
| Office supplies inventory. . . . . . . . . . . . . . . . . . . . . . . . . . . . . . . . . . . . . . . . | 2,160.00 |
| Store supplies inventory . . . . . . . . . . . . . . . . . . . . . . . . . . . . . . . . . . . . . . . | 2,195.00 |
| Value of prepaid insurance . . . . . . . . . . . . . . . . . . . . . . . . . . . . . . . . . . . . . | 1,320.00 |

# Financial Statements for a Partnership

## ENABLING PERFORMANCE TASKS

After studying Chapter 18, you will be able to:
a. Define accounting terms related to financial statements for a merchandising business organized as a partnership.
b. Identify accounting concepts and practices related to financial statements for a merchandising business organized as a partnership.
c. Prepare an income statement for a merchandising business organized as a partnership.
d. Analyze an income statement using component percentages for a merchandising business organized as a partnership.
e. Prepare a distribution of net income statement for a merchandising business organized as a partnership.
f. Prepare an owners' equity statement for a merchandising business organized as a partnership.
g. Prepare a balance sheet for a merchandising business organized as a partnership.

The financial activities of a business are recorded in journals and ledgers during a fiscal period. At the end of a fiscal period, a work sheet is prepared to organize and summarize this financial information. The completed work sheet is used to prepare financial statements. Financial statements provide the primary source of information needed by owners and managers to make decisions on the future activity of a business.

All financial information must be reported in order to make sound business decisions. The financial statements should provide information about a business' financial condition, changes in this financial condition, and the progress of operations. (CONCEPT: Adequate Disclosure)

Comparing financial condition and progress for more than one fiscal period also helps owners and managers make sound business decisions. Therefore, financial information must be reported the same way from one fiscal period to the next. (CONCEPT: Consistent Reporting)

# FINANCIAL STATEMENTS FOR A PARTNERSHIP

A business organized as a partnership prepares four financial statements to report financial progress and condition. A partnership prepares an income statement and a balance sheet similar to those used by a proprietorship. A partnership also prepares two additional financial statements. One statement reports the distribution of net income or net loss for each partner. The other statement reports the changes in owners' equity for the fiscal period.

# INCOME STATEMENT

An income statement is used to report a business' financial progress. Merchandising businesses report revenue, cost of merchandise sold, gross profit on sales, expenses, and net income or loss. Current and previous income statements can be compared to determine the reasons for increases or decreases in net income. This comparison is helpful in making management decisions about future operations.

## Preparing an income statement

Information from a completed work sheet is used to prepare an income statement. CarLand's income statement information on a work sheet for the year ended December 31 is shown in Illustration 18-1.

Illustration 18-1
Income statement
information on a work
sheet

| | ACCOUNT TITLE | 1 TRIAL BALANCE DEBIT | 2 CREDIT | 3 ADJUSTMENTS DEBIT | 4 CREDIT | 5 INCOME STATEMENT DEBIT | 6 CREDIT | 7 BALANCE SHEET DEBIT | 8 CREDIT | |
|---|---|---|---|---|---|---|---|---|---|---|
| 4 | Merchandise Inventory | 225 4 0 0 00 | | | (b) 13 2 0 0 00 | | | 212 2 0 0 00 | | 4 |
| 22 | Sales | | 352 6 0 0 00 | | | | 352 6 0 0 00 | | | 22 |
| 23 | Purchases | 158 3 0 0 00 | | | | 158 3 0 0 00 | | | | 23 |
| 24 | Advertising Expense | 5 5 0 0 00 | | | | 5 5 0 0 00 | | | | 24 |
| 25 | Credit Card Fee Expense | 2 8 9 0 00 | | | | 2 8 9 0 00 | | | | 25 |
| 26 | Insurance Expense | | | (a) 2 6 4 0 00 | | 2 6 4 0 00 | | | | 26 |
| 27 | Miscellaneous Expense | 2 1 8 2 15 | | | | 2 1 8 2 15 | | | | 27 |
| 28 | Payroll Taxes Expense | 7 2 9 9 75 | | | | 7 2 9 9 75 | | | | 28 |
| 29 | Rent Expense | 18 0 0 0 00 | | | | 18 0 0 0 00 | | | | 29 |
| 30 | Salary Expense | 60 1 5 3 00 | | | | 60 1 5 3 00 | | | | 30 |
| 31 | Supplies Expense—Office | | | (c) 3 9 4 0 00 | | 3 9 4 0 00 | | | | 31 |
| 32 | Supplies Expense—Store | | | (d) 3 2 6 0 00 | | 3 2 6 0 00 | | | | 32 |
| 33 | Utilities Expense | 3 1 8 0 00 | | | | 3 1 8 0 00 | | | | 33 |
| 34 | | 569 7 9 0 47 | 569 7 9 0 47 | 23 0 4 0 00 | 23 0 4 0 00 | 280 5 4 4 90 | 352 6 0 0 00 | 289 2 4 5 57 | 217 1 9 0 47 | 34 |
| 35 | Net Income | | | | | 72 0 5 5 10 | | | 72 0 5 5 10 | 35 |
| 36 | | | | | | 352 6 0 0 00 | 352 6 0 0 00 | 289 2 4 5 57 | 289 2 4 5 57 | 36 |

The income statement of a merchandising business has three main sections. (1) Revenue section. (2) Cost of merchandise sold section. (3) Expenses section. The total original price of all merchandise sold during a fiscal period is called the cost of merchandise sold. *(CONCEPT: Historical Cost)* Cost of merchandise sold is sometimes known as cost of goods sold or cost of sales. CarLand's completed income statement is shown in Illustration 18-2.

| CarLand | | | | |
|---|---|---|---|---|
| *Income Statement* | | | | |
| *For Year Ended December 31, 19--* | | | | |
| | | | | % OF SALES |
| Revenue: | | | | |
| Sales | | | 352 6 0 0 00 | 100.0 |
| Cost of Merchandise Sold: | | | | |
| Merchandise Inventory, January 1, 19-- | 225 4 0 0 00 | | | |
| Purchases | 158 3 0 0 00 | | | |
| Total Cost of Mdse. Available for Sale | 383 7 0 0 00 | | | |
| Less Mdse. Inventory, December 31, 19-- | 212 2 0 0 00 | | | |
| Cost of Merchandise Sold | | | 171 5 0 0 00 | 48.6 |
| Gross Profit on Sales | | | 181 1 0 0 00 | 51.4 |
| Expenses: | | | | |
| Advertising Expense | 5 5 0 0 00 | | | |
| Credit Card Fee Expense | 2 8 9 0 00 | | | |
| Insurance Expense | 2 6 4 0 00 | | | |
| Miscellaneous Expense | 2 1 8 2 15 | | | |
| Payroll Taxes Expense | 7 2 9 9 75 | | | |
| Rent Expense | 18 0 0 0 00 | | | |
| Salary Expense | 60 1 5 3 00 | | | |
| Supplies Expense—Office | 3 9 4 0 00 | | | |
| Supplies Expense—Store | 3 2 6 0 00 | | | |
| Utilities Expense | 3 1 8 0 00 | | | |
| Total Expenses | | | 109 0 4 4 90 | 30.9 |
| Net Income | | | 72 0 5 5 10 | 20.4 |

Illustration 18-2
Income statement for a
merchandising business

CarLand uses seven steps in preparing an income statement.

1 Write the income statement heading on three lines.

2 Prepare the revenue section. Use the information from the Income Statement Credit column of the work sheet.

- Write the name of this section, *Revenue:*, at the extreme left of the wide column on the first line.
- Write the title of the revenue account, Sales, on the next line, indented about one centimeter.
- Write the balance of the sales account, *$352,600.00*, in the second amount column. For CarLand, this amount is also the total of the revenue section.

> For businesses with more than one source of revenue, each revenue account title is listed in the wide column. Each account balance is written in the first amount column. The words *Total Revenue* are written in the wide column on the next line below the last revenue account title. The total amount of revenue is written in the second amount column.

3   Prepare the cost of merchandise sold section.

- Write the name of this section, *Cost of Merchandise Sold:*, at the extreme left of the wide column.
- Indent about one centimeter on the next line, and write the items needed to figure cost of merchandise sold. Write the amount of each item in the first amount column.

Beginning merchandise inventory, January 1.......... $  225,400.00
(This amount is the debit balance of Merchandise Inventory in the Trial Balance Debit Column of the work sheet.)

*Plus* purchases made during the fiscal period ........   +158,300.00
(This amount is the debit balance of Purchases in the Income Statement Debit column of the work sheet.)

*Equals* total cost of merchandise available for sale
during the fiscal period ........................   $  383,700.00
*Less* ending merchandise inventory, December 31......   −212,200.00
(This amount is the debit balance of Merchandise Inventory in the Balance Sheet Debit column of the work sheet.)

*Equals* cost of merchandise sold during the fiscal
period ..........................................   $  171,500.00

- Indent about one centimeter on the next line, and write the words *Cost of Merchandise Sold*. Write the cost of merchandise sold amount, *$171,500.00*, in the second amount column.

4   Figure the gross profit on sales. The revenue remaining after cost of merchandise sold has been deducted is called gross profit on sales.

- Write the words *Gross Profit on Sales* on the next line at the extreme left of the wide column.
- Write the gross profit on sales amount, *$181,100.00*, in the second amount column. (Total revenue, $352,600.00, *less* cost of merchandise sold, $171,500.00, *equals* gross profit on sales, $181,100.00.)

5 Prepare the expenses section. Use the information from the Income
Statement Debit column of the work sheet.

- Write the name of this section, *Expenses:*, at the extreme left of the
  wide column.

- Indent about one centimeter on the next line, and list the expense account titles in the order in which they appear on the work sheet.
  Write the amount of each expense account balance in the first
  amount column.

- Indent about one centimeter, and write the words *Total Expenses* on
  the next line in the wide column below the last expense account title.
  Total the individual expense amounts and write the total, *$109,044.90,*
  in the second amount column on the total line.

6 Figure the net income.

- Write the words *Net Income* on the next line at the extreme left of the
  wide column.

- Write the net income amount, *$72,055.10,* in the second amount
  column on the net income line. (Gross profit on sales, $181,100.00, *less*
  total expenses, $109,044.90, *equals* net income, $72,055.10.)

  Verify accuracy by comparing the amount of net income figured
  on the income statement, $72,055.10, with the amount on the work
  sheet, $72,055.10. The two amounts must be the same.

7 Rule double lines across both amount columns to show that the income
statement has been verified as correct.

## Analyzing an income statement showing a net income

For a merchandising business, every sales dollar reported on the income statement includes four components. (1) Cost of merchandise sold.
(2) Gross profit on sales. (3) Total expenses. (4) Net income. To help make
decisions about future operations, CarLand analyzes relationships between these four income statement components and sales. The percentage
relationship between one financial statement item and the total that includes that item is known as a component percentage. On an income statement, component percentages are figured by dividing the amount of each
component by the amount of sales. CarLand figures a component percentage for cost of merchandise sold, gross profit on sales, total expenses, and
net income. The relationship between each component and sales is shown
in a separate column on the income statement.

## Acceptable component percentages

For a component percentage to be useful, a business must know acceptable percentages. This information is determined by making comparisons
with prior fiscal periods as well as with industry standards that are pub-

lished by industry organizations. Based on these sources, CarLand determines the acceptable component percentages shown in the following table.

| Income Statement Items | Acceptable Component Percentages | Actual Component Percentages |
|---|---|---|
| Sales | 100.0% | 100.0% |
| Cost of merchandise sold | not more than 50.0% | 48.6% |
| Gross profit on sales | not less than 50.0% | 51.4% |
| Total expenses | not more than 32.0% | 30.9% |
| Net income | not less than 18.0% | 20.4% |

Each percentage represents the amount of each sales dollar that is considered acceptable. For example, CarLand determines that no more than 50 cents, or 50.0%, of each sales dollar should be devoted to cost of merchandise sold.

**Cost of merchandise sold component percentage.** The cost of merchandise sold is a major cost. Therefore, this cost must be kept as low as possible. Analysis of CarLand's income statement, Illustration 18-2, shows that the cost of merchandise sold is 48.6% of sales. This component percentage is calculated as shown below.

| Cost of Merchandise Sold | ÷ | Sales | = | Cost of Merchandise Sold Component Percentage |
|---|---|---|---|---|
| $171,500.00 | ÷ | $352,600.00 | = | 48.6% |

The component percentage for cost of merchandise sold, 48.6%, is *less than* the maximum acceptable percentage, 50.0%. Therefore, CarLand's component percentage for cost of merchandise sold is considered acceptable.

**Gross profit on sales component percentage.** Gross profit must be large enough to cover total expenses and the desired amount of net income. CarLand determines that at least 50 cents, or 50.0%, of each sales dollar should result in gross profit. Analysis of CarLand's income statement shows that the component percentage for gross profit on sales is 51.4%. This component percentage is calculated as shown below.

| Gross Profit on Sales | ÷ | Sales | = | Gross Profit on Sales Component Percentage |
|---|---|---|---|---|
| $181,100.00 | ÷ | $352,600.00 | = | 51.4% |

The component percentage for gross profit on sales, 51.4%, is *not less than* the minimum acceptable percentage, 50.0%. Therefore, CarLand's component percentage for gross profit on sales is considered acceptable.

**Total expenses component percentage.** Total expenses must be less than gross profit on sales to provide a desirable net income. CarLand determines that no more than 32 cents, or 32.0%, of each sales dollar should be devoted to total expenses. Analysis of CarLand's income statement shows that the component percentage for total expenses is 30.9%. This component percentage is calculated as shown below.

| Total Expenses | ÷ | Sales | = | Total Expenses Component Percentage |
|---|---|---|---|---|
| $109,044.90 | ÷ | $352,600.00 | = | 30.9% |

The component percentage for total expenses, 30.9%, is *not more than* the maximum acceptable percentage, 32.0%. Therefore, CarLand's component percentage for total expenses is considered acceptable.

**Net income component percentage.** The component percentage for net income shows the progress being made by a business. CarLand determines that at least 18 cents, or 18.0%, of each sales dollar should result in net income. Analysis of CarLand's income statement shows that the component percentage for net income is 20.4%. This component percentage is calculated as shown below.

| Net Income | ÷ | Sales | = | Net Income Component Percentage |
|---|---|---|---|---|
| $72,055.10 | ÷ | $352,600.00 | = | 20.4% |

The component percentage for net income, 20.4%, is *not less than* the minimum acceptable percentage, 18.0%. Therefore, CarLand's component percentage for net income is considered acceptable.

## Analyzing an income statement showing a net loss

When a business' total expenses are greater than the gross profit on sales, the difference is known as a net loss. For example, the income statement shown in Illustration 18-3 shows a net loss of $3,770.00 for the fiscal period.

Total expenses, $109,120.00, *less* gross profit on sales, $105,350.00, *equals* net loss, $3,770.00. The net loss amount, *$3,770.00,* is written in parentheses in the second amount column on the line with the words *Net Loss.* An amount written in parentheses on a financial statement indicates a negative amount.

Autoworks uses the same acceptable component percentages as CarLand. Analysis of the income statement, Illustration 18-3, indicates unacceptable component percentages. (1) The component percentage for cost of merchandise sold, 53.3%, is *more than* the maximum acceptable component percentage, 50.0%. (2) The component percentage for gross profit on sales, 46.7%, is *less than* the minimum acceptable component percentage, 50.0%. (3) The component percentage for total expenses, 48.4%, is *more than* the

| Autoworks Income Statement For Year Ended December 31, 19-- | | | | % OF SALES |
|---|---|---|---|---|
| **Revenue:** | | | | |
| Sales | | | 225 4 0 0 00 | 100.0 |
| **Cost of Merchandise Sold:** | | | | |
| Merchandise Inventory, Janaury 1, 19-- | 243 2 0 0 00 | | | |
| Purchases | 138 9 0 0 00 | | | |
| Total Cost of Mdse. Available for Sale | 382 1 0 0 00 | | | |
| Less Mdse. Inventory, December 31, 19-- | 262 0 5 0 00 | | | |
| Cost of Merchandise Sold | | | 120 0 5 0 00 | 53.3 |
| **Gross Profit on Sales** | | | 105 3 5 0 00 | 46.7 |
| **Expenses:** | | | | |
| Advertising Expense | 5 2 0 0 00 | | | |
| Credit Card Fee Expense | 3 1 2 0 00 | | | |
| Insurance Expense | 1 0 5 0 00 | | | |
| Miscellaneous Expense | 2 3 9 0 00 | | | |
| Payroll Taxes Expense | 8 3 4 0 00 | | | |
| Rent Expense | 14 4 0 0 00 | | | |
| Salary Expense | 62 3 1 0 00 | | | |
| Supplies Expense—Office | 4 6 2 0 00 | | | |
| Supplies Expense—Store | 4 2 8 0 00 | | | |
| Utilities Expense | 3 4 1 0 00 | | | |
| Total Expenses | | | 109 1 2 0 00 | 48.4 |
| **Net Loss** | | | (3 7 7 0 00) | (1.67) |

Illustration 18-3
Income statement showing a net loss

maximum acceptable component percentage, 32.0%. (4) Because a net loss occurred, the component percentage for net income, (1.67%), means that Autoworks lost 1.67 cents on each sales dollar. The net loss amount, $3,770.00, is considered unacceptable.

## Actions to correct unacceptable component percentages

The goal of any business is to earn an acceptable net income. When component percentages are not acceptable, regardless of whether a net income or net loss occurred, management action is necessary.

**Unacceptable component percentage for gross profit on sales.** The component percentage for gross profit on sales is directly related to sales revenue and cost of merchandise sold. An unacceptable component percentage for gross profit on sales requires one of three actions. (1) Increase sales revenue. (2) Decrease cost of merchandise sold. (3) Increase sales revenue and also decrease cost of merchandise sold.

Increasing sales revenue while keeping the cost of merchandise sold the same will increase gross profit on sales. To increase sales revenue, management may consider increasing the markup on merchandise purchased for sale. However, a business must be cautious on the amount of the markup increase. If the increase in markup is too large, a decrease in sales revenue could occur for two reasons. (1) The sales price is beyond what customers are willing to pay. (2) The sales price is higher than what competing businesses charge for the same merchandise.

Decreasing the cost of merchandise sold while keeping the sales revenue the same will also increase gross profit on sales. To decrease cost of merchandise sold, management should review purchasing practices. For example, would purchasing merchandise in larger quantities or from other vendors result in a lower cost?

Combining a small increase in sales revenue and a small decrease in the cost of merchandise sold may also result in an acceptable component percentage for gross profit on sales.

**Unacceptable component percentage for total expenses.** Each expense account balance must be reviewed to determine if major increases have occurred. This review should include comparisons with prior fiscal periods as well as with industry standards. Actions must then be taken to reduce any expenses for which major increases have occurred or that are beyond industry standards.

**Unacceptable component percentage for net income.** If the component percentages for cost of merchandise sold, gross profit on sales, and total expenses are brought within acceptable ranges, net income will also be acceptable.

## DISTRIBUTION OF NET INCOME STATEMENT

A partnership's net income or net loss may be divided in any way agreed upon by the partners. Amy Kramer and Dario Mesa, partners in CarLand, agreed to share net income or net loss equally.

A partnership distribution of net income or net loss is usually shown on a separate financial statement. A partnership financial statement showing net income or loss distribution to partners is called a distribution of net income statement.

### Preparing a distribution of net income statement

The net income, $72,055.10, from the income statement shown in Illustration 18-2 is used to prepare the distribution of net income statement. CarLand's distribution of net income statement is shown in Illustration 18-4.

| CarLand | | | | | |
|---|---|---|---|---|---|
| Distribution of Net Income Statement | | | | | |
| For Year Ended December 31, 19-- | | | | | |
| Amy Kramer | | | | | |
| 50.0% of Net Income | 36 | 0 | 2 | 7 | 55 |
| Dario Mesa | | | | | |
| 50.0% of Net Income | 36 | 0 | 2 | 7 | 55 |
| Net Income | 72 | 0 | 5 | 5 | 10 |

Illustration 18-4
Distribution of net income
statement for a partnership

CarLand uses seven steps in preparing a distribution of net income statement.

1  Write the heading of the distribution of net income statement on three lines.

2  Write one partner's name, *Amy Kramer*, on the first line at the extreme left of the wide column.

3  Indent about one centimeter on the next line, and write Amy Kramer's share of net income as a percentage, *50.0% of Net Income*. Write Miss Kramer's share of net income, *$36,027.55* (50.0% × $72,055.10), in the amount column on the same line.

4  Write the other partner's name, *Dario Mesa*, on the next line at the extreme left of the wide column.

5  Indent about one centimeter on the next line, and write Dario Mesa's share of net income as a percentage, *50.0% of Net Income*. Write Mr. Mesa's share of net income, *$36,027.55* (50.0% × $72,055.10), in the amount column on the same line.

6  Write the words *Net Income* on the next line at the extreme left of the wide column. Add the distribution of net income for Amy Kramer, $36,027.55, and for Dario Mesa, $36,027.55. Write the total amount, *$72,055.10*, in the amount column. Verify accuracy by comparing the total amount, $72,055.10, with the net income reported on the income statement, $72,055.10. The two amounts must be the same.

7  Rule double lines across the amount column to show that the distribution of net income statement has been verified as correct.

## Distribution of net income statement with unequal distribution of earnings

Regardless of how earnings are shared, the steps in preparing a distribution of net income statement are the same. The only difference is the description of how the earnings are to be shared by the partners. A distribution of net income statement with unequal shares of earnings is shown in Illustration 18-5.

Illustration 18-5
Distribution of net income
statement with unequal
distribution of earnings

| Central Sporting Goods | | | | | |
|---|---|---|---|---|---|
| Distribution of Net Income Statement | | | | | |
| For Year Ended December 31, 19-- | | | | | |
| Dolores Demski | | | | | |
| 60.0% of Net Income | | | | 40 8 0 0 00 | |
| Linda Kemp | | | | | |
| 40.0% of Net Income | | | | 27 2 0 0 00 | |
| Net Income | | | | 68 0 0 0 00 | |

Dolores Demski and Linda Kemp are partners in a business. Because Mrs. Demski spends more time in the business than Ms. Kemp, the partners agree to share net income or loss unequally. Mrs. Demski gets 60.0% of net income or loss. Ms. Kemp gets 40.0% of net income or loss. With a net income of $68,000.00, Mrs. Demski receives 60.0%, or $40,800.00. Ms. Kemp receives 40.0%, or $27,200.00.

# OWNERS' EQUITY STATEMENT

The amount of net income earned is important to business owners. Owners are also interested in changes that occur in owners' equity during a fiscal period. A financial statement that summarizes the changes in owners' equity during a fiscal period is called an owners' equity statement. Business owners can review an owners' equity statement to determine if owners' equity is increasing or decreasing and what is causing the change. Three factors can change owners' equity. (1) Additional investments. (2) Withdrawals. (3) Net income or net loss.

## Preparing an owners' equity statement

An owners' equity statement shows information about changes during a fiscal period in each partner's capital. Information needed to prepare an owners' equity statement is obtained from the distribution of net income statement and the general ledger capital and drawing accounts. The distribution of net income statement shows each partner's share of net income or net loss. Three kinds of information are obtained from each partner's capital and drawing account. (1) Beginning capital amount. (2) Any additional investments made during the fiscal period. (3) Each partner's withdrawal of assets during the fiscal period.

The general ledger capital and drawing accounts of Amy Kramer and Dario Mesa, partners, are shown in Illustration 18-6.

Illustration 18-6
Partners' capital and
drawing accounts

ACCOUNT **Amy Kramer, Capital**                      ACCOUNT NO. **3110**

| DATE | | ITEM | POST. REF. | DEBIT | CREDIT | BALANCE DEBIT | BALANCE CREDIT |
|---|---|---|---|---|---|---|---|
| Jan. | 1 | Balance | √ | | | | 101 1 1 8 00 |

ACCOUNT **Amy Kramer, Drawing**                      ACCOUNT NO. **3120**

| DATE | | ITEM | POST. REF. | DEBIT | CREDIT | BALANCE DEBIT | BALANCE CREDIT |
|---|---|---|---|---|---|---|---|
| Dec. | 1 | Balance | √ | | | 16 7 0 0 00 | |
| | 15 | | 24 | 1 5 0 0 00 | | 18 2 0 0 00 | |

ACCOUNT **Dario Mesa, Capital**                      ACCOUNT NO. **3130**

| DATE | | ITEM | POST. REF. | DEBIT | CREDIT | BALANCE DEBIT | BALANCE CREDIT |
|---|---|---|---|---|---|---|---|
| Jan. | 1 | Balance | √ | | | | 101 2 2 8 00 |

ACCOUNT **Dario Mesa, Drawing**                      ACCOUNT NO. **3140**

| DATE | | ITEM | POST. REF. | DEBIT | CREDIT | BALANCE DEBIT | BALANCE CREDIT |
|---|---|---|---|---|---|---|---|
| Dec. | 1 | Balance | √ | | | 17 1 0 0 00 | |
| | 15 | | 24 | 1 5 0 0 00 | | 18 6 0 0 00 | |

Neither Amy Kramer nor Dario Mesa invested any additional capital during the year ended December 31. The beginning and ending capital balances, therefore, are the same as recorded in the accounts on January 1. Both partners withdrew cash and merchandise during the year ended December 31.

CarLand's owners' equity statement, prepared for the year ended December 31, is shown in Illustration 18-7.

| CarLand | | | | |
|---|---|---|---|---|
| Owners' Equity Statement | | | | |
| For Year Ended December 31, 19-- | | | | |
| Amy Kramer | | | | |
|    Capital, January 1, 19-- | | 101 1 1 8 00 | | |
|    Share of Net Income | 36 0 2 7 55 | | | |
|    Less Withdrawals | 18 2 0 0 00 | | | |
|    Net Increase in Capital | | 17 8 2 7 55 | | |
|    Capital, December 31, 19-- | | | 118 9 4 5 55 | |
| Dario Mesa | | | | |
|    Capital, January 1, 19-- | | 101 2 2 8 00 | | |
|    Share of Net Income | 36 0 2 7 55 | | | |
|    Less Withdrawals | 18 6 0 0 00 | | | |
|    Net Increase in Capital | | 17 4 2 7 55 | | |
|    Capital, December 31, 19-- | | | 118 6 5 5 55 | |
| Total Owners' Equity, December 31, 19-- | | | 237 6 0 1 10 | |

Illustration 18-7
Owners' equity statement

CarLand uses seven steps in preparing an owners' equity statement.

1 Write the heading of the owners' equity statement on three lines.

2 Write the name, *Amy Kramer*, on the first line at the extreme left of the wide column.

3 Figure the net increase in capital for Amy Kramer.

- Indent about one centimeter on the next line, and write the words *Capital, January 1, 19--*. Write the beginning capital amount, *$101,118.00*, in the second amount column on the same line. (This amount is obtained from Miss Kramer's capital account in the general ledger.)

- Indent about one centimeter on the next line, and write the words *Share of Net Income*. On the same line, write Miss Kramer's share of net income amount, *$36,027.55*, in the first amount column. (This amount is obtained from the distribution of net income statement.)

- Indent about one centimeter on the next line, and write the words *Less Withdrawals*. On the same line, write the withdrawals amount, *$18,200.00*, in the first amount column. (This amount is obtained from Miss Kramer's drawing account in the general ledger.)

- Indent about one centimeter on the next line, and write the words *Net Increase in Capital*. Write the net increase in capital amount,

*$17,827.55*, on the same line in the second amount column. (The share of net income, $36,027.55, *less* withdrawals, $18,200.00, *equals* the net increase in capital, $17,827.55.)

- Indent about one centimeter on the next line, and write the words *Capital, December 31, 19--*. Write the December 31 capital amount, *$118,945.55*, on the same line in the third amount column. (The January 1 capital, $101,118.00, *plus* the net increase in capital, $17,827.55, *equals* the December 31 capital, $118,945.55.)

4 Write the name, *Dario Mesa*, on the next line at the extreme left of the wide column.

5 Figure the net increase in capital for Dario Mesa.
- Indent about one centimeter on the next line, and write the words *Capital, January 1, 19--*. On the same line, write the beginning capital amount, *$101,228.00*, in the second amount column.
- Indent about one centimeter on the next line, and write the words *Share of Net Income*. On the same line, write Mr. Dario's share of net income amount, *$36,027.55*, in the first amount column.
- Indent about one centimeter on the next line, and write the words *Less Withdrawals*. On the same line, write the withdrawals amount, *$18,600.00*, in the first amount column.
- Indent about one centimeter on the next line, and write the words *Net Increase in Capital*. On the same line, write the difference, *$17,427.55*, in the second amount column.
- Indent about one centimeter on the next line, and write the words *Capital, December 31, 19--*. On the same line, write the December 31 capital amount, *$118,655.55*, in the third amount column.

6 Write the words *Total Owners' Equity, December 31, 19--* on the next line at the extreme left of the wide column. On the same line, write the total amount, *$237,601.10*, in the third amount column.

7 Rule double lines across the three amount columns to show that the totals have been verified as correct.

Some businesses include the owners' equity statement information as part of the balance sheet. An example of this method of reporting changes in owner's equity is shown in Illustration 8-13, Chapter 8.

## Owners' equity statement with an additional investment and a net loss

On December 31 the capital accounts of Kevin Blaine and David Lamont showed additional investments of $10,000.00 each. Also, the income statement, Illustration 18-3, showed a net loss of $3,770.00. The partners agreed to share net income or net loss equally. The owners' equity statement for Autoworks is shown in Illustration 18-8.

| Autoworks | | | | | |
|---|---|---|---|---|---|
| Owners' Equity Statement | | | | | |
| For Year Ended December 31, 19-- | | | | | |
| *Kevin Blaine* | | | | | |
| Capital, January 1, 19-- | 104 3 0 0 00 | | | | |
| Plus Additional Investment | 10 0 0 0 00 | | | | |
| Total | | 114 3 0 0 00 | | | |
| Share of Net Loss | 1 8 8 5 00 | | | | |
| Plus Withdrawals | 14 8 0 0 00 | | | | |
| Net Decrease in Capital | | 16 6 8 5 00 | | | |
| Capital, December 31, 19-- | | | 97 6 1 5 00 | | |
| *David Lamont* | | | | | |
| Capital, January 1, 19-- | 102 8 0 0 00 | | | | |
| Plus Additional Investment | 10 0 0 0 00 | | | | |
| Total | | 112 8 0 0 00 | | | |
| Share of Net Loss | 1 8 8 5 00 | | | | |
| Plus Withdrawals | 15 1 0 0 00 | | | | |
| Net Decrease in Capital | | 16 9 8 5 00 | | | |
| Capital, December 31, 19-- | | | 95 8 1 5 00 | | |
| Total Owners' Equity, December 31, 19-- | | | 193 4 3 0 00 | | |

Illustration 18-8
Owners' equity statement
showing an additional
investment and a net loss

# BALANCE SHEET

Some management decisions can best be made after owners have determined the amount of assets, liabilities, and owners' equity. Owners could obtain some of the information needed by inspecting general ledger accounts. The information needed might also be found on a work sheet. However, the information is easier to use when organized and reported on a balance sheet. A balance sheet reports a business' financial condition on a specific date. A balance sheet may be prepared in account form or report form. Rugcare, described in Chapter 8, uses the account form. Petlodge, described in Chapter 11, uses the report form. CarLand also uses the report form.

## Preparing a balance sheet

The information used to prepare a balance sheet is obtained from two sources. (1) The Balance Sheet columns of a work sheet, as shown in Illustration 18-9. (2) The owners' equity statement, as shown in Illustration 18-7.

| | | 1 | 2 | 3 | 4 | 5 | 6 | 7 | 8 | |
|---|---|---|---|---|---|---|---|---|---|---|
| | ACCOUNT TITLE | TRIAL BALANCE | | ADJUSTMENTS | | INCOME STATEMENT | | BALANCE SHEET | | |
| | | DEBIT | CREDIT | DEBIT | CREDIT | DEBIT | CREDIT | DEBIT | CREDIT | |
| 1 | Cash | 24 2 3 3 57 | | | | | | 24 2 3 3 57 | | 1 |
| 2 | Petty Cash | 5 0 0 00 | | | | | | 5 0 0 00 | | 2 |
| 3 | Accounts Receivable | 9 3 3 2 00 | | | | | | 9 3 3 2 00 | | 3 |
| 4 | Merchandise Inventory | 225 4 0 0 00 | | | (a) 13 2 0 0 00 | | | 212 2 0 0 00 | | 4 |
| 5 | Supplies—Office | 5 4 0 0 00 | | | (b) 3 9 4 0 00 | | | 1 4 6 0 00 | | 5 |
| 6 | Supplies—Store | 5 7 8 0 00 | | | (c) 3 2 6 0 00 | | | 2 5 2 0 00 | | 6 |
| 7 | Prepaid Insurance | 4 8 4 0 00 | | | (d) 2 6 4 0 00 | | | 2 2 0 0 00 | | 7 |
| 8 | Accounts Payable | | 10 4 5 1 90 | | | | | | 10 4 5 1 90 | 8 |
| 9 | Employee Income Tax Payable | | 4 0 2 00 | | | | | | 4 0 2 00 | 9 |
| 10 | FICA Tax Payable | | 8 3 2 16 | | | | | | 8 3 2 16 | 10 |
| 11 | Sales Tax Payable | | 1 7 6 0 00 | | | | | | 1 7 6 0 00 | 11 |
| 12 | Unemployment Tax Payable—Fed. | | 5 9 15 | | | | | | 5 9 15 | 12 |
| 13 | Unemployment Tax Payable—State | | 3 9 9 26 | | | | | | 3 9 9 26 | 13 |
| 14 | Health Insurance Premiums Pay. | | 8 4 0 00 | | | | | | 8 4 0 00 | 14 |
| 15 | U.S. Savings Bonds Payable | | 4 0 00 | | | | | | 4 0 00 | 15 |
| 16 | United Way Donations Payable | | 6 0 00 | | | | | | 6 0 00 | 16 |
| 17 | | | | | | | | | | 17 |

CarLand's completed balance sheet on December 31, the last day of the fiscal year, is shown in Illustration 18-10 on page 428.

Illustration 18-9
Balance sheet information on a work sheet

CarLand uses six steps in preparing a balance sheet.

**1** Write the balance sheet heading on three lines.

**2** Prepare the assets section of the balance sheet. Use information from the work sheet given in Illustration 18-9.

- Write the section title, *Assets*, on the first line in the middle of the wide column.

- Beginning on the next line, at the extreme left of the wide column, write the asset account titles in the order in which they appear on the work sheet. Write the balance of each asset account in the first amount column.

- Write the words *Total Assets* on the next line below the last asset account title. Total the individual asset amounts, and write the total assets, $252,445.57, on the same line in the second amount column.

**3** Prepare the liabilities section of the balance sheet. Use information from the work sheet given in Illustration 18-9.

- Write the section title, *Liabilities*, on the next line in the middle of the wide column.

| CarLand | | | | | | | | | | | | | | |
|---|---|---|---|---|---|---|---|---|---|---|---|---|---|---|
| **Balance Sheet** | | | | | | | | | | | | | | |
| **December 31, 19--** | | | | | | | | | | | | | | |
| *Assets* | | | | | | | | | | | | | | |
| Cash | 24 | 2 | 3 | 3 | 57 | | | | | | | | | |
| Petty Cash | | 5 | 0 | 0 | 00 | | | | | | | | | |
| Accounts Receivable | 9 | 3 | 3 | 2 | 00 | | | | | | | | | |
| Merchandise Inventory | 212 | 2 | 0 | 0 | 00 | | | | | | | | | |
| Supplies—Office | 1 | 4 | 6 | 0 | 00 | | | | | | | | | |
| Supplies—Store | 2 | 5 | 2 | 0 | 00 | | | | | | | | | |
| Prepaid Insurance | 2 | 2 | 0 | 0 | 00 | | | | | | | | | |
| Total Assets | | | | | | 252 | 4 | 4 | 5 | 57 | | | | | |
| *Liabilities* | | | | | | | | | | | | | | |
| Accounts Payable | 10 | 4 | 5 | 1 | 90 | | | | | | | | | |
| Employee Income Tax Payable | | 4 | 0 | 2 | 00 | | | | | | | | | |
| FICA Tax Payable | | 8 | 3 | 2 | 16 | | | | | | | | | |
| Sales Tax Payable | 1 | 7 | 6 | 0 | 00 | | | | | | | | | |
| Unemployment Tax Payable—Federal | | | 5 | 9 | 15 | | | | | | | | | |
| Unemployment Tax Payable—State | | 3 | 9 | 9 | 26 | | | | | | | | | |
| Health Insurance Premiums Payable | | 8 | 4 | 0 | 00 | | | | | | | | | |
| U.S. Savings Bonds Payable | | | 4 | 0 | 00 | | | | | | | | | |
| United Way Donations Payable | | | 6 | 0 | 00 | | | | | | | | | |
| Total Liabilities | | | | | | 14 | 8 | 4 | 4 | 47 | | | | | |
| *Owners' Equity* | | | | | | | | | | | | | | |
| Amy Kramer, Capital | 118 | 9 | 4 | 5 | 55 | | | | | | | | | |
| Dario Mesa, Capital | 118 | 6 | 5 | 5 | 55 | | | | | | | | | |
| Total Owners' Equity | | | | | | 237 | 6 | 0 | 1 | 10 | | | | | |
| Total Liabilities and Owners' Equity | | | | | | 252 | 4 | 4 | 5 | 57 | | | | | |

Illustration 18-10
Balance sheet for a
partnership

- Beginning on the next line, at the extreme left of the wide column, write the liability account titles in the order in which they appear on the work sheet. Write the balance of each liability account in the first amount column.

- Write the words *Total Liabilities* on the next line below the last liability account title. Total the individual liability amounts, and write the total liabilities, *$14,844.47*, on the same line in the second amount column.

4 Prepare the owners' equity section of the balance sheet. Use information from the owners' equity statement given in Illustration 18-7.

- Write the section title, *Owners' Equity,* on the next line in the middle of the wide column.

- Write the account title, Amy Kramer, Capital, on the next line at the extreme left of the wide column. On the same line, write the amount of Amy Kramer's current capital, *$118,945.55,* in the first amount column.

- Write the account title, Dario Mesa, Capital, on the next line at the extreme left of the wide column. On the same line, write the amount of Dario Mesa's current capital, *$118,655.55,* in the first amount column.

- Write the words *Total Owners' Equity* on the next line at the extreme left of the wide column. Add the two capital amounts, and write the total, *$237,601.10,* on the same line in the second amount column.

5 Total the liabilities and owners' equity sections of the balance sheet.

- Write the words *Total Liabilities and Owners' Equity* on the next line at the extreme left of the wide column. Total the liabilities and owners' equity, and write the total, *$252,445.57,* on the same line in the second amount column.

   Verify accuracy by comparing the total amount of assets and the total amount of liabilities and owners' equity. These two amounts must be the same. The two amounts, $252,445.57, are the same. The balance sheet is assumed to be correct.

6 Rule double lines across both amount columns below Total Assets and below Total Liabilities and Owners' Equity. These two sets of double lines show that the amounts have been verified as correct.

## Supporting schedules for a balance sheet

A report prepared to give details about an item on a principal financial statement is called a supporting schedule. A supporting schedule is sometimes known as a supplementary report or an exhibit.

CarLand prepares two supporting schedules to accompany the balance sheet. The supporting schedules are a schedule of accounts payable and a schedule of accounts receivable. A balance sheet shows only the accounts payable total amount. The account balance for each vendor is not shown. When detailed information is needed, a supporting schedule of accounts payable is prepared showing the balance for each vendor. A balance sheet also shows only the accounts receivable total amount. When information about the account balance for each customer is needed, a supporting schedule of accounts receivable is prepared. CarLand's supporting schedules on December 31 are similar to the supporting schedules for November 30 shown in Chapter 14.

# SUMMARY OF FINANCIAL STATEMENTS FOR A PARTNERSHIP

The chart shown in Illustration 18-11 summarizes the financial statements for a partnership.

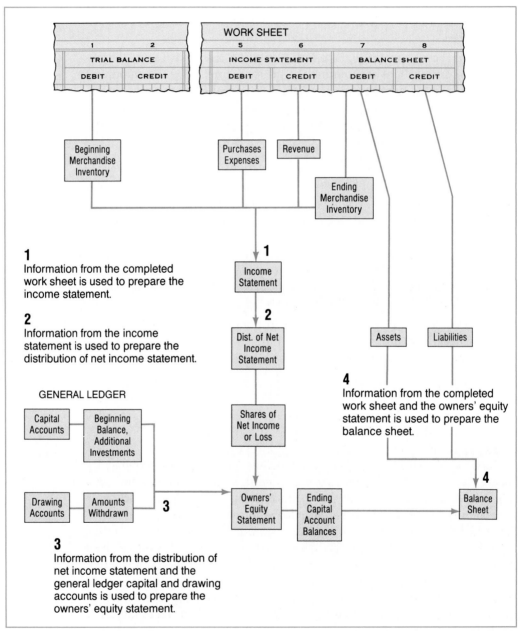

Illustration 18-11      Summary of financial statements for a partnership

# ACCOUNTING TERMS

What is the meaning of each of the following?

1. cost of merchandise sold
2. gross profit on sales
3. distribution of net income statement
4. owners' equity statement
5. supporting schedule

# QUESTIONS FOR INDIVIDUAL STUDY

1. Why is a work sheet prepared at the end of a fiscal period?
2. What is the primary source of information needed by owners and managers to make decisions on future activities of a business?
3. Which accounting concept is being applied when financial statements contain all information necessary for a reader to understand a business' financial condition and progress?
4. Which accounting concept is being applied when accounting principles are applied the same way in preparing financial statements from one fiscal period to the next?
5. Which financial statement reports the financial progress of a business?
6. How may income statements be used to determine reasons for increases or decreases in net income?
7. Where does a business find the information needed to prepare an income statement?
8. What are the three main sections of an income statement for a merchandising business?
9. How is the cost of merchandise sold calculated?
10. How is the gross profit on sales calculated?
11. How is net income calculated?
12. What four component percentages does CarLand calculate to analyze its income statement?
13. How does a business determine acceptable component percentages?
14. How is net loss calculated?
15. What are two reasons why an increase in markup could result in a decrease in sales revenue?
16. Why does a partnership prepare a distribution of net income statement?
17. Why do businesses prepare an owners' equity statement?
18. What three factors can cause changes in owners' equity to occur?
19. Where does a business find the information needed to prepare an owners' equity statement?
20. Which financial statement reports the financial condition of a business?

# CASES FOR MANAGEMENT DECISION

**CASE 1** Jun Mori and Victoria Leben, partners, compared their current income statement with their income statement of a year ago. They noted that sales were 15.0% higher than a year ago. They also noted that the total expenses were 20.0% higher than a year ago. What type of analysis should be done to determine whether the increase in expenses is justified?

**CASE 2** Rhoda Chalupa and Jonathan Fulton are partners in a paint and decorating store. The store operates on a yearly fiscal period. At the end of each year, an accountant is hired to prepare financial statements. At the end of each month during the year, Mrs. Chalupa prepares a work sheet. The work sheet is prepared to determine if the business made or lost money that month. The accountant suggests that monthly financial statements also be prepared. Mrs. Chalupa believes, however, that the monthly work sheet is sufficient to determine how the business is doing. Do you agree with Mrs. Chalupa or the accountant? Why?

## ■ DRILLS FOR UNDERSTANDING

### DRILL 18-D1   Figuring the cost of merchandise sold

The work sheets of three businesses show the following information.

| Business | Account Title | Trial Balance Debit | Income Statement Debit | Balance Sheet Debit |
|---|---|---|---|---|
| A | Merchandise inventory . . .<br>Purchases . . . . . . . . . . . . . | $118,000.00 | $23,800.00 | $124,000.00 |
| B | Merchandise inventory . . .<br>Purchases . . . . . . . . . . . . . | $174,000.00 | $38,200.00 | $192,000.00 |
| C | Merchandise inventory . . .<br>Purchases . . . . . . . . . . . . . | $152,000.00 | $29,400.00 | $144,000.00 |

**Instructions:** Figure the cost of merchandise sold for each business.

### DRILL 18-D2   Figuring net income or loss

The work sheets of three businesses show the following information.

| Business | Account Title | Trial Balance Debit | Income Statement Debit | Income Statement Credit | Balance Sheet Debit |
|---|---|---|---|---|---|
| A | Merchandise Inventory . .<br>Sales. . . . . . . . . . . . . . . .<br>Purchases . . . . . . . . . . . .<br>Total Expenses. . . . . . . . | $225,000.00 | $64,600.00<br>42,300.00 | $162,400.00 | $214,000.00 |
| B | Merchandise Inventory . .<br>Sales. . . . . . . . . . . . . . . .<br>Purchases . . . . . . . . . . . .<br>Total Expenses. . . . . . . . | $186,400.00 | $82,000.00<br>53,800.00 | $122,000.00 | $198,000.00 |
| C | Merchandise Inventory . .<br>Sales. . . . . . . . . . . . . . . .<br>Purchases . . . . . . . . . . . .<br>Total Expenses. . . . . . . . | $210,000.00 | $58,800.00<br>29,600.00 | $135,400.00 | $202,600.00 |

**Instructions:** Figure the net income or loss for each business.

### DRILL 18-D3   Figuring component percentages

The income statements of three businesses show the following information.

| Business | Component | Amount |
|----------|-----------|--------|
| A | Sales<br>Cost of Merchandise Sold<br>Gross Profit on Sales<br>Total Expenses<br>Net Income | $186,000.00<br>91,000.00<br>95,000.00<br>41,000.00<br>54,000.00 |
| B | Sales<br>Cost of Merchandise Sold<br>Gross Profit on Sales<br>Total Expenses<br>Net Income | $164,000.00<br>78,000.00<br>86,000.00<br>48,000.00<br>38,000.00 |
| C | Sales<br>Cost of Merchandise Sold<br>Gross Profit on Sales<br>Total Expenses<br>Net Income | $226,000.00<br>121,000.00<br>105,000.00<br>68,000.00<br>37,000.00 |

**Instructions:** Figure component percentages for cost of merchandise sold, gross profit on sales, total expenses, and net income for each business. Round percentage calculations to the nearest 0.1%.

DRILL 18-D4   **Figuring the distribution of net income or loss**

The following information concerns net income or loss distribution for three businesses.

| Business | Partner | Agreement on Sharing Income or Loss |
|----------|---------|--------------------------------------|
| A | 1<br>2 | 50.0% of income or loss<br>50.0% of income or loss |
| B | 1<br>2 | 40.0% of income or loss<br>60.0% of income or loss |
| C | 1<br>2<br>3 | 25.0% of income or loss<br>30.0% of income or loss<br>45.0% of income or loss |

**Instructions: 1.** Assume that each business earned a net income of $64,000.00. What is the amount of income to be distributed to each partner in each business?

**2.** Assume that each business had a net loss of $8,000.00. What is the amount of loss to be distributed to each partner in each business?

 APPLICATION PROBLEMS

PROBLEM 18-1   **Preparing financial statements**

The work sheet for Midwest Supply for the year ended December 31 of the current year is provided in the working papers accompanying this textbook.

**Instructions: 1.** Prepare an income statement. Figure and record the following component percentages: (a) cost of merchandise sold, (b) gross profit on sales, (c) total expenses, and (d) net income or loss. Round percentage calculations to the nearest 0.1%.

    **2.** Prepare a distribution of net income statement. Net income or loss is to be shared equally.

    **3.** Prepare an owners' equity statement. No additional investments were made.

    **4.** Prepare a balance sheet in report form.

PROBLEM 18-2  **Preparing a distribution of net income statement and an owners' equity statement (net income)**

Louise Cova and Diane Landon are partners in a merchandising business. The following information was taken from the records on December 31 of the current year.

| Partner | Balance of Capital Account January 1 | Balance of Drawing Account | Distribution of Net Income |
|---------|-----------|-----------|-----------|
| Cova | $138,000.00 | $15,260.00 | 60.0% |
| Landon | $124,000.00 | $16,340.00 | 40.0% |

**Instructions: 1.** On December 31 the partnership had a net income of $72,400.00. Prepare a distribution of net income statement for the partnership of C.L. Sales.

    **2.** Prepare an owners' equity statement. No additional investments were made.

PROBLEM 18-3  **Preparing an owners' equity statement (net loss)**

Paul Chapman and Lawrence Jaffa are partners in a merchandising business. The following information was taken from the records on December 31 of the current year.

| Partner | Balance of Capital Account January 1 | Balance of Drawing Account | Distribution of Net Loss |
|---------|-----------|-----------|-----------|
| Chapman | $113,000.00 | $12,680.00 | $3,400.00 |
| Jaffa | $107,000.00 | $13,540.00 | $3,400.00 |

**Instructions:** Prepare an owners' equity statement for Riverside Supply. Additional investments made during the year: Paul Chapman, $11,000.00; Lawrence Jaffa, $9,000.00.

# ENRICHMENT PROBLEMS

MASTERY PROBLEM 18-M  **Preparing financial statements**

Gallery Furniture prepared the following work sheet for the year ended December 31 of the current year.

**Instructions: 1.** Prepare an income statement. Figure and record the following component percentages: (a) cost of merchandise sold, (b) gross profit on sales, (c) total expenses, and (d) net income or loss. Round percentage calculations to the nearest 0.1%.

    **2.** Prepare a distribution of net income statement. Net income or loss is to be shared equally.

    **3.** Prepare an owners' equity statement. No additional investments were made.

    **4.** Prepare a balance sheet in report form.

Gallery Furniture

Work Sheet

For Year Ended December 31, 19--

| | | | 1 | 2 | 3 | 4 | 5 | 6 | 7 | 8 | |
|---|---|---|---|---|---|---|---|---|---|---|---|
| | ACCOUNT TITLE | | TRIAL BALANCE | | ADJUSTMENTS | | INCOME STATEMENT | | BALANCE SHEET | | |
| | | | DEBIT | CREDIT | DEBIT | CREDIT | DEBIT | CREDIT | DEBIT | CREDIT | |
| 1 | Cash | | 28 7 9 2 00 | | | | | | 28 7 9 2 00 | | 1 |
| 2 | Petty Cash | | 5 0 0 00 | | | | | | 5 0 0 00 | | 2 |
| 3 | Accounts Receivable | | 12 8 3 5 00 | | | | | | 12 8 3 5 00 | | 3 |
| 4 | Merchandise Inventory | | 290 6 0 0 00 | | | (a)14 5 1 0 00 | | | 276 0 9 0 00 | | 4 |
| 5 | Supplies—Office | | 5 3 7 5 00 | | | (b)3 3 6 0 00 | | | 2 0 1 5 00 | | 5 |
| 6 | Supplies—Store | | 5 8 4 0 00 | | | (c)3 7 2 0 00 | | | 2 1 2 0 00 | | 6 |
| 7 | Prepaid Insurance | | 5 1 4 5 00 | | | (d)2 9 4 0 00 | | | 2 2 0 5 00 | | 7 |
| 8 | Accounts Payable | | | 9 1 3 0 00 | | | | | | 9 1 3 0 00 | 8 |
| 9 | Sales Tax Payable | | | 1 0 7 2 00 | | | | | | 1 0 7 2 00 | 9 |
| 10 | Jennifer Faust, Capital | | | 142 9 6 0 00 | | | | | | 142 9 6 0 00 | 10 |
| 11 | Jennifer Faust, Drawing | | 18 9 1 0 00 | | | | | | 18 9 1 0 00 | | 11 |
| 12 | David Mason, Capital | | | 137 4 5 0 00 | | | | | | 137 4 5 0 00 | 12 |
| 13 | David Mason, Drawing | | 18 3 6 0 00 | | | | | | 18 3 6 0 00 | | 13 |
| 14 | Income Summary | | | | (a)14 5 1 0 00 | | 14 5 1 0 00 | | | | 14 |
| 15 | Sales | | | 257 3 0 0 00 | | | | 257 3 0 0 00 | | | 15 |
| 16 | Purchases | | 129 2 8 0 00 | | | | 129 2 8 0 00 | | | | 16 |
| 17 | Advertising Expense | | 5 5 8 5 00 | | | | 5 5 8 5 00 | | | | 17 |
| 18 | Credit Card Fee Expense | | 2 3 6 0 00 | | | | 2 3 6 0 00 | | | | 18 |
| 19 | Insurance Expense | | | | (d)2 9 4 0 00 | | 2 9 4 0 00 | | | | 19 |
| 20 | Miscellaneous Expense | | 2 6 4 0 00 | | | | 2 6 4 0 00 | | | | 20 |
| 21 | Rent Expense | | 19 2 0 0 00 | | | | 19 2 0 0 00 | | | | 21 |
| 22 | Supplies Expense—Office | | | | (b)3 3 6 0 00 | | 3 3 6 0 00 | | | | 22 |
| 23 | Supplies Expense—Store | | | | (c)3 7 2 0 00 | | 3 7 2 0 00 | | | | 23 |
| 24 | Utilities Expense | | 2 4 9 0 00 | | | | 2 4 9 0 00 | | | | 24 |
| 25 | | | 547 9 1 2 00 | 547 9 1 2 00 | 24 5 3 0 00 | 24 5 3 0 00 | 186 0 8 5 00 | 257 3 0 0 00 | 361 8 2 7 00 | 290 6 1 2 00 | 25 |
| 26 | Net Income | | | | | | 71 2 1 5 00 | | | 71 2 1 5 00 | 26 |
| 27 | | | | | | | 257 3 0 0 00 | 257 3 0 0 00 | 361 8 2 7 00 | 361 8 2 7 00 | 27 |
| 28 | | | | | | | | | | | 28 |

CHALLENGE PROBLEM 18-C **Preparing financial statements (unequal distribution of net income; additional investment)**

*Gallery Furniture's work sheet is shown in Mastery Problem 18-M.*

**Instructions: 1.** Prepare a distribution of net income statement. The net income is to be shared as follows: Jennifer Faust, 75.0%; David Mason, 25.0%.

**2.** Prepare an owners' equity statement. Mr. Mason made an additional investment of $15,000.00 during the year. He had a beginning capital of $122,450.00.

# Recording Adjusting and Closing Entries for a Partnership

ENABLING PERFORMANCE TASKS

After studying Chapter 19, you will be able to:
a. Identify accounting concepts and practices related to adjusting and closing entries for a merchandising business organized as a partnership.
b. Record adjusting entries for a merchandising business organized as a partnership.
c. Record closing entries for a merchandising business organized as a partnership.
d. Prepare a post-closing trial balance for a merchandising business organized as a partnership.

General ledger account balances are changed only by posting journal entries. Two types of journal entries change general ledger account balances at the end of a fiscal period. (1) Adjusting entries bring general ledger account balances up to date. (2) Closing entries prepare temporary accounts for the next fiscal period. *(CONCEPT: Matching Expenses with Revenue)* Information needed for journalizing adjusting entries is taken from the Adjustments columns of a work sheet. Information needed for journalizing closing entries is taken from the Income Statement and Balance Sheet columns of a work sheet and a distribution of net income statement.

## RECORDING ADJUSTING ENTRIES

Four adjustments in the partial work sheet's Adjustments columns are shown in Illustration 19-1.

| | ACCOUNT TITLE | TRIAL BALANCE | | ADJUSTMENTS | |
|---|---|---|---|---|---|
| | | **1** DEBIT | **2** CREDIT | **3** DEBIT | **4** CREDIT |
| 4 | *Merchandise Inventory* | 225 4 0 0 00 | | | (a)13 2 0 0 00 |
| 5 | *Supplies—Office* | 5 4 0 0 00 | | | (b) 3 9 4 0 00 |
| 6 | *Supplies—Store* | 5 7 8 0 00 | | | (c) 3 2 6 0 00 |
| 7 | *Prepaid Insurance* | 4 8 4 0 00 | | | (d) 2 6 4 0 00 |
| 21 | *Income Summary* | | | (a)13 2 0 0 00 | |
| 26 | *Insurance Expense* | | | (d) 2 6 4 0 00 | |
| 31 | *Supplies Expense—Office* | | | (b) 3 9 4 0 00 | |
| 32 | *Supplies Expense—Store* | | | (c) 3 2 6 0 00 | |
| 33 | | | | | |

Adjusting entries are recorded on the next journal page following the page on which the last daily transaction for the month is recorded. The adjusting entries are entered in the General Debit and Credit columns of a journal. CarLand's four adjusting entries are recorded in a journal as shown in Illustration 19-2.

*Illustration 19-1*
*Partial work sheet showing adjustments*

PAGE 26

### JOURNAL

| | DATE | | ACCOUNT TITLE | DOC. NO. | POST. REF. | GENERAL DEBIT | GENERAL CREDIT | ACCOUNTS RECEIVABLE DEBIT | ACCOUNTS RECEIVABLE CREDIT | |
|---|---|---|---|---|---|---|---|---|---|---|
| 1 | | | *Adjusting Entries* | | | | | | | 1 |
| 2 | 19-- Dec. | 31 | *Income Summary* | | | 13 2 0 0 00 | | | | 2 |
| 3 | | | *Merchandise Inventory* | | | | 13 2 0 0 00 | | | 3 |
| 4 | | 31 | *Supplies Expense—Office* | | | 3 9 4 0 00 | | | | 4 |
| 5 | | | *Supplies—Office* | | | | 3 9 4 0 00 | | | 5 |
| 6 | | 31 | *Supplies Expense—Store* | | | 3 2 6 0 00 | | | | 6 |
| 7 | | | *Supplies—Store* | | | | 3 2 6 0 00 | | | 7 |
| 8 | | 31 | *Insurance Expense* | | | 2 6 4 0 00 | | | | 8 |
| 9 | | | *Prepaid Insurance* | | | | 2 6 4 0 00 | | | 9 |

The heading, *Adjusting Entries,* is written in the middle of the journal's Account Title column. This heading explains all of the adjusting entries that follow. Therefore, indicating a source document is unnecessary. The first adjusting entry is recorded on the first two lines below the heading.

*Illustration 19-2*
*Adjusting entries recorded in a journal*

## Adjusting entry for merchandise inventory

The debit and credit parts of the merchandise inventory adjustment are identified on the work sheet by the letter (a), Illustration 19-1. The merchandise inventory adjustment includes a debit to Income Summary and a credit to Merchandise Inventory of $13,200.00.

CarLand's adjusting entry for merchandise inventory is shown on lines 2 and 3 of the journal, Illustration 19-2.

The effect of posting the adjusting entry for merchandise inventory is shown in the T accounts.

| Income Summary | |
|---|---|
| Adj. (a)  13,200.00 | |

| Merchandise Inventory | |
|---|---|
| Bal.         225,400.00 | Adj. (a)        13,200.00 |
| (New Bal.    212,200.00) | |

## Adjusting entry for office supplies inventory

The debit and credit parts of the office supplies adjustment are identified on the work sheet by the letter (b), Illustration 19-1. The office supplies inventory adjustment includes a debit to Supplies Expense—Office and a credit to Supplies—Office of $3,940.00.

CarLand's adjusting entry for office supplies inventory is shown on lines 4 and 5 of the journal, Illustration 19-2.

The effect of posting the adjusting entry for office supplies inventory is shown in the T accounts.

| Supplies Expense—Office | |
|---|---|
| Adj. (b)   3,940.00 | |

| Supplies—Office | |
|---|---|
| Bal.        5,400.00 | Adj. (b)        3,940.00 |
| (New Bal.   1,460.00) | |

## Adjusting entry for store supplies inventory

The debit and credit parts of the store supplies adjustment are identified on the work sheet by the letter (c), Illustration 19-1. The store supplies inventory adjustment includes a debit to Supplies Expense—Store and a credit to Supplies—Store of $3,260.00.

CarLand's adjusting entry for store supplies inventory is shown on lines 6 and 7 of the journal, Illustration 19-2.

The effect of posting the adjusting entry for store supplies inventory is shown in the T accounts.

| Supplies Expense—Store | |
|---|---|
| Adj. (c)   3,260.00 | |

| Supplies—Store | |
|---|---|
| Bal.        5,780.00 | Adj. (c)        3,260.00 |
| (New Bal.   2,520.00) | |

## Adjusting entry for prepaid insurance

The debit and credit parts of the prepaid insurance adjustment are identified on the work sheet by the letter (d), Illustration 19-1. The prepaid insurance adjustment includes a debit to Insurance Expense and a credit to Prepaid Insurance of $2,640.00.

CarLand's adjusting entry for prepaid insurance is shown on lines 8 and 9 of the journal, Illustration 19-2.

The effect of posting the adjusting entry for prepaid insurance is shown in the T accounts.

| Insurance Expense | |
|---|---|
| Adj. (d)   2,640.00 | |

| Prepaid Insurance | |
|---|---|
| Bal.        4,840.00 | Adj. (d)        2,640.00 |
| (New Bal.   2,200.00) | |

# SUMMARY OF ADJUSTING ENTRIES FOR A MERCHANDISING BUSINESS ORGANIZED AS A PARTNERSHIP

The four adjusting entries for a merchandising business organized as a partnership are summarized in Illustration 19-3.

| ADJUSTING ENTRY | JOURNAL | | |
|---|---|---|---|
| | ACCOUNT TITLE | GENERAL | |
| | | DEBIT | CREDIT |
| 1. Adjust merchandise inventory (increase in inventory) | Merchandise Inventory<br>Income Summary | X | X |
| (decrease in inventory) | Income Summary<br>Merchandise Inventory | X | X |
| 2. Adjust office supplies inventory | Supplies Expense—Office<br>Supplies—Office | X | X |
| 3. Adjust store supplies inventory | Supplies Expense—Store<br>Supplies—Store | X | X |
| 4. Adjust prepaid insurance | Insurance Expense<br>Prepaid Insurance | X | X |

Illustration 19-3
Summary of adjusting entries for a merchandising business organized as a partnership

# RECORDING CLOSING ENTRIES

At the end of a fiscal period, the temporary accounts are closed to prepare the general ledger for the next fiscal period. *(CONCEPT: Matching Expenses with Revenue)* To close a temporary account, an amount equal to its balance is recorded on the side opposite the balance. CarLand records four kinds of closing entries.

1 An entry to close income statement accounts with credit balances.
2 An entry to close income statement accounts with debit balances.
3 An entry to record net income or loss and close the income summary account.
4 Entries to close the partners' drawing accounts.

## The income summary account

A temporary account is used to summarize the closing entries for revenue, cost, and expenses. The account is titled *Income Summary* because it is used to summarize information about net income. Income Summary is used only at the end of a fiscal period to help prepare other accounts for a new fiscal period. The income summary account is a unique account because it does not have a normal balance side.

Amounts needed for the closing entries are obtained from the Income Statement and Balance Sheet columns of the work sheet and from the distribution of net income statement.

Closing entries are entered in the General Debit and Credit columns of a journal. The heading, *Closing Entries*, is written in the middle of the journal's Account Title column on the next line following the last adjusting entry. This heading explains all of the closing entries that follow. Therefore, indicating a source document is unnecessary. The first closing entry is recorded on the first two lines below the heading.

## Closing entry for an income statement account with a credit balance

CarLand's work sheet has one income statement account with a credit balance, Sales, as shown in Illustration 19-4. This revenue account has a normal credit balance at the end of a fiscal period. This credit balance must be reduced to zero to prepare the account for the next fiscal period. *(CONCEPT: Matching Expenses with Revenue)* The closing entry for Sales is journalized as shown in Illustration 19-4.

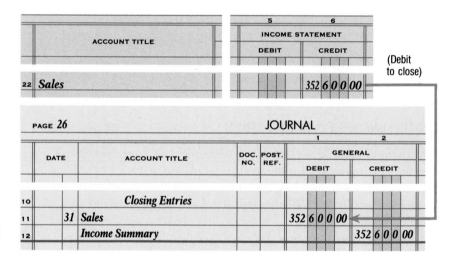

Illustration 19-4
Closing entry for an income statement account with a credit balance

To reduce the balance to zero, Sales is debited for the amount of the balance, $352,600.00. Income Summary is credited for $352,600.00 so that debits equal credits in this entry.

The effect of this closing entry on the general ledger accounts is shown in the T accounts.

|  | Sales |  |  |
| --- | --- | --- | --- |
| Closing | 352,600.00 | Bal. | 352,600.00 |
|  |  | (New Bal. zero) |  |

|  | Income Summary |  |  |
| --- | --- | --- | --- |
| Adj. (mdse. inv.) | 13,200.00 | Closing (revenue) | 352,600.00 |

The balance of Sales is now zero, and the account is ready for the next fiscal period.

## Closing entry for income statement accounts with debit balances

CarLand's work sheet has eleven income statement accounts with debit balances, as shown in Illustration 19-5. These eleven accounts are the cost account, Purchases, and the ten expense accounts. The cost and expense accounts have normal debit balances at the end of a fiscal period. These debit balances must be reduced to zero to prepare the accounts for the next

| | | | 5 | 6 |
|---|---|---|---|---|
| | ACCOUNT TITLE | | INCOME STATEMENT | |
| | | | DEBIT | CREDIT |
| 21 | Income Summary | | 13 2 0 0 00 | |
| 22 | Sales | | | 352 6 0 0 00 |
| 23 | Purchases | | 158 3 0 0 00 | |
| 24 | Advertising Expense | | 5 5 0 0 00 | |
| 25 | Credit Card Fee Expense | | 2 8 9 0 00 | |
| 26 | Insurance Expense | | 2 6 4 0 00 | |
| 27 | Miscellaneous Expense | | 2 1 8 2 15 | |
| 28 | Payroll Taxes Expense | | 7 2 9 9 75 | |
| 29 | Rent Expense | | 18 0 0 0 00 | |
| 30 | Salary Expense | | 60 1 5 3 00 | |
| 31 | Supplies Expense—Office | | 3 9 4 0 00 | |
| 32 | Supplies Expense—Store | | 3 2 6 0 00 | |
| 33 | Utilities Expense | | 3 1 8 0 00 | |

(Credit to close)

PAGE 26    JOURNAL

| | DATE | ACCOUNT TITLE | DOC. NO. | POST. REF. | GENERAL DEBIT | GENERAL CREDIT |
|---|---|---|---|---|---|---|
| 13 | 31 | Income Summary | | | 267 3 4 4 90 | |
| 14 | | Purchases | | | | 158 3 0 0 00 |
| 15 | | Advertising Expense | | | | 5 5 0 0 00 |
| 16 | | Credit Card Fee Expense | | | | 2 8 9 0 00 |
| 17 | | Insurance Expense | | | | 2 6 4 0 00 |
| 18 | | Miscellaneous Expense | | | | 2 1 8 2 15 |
| 19 | | Payroll Taxes Expense | | | | 7 2 9 9 75 |
| 20 | | Rent Expense | | | | 18 0 0 0 00 |
| 21 | | Salary Expense | | | | 60 1 5 3 00 |
| 22 | | Supplies Expense—Office | | | | 3 9 4 0 00 |
| 23 | | Supplies Expense—Store | | | | 3 2 6 0 00 |
| 24 | | Utilities Expense | | | | 3 1 8 0 00 |

Illustration 19-5
Closing entry for income statement accounts with debit balances

fiscal period. *(CONCEPT: Matching Expenses with Revenue)* To reduce the balances to zero, the cost and expense accounts are credited for the amount of their balances. The account used for the debit of this closing entry is Income Summary. The closing entry for the cost and expense accounts is journalized as shown in Illustration 19-5.

The income summary amount shown on the work sheet, $13,200.00, is the amount of the adjustment for merchandise inventory. Income Summary is used to summarize the amounts that contribute to net income. The adjustment for merchandise inventory contributes to net income. However, Income Summary is not closed as part of this closing entry. Instead, the account is closed with the third closing entry when net income is recorded.

The debit to Income Summary is not entered in the amount column until all cost and expense balances have been journalized and the total amount calculated. The account title and balance of each cost and expense account is written in the Account Title and General Credit columns. After all cost and expense accounts and their balances have been written in the journal, add the credit amounts for this entry. Write the total of the cost and expense accounts, *$267,344.90,* in the General Debit column on the same line as the account title Income Summary.

The effect of this closing entry on the general ledger accounts is shown in the T accounts.

### Income Summary

| Adj. (mdse. inv.)<br>Closing (cost and<br>expenses) | 13,200.00<br><br>267,344.90 | Closing (revenue)<br>*(New Bal.* | 352,600.00<br>*72,055.10)* |
|---|---|---|---|

| Purchases | | Rent Expense | |
|---|---|---|---|
| Bal. 158,300.00 *(New Bal. zero)* | Closing 158,300.00 | Bal. 18,000.00 *(New Bal. zero)* | Closing 18,000.00 |

| Advertising Expense | | Salary Expense | |
|---|---|---|---|
| Bal. 5,500.00 *(New Bal. zero)* | Closing 5,500.00 | Bal. 60,153.00 *(New Bal. zero)* | Closing 60,153.00 |

| Credit Card Fee Expense | | Supplies Expense—Office | |
|---|---|---|---|
| Bal. 2,890.00 *(New Bal. zero)* | Closing 2,890.00 | Bal. 3,940.00 *(New Bal. zero)* | Closing 3,940.00 |

| Insurance Expense | | Supplies Expense—Store | |
|---|---|---|---|
| Bal. 2,640.00 *(New Bal. zero)* | Closing 2,640.00 | Bal. 3,260.00 *(New Bal. zero)* | Closing 3,260.00 |

| Miscellaneous Expense | | Utilities Expense | |
|---|---|---|---|
| Bal. 2,182.15 *(New Bal. zero)* | Closing 2,182.15 | Bal. 3,180.00 *(New Bal. zero)* | Closing 3,180.00 |

| Payroll Taxes Expense | |
|---|---|
| Bal. 7,299.75 *(New Bal. zero)* | Closing 7,299.75 |

The cost account, Purchases, and the expense accounts are now closed and have zero balances. Income Summary has three amounts. (1) A debit of $13,200.00, the amount of the merchandise inventory adjustment. (2) A credit of $352,600.00, the amount of the entry to close the revenue account. (3) A debit of $267,344.90, the total amount of the entry to close the cost and expense accounts. The balance of Income Summary is the net income for the fiscal period, $72,055.10.

## Closing entry to record net income or loss and close the income summary account

Net income increases the partners' equity and, therefore, must be credited to the partners' capital accounts. The share of the net income to be recorded for each partner is shown on the distribution of net income statement. The balance of the temporary account Income Summary must be reduced to zero to prepare the account for the next fiscal period. The distribution of net income statement and the closing entry to record net income and close Income Summary are shown in Illustration 19-6.

Illustration 19-6
Closing entry to record net income and close the income summary account

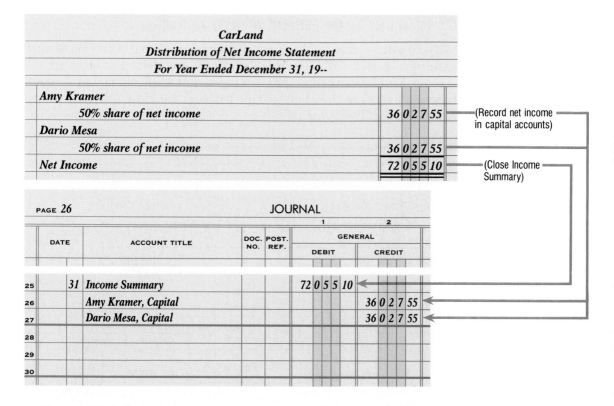

The effect of this closing entry on the general ledger accounts is shown in the T accounts.

### Income Summary

| | | | |
|---|---|---|---|
| Adj. (mdse. inv.) | 13,200.00 | Closing (revenue) | 352,600.00 |
| Closing (cost and | | | |
| expenses | 267,344.90 | | |
| Closing (net income) | 72,055.10 | *(New Bal. zero)* | |

### Amy Kramer, Capital

| | | | |
|---|---|---|---|
| | | Bal. | 101,118.00 |
| | | Closing (net income) | 36,027.55 |

### Dario Mesa, Capital

| | | | |
|---|---|---|---|
| | | Bal. | 101,228.00 |
| | | Closing (net income) | 36,027.55 |

The credits to the two partners' capital accounts, $36,027.55, record the partners' share of the net income. The debit to the income summary account, $72,055.10, reduces the account balance to zero and prepares the account for the next fiscal period.

If the business has a net loss, the partners' capital accounts are debited for their share of the net loss. Income Summary is credited for the total net loss.

## Closing entries for the partners' drawing accounts

The partners' drawing accounts are temporary accounts and must begin each fiscal period with zero balances. Because withdrawals are neither a revenue, cost, nor expense, the drawing accounts are not closed through Income Summary. The drawing account balances are closed directly to the partners' capital accounts.

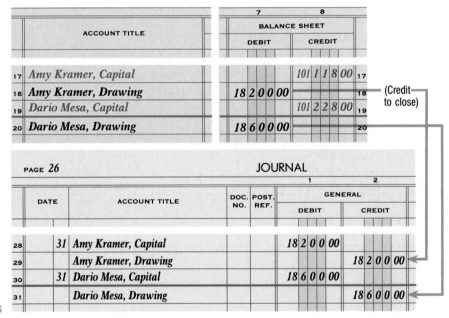

Illustration 19-7
Closing entries for the
partners' drawing accounts

A partial work sheet and the closing entries for the partners' drawing accounts are shown in Illustration 19-7. The closing entry is on lines 28-31 of the journal.

The credits to Amy Kramer, Drawing and Dario Mesa, Drawing reduce the account balances to zero. The accounts are prepared for the next fiscal period. The debits to Amy Kramer, Capital and Dario Mesa, Capital reduce the balances of these accounts by the amount of the partners' withdrawals during the fiscal period.

The effect of these closing entries on the general ledger accounts is shown in the T accounts.

### Amy Kramer, Capital

| Closing (drawing) | 18,200.00 | Bal. | 101,118.00 |
| | | Closing (net income) | 36,027.55 |
| | | *(New Bal.* | *118,945.55)* |

### Amy Kramer, Drawing

| Bal. | 18,200.00 | Closing | 18,200.00 |
| *(New Bal. zero)* | | | |

### Dario Mesa, Capital

| Closing (drawing) | 18,600.00 | Bal. | 101,228.00 |
| | | Closing (net income) | 36,027.55 |
| | | *(New Bal.* | *118,655.55)* |

### Dario Mesa, Drawing

| Bal. | 18,600.00 | Closing | 18,600.00 |
| *(New Bal. zero)* | | | |

After the closing entry for the partners' drawing accounts, the balances of the partners' capital accounts are the same as reported in the owners' equity section of the balance sheet, Illustration 19-8.

| *CarLand* | | | | | | | | | | | |
|---|---|---|---|---|---|---|---|---|---|---|---|
| *Balance Sheet* | | | | | | | | | | | |
| *December 31, 19--* | | | | | | | | | | | |
| | | | | | | | | | | | |
| *Owners' Equity* | | | | | | | | | | | |
| *Amy Kramer, Capital* | 118 | 9 | 4 | 5 | 55 | | | | | | |
| *Dario Mesa, Capital* | 118 | 6 | 5 | 5 | 55 | | | | | | |
| *Total Owners' Equity* | | | | | | 237 | 6 | 0 | 1 | 10 | |
| *Total Liabilities and Owners' Equity* | | | | | | 252 | 4 | 4 | 5 | 57 | |

Illustration 19-8
Owners' equity section of a balance sheet

CarLand's closing entries recorded in a journal are shown in Illustration 19-9.

| | | | | | GENERAL | | ACCOUNTS RECEIVABLE | |
| | DATE | ACCOUNT TITLE | DOC. NO. | POST. REF. | DEBIT | CREDIT | DEBIT | CREDIT | |
|---|---|---|---|---|---|---|---|---|---|
| 10 | | *Closing Entries* | | | | | | | 10 |
| 11 | 31 | *Sales* | | | 352 6 0 0 00 | | | | 11 |
| 12 | | *Income Summary* | | | | 352 6 0 0 00 | | | 12 |
| 13 | 31 | *Income Summary* | | | 267 3 4 4 90 | | | | 13 |
| 14 | | *Purchases* | | | | 158 3 0 0 00 | | | 14 |
| 15 | | *Advertising Expense* | | | | 5 5 0 0 00 | | | 15 |
| 16 | | *Credit Card Fee Expense* | | | | 2 8 9 0 00 | | | 16 |
| 17 | | *Insurance Expense* | | | | 2 6 4 0 00 | | | 17 |
| 18 | | *Miscellaneous Expense* | | | | 2 1 8 2 15 | | | 18 |
| 19 | | *Payroll Taxes Expense* | | | | 7 2 9 9 75 | | | 19 |
| 20 | | *Rent Expense* | | | | 18 0 0 0 00 | | | 20 |
| 21 | | *Salary Expense* | | | | 60 1 5 3 00 | | | 21 |
| 22 | | *Supplies Expense—Office* | | | | 3 9 4 0 00 | | | 22 |
| 23 | | *Supplies Expense—Store* | | | | 3 2 6 0 00 | | | 23 |
| 24 | | *Utilities Expense* | | | | 3 1 8 0 00 | | | 24 |
| 25 | 31 | *Income Summary* | | | 72 0 5 5 10 | | | | 25 |
| 26 | | *Amy Kramer, Capital* | | | | 36 0 2 7 55 | | | 26 |
| 27 | | *Dario Mesa, Capital* | | | | 36 0 2 7 55 | | | 27 |
| 28 | 31 | *Amy Kramer, Capital* | | | 18 2 0 0 00 | | | | 28 |
| 29 | | *Amy Kramer, Drawing* | | | | 18 2 0 0 00 | | | 29 |
| 30 | 31 | *Dario Mesa, Capital* | | | 18 6 0 0 00 | | | | 30 |
| 31 | | *Dario Mesa, Drawing* | | | | 18 6 0 0 00 | | | 31 |
| 32 | | | | | | | | | 32 |
| 33 | | | | | | | | | 33 |
| 34 | | | | | | | | | 34 |
| 35 | | | | | | | | | 35 |
| 36 | | | | | | | | | 36 |

PAGE 26     JOURNAL

Illustration 19-9
Closing entries for a
partnership recorded in a
journal

# SUMMARY OF CLOSING ENTRIES FOR A MERCHANDISING BUSINESS ORGANIZED AS A PARTNERSHIP

The closing entries for a merchandising business organized as a partnership are summarized in Illustration 19-10.

| CLOSING ENTRY | JOURNAL | | |
|---|---|---|---|
| | ACCOUNT TITLE | GENERAL | |
| | | DEBIT | CREDIT |
| 1. Transfers income statement accounts with credit balances to Income Summary | Revenue account<br>Income Summary | X | X |
| 2. Transfers income statement accounts with debit balances to Income Summary | Income Summary<br>Cost and expense accounts | X | X |
| 3. Transfers net income or loss to partners' capital accounts and closes Income Summary | Income Summary<br>Partners' capital accounts<br>(net income) | X | X |
| | Partners' capital accounts<br>Income Summary<br>(net loss) | X | X |
| 4. Transfers partners' drawing account balances to partners' capital accounts | Partners' capital accounts<br><br>Partners' drawing accounts | X | X |

Illustration 19-10
Summary of closing entries

# CHECKING A GENERAL LEDGER'S ACCURACY AFTER POSTING ADJUSTING AND CLOSING ENTRIES

CarLand's 4-column general ledger account form has separate Balance Debit and Balance Credit columns. Each time an entry is posted to a general ledger account, the account balance is figured. The balance is then recorded in the appropriate balance column. Each general ledger account shows its current balance at all times. When an account is closed, a short line is drawn in both the Balance Debit and Credit columns. The ending balance for one fiscal period is the beginning balance for the next fiscal period.

## Completed general ledger

CarLand's completed general ledger after adjusting and closing entries are posted is shown in Illustration 19-11.

| ACCOUNT *Cash* | | | | | | | | |
|---|---|---|---|---|---|---|---|---|
| | | | | | | ACCOUNT NO. *1110* | | |
| DATE | ITEM | POST. REF. | DEBIT | CREDIT | BALANCE | | | |
| | | | | | DEBIT | | CREDIT | |
| *Dec.* 31 | *Balance* | √ | | | 24 2 3 3 57 | | | |

Illustration 19-11
General ledger after adjusting and closing entries are posted

| ACCOUNT *Petty Cash* | | | | | ACCOUNT NO. *1120* | |
|---|---|---|---|---|---|---|
| DATE | ITEM | POST. REF. | DEBIT | CREDIT | BALANCE | |
| | | | | | DEBIT | CREDIT |
| Dec.[19--] 31 | Balance | ✓ | | | 5 0 0 00 | |

| ACCOUNT *Accounts Receivable* | | | | | ACCOUNT NO. *1130* | |
|---|---|---|---|---|---|---|
| DATE | ITEM | POST. REF. | DEBIT | CREDIT | BALANCE | |
| | | | | | DEBIT | CREDIT |
| Dec.[19--] 31 | Balance | ✓ | | | 9 3 3 2 00 | |

| ACCOUNT *Merchandise Inventory* | | | | | ACCOUNT NO. *1140* | |
|---|---|---|---|---|---|---|
| DATE | ITEM | POST. REF. | DEBIT | CREDIT | BALANCE | |
| | | | | | DEBIT | CREDIT |
| Jan.[19--] 1 | Balance | ✓ | | | 225 4 0 0 00 | |
| Dec. 31 | | 26 | | 13 2 0 0 00 | 212 2 0 0 00 | |

| ACCOUNT *Supplies—Office* | | | | | ACCOUNT NO. *1145* | |
|---|---|---|---|---|---|---|
| DATE | ITEM | POST. REF. | DEBIT | CREDIT | BALANCE | |
| | | | | | DEBIT | CREDIT |
| Dec.[19--] 31 | Balance | ✓ | | | 5 4 0 0 00 | |
| 31 | | 26 | | 3 9 4 0 00 | 1 4 6 0 00 | |

| ACCOUNT *Supplies—Store* | | | | | ACCOUNT NO. *1150* | |
|---|---|---|---|---|---|---|
| DATE | ITEM | POST. REF. | DEBIT | CREDIT | BALANCE | |
| | | | | | DEBIT | CREDIT |
| Dec.[19--] 31 | Balance | ✓ | | | 5 7 8 0 00 | |
| 31 | | 26 | | 3 2 6 0 00 | 2 5 2 0 00 | |

| ACCOUNT *Prepaid Insurance* | | | | | ACCOUNT NO. *1160* | |
|---|---|---|---|---|---|---|
| DATE | ITEM | POST. REF. | DEBIT | CREDIT | BALANCE | |
| | | | | | DEBIT | CREDIT |
| Dec.[19--] 31 | Balance | ✓ | | | 4 8 4 0 00 | |
| 31 | | 26 | | 2 6 4 0 00 | 2 2 0 0 00 | |

Illustration 19-11
General ledger after
adjusting and closing
entries are posted
(continued)

ACCOUNT *Accounts Payable*  ACCOUNT NO. *2110*

| DATE | ITEM | POST. REF. | DEBIT | CREDIT | BALANCE DEBIT | BALANCE CREDIT |
|---|---|---|---|---|---|---|
| Dec. 31 | Balance | √ | | | | 10 4 5 1 90 |

ACCOUNT *Employee Income Tax Payable*  ACCOUNT NO. *2120*

| DATE | ITEM | POST. REF. | DEBIT | CREDIT | BALANCE DEBIT | BALANCE CREDIT |
|---|---|---|---|---|---|---|
| Dec. 31 | Balance | √ | | | | 4 0 2 00 |

ACCOUNT *FICA Tax Payable*  ACCOUNT NO. *2130*

| DATE | ITEM | POST. REF. | DEBIT | CREDIT | BALANCE DEBIT | BALANCE CREDIT |
|---|---|---|---|---|---|---|
| Dec. 31 | Balance | √ | | | | 8 3 2 16 |

ACCOUNT *Sales Tax Payable*  ACCOUNT NO. *2140*

| DATE | ITEM | POST. REF. | DEBIT | CREDIT | BALANCE DEBIT | BALANCE CREDIT |
|---|---|---|---|---|---|---|
| Dec. 31 | Balance | √ | | | | 1 7 6 0 00 |

ACCOUNT *Unemployment Tax Payable—Federal*  ACCOUNT NO. *2150*

| DATE | ITEM | POST. REF. | DEBIT | CREDIT | BALANCE DEBIT | BALANCE CREDIT |
|---|---|---|---|---|---|---|
| Dec. 31 | Balance | √ | | | | 5 9 15 |

ACCOUNT *Unemployment Tax Payable—State*  ACCOUNT NO. *2160*

| DATE | ITEM | POST. REF. | DEBIT | CREDIT | BALANCE DEBIT | BALANCE CREDIT |
|---|---|---|---|---|---|---|
| Dec. 31 | Balance | √ | | | | 3 9 9 26 |

Illustration 19-11
General ledger after adjusting and closing entries are posted (continued)

ACCOUNT *Health Insurance Premiums Payable*                          ACCOUNT NO. *2170*

| DATE | ITEM | POST. REF. | DEBIT | CREDIT | BALANCE DEBIT | BALANCE CREDIT |
|------|------|-----------|-------|--------|-------|--------|
| *Dec.* *31* *Balance* | | √ | | | | 8 4 0 00 |

ACCOUNT *U.S. Savings Bonds Payable*                          ACCOUNT NO. *2180*

| DATE | ITEM | POST. REF. | DEBIT | CREDIT | BALANCE DEBIT | BALANCE CREDIT |
|------|------|-----------|-------|--------|-------|--------|
| *Dec.* *31* *Balance* | | √ | | | | 4 0 00 |

ACCOUNT *United Way Donations Payable*                          ACCOUNT NO. *2190*

| DATE | ITEM | POST. REF. | DEBIT | CREDIT | BALANCE DEBIT | BALANCE CREDIT |
|------|------|-----------|-------|--------|-------|--------|
| *Dec.* *31* *Balance* | | √ | | | | 6 0 00 |

ACCOUNT *Amy Kramer, Capital*                          ACCOUNT NO. *3110*

| DATE | ITEM | POST. REF. | DEBIT | CREDIT | BALANCE DEBIT | BALANCE CREDIT |
|------|------|-----------|-------|--------|-------|--------|
| *Dec.* *31* *Balance* | | √ | | | | 101 1 1 8 00 |
| *31* | | 26 | | 36 0 2 7 55 | | 137 1 4 5 55 |
| *31* | | 26 | 18 2 0 0 00 | | | 118 9 4 5 55 |

ACCOUNT *Amy Kramer, Drawing*                          ACCOUNT NO. *3120*

| DATE | ITEM | POST. REF. | DEBIT | CREDIT | BALANCE DEBIT | BALANCE CREDIT |
|------|------|-----------|-------|--------|-------|--------|
| *Dec.* *31* *Balance* | | √ | 18 2 0 0 00 | | | |
| *31* | | 26 | | 18 2 0 0 00 | —— | —— |

Illustration 19-11
General ledger after
adjusting and closing
entries are posted
(continued)

Illustration 19-11
General ledger after
adjusting and closing
entries are posted
(continued)

ACCOUNT *Dario Mesa, Capital*                                        ACCOUNT NO. *3130*

| DATE | | ITEM | POST. REF. | DEBIT | CREDIT | BALANCE DEBIT | BALANCE CREDIT |
|---|---|---|---|---|---|---|---|
| Dec.<sup>19--</sup> | 31 | Balance | ✓ | | | | 101 2 2 8 00 |
| | 31 | | 26 | | 36 0 2 7 55 | | 137 2 5 5 55 |
| | 31 | | 26 | 18 6 0 0 00 | | | 118 6 5 5 55 |

ACCOUNT *Dario Mesa, Drawing*                                        ACCOUNT NO. *3140*

| DATE | | ITEM | POST. REF. | DEBIT | CREDIT | BALANCE DEBIT | BALANCE CREDIT |
|---|---|---|---|---|---|---|---|
| Dec.<sup>19--</sup> | 31 | Balance | ✓ | | | 18 6 0 0 00 | |
| | 31 | | 26 | | 18 6 0 0 00 | —— | —— |

ACCOUNT *Income Summary*                                             ACCOUNT NO. *3150*

| DATE | | ITEM | POST. REF. | DEBIT | CREDIT | BALANCE DEBIT | BALANCE CREDIT |
|---|---|---|---|---|---|---|---|
| Dec.<sup>19--</sup> | 31 | | 26 | 13 2 0 0 00 | | 13 2 0 0 00 | |
| | 31 | | 26 | | 352 6 0 0 00 | | 339 4 0 0 00 |
| | 31 | | 26 | 267 3 4 4 90 | | | 72 0 5 5 10 |
| | 31 | | 26 | 72 0 5 5 10 | | —— | —— |

ACCOUNT *Sales*                                                      ACCOUNT NO. *4110*

| DATE | | ITEM | POST. REF. | DEBIT | CREDIT | BALANCE DEBIT | BALANCE CREDIT |
|---|---|---|---|---|---|---|---|
| Dec.<sup>19--</sup> | 31 | Balance | ✓ | | | | 352 6 0 0 00 |
| | 31 | | 26 | 352 6 0 0 00 | | —— | —— |

ACCOUNT *Purchases*                                                  ACCOUNT NO. *5110*

| DATE | | ITEM | POST. REF. | DEBIT | CREDIT | BALANCE DEBIT | BALANCE CREDIT |
|---|---|---|---|---|---|---|---|
| Dec.<sup>19--</sup> | 31 | Balance | ✓ | | | 158 3 0 0 00 | |
| | 31 | | 26 | | 158 3 0 0 00 | —— | —— |

## ACCOUNT Advertising Expense                    ACCOUNT NO. 6110

| DATE | | ITEM | POST. REF. | DEBIT | CREDIT | BALANCE DEBIT | BALANCE CREDIT |
|---|---|---|---|---|---|---|---|
| 19-- Dec. | 31 | Balance | ✓ | | | 5 5 0 0 00 | |
| | 31 | | 26 | | 5 5 0 0 00 | | |

## ACCOUNT Credit Card Fee Expense                    ACCOUNT NO. 6120

| DATE | | ITEM | POST. REF. | DEBIT | CREDIT | BALANCE DEBIT | BALANCE CREDIT |
|---|---|---|---|---|---|---|---|
| 19-- Dec. | 31 | Balance | ✓ | | | 2 8 9 0 00 | |
| | 31 | | 26 | | 2 8 9 0 00 | | |

## ACCOUNT Insurance Expense                    ACCOUNT NO. 6130

| DATE | | ITEM | POST. REF. | DEBIT | CREDIT | BALANCE DEBIT | BALANCE CREDIT |
|---|---|---|---|---|---|---|---|
| 19-- Dec. | 31 | | 26 | 2 6 4 0 00 | | 2 6 4 0 00 | |
| | 31 | | 26 | | 2 6 4 0 00 | | |

## ACCOUNT Miscellaneous Expense                    ACCOUNT NO. 6140

| DATE | | ITEM | POST. REF. | DEBIT | CREDIT | BALANCE DEBIT | BALANCE CREDIT |
|---|---|---|---|---|---|---|---|
| 19-- Dec. | 31 | Balance | ✓ | | | 2 1 8 2 15 | |
| | 31 | | 26 | | 2 1 8 2 15 | | |

## ACCOUNT Payroll Taxes Expense                    ACCOUNT NO. 6150

| DATE | | ITEM | POST. REF. | DEBIT | CREDIT | BALANCE DEBIT | BALANCE CREDIT |
|---|---|---|---|---|---|---|---|
| 19-- Dec. | 31 | Balance | ✓ | | | 7 2 9 9 75 | |
| | 31 | | 26 | | 7 2 9 9 75 | | |

Illustration 19-11
General ledger after
adjusting and closing
entries are posted
(continued)

Illustration 19-11
General ledger after
adjusting and closing
entries are posted
(concluded)

**ACCOUNT** *Rent Expense*      **ACCOUNT NO.** *6160*

| DATE | | ITEM | POST. REF. | DEBIT | CREDIT | BALANCE DEBIT | BALANCE CREDIT |
|---|---|---|---|---|---|---|---|
| Dec. 19-- | 31 | Balance | √ | | | 18 0 0 0 00 | |
| | 31 | | 25 | | 18 0 0 0 00 | | |

**ACCOUNT** *Salary Expense*      **ACCOUNT NO.** *6170*

| DATE | | ITEM | POST. REF. | DEBIT | CREDIT | BALANCE DEBIT | BALANCE CREDIT |
|---|---|---|---|---|---|---|---|
| Dec. 19-- | 31 | Balance | √ | | | 60 1 5 3 00 | |
| | 31 | | 25 | | 60 1 5 3 00 | | |

**ACCOUNT** *Supplies Expense—Office*      **ACCOUNT NO.** *6175*

| DATE | | ITEM | POST. REF. | DEBIT | CREDIT | BALANCE DEBIT | BALANCE CREDIT |
|---|---|---|---|---|---|---|---|
| Dec. 19-- | 31 | | 26 | 3 9 4 0 00 | | 3 9 4 0 00 | |
| | 31 | | 26 | | 3 9 4 0 00 | | |

**ACCOUNT** *Supplies Expense—Store*      **ACCOUNT NO.** *6180*

| DATE | | ITEM | POST. REF. | DEBIT | CREDIT | BALANCE DEBIT | BALANCE CREDIT |
|---|---|---|---|---|---|---|---|
| Dec. 19-- | 31 | | 26 | 3 2 6 0 00 | | 3 2 6 0 00 | |
| | 31 | | 26 | | 3 2 6 0 00 | | |

**ACCOUNT** *Utilities Expense*      **ACCOUNT NO.** *6190*

| DATE | | ITEM | POST. REF. | DEBIT | CREDIT | BALANCE DEBIT | BALANCE CREDIT |
|---|---|---|---|---|---|---|---|
| Dec. 19-- | 31 | Balance | √ | | | 3 1 8 0 00 | |
| | 31 | | 26 | | 3 1 8 0 00 | | |

Balance sheet accounts (asset, liability, and capital accounts) have up-to-date balances to begin the new fiscal period. Balances in the balance sheet accounts agree with the amounts on the balance sheet, Illustration 18-10, Chapter 18. General ledger account balances on December 31 of one year are the beginning balances for January 1 of the next year.

Income statement accounts (revenue, cost, and expense accounts) have zero balances to begin the new fiscal period. *(CONCEPT: Matching Expenses with Revenue)*

## Post-closing trial balance

After adjusting and closing entries have been posted, a post-closing trial balance is prepared. The post-closing trial balance is prepared to prove the equality of debits and credits in the general ledger. CarLand's post-closing trial balance prepared on December 31 is shown in Illustration 19-12.

| ACCOUNT TITLE | DEBIT | CREDIT |
|---|---:|---:|
| *Cash* | 24 2 3 3 57 | |
| *Petty Cash* | 5 0 0 00 | |
| *Accounts Receivable* | 9 3 3 2 00 | |
| *Merchandise Inventory* | 212 2 0 0 00 | |
| *Supplies—Office* | 1 4 6 0 00 | |
| *Supplies—Store* | 2 5 2 0 00 | |
| *Prepaid Insurance* | 2 2 0 0 00 | |
| *Accounts Payable* | | 10 4 5 1 90 |
| *Employee Income Tax Payable* | | 4 0 2 00 |
| *FICA Tax Payable* | | 8 3 2 16 |
| *Sales Tax Payable* | | 1 7 6 0 00 |
| *Unemployment Tax Payable—Federal* | | 5 9 15 |
| *Unemployment Tax Payable—State* | | 3 9 9 26 |
| *Health Insurance Premiums Payable* | | 8 4 0 00 |
| *U.S. Savings Bonds Payable* | | 4 0 00 |
| *United Way Donations Payable* | | 6 0 00 |
| *Amy Kramer, Capital* | | 118 9 4 5 55 |
| *Dario Mesa, Capital* | | 118 6 5 5 55 |
| *Totals* | 252 4 4 5 57 | 252 4 4 5 57 |

*CarLand*
*Post-Closing Trial Balance*
*December 31, 19--*

Illustration 19-12
Post-closing trial balance

All general ledger accounts that have balances are listed on a post-closing trial balance. Accounts are listed in the same order as they appear in the general ledger. Accounts with zero balances are not listed on a post-closing trial balance.

Account balances on the post-closing trial balance, Illustration 19-12, agree with the balances on the balance sheet, Illustration 18-10, Chapter 18. Also, because the post-closing trial balance debit and credit balance totals are the same, $252,445.57, the equality of debits and credits in the general ledger is proved. The general ledger is ready for the next fiscal period. (CONCEPT: *Accounting Period Cycle*)

## SUMMARY OF AN ACCOUNTING CYCLE FOR A MERCHANDISING BUSINESS

Service and merchandising businesses use a similar accounting cycle. The accounting cycles are also similar for a proprietorship and a partnership. Variations occur when subsidiary ledgers are used. Variations also occur in preparing financial statements. CarLand's accounting cycle for a merchandising business is summarized in Illustration 19-13.

Illustration 19-13
Summary of an accounting cycle for a merchandising business

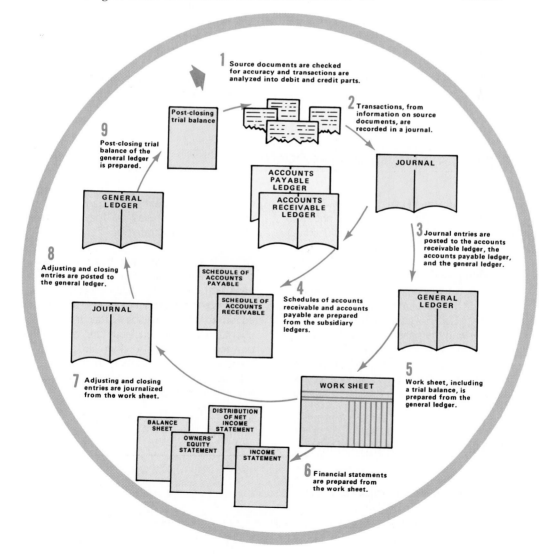

## ■ QUESTIONS FOR INDIVIDUAL STUDY

1. What two types of journal entries change general ledger account balances at the end of a fiscal period?
2. Where is the information obtained for journalizing adjusting entries?
3. Where is the information obtained for journalizing closing entries?
4. Where is the explanation for adjusting entries written in a journal?
5. Which accounting concept is being applied when temporary accounts are closed at the end of a fiscal period?
6. What four kinds of closing entries are recorded at the end of a fiscal period?
7. What is the title of the temporary account used to summarize information about net income at the end of a fiscal period?
8. Why is the income summary account considered a unique account?
9. Where is the explanation for closing entries written in a journal?
10. What are the three amounts recorded in the income summary account after closing the revenue, cost, and expense accounts?
11. Why are partners' withdrawals not closed to the income summary account?
12. What is recorded in the Balance Debit and Credit columns of a general ledger account when an account is closed?
13. Which accounting concept is being applied when revenue, cost, and expense accounts begin a new fiscal period with zero balances?
14. What accounts are listed on a post-closing trial balance?

## ■ CASES FOR MANAGEMENT DECISION

**CASE 1** Household Furniture's Trial Balance Debit column of the work sheet shows a debit balance of $2,400.00 for the office supplies account. The ending office supplies inventory is determined to be $1,800.00. The accounting clerk journalized the following adjusting entry: debit Supplies Expense—Office, $1,800.00; credit Supplies—Office, $1,800.00. Susan Gray, partner, discussed the entry with the accounting clerk and suggested that the adjusting entry should have been for $600.00 instead of $1,800.00. The clerk indicates that there is no problem because the amounts will be adjusted again at the end of the next fiscal period. Do you agree with Miss Gray or the accounting clerk? Explain your answer.

**CASE 2** Two businesses have been using different accounting practices. One business first closes the income summary account to record the net income in the capital accounts and then closes the drawing accounts. The other business first closes the drawing accounts and then closes the income summary account to record the net income in the capital accounts. Which practice is correct? Explain.

## ■ DRILLS FOR UNDERSTANDING

**DRILL 19-D1**   **Analyzing adjusting entries**

The following information is from the work sheet of Chaney's Giftware.

| | | 1 | 2 | 3 | 4 |
|---|---|---|---|---|---|
| | ACCOUNT TITLE | TRIAL BALANCE | | ADJUSTMENTS | |
| | | DEBIT | CREDIT | DEBIT | CREDIT |
| 4 | *Merchandise Inventory* | 248 0 0 0 00 | | | (a)16 0 0 0 00 |
| 5 | *Supplies—Office* | 3 9 4 0 00 | | | (b) 2 3 4 0 00 |
| 6 | *Supplies—Store* | 4 3 1 0 00 | | | (c) 2 6 8 0 00 |
| 7 | *Prepaid Insurance* | 4 3 7 0 00 | | | (d) 2 8 4 0 00 |
| 21 | *Income Summary* | | | (a)16 0 0 0 00 | |
| 26 | *Insurance Expense* | | | (d) 2 8 4 0 00 | |
| 31 | *Supplies Expense—Office* | | | (b) 2 3 4 0 00 | |
| 32 | *Supplies Expense—Store* | | | (c) 2 6 8 0 00 | |

**Instructions: 1.** Prepare a T account for each account. For those accounts that have a balance, enter the balance on the proper side of the T account.
   **2.** Enter the adjusting entries in the appropriate T accounts.

## DRILL 19-D2   Analyzing adjusting entries

The following information is related to adjustments needed at the end of a fiscal period for three businesses.

| Business | Account Title | Account Balance in General Ledger | Adjustment Information | |
|---|---|---|---|---|
| | | | Ending Inventories | Ending Value |
| 1 | Merchandise Inventory | $388,000.00 | $365,000.00 | |
| | Supplies—Office | 4,730.00 | 2,910.00 | |
| | Supplies—Store | 5,230.00 | 3,470.00 | |
| | Prepaid Insurance | 3,360.00 | | $840.00 |
| 2 | Merchandise Inventory | $274,000.00 | $286,000.00 | |
| | Supplies—Office | 3,620.00 | 1,840.00 | |
| | Supplies—Store | 3,950.00 | 2,110.00 | |
| | Prepaid Insurance | 2,850.00 | | $570.00 |
| 3 | Merchandise Inventory | $292,000.00 | $278,000.00 | |
| | Supplies—Office | 4,480.00 | 2,250.00 | |
| | Supplies—Store | 4,130.00 | 2,320.00 | |
| | Prepaid Insurance | 3,200.00 | | $800.00 |

**Instructions: 1.** Prepare eight T accounts for each of the three businesses. (1) Merchandise Inventory. (2) Supplies—Office. (3) Supplies—Store. (4) Prepaid Insurance. (5) Income Summary. (6) Insurance Expense. (7) Supplies Expense—Office. (8) Supplies Expense—Store. For those accounts that have a balance, enter the balance on the proper side of the T account.
   **2.** Enter the adjusting entries in the appropriate T accounts for each business.

DRILL 19-D3   **Analyzing closing entries**

The following information is from the work sheet of Novak's Sport Center.

| | | 5 | 6 |
|---|---|---|---|
| | ACCOUNT TITLE | INCOME STATEMENT | |
| | | DEBIT | CREDIT |
| 21 | *Income Summary* | 12 00 0 00 | |
| 22 | *Sales* | | 236 0 0 0 00 |
| 23 | *Purchases* | 94 4 0 0 00 | |
| 24 | *Advertising Expense* | 3 2 5 0 00 | |
| 25 | *Credit Card Fee Expense* | 2 1 3 0 00 | |
| 26 | *Insurance Expense* | 2 5 2 0 00 | |
| 27 | *Miscellaneous Expense* | 1 3 8 0 00 | |
| 28 | *Rent Expense* | 14 4 0 0 00 | |
| 29 | *Supplies Expense—Office* | 2 9 8 0 00 | |
| 30 | *Supplies Expense—Store* | 3 1 2 0 00 | |
| 31 | | | |
| 32 | | | |
| 33 | | | |
| 34 | | | |
| 35 | | | |
| 36 | | | |
| 37 | | | |
| 38 | | | |
| 39 | | | |
| 40 | | | |
| 41 | | | |
| 42 | | | |
| 43 | | | |
| 44 | | | |
| 45 | | | |
| 46 | | | |
| 47 | | | |
| 48 | | | |

**Instructions: 1.** Prepare a T account for each account. In each T account, enter the amount that is shown in the Income Statement columns.

**2.** Enter the debit and credit amounts to close the income statement credit balance account. Enter the debit and credit amounts to close the income statement debit balance accounts.

## ▉ APPLICATION PROBLEM

**PROBLEM 19-1  Journalizing and posting adjusting and closing entries; preparing a post-closing trial balance**

Use the following partial work sheet of Jewel Box Company for the year ended December 31 of the current year. The general ledger accounts and their balances are in the working papers accompanying this textbook.

| | ACCOUNT TITLE | 3 ADJUSTMENTS DEBIT | 4 ADJUSTMENTS CREDIT | 5 INCOME STATEMENT DEBIT | 6 INCOME STATEMENT CREDIT |
|---|---|---|---|---|---|
| 4 | *Merchandise Inventory* | | (a)13 0 0 0 00 | | |
| 5 | *Supplies—Office* | | (b) 2 1 4 0 00 | | |
| 6 | *Supplies—Store* | | (c) 2 4 5 0 00 | | |
| 7 | *Prepaid Insurance* | | (d) 2 6 4 0 00 | | |
| 21 | *Income Summary* | (a)13 0 0 0 00 | | 13 0 0 0 00 | |
| 22 | *Sales* | | | | 316 0 0 0 00 |
| 23 | *Purchases* | | | 126 4 5 0 00 | |
| 24 | *Advertising Expense* | | | 4 7 2 0 00 | |
| 25 | *Credit Card Fee Expense* | | | 3 2 6 0 00 | |
| 26 | *Insurance Expense* | (d) 2 6 4 0 00 | | 2 6 4 0 00 | |
| 27 | *Miscellaneous Expense* | | | 1 9 3 0 00 | |
| 28 | *Payroll Taxes Expense* | | | 6 7 7 3 00 | |
| 29 | *Rent Expense* | | | 15 6 0 0 00 | |
| 30 | *Salary Expense* | | | 56 7 8 7 00 | |
| 31 | *Supplies Expense—Office* | (b) 2 1 4 0 00 | | 2 1 4 0 00 | |
| 32 | *Supplies Expense—Store* | (c) 2 4 5 0 00 | | 2 4 5 0 00 | |
| 33 | *Utilities Expense* | | | 2 9 4 0 00 | |
| 34 | | 20 2 3 0 00 | 20 2 3 0 00 | 238 6 9 0 00 | 316 0 0 0 00 |
| 35 | *Net Income* | | | 77 3 1 0 00 | |
| 36 | | | | 316 0 0 0 00 | 316 0 0 0 00 |

**Instructions: 1.** Use page 25 of a journal. Journalize the adjusting entries using information from the partial work sheet.

**2.** Post the adjusting entries.

**3.** Continue using page 25 of the journal. Journalize the closing entries using information from the work sheet. The distribution of net income statement shows equal distribution of earnings. The partners' drawing accounts show the following debit balances in the work sheet's Balance Sheet Debit column: Paula Chaney, Drawing, $14,580.00; Scott Chaney, Drawing, $14,720.00.

**4.** Post the closing entries.

**5.** Prepare a post-closing trial balance.

## ■ ENRICHMENT PROBLEMS

**MASTERY PROBLEM 19-M**   **Journalizing and posting adjusting and closing entries; preparing a post-closing trial balance**

Use the following partial work sheet of Robco Toys for the year ended December 31 of the current year. The general ledger accounts and their balances are in the working papers accompanying this textbook.

| | ACCOUNT TITLE | | ADJUSTMENTS 3 DEBIT | ADJUSTMENTS 4 CREDIT | INCOME STATEMENT 5 DEBIT | INCOME STATEMENT 6 CREDIT |
|---|---|---|---|---|---|---|
| 4 | Merchandise Inventory | | | (a)12 5 0 0 00 | | |
| 5 | Supplies—Office | | | (b) 2 4 3 0 00 | | |
| 6 | Supplies—Store | | | (c) 2 2 7 0 00 | | |
| 7 | Prepaid Insurance | | | (d) 2 2 8 0 00 | | |
| 21 | Income Summary | | (a)12 5 0 0 00 | | 12 5 0 0 00 | |
| 22 | Sales | | | | | 325 6 3 0 00 |
| 23 | Purchases | | | | 130 4 5 0 00 | |
| 24 | Advertising Expense | | | | 5 1 8 0 00 | |
| 25 | Credit Card Fee Expense | | | | 3 4 2 0 00 | |
| 26 | Insurance Expense | | (d) 2 2 8 0 00 | | 2 2 8 0 00 | |
| 27 | Miscellaneous Expense | | | | 2 0 6 0 00 | |
| 28 | Payroll Taxes Expense | | | | 7 1 2 4 00 | |
| 29 | Rent Expense | | | | 15 6 0 0 00 | |
| 30 | Salary Expense | | | | 59 3 6 0 00 | |
| 31 | Supplies Expense—Office | | (b) 2 4 3 0 00 | | 2 4 3 0 00 | |
| 32 | Supplies Expense—Store | | (c) 2 2 7 0 00 | | 2 2 7 0 00 | |
| 33 | Utilities Expense | | | | 2 8 8 0 00 | |
| 34 | | | 19 4 8 0 00 | 19 4 8 0 00 | 245 5 5 4 00 | 325 6 3 0 00 |
| 35 | Net Income | | | | 80 0 7 6 00 | |
| 36 | | | | | 325 6 3 0 00 | 325 6 3 0 00 |
| 37 | | | | | | |

**Instructions: 1.** Use page 25 of a journal. Journalize the adjusting entries using information from the partial work sheet.

**2.** Post the adjusting entries.

**3.** Continue using page 25 of the journal. Journalize the closing entries using information from the work sheet. The distribution of net income statement shows equal distribution of earnings. The partners' drawing accounts show the following debit balances in the work sheet's Balance Sheet Debit column: Marcus Florie, Drawing, $18,230.00; Karen Rader, Drawing, $18,710.00.

**4.** Post the closing entries.

**5.** Prepare a post-closing trial balance.

## CHALLENGE PROBLEM 19-C   Completing end-of-fiscal-period work

Plaza Book Center's trial balance is recorded on a 10-column work sheet in the working papers accompanying this textbook. The general ledger accounts and their balances are also given.

**Instructions: 1.** Use the following adjustment information. Complete the 10-column work sheet.

### Adjustment Information, December 31

| | |
|---|---:|
| Merchandise inventory................................. | $204,680.00 |
| Office supplies inventory............................... | 2,635.00 |
| Store supplies inventory............................... | 2,310.00 |
| Value of prepaid insurance ........................... | 2,200.00 |

**2.** Prepare an income statement from the information on the work sheet. Calculate and record the following component percentages: (a) cost of merchandise sold, (b) gross profit on sales, (c) total expenses, and (d) net income or loss. Round percentage calculations to the nearest 0.1%.

**3.** Prepare a distribution of net income statement. Net income or loss is to be shared equally.

**4.** Prepare an owners' equity statement. No additional investments were made.

**5.** Prepare a balance sheet in report form.

**6.** Use page 25 of a journal. Journalize the adjusting entries.

**7.** Post the adjusting entries.

**8.** Continue using page 25 of the journal. Journalize the closing entries.

**9.** Post the closing entries.

**10.** Prepare a post-closing trial balance.

# Reinforcement Activity 2, Part B

# An Accounting Cycle for a Partnership: End-of-Fiscal-Period Work

*The ledgers used in Reinforcement Activity 2, Part A, are needed to complete Reinforcement Activity 2, Part B.*

Reinforcement Activity 2, Part B, includes those accounting activities needed to complete the accounting cycle of ClearView Optical.

## END-OF-FISCAL-PERIOD WORK

**Instructions: 10.** Prepare a trial balance on a work sheet. Use December 31 of the current year as the date.

**11.** Complete the work sheet using the following adjustment information.

### Adjustment Information, December 31

| | |
|---|---:|
| Merchandise inventory | $203,200.00 |
| Office supplies inventory | 2,370.00 |
| Store supplies inventory | 3,240.00 |
| Value of prepaid insurance | 260.00 |

**12.** Prepare an income statement. Figure and record the following component percentages: (a) cost of merchandise sold, (b) gross profit on sales, (c) total expenses, and (d) net income or loss. Round percentage calculations to the nearest 0.1%.

**13.** Prepare a distribution of net income statement. Net income or loss is to be shared equally.

**14.** Prepare an owners' equity statement. No additional investments were made.

**15.** Prepare a balance sheet in report form.

**16.** Use page 25 of a journal. Journalize and post the adjusting entries.

**17.** Continue using page 25 of the journal. Journalize and post the closing entries.

**18.** Prepare a post-closing trial balance.

# Computer Application 4
# Automated Accounting Cycle for a
# Partnership: End-of-Fiscal-Period Work

Chapters 17 through 19 describe CarLand's manual accounting procedures for completing end-of-fiscal-period work. Computer Application 4 describes procedures for using a microcomputer to complete CarLand's end-of-fiscal-period work. Computer Application Problem 4 contains instructions for using a microcomputer to solve Challenge Problem 19-C, Chapter 19.

## PLANNING ADJUSTMENTS

Procedures for bringing CarLand's general ledger account balances up to date are similar to those described for Petlodge in Chapter 11.

Option K is selected from the General Ledger Main Menu, Illustration C4-1, page 464, to direct the computer to prepare a trial balance.

A trial balance is prepared to check the equality of debits and credits in the general ledger and to plan adjusting entries. CarLand's trial balance is shown in Illustration C4-2, page 464.

### Recording adjusting entries

Adjusting entries are journalized on a general ledger input form (FORM GL-2). CarLand's completed general ledger input form for the adjusting entries is shown in Illustration C4-3, page 465.

Illustration C4-1
General ledger
main menu

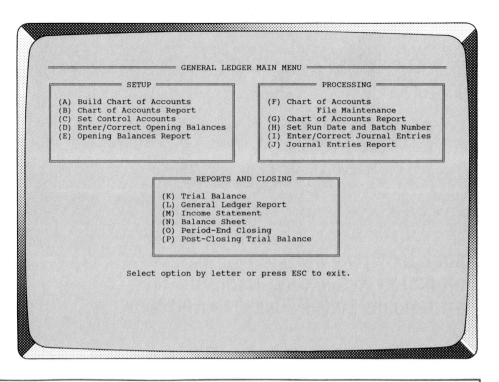

```
================= GENERAL LEDGER MAIN MENU =================

 === SETUP ===                        === PROCESSING ===
 (A)  Build Chart of Accounts         (F)  Chart of Accounts
 (B)  Chart of Accounts Report                File Maintenance
 (C)  Set Control Accounts            (G)  Chart of Accounts Report
 (D)  Enter/Correct Opening Balances  (H)  Set Run Date and Batch Number
 (E)  Opening Balances Report         (I)  Enter/Correct Journal Entries
                                      (J)  Journal Entries Report


              === REPORTS AND CLOSING ===
              (K)  Trial Balance
              (L)  General Ledger Report
              (M)  Income Statement
              (N)  Balance Sheet
              (O)  Period-End Closing
              (P)  Post-Closing Trial Balance


         Select option by letter or press ESC to exit.
```

Illustration C4-2
Trial balance

```
RUN DATE: 12/31/--                    CARLAND
                                   TRIAL BALANCE

------------------------------------------------------------------------
ACCOUNT      ACCOUNT
NUMBER       TITLE                    DEBIT AMOUNT         CREDIT AMOUNT
------------------------------------------------------------------------
1110         Cash                       24233.57
1120         Petty Cash                   500.00
1130         Accounts Receivable         9332.00
1140         Merchandise Inventory     225400.00
1145         Supplies--Office            5400.00
1150         Supplies--Store             5780.00
1160         Prepaid Insurance           4840.00
2110         Accounts Payable                                 10451.90
2120         Empl. Income Tax Payable                           402.00
2130         FICA Tax Payable                                   832.16
2140         Sales Tax Payable                                 1760.00
2150         Unempl. Tax Pay.--Federal                           59.15
2160         Unempl. Tax Pay.--State                            399.26
2170         Health Ins. Prem. Payable                          840.00
2180         U.S. Savings Bonds Pay.                             40.00
2190         United Way Don. Payable                             60.00
3110         Amy Kramer, Capital                             101118.00
3120         Amy Kramer, Drawing         18200.00
3130         Dario Mesa, Capital                             101228.00
3140         Dario Mesa, Drawing         18600.00
4110         Sales                                           352600.00
5110         Purchases                  158300.00
6110         Advertising Expense          5500.00
6120         Credit Card Fee Expense      2890.00
6140         Miscellaneous Expense        2182.15
6150         Payroll Taxes Expense        7299.75
6160         Rent Expense                18000.00
6170         Salary Expense              60153.00
6190         Utilities Expense            3180.00
                                     --------------       --------------
             TOTALS                    569790.47            569790.47
                                     ==============       ==============
```

| RUN DATE 12/31/-- MM DD YY | | GENERAL LEDGER Input Form | | FORM GL-2 | |
|---|---|---|---|---|---|
| BATCH NO. 4 | | | | | |

| | 1 DAY | 2 DOC. NO. | 3 ACCOUNT NUMBER | 4 DEBIT AMOUNT | 5 CREDIT AMOUNT | |
|---|---|---|---|---|---|---|
| 1 | 31 | Adj.Ent. | 3150 | 13200 00 | | 1 |
| 2 | | | 1140 | | 13200 00 | 2 |
| 3 | 31 | Adj.Ent. | 6175 | 3940 00 | | 3 |
| 4 | | | 1145 | | 3940 00 | 4 |
| 5 | 31 | Adj.Ent. | 6180 | 3260 00 | | 5 |
| 6 | | | 1150 | | 3260 00 | 6 |
| 7 | 31 | Adj.Ent. | 6130 | 2640 00 | | 7 |
| 8 | | | 1160 | | 2640 00 | 8 |
| 20 | | | | | | 20 |
| 21 | | | | | | 21 |
| 22 | | | | | | 22 |
| 23 | | | | | | 23 |
| 24 | | | | | | 24 |
| 25 | | | | | | 25 |
| | | | BATCH TOTALS | 23040 00 | 23040 00 | |

Illustration C4-3
General ledger input form
with adjusting entries
entered

CarLand has the following adjustment data on December 31.

**Adjustment Information, December 31**

| | |
|---|---|
| Merchandise inventory . . . . . . . . . . . . . . . . . . . . . . . . . . . . . . . . . . . . . . . . | $212,200.00 |
| Office supplies inventory . . . . . . . . . . . . . . . . . . . . . . . . . . . . . . . . . . . . . | 1,460.00 |
| Store supplies inventory . . . . . . . . . . . . . . . . . . . . . . . . . . . . . . . . . . . . . . | 2,520.00 |
| Value of prepaid insurance . . . . . . . . . . . . . . . . . . . . . . . . . . . . . . . . . . | 2,200.00 |

After all adjusting entries have been journalized, the Debit Amount and Credit Amount columns are totaled. The totals are entered on the Batch Totals line provided at the bottom of the input form. The two totals are compared to assure that debits equal credits. As the two totals are the same, $23,040.00, the adjusting entries journalized on the general ledger input form are assumed to be correct.

## Processing adjusting entries

Option H is selected from the General Ledger Main Menu, Illustration C4-1, to set the run date, 12/31/--, and the batch number, 4. Option I is selected from the General Ledger Main Menu to display spaces for entering the adjusting entries. After all lines on the input form have been entered and posted, Option J is selected from the General Ledger Main Menu. This option directs the computer to prepare a journal entries report for the adjusting entries. CarLand's journal entries report for adjusting entries is shown in Illustration C4-4.

Illustration C4-4
Journal entries report for adjusting entries

```
RUN DATE: 12/31/--                    CARLAND
                             JOURNAL ENTRIES BATCH# 4
       --------------------------------------------------------------------
 JE#    DATE    ACCOUNT NUMBER & TITLE         DEBIT AMOUNT   CREDIT AMOUNT
       --------------------------------------------------------------------
 0050  12/31/-- 3150   Income Summary             13200.00
                1140     Merchandise Inventory                   13200.00
                       DOCUMENT: Adj.Ent.

 0051  12/31/-- 6175   Supplies Expense--Office    3940.00
                1145     Supplies--Office                         3940.00
                       DOCUMENT: Adj.Ent.

 0052  12/31/-- 6180   Supplies Expense--Store     3260.00
                1150     Supplies--Store                          3260.00
                       DOCUMENT: Adj.Ent.

 0053  12/31/-- 6130   Insurance Expense           2640.00
                1160     Prepaid Insurance                        2640.00
                       DOCUMENT: Adj.Ent.

                                             ---------------  ---------------
                TOTALS                           23040.00        23040.00
                                             ===============  ===============
                IN BALANCE
```

The journal entries report for adjusting entries is checked against the general ledger input form for adjusting entries. The totals shown on the report, $23,040.00, are the same as on the general ledger input form. Therefore, the journal entries report is assumed to be correct.

# PREPARING END-OF-FISCAL-PERIOD REPORTS

In automated accounting end-of-fiscal-period reports are prepared by a computer based on instructions in computer software.

## Processing financial statements

After the journal entries report for adjusting entries has been prepared and checked for accuracy, Option M is selected from the General Ledger

Main Menu. This option directs the computer to print an income statement. CarLand's income statement is shown in Illustration C4-5.

Illustration C4-5
Income statement prepared by computer

```
                              CARLAND
                         INCOME STATEMENT
                    FOR PERIOD ENDED 12/31/--
                                                              % OF NET
  R E V E N U E                                               REVENUE
  -------------                                               --------
  Sales                          352600.00                      100.00
                                ---------------
  NET REVENUE                                     352600.00     100.00

  C O S T   O F   M D S E .   S O L D
  -----------------------------------
  BEGINNING INVENTORY            225400.00                       63.93
  Purchases                      158300.00                       44.90
                                ---------------
  MDSE. AVAILABLE FOR SALE       383700.00                      108.82
  LESS ENDING INVENTORY          212200.00                       60.18
                                ---------------
  COST OF MDSE. SOLD                              171500.00      48.64
                                               ---------------
  GROSS PROFIT ON OPERATIONS                      181100.00      51.36

  E X P E N S E S
  ---------------
  Advertising Expense              5500.00                        1.56
  Credit Card Fee Expense          2890.00                         .82
  Insurance Expense                2640.00                         .75
  Miscellaneous Expense            2182.15                         .62
  Payroll Taxes Expense            7299.75                        2.07
  Rent Expense                    18000.00                        5.10
  Salary Expense                  60153.00                       17.06
  Supplies Expense--Office         3940.00                        1.12
  Supplies Expense--Store          3260.00                         .92
  Utilities Expense                3180.00                         .90
                                ---------------
  TOTAL EXPENSES                                  109044.90      30.93
                                               ---------------
  NET INCOME                                       72055.10      20.44
                                               ===============
```

CarLand's net income or net loss is distributed equally to each partner based on the partnership agreement. In CarLand's manual accounting system, a distribution of net income statement is prepared to show how the net income or net loss is divided. Then, an owners' equity statement is prepared to show changes in each partner's capital during a fiscal period. In CarLand's automated accounting system, distribution of income and changes in capital are both shown on the balance sheet.

Illustration C4-6
Balance sheet prepared by
computer

Option N is selected from the General Ledger Main Menu to direct the computer to print a balance sheet. CarLand's balance sheet is shown in Illustration C4-6.

```
                              CARLAND
                           BALANCE SHEET
                             12/31/--

  A S S E T S
  -----------
  Cash                          24233.57
  Petty Cash                      500.00
  Accounts Receivable            9332.00
  Merchandise Inventory        212200.00
  Supplies--Office               1460.00
  Supplies--Store                2520.00
  Prepaid Insurance              2200.00
                              ----------------
  TOTAL ASSETS                                  252445.57
                                                ================

  L I A B I L I T I E S
  ---------------------
  Accounts Payable              10451.90
  Empl. Income Tax Payable        402.00
  FICA Tax Payable                832.16
  Sales Tax Payable              1760.00
  Unempl. Tax Pay.--Federal        59.15
  Unempl. Tax Pay.--State         399.26
  Health Ins. Prem. Payable       840.00
  U.S. Savings Bonds Pay.          40.00
  United Way Don. Payable          60.00
                              ----------------
  TOTAL LIABILITIES                               14844.47

  O W N E R ' S   E Q U I T Y
  ---------------------------
  Amy Kramer, Capital          101118.00
  Amy Kramer, Drawing          -18200.00
  SHARE OF NET INCOME @ 50%     36027.55
  Dario Mesa, Capital          101228.00
  Dario Mesa, Drawing          -18600.00
  SHARE OF NET INCOME @ 50%     36027.55
                              ----------------
  TOTAL CAPITAL                                  237601.10
                                                ----------------
  TOTAL LIABILITIES & CAPITAL                    252445.57
                                                ================
```

In manual accounting closing entries for all temporary accounts are manually entered in a journal and posted to general ledger accounts. In automated accounting the computer software contains instructions for closing temporary accounts. After the balance sheet has been prepared, Option O is selected from the General Ledger Main Menu to perform period-end closing.

After completing period-end closing, Option P is selected from the General Ledger Main Menu. This option directs the computer to print a post-closing trial balance. CarLand's post-closing trial balance is shown in Illustration C4-7.

Illustration C4-7
Post-closing trial balance
prepared by computer

```
RUN DATE: 12/31/--                        CARLAND
                                 POST-CLOSING TRIAL BALANCE

------------------------------------------------------------------------------
ACCOUNT       ACCOUNT
NUMBER        TITLE                       DEBIT AMOUNT        CREDIT AMOUNT
------------------------------------------------------------------------------
 1110         Cash                          24233.57
 1120         Petty Cash                      500.00
 1130         Accounts Receivable            9332.00
 1140         Merchandise Inventory        212200.00
 1145         Supplies--Office               1460.00
 1150         Supplies--Store                2520.00
 1160         Prepaid Insurance              2200.00
 2110         Accounts Payable                                   10451.90
 2120         Empl. Income Tax Payable                             402.00
 2130         FICA Tax Payable                                     832.16
 2140         Sales Tax Payable                                   1760.00
 2150         Unempl. Tax Pay.--Federal                             59.15
 2160         Unempl. Tax Pay.--State                              399.26
 2170         Health Ins. Prem. Payable                            840.00
 2180         U.S. Savings Bonds Pay.                               40.00
 2190         United Way Don. Payable                               60.00
 3110         Amy Kramer, Capital                               118945.55
 3130         Dario Mesa, Capital                               118655.55
                                          --------------      --------------
              TOTALS                         252445.57           252445.57
                                          ==============      ==============
```

## ■ COMPUTER APPLICATION PROBLEM

**COMPUTER APPLICATION PROBLEM 4**   **End-of-fiscal-period work**

**Instructions: 1.** Load the *Automated Accounting for the Microcomputer* software. Select Computer Application 4 (CA-4) from the CENTURY 21 ACCOUNTING Template Disk. The general ledger chart of accounts and current balances have been entered and stored on the Template Disk.

**2.** Display/Print a trial balance.

**3.** Refer to the adjustment information given in Challenge Problem 19-C, Chapter 19. Journalize the adjusting entries on a general ledger input form. Use December 31 of the current year as the run date. Batch No. 3. Use the following account numbers and titles.

| Acct. No. | Account Title | Balance before Adjustments |
|---|---|---|
| 1130 | Merchandise Inventory ....................... | $218,320.00 |
| 1140 | Supplies—Office ............................ | 5,180.00 |
| 1150 | Supplies—Store ............................. | 4,275.00 |
| 1160 | Prepaid Insurance .......................... | 3,960.00 |
| 3150 | Income Summary............................ | — |
| 6120 | Insurance Expense .......................... | — |
| 6150 | Supplies Expense—Office..................... | — |
| 6160 | Supplies Expense—Store...................... | — |

**4.** Key-enter the adjusting entries from the completed general ledger input form.

**5.** Display/Print the journal entries report.

**6.** Display/Print the income statement.

**7.** Display/Print the balance sheet.

**8.** Close the general ledger.

**9.** Display/Print the post-closing trial balance.

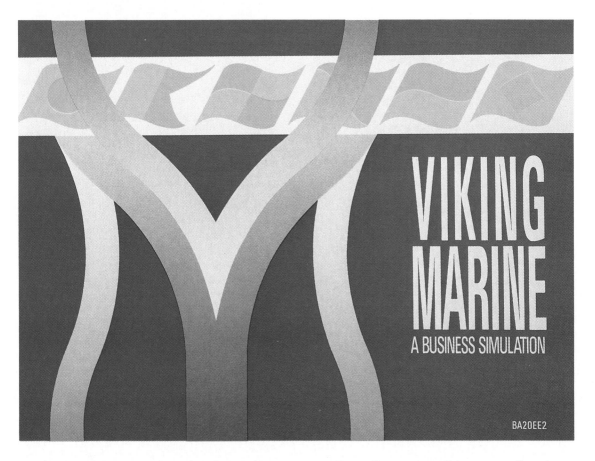

VIKING MARINE

A BUSINESS SIMULATION

BA20EE2

Viking Marine is a merchandising business organized as a partnership. This business simulation covers the realistic transactions completed by Viking Marine, which sells personal watercraft and water sports items. Transactions are recorded in a journal similar to the one used by CarLand in Part 3. The following activities are included in the accounting cycle for Viking Marine. This business simulation is available from the publisher in either manual or automated versions.

## Activities in Viking Marine

1. Recording transactions in a journal from source documents.
2. Posting items to be posted individually to a general ledger and subsidiary ledger.
3. Recording a payroll in a payroll register. Updating the employee earnings record. Recording payroll journal entries.
4. Posting column totals to a general ledger.
5. Preparing schedules of accounts receivable and accounts payable from subsidiary ledgers.
6. Preparing a trial balance on a work sheet.
7. Planning adjustments and completing a work sheet.
8. Preparing financial statements.
9. Journalizing and posting adjusting entries.
10. Journalizing and posting closing entries.
11. Preparing a post-closing trial balance.

# Accounting Concepts

The following accounting concepts and their definitions are provided in this appendix for ready reference.

## ACCOUNTING CONCEPTS

Accounting personnel are guided in their work by generally accepted accounting concepts. Ten commonly accepted accounting concepts are described in this appendix. Each concept is fully explained in the text the first time an application of the concept is described. Throughout the textbook, each time a concept application occurs, a concept reference is given, such as (CONCEPT: Business Entity).

1. ACCOUNTING PERIOD CYCLE. [Chapter 7]
   Changes in financial information are reported for a specific period of time in the form of financial statements.
2. ADEQUATE DISCLOSURE. [Chapter 8]
   Financial statements contain all information necessary to understand a business' financial condition.
3. BUSINESS ENTITY. [Chapter 1]
   Financial information is recorded and reported separately from the owner's personal financial information.
4. CONSISTENT REPORTING. [Chapter 7]
   The same accounting procedures are followed in the same way in each accounting period.
5. GOING CONCERN. [Chapter 1]
   Financial statements are prepared with the expectation that a business will remain in operation indefinitely.
6. HISTORICAL COST. [Chapter 12]
   The actual amount paid for merchandise or other items bought is recorded.

7. MATCHING EXPENSES WITH REVENUE. [Chapter 7]
   Revenue from business activities and expenses associated with earning that revenue are recorded in the same accounting period.
8. OBJECTIVE EVIDENCE. [Chapter 4]
   A source document is prepared for each transaction.
9. REALIZATION OF REVENUE. [Chapter 13]
   Revenue is recorded at the time goods or services are sold.
10. UNIT OF MEASUREMENT. [Chapter 1]
    Business transactions are stated in numbers that have common values, that is, using a common unit of measurement.

# Recycling Problems

**RECYCLING PROBLEM 1-R   Determining how transactions change an accounting equation and preparing a balance sheet**

Kim Suomi is starting Suomi Service Center, a telephone-answering business. Suomi Service Center uses the accounts shown in the following accounting equation. Use a form similar to the following to complete this problem.

| Trans. No. | Assets | | | = Liabilities | + Owner's Equity |
|---|---|---|---|---|---|
| | Cash + | Supplies + | Prepaid Insurance | = Olson Office Supply | + Kim Suomi, Capital |
| Beg. Bal. | 0 | 0 | 0 | 0 | 0 |
| 1. | +700 | | | | +700 (investment) |
| New Bal. | 700 | 0 | 0 | 0 | 700 |
| 2. | | | | | |

*Transactions*
1. Received cash from owner as an investment, $700.00.
2. Bought supplies on account from Olson Office Supply, $100.00.
3. Paid cash for insurance, $150.00.
4. Paid cash for supplies, $50.00.
5. Paid cash on account to Olson Office Supply, $50.00.

**Instructions: 1.** For each transaction, complete the following. Transaction 1 is given as an example.
a. Analyze the transaction to determine which accounts in the accounting equation are affected.
b. Write the amount in the appropriate columns, using a plus ( + ) if the account increases or a minus (−) if the account decreases.
c. For transactions that change owner's equity, write in parentheses a description of the transaction to the right of the amount.
d. Calculate the new balance for each account in the accounting equation.
e. Before going on to the next transaction, determine that the accounting equation is still in balance.

**2.** Using the final balances in the accounting equation, prepare a balance sheet. Use February 7 of the current year as the date of the balance sheet.

RECYCLING PROBLEM 2-R  **Determining how transactions change an accounting equation and preparing a balance sheet**

Steve Bird operates a service business called Office Plants Company. Office Plants Company uses the accounts shown in the following accounting equation. Use a form similar to the following to complete the problem.

| Trans. No. | Assets | | | = | Liabilities | + | Owner's Equity |
|---|---|---|---|---|---|---|---|
| | Cash + | Supplies + | Prepaid Insurance | = | Stanton Company | + | Steve Bird, Capital |
| Beg. Bal. | 1,600 | 200 | 400 | | 500 | | 1,700 |
| 1. | −90 | | | | | | −90 (expense) |
| New Bal. | 1,510 | 200 | 400 | | 500 | | 1,610 |
| 2. | | | | | | | |

*Transactions*
1. Paid cash for telephone bill, $90.00.
2. Received cash from sales, $230.00.
3. Paid cash for equipment repair, $25.00.
4. Received cash from owner as an investment, $300.00.
5. Paid cash for rent, $400.00.
6. Received cash from sales, $250.00.
7. Paid cash for advertising, $100.00.
8. Paid cash on account to Stanton Company, $500.00.
9. Paid cash for water bill, $60.00.
10. Paid cash for miscellaneous expense, $10.00.
11. Bought supplies on account from Stanton Company, $300.00.
12. Paid cash for supplies, $200.00.
13. Received cash from sales, $270.00.
14. Paid cash to owner for personal use, $600.00.
15. Paid cash for insurance, $150.00.

**Instructions: 1.** For each transaction, complete the following. Transaction 1 is given as an example.
a. Analyze the transaction to determine which accounts in the accounting equation are affected.
b. Write the amount in the appropriate columns, using a plus (+) if the account increases or a minus (−) if the account decreases.
c. For transactions that change owner's equity, write in parentheses a description of the transaction to the right of the amount.
d. Calculate the new balance for each account in the accounting equation.
e. Before going on to the next transaction, determine that the accounting equation is still in balance.
**2.** Using the final balances in the accounting equation, prepare a balance sheet. Use the date November 15 of the current year.

## RECYCLING PROBLEM 3-R   Analyzing transactions into debit and credit parts

Alicia Valdez owns a business called QuickWash. QuickWash uses the following accounts.

Cash
Supplies
Prepaid Insurance
Kishler Office Supplies
Travis Office Supplies
Alicia Valdez, Capital
Alicia Valdez, Drawing

Sales
Advertising Expense
Miscellaneous Expense
Rent Expense
Repair Expense
Utilities Expense

*Transactions*

Mar.  1. Received cash from owner as an investment, $3,000.00.
   2. Paid cash for supplies, $60.00.
   5. Paid cash for rent, $200.00.
   5. Received cash from sales, $350.00.
   6. Bought supplies on account from Travis Office Supplies, $500.00.
   9. Paid cash for repairs, $10.00.
   12. Received cash from sales, $200.00.
   13. Paid cash for insurance, $100.00.
   17. Bought supplies on account from Kishler Office Supplies, $50.00.
   19. Paid cash for miscellaneous expense, $5.00.
   19. Received cash from owner as an investment, $800.00.
   19. Received cash from sales, $300.00.
   20. Paid cash on account to Travis Office Supplies, $50.00.
   24. Paid cash for telephone bill (utilities expense), $25.00.
   25. Paid cash for advertising, $35.00.
   26. Received cash from sales, $320.00.
   30. Paid cash to owner for personal use, $500.00.
   31. Received cash from sales, $100.00.

**Instructions: 1.** Prepare a T account for each account.
**2.** Analyze each transaction into its debit and credit parts. Write the debit and credit amounts in the proper T accounts to show how each transaction changes account balances. Write the date of the transaction in parentheses before each amount.

## RECYCLING PROBLEM 4-R   Journalizing transactions

Mary Ching owns a service business called Ching's Accounting. Ching's Accounting uses the following accounts.

Cash
Supplies
Prepaid Insurance
West Supplies
Wilson's Office Supplies
Mary Ching, Capital
Mary Ching, Drawing

Sales
Advertising Expense
Miscellaneous Expense
Rent Expense
Repair Expense
Utilities Expense

**Instructions: 1.** Journalize the following transactions completed during October of the current year. Use page 1 of a journal similar to the one described in Chapter 4 for Rugcare. Source documents are abbreviated as follows: check, C; memorandum, M; receipt, R; calculator tape, T.

Oct.  1. Received cash from owner as an investment, $14,000.00. R1.
       2. Paid cash for rent, $700.00. C1.
       5. Paid cash for supplies, $500.00. C2.
       6. Paid cash for insurance, $1,500.00. C3.
       7. Bought supplies on account from West Supplies, $2,000.00. M1.
       9. Paid cash for miscellaneous expense, $5.00. C4.
      12. Paid cash on account to West Supplies, $1,000.00. C5.
      12. Received cash from sales, $450.00. T12.
      13. Received cash from sales, $400.00. T13.
      14. Paid cash for telephone bill, $60.00. C6.
      14. Received cash from sales, $480.00. T14.
      15. Paid cash for repairs, $80.00. C7.
      15. Paid cash to owner for personal use, $400.00. C8.
      15. Received cash from sales, $550.00. T15.
      16. Received cash from sales, $480.00. T16.
      19. Received cash from sales, $380.00. T19.
      20. Received cash from sales, $520.00. T20.
      21. Bought supplies on account from Wilson's Office Supplies, $600.00. M2.
      21. Received cash from sales, $400.00. T21.
      22. Paid cash for supplies, $1,200.00. C9.
      22. Received cash from sales, $550.00. T22.
      23. Received cash from sales, $450.00. T23.

**2.** Prove and rule page 1 of the journal. Carry the column totals forward to page 2 of the journal.
**3.** Use page 2 of the journal. Journalize the following transactions completed during October of the current year.

Oct. 26. Paid cash for advertising, $100.00. C10.
      26. Bought supplies on account from West Supplies, $60.00. M3.
      26. Received cash from sales, $460.00. T26.
      27. Received cash from sales, $370.00. T27.
      28. Paid cash for electric bill, $40.00. C11.
      28. Received cash from sales, $400.00. T28.
      29. Paid cash on account to West Supplies, $60.00. C12.
      29. Received cash from sales, $330.00. T29.
      30. Paid cash for supplies, $50.00. C13.
      30. Received cash from sales, $550.00. T30.
      31. Paid cash to owner for personal use, $400.00. C14.

**4.** Prove page 2 of the journal.
**5.** Prove cash. The beginning cash balance on October 1 is zero. The balance on the next unused check stub is $14,675.00.
**6.** Rule page 2 of the journal.

## RECYCLING PROBLEM 5-R   Journalizing and posting to a general ledger

Al Burns owns a service business called Burns Cleaning. Burns Cleaning uses the same journal used by Rugcare in Chapter 4.

**Instructions: 1.** Open a general ledger account for each of the following accounts.

| Assets | | Revenue | |
|---|---|---|---|
| 110 | Cash | 410 | Sales |
| 120 | Supplies | | Expenses |
| 130 | Prepaid Insurance | 510 | Advertising Expense |
| | Liabilities | 520 | Miscellaneous Expense |
| 210 | Mitchell Office Supplies | 530 | Rent Expense |
| | Owner's Equity | 540 | Utilities Expense |
| 310 | Al Burns, Capital | | |
| 320 | Al Burns, Drawing | | |

**2.** Journalize the following transactions completed during November of the current year. Use page 1 of a journal. Source documents are abbreviated as follows: check, C; memorandum, M; receipt, R; calculator tape, T.

Nov.  1. Received cash from owner as an investment, $7,000.00. R1.
     3. Paid cash for insurance, $250.00. C1.
     5. Paid cash for miscellaneous expense, $5.00. C2.
     6. Received cash from sales, $410.00. T6.
     9. Paid cash for rent, $400.00. C3.
    11. Paid cash for supplies, $550.00. C4.
    13. Bought supplies on account from Mitchell Office Supplies, $700.00.   M1.
    13. Received cash from sales, $380.00. T13.
    16. Paid cash for electric bill, $50.00. C5.
    18. Paid cash on account to Mitchell Office Supplies, $350.00. C6.
    20. Paid cash for advertising, $35.00. C7.
    20. Received cash from sales, $1,020.00. T20.
    25. Paid cash for supplies, $100.00. C8.
    27. Paid cash for supplies, $120.00. C9.
    27. Received cash from sales, $1,660.00. T27.
    30. Paid cash to owner for personal use, $500.00. C10.
    30. Received cash from sales, $450.00. T30.

   **3.** Prove the journal.
   **4.** Prove cash. The beginning cash balance on November 1 is zero. The balance on the next unused check stub is $8,560.00.
   **5.** Rule the journal.
   **6.** Post from the journal to the general ledger.

## RECYCLING PROBLEM 6-R   Reconciling a bank statement; journalizing a bank service charge, a dishonored check, and petty cash transactions

Sarah Getz owns a business called Quick Service. Quick Service completed the following transactions during August of the current year.

**Instructions: 1.** Journalize the following transactions completed during August of the current year. Use page 8 of a journal. Source documents are abbreviated as follows: check, C; memorandum, M.

Aug. 24. Paid cash to establish a petty cash fund, $200.00. C81.
25. Received notice from the bank of a dishonored check, $50.00, plus $5.00 fee; total, $55.00. M28.
26. Paid cash for miscellaneous expense, $18.00. C82.
27. Paid cash for supplies, $60.00. C83.
28. Paid cash for repairs, $35.00. C84.
31. Paid cash to owner for personal use, $500.00. C85.
31. Paid cash to replenish the petty cash fund, $105.00: supplies, $65.00; miscellaneous expense, $40.00. C86.

**2.** On August 31 of the current year, Quick Service received a bank statement dated August 30. Prepare a bank statement reconciliation. Use August 31 of the current year as the date. The following information is obtained from the August 30 bank statement and from the records of the business.

| | |
|---|---|
| Bank statement balance. . . . . . . . . . . . . . . . . . . . . . . . . . . . . . . . . . . . . . . . . . . . . . . . . . . . . . . . . . . . . | $1,970.00 |
| Bank service charge . . . . . . . . . . . . . . . . . . . . . . . . . . . . . . . . . . . . . . . . . . . . . . . . . . . . . . . . . . . . | 6.00 |
| Outstanding deposit, August 31 . . . . . . . . . . . . . . . . . . . . . . . . . . . . . . . . . . . . . . . . . . . . . . . . . | 520.00 |
| Outstanding checks, Nos. 85 and 86. | |
| Checkbook balance on Check Stub No. 87 . . . . . . . . . . . . . . . . . . . . . . . . . . . . . . . . . . . . . | 1,891.00 |

**3.** Continue using the journal and journalize the following transaction.

Aug. 31. Received bank statement showing August bank service charge, $6.00. M29.

RECYCLING PROBLEM 7-R   **Completing a work sheet**

On May 31 of the current year, ServiceAll has the following general ledger accounts and balances.  The business uses a monthly fiscal period.

|  | Account Balances | |
|---|---|---|
| **Account Titles** | **Debit** | **Credit** |
| Cash. . . . . . . . . . . . . . . . . . . . . . . . . . . . . . . . . . . . . . . . . . . . . . | $3,900.00 | |
| Petty Cash . . . . . . . . . . . . . . . . . . . . . . . . . . . . . . . . . . . . . | 100.00 | |
| Supplies . . . . . . . . . . . . . . . . . . . . . . . . . . . . . . . . . . . . . . . | 3,400.00 | |
| Prepaid Insurance . . . . . . . . . . . . . . . . . . . . . . . . . . . . . . . | 850.00 | |
| Gordon Supplies . . . . . . . . . . . . . . . . . . . . . . . . . . . . . . . . | | $  170.00 |
| Weil Company . . . . . . . . . . . . . . . . . . . . . . . . . . . . . . . . . . | | 90.00 |
| James McCurdy, Capital . . . . . . . . . . . . . . . . . . . . . . . . . | | 6,000.00 |
| James McCurdy, Drawing . . . . . . . . . . . . . . . . . . . . . . . . | 340.00 | |
| Income Summary . . . . . . . . . . . . . . . . . . . . . . . . . . . . . . . . | — | — |
| Sales . . . . . . . . . . . . . . . . . . . . . . . . . . . . . . . . . . . . . . . . . . | | 3,500.00 |
| Advertising Expense. . . . . . . . . . . . . . . . . . . . . . . . . . . . . | 270.00 | |
| Insurance Expense . . . . . . . . . . . . . . . . . . . . . . . . . . . . . . | — | |
| Miscellaneous Expense . . . . . . . . . . . . . . . . . . . . . . . . . . | 120.00 | |
| Rent Expense. . . . . . . . . . . . . . . . . . . . . . . . . . . . . . . . . . . | 400.00 | |
| Supplies Expense . . . . . . . . . . . . . . . . . . . . . . . . . . . . . . . | — | |
| Utilities Expense . . . . . . . . . . . . . . . . . . . . . . . . . . . . . . . . | 380.00 | |

**Instructions:  1.** Prepare the heading and trial balance on a work sheet.

**2.** Analyze the following adjustment information into debit and credit parts.  Record the adjustments on the work sheet.

Adjustment Information, May 31

Supplies on hand . . . . . . . . . . . . . . . . . . . . . . . . . . . . . . . . . . . . . . . . . . . . . . . $2,000.00
Value of prepaid insurance . . . . . . . . . . . . . . . . . . . . . . . . . . . . . . . . . . . .      350.00

**3.** Extend the up-to-date account balances to the Balance Sheet or Income Statement columns.

**4.** Complete the work sheet.

## RECYCLING PROBLEM 8-R   Preparing financial statements

The following information is obtained from the work sheet of Best Delivery Service for the month ended December 31 of the current year.

| | ACCOUNT TITLE | INCOME STATEMENT | | BALANCE SHEET | | |
| --- | --- | --- | --- | --- | --- | --- |
| | | DEBIT | CREDIT | DEBIT | CREDIT | |
| 1 | Cash | | | 6 0 7 5 00 | | 1 |
| 2 | Petty Cash | | | 2 0 0 00 | | 2 |
| 3 | Supplies | | | 6 3 0 0 00 | | 3 |
| 4 | Prepaid Insurance | | | 2 1 0 0 00 | | 4 |
| 5 | Dale Supplies | | | | 3 8 0 0 00 | 5 |
| 6 | Niles Office Supplies | | | | 9 7 0 00 | 6 |
| 7 | Evert Pole, Capital | | | | 9 7 0 0 00 | 7 |
| 8 | Evert Pole, Drawing | | | 1 0 0 0 00 | | 8 |
| 9 | Income Summary | | | | | 9 |
| 10 | Sales | | 4 5 6 0 00 | | | 10 |
| 11 | Advertising Expense | 3 0 0 00 | | | | 11 |
| 12 | Insurance Expense | 1 5 0 00 | | | | 12 |
| 13 | Miscellaneous Expense | 1 2 0 00 | | | | 13 |
| 14 | Rent Expense | 2 5 0 0 00 | | | | 14 |
| 15 | Supplies Expense | 1 6 5 00 | | | | 15 |
| 16 | Utilities Expense | 1 2 0 00 | | | | 16 |
| 17 | | 3 3 5 5 00 | 4 5 6 0 00 | 15 6 7 5 00 | 14 4 7 0 00 | 17 |
| 18 | Net Income | 1 2 0 5 00 | | | 1 2 0 5 00 | 18 |
| 19 | | 4 5 6 0 00 | 4 5 6 0 00 | 15 6 7 5 00 | 15 6 7 5 00 | 19 |

**Instructions: 1.** Prepare an income statement for the month ended December 31 of the current year. Figure and record the component percentages for total expenses and net income. Round percentage calculations to the nearest 0.1%.

**2.** Prepare a balance sheet for December 31 of the current year.

## RECYCLING PROBLEM 9-R   Journalizing adjusting and closing entries

The following information is obtained from the partial work sheet of Lawn Services for the month ended September 30 of the current year.

| | | 3 | 4 | 5 | 6 | 7 | 8 | |
|---|---|---|---|---|---|---|---|---|
| | | ADJUSTMENTS | | INCOME STATEMENT | | BALANCE SHEET | | |
| | ACCOUNT TITLE | DEBIT | CREDIT | DEBIT | CREDIT | DEBIT | CREDIT | |
| 1 | Cash | | | | | 3150 00 | | 1 |
| 2 | Supplies | | (a) 175 00 | | | 675 00 | | 2 |
| 3 | Prepaid Insurance | | (b) 230 00 | | | 250 00 | | 3 |
| 4 | Lodge Supplies | | | | | | 450 00 | 4 |
| 5 | Verner Supplies | | | | | | 100 00 | 5 |
| 6 | Norman Eli, Capital | | | | | | 3130 00 | 6 |
| 7 | Norman Eli, Drawing | | | | | 315 00 | | 7 |
| 8 | Income Summary | | | | | | | 8 |
| 9 | Sales | | | | 1615 00 | | | 9 |
| 10 | Insurance Expense | (b) 230 00 | | 230 00 | | | | 10 |
| 11 | Miscellaneous Expense | | | 75 00 | | | | 11 |
| 12 | Rent Expense | | | 425 00 | | | | 12 |
| 13 | Supplies Expense | (a) 175 00 | | 175 00 | | | | 13 |
| 14 | | 405 00 | 405 00 | 905 00 | 1615 00 | 4390 00 | 3680 00 | 14 |
| 15 | Net Income | | | 710 00 | | | 710 00 | 15 |
| 16 | | | | 1615 00 | 1615 00 | 4390 00 | 4390 00 | 16 |
| 17 | | | | | | | | 17 |
| 18 | | | | | | | | 18 |
| 19 | | | | | | | | 19 |
| 20 | | | | | | | | 20 |
| 21 | | | | | | | | 21 |
| 22 | | | | | | | | 22 |
| 23 | | | | | | | | 23 |
| 24 | | | | | | | | 24 |

**Instructions: 1.** Use page 3 of a journal. Journalize the adjusting entries.
**2.** Continue to use page 3 of the journal. Journalize the closing entries.

## RECYCLING PROBLEM 10-R   Preparing a general ledger file maintenance input form and journalizing opening balances

Carpet Magic has the following general ledger chart of accounts and post-closing trial balance on August 31 of the current year.

| Balance Sheet Accounts | | Income Statement Accounts | |
| --- | --- | --- | --- |
| **(100) ASSETS** | | **(400) REVENUE** | |
| 110 | Cash | 410 | Cleaning Fees |
| 120 | Petty Cash | | |
| 130 | Supplies—Cleaning | | **(500) EXPENSES** |
| 140 | Supplies—Office | | |
| 150 | Prepaid Insurance | 510 | Advertising Expense |
| | | 520 | Insurance Expense |
| | **(200) LIABILITIES** | 530 | Miscellaneous Expense |
| | | 540 | Rent Expense |
| 210 | Decker Cleaning Supplies | 550 | Supplies Expense—Cleaning |
| 220 | McKenna Office Supply | 560 | Supplies Expense—Office |
| | | 570 | Utilities Expense |
| | **(300) OWNER'S EQUITY** | | |
| 310 | Charles Dietz, Capital | | |
| 320 | Charles Dietz, Drawing | | |
| 330 | Income Summary | | |

*Carpet Magic*

*Post-Closing Trial Balance*

*August 31, 19--*

| ACCOUNT TITLE | DEBIT | CREDIT |
| --- | --- | --- |
| Cash | 12 9 2 0 00 | |
| Petty Cash | 4 0 0 00 | |
| Supplies—Cleaning | 2 6 1 0 00 | |
| Supplies—Office | 1 2 4 0 00 | |
| Prepaid Insurance | 1 2 0 0 00 | |
| Decker Cleaning Supplies | | 1 3 1 5 00 |
| McKenna Office Supply | | 6 6 5 00 |
| Charles Dietz, Capital | | 16 3 9 0 00 |
| Totals | 18 3 7 0 00 | 18 3 7 0 00 |

**Instructions: 1.** Prepare a general ledger file maintenance input form (FORM GL-1) for the general ledger chart of accounts. Use September 1 of the current year as the run date.

**2.** Journalize the opening balances for Carpet Magic on a general ledger input form (FORM GL-2). Use September 1 of the current year as the run date and the date of the opening balances. Batch No. 1; Memorandum No. 1.

**3.** Total and prove the Debit Amount and Credit Amount columns. Record the batch totals.

## RECYCLING PROBLEM 11-R   Preparing input forms for an automated accounting system

Tien's Hairstyling has the following general ledger chart of accounts.

| Balance Sheet Accounts | | Income Statement Accounts | |
|---|---|---|---|
| **(100) ASSETS** | | **(400) REVENUE** | |
| 110 | Cash | 410 | Sales |
| 120 | Petty Cash | | |
| 130 | Supplies—Beauty | **(500) EXPENSES** | |
| 140 | Supplies—Office | | |
| 150 | Prepaid Insurance | 510 | Advertising Expense |
| | | 520 | Insurance Expense |
| **(200) LIABILITIES** | | 530 | Miscellaneous Expense |
| | | 540 | Rent Expense |
| 210 | Comair Beauty Supplies | 550 | Supplies Expense—Beauty |
| 220 | Eagle Office Supplies | 560 | Supplies Expense—Office |
| 230 | Monaco Beauty Supplies | | |
| **(300) OWNER'S EQUITY** | | | |
| 310 | Damien Tien, Capital | | |
| 320 | Damien Tien, Drawing | | |
| 330 | Income Summary | | |

Tien's Hairstyling performed the following file maintenance activities.

| Account Deleted | Account Title Change | Accounts Added |
|---|---|---|
| Comair Beauty Supplies | Rent Expense | Grandy Beauty Supplies |
| | TO | Rent Expense—Computer |
| | Rent Expense—Building | Utilities Expense |

**Instructions: 1.** Assign account numbers to the new accounts using the unused middle number method.

**2.** Prepare a general ledger file maintenance input form (FORM GL-1). Use July 1 of the current year as the run date.

**3.** Journalize the following transactions on a general ledger input form (FORM GL-2). Use July 31 of the current year as the run date. Batch No. 6. Source documents are abbreviated as follows: check, C; receipt, R; cash register tape, T.

*Transactions*

July 27. Paid cash for advertising, $125.00. C185.
  27. Paid cash for beauty supplies, $175.00. C186.
  28. Paid cash for office supplies, $103.00. C187.
  29. Paid cash on account to Eagle Office Supplies, $297.00. C188.
  29. Received cash from owner as an investment, $2,500.00. R10.
  30. Paid cash for miscellaneous expense, $65.00. C189.
  30. Paid cash to replenish the petty cash fund, $201.00: beauty supplies, $82.00; office supplies, $67.00; miscellaneous, $52.00. C190.
  30. Paid cash for electric bill, $126.00. C191.
  31. Paid cash for computer rent, $880.00. C192.
  31. Paid cash to owner for personal use, $800.00. C193.
  31. Received cash from sales, $1,830.00. T31.

**4.** Total and prove the Debit Amount and Credit Amount columns. Record the batch totals.

**5.** The following accounts need adjustment at the end of the fiscal period. Journalize the adjusting entries on a general ledger input form (FORM GL-2). Use July 31 of the current year as the run date. Batch No. 7.

| Account Title | Account Balance |
|---|---|
| Supplies—Beauty . . . . . . . . . . . . . . . . . . . . . . . . . . . . . . . . . . | $2,130.00 |
| Supplies—Office . . . . . . . . . . . . . . . . . . . . . . . . . . . . . . . . . . . | 1,427.00 |
| Prepaid Insurance . . . . . . . . . . . . . . . . . . . . . . . . . . . . . . . . . | 1,575.00 |

**Adjustment Information, July 31**

| | |
|---|---|
| Value of beauty supplies on hand . . . . . . . . . . . . . . . . . . . . . . | $1,560.00 |
| Value of office supplies on hand . . . . . . . . . . . . . . . . . . . . . . | 1,160.00 |
| Value of prepaid insurance . . . . . . . . . . . . . . . . . . . . . . . . . . | 1,400.00 |

**6.** Total and prove the Debit Amount and Credit Amount columns. Record the batch totals.

## RECYCLING PROBLEM 12-R   Journalizing purchases, cash payments, and other transactions

Eva Akemi and Daniel Marino, partners, own a furniture store.

**Instructions:** Journalize the following transactions completed during November of the current year. Use page 19 of a journal similar to the one described in Chapter 12. Source documents are abbreviated as follows: check, C; memorandum, M; purchase invoice, P.

Nov. 2. Paid cash for rent, $1,200.00. C251.
 2. Purchased merchandise on account from Baines Furniture Co., $2,335.00. P88.
 3. Paid cash for office supplies, $66.00. C252.
 5. Paid cash on account to Decor-Concepts, $985.00, covering P85. C253.
 7. Purchased merchandise for cash, $130.00. C254.
 9. Purchased merchandise on account from Metaline Co., $950.00. P89.
 9. Bought store supplies on account from Gateway Supply, $140.00. M40.
 10. Purchased merchandise for cash, $83.00. C255.
 12. Paid cash on account to Furniture Industries, $1,400.00, covering P86. C256.
 12. Bought office supplies on account from Scott Supply, $95.00. M41.
 14. Discovered that a transaction for store supplies bought in October was journalized and posted in error as a debit to Purchases instead of Supplies—Store, $74.00. M42.
 16. Eva Akemi, partner, withdrew cash for personal use, $1,000.00. C257.
 17. Daniel Marino, partner, withdrew cash for personal use, $1,000.00. C258.
 17. Paid cash for advertising, $75.00. C259.
 19. Paid cash on account to Classic Furniture, $1,345.00, covering P87. C260.
 19. Purchased merchandise on account from Metaline Co., $1,250.00. P90.
 20. Daniel Marino, partner, withdrew merchandise for personal use, $152.00. M43.
 22. Purchased merchandise for cash, $60.00. C261.
 24. Paid cash on account to Baines Furniture Co., $2,335.00, covering P88. C262.
 25. Eva Akemi, partner, withdrew merchandise for personal use, $225.00. M44.
 27. Paid cash for store supplies, $78.00. C263.
 30. Paid cash to replenish the petty cash fund, $301.00: office supplies, $78.00; store supplies, $52.00; advertising, $125.00; miscellaneous, $46.00. C264.
 30. Paid cash on account to Metaline Co., $950.00, covering P89. C265.

RECYCLING PROBLEM 13-R   **Journalizing sales and cash receipts**

Ana Lamas and Alex Keyser, partners, own an office supply store.

**Instructions: 1.** Journalize the following transactions completed during September of the current year. Use page 21 of a journal similar to the one described in Chapter 13. A 4% sales tax has been added to each sale. Source documents are abbreviated as follows: receipt, R; sales invoice, S; cash register tape, T.

Sept.  1. Sold merchandise on account to Samuel Quist, $75.00, plus sales tax, $3.00; total, $78.00. S53.
    1. Received cash on account from David Plouff, $85.28, covering S49. R85.
    2. Sold merchandise on account to Carmen Estevez, $125.00, plus sales tax, $5.00; total, $130.00. S54.
    5. Sold merchandise on account to Keith Aldrich, $265.00, plus sales tax, $10.60; total, $275.60. S55.
    5. Recorded cash and credit card sales, $1,940.00, plus sales tax, $77.60; total, $2,017.60. T5.
    7. Received cash on account from Edward Jarmen, $249.60, covering S50. R86.
    9. Sold merchandise on account to Perez Accounting Co., $345.00, plus sales tax, $13.80; total, $358.80. S56.
    10. Sold merchandise on account to Nancy Cain, $85.00, plus sales tax, $3.40; total, $88.40. S57.
    11. Received cash on account from Bonner Secretarial Service, $249.60, covering S51. R87.
    12. Recorded cash and credit card sales, $2,350.00, plus sales tax, $94.00; total, $2,444.00. T12.
    14. Received cash on account from David Doran, $187.20, covering S52. R88.
    15. Sold merchandise on account to Hazel Ervin, $65.00, plus sales tax, $2.60; total, $67.60. S58.
    18. Received cash on account from Samuel Quist, $78.00, covering S53. R89.
    19. Recorded cash and credit card sales, $2,450.00, plus sales tax, $98.00; total, $2,548.00. T19.
    21. Received cash on account from Carmen Estevez, $130.00, covering S54. R90.
    25. Received cash on account from Keith Aldrich, $275.60, covering S55. R91.
    26. Recorded cash and credit card sales, $2,140.00, plus sales tax, $85.60; total, $2,225.60. T26.
    29. Sold merchandise on account to Susan Gates, $145.00, plus sales tax, $5.80; total, $150.80. S59.
    30. Recorded cash and credit card sales, $1,285.00, plus sales tax, $51.40; total, $1,336.40. T30.

**2.** Total the journal. Prove the equality of debits and credits.
**3.** Rule the journal.


RECYCLING PROBLEM 14-R   **Opening accounts and journalizing and posting business transactions**

**Instructions: 1.** Open new pages for the following accounts in the general ledger of Catalina Shoes. Record the balances as of September 1 of the current year.

| Account No. | Account Title | Account Balance |
|---|---|---|
| 1110 | Cash ............................................... | $ 13,200.00 |
| 1130 | Accounts Receivable ................................ | 441.00 |
| 1140 | Supplies—Office..................................... | 1,830.00 |
| 1150 | Supplies—Store .................................... | 1,560.00 |
| 2110 | Accounts Payable.................................... | 3,820.00 |
| 2120 | Sales Tax Payable................................... | 937.50 |
| 3120 | Sophia Kizer, Drawing .............................. | 9,820.00 |
| 3140 | Brian Rankin, Drawing............................... | 9,600.00 |
| 4110 | Sales ............................................. | 150,000.00 |
| 5110 | Purchases.......................................... | 88,000.00 |
| 6110 | Advertising Expense................................. | 2,310.00 |
| 6140 | Miscellaneous Expense .............................. | 1,260.00 |
| 6160 | Rent Expense....................................... | 7,600.00 |
| 6190 | Utilities Expense ................................... | 1,620.00 |

**2.** Open new pages for the following vendor accounts in the accounts payable ledger. Record the balances as of September 1 of the current year.

| Vendor No. | Vendor Name | Purchase No. | Account Balance |
|---|---|---|---|
| 210 | A & J Shoes ................................. | P66 | $1,480.00 |
| 220 | Colormate Shoes............................. | — | — |
| 230 | Sanz Supply ................................. | — | — |
| 240 | Suave Shoe Co.............................. | P65 | 2,340.00 |

**3.** Open new pages for the following customer accounts in the accounts receivable ledger. Record the balances as of September 1 of the current year.

| Customer No. | Customer Name | Sales No. | Account Balance |
|---|---|---|---|
| 110 | Joyce Abler .................................... | S53 | $178.50 |
| 120 | Helen Gorthy................................... | — | — |
| 130 | Joshua Lentz................................... | — | — |
| 140 | Earl Ward ..................................... | S52 | 262.50 |

**4.** Journalize the following transactions completed during September of the current year. Use page 15 of a journal similar to the one described in Chapter 14. A 5% sales tax has been added to each sale. Source documents are abbreviated as follows: check, C; memorandum, M; purchase invoice, P; receipt, R; sales invoice, S; cash register tape, T.

Sept. 1. Paid cash for rent, $950.00. C225.
   2. Purchased merchandise on account from Colormate Shoes, $1,650.00. P67.
   4. Received cash on account from Earl Ward, $262.50, covering S52. R33.
   5. Recorded cash and credit card sales, $3,350.00, plus sales tax, $167.50; total, $3,517.50. T5.
      *Posting.* Post the items that are to be posted individually.
   7. Paid cash for electric bill, $158.10. C226.
   9. Bought office supplies on account from Sanz Supply, $135.00. M32.
   10. Paid cash on account to Suave Shoe Co., $2,340.00, covering P65. C227.
   12. Recorded cash and credit card sales, $4,140.00, plus sales tax, $207.00; total, $4,347.00. T12.
      *Posting.* Post the items that are to be posted individually.
   14. Sold merchandise on account to Helen Gorthy, $260.00, plus sales tax, $13.00; total, $273.00. S54.

Sept. 15. Sold merchandise on account to Joshua Lentz, $125.00, plus sales tax, $6.25; total, $131.25. S55.

15. Sophia Kizer, partner, withdrew cash for personal use, $1,200.00. C228.

15. Brian Rankin, partner, withdrew cash for personal use, $1,200.00. C229.

18. Purchased merchandise on account from A & J Shoes, $940.00. P68.

19. Recorded cash and credit card sales, $4,080.00, plus sales tax, $204.00; total, $4,284.00. T19.

    *Posting.* Post the items that are to be posted individually.

21. Discovered that office supplies bought for cash was journalized and posted in error as a debit to Supplies—Store instead of Supplies—Office, $118.00. M33.

22. Sophia Kizer, partner, withdrew merchandise for personal use, $125.00. M34.

24. Sold merchandise on account to Earl Ward, $135.00, plus sales tax, $6.75; total, $141.75. S56.

25. Sold merchandise on account to Joyce Abler, $95.00, plus sales tax, $4.75; total, $99.75. S57.

26. Recorded cash and credit card sales, $4,530.00, plus sales tax, $226.50; total, $4,756.50. T26.

    *Posting.* Post the items that are to be posted individually.

28. Received cash on account from Joyce Abler, $178.50, covering S53. R34.

28. Paid cash on account to A & J Shoes, $1,480.00, covering P66. C230.

30. Paid cash to replenish the petty cash fund, $201.50: office supplies, $42.00; store supplies, $57.50; advertising, $64.00; miscellaneous, $38.00. C231.

30. Purchased merchandise on account from Suave Shoe Co., $860.00. P69.

30. Recorded cash and credit card sales, $1,970.00, plus sales tax, $98.50; total, $2,068.50. T30.

    *Posting.* Post the items that are to be posted individually.

**5.** Total the journal. Prove the equality of debits and credits.

**6.** Prove cash. The balance on the next unused check stub is $25,084.90.

**7.** Rule the journal.

**8.** Post the totals of the special columns of the journal.

**9.** Prepare a schedule of accounts payable and a schedule of accounts receivable. Prove the accuracy of the subsidiary ledgers by comparing the schedule totals with the balances of the controlling accounts in the general ledger. If the totals are not the same, find and correct the errors.

## RECYCLING PROBLEM 15-R  Preparing a semimonthly payroll

The following information is for the semimonthly pay period June 1-15 of the current year.

| Employee | | Marital Status | No. of Allowances | Earnings | | Deductions |
|---|---|---|---|---|---|---|
| No. | Name | | | Regular | Overtime | Health Insurance |
| 3 | Cahill, Bryan | S | 2 | $598.40 | $40.00 | $25.00 |
| 4 | Dykes, Eleanor | M | 3 | 525.60 | | 30.00 |
| 7 | Holcomb, David | S | 1 | 624.00 | | |
| 1 | Kirby, Sharon | S | 1 | 552.00 | 9.30 | |
| 5 | Mendez, Thomas | M | 2 | 545.60 | | 25.00 |
| 6 | Salassi, Carol | M | 3 | 576.00 | | 30.00 |
| 8 | Tsang, Elaine | M | 2 | 651.20 | 44.40 | 25.00 |

**Instructions: 1.** Prepare a payroll register. The date of payment is June 16. Use the income tax withholding tables in Illustration 15-4 to find the income tax withholding for each employee. Calculate FICA tax withholding using an 8% tax rate. None of the employee accumulated earnings has exceeded the FICA tax base.

**2.** Prepare a check for the total amount of the net pay. Make the check payable to Payroll Account, and sign your name as a partner of Riddley Company. The beginning check stub balance is $7,687.89.

**3.** Prepare payroll checks for David Holcomb, Check No. 332, and Carol Salassi, Check No. 335. Sign your name as a partner of Riddley Company. Record the two payroll check numbers in the payroll register.

## RECYCLING PROBLEM 16-R   Journalizing payroll taxes

Johnson Manufacturing completed payroll transactions during the period February 28 to April 30 of the current year. Payroll tax rates are as follows: FICA, 8%; federal unemployment, 0.8%; and state unemployment, 5.4%. No total earnings have exceeded the tax base for calculating unemployment taxes.

**Instructions: 1.** Journalize the following transactions on page 4 of a journal. Source documents are abbreviated as follows: check, C, and memorandum, M.

Feb. 28. Paid cash for monthly payroll, $3,312.16 (total payroll, $4,298.00, less deductions: employee income tax, $642.00; FICA tax, $343.84). C167.
   28. Recorded employer payroll taxes expense. M34.
Mar. 15. Paid cash for liability for employee income tax, $642.00, and for FICA tax, $687.68; total, $1,329.68. C192.
   31. Paid cash for monthly payroll, $3,328.84 (total payroll, $4,327.00, less deductions: employee income tax, $652.00; FICA tax, $346.16). C235.
   31. Recorded employer payroll taxes expense. M39.
Apr. 15. Paid cash for liability for employee income tax, $652.00, and for FICA tax, $692.32; total, $1,344.32. C251.
   30. Paid cash for federal unemployment tax liability for quarter ended March 31, $103.62. C272.
   30. Paid cash for state unemployment tax liability for quarter ended March 31, $699.41. C273.

**2.** Prove and rule the journal.

## RECYCLING PROBLEM 17-R   Completing a work sheet

On December 31 of the current year, Klimer has the following general ledger accounts and balances.

| Account Title | Balance |
|---|---|
| Cash | $ 19,865.00 |
| Petty Cash | 500.00 |
| Accounts Receivable | 9,260.00 |
| Merchandise Inventory | 226,320.00 |
| Supplies—Office | 5,085.00 |
| Supplies—Store | 5,420.00 |
| Prepaid Insurance | 4,300.00 |
| Accounts Payable | 9,720.00 |
| Sales Tax Payable | 950.00 |
| Dorothy Klimer, Capital | 107,365.00 |
| Dorothy Klimer, Drawing | 15,880.00 |
| Howard Klimer, Capital | 106,190.00 |
| Howard Klimer, Drawing | 15,730.00 |
| Income Summary | — |
| Sales | 189,540.00 |
| Purchases | 85,250.00 |
| Advertising Expense | 4,735.00 |
| Credit Card Fee Expense | 1,930.00 |
| Insurance Expense | — |
| Miscellaneous Expense | 2,360.00 |
| Rent Expense | 14,400.00 |
| Supplies Expense—Office | — |
| Supplies Expense—Store | — |
| Utilities Expense | 2,730.00 |

**Instructions:** Prepare Klimer's work sheet for the fiscal period ended December 31 of the current year.

### Adjustment Information, December 31

| | |
|---|---|
| Merchandise inventory | $218,770.00 |
| Office supplies inventory | 2,195.00 |
| Store supplies inventory | 2,205.00 |
| Value of prepaid insurance | 1,720.00 |

## RECYCLING PROBLEM 18-R  Preparing financial statements

Discount Footwear prepared the work sheet shown on page C-17 for the year ended December 31 of the current year.

**Instructions: 1.** Prepare an income statement. Figure and record the following component percentages: (a) cost of merchandise sold, (b) gross profit on sales, (c) total expenses, and (d) net income or loss. Round percentage calculations to the nearest 0.1%.

    **2.** Prepare a distribution of net income statement. Net income or loss is to be shared equally.

    **3.** Prepare an owners' equity statement. No additional investments were made.

    **4.** Prepare a balance sheet in report form.

Discount Footwear

Work Sheet

For Year Ended December 31, 19--

| | ACCOUNT TITLE | TRIAL BALANCE | | ADJUSTMENTS | | INCOME STATEMENT | | BALANCE SHEET | | |
|---|---|---|---|---|---|---|---|---|---|---|
| | | DEBIT | CREDIT | DEBIT | CREDIT | DEBIT | CREDIT | DEBIT | CREDIT | |
| 1 | Cash | 19 395 00 | | | | | | 19 395 00 | | 1 |
| 2 | Petty Cash | 300 00 | | | | | | 300 00 | | 2 |
| 3 | Accounts Receivable | 893 00 | | | | | | 893 00 | | 3 |
| 4 | Merchandise Inventory | 257 200 00 | | | (a)9 750 00 | | | 247 450 00 | | 4 |
| 5 | Supplies-Office | 512 00 | | | (b)298 00 | | | 214 00 | | 5 |
| 6 | Supplies-Store | 487 50 | | | (c)314 00 | | | 173 50 | | 6 |
| 7 | Prepaid Insurance | 483 00 | | | (d)276 00 | | | 207 00 | | 7 |
| 8 | Accounts Payable | | 836 00 | | | | | | 836 00 | 8 |
| 9 | Sales Tax Payable | | 98 00 | | | | | | 98 00 | 9 |
| 10 | Joseph Kane, Capital | | 111 640 00 | | | | | | 111 640 00 | 10 |
| 11 | Joseph Kane, Drawing | 15 840 00 | | | | | | 15 840 00 | | 11 |
| 12 | Gail Miles, Capital | | 110 360 00 | | | | | | 110 360 00 | 12 |
| 13 | Gail Miles, Drawing | 15 930 00 | | | | | | 15 930 00 | | 13 |
| 14 | Income Summary | | | (a)9 750 00 | | 9 750 00 | | | | 14 |
| 15 | Sales | | 235 450 00 | | | | 235 450 00 | | | 15 |
| 16 | Purchases | 105 950 00 | | | | 105 950 00 | | | | 16 |
| 17 | Advertising Expense | 4 965 00 | | | | 4 965 00 | | | | 17 |
| 18 | Credit Card Fee Expense | 2 130 00 | | | | 2 130 00 | | | | 18 |
| 19 | Insurance Expense | | | (d)276 00 | | 276 00 | | | | 19 |
| 20 | Miscellaneous Expense | 2 285 00 | | | | 2 285 00 | | | | 20 |
| 21 | Rent Expense | 16 800 00 | | | | 16 800 00 | | | | 21 |
| 22 | Supplies Expense-Office | | | (b)298 00 | | 298 00 | | | | 22 |
| 23 | Supplies Expense-Store | | | (c)314 00 | | 314 00 | | | | 23 |
| 24 | Utilities Expense | 2 240 00 | | | | 2 240 00 | | | | 24 |
| 25 | | 466 790 00 | 466 790 00 | 1 863 00 | 1 863 00 | 153 000 00 | 235 450 00 | 313 790 00 | 231 340 00 | 25 |
| 26 | Net Income | | | | | 82 450 00 | | | 82 450 00 | 26 |
| 27 | | | | | | 235 450 00 | 235 450 00 | 313 790 00 | 313 790 00 | 27 |
| 28 | | | | | | | | | | 28 |

## RECYCLING PROBLEM 19-R   Journalizing adjusting and closing entries

Use the following partial work sheet of Cook & Latzco Paints for the year ended December 31 of the current year.

| | | 3 | 4 | 5 | 6 |
| --- | --- | --- | --- | --- | --- |
| ACCOUNT TITLE | | ADJUSTMENTS | | INCOME STATEMENT | |
| | | DEBIT | CREDIT | DEBIT | CREDIT |
| 4 | Merchandise Inventory | | (a) 9 8 4 0 00 | | |
| 5 | Supplies—Office | | (b) 2 5 1 0 00 | | |
| 6 | Supplies—Store | | (c) 2 6 3 0 00 | | |
| 7 | Prepaid Insurance | | (d) 2 5 8 0 00 | | |
| 21 | Income Summary | (a) 9 8 4 0 00 | | 9 8 4 0 00 | |
| 22 | Sales | | | | 310 9 2 0 00 |
| 23 | Purchases | | | 124 3 5 0 00 | |
| 24 | Advertising Expense | | | 4 7 8 0 00 | |
| 25 | Credit Card Fee Expense | | | 3 9 8 0 00 | |
| 26 | Insurance Expense | (d) 2 5 8 0 00 | | 2 5 8 0 00 | |
| 27 | Miscellaneous Expense | | | 2 1 4 0 00 | |
| 28 | Payroll Taxes Expense | | | 7 0 7 0 00 | |
| 29 | Rent Expense | | | 13 2 0 0 00 | |
| 30 | Salary Expense | | | 58 9 2 0 00 | |
| 31 | Supplies Expense—Office | (b) 2 5 1 0 00 | | 2 5 1 0 00 | |
| 32 | Supplies Expense—Store | (c) 2 6 3 0 00 | | 2 6 3 0 00 | |
| 33 | Utilities Expense | | | 2 7 6 0 00 | |
| 34 | | 17 5 6 0 00 | 17 5 6 0 00 | 234 7 6 0 00 | 310 9 2 0 00 |
| 35 | Net Income | | | 76 1 6 0 00 | |
| 36 | | | | 310 9 2 0 00 | 310 9 2 0 00 |
| 37 | | | | | |
| 38 | | | | | |
| 39 | | | | | |
| 40 | | | | | |
| 41 | | | | | |

**Instructions: 1.** Use page 25 of a journal. Journalize the adjusting entries using information from the partial work sheet.

**2.** Continue using page 25 of the journal. Journalize the closing entries using information from the work sheet. The distribution of net income statement shows equal distribution of earnings. The partners' drawing accounts show the following debit balances in the work sheet's Balance Sheet Debit column: Angela Cook, Drawing, $14,780.00; Alan Latzco, Drawing, $15,120.00.

# Index

Bold page numbers indicate illustrations.